THE

WILLARD J. GRAHAM SERIES

IN ACCOUNTING

BOOKS IN THE WILLARD J. GRAHAM SERIES IN ACCOUNTING

ANDERSON & SCHMIDT *Practical Controllership* rev. ed.
ANTHONY *Management Accounting: Text and Cases* 4th ed.
ANTHONY *Management Accounting Principles* rev. ed.
BARR & GRINAKER *Short Audit Case*
FREMGEN *Managerial Cost Analysis*
GORDON & SHILLINGLAW *Accounting: A Management Approach* 4th ed.
GRIFFIN, WILLIAMS, & WELSCH *Advanced Accounting*
GRINAKER & BARR *Audit Practice Case*
GRINAKER & BARR *Auditing: The Examination of Financial Statements*
HENDRIKSEN *Accounting Theory* rev. ed.
HOLMES *Auditing: Principles and Procedure* 6th ed.
HOLMES *Basic Auditing Principles* 3d ed.
HOLMES, MAYNARD, EDWARDS, & MEIER *Elementary Accounting* 3d ed.
KENNEDY & MCMULLEN *Financial Statements: Form, Analysis, and Interpretation* 5th ed.
LADD *Contemporary Corporate Accounting and the Public*
MEIGS & LARSEN *Principles of Auditing* 4th ed.
MIKESELL & HAY *Governmental Accounting* 4th ed.
MOORE & STETTLER *Accounting Systems for Management Control*
MURPHY *Advanced Public Accounting Practice*
MURPHY *Auditing and Theory: A CPA Review*
NEUNER & FRUMER *Cost Accounting: Principles and Practice* 7th ed.
NIELSEN *Cases in Auditing*
O'NEIL, FARWELL, & BOYD *Quantitative Controls for Business: An Introduction*
PATON *Corporate Profits*
PYLE & WHITE *Fundamental Accounting Principles* 5th ed.
SCHRADER, MALCOLM, & WILLINGHAM *Financial Accounting: An Input/Output Approach*
SHILLINGLAW *Cost Accounting: Analysis and Control* rev. ed.
SPILLER *Financial Accounting: Basic Concepts*
WELSCH, ZLATKOVICH, & WHITE *Intermediate Accounting* rev. ed.
WILLIAMS & GRIFFIN *Management Information: A Quantitative Accent*

MANAGERIAL COST ANALYSIS

MANAGERIAL COST ANALYSIS

By

JAMES M. FREMGEN, D.B.A., C.P.A.

Associate Professor of Accounting
U.S. Naval Postgraduate School

1966

RICHARD D. IRWIN, INC.

HOMEWOOD, ILLINOIS

First Printing, January, 1966
Second Printing, January, 1968
Third Printing, January, 1969
Fourth Printing, December, 1969
Fifth Printing, July, 1970

PRINTED IN THE UNITED STATES OF AMERICA
Library of Congress Catalog Card No. 66–11810

To Eleanor, Jim, and Steve

PREFACE

The Theme of the Text

The basic premise underlying this text is that a wide range of cost data is useful to management in the efficient operation of a business enterprise. Many other data, both financial and nonfinancial, are also useful, of course. Nevertheless, there are sufficient applications of cost data to business problems and enough difficulties involved in the development and analysis of appropriate costs to warrant a separate volume devoted to them. The essential theme of this book, then, is the use of costs in business planning, control, and decision making. Effective implementation of this theme demands that the student understand the nature of costs and the basic procedures by which costs are accumulated and accounted for in a business firm. A detailed study of cost accumulation and processing is avoided, however, in favor of a more extensive examination of the uses of costs by management. The only course prerequisite to effective use of this text is a college-level introduction to the principles of financial accounting (one or two semesters or quarters).

Organization and Content

The text is organized into three basic parts, following an introductory first chapter. Part I (three chapters) introduces the student to various concepts of costs and to the fundamentals of cost accounting. Chapter 2 defines and explains the cost concepts and classifications that are used throughout the text. Chapters 3 and 4 present the basic cost accounting cycle and explain the costing of inventories in a manufacturing firm. Both absorption costing and variable (direct) costing are explained and illustrated here, and the arguments in favor of each are examined. No attempt is made to convince the student of the merit of one or the other of these alternatives. Rather, the objective is to make him recognize the existence of the alternatives and comprehend their similarities and differences.

Part II (eight chapters) explores the uses of costs in the planning and control of business operations. Chapter 5 introduces standards and standard costs and discusses their development and use. Chapters 6, 7, and 8 discuss and illustrate comprehensive business budgeting, including the planning of operations and resources. Chapter 9 deals with flexible budgets for overhead. Chapters 10 and 11 explain the use of standard costs in the accounting system and the computation and analysis of variances. Finally, Chapter 12 discusses some of the peculiar problems of planning and controlling nonmanufacturing costs.

Part III (seven chapters) discusses the uses of cost data in specific decision-making situations. The emphasis here is on the identification and analysis of relevant costs. Chapter 13 deals with cost-volume-profit relationships and break-even analysis. Chapter 14 explains and illustrates the incremental profit approach to short-term decision making. Chapter 15 is concerned with the analysis of rates of return on investments, both in retrospect and in prospect. Chapter 16 explains and evaluates procedures for determining the profitability of long-term investment proposals. Chapter 17 discusses the relevance of costs to pricing decisions. Chapter 18 examines the special problems involved in measuring the profit of a segment of a firm. Finally, Chapter 19 considers some general rules for the preparation of effective reports to management.

The text has been tested in a one-semester (fifteen weeks) course following the introductory course in principles of financial accounting. For such a course, it is practical to cover certain chapters, notably Chapters 1, 12, and 19, with little direct attention in class. Chapters 6, 7, and 8 on budgeting may be covered in as much or as little time as the instructor wishes, without prejudice to the study of subsequent chapters. With more extensive use of problems and cases and, perhaps, with the assignment of additional readings, the text should be adaptable to the needs of a two-semester or two-quarter course as well.

The questions for discussion at the end of the chapter are designed to stimulate the student's thinking about the concepts presented in the chapter and their implications for the total management process. A deliberate effort has been made to avoid questions that merely require the student to find and repeat a passage in the text. A variety of problems is included to test the student's understanding of the concepts presented and his ability to apply them to specific situations. To the extent feasible, these problems avoid lengthy calculations and tedious repetition of mechanical processes. Some questions and problems have no unique correct answers but test the student's ability to recognize and deal with all facets of a business problem and to produce a reasonable solution to it.

The cases in Appendix A are designed to elicit a careful study and reasoned analysis of a particular business situation. They seek to integrate the materials discussed in several chapters. The introductory note in each case indicates the earliest point in the sequence of text material at which the student may reasonably be expected to analyze the case effectively.

Acknowledgments

The appearance of a single name on the cover of this book belies the many who have contributed to its development and production; yet it would be impossible for me to recognize all who have aided and guided me in the preparation of the text. However, for me not to express my appreciation to some of them would be unthinkable. My debt of gratitude begins with Professor Bernard B. Finnan of the University of Notre Dame, a former instructor and more recently a colleague. It was after his course in cost accounting that I chose accounting as my major area of study. It was his counsel that nurtured my earliest interests in the teaching profession. The original idea for this particular book was developed in discussions with Professor Ray H. McClary of Bradley University. Special appreciation is due Professor Ray M. Powell of the University of Notre Dame. He read and criticized several chapters and, as my department head, graciously offered administrative encouragement and assistance that materially accelerated the completion of the manuscript.

Professors Willard J. Graham of the University of North Carolina, John Burke of Western Michigan University, Allan R. Drebin of Cornell University, and Howard Jensen of the University of Colorado read the entire manuscript and made numerous invaluable comments and suggestions. Mr. Charles Smith of the Pennsylvania State University reviewed the problems and the instructor's manual. Two of my student assistants at Notre Dame—Michael P. Bohan, now with Touche, Ross, Bailey & Smart, and Thomas Numainville, now with Arthur Andersen & Co.—assisted with the production of the manuscript. Mrs. June Locke and Mrs. Peggy Swain typed most of the successive drafts of the manuscript. Finally, I must express my gratitude to my students who used the text in class in preliminary form. They graciously endured and helped identify many of the shortcomings now eliminated from the text. The shortcomings that remain, however, are entirely my own responsibility.

JAMES M. FREMGEN

MONTEREY, CALIFORNIA
November, 1965

TABLE OF CONTENTS

APPENDIXES

INDEX

INTRODUCTION

Chapter 1

THE ROLE OF THE INDUSTRIAL ACCOUNTANT

IN ADDITION to his many sins against Christmas, Ebenezer Scrooge may be held accountable for a notable disservice to the profession of accountancy. By placing Bob Cratchit on a high stool, bent over a dusty ledger with a long quill pen in his hand and a green eyeshade over his brow, Scrooge perpetuated a caricature of the accountant which persisted long after that miser's reconciliation with his fellowmen. Happily, this image has been dispelled. Today, accountants guide the fortunes of some of the largest industrial corporations in America, and they have filled creditably some of the most responsible positions in the government. The basic reason for this advancement of the accountant's role in society is the fact that business managers have come to appreciate the importance of accounting data and analyses in the effective administration of an enterprise. Accountants have become members in good standing of the business management team. The central theme of this book is the usefulness of accounting information in the management of a business enterprise.

Managerial applications of accounting data are not the only important aspects of modern accounting development, of course. The responsibilities of the accountant, and particularly of the independent certified public accountant, extend far beyond the limits of a single business firm. However, the uses of accounting information in business management are sufficiently important and varied that it is appropriate to study them separately from other accounting practices. Thus, the accountant holding the center of the stage in this volume is the industrial accountant, whose primary concern is with the particular problems and needs of a specific firm. Various aspects of his job and his responsibilities will be considered in the pages that follow.

FUNCTIONS AND RESPONSIBILITIES OF THE INDUSTRIAL ACCOUNTANT

The Controller

The controller, or comptroller, of a business enterprise is typically the top accounting executive in the firm. To be sure, the accountant may rise beyond the position of controller to those of executive vice-president, president, and chairman of the board. In these latter positions, however, his areas of responsibility and authority would be so broad that it would not be accurate to continue to describe him as an accounting executive. While the role of the controller varies somewhat among firms, typically he occupies a staff position and reports directly to top management. Under his cognizance there is likely to be a large and diverse staff, responsible to him for the timely and efficient accomplishment of the various accounting functions of the firm. There is no single accepted listing of the functions of the controller's staff, but the following list is typical of most business enterprises:

1. Financial accounting.
2. Tax accounting.
3. Internal control.
4. Accounting systems design.
5. Management accounting.

Each of these will be considered briefly below.

Financial Accounting

Financial accounting encompasses a broad range of accounting practices and procedures related to the proper recording and reporting of the assets, liabilities, equities, revenues, and expenses of the firm. The end product of financial accounting is the financial report, the basic means of communicating financial information about the firm to those outside it. For this purpose, stockholders are regarded as "outsiders." In one sense, stockholders might be viewed as the most important "insiders"; for they own the corporation. However, the corporate sector of our economy has developed to such an extent that the stockholders of most large companies are merely investors who provide a portion of the capital employed by corporate management in the conduct of the affairs of the firm. In this situation, it is reasonable to regard shareholders as outside parties; for their direct control over corporate activities is normally minimal.

Financial reporting is commonly accomplished in the form of published income statements and balance sheets, along with supporting data and explanations. These reports are prepared in accordance with generally accepted accounting principles. These principles are derived chiefly from their wide acceptance in the accounting profession, although some of them stem from legal pronouncements. The Securities and Exchange Commission, for example, has rather broad powers to regulate accounting practices, although it has chosen to leave the selection of accounting principles, for the most part, to the accounting profession. Thus, the procedures of financial reporting are determined primarily by factors outside the firm. A certain degree of discretion is left to the reporting corporation, but the constraints upon individual firms' practices are fairly strict. It is entirely reasonable to demand that financial reports conform to specific accounting and reporting standards so that readers may interpret them in the light of accepted practices.

Financial accounting involves so many facets of a firm's operations that it is impossible to separate it from the other functions of the industrial accountant. Indeed, all of the functions discussed here are interrelated and overlapping. The separate discussions should not be interpreted as suggesting that these functions are wholly separable in practice.

Tax Accounting

For most businesses, tax accounting is concerned primarily with the federal income tax. This is not the only tax to which firms are subject, of course. Taxes imposed by states, municipalities, and foreign governments may be quite important also. Business enterprises are subject to property taxes, excise taxes, and others. The federal income tax is different from these, however, in that the firm not only pays the tax but also assesses it. That is, the firm must determine how much tax is payable for a given tax period. The determination of the income tax liability is chiefly a function of the Internal Revenue Code and the supporting regulations, but there is some room for judgment and choice on the part of the taxpayer. It is, therefore, the responsibility of the tax accountant to determine the lowest possible income tax liability consistent with the law and regulations. Tax minimization (very different from tax evasion) is a perfectly legitimate objective of business management, and a great deal of time and effort is expended by accounting personnel to achieve that objective.

Except in those areas where the provisions of the income tax law conflict with generally accepted accounting principles for financial reporting, tax accounting is dependent largely upon the data developed within the financial accounting function.

Internal Control

The purposes of internal control are many and they involve matters which extend beyond the scope of accounting, as such. The basic objectives of internal control are

1. The safeguarding of assets,
2. The accuracy and reliability of accounting data,
3. The promotion of operating efficiency, and
4. The adherence to prescribed managerial policies.[1]

The safeguarding of assets, and particularly those assets, such as cash, which are especially susceptible to misappropriation, is a very important responsibility of the industrial accountant. Control of the recording and reporting of accounting data is quite obviously essential to the effective fulfillment of any accounting function. The promotion of operating efficiency and compliance with established management policies should be regarded as responsibilities of every employee of a firm. The accountant's comprehensive overview of the firm's total operations, however, makes him peculiarly qualified to assume such responsibilities. In large firms, internal control may be so extensive and formalized that a separate subdivision of the controller's staff may be charged with the responsibility of maintaining its effectiveness. The specific responsibilities of this subdivision are commonly referred to as internal auditing. In some corporations, the internal auditing function is independent of the controller and the chief internal auditor reports directly to top management.

Accounting Systems Design

Integrally related to all of the other accounting functions listed here is that of accounting systems design. The primary purpose of this function is to develop systems which will efficiently and economically facilitate the other four functions. Systems design includes the structure of accounts within the firm and the processing of data through those accounts. The methods by which data are processed are also part of the job of systems design. As far as financial accounting is concerned, an accounts receivable ledger is the same regardless of how it is handled mechanically—handwritten in a bound ledger, machine punched on cards, or prepared by an electronic computer on magnetic tape. The mechanics are within the scope of the systems design function. The basic

[1] Committee on Auditing Procedure, American Institute of Certified Public Accountants, *Auditing Standards and Procedures* (New York, 1963), p. 27.

objective of systems design should be the most efficient recording, processing, and reporting of data at the lowest possible cost.

Management Accounting

Discussion of the management accounting function has been deferred to the last here not because of the relative unimportance of the subject but to serve as a link to the main theme of the book. Management accounting is the function of the industrial accountant with which most of this volume will be concerned. Once again, this function cannot be separated completely from the other four. Many of the data relevant to financial accounting and to tax accounting are also pertinent to management accounting. The important feature which distinguishes management accounting from financial accounting is its point of view. Financial accounting is intended to serve as a means of communicating financial information to outsiders. Management accounting is a means of communicating financial data to business managers. It need not be guided by generally accepted accounting principles but only by what the particular firm's management wants and needs. Any procedure or practice that proves helpful to management in the operation and control of the enterprise is good management accounting. It is in connection with this function that the industrial accountant is most importantly a member of the management team. His view here is focused on the interests and needs of his firm and not upon those of outside parties. This is as it should be. If accounting were of no direct use to management in the operation of the firm, then, from the point of view of management, it would be little more than a burden, a necessary evil. But accounting data are useful to management, and it is the responsibility of the management accountant to make them available in the form and at the time required by management.

COST ACCOUNTING

Cost accounting is an important part of the total accounting activities of a business firm, and particularly of a manufacturing company. It is not a sixth distinct function of accounting but, rather, a separate activity related to the five functions discussed in the preceding section. Cost accounting is concerned with the proper recording, analysis, and reporting of the various costs incurred in the operation of an enterprise. Accounting systems design must conceive and structure procedures for the efficient accomplishment of these objectives. Internal control of costs and cost records is essential. It is in connection with the functions of financial and management accounting, however, that cost accounting is most often studied and employed. Through its financial accounting implications, cost accounting also relates to the tax accounting function.

It is impossible to draw a sharp and clear line between the financial and management accounting facets of cost accounting. Many of the cost data necessary for accurate financial reporting are of equal importance to management. However, there are some significant differences in points of view between financial and managerial reporting.

Financial Accounting Applications

As regards financial accounting, cost accounting activities are directed primarily toward the correct classification and measurement of the cost data which are reported on the income statement and on the balance sheet. These activities relate to the determination of periodic net income and to the valuation of inventories. They are guided by the dictates of generally accepted accounting principles. While financial reporting is not the central theme of the book, it is essential that the student have a basic knowledge of cost accounting as related to that function; for many of the managerial applications of cost information are derived from financial accounting practices. Chapters 3 and 4 present the fundamental concepts and procedures for the financial reporting aspects of cost accounting.

Management Accounting Applications

The managerial applications of cost accounting derive from and are determined by the needs of management in particular instances. Cost data are very useful to managers in planning, controlling, and evaluating business operations and in making specific decisions among alternative courses of action. In this context, costs should be reported in whatever manner best satisfies the requirements of management, regardless of compliance with or deviation from generally accepted accounting principles. Parts II and III of this book are concerned principally with the management accounting applications of costs. Particularly in Part II, however, the management and financial accounting aspects are so interwoven that their separate discussion can be based upon different points of view only, and not upon wholly different concepts.

Profit Motive

A great deal has been said in recent years on the subject of the motivation underlying business activities. In traditional economic theory, enterprises are assumed to be motivated by the desire for profit and to act in such a manner as to maximize their profits. This profit maximization is a short-run concept; that is, it is assumed that the firm seeks to obtain the maximum profit possible under the presently existing circumstances. While short-run profit maximization is a necessary assumption for purposes of certain economic analyses, it need not be applied strictly to actual business behavior. Modern business operations are conducted in a dynamic society; circumstances are almost constantly changing. Further, most enterprises look forward to indefinite lives and, hence, must conduct current operations with a view to their long-run implications. Thus, the business manager is likely to be concerned with obtaining the maximum profit in the long run, even if this suggests the acceptance of something less than the maximum profit in the short run. For example, a monopolist can obtain whatever price he wishes for his product (within the limits imposed by the demand for it, of course) and has the power to set a price that will maximize his short-run profit. He may elect to set a somewhat lower price, however, and forego the maximum short-run return in order to attain what he anticipates will be the greatest long-run return. The lower price, while not consistent with the highest possible immediate profit, may tend to discourage entry of competitors into his market and may also forestall possible governmental action designed to deprive him of his monopoly power.

Because of the traditional short-run connotation of the term profit maximization, it might be desirable to describe the long-run profit objective as profit optimization. This is a matter of semantics and not critical to the discussions in this book. However termed, the profit motive here will always be viewed in a long-run perspective unless the contrary is specifically indicated.

Some businessmen and observers of business activities have suggested that the basic objective of a business firm ought not be profit but service. The service objective is normally interpreted as a purposeful effort to provide efficiently an economic good, whether commodity or service, to society. In a free enterprise system, the service objective is not really an alternative to the profit motive, however, but a necessary prerequisite to it. Obviously, profits can be obtained only if the firm renders a valuable service to its customers. But to deny the validity of the profit motive is to deny the free enterprise system. In a competitive economy, the profit motive is the key to the efficient allocation of resources. Even in communist Russia, the managers of the state-controlled economy have recognized the need for some form of profit motivation (carefully limited in this instance, of course) in their striving for efficient production.

The profit motive underlies many of the management accounting practices which will be discussed in this volume. Such objectives as the control of costs, the planning of future operations, and the selection of the most advantageous available alternatives would have to be viewed in a wholly different light if the profit motive were removed. Thus, the discussions here will presume that management's basic objective is to obtain the greatest possible profit in the long-run operations of the enterprise. Because of the uncertainties and risks which attend business activities in a free society, long-run profit cannot necessarily be measured in advance and the implications of specific decisions for that profit can only be predicted, not known positively. Nevertheless, however hazy it may appear in a particular instance, the profit motive is still the basic stimulus and purpose of managerial action.

PROFESSIONAL DEVELOPMENT IN MANAGEMENT ACCOUNTING

Recent years have witnessed considerable debate as to whether or not business management may be regarded as a professional activity. The answer to this question depends upon how "professional" is defined, and there does not appear to be any general agreement on this point. The author is not interested in pursuing this particular argument here. He would be willing to substitute "occupational" for "professional" in the heading of this section if that would provide a better common ground for the ensuing discussion.

Whether management is viewed as a profession, an art, or an occupation, it is unquestionably an important function in any business enterprise and in any economically developed society. Management affords a challenging and, potentially, very rewarding (in both the personal sense and the pecuniary sense) career. As already mentioned, accountants have become indispensable members of the top management team in any large enterprise. And they are more and more assuming additional responsibilities which encompass far more than their own area of specialization. In keeping with this development, organizations of management accountants have developed to further the interests and personal effectiveness of their members. The three principal organizations in this area are the National Association of Accountants (formerly called the National Association of Cost Accountants), the Financial Executives Institute (formerly the Controllers Institute), and the Institute of Internal Auditors. Each of these associations has a widespread membership that participates in the activities of local chapters as well as in the national organization. Each publishes a monthly (quarterly in the case of the Institute of Internal Auditors) journal, containing articles and news items of particular interest to management accountants. In addition to these, such other organizations as the American Accounting Association and the American Management Association have turned their attentions to matters related specifically to management accounting.

In light of recent and prospective developments in American (and, for that matter, worldwide) business, it is difficult to imagine that the role of the accountant and of accounting analysis will do anything but increase in importance in enterprise management. These developments do not mean that all managers will be accountants or that the business roles of other specialists will be eclipsed. The need for specialized knowledge and skill in such areas as production, distribution, engineering, research, and personnel administration will continue to grow also. Further, the role of the accountant as a specialist will not cease to exist as such; but his special functions will pervade more and more of the general operation of and decision making in business firms. Thus, while the manager need not be an accountant himself, he must be able to understand and interpret accounting information with considerable facility. The development and processing of accounting data are technical functions, but they are designed to support the more general managerial functions of planning, organization, and control. The accountant and the manager must be able to communicate freely and effectively. This requires that the manager be familiar with accounting practices and concepts, including their limitations, and that the accountant be conversant with all of the operations and problems of the firm. It is the author's hope that this volume will contribute to the manager's appreciation of how accounting can aid in his intelligent pursuit of the basic objective of the firm, to the accountant's understanding of the needs of management in various instances, and to the ability of both to adapt accounting procedures to meet the changing needs of business management.

Part I
COSTS AND COST ACCOUNTING

Chapter 2

COST CONCEPTS AND CLASSIFICATIONS

IN FINANCIAL accounting, the term cost, used without modifiers, has a fairly generally accepted meaning. In management accounting, however, there are a great many different concepts of "cost," each intended to convey a very specific and distinct meaning. Unfortunately, cost terminology in this latter area has not been established with complete agreement. Different accountants use different terms to describe the same concept of cost, and a single term may be used to denote different concepts. The terminology employed in this volume follows that which appears to have attained a substantial degree of acceptance and which seems to the author to be most useful.

HISTORICAL AND FUTURE COSTS

Historical Costs

Within the scope of the data-recording function of accounting, the term cost almost invariably means *historical cost,* or *actual cost.* This is defined by the Committee on Terminology of the American Institute of Certified Public Accountants as follows:

> *Cost* is the amount, measured in money, of cash expended or other property transferred, capital stock issued, services performed, or a liability incurred, in consideration of goods or services received or to be received.[1]

In other words, historical cost is the measurable monetary value of goods or services given up in exchange for other goods or services. The measurability of the cost in monetary terms is essential to the concept. One of the traditional requisites of the recording function in accounting has been the existence of objective, verifiable evidence in support of each transaction to be recorded. As accounting deals with business information in terms of money, this objective evidence must not only demon-

[1] Committee on Terminology, American Institute of Certified Public Accountants, *Accounting Terminology Bulletin No. 4: Cost, Expense, and Loss* (New York, 1957), p. 1.

strate the reality of the transaction but also provide for its accurate measurement in monetary terms. The cost data reported in conventional financial statements are almost exclusively historical costs. The accurate measurement of the costs incurred is not the only problem concerning them, however. There is also the very important question of in which financial statement, the balance sheet or the income statement, they are to be reported.

Expired and Unexpired Costs. All historical costs may be classified as either unexpired or expired. An *unexpired cost* is one which has the capacity of contributing to the production of revenue in the future. It is the measured monetary value of the expenditure for goods or services which can be of use in the future revenue-producing activities of the firm. Thus, an unexpired cost is an asset and is reported on the balance sheet as of the end of an accounting period. The cost of salable merchandise on hand affords a good example of an unexpired cost. Such cost can contribute to the production of revenue in the future because the merchandise acquired at that cost can subsequently be sold. An *expired cost* is one which cannot contribute to the production of future revenues. Such revenue-producing capacity as this cost had has either already been consumed in the production of revenue or has been lost without benefit to the firm. The first type of expired cost, that which has been consumed in the production of revenue, is called an *expense.* An example is the cost of merchandise which has been sold. The second type, which has expired with no benefit to the enterprise, is generally described as a *loss.* An illustration of a loss is the cost of uninsured merchandise destroyed by fire. Both expenses and losses are conventionally reported on the income statement.

Many of the most complex and controversial accounting problems relate to the separation of expired and unexpired costs in preparing financial reports. Alternative accounting procedures may resolve these problems differently. The measurement of cost expiration depends not only upon the occurrence of transactions but also upon the particular accounting theories and practices employed by a firm. In exactly the same circumstances, different procedures for handling a particular type of cost may result in materially different figures for expired and unexpired costs. The professional accountant must become very familiar with the various alternative procedures and, more importantly, must learn to evaluate them critically in light of specific facts and conditions. While the manager need not have as complete a technical understanding of alternative accounting techniques, he must have a basic knowledge of them in order for him to appreciate the significance and limitations of the accounting data with which he must work and upon which, in part, he must base his decisions. Some of these alternative techniques will be considered, as appropriate, in subsequent chapters.

Future Costs

If the preoccupation of financial accounting is with historical costs, that of management accounting is more likely to be with future costs. *Future costs* may be defined as those costs which are reasonably expected to be incurred in some future period or periods. Because these costs are expectations rather than accomplished facts, their actual incurrence is a forecast and their measurement, an estimate. Management is vitally concerned with future costs for the simple reason that they are the only costs over which managers can exercise any control. Historical costs can merely be observed and evaluated in retrospect. If they are regarded as excessive, management can ask only, "What went wrong?" Future costs, on the other hand, can be planned for—and planned to be avoided. If future costs are considered too high, management can ask the very important question, "What can be done about this?" If necessary, resources can be planned to meet the high costs; if feasible, plans can be made to reduce them. Despite the estimation inherent in the concept of future costs, the measurement of such costs is no less important than the measurement of historical costs. If anything, it is more important to management. The measurement of historical costs is basically a record-keeping activity, an essentially passive function insofar as management is concerned. The measurement of future costs, however, is critically associated with the active management functions of planning and control.

When a future cost is not merely expected but is incorporated formally into the overall operating plans for a specific period in the future, it is referred to as a *budgeted cost.* A detailed examination of budgeting will be deferred until later chapters. For the present it is sufficient to observe that budgets are formal, comprehensive, and coordinated plans relative to operations in specific future periods. Budgeted costs are important elements in these overall plans.

DIRECT AND INDIRECT COSTS

All costs incurred are, of course, identified with the particular business enterprise. But this broad identification of costs with the firm is typically insufficient for purposes of determining periodic income and measuring asset values and for purposes of managerial analyses. For these purposes, it is necessary to associate costs with subcomponents or segments of the firm. These segments are referred to, in this context, as *costing units.* A costing unit is simply anything within a business enterprise to which it is both significant and practical to assign costs. Both criteria of significance and practicality are important here. For example, it might prove practical to associate certain costs with rainy days; but such association may be of no significance whatever to anyone concerned with the enterprise. Conversely, it might appear significant to identify costs with moments of imaginative thinking by executives; but no practical means of doing so may be available. Some fairly common illustrations of costing units are the following:

1. An individual unit of product: for example, a 1,000 gallon batch of "Silverthorn Grey" latex interior wall paint.
2. A product line: for example, commercial paints.
3. A division of a corporation: for example, the Pontiac Division of General Motors Corporation.
4. A department within a plant: for example, the spray-paint shop of a major appliance manufacturer.
5. A sales territory: for example, the Washington-Oregon-Northern California territory.
6. A particular channel, or method of distribution: for example, sales to wholesalers.

There are three possibilities with respect to the relationship between a particular cost and a given costing unit. Certain costs can be traced logically and practically in their entirety to a costing unit; there is a directly determinable relationship. Such costs are called *direct costs.* An example of a direct cost would be the monthly salary of a divisional manager, where the division is the costing unit under consideration. Other costs can be identified partially with a costing unit, but not entirely. That is, they relate to the unit under study; but they also relate to other costing units. The amount of the cost which is properly identifiable with one unit is not readily determinable. Such costs are termed *indirect costs.* An example would be the monthly salary of a corporation's president, where one of several divisions is the relevant costing unit. The president's services benefit each division, but the proportion of his salary assignable to one particular division cannot be directly determined. Indirect costs are frequently called *common costs,* that is, costs which are common to, or shared by, two or more costing units. Finally, there are some costs which bear no identifiable relationship to a particular costing unit. Continuing the example of a corporate division, the salary of the manager of division B is neither a direct nor an indirect cost of division A. Thus, the direct and indirect costs of a particular costing unit do not necessarily include all of the costs incurred by the firm. Some costs may be totally unrelated to the costing unit in question.

From the foregoing discussion, it should be clear that whether a specific cost is direct or indirect depends upon the costing unit under consideration. Certain costs may be direct with respect to one costing unit and indirect with respect to another. Hence, the concepts of direct and indirect costs are meaningless without identification, at least implicitly, of the relevant costing unit. In financial accounting, the terms direct and indirect costs are sometimes used in such a way that the only costing unit suggested as being associated with them is the unit of product. To be sure, this is a very important costing unit in a business and one for which direct and indirect costs are typically ascertained. However, these concepts are also very useful with respect to many other costing units and will be used in their broader contexts throughout this volume. Thus, whenever direct and indirect costs are discussed, the relevant costing unit will be indicated.

COST ELEMENTS IN A MANUFACTURING ENTERPRISE

Manufacturing Costs

At one time, the study of cost accounting was concerned almost exclusively with the subject of manufacturing costs. While recent years have seen much greater attention devoted to nonmanufacturing costs, the costs of manufacturing remain the principal concern of both students and practicing cost accountants. There are two chief reasons for this emphasis on manufacturing costs. The first is the traditional practice of including only the costs incurred to manufacture goods in the valuation of the inventories thereof. The importance of accurate inventory valuation in financial accounting necessitates considerable detail in the development and classification of factory costs. The second reason is the fact that the processes of manufacture have become much more standardized and routinized than those of distribution, research, and administration. The greater uniformity of operations permits a higher degree of planning and control and, consequently, requires more detailed cost information. The manufacture of a large and diverse line of products, typical of so many modern corporations, involves the use of a wide variety of goods and services. For accounting purposes, however, each of these items is classified as one of three manufacturing cost elements, *materials, labor,* or *overhead.*

Materials. Materials include a wide range of physical commodities that go into the making of a product. These are commonly described as raw materials. This term is by no means limited to basic natural resources. The raw material of one firm may be the finished product of another. For example, automobile tires are a finished product of a rubber company but a raw material of an automobile manufacturer.

For purposes of the accounting record-keeping function, the most important classification of materials cost is the distinction between direct and indirect materials, the product being the relevant costing unit. *Direct materials* are those which can be identified, logically and practically, with the product. Only direct materials are included in the classification of "materials." *Indirect materials,* those which cannot be traced directly to the product, are included in the classification of "overhead."

The line between direct and indirect materials is not always an easy one to draw. To begin with, different cost accounting systems may result in different treatments of the same item. (Cost accounting systems will be discussed in Chapter 4.) Further, the direct identification of some materials with the product may be practical only at a prohibitively high cost. Hence, the distinction is commonly drawn on pragmatic as well as theoretic grounds. For example, in the manufacture of wooden chairs, the cost of the wood may be the only recognized direct material. Such materials as glue and screws, while logically traceable to the finished chair, may be treated as indirect simply because the expense of direct identification with the product would exceed the value to the firm of the added informational precision. This illustration points out a cardinal rule of accounting systems design. The benefit derived from an accounting technique must always at least equal the expense of that technique. A procedure that saves costs of $10,000 annually but itself costs $12,000 annually is clearly not justifiable on financial grounds.

Labor. Like materials, the cost element "labor" includes only *direct labor,* that which can be identified directly with the product. *Indirect labor* is treated as a part of overhead. A simple illustration may assist in explaining the distinction here. A punch-press operator works directly on the product. He spends, on the average, a certain amount of time on each piece. His efforts can be logically traced to and reasonably measured in terms of the product. Hence, his wages are accounted for as direct labor. Other workers in the same plant, such as foremen, janitors, and watchmen, do not work directly with the product. While their services are essential to production, there is no reasonable basis for measuring their efforts in terms of units of product. Hence, their wages and salaries are regarded as indirect labor cost, a part of overhead. In practice, there is considerable diversity with respect to the definition of direct labor. In some firms, such labor-related costs as fringe benefits are treated as direct labor; in others, these costs are regarded as indirect. Supplementary unemployment benefit payments and guaranteed annual wage contracts present further complications in the classification of labor costs. All of these complications, however, are problems of practical application, not of basic concepts. Thus, the simplified presentation of labor cost accounting employed in this text will in no way limit the student's knowledge of the fundamental concepts involved.

Overhead. For practical purposes, the cost classification of *overhead* may be defined simply as including all manufacturing costs other than direct materials and direct labor. Alternatively, overhead may be defined as indirect manufacturing costs. Among the items commonly included in this classification are the following: indirect materials, factory supplies, indirect labor, heat and power, depreciation on factory equipment, insurance on factory equipment, and machinery repairs and maintenance.

Perhaps the most perplexing aspect of overhead is the great diversity of terms which have been used to describe the concept. *Manufacturing expense, factory expense, burden, factory burden, loading, indirect expense, overhead, manufacturing overhead,* and other terms have all been used to denote exactly the same concept. The term overhead will be used consistently in this book. The student should, however, be aware of some of the different terms used and should recognize them when they are encountered. In view of the colloquial use of the term overhead to indicate operating costs in all types of enterprises, manufacturing and nonmanufacturing, profit and nonprofit, it might be considered preferable to prefix the word "overhead" with the qualifying adjective "manufacturing" to denote the indirect manufacturing costs discussed here. However, in cost accounting the term overhead, without a modifier, has a generally recognized technical meaning—indirect manufacturing costs—and will be used here in this way.

For certain purposes, it is useful to group materials and labor costs together and to identify this combination by a single term, *prime costs.* Similarly, labor and overhead costs together are commonly referred to as *conversion costs.* This latter term stems from the fact that labor and overhead costs are incurred in the process of converting raw materials into finished products.

Nonmanufacturing Costs

Despite their traditional preoccupation with manufacturing costs, cost accountants have come to devote more attention and effort to the nonmanufacturing costs incurred by business firms. One of the chief reasons for this change has been the recognition of the fact that nonmanufacturing costs account for the largest portion of every dollar spent by consumers. In other words, the sheer magnitude of the items involved makes it impossible to treat them too casually. As more and more dollars are channeled into these nonmanufacturing activities, business managers are becoming increasingly aware of the need for efficient planning and control of such costs and, hence, for more complete and analytical data concerning them.

The subclassifications of nonmanufacturing costs are not as well defined as those of manufacturing costs. For purposes of discussion in this text, four such classifications are here proposed.

1. *Distribution costs* are those incurred in the performance of a wide range of activities generally categorized as marketing. These include selling, shipping, advertising, sales salaries, salesmen's travel expenses, etc.

2. *Administration costs* include both executive and clerical costs which do not fit logically into some other classification (such as manufacturing or distribution). Examples are the salaries of top managers (president, executive vice-president), directors' fees, general accounting costs, public relations' costs, etc.

3. *Research and development costs* have frequently been included in administrative costs for want of a better classification. Recent years have witnessed a marked rise in overall business spending for these activities, however; and it is desirable to give them more individual attention. Especially in instances where efforts are directed toward basic research rather than simply toward product development, these costs seem to be sufficiently unique and significant to deserve separate classification.

4. *Financial costs* also have often been treated as part of administrative costs. These consist primarily of interest costs of one type or another. Also included in this classification are such costs as bank service charges, purchase discounts not taken, and stock and bond issue costs. Again, separate identification and treatment appear desirable.

The main focus of attention in this volume will be on manufacturing costs. However, special consideration will be given to nonmanufacturing items throughout the text as appropriate and especially in Chapter 12. Many of the concepts and techniques widely applied to manufacturing costs are applicable also to nonmanufacturing costs with more or less modification.

THE BEHAVIOR OF COSTS WITH CHANGES IN VOLUME

One of the most commonly employed and useful of cost classifications is that on the basis of cost behavior with respect to changes in the volume of business activity. As volume changes, costs may either change with it or remain constant. Further, those costs which do change with volume may do so in different ways. Thus, classification of costs according to their behavior patterns with respect to changes in volume greatly facilitates the managerial functions of planning, controlling, and decision making. In this connection, costs are classified as *variable, fixed,* or *semivariable.*

Strict Definitions of Cost-Volume Relationships

In accounting literature, the three cost classifications relative to volume changes are typically defined as follows:

1. *Variable costs* are those costs which vary, or change, in total in direct proportion to changes in volume. Successive increases in units of volume result in parallel and proportionate increases in variable costs. Similarly, decreases in volume produce proportionate cost decreases. As an illustration, observe the following relationship between the cost of raw materials and the units of a particular product produced:

Units of Product	*Raw Materials Cost*
1	$ 2.50
10	25.00
100	250.00
500	1,250.00
842	2,105.00
2,400	6,000.00

Each change of one unit of product causes a change of $2.50 of materials cost. Materials cost in the illustration—and variable costs in general—change in direct proportion to volume. Expressed mathematically, there is a linear relationship between volume and cost. As is apparent in the foregoing example, the direct proportional relationship between total materials cost and volume means that each additional unit of product has exactly the same cost per unit as all other units. Thus, *variable costs vary in total in direct proportion to volume and, consequently, are constant per unit of volume.*

2. *Fixed costs* remain constant in total regardless of changes in volume. They are unaffected by volume changes. For example, the monthly rent on a computer installation may be $24,000 regardless of how many hours the equipment is used per month. Volume of operation may vary from no use at all to maximum monthly volume without altering the rental cost by one cent. Because it is fixed in total for the rental period, the rental cost of the equipment per hour of use decreases as the number of operating hours increases. This is apparent in the following comparison of several alternative monthly volumes of computer operation:

Total Monthly Rental	*Hours Operated per Month*	*Average Hourly Cost*
$24,000	1,000	$24.00
24,000	6,000	4.00
24,000	8,000	3.00
24,000	12,000	2.00

There is an inverse relationship between volume and fixed cost per unit of volume. Hence, *fixed costs are constant in total as volume changes but vary per unit of volume inversely with volume.*

3. *Semivariable costs* are simply all costs which are neither perfectly variable nor absolutely fixed with respect to volume changes. Semivariable costs change in the same direction as volume but not in direct proportion thereto. They may remain constant over relatively small ranges of volume but increase as volume increases beyond these limited ranges. Hence, they might just as well be called semifixed costs. The term semivariable is more widely used, however, and will be employed consistently here.

These three cost concepts are depicted graphically in Figure 2–1. Volume is measured on the x (horizontal) axis of the chart and dollars of cost, on the y (vertical) axis. Variable costs increase with volume in a steady, linear pattern. Fixed costs are totally unaffected by volume changes; they are the same at maximum volume as at none at all. (This, of course, assumes that the firm will continue to exist while not producing. All costs may be eliminated by going out of business.) Semivariable costs increase with volume but not in the same regular manner as the variable costs. The stair step progression of these costs in Figure 2–1 is not necessarily typical. The various steps might be of less regular length and/or height, or the overall pattern of a particular semivariable cost might be better depicted by a nonlinear curve.

Relevant Concepts of Volume. In the foregoing discussion of cost-volume relationships, the term volume has been used in a general sense to denote business activity of some kind. It is readily apparent that the same concept of volume is not applicable to every cost item. Thus, raw materials cost was viewed as variable with respect to the volume of goods produced. Computer equipment rental was regarded as fixed with respect to the volume of use of the equipment. This rental charge would also be fixed with respect to the volume of goods produced, but such relationship might not be considered relevant. Materials cost could

FIGURE 2–1

COST-VOLUME RELATIONSHIPS: PERFECT

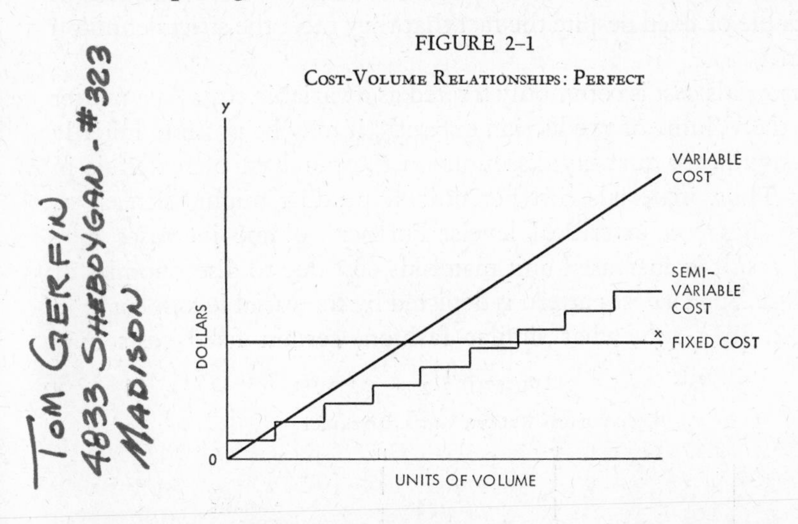

hardly be regarded as either fixed or variable with respect to computer hours. There simply is no significant relationship between the two quantities. Costs can be identified as variable, semivariable, or fixed only with reference to the volume of some activity to which those costs are pertinent. Manufacturing costs are typically evaluated in this connection in the light of the volume of goods produced. Selling costs are appraised with reference to the volume of goods sold. Administrative costs are usually viewed in relation to some relevant measure of work, such as the number of lines in letters typed or the number of payroll checks prepared. Throughout this text, the terms variable or fixed, when applied to manufacturing costs, will have reference to cost behavior with respect to changes in the volume of units of product manufactured, unless otherwise indicated.

Cost-Volume Relationships in Practice

The definitions of variable and fixed costs in the previous section are very rigid. Any cost that is neither perfectly variable nor absolutely fixed would be classified as semivariable. As will be evident in subsequent discussions, these rigid definitions are necessary for the analytical employment of the concepts. However, in practice, it is likely that there are comparatively few costs which would be perfectly variable or absolutely fixed over *all* ranges of volume. Hence, the preponderance of costs in real business firms might well fall into the semivariable class. Because of the indefinite nature of this category, however, such classification of most business costs would greatly impair the analytical usefulness of cost-volume relations. Hence, in practice, many costs are classified as either variable or fixed despite the fact that they meet the strict definition of neither.

Raw materials cost is commonly treated as a variable cost. As a matter of fact, as the volume of production expands, it may be possible initially to obtain significant quantity discounts on the purchase of materials in large lots. Thus, materials cost per unit of product might decrease as volume reaches certain critical levels. Further volume increases may ultimately result in increased unit materials cost due to diseconomies of excessive size. Such a cost pattern is depicted by the variable cost curve in Figure 2–2. In a somewhat similar fashion, certain fixed costs may

FIGURE 2–2

COST-VOLUME RELATIONSHIPS: IMPERFECT

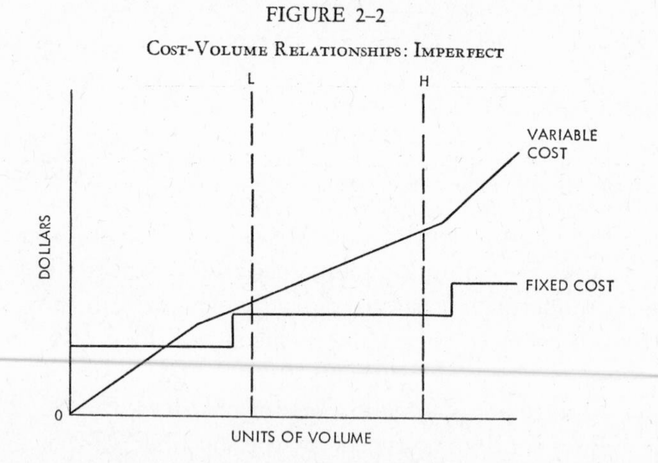

remain constant in total over significant ranges of volume. Again, however, there may be critical points beyond which additional costs may have to be incurred. This may be illustrated by the cost of supervision in a factory. There are critical points of operating volume at which it becomes necessary to employ additional supervisors to assure adequate control over expanding production. Such cost behavior is shown by the fixed cost curve in Figure 2–2.

Lest it appear that the variable and fixed cost classifications have no practical validity, it must be pointed out that, while a particular cost may not fit the strict definition of either classification, it may be both useful and operationally valid to treat it as variable or fixed, whichever is more nearly the case, for purposes of managerial analyses. First of all, identification of costs as either variable or fixed is useful. It permits analyses which otherwise would not be feasible. Second, such identification may be valid for analytical purposes within limited ranges of volume. Notice that the cost curves in Figure 2–2, while not conforming to the strict definitions of "variable" and "fixed" over the entire range of volume, do so conform over significant ranges. It is quite possible that most cost items will prove to be very nearly perfectly variable or absolutely fixed over the relevant range of volume, that within which the firm is most likely to operate. Thus, in Figure 2–2, if the firm could reasonably expect that its volume of production would be no less than that indicated by the point L and no greater than that indicated by the point H, it is apparent that the costs whose behavior is charted would conform to the strict definitions of "variable" and "fixed" over the relevant range of activity. To be sure, Figure 2–2 is so constructed as to make this so; it could well be that the breaks in either or both cost curves would occur within the relevant range of output. Nevertheless, this chart serves to illustrate an important point, namely, that cost behavior in the extreme ranges of activity may not be relevant for purposes of management analysis. Within the bounds of the minimum and maximum practical levels of output, many more cost items may prove to be either variable or fixed than would be so over the full range of technically possible (but practically improbable) operations.

The semivariable cost classification presents some peculiar problems. Certain costs fail to meet the criteria of either variable or fixed costs over any significant range of activity. Treating them as semivariable, however, does not admit of any definite analysis of their behavior in response to volume changes. But it is this very analysis that makes cost classifications with respect to volume changes so important to management. Thus, as a practical matter, many costs which actually appear to be genuinely semivariable are treated as though they were either variable or fixed, whichever they more nearly approximate, or as though they were made up of separable variable and fixed components. In other words, to meet the needs of management in analyzing cost behavior, the semivariable cost classification is not uncommonly completely eliminated. The procedures to accomplish this end will be discussed in Chapter 9, along with some consideration of the limitations which such practice places upon subsequent analyses.

COST CONCEPTS FOR DECISION MAKING

Responsibility Costing

Historically, accounting was concerned largely with the reporting of economic facts relevant to an entire enterprise. Recent years have seen increased interest in the subdivision of the enterprise along responsibility lines for purposes of reporting to management. More and more management reports are emphasizing the association of economic facts with the persons responsible therefor. This involves both the reporting of information to the executive responsible for the particular area of a business and also the reporting to higher management levels the results of operations in such a manner as to identify them with the responsible subordinates. This development has commonly been referred to as *responsibility accounting.* In cost accounting, it has resulted in the classification of costs along responsibility lines. Cost data are accumulated and reported according to areas of responsibility within a firm. These areas are commonly referred to as *responsibility centers.* Thus, reports indicate not only what costs have been incurred but also who is responsible for them. This specific subdevelopment of responsibility accounting may be termed *responsibility costing* and is one of the most important cost classification schemes as far as business management is concerned. Responsibility costing facilitates greatly the practical implementation of management's cost control objective. It permits the translation of the basic objective into a program of action centered around people, and, after all, only people can make cost control a reality.

Controllable Costs. The concept of responsibility costing leads directly to the classification of costs as controllable or uncontrollable. Obviously, the controllability of a cost depends upon the level of responsibility under consideration. A *controllable cost* may be defined as one which is reasonably subject to regulation by the executive with whose responsibility that cost is being identified. Thus, a cost which is uncontrollable at one level of responsibility may be regarded as controllable at some other, usually higher, level. For example, the cost of factory maintenance may be uncontrollable at the level of the department supervisor, even though it may appear reasonable to trace some portion of that cost to the individual departments. At the level of the factory manager, on the other hand, maintenance costs may be viewed as controllable, at least in part.

The controllability of certain costs may be shared by two or more executives. Thus, raw materials cost is generally considered to be a controllable cost. However, there are two distinct factors involved in materials cost. One is the price paid for the materials and the other is the usage of those materials. The responsibilities for these two factors may not be coincidental. The responsibility for prices may rest with the purchasing agent, while that for usage, with the respective production department supervisors.

It is important that cost controllability be understood in the proper sense. It does not involve eliminating costs, but rather keeping costs as close as possible to some desirable and reasonably attainable levels, or standards. Further, all deviations of actual costs from such standards must not be presumed to be controllable simply because the particular cost items in question are normally regarded as controllable. For example, raw materials cost in one period may be higher than normal because of unusually high prices. If these high prices were paid because materials were obtained from a distant supplier at higher than normal freight charges when local sources of supply were available, the deviation may be treated as positively controllable at the responsibility level of the purchasing agent. However, if the high prices can be traced to a market shortage due to the sudden discontinuance of certain foreign sources of supply, the deviation can hardly be considered controllable at any responsibility level within the firm. In summary then, it may be said that controllable costs are those which may be controlled by executives at a given responsibility level; but specific deviations from standards must be analyzed individually before they can be adjudged controllable or uncontrollable.

Costs Relevant to Alternative Choices

Business managers are frequently faced with decisions among two or more alternatives. These decisions may be fairly complex in terms of numbers of possible choices—for example, choosing among alternatives A, B, C, D, and E, all of which are mutually exclusive. Other decisions may involve simply the alternatives of accepting or rejecting a single proposal. Regardless of the degree of complexity of a particular decision, management must obtain all of the information relevant to the alternatives. This information will include, very importantly, cost data. It will also include many other facts which cannot be expressed quantitatively, as are cost data. For example, the impact of a decision upon employee relations or upon the corporate image is a crucial factor but is not normally subject to quantitative measurement. Thus, it must be kept in mind that, while cost data are important to a business decision, they are still only part of the basis for the final decision; they do not make the decision by themselves.

As is already apparent from the limited discussion in this chapter, there is a great variety of cost data available within a business firm. Not all of these data are likely to be relevant to the alternatives in a specific decision and, hence, not all should be reported to management for decision-making purposes. A surfeit of irrelevant information can be just as useless and misleading as a lack of significant facts. Accountants, therefore, must be able to develop those cost data which are relevant to the particular decision at hand and to report them to management in a manner which will facilitate analysis of the alternatives and formulation of a decision.

Differential and Sunk Costs. A *differential cost* may be defined as one which will be affected by a decision among alternatives. In other words, such a cost will be different depending upon which of the alternatives is chosen. Hence, it is relevant to management in the analysis for decision making. A *sunk cost* is one which will be unaffected by a particular decision. It will be the same regardless of which alternative is selected. Thus, it need not be considered by management in evaluating the alternatives, as it is common to all of them. To illustrate these concepts, consider a decision between purchasing or renting an electronic computer and auxiliary equipment (assuming that the decision to install a computer has already been finalized). The rental contract would include installation, servicing, and maintenance by the manufacturer. The purchase price would include only the equipment, delivered to the buyer's plant. For the sake of simplicity, assume that all costs associated with this equipment can be classified as one of the following:

1. Acquisition cost.
2. Service and maintenance costs.
3. Operating costs (labor, power, etc.).
4. Space occupancy costs (depreciation, taxes, insurance, etc., on the portion of the plant in which the computer will be housed).

From the information given concerning the rental and purchase contracts, it is apparent that acquisition costs will differ as between the alternatives. Under the rental contract, the only acquisition cost will be the sum of the periodic rent payments. Under the purchase agreement, the acquisition costs will include the invoice price of the equipment plus the costs of installation and "de-bugging." Service and maintenance costs will exist, as such, only if the equipment is purchased; the rent would include these items. The operating costs and space occupancy costs will be the same regardless of which alternative is selected. Therefore, the acquisition and the service and maintenance costs are differential costs, while operating and space occupancy costs are sunk costs. The former are relevant to the rent or buy decision; the latter are not.

The reader should be careful to avoid the mistake sometimes made of thinking of differential costs as synonymous with variable costs and sunk costs as synonymous with fixed costs. In the illustration of the computer installation, observe that monthly rental, a typical fixed cost, is a differential cost in the decision-making analysis. The operating costs of labor and power, which would, at least in part, be variable with the volume of computer hours, are sunk costs with respect to this decision. Incidentally, the term sunk cost is somewhat unfortunate in view of the common unpleasant connotations of the word "sunk," especially in maritime activities. Nevertheless, the term is quite widely used in the context explained above; and the student should become familiar with it. But he must avoid thinking of sunk costs as costs which are unrecoverable or as mistakes of the past.

Incremental Cost. The term incremental cost is often used as a synonym for differential cost. There is no serious objection to such usage, so long as the meanings of the terms employed are clear in the context of the particular discussion. However, the author believes that a useful distinction can be made between the two terms. In this text, therefore, *incremental cost* will be used to mean the excess of the differential cost of one alternative over the differential cost of the least costly alternative. Thus, incremental cost may be described as *net* differential cost. The distinction may be made clear by a simple illustration. A factory now uses method A to move goods from one department to another. Method B has been proposed as being more efficient technically and safer for personnel. Analysis reveals that the differential costs of method A total $3,500 per month; those of method B amount to $3,800 per month. The incremental cost of method B is $300; that of method A is —$300. Alternatively, one could say that the incremental cost *saving* of method A is $300. Thus, differential costs are all costs which would be affected by a particular decision. The incremental cost of one alternative is the excess of that alternative's differential costs over those of the least costly alternative. As can be seen in the foregoing illustration, incremental cost may be negative as well as positive, though it is more commonly expressed as a positive quantity.

Marginal Cost. Some writers have suggested that the term marginal cost may be used as a synonym for incremental cost in analyses for decision making. While the literal meaning of the term marginal would permit this usage, "marginal cost" has come to have so specific a meaning in short-run economic analysis—the cost incurred in the production of one additional unit of output—that the author feels its use in accounting is more likely to confuse than to facilitate communication. Hence, "marginal cost" will not be used at all in this book in reference to accounting cost concepts.

Avoidable Cost. An *avoidable cost* is simply one particular type of differential cost. It is a cost which would be obviated entirely as a result of a decision to eliminate some segment of a business enterprise. For example, the decision to discontinue the sale of a manufactured product to wholesalers would permit the elimination of distribution costs exclusively related to wholesale sales—advertising in wholesaling periodicals, sales calls on wholesalers, etc. These would be avoidable costs with respect to such a decision. However, other distribution costs—the sales manager's salary, institutional advertising, etc.—would be unaffected by the discontinuance of this one channel of distribution. These would be *unavoidable costs,* particular types of sunk costs.

Out-of-Pocket Cost. Any cost which will require the expenditure of cash as a consequence of a management decision may be referred to as an *out-of-pocket cost.* For example, the decision to exploit a mineral deposit presently owned by the company will result in certain costs such as wages and supplies which will require cash outlays. The same decision also results in the incurrence of the cost item "depletion," the cost of the mineral resources exhausted as a result of mining operations. This cost, however, does not involve current cash expenditures. The cash payment (or at least the commitment to make a cash payment) for the mineral deposit was made earlier, at the time of acquisition of the property. Once the property has been obtained, such costs as depletion and depreciation are not out-of-pocket costs. Prior to purchase, however, the cost of the property does constitute an out-of-pocket cost of the decision to purchase. This particular cost concept is especially useful in analyses of future cash flows related to proposed investments.

MISCELLANEOUS COST CONCEPTS

Replacement Cost

The sustained and substantial price inflation in the United States since 1939 has given rise to considerable dissatisfaction with the traditional use of historical cost in financial reports. Many have argued that the actual cost of an asset, in terms of dollars expended at the time of its acquisition, is not significant at some later date when the purchasing power of the dollar has changed materially. The merit of this argument is evidenced by the widespread and still growing concern among accountants and businessmen generally with the problem of appropriate recognition of price-level changes in accounting. One of the most frequently proposed solutions to this problem is the use of replacement cost instead of historical cost in financial reports. Unfortunately, such suggestions have largely failed to produce changes in business practice, partly because of a lack of general agreement as to the measurement of replacement cost.

Replacement cost is the current market value of a specific asset, that is, what that asset would cost if it were to be acquired in its present condition in a free market transaction. It is the market value of the asset in its present condition, not the cost of the same asset when new or of some improved substitute asset. The fact that no market presently exists for a particular asset may make any measurement of replacement cost extremely difficult, but it does not alter the basic concept involved. The most familiar use of replacement cost in accounting practice today is in connection with the popular valuation of inventories at cost or market, whichever is lower, "market" here defined as the current replacement cost of that inventory, whether replacement would be effected by purchase or by production.

Opportunity Cost

In economic analysis, the word cost most commonly means opportunity cost. The *opportunity cost* of an economic good or service is the maximum amount which that good or service could yield if applied to some other purpose. Hence, opportunity cost is frequently defined as the revenue foregone in the most advantageous alternative application as a result of employing capital in its present use. So long as transactions take place in a basically free market, it is reasonable to assume that the actual cost (in the accounting sense of the term) of an asset is equal to its opportunity cost at the moment of acquisition. However, as economic conditions change, the cost of that asset as reported on the balance sheet at some future date (i.e., actual cost minus accumulated depreciation to date) is not necessarily equal to the opportunity cost of retaining it. Rather, the current fair market value, or replacement cost, of the asset may be taken as its opportunity cost then.

Obviously, the concept of opportunity cost is extremely important and useful to management in making decisions among alternatives. As a practical matter, however, it is normally impossible to identify with certainty the most advantageous alternative use of capital and, hence, impossible to determine opportunity cost, as such, quantitatively. Thus, practical business analyses must rely on such concepts as replacement cost and incremental cost to indicate the most advantageous uses of capital.

Imputed costs are particular types of opportunity cost. They are costs not actually incurred in an exchange transaction but still relevant to a particular business operation. For example, the use of cash already held in the company bank account to increase inventory levels results in certain actual costs, measured in exchange transactions. The price of the goods, the freight charges on them, and the rental of additional warehouse space for them are examples. Since cash was not borrowed to finance the inventory build-up, no actual interest payments will be made. However, if the cash on hand had been invested in some other way, it could have resulted in the receipt of interest revenue. This interest foregone on an alternative investment is referred to as imputed interest and is one of the most familiar illustrations of an imputed cost. An imputed cost is a real cost, even though current accounting practice would not record it in the accounts; and management must not ignore it in making business decisions. Happily, there are quantitative techniques for analyzing investment decisions which "automatically" include imputed interest in the analysis without requiring special treatment of it. These techniques will be discussed at length in Chapters 15 and 16.

QUESTIONS FOR DISCUSSION

1. "Management is vitally concerned with future costs for the simple reason that they are the only costs over which managers can exercise any control. Hence, historical costs are of no interest to management except as bases for evaluating past operations." Do you agree or disagree with this statement? Explain your position.
2. Define the concepts of direct and indirect costs. Can all of the costs incurred by a business enterprise be classified as either direct or indirect?
3. "As regards manufacturing costs where the product is the relevant costing unit, all direct costs are variable and all indirect costs are fixed." Do you agree or disagree with this assertion? Why?
4. The Upsilon Corporation manufactures three products, Alpha, Beta, and Gamma, in its plant. Indicate whether you would expect each of the following cost items to be direct, indirect, or unrelated to product Beta, where Beta is the costing unit in question:
   a. Raw materials used to manufacture Beta.
   b. Depreciation on plant and equipment.
   c. Salary of plant manager.
   d. Companywide advertising.
   e. Wages of workers who package Beta.

f. Raw materials used to manufacture Gamma.
g. Federal income tax.

5. For each cost item listed below, state whether you would expect it to be (1) variable in relation to production volume, (2) variable in relation to sales volume, (3) semivariable in relation to production, (4) semivariable in relation to sales, or (5) fixed. Briefly explain your reasoning in each case.
   a. Factory supervision.
   b. Maintenance of office equipment.
   c. Wages of production machine operators.
   d. Bad debts.
   e. Depreciation on factory equipment.
   f. Manufacturer's federal excise tax on goods produced.
   g. Janitors' wages.
6. "Both variable and fixed costs may be either controllable or uncontrollable costs." Do you agree or disagree with this statement? Explain your position and use examples if you feel they will help support your answer.
7. What are the basic requisites of effective responsibility costing?
8. The following costs are expected to be incurred at the indicated monthly production volumes (in terms of units of product):

Monthly Volume	*Factory Wages*	*Equipment Maintenance*	*Factory Supplies*
1,000	$10,000	$2,000	$ 1,000
5,000	15,000	2,000	4,500
10,000	24,000	3,000	8,000
15,000	30,000	3,000	10,500
20,000	40,000	4,000	12,000
25,000	50,000	4,000	14,400
30,000	60,000	4,000	15,000
35,000	70,000	4,000	16,000
40,000	82,000	5,000	17,500

Barring some unusual occurrence, such as a strike, monthly production volume can be expected to fall somewhere between 20,000 and 30,000 units of product. As a practical matter, how would you recommend each of these three cost items be regarded—as variable, semivariable, or fixed? Give reasons for your answers.

9. A. B. Crow is considering trading his old car in on a new one. He bought the old car 18 months ago for $3,000. He still owes $900 on it; thus, his equity is $2,100. The new car he wants sells for $3,600, and he would be allowed $1,500 on the trade-in of his old car. He would finance the balance of the price in the same way that he financed the purchase of the old car, by borrowing from his bank at an interest rate of 8%. With respect to Mr. Crow's decision, which costs are differential and which are sunk? What would be the incremental cost (or cost saving) of the decision to buy the new car rather than to keep the old one?
10. Michael Wren has invented an automatic pancake turner. He plans to go into the business of making and selling this device, which he has patented. He estimates that each turner will cost $.75 for materials. He anticipates

no labor cost, for he plans to do all the work himself. To this end, he will quit his present job in which he earns $600 per month. He will rent Patrick McDonough's garage as his workshop at a monthly rental of $45. He has already purchased the tools needed for this work for $75. To buy the same tools today, Wren would have to pay $90.

In the foregoing paragraph, identify one or more examples of each of the following types of costs: (A single cost item may be identified as more than one type of cost.)

a. Historical cost.
b. Future cost.
c. Variable cost.
d. Fixed cost.
e. Out-of-pocket cost.
f. Differential cost.
g. Sunk cost.
h. Opportunity cost.
i. Replacement cost.
j. Unexpired cost.

11. "All out-of-pocket costs are avoidable costs." Discuss the validity of this statement. Is it completely true, true under certain circumstances only, or wholly false?

12. If all of a firm's costs are either perfectly variable or absolutely fixed and its selling price remains unchanged no matter how many units of product are sold, will the firm's profit before tax decrease as volume increases, increase at a slower rate than volume, increase in direct proportion to volume, or increase at a faster rate than volume? Explain your answer.

Chapter 3

THE COST ACCOUNTING CYCLE

THIS CHAPTER and the following one are concerned with the basic mechanics of recording and processing manufacturing cost data. These mechanics relate primarily to the financial accounting aspects of cost accounting—specifically, the valuation of inventories and the measurement of income in a manufacturing enterprise. At the same time, however, the manner of recording and classifying costs provides the key to effective cost control. Hence, cost accounting systems must be constructed with two important objectives in mind—accurate financial reports and effective cost control.

THE FLOW OF COSTS IN MANUFACTURING

At the moment of their incurrence, all costs may be regarded as essentially identical. They are all unexpired costs, incurred in the expectation that they will contribute to the production of revenue. What happens to costs after their incurrence depends upon their natures and also upon the particular accounting practices employed by the firm. With a very few exceptions (e.g., the cost of land), all costs ultimately expire, or become expenses. The exact manner of their expiration, however, is determined by a number of factors, some of which are considered in the paragraphs that follow.

Cost Expiration in General

Long-Lived Assets. Some costs are incurred in order to acquire assets which can be expected to contribute to the production of revenues over fairly long periods of time. The cost of a factory building, for example, will remain a positive factor in the generation of revenue so long as the building is used in the manufacture of a salable product. The objective of income measurement requires that an appropriate portion of the cost of that building be charged to, or matched with, each dollar of revenue stemming from the sale of goods produced within its walls. Thus, only a portion of the building's cost will be matched with revenue in any one accounting period (whether one year, one month, or any other unit of time). The amount of such cost matched with revenue during any one period is the amount of the cost that expires during the period, that is, the amount which ceases to be an asset and becomes an expense. The process of periodically charging part of the cost of a long-lived asset to revenue is called *amortization.* The amortization of the cost of physical plant and equipment—buildings, machinery, vehicles, furniture and fixtures, etc.—is called depreciation.

Current Operating Expenses. Certain other costs follow a path almost diametrically opposed to that taken by long-lived assets. Such costs as salesmen's commissions and delivery costs are normally assumed to have contributed to the creation of revenue at the moment of their incurrence. Hence, they are charged immediately to expense accounts without their ever being classified as assets. Many costs are typically accorded this same treatment, even though their direct relationship to current revenues is not as obvious as in the case of, say, salesmen's commissions. Thus, such cost items as advertising, executives' salaries, and product development are generally treated as expenses in the period in which they are incurred, even though a careful examination of their natures might suggest that they will enhance revenues in future periods as well as in the current one. Such treatment is a matter of practical convenience in most cases; in some instances, it is likely no more than a matter of habit. Whatever the reason, it is a fact that a great many costs are, as a matter of practice, expensed as soon as they are incurred.

Expiration of Manufacturing Costs

Cost Transformations. In manufacturing accounting, it is a generally accepted practice that the costs of manufacturing a product are treated as an asset—inventory—until the product is sold, at which time those costs are matched with the revenue from the sale in the process of measuring income. This means that certain costs, such as materials and plant property, which are initially recorded as separate assets, are transformed into a new type of asset before they ultimately become expenses. The process by which an asset cost is transferred to another asset category, the cost of manufactured goods, is referred to as *cost transformation.* This amounts to a temporary change of asset classification pending the sale of the product. For example, the amortization of the cost of long-lived manufacturing facilities involves an intermediate cost transformation prior to ultimate cost expiration when the manufactured product is sold.

The concept that the costs incurred in the manufacture of a product are combined in a new asset and expire only when that product is sold (or in some way damaged or otherwise rendered unsalable) is commonly stated as the principle that *costs attach.* Under this principle, elements of cost which could not be stored in an asset account in and of themselves—such as labor cost—may become parts of the asset representing the cost of the manufactured product. Thus, manufacturing inventory accounts contain elements of cost which are not inventoriable separately. Labor cannot be stored as a commodity awaiting employment (except, perhaps, if it is performed by a slave labor force), but the cost of labor already employed can be seen in the form of a manufactured product and be regarded as part of the total cost of that product.

Product and Period Costs. The foregoing paragraphs have explained how some costs in a manufacturing firm are charged to the cost of the product and can be regarded as part of the total cost of that product. Other costs are treated as expiring in the accounting period in which they are incurred. The former type of cost is called a *product cost;* the latter, a *period cost.* It has already been observed that current manufacturing costs are generally accepted as product costs. Nonmanufacturing costs, on the other hand, are treated as period costs. This distinction is generally accepted in current accounting practice, but it has not gone unchallenged. In recent years there has developed a significant movement away from this traditional approach to the product/period cost distinction and toward an approach which treats as product costs only those manufacturing costs that vary in proportion to the volume of goods produced. In this newer approach, fixed manufacturing costs, along with nonmanufacturing costs, are treated as period costs.

Absorption Costing. The traditional method of accounting for manufacturing costs has included all such costs, regardless of their behavior with respect to changes in volume, as costs of the product. This method is called *absorption costing,* or *full costing;* for the product "absorbs" the full amount of manufacturing costs. Fixed and variable factory costs are handled in exactly the same manner. The distinction between product and period costs is made only on the basis of the different functional areas of business activity, manufacturing costs being product costs and distribution, administrative, research, and financial costs being period costs. (Of course, certain nonmanufacturing costs, while not included as part of the cost of the product, may be deferred to future periods as assets rather than being treated as expenses of the current period. Costs of office furniture and of unexpired insurance on office buildings are examples.)

Variable Costing. In an increasing number of manufacturing enterprises, the traditional absorption costing technique is being replaced by the more recent innovation, *variable costing.* Under the variable costing method, only those manufacturing costs which vary with output are included in the cost of the product; fixed manufacturing costs are accounted for as period costs. Thus, this method distinguishes between product and period costs on the basis of cost-volume relationships as well as on the basis of the functional areas of business operations. Variable nonmanufacturing costs, it must be understood, are treated as period costs under variable costing, just as they are under absorption costing. In practice, direct materials and direct labor are almost always treated as variable costs. Hence, the actual distinction between absorption and variable costing lies in the accounting treatment of overhead and, specifically, fixed overhead. Variable overhead, like

FIGURE 3–1

Flow of Manufacturing Costs in Absorption Costing

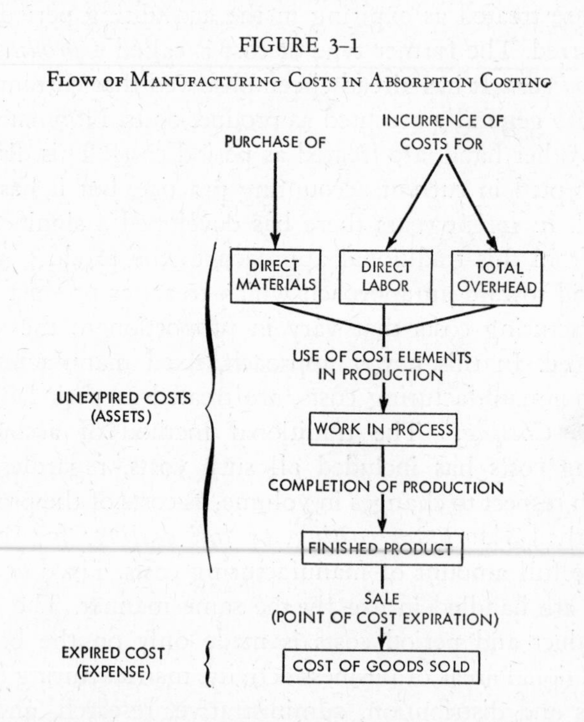

materials and labor, is treated as a product cost under both methods. Fixed overhead is treated as a product cost in absorption costing, but as a period cost in variable costing.

In this chapter, the methodologies of both absorption and variable costing will be illustrated. A critical appraisal and comparison of the two will be presented in the following chapter.

Manufacturing Inventory Accounts

In a merchandising enterprise, a single inventory account for all merchandise on hand is typical. This single account in the general ledger is supported by detailed records for stocks of each individual item in inventory. But only one general ledger, or control, account is needed for merchandise inventory from the time it is purchased until it is sold. In a manufacturing firm, however, a single inventory control account is not suitable. The function that distinguishes manufacturing from merchandising is the alteration of the form of materials purchased by the manufacturer and the conversion thereof into a new product. Thus, pig iron is converted to sheet steel; sheet steel, to automobile fenders; etc. At any one time, a manufacturing enterprise is likely to have on hand raw materials as yet unprocessed, goods in the process of manufacture but not yet completed, and finished products awaiting sale. Each of these stages of goods is normally accounted for in a separate inventory account. Raw

FIGURE 3–2

Flow of Manufacturing Costs in Variable Costing

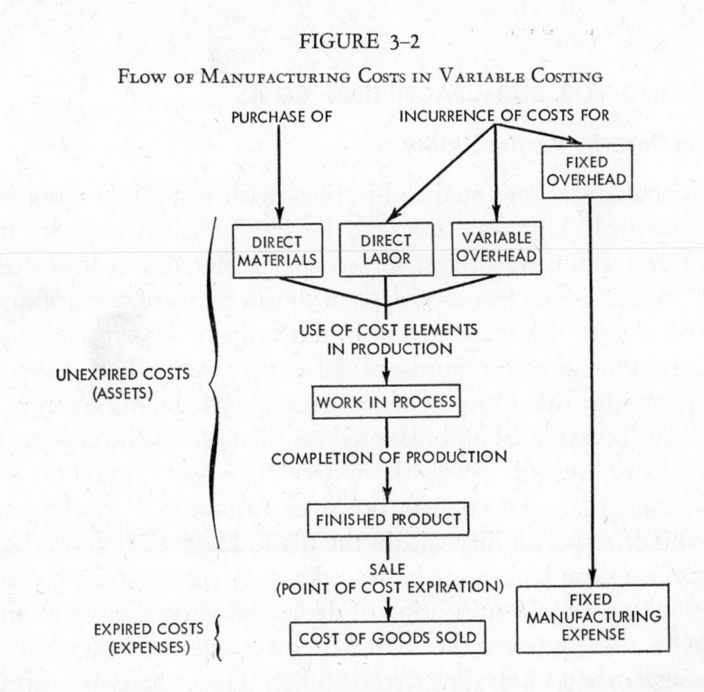

materials are reported in a Materials Inventory account; uncompleted production, in a Work in Process account; and completed production, in a Finished Product account. Each of these is an inventory account and an asset. Each is a part of the sequential flow of manufacturing costs. Materials, as such, appear when they are purchased from suppliers. They become part of Work in Process at the time they are issued from the storeroom to the factory for use. Work in Process becomes Finished Product when the process of manufacture is completed. Finally, Finished Product is transferred to the Cost of Goods Sold account at the point of sale of the items in inventory. Sale is the point at which manufacturing costs expire (excepting fixed manufacturing costs under the variable costing method); hence, Cost of Goods Sold is an expense account.

This flow of manufacturing costs in the absorption costing method is presented diagrammatically in Figure 3–1. Notice that labor and overhead are included in this diagram in a position parallel to that of materials. While these two cost elements cannot be stored in inventory themselves, as can materials, they are costs of the product and are stored in the inventories of Work in Process and Finished Product. All three manufacturing cost elements finally become expenses as part of Cost of Goods Sold. Figure 3–2 repeats this cost flow diagram for variable costing. The only difference between the two is in the handling of fixed overhead.

ACCOUNTING FOR MANUFACTURING COSTS

Recording Costs by Responsibility

One of management's main objectives with respect to costs is their effective control. This objective can be implemented only by tracing costs to responsible executives, for cost control requires knowledge of who is responsible for costs as well as of the amounts of costs. Thus, costs are identified with the smallest significant units of managerial responsibility; these units are commonly called *cost centers* when cost analysis and control are the objects of attention. All manufacturing costs incurred are accumulated and recorded on the basis of the cost centers to which they are logically traceable. Often these cost centers are departments within a plant. Some costs, however, cannot logically be traced to any subunit of responsibility within the plant. Depreciation on the plant building, for example, cannot be traced to any cost center smaller than the entire plant. Any identification of depreciation on the plant with one department therein must be based upon some arbitrary allocation scheme rather than upon direct traceability. Thus, there are commonly large cost centers which embrace two or more smaller ones. Normally, these larger cost centers correspond to higher levels of managerial responsibility.

The actual accounting processes for tracing costs to the pertinent cost centers may vary among firms. It is possible, for example, to have separate accounts for each cost element (i.e., materials, labor, and overhead) for each cost center. Alternatively, a single account may include all items of one cost element, subsidiary records and reports being employed to fix responsibility for costs by cost centers. In a large, decentralized firm, the former alternative would seem preferable. Whatever the methods used to accomplish it, the identification of costs with responsible executives and supervisors must be regarded as an imperative of good management accounting.

Accounting for Materials

Purchase. Accounting for materials begins when a need for a particular material is determined at some level of responsibility within the firm and a formal request is made that such material be purchased in the required amount. This formal request is commonly made on a standard form called a *purchase requisition.* This is an internal document, submitted by the department requesting the material to the purchasing department. A requisition may be initiated by one of the production departments which uses the item in question. More commonly, however, the requisition would be initiated by the materials storeroom when existing stocks of the material reach a pre-established minimum level which serves as a signal to re-order. No formal journal entry is prepared to record the issuance of a purchase requisition. However, the requisition sets into motion the activities which will ultimately result in the journalizing of a purchase.

If the purchase requisition is approved, the purchasing department will select the most advantageous supplier of the material needed and will issue a *purchase order* for the item. (It should be noted here that efficient purchasing normally involves issuance of purchase orders for several items at one time, where the orders for individual items are not large.) A purchase order is a document sent by the purchasing department to the supplier. It includes materials specifications, quantities ordered, and the date the items are needed. The supplier fills this order by shipping the materials requested and billing the purchaser for them by sending an invoice, which details the items purchased, the quantities shipped, and the prices. After the actual shipment has been compared with the invoice, called a *purchase invoice* in the hands of the purchaser, the invoice becomes the basis for the preparation of a journal entry to record the purchase, the invoice price (including freight charges, etc. where applicable) being the measured cost of the materials purchased. Such an entry follows:

Materials Inventory...........................	xxx	
Vouchers Payable......................		xxx

In this entry and in similar ones throughout this text, it is assumed that a voucher system is used to control cash disbursements and, hence, that all obligations incurred in the purchase of goods or services are credited to an account titled Vouchers Payable.

Usage. As materials are needed in the factory, the production departments issue *materials requisitions* (not to be confused with purchase requisitions) to the materials storeroom for the required quantities of the particular items. These materials requisitions, indicating the department requesting the items, are the bases for tracing materials costs to cost centers within the plant. The issuance of the materials to the factory by the storeroom signals a change in the inventory classification of those items. They now cease to be materials, as such, and become a part of the product in the process of manufacture. Accountingwise, this results in a cost transformation from Materials Inventory to Work in Process. The following entry is made:

Work in Process	xxx	
Materials Inventory		xxx

The foregoing entry assumes that the materials requisitioned are direct materials. This is not always the case. At the time of purchase, it is not always possible to distinguish between items that will be used as direct materials and those which will be used as indirect materials. And even if such distinction is possible, both direct and indirect materials may be included in the Materials Inventory account when purchased. When issued, however, indirect materials are not charged directly to the Work in Process account. To be sure, they will ultimately be charged to that account; but they are first accumulated along with other indirect manufacturing costs in an account for overhead costs in general. Thus, the requisition of indirect materials would be recorded as follows:

Overhead Control	xxx	
Materials Inventory		xxx

At this point, the Overhead Control account may be taken simply as a temporary account for the accumulation of all indirect factory costs.

Accounting for Labor

For purposes of discussion, problems of accounting for labor may be classified in two categories. *Labor cost accounting* is concerned with the accounts and amounts to be charged (debited) for labor costs. *Payroll accounting* is concerned with the accounts and amounts to be credited in the recording and paying of obligations to employees for labor services. Because of the traditional emphasis in cost accounting upon manufacturing costs, labor cost accounting is concerned chiefly with manufacturing, or factory labor. Payroll accounting, however, is just as concerned with administrative and sales employees as with factory workers.

In large firms, it is economically feasible to departmentalize many different activities and to accomplish considerable division of work. In such a firm, labor cost accounting may be handled by a factory accounting department and payroll accounting, by a payroll department. In such cases, some account common to both departments is needed so that the two separate accounting operations may be tied together and reconciled, to the extent that they both deal with the same basic data. This account may have different titles in different companies. In this text, it will be referred to as the Payroll Summary account. This is the account credited by the factory accounting department for the total of amounts debited to the various manufacturing cost accounts affected and the account debited by the payroll department for the total of credits representing obligations to employees and other parties entitled to some portion of the employees' earnings (e.g., the federal government). Obviously, except for lags in bookkeeping procedures in the two departments, the debits and credits to the Payroll Summary account for any period of time will be equal (assuming no errors are made).

Labor Cost Accounting. The proper charging of labor costs to manufacturing cost accounts requires that distinctions be made between direct and indirect labor costs and between labor costs incurred in different cost centers. The former distinction is largely a matter of definition; the latter, a matter of accurate record keeping. The maintenance of records which show the amounts of time worked by employees in various cost centers and the availability of hourly wage rate data permit the charging of factory labor costs by areas of responsibility. For the sake of simplicity, the discussions and illustrations in this chapter will assume that there is only one cost center—the entire factory—in the plant under study. This assumption will not alter the basic concepts involved or the mechanics of recording labor costs; it merely reduces the number of accounts to be handled.

As stated in Chapter 2, direct labor is that labor which can be traced logically and practically to the product. All other labor costs are regarded as indirect and are included in overhead. The wages of foremen, janitors, watchmen, factory clerks, and others whose work is not concerned directly with the product are usually treated as indirect costs. In addition, a number of payments made to direct laborers are commonly included in overhead rather than in direct labor. Wages paid to direct laborers while they are not actually performing productive work are usually accounted for as overhead. Examples of such wages are vacation pay, holiday pay, and idle-time pay for periods when workers are idled because of machinery breakdowns or production bottlenecks. The reason for treating as overhead such payments to workers whose labor is normally regarded as direct is that these payments cannot be traced directly to units of product. Vacation pay and idle-time pay could hardly be charged directly to particular units of product, as no units are produced during the periods for which those costs are incurred. Premiums paid to direct laborers for overtime and double-time work and for night-shift work are normally included in overhead. If such premiums were charged directly to the units produced during overtime or night shifts, those units would have higher costs than those produced during the regular forty-hour week. Yet, the overtime and night-shift work is usually necessitated by a generally high level of production, not by specific units or jobs. Hence, it would not be meaningful to report units manufactured during overtime or night hours as more costly than their counterparts produced during the regular eight-hour day. Rather, overtime and night-shift premiums should be viewed as costs incurred because total production exceeds the capacity of the plant during a straight forty-hour week. As such, these costs are applicable to all units produced but directly traceable to none.

The following journal entry illustrates the distribution of factory labor costs to the appropriate manufacturing cost accounts:

Work in Process	xxx	
Overhead Control	xxx	
Payroll Summary		xxx

The debit to Work in Process is to charge the direct labor cost to the product. Overhead Control is debited for indirect labor costs, overtime premiums, vacation pay, etc. The detail supporting this entry would be accumulated and classified on a labor cost distribution sheet.

Labor-Related Costs. In addition to wage and salary payments made to workers, employers incur a number of costs incidental to the employment of workers. These include such items as the employer's share of social security taxes, unemployment compensation taxes, insurance premiums, contributions to pension funds, and supplementary unemployment benefits. These are *labor-related costs* or *fringe benefits.* They are most often treated as part of overhead, to the extent that they relate to manufacturing workers. Labor-related costs are incurred in connection with nonmanufacturing workers also. These, logically, are charged to nonmanufacturing expense accounts rather than to overhead. The entry to record labor-related costs applicable to factory employees is illustrated below:

Overhead Control	xxx	
Social Security Taxes Payable		xxx
Unemployment Compensation Taxes Payable		xxx
Health Insurance Premiums Payable		xxx
Etc.		xxx

There is no credit to the Payroll Summary account in this entry, for the labor-related costs do not involve direct payments to workers or withholdings from workers' earnings. Thus, labor-related costs are not involved in the payroll accounting process.

Some firms include labor-related costs in the classification of direct labor. This is accomplished by estimating the total average labor-related cost per direct labor hour and adding that average to the hourly wage rate to determine the total direct labor charge per hour. For example, assume that the direct labor wage rate in a plant is $2.50 per hour and that the average total labor-related cost is estimated to be $.65 per hour. Direct labor is then charged at a rate of $3.15 per hour. Since the $.65 portion of this charge is an estimate, it is likely that the total actual labor-related costs incurred would be somewhat more or less than the total charged to Work in Process. Such a difference would be disposed of by an adjustment at the end of the accounting perod.[1] Including the labor-related costs applicable to direct labor wages in the classification of direct labor cost is unquestionably valid, and many accountants argue that it is distinctly preferable to including them in overhead. Nevertheless, most firms continue to treat labor-related costs as part of overhead. They will consistently be included in overhead in this text.

Regardless of how labor-related costs are classified for cost accounting purposes, their nature remains the same. The same procedures for controlling these costs would be employed no matter how they were classified in the accounts, and their significance in decision making is unaffected by their classification. Any decision that will have a direct impact upon direct labor cost will have a similar impact upon labor-related costs, and the latter are pertinent to that decision whether classified as direct labor or as overhead.

[1] The manner of disposing of the difference between actual and estimated labor-related costs would be essentially the same as that illustrated later in this chapter for disposing of differences between actual overhead costs and normal overhead costs charged to production.

Evolving Problems of Labor Cost Accounting. Traditionally, labor has been regarded as a direct cost, incurred specifically because of the units of product manufactured. Likewise, it has generally been considered to be a variable cost, fluctuating in direct proportion to the volume of production. Where labor cost is incurred on a piece-rate basis—so much per unit of product manufactured—it clearly is both direct and variable with respect to production. Even where direct laborers are paid on an hourly basis, labor cost is essentially direct and variable if the workers are laid off when no production work is being done. However, if workers are regularly paid for a full forty-hour week, regardless of the amount of production, then labor cost would appear to be a fixed cost directly traceable to the firm's being in operation. It would not then vary with the volume of production nor would it be directly traceable to units of product.

At the time of this writing, it would not be accurate to say that labor has truly become a fixed cost in American industry. There is a definite movement in that direction, however. Supplementary unemployment benefit payments and other wage continuation plans require employers to pay workers for time when they are not working. The demands for a guaranteed annual wage, or annual salary for production workers, recur in many labor contract negotiations. It is not unlikely that these demands will one day be met. Nor is this movement caused entirely by bargaining demands. Many employers have found numerous advantages in having a stable work force, even if it necessitates paying employees for nonproductive time.

Even if labor were, in effect, a fixed cost, it could be made to appear as a variable cost in the accounts. Direct labor could be charged to each unit of product at some normal rate; and labor cost of nonproductive time could be charged to overhead. In this case, however, labor cost is artificially made to appear direct and variable. The nature of the cost cannot be altered by the way in which it is accounted for. Charging idle-time labor costs to overhead is reasonable only when idle time is not a regular part of total labor cost. If labor were to become a true fixed cost, as in the case of annual salaries for production workers, it should be accounted for as such. It would then be an indirect cost insofar as the individual units of product are concerned and ought to be accounted for in the same way as fixed overhead costs. Such a method of accounting for labor cost would not change materially the final cost of manufactured products where absorption costing is used. Labor would still be charged to production, except that it would now be considered an indirect rather than a direct cost. If variable costing were used, however, labor, now being a fixed cost, would be treated as a period cost rather than as a cost of the product.

The problems associated with labor becoming a fixed cost are still beyond the frontier of accounting practice. Cost accountants have not given any great amount of attention to their solution. It may be that the present trend toward fixed labor costs will be halted and even reversed, but this does not now seem likely. Rather, it is likely that the trend will accelerate and that accountants will have to deal directly with the consequent problems.

Payroll Accounting. The mechanics of payroll accounting are common to all enterprises which employ a significant number of workers. The payroll department handles the pay records of all employees, whether they receive hourly wages or weekly salaries, whether they are employed in production or in some nonmanufacturing activity. Basically, the payroll department's task is to determine who is to receive what amount of each employee's gross earnings and to prepare payroll checks. The federal government receives a portion of each worker's earnings in the form of income tax withheld from the worker's pay and also in the form of social security[2] tax withheld. In some states, income tax is also withheld for the account of the state government. Union dues are frequently "checked," or withheld by the employer for the union. There may be withholdings for insurance programs to which employees contribute, United Fund and similar donations pledged by the employees, and investment programs such as the "bond-a-month" plan for the purchase of U.S. savings bonds. Finally, after all withholdings, the balance is paid to the employee; this is his "take-home" pay. Following is a general journal entry to record the payment of a payroll in accordance with the foregoing discussion:

	Debit	Credit
Payroll Summary	xxx	
Federal Income Tax Withheld		xxx
Social Security Taxes Payable		xxx
Union Dues Withheld		xxx
United Fund Contributions Withheld		xxx
Etc.		xxx
Vouchers Payable		xxx

The credit to Vouchers Payable is for the amount of the employees' net "take-home" pay. This liability will be discharged when the payroll checks are drawn and disbursed. The liabilities for the amounts withheld will be discharged when remittances are made to the government, the union, the United Fund, etc.

---

[2] The social security tax is also referred to as the OASI (Old Age and Survivors' Insurance) tax and as the FICA (Federal Insurance Contributions Act) tax.

Accounting for Overhead

Thus far, we have observed the actual recording of three items of overhead cost—indirect materials, indirect labor, and labor-related costs. There are a great many other items in the overhead classification, all of which must be accounted for as have these three. It is also necessary to charge overhead costs to the product, that is, to Work in Process. In this section, we shall examine first the accumulation and classification of overhead cost items and then the charging of overhead costs to the product.

Recording Variable and Fixed Overhead Costs. In the entries already illustrated, the three overhead items encountered were charged to a single account, Overhead Control. As already mentioned, it is desirable to accumulate these costs according to responsibility. Hence, each distinct cost center ought to have its own overhead account. Again, for simplicity, we shall pusue the discussion of overhead costs under an assumption that there is only one cost center in the plant under study. There is still a further classification of overhead costs which should be observed, however. Traditionally, all overhead costs have been included in one account for each cost center. Recent years, however, have witnessed increasing interest on the part of management in having manufacturing cost data identified and recorded in the accounts as variable or fixed with respect to changes in output. Since materials and labor are almost universally regarded as variable costs, as a practical matter only overhead costs must be segregated into variable and fixed classifications. This can be accomplished by having two overhead control accounts for each cost center—Variable Overhead Control and Fixed Overhead Control. This separate recording of variable and fixed overhead can and should be effected under either an absorption costing or a variable costing system. From an accounting viewpoint, separate recording is essential only in variable costing. But, for purposes of management, it is equally desirable under both methods.

There is still the very important problem of identifying those costs which are variable and those which are fixed. In a practical situation, this distinction may present some very perplexing problems. Nevertheless, as mentioned in the previous chapter, the distinction is so useful to management that it must be made even if it involves a number of approximations. For purposes of illustration in this chapter, we shall consider only eight overhead cost items, including the three already encountered in connection with accounting for materials and labor. These eight items are listed below and classified as variable or fixed. The classifications of the individual cost items here are for illustrative purposes and do not purport to be applicable in manufacturing enterprises generally.

Variable Costs	*Fixed Costs*
Indirect materials	Indirect labor
Labor-related costs	Labor-related costs
Power and light	Depreciation
	Insurance
	Property taxes
	Repairs and maintenance

Labor-related costs are unique in this listing, as they are included both as variable and as fixed. To the extent that they relate to direct labor, a variable cost here, they are variable. To the extent that they relate to indirect labor, a fixed cost here, they are fixed.

We must now retrace our steps and reconstruct some of the entries prepared earlier so that all overhead items will be identified and recorded as variable or fixed. The entry for the requisition of indirect materials now appears as follows:

Variable Overhead Control	xxx	
Materials Inventory		xxx

The entry to record the distribution of labor costs, including indirect labor, is now prepared thus:

Work in Process	xxx	
Fixed Overhead Control	xxx	
Payroll Summary		xxx

The labor-related costs are now recorded as follows:

Variable Overhead Control	xxx	
Fixed Overhead Control	xxx	
Social Security Taxes Payable		xxx
Unemployment Compensation Taxes Payable		xxx
Health Insurance Premiums Payable		xxx
Etc.		xxx

Note that the only change in each of the three entries above is in the title(s) of the overhead account(s) debited. The remaining overhead items in our lists may be recorded by the following entries:

Variable Overhead Control	xxx	
Vouchers Payable (power and light bills)		xxx
Fixed Overhead Control	xxx	
Accumulated Depreciation–Plant and Equipment		xxx
Unexpired Insurance		xxx
Accrued Property Taxes Payable		xxx
Vouchers Payable (repair and maintenance bills)		xxx

These two entries assume that power and light and repair and maintenance bills are paid currently, that insurance is paid for in advance, and that property taxes are accrued and paid subsequently.

Charging Actual Overhead Costs to Production. Because overhead is indirect and, in total, is not perfectly variable with output, it is not possible to charge overhead costs to production in the same way as materials and labor. The materials and labor costs associated with a particular product or batch of production are determinable when the materials are used and the labor time recorded. The overhead costs associated with a particular product, however, can be determined only by some arbitrary allocation scheme, the total overhead costs being spread among total production in some manner which appears reasonable. Total actual overhead cost, of course, cannot be determined until the end of the accounting period and, hence, cannot be allocated to the products until then. If there is no objection to such a delay in charging overhead costs, an entry can be prepared as of the end of each period to charge that period's production with its overhead costs. The entry depends upon the costing method employed in the firm—absorption costing or variable costing. Under absorption costing, both variable and fixed overhead are charged to production.

Work in Process	xxx	
Variable Overhead Control		xxx
Fixed Overhead Control		xxx

Under variable costing, only the variable overhead is treated as a product cost.

Work in Process	xxx	
Variable Overhead Control		xxx

Fixed overhead is treated as an expense of the current period, and Fixed Overhead Control would be closed to the Revenue and Expense Summary account.

Charging Normal Overhead Cost to Production. The practice of charging actual overhead to production after the end of the accounting period involves a number of difficulties. These stem from the facts that overhead is indirect and is composed, in part at least, of fixed costs. If all overhead were directly traceable to and perfectly variable with output, it could be charged to production in the same way as materials and labor. It is a fact, however, that overhead is partly fixed; and, as American manufacturers move more toward automation, it is reasonable to expect that the fixed-cost component of total overhead will become increasingly larger. Variable overhead is not readily traced to individual products either, even though it does vary in proportion to output. For example, the usage of indirect materials is commonly a function of the volume of production; but the usage of specific indirect materials cannot ordinarily be traced to specific products. Two of the most notable difficulties attendant upon the charging of actual overhead to production are discussed in the paragraphs which follow.

If a firm contracts to produce special equipment for the federal government and to bill the equipment at the cost to manufacture plus a fixed fee (profit),[3] no billing can be made until the total cost of the equipment, including overhead, is known. Thus, if actual overhead is charged to production at the end of the accounting period, say, one month, and the work on the contract is completed early in the month, the billing must be delayed until after the end of the month. Clearly, this is not a satisfactory arrangement for either party concerned. There must be some way of determining overhead when the contract is completed.

Another disadvantage of charging actual overhead cost to production may be seen from an examination of a firm that experiences significant seasonal variations in the volume of its production. Such a situation is depicted in Table 3–1. For purposes of this illustration, all variable

TABLE 3–1

IMPACT OF SEASONAL OUTPUT ON UNIT COST

Month	*Units of Product Produced*	*Fixed Cost in Total*	*Fixed Cost per Unit*	*Variable Cost per Unit*	*Total Cost per Unit of Product*
January	1,000	$ 8,000	$8.00	$6.00	$14.00
February	2,000	8,000	4.00	6.00	10.00
March	2,500	8,000	3.20	6.00	9.20
April	4,000	8,000	2.00	6.00	8.00
May	6,000	8,000	1.33	6.00	7.33
June	8,000	8,000	1.00	6.00	7.00
July	8,000	8,000	1.00	6.00	7.00
August	6,000	8,000	1.33	6.00	7.33
September	4,000	8,000	2.00	6.00	8.00
October	3,500	8,000	2.29	6.00	8.29
November	2,000	8,000	4.00	6.00	10.00
December	1,000	8,000	8.00	6.00	14.00
	48,000	$96,000			

costs—materials, labor, and variable overhead—are included in a single figure *per unit of product;* it is the same each month. Fixed overhead, on

[3] Cost-plus-fixed-fee contracts are quite common in the production of goods for the government, and the government is a major purchaser of industrial production in the United States.

the other hand, is the same in total each month. Therefore, it varies, per unit of output, inversely with the volume of production. In months of low production, unit fixed cost and, consequently, total unit cost are relatively high. Conversely, in months of high production, unit cost is relatively low. Thus, marked differences in the unit cost of the product appear from month to month even though the product remains unchanged; only the quantities in which it is produced change. These variations in unit cost are likely to be misleading and to result in meaningless fluctuations in income from month to month, for selling price is not likely to change as unit cost changes. While the extent of the fluctuations in monthly output in Table 3–1 is admittedly extreme, it serves to illustrate the problem of charging actual overhead costs to production when output varies seasonally.

The reader should by now have recognized that the problem of seasonal variations in output exists only under absorption costing. Under variable costing, since no fixed costs are charged to the product, unit cost will be unaffected by volume fluctuations. The problem discussed with reference to the cost-plus-fixed-fee contract, however, is common to both absorption and variable costing.

If some overhead cost per unit that would be valid over the whole year could be determined in advance, it would solve the two problems described above. First, it would permit the charging of overhead cost to products as soon as they are completed. Hence, the cost-plus-fixed-fee contract could be billed as soon as the work is finished. Second, it would eliminate the seasonal fluctuations in unit cost due to the seasonal variations in output. For example, in Table 3–1, if the firm's accountant could have foreseen that a total of 48,000 units of product would have been produced during the year and that a total of $96,000 in fixed costs would have been incurred in that year, he could have predetermined that the fixed cost of producing each unit would be, as an average for the entire year, $2.00. Therefore, the total unit cost would be $8.00 in each month. But can annual output and fixed costs be known in advance? While they cannot be predicted with certainty, they typically can be estimated in advance with reasonable confidence. As a matter of fact, if management is to plan business operations for a year, such estimates must be made. When these estimates are formalized, they are generally called budgets. For the present, we are concerned only with budgets for output and for fixed overhead. Given these two budgeted data, we can determine by simple division the budgeted unit fixed cost of the product for a period. When this budgeted unit cost is used in charging fixed overhead to production in the accounts, it is referred to as a *normal fixed overhead rate.*

A *normal variable overhead rate* may be determined quite readily from observations of the variable overhead costs incurred per unit of output in the past, with adjustments for changing prices and circumstances. By virtue of the fact that it is variable, the variable overhead rate logically would be budgeted initially as an amount per unit of product. However, formal budgets are often prepared to show the total planned variable overhead cost. This total would, of course, be based upon a rate per unit and a budget of total unit output. In this case, the cost accountant would compute the normal variable overhead rate apparently in the same way as the fixed rate, that is, by dividing total budgeted variable cost by budgeted output. This calculation actually would only be returning to the starting point in the process of budgeting variable overhead cost. The variable overhead rate will be the same at any level of output, whereas the fixed overhead rate will decline as higher levels of output are budgeted.

It must be understood that the use of normal overhead rates, derived from budgeted data, does not mean that the budget itself is recorded by means of a journal entry. The overhead charged to production in this case is the normal overhead rate(s) multiplied by the actual output for the period. Budgeted output is used only to determine the normal fixed overhead rate, not to charge overhead to production. The normal overhead rates are, in effect, estimates of what actual overhead per unit of output will be. The overhead cost charged to Work in Process, thus, is a function of the normal overhead rates and the actual output for the period.

Charging overhead costs to production at a normal rate means that the Work in Process account will not consist entirely of literally *actual* costs. The normal cost element will carry through to the Finished Product and Cost of Goods Sold accounts. (Refer again to Figures 3–1 and 3–2 to see why this must be so.) This minor deviation from actual cost is widely accepted in business and, as a matter of fact, is probably typical of most actual cost systems. Because the use of normal overhead rates results in the charging to Work in Process of something other than actual overhead costs incurred, it is general practice to make the offsetting credits for that charge to accounts other than the overhead control accounts. These credits may be made to accounts titled Variable Overhead Applied and, under absorption costing only, Fixed Overhead Applied. Journal entries to record the charging of overhead at normal rates are illustrated below. Under absorption costing, both variable and fixed overhead are charged to the product.

Work in Process	xxx	
Variable Overhead Applied		xxx
Fixed Overhead Applied		xxx

Under variable costing, only variable costs enter into the cost of the manufactured product.

Work in Process	xxx	
Variable Overhead Applied		xxx

The Fixed Overhead Control account would again be closed directly to the Revenue and Expense Summary account, just as any other current expense.

As a result of the procedure described in the previous paragraph, there will be two accounts for variable overhead and, again only under absorption costing, two accounts for fixed overhead in the general ledger—the overhead control accounts with debit balances representing the actual costs incurred and the overhead applied accounts with credit balances representing the overhead cost charged to the product for the period. The balances in the two accounts for variable costs and, when appropriate, in the two accounts for fixed costs will be equal and offsetting only if the budgeted cost and output data prove to be exactly equal to the comparable actual data. Obviously, it is very unlikely that the budgeted and actual data will be identical. They may be very close to each other, but some discrepancy is virtually inevitable. Consequently, there will almost always be some differences between the debit balances in the overhead control accounts and the respective credit balances in the overhead applied accounts. These differences are termed *underapplied overhead* when actual costs exceed the costs applied and *overapplied overhead* when the costs applied are greater than the actual costs incurred. While there are alternative methods of disposing of under- or overapplied overhead, at this point we shall simply observe that it may be closed directly to the Revenue and Expense Summary account. This would be accomplished by closing both the overhead control accounts and the overhead applied accounts to Revenue and Expense Summary at the end of the fiscal year. The reporting of under- or overapplied overhead in financial statements is illustrated later in this chapter.

Comprehensive Illustration

At this point, it may be helpful in understanding the basic cost accounting cycle, that is, the flow of manufacturing costs through the successive accounts, to study a single illustration with specific production and cost data. These data relate to the Wedgewood Products Company for the year 1965. Both absorption costing and variable costing will be illustrated in this example.

The company's experience indicates that each unit of product will involve the incurrence of an average of $.80 of variable overhead costs; hence, variable overhead will be applied to the product at a normal rate of $.80 per unit. Fixed overhead costs are budgeted at $800,000 for the year and output, at 400,000 units. Thus, under absorption costing only, fixed overhead will be applied to production at a normal rate of $2.00 per unit. The variable and fixed cost items in this illustration will be those listed and classified on page 51. Although no entries are needed to record the inventory balances at the beginning of the year, since those balances are carried forward from the previous year, it is useful to show such balances. This information will serve to explain how more materials than were purchased currently could be used during the year. The inventory account balances for Work in Process and Finished Product will be greater under absorption costing than under variable costing, of course; for the former method includes fixed overhead in inventory, while the latter method does not. Inventory balances of the Wedgewood Products Company as of December 31, 1964, are as follows:

	Absorption Costing	*Variable Costing*
Materials Inventory	$200,000	$200,000
Work in Process	168,000	120,000
Finished Product	462,000	330,000

Following are the transactions relevant to manufacturing operations during 1965 and general journal entries to record them:

1. Raw materials costing $1,200,000 were purchased.

		Dr.	Cr.
(1)	Materials Inventory	1,200,000	
	Vouchers Payable		1,200,000

2. Materials costing $1,285,000 were issued to the factory. Of these, $1,185,000 were direct materials and $100,000 were indirect materials.

(2)	Work in Process	1,185,000	
	Variable Overhead Control	100,000	
	Materials Inventory		1,285,000

3. The factory payroll for 1965 totaled $600,000. Of this total, $474,000 represents the cost of direct labor; the balance is indirect.

(3)	Work in Process	474,000	
	Fixed Overhead Control	126,000	
	Payroll Summary		600,000

4. Labor-related costs totaled $48,000; this included $38,000 related to variable direct labor and $10,000 related to fixed indirect labor. The individual items include the company's share of social security taxes ($17,000), unemployment compensation taxes ($15,000), and health insurance premiums ($16,000).

(4)	Variable Overhead Control	38,000	
	Fixed Overhead Control	10,000	
	Social Security Taxes Payable		17,000
	Unemployment Compensation Taxes Payable		15,000
	Insurance Premiums Payable		16,000

5. In the payroll department, the gross payroll for the year was distributed. Amounts withheld included $95,000 for employees' federal incomes taxes, $17,000 for the employees' share of social security taxes, $8,500 for union dues, and $12,000 for United Fund donations.

(5)	Payroll Summary	600,000	
	Federal Income Tax Withheld		95,000
	Social Security Taxes Payable		17,000
	Union Dues Withheld		8,500
	United Fund Contributions Withheld		12,000
	Vouchers Payable		467,500

The credit to Vouchers Payable represents the employees' take-home pay for the year. The reader should note that this entry is not essential to the depiction of the cost accounting cycle. Payroll accounting is common to financial accounting generally; it is not peculiar to cost accounting. The entry is included here for the sake of illustrative completeness.

6. Additional overhead costs incurred were as follows:

Power and light	$138,000
Depreciation on plant and equipment	350,000
Insurance on plant	80,000
Property taxes on plant	76,000
Repairs and maintenance	170,000

These items are recorded as follows:

(6–1)	Variable Overhead Control	138,000	
	Vouchers Payable*		138,000
(6–2)	Fixed Overhead Control	676,000	
	Accumulated Depreciation–Plant and Equipment		350,000
	Unexpired Insurance		80,000
	Accrued Property Taxes		76,000
	Vouchers Payable†		170,000

* Power and light.
† Repairs and maintenance.

7. To this point in the illustration, all of the entries made are identical under both absorption and variable costing. The remaining entries, however, dealing either with overhead specifically or with the full cost of the product, including overhead, will be different under the alternative costing methods. Actual output for 1965 (i.e., work done during the year, not including work already done on the beginning inventory of Work in Process) was 395,000 units of product. Overhead is charged to production at normal rates. Variable overhead is charged at a rate of $.80 for each of the 395,000 units produced. Under absorption costing, fixed overhead is charged at a rate of $2.00 per unit.

(7A)	Work in Process	1,106,000	
	Variable Overhead Applied		316,000
	Fixed Overhead Applied		790,000

Under variable costing, only the variable overhead is applied to production. Notice that this results in a materially lower cost of the Work in Process inventory.

(7V)	Work in Process	316,000	
	Variable Overhead Applied		316,000

8. The total cost of production completed during a period is normally computed by determining the unit cost of production for the period and multiplying that unit cost by the number of units completed. The determination of unit cost is discussed and illustrated in Chapter 4. At this point, we shall merely assume total costs of completed production to be $2,688,000 under absorption costing and $1,920,000 under variable costing. The difference between these two amounts should be equal to the number of units completed multiplied by the normal fixed overhead rate of $2 per unit, for the only difference between absorption and variable costing is in the treatment of fixed overhead. The entries to record the cost of completed production during 1965 under absorption costing and variable costing, respectively, are as follows:

(8A)	Finished Product	2,688,000	
	Work in Process		2,688,000
(8V)	Finished Product	1,920,000	
	Work in Process		1,920,000

9. Total sales in 1965 amounted to $4,872,000; all of these sales were made on account. The cost of the goods sold amounted to $2,842,000 under absorption costing and $2,030,000 under variable costing. Once again, the cost of goods sold would actually be determined by reference to the unit costs of finished products and the quantities of products sold. These determinations are deferred here until the following chapter, however. Two entries are necessary to record the sales. The first records the sales on account to customers; it records the selling prices of the goods sold.

(9–1)	Accounts Receivable	4,872,000	
	Sales		4,872,000

This entry is the same regardless of the costing method employed. The second entry records the expiration of the cost of the goods sold. It is the entry which reflects the transfer of product costs from the asset category (inventory) to the expense classification. This entry will be different under the alternative costing methods. Under absorption costing, the entry for the cost of goods sold is as follows:

(9–2A)	Cost of Goods Sold	2,842,000	
	Finished Product		2,842,000

Under variable costing, the entry appears as follows:

(9–2V)	Cost of Goods Sold	2,030,000	
	Finished Product		2,030,000

10. The entries made to this point in the illustration reflect the complete flow of manufacturing costs through the accounts, from acquisition of the factors of production through the expiration of the costs of those factors at the time of sale of the manufactured product. Some of the manufacturing cost accounts which have been used are nominal accounts that must be closed at the end of the fiscal year. These include the overhead control accounts, the overhead applied accounts, and Cost of Goods Sold. Under absorption costing, these closing entries would be as follows:

(10–1A)	Variable Overhead Applied	316,000	
	Fixed Overhead Applied	790,000	
	Variable Overhead Control		276,000
	Fixed Overhead Control		812,000
	Revenue and Expense Summary		18,000

(10–2A)	Revenue and Expense Summary	2,842,000	
	Cost of Goods Sold		2,842,000

In Entry 10–1A, the only amount of overhead cost that is actually closed directly to Revenue and Expense Summary and, hence, treated as a period cost is the net amount of overapplied overhead. The reader will observe that variable overhead was overapplied in the amount of $40,000, while fixed overhead was underapplied by $22,000. For purposes of cost analysis and control, these two separate figures are significant; but it is unlikely that there would be any real advantage in their being shown separately in the accounts or in the financial statements.

Under variable costing, only variable overhead has been applied to production. Fixed overhead has merely been accumulated in an expense account, which must be closed at the end of the period. The closing entries would appear as follows:

(10–1V)	Variable Overhead Applied	316,000	
	Variable Overhead Control		276,000
	Revenue and Expense Summary		40,000
(10–2V)	Revenue and Expense Summary	2,842,000	
	Cost of Goods Sold		2,030,000
	Fixed Overhead Control		812,000

After all entries have been posted and the books closed, the following inventory balances as of December 31, 1965, remain:

	Absorption Costing	*Variable Costing*
Materials Inventory	$115,000	$115,000
Work in Process	245,000	175,000
Finished Product	308,000	220,000

These will be the beginning inventory balances of the year 1966.

OPERATING STATEMENTS FOR A MANUFACTURING ENTERPRISE

In a manufacturing concern, as in a merchandising firm, the principal operating statement is the income statement. However, in manufacturing, the development of the cost of goods sold figure is considerably more complex. Hence, it is typical of manufacturing companies' financial statements that the income statement is supported by a detailed *statement of costs of goods manufactured and sold.* The latter statement summarizes the results of manufacturing operations for the period; it is a formal presentation of the data processed through the cost accounting cycle during one period. Both this statement and the income statement for the Wedgewood Products Company for 1965 are illustrated below. The basic data are those from the comprehensive illustration in the preceding section.

Operating Statements under Absorption Costing

Table 3–2 is a statement of cost of goods manufactured and sold

TABLE 3–2
WEDGEWOOD PRODUCTS COMPANY
Statement of Cost of Goods Manufactured and Sold
For the Year Ended December 31, 1965

Direct materials:			
Inventory, Jan. 1, 1965		$ 200,000	
Purchases		1,200,000	
Available for use		1,400,000	
Deduct:			
Inventory, Dec. 31, 1965	$115,000		
Indirect materials used	100,000	215,000	$1,185,000
Direct labor			474,000
Overhead applied			1,106,000
Total current production costs			$2,765,000
Deduct: Increase in Work Process			
Inventory, Dec. 31, 1965		245,000	
Inventory, Jan. 1, 1965		168,000	77,000
Cost of goods manufactured			$2,688,000
Add: Decrease in Finished Product			
Inventory, Jan. 1, 1965		462,000	
Inventory, Dec. 31, 1965		308,000	154,000
Cost of goods sold			$2,842,000

prepared in accordance with the absorption costing method. Table 3–3 is the income statement following from that supporting statement. The reader should note that the format of the statements presented here is not suggested as a standard format to be followed in all cases. There is a considerable variety of forms used in business practice. Those illustrated in this chapter are widely employed.

In Table 3–2, the cost of goods manufactured is equal to the cost of goods completed during 1965, that is, the cost transferred from Work in Process to Finished Product (cf., Entry 8A in the previous section). The final figure in Table 3–2, the cost of goods sold, is the same figure transferred from Finished Product to the Cost of Goods Sold account in the comprehensive illustration (cf., Entry 9–2A). In the calculation of the direct materials used, it is necessary to deduct the cost of indirect materials used from the cost of available materials. The cost of indirect materials is intended to be included in the overhead cost applied. Separate identification of variable and fixed overhead applied might be made, but it is probably not too important in a summary statement of this type.

In order to prepare an income statement, we need some additional data not yet specified. Distribution expenses for the year total $840,000; administrative expenses amount to $690,000. All income is subject to a flat federal income tax rate of 47%. The income statement in Table 3–3 appears in the familiar form widely used currently.

TABLE 3–3
WEDGEWOOD PRODUCTS COMPANY
Income Statement
For the Year Ended December 31, 1965

Sales		$4,872,000
Cost of goods sold (cf. Table 3–2)	$2,842,000	
Less: Net overapplied overhead	18,000	2,824,000
Gross margin		$2,048,000
Nonmanufacturing expenses:		
Distribution	$ 840,000	
Administration	690,000	1,530,000
Net operating income		$ 518,000
Federal income tax		243,460
Net income		$ 274,540

The net overapplied overhead here is deducted from the cost of goods sold before computing the gross margin. A net underapplied overhead figure would be added to cost of goods sold. Some accountants prefer to show this deduction or addition at the end of the statement of cost of goods manufactured and sold. Either alternative is acceptable, and the difference between the two is a minor one. In either case, the under- or overapplied overhead is reported as an adjustment to the expired manufacturing costs of the period (i.e., the cost of goods sold). As under- or overapplied overhead relates to manufacturing costs, such an adjustment seems to be the most appropriate method of reporting the item.

Operating Statements under Variable Costing

The statement of cost of goods manufactured and sold under variable costing is nearly identical to that prepared under absorption costing. The only difference is that no fixed overhead is included in any of the data in the statement. Table 3–4 illustrates such a statement, prepared from the data under variable costing in the comprehensive illustration of the preceding section.

The income statement for variable costing differs very significantly from that for absorption costing. Not only are different data involved in the determination of cost of goods sold, but the entire form of

TABLE 3–4
WEDGEWOOD PRODUCTS COMPANY
Statement of Cost of Goods Manufactured and Sold
For the Year Ended December 31, 1965

Direct materials:			
Inventory, Jan. 1, 1965		$ 200,000	
Purchases		1,200,000	
Available for use		$1,400,000	
Deduct:			
Inventory, Dec. 31, 1965	$115,000		
Indirect materials used	100,000	215,000	$1,185,000
Direct labor			474,000
Variable overhead applied			316,000
Total variable production costs			$1,975,000
Deduct: Increase in Work in Process			
Inventory, Dec. 31, 1965		175,000	
Inventory, Jan. 1, 1965		120,000	55,000
Cost of goods manufactured			$1,920,000
Add: Decrease in Finished Product			
Inventory, Jan. 1, 1965		330,000	
Inventory, Dec. 31, 1965		220,000	110,000
Cost of goods sold			$2,030,000

presentation is different. The principal intermediate profit figure in the absorption costing statement is the gross margin. Under variable costing, the basic intermediate profit figure is the *variable profit,* the excess of revenues over variable expenses of the period. The variable profit figure is one which is particularly useful to management in various cost analyses for decision making. The variable costing income statement is illustrated in Table 3–5. For this statement, it is necessary to distinguish between variable and fixed nonmanufacturing costs as well as between variable and fixed production costs. Thus, of the total $840,000 of

TABLE 3–5
WEDGEWOOD PRODUCTS COMPANY
Income Statement
For the Year Ended December 31, 1965

Sales			$4,872,000
Variable expenses:			
Variable cost of goods sold (cf., Table 3–4)	$2,030,000		
Less: Overapplied variable overhead	40,000	$1,990,000	
Variable distribution expense		340,000	
Variable administrative expense		90,000	2,420,000
Variable profit			$2,452,000
Fixed expenses:			
Fixed overhead		$ 812,000	
Fixed distribution expense		500,000	
Fixed administrative expense		600,000	1,912,000
Net operating income			$ 540,000
Federal income tax			253,800
Net income			$ 286,200

distribution expenses, $340,000 are variable and $500,000 are fixed. The total administrative expenses of $690,000 consist of $90,000 of variable costs and $600,000 of fixed costs. It is important to note that the differences in the income statements under absorption costing and variable costing are not only differences of form. The reported net incomes differ because of the different methods of accounting for fixed overhead.

The presentations of absorption and variable costing in this chapter have been limited to the accounting procedures for the two methods. A critical comparison and appraisal of these two costing techniques will be made in the next chapter.

QUESTIONS FOR DISCUSSION

1. What is meant by the concept that *costs attach?* Which costs attach in absorption costing? Which costs attach in variable costing?
2. Distinguish between product costs and period costs. How does each type of cost expire?
3. Which accounts in the general ledger of a manufacturing firm may be expected to be different under variable costing as compared with absorption costing?
4. Several different schemes of classification of costs have been discussed in this chapter. It is desirable that these several classifications be incorporated in the recording of costs in the accounts. Identify these different cost classification schemes and state the objective(s) of recording costs according to each scheme.
5. Should vacation pay and labor-related costs be included as part of direct labor cost or should they be accounted for as part of overhead? Explain your answer.
6. If the direct labor costs of production were true fixed costs of the period, how would they be accounted for? How would these procedures differ, if at all, from the current practices with respect to labor cost accounting?
7. What are the advantages of using normal overhead rates instead of actual rates? What are the disadvantages? On balance, do you feel the advantages outweigh the disadvantages or vice versa? Why?
8. "The use of a normal fixed overhead rate results in an artificial smoothing of unit production costs over the period of a year in which there occur significant seasonal fluctuations in output." To what does this allegation refer? How would you respond to it?
9. Why might the net income of a firm in one period be reported differently under absorption costing as compared with variable costing in the same firm and the same period?
10. "Variable costing is preferable to absorption costing in that it results in lower inventory values and, therefore, lower inventory carrying costs (i.e., imputed interest on the investment in inventory)." Comment on this statement.

11. Describe the flow of manufacturing costs through the cost accounting cycle without making any reference to accounts.

PROBLEMS

1. The operations of the Raritan Corporation for the year ended December 31, 1965, are summarized below. The corporation uses absorption costing.

a. Inventory balances, Jan. 1, 1965:

Materials	$ 10,000
Work in Process	12,000
Finished Product	30,000

b. Purchases of raw materials	150,000
c. Direct materials used	144,000
d. Direct labor cost incurred	120,000

e. Actual overhead costs incurred:

Variable	35,000
Fixed	62,000

(Credit "various accounts")

f. Variable overhead is applied to production at a normal rate of $1.50 per unit of product. Fixed overhead is applied to production at a normal rate of $2.50 per unit of product. During 1965, a total of 24,000 units of product were manufactured.

g. Cost of completed production	$352,000
h. Cost of products sold	370,000
i. Revenue from product sales	500,000

Required:

1. Prepare general journal entries to record all of the operating transactions for 1965. Do not prepare closing entries.
2. Compute the ending balances in the three inventory accounts at Dec. 31, 1965.
3. Compute the amount of under- or overapplied overhead for the year.

2. The Bonham Manufacturing Company uses variable costing in accounting for its production costs. Following is a summary of the company's operations for the year ended December 31, 1966:

a. Inventories, Jan. 1, 1966:

Materials	$ 12,000
Work in Process	24,000
Finished Product	40,000

b. Purchases of materials	220,000
c. Direct materials used	208,000
d. Direct labor cost incurred	185,000

e. Actual overhead costs incurred:

Variable	110,000
Fixed	90,000

(Credit "various accounts.")

f. Variable overhead is applied to production at a normal rate of $.25 per unit of product. 400,000 units of product were manufactured during 1966.

g. Cost of goods completed	$509,000

h. Sales

At selling price	700,000
At cost	525,000

Required:

1. Prepare general journal entries to record all of the operations for 1966. Do not prepare closing entries.
2. Compute the ending balances in the inventory accounts at December 31, 1966.
3. Compute the amount of under- or overapplied overhead for 1966.

3. The Winona Manufacturing Company charges overhead to production at normal rates and employs the absorption costing method. Past experience, adjusted for anticipated price changes, indicated that variable overhead would average $.80 per unit of product. For 1966, fixed overhead was budgeted at $3,000,000. Output for 1966 was budgeted at 2,500,000 units of product. Actual output for 1966 proved to be only 2,250,000 units. Actual overhead for the year included variable costs of $1,865,000 and fixed costs of $2,850,000.

Required:

1. Compute the under- or overapplied overhead for variable and fixed costs separately. State briefly what facts or conditions appear to have caused these under- or overapplied amounts.
2. Prepare a general journal entry (or entries) to close all accounts relative to overhead at December 31, 1966.

4. The Naugatuck Products Corporation charges overhead to production at a normal rate and uses the variable costing method in accounting for production. Budgeted variable overhead for 1966 was $1.45 per unit of product. Budgeted fixed overhead was $720,000. Budgeted output for the year was set at 600,000 units of product. Actual output for 1966 totaled 660,000 units. Actual variable overhead amounted to $925,000 and actual fixed overhead, to $735,000.

Required:

1. Show all balances in overhead control and overhead applied accounts, before closing, as of December 31, 1966. Compute any under- or overapplied overhead.
2. Prepare a general journal entry (or entries) to close all accounts relative to overhead at December 31, 1966.

5. The total factory labor cost of the Coos Bay Milling Company for the two-week period ended September 30, 1965, is $36,458. Of this amount, $29,754 is direct labor; the balance is indirect and is regarded by the company as a fixed cost. The payroll department withholds a total of $5,180 from this payroll for federal income taxes. The entire payroll is subject to the social security withholding rate of 3.8%. The only other item withheld is 2% of the payroll; this represents the employees' contributions to a company pension plan. The company must match the employees' social security tax payments, must contribute 4% of the payroll to the pension plan, and must pay unemployment compensation tax in the amount of 3.5% of the gross payroll.

Required:

Prepare general journal entries to record (1) the charging of labor costs and labor-related costs to the appropriate manufacturing cost accounts by the cost accounting department and (2) the distribution of the biweekly payroll by the payroll department.

6. The Wachusett Corporation manufactures ceramic ashtrays. The variable costing method is used in product cost accounting. The company began operations in January, 1965. Budgeted output for 1965 called for production of 4,000,000 ashtrays. Budgeted overhead costs included $320,000 of fixed overhead and $.05 of variable overhead per ashtray. Actual production data for 1965 are summarized below:
   a. 6,000,000 pounds of raw materials were purchased at an average cost of $.02 per pound. 5,850,000 pounds were issued to the factory for production.
   b. The total factory payroll for the year amounted to $550,000. Of this total, $468,000 was direct labor and the balance was indirect. Federal income tax withheld totaled $80,000. The entire payroll is subject to the FICA tax rate of 3.8%. The employer must match the employees' FICA tax payments and must also pay 3.5% of the payroll in unemployment compensation tax.
   c. Actual variable overhead costs incurred during 1965 were as follows:
   Factory supplies purchased and used—$35,000.
   Electric power bills paid—$21,100.
   Indirect labor.
   Labor-related costs.
   d. Actual fixed overhead costs incurred during the year included the following items:
   Depreciation on plant and equipment—$200,000.
   Taxes on plant and equipment—$24,000. (Half of these taxes have already been paid; the remaining half is due and payable on or before March 15, 1966.)
   Insurance on plant and equipment—$18,000. (This is the current year's portion of a three-year insurance policy purchased on June 30, 1964.)
   Repairs and maintenance—$65,000. (All paid currently.)
   e. A total of 3,900,000 ashtrays were produced in 1965. No uncompleted work was in process at December 31. Production records reveal that each ashtray produced had an average cost of $.20. Of the completed units, 3,600,000 were shipped to customers and billed at a selling price of $.45 per ashtray.

Required:

Prepare general journal entries to record the operations of the Wachusett Corporation for 1965 and to close the nominal accounts at the end of the year.

7. The Klamath Cabinet Works manufactures wooden cabinets for television and stereo sets. Absorption costing is used. Budgeted production for 1966 was set at 70,000 cabinets. Fixed overhead was budgeted at $1,260,000 for

the year and variable overhead, at $2 per cabinet. Actual operating data for 1966 are summarized below:

a. The cost of raw materials purchased during 1966 totaled $3,000,000. The cost of raw materials issued to the factory totaled $3,150,000.

b. The factory payroll for the year included $2,100,000 of direct labor and $400,000 of indirect labor. Federal income tax withheld totaled $350,000. The entire payroll is subject to the 3.8% FICA withholding tax, which the employer must match. In addition, the employer pays unemployment compensation tax in the amount of 3.5% of the total payroll.

c. The actual variable overhead costs incurred during 1966 were as follows:
Indirect materials used—$108,500. (This amount is included in the total cost of raw materials issued to the factory.)
Labor-related costs.

d. Actual fixed overhead costs included the following items:
Depreciation on factory facilities—$500,000.
Heat, light, and power—$80,000. (All paid currently.)
Property taxes on factory—$40,000. (These taxes are due and payable in 1967.)
Maintenance—$250,000. (All paid currently.)
Indirect labor.
Labor-related costs.

e. A total of 75,000 cabinets were produced during 1966. There was no inventory of Work in Process at either the beginning or the end of the year. All units completed were shipped to customers on the same day. The selling price is $130 per cabinet.

Required:

Prepare general journal entries to record all of the operating transactions of 1966 and to close the nominal accounts at the end of the year.

8. The following data are taken from the accounting records of the SJF Products Company for the year ended December 31, 1965:

Inventories, Jan. 1:	
Raw materials	$ 15,000
Work in process	9,000
Finished products	33,000
Sales	350,000
Purchases of raw materials	100,000
Materials issued to the factory:	
As direct materials	88,000
As indirect materials (variable cost)	7,000
Factory payroll:	
Direct labor	84,000
Indirect labor (variable cost)	34,000
Salesmen's salaries (variable cost)	45,000
Factory power and utilities (fixed cost)	22,000
Advertising (fixed cost)	10,000
Depreciation on factory equipment (fixed cost)	30,000
Inventories, Dec. 31:	
Raw materials	?
Work in process	12,000
Finished products	26,000

Overhead is applied to production at normal rates of $.90 per unit of product for variable costs and $1.10 per unit of product for fixed costs. The actual output of 1965 totaled 45,000 units of product. The applicable federal income tax rate is 40%.

Required:

Prepare an income statement and a supporting statement of cost of goods manufactured and sold for the year ended December 31, 1965.

9. The data below represent a summarization of the manufacturing and selling operations of the Alert Automotive Company for the year 1966.

Sales	$410,000
Purchases of materials	80,000
Payroll:	
Direct labor	120,000
Indirect labor (fixed cost)	50,000
Office payroll (fixed cost)	70,000
Depreciation (fixed cost):	
On factory equipment	40,000
On office equipment	10,000
Repairs and maintenance (fixed cost):	
On factory equipment	15,000
On office equipment	5,000
Supplies used (variable cost):	
In factory	25,000
In office	5,000
Labor-related costs	8% of payroll

Output for 1966 totaled 180,000 units of product. Variable overhead is applied to production at the normal rate of $.20 per unit of product. Fixed overhead is accounted for as a period expense.

Inventories at the beginning and end of the year were as follows:

	Jan. 1	*Dec. 31*
Materials	$16,000	$ 6,000
Work in process	8,000	10,000
Finished product	30,000	35,000

The applicable income tax rate is 48%.

Required:

Prepare an income statement and a supporting schedule of cost of goods manufactured and sold for the year 1966.

10. Following is the adjusted trial balance of the Yeaton Manufacturing Corporation as of December 31, 1966:

	Debit	Credit
Cash	$ 18,000	
Accounts receivable	26,000	
Inventories:		
Materials	30,000	
Work in process	12,000	
Finished product	44,000	
Land	60,000	
Plant property and equipment	280,000	
Accumulated depreciation—plant property and equipment		$ 60,000
Patents	21,000	
Vouchers payable		30,000
Accrued expenses		25,000
Mortgage bonds payable		150,000
Common stock		200,000
Retained earnings		10,000
Sales		304,000
Cost of goods sold	165,000	
Variable overhead control	32,000	
Fixed overhead control	28,000	
Selling expenses	35,000	
General and administrative expenses	60,000	
Variable overhead applied		30,000
Fixed overhead applied		25,000
Interest expense	9,000	
Federal income tax	14,000	
	$834,000	$834,000

In addition, the cost records show that materials costing $80,000 were purchased during 1966 and that the inventories at January 1, 1966, were as follows:

Materials	$25,000
Work in process	2,000
Finished product	39,000

Required:

Prepare an income statement and a statement of cost of goods manufactured and sold for the year ended December 31, 1966.

11. The adjusted trial balance of the Taney Milling Company as of December 31, 1966, appears as follows:

	Debit	Credit
Cash	$ 3,500	
Accounts receivable	12,400	
Inventories:		
Materials	22,200	
Work in process	4,800	
Finished product	11,700	
Land	29,000	
Buildings	68,500	
Accumulated depreciation—buildings		$ 34,900

	Debit	Credit
Machinery and equipment	114,000	
Accumulated depreciation—machinery and equipment		52,60C
Accounts payable		9,400
Accrued expenses		1,800
Bank notes payable		15,000
C. G. Taney, capital		172,200
Sales		401,600
Cost of goods sold	253,800	
Variable overhead control	31,300	
Fixed overhead control	84,400	
Variable distribution expenses	16,200	
Fixed distribution expenses	28,000	
Fixed administrative expenses	42,000	
Variable overhead applied		35,200
Interest expenses	900	
	$722,700	$722,700

Materials were purchased at a total cost of $145,000 during 1966. The direct labor charges for the year were $76,400. Inventories at January 1, 1966, were as follows:

Materials	$19,400
Work in process	7,100
Finished product	9,400

Required:

Prepare an income statement and a supporting statement of cost of goods manufactured and sold for the year ended December 31, 1966.

12. The Hawthorn Metal Products Corporation manufactures a variety of small machined parts. Output is measured in terms of pounds of finished product. The budgeted output for the year 1965 was set at 6,000,000 pounds. Actual output for that year proved to be only 5,600,000 pounds. The overhead cost budget for 1965 was developed as follows:

Variable cost items:		
Indirect materials and supplies	$ 30,000	
Indirect labor	150,000	
Labor-related costs	36,000	
Power and light	54,000	$270,000
Fixed cost items:		
Depreciation	$400,000	
Plant supervisors' salaries	80,000	
Labor-related costs	4,000	
Maintenance	180,000	
Property taxes	26,000	
Property insurance	30,000	720,000
		$990,000

The corporation uses absorption costing.

The following inventory balances appeared in the firm's balance sheet at December 31, 1964:

Materials	$55,000
Work in process	28,000
Finished product	88,000

Raw materials purchases for the year totaled $1,200,000. A summary of storeroom issue slips for the year show that $1,185,000 of direct materials and $28,000 of indirect materials and supplies were issued to the factory.

Following is the distribution of the total payroll for 1965:

Direct labor	$435,000
Indirect labor	145,000
Plant supervisors' salaries	85,000
Salesmen's commissions	125,000
Administrative salaries	200,000
	$990,000

Federal income tax in the amount of $170,000 was withheld from employees' earnings. Social security taxes were withheld in an amount equal to 3.8% of the total payroll. Union dues totaling $8,000 were withheld from factory workers' checks. The company matches the employees' social security contributions and pays unemployment compensation tax equal to 3.5% of the total payroll.

The following expenses were paid in cash during 1965:

Power and light	$ 53,000
Maintenance bills	160,000
Property taxes for 1965	26,000
Property insurance premiums for the years 1965, 1966, and 1967	84,000
Advertising bills	78,000
Miscellaneous administrative expenses	52,000
Interest	6,000

Depreciation on factory building and equipment and on office furniture and fixtures was recorded in the amounts of $410,000 and $50,000, respectively.

The production records show that $2,530,000 of goods were completed and transferred to the finished stock warehouse during 1965. The costs of goods shipped and billed to customers during the year was $2,500,000. These shipments were billed at prices aggregating $3,468,100. The applicable federal income tax rate is 48% of all income.

Required:

1. Prepare general journal entries to record all of the operating transactions of the Hawthorn Metal Products Corporation for 1965.
2. Prepare an income statement and a statement of cost of goods manufactured and sold for the year ended December 31, 1965.
3. Prepare closing entries at December 31, 1965.

4. Explain in as much detail as you can why overhead was under- or over-applied in the amount that it was.

13. The Gresham Company produces concrete funeral vaults. Only variable production costs are charged to the inventories of goods produced. Budgeted sales and production volumes for 1966 were set at 300,000 units of product. Expenses for the year were budgeted as follows:

Raw materials	$11.50 per unit produced
Direct labor	$2.25 per unit produced
Indirect labor	$.50 per unit produced
Indirect materials	$.40 per unit produced
Salesmen's commissions	10% of sales
Shipping and billing expenses	$.25 per unit sold
Administrative salaries	$165,000
General office expenses	$75,000
Labor-related costs	7.3% of total payroll
Depreciation on factory	$360,000
Depreciation on office	$60,000

Variable overhead costs are charged to production at a normal rate of $.98 per unit of product. A total of 315,000 units were actually produced during 1966. 320,000 units were sold at a price of $24 each. The total cost of these units sold was $4,687,000.

The following inventory balances were reported as of December 31, 1965:

Materials	$210,000
Work in process	90,000
Finished product	147,000

Materials costing $3,600,000 were purchased during 1966. Direct materials issued cost $3,625,000; indirect materials issued cost $130,000.

The following expenses of the year 1966 were paid in cash:

Payroll:	
Direct labor	$710,000
Indirect labor	160,000
Salesmen's commissions	700,000
Administrative salaries	152,000
Shipping and billing expenses	80,000
General office expenses	84,000

The entire payroll is subject to social security payments of 3.8% by both the employees and the company. In addition, the company withheld $300,000 of federal income taxes from employees' earnings. Unemployment compensation tax in the amount of 3.5% of the payroll must be paid by the company.

Depreciation charges for the year were recorded as follows:

Factory	$345,000
Office	60,000

The cost of production completed during 1966 totaled $4,613,200.

Federal income tax accrues at a flat rate of 48% of taxable income.

Required:

1. Prepare general journal entries to record all of the operating transactions for the year 1966.
2. Prepare an income statement and a statement of cost of goods manufactured and sold for the year.
3. Prepare closing entries at December 31, 1966.

Chapter 4

INVENTORY COSTING

FROM THE discussion of the cost accounting cycle in the previous chapter, the reader can see that one of the most important implications of that cycle for financial accounting is the assignment of manufacturing costs to inventory accounts. This chapter will treat several aspects of accounting for costs in inventory. Specifically, the following matters will be considered:

1. Inventory accounting methods.
2. Inventory cost flow assumptions.
3. Cost accounting systems.
4. Absorption and variable costing compared—a critical comparison.

The latter two points involve considerably more than just inventory accounting and will be considered in broader contexts.

INVENTORY ACCOUNTING METHODS

Perpetual, or Book, Inventory Method

The illustrations of the cost accounting cycle in Chapter 3 were prepared, without specific mention of the fact, in accordance with the *perpetual inventory method.* Under a perpetual, or book, inventory method, the costs of all items placed into inventory are debited immediately to the inventory account and the costs of items removed from inventory are credited promptly to that account. Thus, so long as all postings are complete, the inventory account will, at all times, show the cost of the inventory on hand. There is a perpetual record in the books of account of the balance in inventory. This method measures directly the flows of costs into and out of inventory. A perpetual inventory record can be incorporated effectively in a system of inventory control. Accurate and up-to-date records of inventory receipts and issues, coupled with adequate physical safeguarding of stocks on hand, provide simultaneously the bases for good inventory control and correct inventory cost data.

Periodic, or Physical, Inventory Method

In a *periodic inventory method,* actual stocks on hand are counted at the close of each accounting period (typically one year). The sum of the stock at the close of the previous year and the purchases during the current year is the amount of inventory available for use or sale (depending upon the nature of the inventory) during the current period. Subtracting from this sum the stock counted as of the end of the current year, one determines the amount of the inventory issued—whether for use or for sale—during the current year. This method does not provide information as to inventory balances except when physical counts of inventories are taken. Between physical counts, existing inventory balances can only be estimated. This does not imply that no physical control over inventory is exercised during the period. On the contrary, physical control may be just as sound under a periodic inventory method as under a perpetual method.

Comparison of Perpetual and Periodic Inventory Methods

In general, the perpetual and periodic inventory methods may be viewed as alternative approaches to the same end, not as alternative ends. The periodic inventory method involves an absolutely essential physical count of stocks on hand as of the end of the accounting period. The perpetual inventory method does not. Thus, the end-of-year closing procedures may be substantially simplified by the use of the perpetual method. This does not mean, however, that no physical counts need be taken under the perpetual inventory method. Such counts must be made annually in either method, but, in the perpetual method, they may be made at any time and not necessarily as of the end of the period. The inventory count in the perpetual method may be made continually throughout the year—different classes of inventory being counted each month. This practice tends to avoid delays or shutdowns due to a full-scale annual physical count. The book inventory accounts should be adjusted for any discrepancies revealed by the physical count. Such discrepancies are almost inevitable in any business firm; hopefully, they will not be material in amount.

INVENTORY COST FLOW ASSUMPTIONS

To this point, the flow of costs through inventory accounts has been considered in a very general way, and primarily in terms of aggregate dollar amounts. As a matter of fact, however, those aggregate quantities typically are comprised of individual items in inventory and their individual costs. If each item that passed through a particular inventory account bore exactly the same cost per unit, the determination of the aggregate costs charged and credited to the account would be a simple matter of multiplying physical quantities by the uniform unit cost. Business experience, however, has shown that unit costs are not likely to remain unchanged indefinitely. Changes in the general price level, in prices in specific commodity markets, and in the physical quality and composition of commodities all tend to produce variations in unit costs over time. Thus, at any one time, an inventory may comprise physically homogeneous items having different unit costs. For example, suppose that the inventory of raw materials of a manufacturing company includes 500 pounds of material X, purchased at different times and different prices, as follows:

Purchase on April 26	100 lbs. @ $3.03 =	$ 303
Purchase on May 8	250 lbs. @ $3.08 =	770
Purchase on May 15	150 lbs. @ $3.18 =	477
	500 lbs.	$1,550

On May 20, 250 pounds of material X are issued to the factory. From Chapter 3, we know that the cost of these 250 pounds will be charged to Work in Process and credited to Materials Inventory. The question now is which pounds at which unit cost were issued.

One way of determining which units are issued from inventory is *specific identification.* This would require that each physical unit of material be separately identified with its unique unit cost. Then, as that physical unit is removed from inventory, its cost would be charged to Work in Process. Specific identification is feasible where the inventory consists of small quantities of physically separable items. It becomes impractical where the quantity of items is large, as in the case of a bin of bolts. It is impossible in inventories of fungible goods, such as liquids and grains stored in a single tank, elevator, or other container. Even where specific identification is possible, it is questionable whether it is desirable. If there are marked differences among the unit costs of goods in inventory, management might be able to manipulate income from period to period by judicious selection of the specific items to be drawn from stock.

What then is the alternative to specific identification? As a practical matter, some assumption must be made as to the sequence in which costs flow out of inventory. Current accounting practice recognizes three basic cost flow assumptions as generally acceptable. These will be discussed in turn below. It must be emphasized that these are *cost flow* assumptions. Their whole purpose is to determine the costs to be credited to inventory accounts for items removed from stock and, consequently, cost balances remaining in inventory. They are not intended to depict nor should they be interpreted as depicting the physical flow of goods in inventory. Physical and cost flows may parallel each other, but generally accepted accounting principles allow the use of a cost flow assumption which is clearly at variance with the observable physical flow.

First-in, First-out Assumption

The first inventory cost flow assumption to be considered here is the *first-in, first-out* assumption, or FIFO. As the name implies, FIFO assumes that the earliest units received in inventory are the first ones to be issued. Thus, under FIFO, the 250 pounds of material X issued in the illustration above would be assumed to consist of the 100 pounds from the purchase of April 26 and 150 pounds from the purchase of May 8. The costs of materials issued and of materials left in inventory after the issue on May 20 would then be determined as follows:

Materials issued:		
100 lbs. @ $3.03	$303	
150 lbs. @ $3.08	462	$ 765
Materials remaining in inventory:		
100 lbs. @ $3.08	308	
150 lbs. @ $3.18	477	785
Total		$1,550

Each purchase is kept separate in the inventory records, and the order in which it was received determines the order of its issuance. Perhaps the principal appeal of the FIFO assumption is that it is likely to conform to the physical flow of goods in the majority of instances. However, it must be remembered that the selection of a cost flow assumption is not necessarily tied to the physical flow of the goods in the inventory under current accounting principles. Some accountants have argued that the cost flow should follow the physical flow, but this position has not become generally accepted.

Average Cost

A second cost flow assumption states, in effect, that all units in inventory are so commingled as to render identification of specific purchases insignificant. Consequently, all additional purchases are added in with the inventory already on hand to determine an average unit cost for all of the units in stock. This is the *average cost* assumption. Since each new purchase is averaged with the goods already on hand to determine unit cost, there is only one unit cost in an inventory account at any one time; and all units issued from that inventory are credited to the account at the then current average unit cost. Continuing with the illustration of material X developed in the previous sections, the unit cost in inventory from April 26 through May 7 would be $3.03; for that is the only unit cost encountered in the limited experience indicated to May 7. The purchase of May 8, however, would require the computation of a new average unit cost. This will be the quotient of the total cost in inventory ($303 + $770 = $1,073) divided by the total physical quantity in stock (100 lbs. + 250 lbs. = 350 lbs.). The new average unit cost, $3.0657 ($1,073 ÷ 350 lbs.), would obtain until the next purchase on May 15. As it happens, neither the unit cost of $3.03 nor that of $3.0657 was ever employed in connection with an issue of materials; for no issues of material X occurred prior to the next purchase on May 15. With the purchase of May 15, the unit cost is once more recomputed, this time at $3.10 ($1,073 + $477 = $1,550; 350 lbs. + 150 lbs. = 500 lbs.; $1,550 ÷ 500 lbs. = $3.10). This unit cost will be employed on May 20 when 250 pounds are issued to the factory. Under the average cost assumption, the costs of material X issued and still on hand would appear as follows:

Materials issued:	
250 lbs. @ $3.10	$ 775
Materials remaining in inventory:	
250 lbs. @ $3.10	775
Total	$1,550

This illustration reveals the basic methodology of the average cost method. Only one unit cost figure appears in each inventory account at one time. This average unit cost is recomputed each time additional units are received in inventory. It is not affected by issues from inventory; issues are credited to the inventory account at the current average unit cost. The average unit cost is always a *weighted average,* that is, the total dollar cost of the inventory is divided by the total number of units on hand. Hence, the unit prices in purchases of large quantities have relatively greater impacts upon average unit costs than the prices in purchases of small quantities. (Observe the unit cost computation on the occasion of the May 8 purchase as a demonstration of this weighting effect.)

Last-in, First-out Assumption

The third cost flow assumption to be considered is the *last-in, first-out,* or LIFO assumption. It is exactly the converse of the FIFO assumption. The most recent acquisitions in inventory are assumed to be issued first. Thus, any ending inventory balance will be assumed to consist of the oldest items purchased, as long as the entire stock has not been liquidated at one time. Obviously, the last-in, first-out assumption is not likely to correspond with the physical flow of goods except in unusual instances. For perishable items, a last-in, first-out physical flow would be impossible. Nevertheless, current accounting practice would accept the use of LIFO in such a situation. LIFO, like FIFO and average cost, is a *cost flow* assumption; and there is no requirement that the assumed cost flow correspond to the observable physical flow.

The mechanics of LIFO are illustrated in connection with the data used in the previous sections. The 250 pounds of material X issued on May 20 would be assumed to consist of the 150 pounds purchased on May 15 and 100 of the pounds purchased on May 8. The balance of 250 pounds would then consist of the remaining 150 pounds from the May 8 purchase and the 100 pounds purchased on April 26. The costs of material X issued and on hand as of May 20 would be as follows:

Materials issued:		
150 lbs. @ $3.18	$477	
100 lbs. @ $3.08	308	$ 785
Materials remaining in inventory:		
100 lbs. @ $3.03	$303	
150 lbs. @ $3.08	462	765
Total		$1,550

The mechanics of the three cost flow assumptions illustrated here, and particularly those of LIFO, can become considerably more complex. The basic concepts, however, are always as shown here. From the viewpoint of management, the consequences of these various cost flow assumptions are of much more interest than the mechanics, although a fundamental understanding of the procedures is obviously essential to any appreciation of the implications thereof.

Comparison and Evaluation of Cost Flow Assumptions

The illustrations of FIFO, average cost, and LIFO above show that the different assumptions produce different figures for the cost of goods issued and for the inventory balance as of the end of a period. In the example of material X, FIFO results in a cost of goods issued of $765; average cost, $775; and LIFO, $785. If the inventory involved were one of finished goods instead of raw materials, the respective costs of goods issued would represent the cost of goods sold. But the greater the cost of materials used, the greater ultimately will be the cost of goods sold. Hence, regardless of the inventory involved, the same general impact upon cost of goods sold will obtain for each cost flow assumption. Consequently—and most important—income will be affected by the selection of an inventory cost flow assumption except in the rare instance where all items acquired for inventory have the same unit price. Since price change rather than price stability has characterized the economic experience of most modern countries, it is a safe generalization that the cost flow assumption used will be a partial determinant of net income and, hence, of income taxes. For purposes of this discussion, we may regard income taxes as a direct function of net income. The direction of the impact upon income and income taxes of the cost flow assumption chosen depends upon the direction of movement of the prices for the inventoried commodities.

In an inflationary period, the LIFO inventory assumption tends generally to produce lower income and income taxes than either FIFO or average cost. The reason for this is that, under LIFO, the most recent costs, which in inflation are normally the higher costs, are charged against revenue in the income determination process. The early, lower costs remain in inventory. Under FIFO these lower costs would be charged to revenue. The average cost assumption lies somewhere between FIFO and LIFO in this connection, but its impact is generally closer to that of FIFO than to that of LIFO. In deflation, of course, the results are just the opposite; LIFO will tend to produce higher income figures than FIFO or average cost. From the standpoint of economic logic, deflation may be regarded as just as much a possibility as inflation. The experience of the American economy since 1939, however, has created an apparent inflationary bias in the thinking of most businessmen and consumers. The combination of inflation and high income tax rates during the decades of the 1940s and 1950s in the United States has led to very wide adoption of LIFO. In the study of accounting practices of 600 American corporations made annually by the American Institute of Certified Public Accountants, the LIFO assumption has been shown to be used more commonly than any other cost flow assumption.[1] Certainly, it makes sense for management to adopt whatever legitimate

[1] American Institute of Certified Public Accountants, *Accounting Trends and Techniques, 1964* (New York, 1964), p. 46.

means are available to minimize income tax payments. The tax savings involved in the use of LIFO may be substantial, particularly when viewed in the aggregate over a period of many years. One large manufacturer has estimated that its use of LIFO resulted in savings of approximately $19,500,000 over a 19-year period. Savings in larger companies may well have been even greater than this.

The tax-saving aspects of LIFO are not completely free of danger for the taxpayer, however. Should inflation halt and deflation set in, the taxpayer may well find that he would then be better off using the FIFO assumption; but he might not be able to secure permission from the Commissioner of Internal Revenue to change his method of inventory accounting. Further, even if inflation continues, a substantial liquidation of inventory in any year might result in the charging to revenue of the old, low costs in inventory and a consequent increase in net income and the income tax. These considerations must be weighed by management, along with the favorable factors, in making the decision to adopt LIFO. And the decision as to the adoption of the LIFO cost flow assumption must be regarded as a management decision, not merely a technical accounting decision. Despite any doubts as to the theoretical validity of LIFO—and many accountants have such doubts—its tax-saving potential (including due consideration of the possible adverse tax implications) should be viewed as the dominant factor in the decision to adopt or reject it.

COST ACCOUNTING SYSTEMS

Any cost accounting system involves the basic cost accounting cycle explained in Chapter 3. However, the mechanics of processing cost data through this cycle and the manner in which these data are accumulated differ between the alternative systems. While many variations exist, the vast majority of cost accounting systems may be classified as one of two types—*job order* or *process.* In both types, manufacturing cost data are accumulated and charged to inventory accounts for the cost of goods produced. The problems of inventory costing differ somewhat between these two types of systems, as do other accounting procedures. More important than these differences, however, are the fundamental objectives common to both systems. They are alternative procedures for accomplishing essentially the same ends—the accurate and meaningful accumulation of cost data, the valuation of inventories, and the determination of income. Both absorption and variable costing, incidentally, can be employed effectively under either type of cost accounting system.

Job Order Cost System

A *job order cost system* is a system in which production is viewed and accounted for as a series of separate and distinct lots, batches, or *jobs.* Costs are accumulated for each individual job, and a unit cost is computed for each job. Job order costing is normally used where production is undertaken to fill specific customers' orders—such as in construction, printing, and shipbuilding. Such a system permits the manufacturer to match the revenue from an order with the costs incurred to produce it. Job order cost systems are by no means limited to instances of production to customers' orders, however. They are implemented in many industries where production is for inventory (to be sold subsequently to as yet undetermined buyers) but is accomplished in a discontinuous series of jobs. For example, in a furniture factory, the productive facilities of the plant may be employed serially for the manufacture of a lot of 100 maple bedsteads, then a lot of 100 maple dressers, then 500 walnut chairs, then 200 oak tables, and finally 100 upholstered couches. Obviously, it is not reasonable to say that 1,000 units of a homogeneous product have been produced. There are significant differences among these various products and the costs of producing them. Simply to identify a certain amount as the total cost of manufacturing these five jobs would not be particularly meaningful. And to divide such a total cost by 1,000 units of product would result in a wholly spurious figure for unit cost. Hence, cost data are developed for and charged to each job order individually. Even where several jobs for the same item are completed during one accounting period, the element of discontinuity of production (time lapses between the several jobs) makes it necessary to accumulate costs by jobs individually. Each job has its own unit cost, the total cost of the job divided by the number of units produced for it. Different job orders for the same product will very likely have slightly different unit costs, for the human element in production and price changes over time can be expected to have some effect upon costs.

Job Order Cost Sheets. The costing unit in a job order system is the particular job. Direct manufacturing costs, therefore, are those which can be traced logically and practically to the units manufactured on a particular job order. Direct materials costs are traced to individual jobs by indicating job order numbers on materials requisitions issued by the plant to the materials storeroom. Direct labor charges to the several jobs are determined by the preparation of labor time tickets which indicate the amount of time spent by a worker on a particular job and his hourly wage rate. Overhead is typically applied at a normal rate when the job is completed.

All manufacturing costs, direct and indirect, are accumulated for each job order on a *job order cost sheet.* This sheet indicates an identifying number for the job so that it may readily be traced, the product being produced, the number of units of product required for the job, the purpose for which the job is undertaken (i.e., for customer's order or for inventory), the date by which completion is necessary, and all of the costs incurred in the production of the job. All costs charged to production during any given period must appear on some job cost sheet. Hence, the total charges to Work in Process during the period will be equal to the total of all charges to job order cost sheets in that period. Similarly, the credits to Work in Process and corresponding debits to Finished Product will represent the sum of all costs charged to job cost sheets for completed jobs. Then, the ending balance in Work in Process will be equal to the sum of all costs accumulated to date on open cost sheets (i.e., sheets for uncompleted jobs) as of the end of the period. The file of job order cost sheets is, in effect, a subsidiary ledger supporting the general ledger account, Work in Process. Unit costs are determined only for completed jobs, and a job may be started in one period and completed in a subsequent one. Consequently, the calculation of unit cost on any one job may involve cost data spanning two or more accounting periods. The only constraint on this calculation is the job.

The necessity for maintaining numerous job order cost sheets and the necessary supporting documents, such as labor time tickets, means that the clerical work involved in a job order cost system is likely to be substantially greater than that required for a process cost system. This does not mean, of course, that a process system is always preferable. In many industries, only the job order system is feasible, regardless of the greater cost of implementing it.

Overhead Costs in Job Order Systems. The use of normal overhead rates, predetermined on the bases of budgeted costs and budgeted volume, is typically regarded as essential to the smooth functioning of a job order cost system. Normal overhead rates permit the determination of the total cost and, hence, unit cost of a job as soon as it is completed. Actual overhead rates could not be applied until the end of the accounting period. As explained in Chapter 3, such a delay is simply not practical.

Where several materially different products are manufactured in the same plant, it is not valid to charge overhead to all of these products by means of one overhead rate or a single set of rates *per unit of product.*

One product may involve considerably more processing for each unit than another product; obviously, the former should be charged for proportionately more overhead. In other words, the unit of product may not be a suitable "common denominator" for the application of overhead costs to production in a multiproduct firm. Where such is the case, the volume of production may be stated in terms of some unit which is common to all products. In business practice today, direct labor hours are widely used as the basis for charging overhead costs to production. Volume is budgeted in terms of expected labor hours and normal rates per hour are set. The overhead charged to any one job is then the product of the number of labor hours actually worked on that job times the normal overhead rates per hour.

Job Order Costing and Responsibility Costing. The fact that cost data are accumulated for job orders does not mean that they are not also accumulated for each cost center in the plant. The choice of a cost accounting system does not change the need for the development of cost data along responsibility lines. Thus, there may be as many charges for labor and overhead on a job order cost sheet as there are cost centers involved in the production of the job. Each cost center would distribute its own costs to the jobs worked on in that center during the period. Since materials are not necessarily added to production in each cost center, there may be fewer charges for materials than there are cost centers.

Job Order Cost Sheet Illustrated. Table 4–1 is an illustration of a job order cost sheet for a manufacturer of paper novelty products. Among the company's products are jigsaw puzzles. The heading of the job cost sheet identifies the job, the product, and other pertinent information. Each job has a distinctive number. In this illustration, the number partially identifies the product. The "P" shows that the job is for puzzles, and the "750" indicates the number of pieces in the puzzles. The final two digits of the job number simply show that this is the sixty-ninth job for 750-piece puzzles. The heading also describes the product and indicates how many units are required for the job. This particular job is being produced for inventory. Others may be produced to a specific customer's order. The production manager initials the cost sheet to authorize production of 1,200 units of this particular product. The date on which the finished units are required is entered along with the date on which the job is started.

All costs incurred in connection with this job are reported on the job order cost sheet. Raw materials costs are traced to the job by means of materials requisitions. Each requisition identifies not only the items being issued and their costs but also the job number for which they were issued. A summary of requisitions for Job No. P750–69 is entered on the

TABLE 4-1

SHERMAN MANUFACTURING COMPANY
Job Order Cost Sheet

Job No. P750–69	Product Series 808 jigsaw puzzle
Date started 8/12/65	Units required 1,200
Date required 8/15/65	Purpose for inventory
Date completed 8/14/65	Job authorized J.F.C.

Job Costs

Raw Materials:				
Item	*Req. No.*		*Cost*	
Picture prints	3607		$180.00	
Cardboard backing	3608		66.00	
Boxes	3612		35.00	
Box labels	3612		48.00	$ 329.00
Direct Labor:				
Department	*Hours*	*Rate*	*Cost*	
Cutting	25	$2.00	$ 50.00	
Boxing	40	$1.75	70.00	120.00
Variable Overhead:				
Department	*Hours*	*Rate*	*Cost*	
Cutting	25	$ .32	$ 8.00	
Boxing	40	$ .40	16.00	24.00
Fixed Overhead:				
Department	*Hours*	*Rate*	*Cost*	
Cutting	25	$ .84	$ 21.00	
Boxing	40	$ .60	24.00	45.00
Total job costs				$ 518.00
Unit cost				$.431667

Inspected and approved R.W.E.

cost sheet. Direct labor time is accumulated in each production department on labor time tickets. These tickets indicate the amount of time spent on a particular job. All tickets for a job are then summarized in each department and the departmental time totals entered on the job cost sheet, along with the departmental wage rates. Variable and fixed overhead are applied on the basis of normal rates per direct labor hour in each department. These normal rates are predetermined at the start of the fiscal year. The actual labor hours to which they are applied are taken from the summary of labor time tickets. The illustration assumes that the Sherman Manufacturing Company uses absorption costing. If variable costing were used, the section for fixed overhead would simply be deleted from the cost sheet; and total job costs would be less. When production is completed, the date is entered in the heading and the factory inspector initials the cost sheet to indicate that the job has been approved and the units transferred to the finished product storeroom.

Process Cost System

Process cost accounting systems regard production as a continuous flow rather than as a series of identifiable lots. Hence, this type of system is employed in industries where production processes are of a continuous and repetitive nature. Examples of such industries are basic steel, cement, flour milling, and petroleum refining. The simplest illustration of a process cost system is in a firm producing a single product or a single line of homogeneous products. However, process costing may be used effectively in a firm which produces a variety of products so long as the overall production process can be broken down into suboperations of a continuous, repetitive nature. For example, the spray-paint shop in a major appliance manufacturer's plant may perform essentially the same operations regardless of whether ranges, refrigerators, or washers are being painted. These suboperations are commonly referred to as *processes,* or *departments* in process costing. For purposes of the present discussion, processes may be identified with cost centers. Hence, the accumulation of cost data by responsibility will also provide the necessary cost information for the process cost accounting system.

Determination of Unit Cost. In a process cost system, the costing unit is the production in a particular department, or cost center, during a specified period of time, commonly one month. Thus, direct manufacturing costs are those which can be traced to the cost center. Consequently, certain costs which would be indirect in a job order system may be direct under process costing. For example, the wages of a janitor whose work is confined to one cost center would be treated as part of direct labor in a process cost system, even though the janitor does not actually work on the product. The important point is that he works directly in the department.

The unit cost under process costing is the quotient of the manufacturing costs incurred in a given center during a given period of time divided by the units of product manufactured in that center during that time period. This calculation is subject to two constraints, the cost center and the time period. The basic formula for unit cost determination is very simple.

$$\text{Unit cost} = \frac{\text{Total costs in department during period}}{\text{Units produced in department during period}}$$

While this basic formula is always valid, the determination of the units produced may be somewhat complex.

Equivalent Units of Production. Since one of the constraints upon the unit cost computation is the time period, the units produced during a particular period must be identified. If there is an inventory of unfinished production (i.e., Work in Process) at the beginning and/or at the end of the period, the determination of units produced involves some additional computations. Obviously, the total number of units of potential finished product in the inventory at the end of the month may not be included among the units produced during that month; for such inclusion would imply that they were completed when this is patently not so. Similarly, the total number of units in beginning inventory cannot be treated as part of current production; to do so would be to ignore the fact that those units were partially completed during the previous month. Thus, some unit is needed to measure the amount of productive work actually done during one period. The unit of measure for this purpose is the *equivalent unit of production.*

Equivalent units of production measure the amount of work accomplished during a given period. They are units of product, but not necessarily exclusively whole units. For example, assume that the drill press department of the ABC Manufacturing Company finished 16,000 units of product during the month of March. The inventory of Work in Process in the department at the end of February consisted of 1,200 units that were then half completed. The inventory of Work in Process at the end of March was comprised of 1,500 units that were one-third complete. The 16,000 units completed during the month do not include any part of the ending inventory, but that inventory was partially manufactured during the month. On the other hand, the 16,000 units do include the 1,200 units in the beginning inventory; but half of the work on those units was completed in the previous month. Hence, the work done (equivalent units) during March consists of the units finished during that month plus the work done on the ending inventory minus the work done in February on the beginning inventory. Equivalent units produced, then, are equal to the total units completed during a period plus the total units in the ending inventory of Work in Process times the fraction that the inventory is completed and minus the total units in the beginning inventory of Work in Process times the fraction that they are already complete at the start of the period. Using the data from the example above, the equivalent units produced in the drill press department during March would be computed as follows:

Units completed during March	16,000
+ Units in ending inventory times fraction completed (1,500 units × $\frac{1}{3}$)	500
	16,500
− Units in beginning inventory times fraction completed (1,200 × $\frac{1}{2}$)	600
= Equivalent units produced	15,900

Unit cost would then be equal to the total costs incurred in the department during March divided by the 15,900 equivalent units.

The problem of equivalent units may be complicated further by the fact that not all of the cost factors of production are the same fraction complete in a given inventory of Work in Process. For example, all of the materials may be put into the production process at its inception; whereas the labor and overhead are added throughout the process. Hence, any inventory of Work in Process would be fully complete with respect to materials but might be any fraction complete with respect to labor and overhead. In such a case, no single figure for equivalent production would be valid. Rather, there would have to be one such figure for materials and a different one for labor and overhead. It should be noted here that labor and overhead will not necessarily be at the same degree of completion in an inventory. If they were not, there would have to be three separate figures for equivalent units. For purposes of the present discussion, we will assume that labor and overhead are always at the same stage of completion. Obviously, this would be the case where overhead is applied to production on the basis of direct labor hours. Thus, a single figure for equivalent units and a single unit cost figure could be used for the combination of labor and overhead, commonly referred to as conversion costs. In the example in the previous paragraph, assume that all materials are placed into production at the start of the process (and, hence, are fully complete in any inventory) and that the fractions of completion indicated apply only to the conversion costs. The calculation of equivalent units would then appear as follows:

	Materials	*Labor and Overhead*
Units completed during March	16,000	16,000
+ Units in ending inventory times fraction completed—		
Materials (1,500 × 1)	1,500	
Labor and overhead (1,500 × $\frac{1}{3}$)		500
	17,500	16,500
− Units in beginning inventory times fraction completed—		
Materials (1,200 × 1)	1,200	
Labor and overhead (1,200 × $\frac{1}{2}$)		600
= Equivalent units produced	16,300	15,900

As a general rule, the concept of equivalent units must be related to a particular cost factor in order for it to be operationally meaningful. Consequently, unit costs typically can be computed only for each cost factor separately. Total unit cost is then the sum of the unit costs for the individual cost factors.

Process Costing Illustration. The determination of unit costs in a process system and the applications of these data are illustrated below for the drill press department of the ABC Manufacturing Company. The equivalent units of production for materials and for labor and overhead in this illustration are those computed in the preceding paragraph. Cost data for the drill press department for March are as follows:

Costs in the beginning inventory		
Materials	$ 22,140	
Labor and overhead	12,912	$ 35,052
Costs charged during March		
Materials	$299,920	
Labor and overhead	343,440	643,360
		$678,412

The equivalent units of production for March, already computed above, include only the work actually accomplished during the current month. The work done on the beginning inventory during February is excluded from the computation of equivalent units. Since total costs will be divided by equivalent units in the calculation of unit costs, logically the total costs used in the computation must parallel the units used. Thus, only the costs incurred during March are included in the determination of unit costs. Costs incurred during February on the beginning inventory of March are excluded. However, these costs incurred during February must be accounted for during March. While they are not employed in the current unit cost computation, they must not be ignored altogether.

The determination of unit cost is not a final end in itself, of course. It serves two fundamental purposes. First, it affords some basis for cost control. Unit costs of several months may be compared, trends noted, and differences evaluated with a view toward cost control. Actual unit costs may also be compared with some standards for unit costs in order to appraise the efficiency of manufacturing operations during the period. Second, the unit cost is necessary to determine the cost of goods completed in the department and transferred to the next step in the production process and also the cost of goods remaining in the departmental inventory of Work in Process at the end of the period. The calculation of unit costs and the application of such unit costs to production are illustrated in Table 4–2, a production cost report for the drill press department for the month of March. This report includes the costs in the beginning inventory, but it does not incorporate them in the computation of unit costs for March. Notice in Table 4–2 that there is no single figure for equivalent units which can be divided into total costs to produce the total unit cost of $40. Individual unit costs are determined for materials and for labor and overhead, and the sum of these is the total unit cost for March.

TABLE 4–2

ABC MANUFACTURING COMPANY
Production Cost Report—Drill Press Department
For the month of March 19—

	Total Costs	*Equivalent Units*	*Unit Cost*
Total costs incurred			
Beginning inventory:			
Materials	$ 22,140		
Labor and overhead	12,912		
	35,052		
Current charges:			
Materials	299,920	16,300	$18.40
Labor and overhead	343,440	15,900	21.60
Total	$678,412		$40.00
Total costs accounted for			
Completed production:			
Units from beginning inventory			
Costs incurred in previous month	$ 35,052		
Cost to complete	12,960	600	$21.60
	48,012	1,200	
Units started currently	592,000	14,800	40.00
	640,012	16,000	
Ending inventory:			
Materials	27,600	1,500	18.40
Labor and overhead	10,800	500	21.60
	38,400		
Total	$678,412		

Obviously, the total costs incurred must be accounted for. There are only two possible dispositions of costs charged to a cost center; they may either be transferred to the next stage of the production process as the cost of completed (in the one department) production or remain in the center as the cost of the ending inventory of Work in Process. Table 4–2 shows the cost of completed production as comprising the cost of the beginning inventory, both the costs incurred in the previous month and the costs incurred currently to complete those units, and the cost of the units which were both started and completed during the current month. The inventory at the end of the month, therefore, consists of units started during the current month, and, consequently, of current costs. The reader should recognize that this illustration employs the first-in, first-out, or FIFO cost flow assumption. The average cost and the last-in, first-out assumptions may also be used in connection with inventories of work in process under a process cost system. While the basic approach is the same regardless of the cost flow assumption employed, there are enough technical distinctions among the three that the elementary picture intended here would be unduly clouded if all three assumptions were illustrated.

The cost report in Table 4–2 is divided into two sections, one showing the total costs incurred and the determination of unit costs and the other showing the disposition of these total costs. Unit costs are computed by dividing the total costs incurred during the current period for each cost factor by the equivalent production of the period for each factor. The costs accounted for include those charged to completed production and those in inventory at the end of the month. The cost of completed production is composed of the costs applied to the beginning inventory during the previous month, the current cost to complete the beginning inventory, and the current costs of units started and finished during the current month. The costs applied to the beginning inventory in February total $35,052. Since the beginning inventory was completed with respect to materials in the previous month, no current materials cost is charged to it. As it was only half completed with respect to labor and overhead, however, an additional 600 equivalent units of labor and overhead must be added during March at the current cost of $21.60 per unit. Adding these costs to complete ($12,960) to the costs of the previous month ($35,052) yields a total cost of $48,012 for the 1,200 units in beginning inventory, now completed. The remaining 14,800 units completed during March were started currently and, hence, can be charged entirely at the current total unit cost of $40.00; the total cost of these units is then $592,000. The single total unit cost figure of $40.00 can be applied to the 14,800 units started and completed currently because they are all at the same degree of completion. The 1,500 units in ending inventory, on the other hand, are fully complete as to materials but only one-third complete as to conversion costs. Consequently, the cost of the ending inventory is the sum of 1,500 equivalent units of materials at the current unit cost of $18.40 plus 500 equivalent units of labor and overhead at the current unit cost of $21.60.

Journal Entries. Unlike the job order system, it is customary in process costs systems that there be as many Work in Process accounts as there are cost centers. Raw materials drawn from the storeroom, direct labor, and overhead are charged to the appropriate Work in Process accounts, as already illustrated in Chapter 3. In addition, the costs of units completed in one department and transferred to another department for further processing are charged to the Work in Process account of the latter department and credited to the account of the former. Referring again to the illustration in the foregoing sections, assume that the drill press department is only the first stage in the production process of the ABC Manufacturing Company. The product proceeds from that department through the stamping and the assembly departments before being placed into the warehouse for finished production. The entries to charge the current costs to the drill press department would be as follows:

Work in Process—Drill Press Dept.	$299,920	
Materials Inventory		$299,920
Work in Process—Drill Press Dept.	343,440	
Payroll Summary		185,360
Variable Overhead Applied		62,780
Fixed Overhead Applied		95,300*

* Separate amounts for labor, variable overhead, and fixed overhead have been assumed here for purposes of the entry. As already explained, they were not necessary for the determination of unit cost in Table 4–2.

These entries assume that the ABC Manufacturing Company uses the absorption costing method and normal overhead rates. Under variable costing, not only the second entry above but also the cost data in Table 4–2 would be different. The advantage, from using normal overhead rates, of being able to cost fully a job upon its completion is not relevant to process costing. However, the advantage of avoiding variations in unit cost from month to month because of seasonal fluctuations in output remains in both systems, job order and process.

The transfer of the semifinished product from the drill press department to the stamping department would be recorded thus:

Work in Process—Stamping Dept.	640,012	
Work in Process—Drill Press Dept.		640,012

Other costs in the stamping department would be recorded in the usual way, as illustrated below without figures.

Work in Process—Stamping Dept.	xxx	
Materials Inventory		xxx
Payroll Summary		xxx
Variable Overhead Applied		xxx
Fixed Overhead Applied		xxx

The total cost in the stamping department will include both costs incurred initially in the drill press department and those incurred directly in the stamping operation. The entries to record all costs charged to the assembly department, again without figures, are as follows:

Work in Process—Assembly Dept.	xxx	
Work in Process—Stamping Dept.		xxx
Work in Process—Assembly Dept.	xxx	
Payroll Summary		xxx
Variable Overhead Applied		xxx
Fixed Overhead Applied		xxx

As can be seen from the last entry above, no additional raw materials are added to the product in the assembly department. The final completion of the product is accomplished in the assembly department and the goods are transferred therefrom to the finished product warehouse.

Finished Product	xxx	
Work in Process—Assembly Dept.		xxx

The entry for the cost of finished product sold is exactly as illustrated in the previous chapter and need not be repeated here.

ABSORPTION AND VARIABLE COSTING COMPARED

The Development of Variable Costing

Absorption costing is generally accepted in current accounting practice as *the* way of accounting for manufacturing costs and, specifically, fixed overhead costs. For many years, in fact, there was not even any significant suggestion of an alternative. During the 1930s, however, the method we know here as variable costing was proposed and given some small notice. But the growth of variable costing was slow in coming. The urgency of World War II caused a great many less critical considerations to be pushed out of men's minds, and the virtual pandemonium of the immediate postwar years was hardly conducive to careful consideration of something so petty as a method of accounting for fixed costs. Thus, the real development of the variable costing technique did not occur until the decade of the 1950s.

To begin with, the author must confess that variable costing is not widely known by that name at all. Rather, the concept has developed and is most popularly known today as *direct costing*. This has been an unfortunate choice of terminology, however; for the distinction which is at the heart of the method is not that between direct and indirect costs, but that between variable and fixed costs. "Variable costing," although not so widely employed, is a much more descriptive term and will be used throughout this volume. The same concept is known as *marginal costing* in Great Britain. Again, the selection of the term seems to be unsatisfactory. Variable costs cannot necessarily be identified with marginal costs, and, as already pointed out, "marginal cost" has so explicit a meaning in economic theory that the author prefers to avoid its use altogether in accounting.

Arguments for and against Variable Costing

The development of variable costing has progressed very rapidly in recent years. Its proponents increase in number almost daily. Advocates of the method have raised a number of arguments in its favor. Some of these will be considered, along with counterarguments where appropriate, in the paragraphs that follow.

Separate Accounting for Variable and Fixed Costs. One argument offered in support of variable costing is that it causes separate identification and recording of variable and fixed costs in the accounts and, hence, greater realization on the part of accountants and managers of the importance of volume in the determination of costs. There can be little question that the separate recording of variable and fixed costs is useful to management. As has been demonstrated in the preceding chapter, this separate recording can be effected just as well under absorption costing as under variable costing. The fact is, however, that a clear distinction between variable and fixed costs has only infrequently been made in the accounts of firms employing absorption costing. In other words, although the separation can be made in either costing method, it typically has accompained only the variable costing method.

Emphasis on Cost-Volume Relationships. Perhaps the most important and unassailable argument in favor of variable costing is that it emphasizes the distinction between variable and fixed costs in reports to management and to others. A comparison of Tables 3–3 and 3–5 in Chapter 3 will testify to the validity of this point. Under absorption costing, the principal intermediate profit figure on the income statement is the gross margin, a residual after the deduction from revenue of both variable and fixed costs of manufacturing. The principal intermediate figure on the variable costing income statement is the variable profit, the difference between revenue (which, of course, varies with sales volume) and those costs which vary with the volume of sales (variable cost of goods sold, variable selling expenses, etc.). Thus, variable profit, in itself, bears a direct relationship to volume. No such relationship exists between gross margin and volume. This undeniable emphasis upon cost-volume relationships is particularly useful to management, which has the power (not without limit, of course) to effect changes in costs and/or in volume. Whether the same emphasis is equally useful to others, such as stockholders and creditors, is problematic.

Some opponents of the variable costing method have pointed out that, by excluding fixed costs from the cost of the product, the method emphasizes variable costs to the prejudice of fixed costs and that fixed costs are likely to be ignored or, at least, minimized in importance by management. This argument is particularly unsatisfactory, however; for it seems to rest upon the unattractive premise that managers are not very bright. But just the opposite would appear to be true. The general prosperity and profitability of American business enterprises hardly suggest the presence of managers who would be likely to overlook fixed costs—or any other costs, for that matter.

Effect of Inventory Changes on Reported Net Income. Under absorption costing, an increase in finished product inventory levels (i.e., ending inventory greater than the beginning balance) in a year of declining sales can have the effect of mitigating a decline in income, because fixed manufacturing costs incurred during the period are partially deferred in inventory until some subsequent period when the goods are sold. Conversely, a reduction in inventory levels (i.e., ending inventory less than the beginning) has the effect of charging to the revenues of that period fixed manufacturing costs incurred in some previous period. In other words, changes in inventory balances from the beginning to the end of a period have an identifiable impact upon income under absorption costing. Advocates of variable costing have argued that such an effect is artificial and may be misleading. They point out that variable costing avoids any income effect resulting from inventory increases or decreases.

The substance of this particular argument can best be seen from a simple illustration. Table 4–3 compares reported incomes under absorption costing and variable costing for the same company for three years. In the first year, more units are manufactured than sold; inventory is increased. In the second year, manufacturing volume and sales volume are identical; inventory balances remain unchanged. Finally, in the third year, sales volume exceeds the volume of production; inventory is decreased. The sales volume is the same (60,000 units) in each year, and the selling price remains stable at $4.00 per unit. The variable manufacturing costs total $2.50 per unit in each year, and the fixed manufacturing costs total $60,000 each year. No nonmanufacturing costs are included in the illustration because, since they are treated in the same way under both absorption and variable costing, they would have no effect upon the comparison.

Certain technical aspects of Table 4–3 must be seen clearly in order to understand fully the comparison being made. Under both costing methods, the variable costs charged to the revenue of the period are $150,000 (the 60,000 units sold each year at the unit variable cost rate of $2.50). Under variable costing, the fixed cost charged to revenue in each year is simply the total of fixed costs incurred in that year—$60,000. Under absorption costing, however, the fixed costs charged to revenue are the fixed costs of the goods sold and may be more or less than the $60,000 of fixed costs incurred in each year. In the first

TABLE 4–3

COMPARATIVE INCOME MEASUREMENTS

	Absorption Costing	*Variable Costing*
First Year:		
Unit sales volume	60,000	60,000
Unit production volume	75,000	75,000
Sales revenue	$240,000	$240,000
Costs charged to revenue:		
Variable	150,000	150,000
Fixed	48,000	60,000
Total costs	198,000	210,000
Net income	$ 42,000	$ 30,000
Second Year:		
Unit sales volume	60,000	60,000
Unit production volume	60,000	60,000
Sales revenue	$240,000	$240,000
Costs charged to revenue:		
Variable	150,000	150,000
Fixed	60,000	60,000
Total costs	210,000	210,000
Net income	$ 30,000	$ 30,000
Third Year:		
Unit sales volume	60,000	60,000
Unit production volume	48,000	48,000
Sales revenue	$240,000	$240,000
Costs charged to revenue:		
Variable	150,000	150,000
Fixed	69,600	60,000
Total costs	219,600	210,000
Net income	$ 20,400	$ 30,000

year, the fixed costs average $.80 per unit ($60,000 ÷ 75,000 units produced). Thus, the fixed cost of goods sold is $48,000 (60,000 units sold at a fixed cost rate of $.80 each). In the second year under absorption costing, fixed costs average $1.00 per unit ($60,000 ÷ 60,000 units produced); and the fixed cost of goods sold is $60,000 (60,000 units sold @ $1.00). Finally, the fixed costs per unit in the third year amount to $1.25 ($60,000 ÷ 48,000 units produced). The fixed costs of goods sold in the third year includes the fixed cost incurred in the third year (48,000 units sold × $1.25 = $60,000) plus some of the fixed costs incurred in the first year and deferred in inventory (12,000 units sold × $.80 = $9,600). This is a total of $69,600. In each year, the first fixed costs charged to revenue are those applicable to the current production. This means that the inventory is accounted for in accordance with the LIFO cost flow assumption. Year-to-year fluctuations in income under absorption costing would appear with either the FIFO or the average cost flow assumption also; only the amounts of the fluctuations would be different.

Table 4–3 presumes that fixed overhead is applied to production at actual rates computed at the end of the year. If a normal rate were used instead, the fluctuations in income under absorption costing would still occur; but they would then be produced, in part, as a result of under- or overapplied overhead. Actual rates were assumed here only because they are simpler to present in the illustration than are normal rates.

The basic point of the illustration can now be seen quite simply. During the three-year period shown, there were no changes in sales volume, selling prices, variable costs per unit, or total fixed costs. The only change was in the volume of production and, consequently, in the levels of inventory. Under variable costing, changes in inventory levels have no effect upon income. Under absorption costing, on the other hand, income is different in each of the three years as a result of the changes in inventory levels. The proponents of variable costing argue that these fluctuations in income are meaningless and potentially misleading and, hence, that variable costing is superior to absorption costing insofar as each is concerned with the measurement of periodic net income.

The validity of this particular argument in favor of variable costing rests upon the validity of the basic premise of the method, namely, that fixed manufacturing costs are period costs and not product costs. Supporters of variable costing contend that such is indeed the case, that fixed overhead is the cost of providing productive capacity, of making production possible during a particular period, but not a part of the cost of the units actually produced in that period. Advocates of absorption costing, on the other hand, argue that the fixed costs of manufacturing are just as much costs of the product as are variable costs. They argue that the utilization of factory facilities as represented by the cost item depreciation is just as essential to the product as are direct materials and labor. Which of these positions is the correct one has been argued frequently and vehemently. As mentioned earlier, absorption costing is generally accepted in current accounting practice, while variable costing is not. This fact does not necessarily demonstrate the theoretic superiority of absorption costing, however. It could be interpreted simply as a reflection of the facts that absorption costing has long been entrenched in accounting practice and that accounting practices are not changed overnight.

It is important that the reader understand that the fluctuations in income shown in Table 4–3 under absorption costing are correct and proper if fixed overhead is truly a product cost as absorption costing suggests. As a matter of fact, if fixed overhead is properly treated as a product cost, then the use of variable costing would result in an artificial equalization of income; and such practice is generally agreed to be improper. Whether income fluctuations caused by changes in inventory levels are valid or not depends upon whether fixed overhead is a product cost or a period cost. At this writing, it is fair to say that the latter question remains a disputed point.

Internal and External Accounting Reports

The development of variable costing has centered around its usefulness in reports to management. Only recently has considerable interest arisen in its use also in reports to stockholders, creditors, and other outside parties. With respect to internal reports submitted to management, the decision as to the use of variable costing is a simple one. The criteria which should guide the selection of accounting techniques in reports to management are utility and efficiency. If variable costing proves to be useful and effective in management reports, then, by all means, it should be used. Variable costing is good management accounting if it facilitates management's achievement of its basic objectives.

Where external reports to stockholders and others are concerned, the criteria determining the selection of accounting practices are *generally accepted accounting principles.* These consist of various concepts, rules, and practices which have attained acceptance in business. At the time of this writing, variable costing has not attained the status of a generally accepted accounting principle. This does not mean that it never will; accounting principles are not immutable.[2] For the present, however, the reader should be aware that variable costing is not considered acceptable in external financial reports.

---

[2] In view of the increasing popularity of variable costing among manufacturing firms, it is not unlikely that it will become generally accepted in external financial reports in the fairly near future. Its acceptance in financial reporting would depend to a considerable extent upon its acceptability in income tax reports also.

A firm which wishes to employ variable costing in its internal reporting system but must adhere to absorption costing for its external reports is not condemned to maintaining two separate sets of books. Costs may be accumulated in the accounts and internal reports prepared in accordance with the variable costing technique. When external reports are prepared, a simple adjustment may be made to add to inventory a proportionate share of the fixed overhead of the period and to remove such amount from the current fixed overhead expense account. For example, if the Fixed Overhead Control account had a balance of $750,000 at the end of a year and it was determined that, under absorption costing, 10% of that total should be deferred in inventory, a simple adjustment would transfer $75,000 of the fixed overhead to the appropriate inventory accounts—Work in Process and/or Finished Product. The remaining $675,000 would be reported as part of the cost of goods sold on the absorption costing income statement. This adjustment would be made only in the external financial statements, of course, not in the ledger accounts, which would be maintained consistently in accordance with variable costing.

QUESTIONS FOR DISCUSSION

1. Has management any interest in the decision as to whether a perpetual or a periodic inventory method is to be used, or is this simply a technical accounting decision? Explain your answer.
2. You have been appointed controller of a newly organized chemical corporation. The firm will manufacture and distribute a variety of chemical products. It will be necessary to maintain fairly large inventories of raw materials and finished products. Which inventory cost flow assumption would you recommend the company use—FIFO, average cost, or LIFO? Why? What implicit assumptions, if any, underlie your recommendation? Might you recommend a different inventory cost flow if these basic underlying assumptions were changed? Explain.
3. "In light of income tax considerations, the LIFO inventory method is, as a practical matter, always preferable to either the FIFO or the average cost method." Comment on the validity of this assertion.
4. "A manufacturer using a job order cost system must use the FIFO inventory cost flow assumption, for the first jobs started would typically be the first ones completed. And no job would ever be left uncompleted for a long period while others were being started and finished (as the LIFO assumption would suggest)." Discuss this statement.
5. What are the comparative merits of using normal overhead rates rather than actual overhead rates in job order cost systems and in process cost systems?

6. Why are equivalent units of production essential to an accurate determination of unit cost in a process cost system but unnecessary for the unit cost computation in a job order cost system?
7. "Process costing is preferable to job order costing because the former is consistent with the objective of responsibility costing while the latter is not." To what does this statement refer? Do you agree or disagree with it? Why?
8. Which is the better method of costing production—absorption costing or variable costing? You may select either method or you may abstain from casting a ballot on the question, but you must carefully explain your selection or the reasons for your abstention.
9. The sales of the Forester Company in 1965 were somewhat disappointing in light of recent years' sales. However, a substantial inventory of finished product was accumulated during that year in anticipation of much improved sales in 1966. Actual sales in 1966 were even better than had been hoped for. All of the current output and most of the inventory accumulated in 1965 were sold. Still, when the financial statements for the year were prepared, the net income for 1966 was less than that for 1965. The chairman of the board was very unhappy at this report and demanded an explanation from the controller. The controller explained that, under the absorption costing method, long used by the company, a major liquidation of the inventory of finished product such as occurred in 1966 tended to reduce income. When the chairman discussed the situation with the firm's auditor, the auditor suggested that he prepare revised statements for 1965 and 1966 under the variable costing method. These revised statements showed a lower income for 1965 than originally reported but a considerably higher income for 1966. The chairman was so pleased with the results reported in the revised statements that he fired the controller and replaced him with the auditor.

   In 1967, sales decline sharply. This decline was believed to be only temporary, however. Upon the recommendations of the sales manager and the new controller, production was maintained at the same level as in the preceding two years. It was agreed that any inventory built up in 1967 would be sold the following year. When the financial statements under variable costing were prepared at the end of 1967, the income statement showed a net loss. The chairman of the board demanded to know why this loss arose. The new controller explained that it was the normal consequence of variable costing in such a year. A new auditor was engaged, and he pointed out to the chairman that a profit for 1967 would have been reported under the old absorption costing method. At this, the chairman bolted from the room, went down to Nick's where he consumed six martinis, and then lay down across the Union Pacific tracks.

   Quick, before the next train comes along, explain to the chairman why the alternative costing methods resulted in such different income figures. Explain to him how he can go on living in reasonable sobriety with one or the other of these two methods.
10. Of what value is an accounting system that records and reports variable and fixed cost data separately?

PROBLEMS

1. The Jaggers Manufacturing Company's inventory records reveal the following information relative to one of the company's principal raw materials:

Balance, Jan. 1	800 units @ $2.00
Purchase, Jan. 8	4,000 units @ $2.06
Issue, Jan. 12	1,800 units
Issue, Jan. 19	2,000 units
Purchase, Jan. 25	1,500 units @ $2.10
Issue, Jan. 30	1,200 units

The company uses a perpetual inventory system.

Required:

Compute the cost of the inventory of this raw material on January 31 under each of the following cost flow assumptions:

1. FIFO.
2. Average cost.
3. LIFO.

2. The Gargery Forge Company's record of finished product shows the following activity during the year 1965:

	Completed Production		*Sales*
Quarter	*Units*	*Unit Cost*	*(Units)*
1st	1,000	$16.40	800
2nd	1,200	16.10	1,200
3rd	1,500	15.80	1,800
4th	1,000	16.50	850

The inventory at January 1, 1965, consisted of 250 units at a unit cost of $16.00.

Required:

1. Assuming that the company uses a perpetual inventory system, compute the ending inventory of Finished Product and the Cost of Goods Sold for 1965 under each of the following cost flow assumptions:
   a. FIFO.
   b. Average cost.
   c. LIFO.
2. Assuming that the company uses a periodic inventory system, compute the ending inventory of Finished Product and the Cost of Goods Sold for 1965 under each of the following cost flow assumptions:
   a. FIFO.
   b. Average cost.
   c. LIFO.

   The ending inventory was counted and found to include 300 units of product.

3. The Havisham Corporation commenced operations in January, 1966. It produces and sells a new type of automobile battery that lasts longer and occupies less space than conventional types. Production and sales data for the first year of operations are summarized below.

Month	*Production*		*Units*
	Units	*Unit Cost*	*Sold*
January	200	$16.25	120
February	500	15.85	380
March	1,200	15.40	1,000
April	2,000	15.10	1,600
May	2,500	15.00	1,800
June	3,000	14.75	2,500
July	4,000	14.55	3,500
August	6,000	13.80	5,000
September	7,500	13.75	6,800
October	8,000	13.50	7,900
November	8,800	13.35	9,600
December	10,000	12.90	11,400

Continued growth in production and sales is anticipated. The company is debating whether to use FIFO or LIFO in the valuation of its inventory of Finished Product. A perpetual inventory record system will be employed in either event.

Required:

1. Compute the cost of the inventory of Finished Product at December 31, 1966, and the Cost of Goods Sold for the year then ended under (*a*) FIFO and (*b*) LIFO.
2. In this case, would you recommend that the Havisham Corporation use FIFO or LIFO? Explain the reasons for your recommendations. Can you envision any circumstances in the future that might suggest that the alternative recommendation would have been wiser? Explain.

4. The Watson Tool Corporation, which commenced operations on August 1, 1965, employs a job order cost system. Overhead is charged to production at normal rates per direct labor hour, as follows:

Variable overhead	$1.40 per hour
Fixed overhead	$1.10 per hour

The acual operations for the month of August, 1965 are summarized as follows:

a. Purchase of raw materials—25,000 pieces @ $1.20
b. Prime costs charged to production:

Job. No.	*Units*	*Materials*	*Direct Labor*	
			Cost	*Hours*
101	10,000	$4,000	$6,000	3,000
102	8,800	3,600	5,400	2,700
103	16,000	7,000	9,000	4,500
104	8,000	3,200	4,800	2,400
105	20,000	8,000	3,600	1,800

c. Actual overhead costs incurred (credit "various accounts"):

Variable	$18,500
Fixed	15,000

d. Completed jobs—101, 102, 103, and 104
e. Sales—$105,000. All units produced on Jobs 101, 102, and 103 were sold; 4,400 units produced on Job 104 were sold.

Required:

1. Prepare general journal entries to record the operations for August, 1965.
2. Compute the unit cost of each completed job.
3. Compute the balance in Work in Process at August 31. Prove the accuracy of this balance by showing the several cost elements (i.e., materials, labor, and overhead) that it comprises.

5. The Holmes Products Company uses a job order cost system and variable costing. Variable overhead is charged to production at a normal rate of $.75 per direct labor hour. The inventories on May 1, 1966, were as follows:

Materials				$34,600
Work in Process:				
Job. No.	*Materials*	*Labor*	*Overhead*	
327	$ 5,000	$ 8,400	$4,200	
329	4,800	7,600	3,800	
330	2,400	3,200	1,600	
	$12,200	$19,200	$9,600	41,000
Finished Product				62,000

Operations for the month of May, 1966 are summarized below.

a. Materials costing $13,800 were purchased on account.
b. A summary of materials requisitions shows the following charges to jobs:

Job. No.	*Materials Cost*
330	$2,700
331	6,120
332	5,500
333	4,400
334	1,800

c. The payroll for the month of May was distributed as follows:

Direct labor:		
Job. No.	*Labor Hours*	*Labor Cost*
327	400	$ 600
329	600	900
330	1,200	1,800
331	3,000	4,500
332	3,600	5,400
333	2,000	3,000
334	200	300
Variable indirect labor	3,300	5,500

d. Other actual variable overhead costs totaled $2,980. Actual fixed overhead amounted to $12,600. (Credit "various accounts.")

e. The following jobs and units were completed during May:

Job. No.	*Units*
327	9,250
329	7,800
330	7,200
331	6,600
332	6,800

f. The cost of products sold during May totaled $70,000.

Required:

1. Prepare journal entries to record the operations for the month of May, 1966.
2. Compute the unit cost of each completed job.
3. Compute the balance in Work in Process at May 31 and show its composition (i.e., materials, labor, and overhead).

6. The Moriarty Manufacturing Corporation produces a variety of power garden tools. A job order cost system is used. On June 1, 1965, the factory ledger showed the following inventory balances:

Materials	$ 70,000
Work in Process	122,000
Finished Product	160,000

Open job order cost sheets on June 1 contained the following charges:

Job No.	*Materials*	*Labor*	*Overhead*
M–1015	$44,000	$12,000	$18,000
C–908	12,000	6,000	9,000
T–750	16,000	2,000	3,000
	$72,000	$20,000	$30,000

Transactions for the month of June are summarized below:

a. Materials costing $130,000 were purchased.

b. A summary of materials issues for the month is as follows:

Job C–908	$ 16,000
Job T–750	8,000
Job M–1016	35,000
Job T–751	19,000
Job M–1017	22,000
Indirect materials (variable cost)	10,000
	$110,000

c. Factory labor costs were distributed as follows:

Job M–1015	$ 18,000
Job C–908	10,000
Job T–750	4,000
Job M–1016	26,000
Job T–751	4,000
Job M–1017	8,000
Indirect labor (variable cost)	30,000
	$100,000

All production workers were paid a uniform wage rate of $2 per hour.

d. The distribution of the factory payroll was as follows:

Payroll checks disbursed	$76,875
Federal income tax withheld	15,325
Social security tax withheld	3,800
Health insurance premiums withheld	4,000

e. Labor-related costs included the following items:

Social security tax	$3,800
Unemployment compensation tax	3,500

f. The actual fixed overhead costs incurred during June included the following charges:

Depreciation on plant and equipment	$45,000
Property taxes payable in 1966	8,000
Property insurance prepaid in 1964	6,000

g. Variable overhead is applied to production at a normal rate of $1.20 per direct labor hour. Fixed overhead is applied at a normal rate of $1.80 per hour.

h. Jobs M-1015, C-908, T-750, and M-1016 were completed during June.

i. Goods costing $375,000 were sold for $500,000.

Required:

1. Prepare general journal entries to record the operations for the month of June.
2. Prepare a statement of cost of goods manufactured and sold for the month ended June 30, 1965.

7. The Lestrade Company manufactures two products, A and B. A job order cost system is employed. The letter prefix to the job number identifies the product being produced on that job. Work in Process is accounted for by individual job orders. Raw Materials and Finished Product are costed under the last-in, first-out assumption.

On January 31, 1966, the company's inventory accounts showed the following balances:

Materials—8,000 lbs. @ $2.00		$16,000
Work in process:		
Job A-29—4,000 units	$12,000	
Job B-33—2,000 units	8,000	20,000
Finished Product:		
Product A—2,500 units @ $4.40	$11,000	
Product B—3,000 units @ $6.00	18,000	29,000

The following raw materials purchases were made during February, 1966.

Feb. 10—10,000 lbs. @ $2.05
Feb. 22—12,000 lbs. @ $2.10

Materials were issued during the month as follows:

Feb. 15—9,000 lbs. for Job A-30
Feb. 25—11,000 lbs. for Job B-34

Direct labor costs of February were charged to jobs as follows:

Job	*Hours*	*Cost*
A-29	2,400	$ 5,000
B-33	1,600	3,300
A-30	6,000	12,500
B-34	4,000	8,400

Actual overhead for the month included $10,000 of variable costs and $15,000 of fixed costs. Variable overhead is applied to production at a normal rate of $.75 per direct labor hour. Fixed overhead is accounted for as a period expense.

Jobs A-29 and B-33 were completed during February. On the last day of the month, 3,000 units of product A and 1,800 units of product B were shipped to customers.

Required:

Prepare analyses of the ledger accounts for Raw Materials, Work in Process, Finished Product, and Cost of Goods Sold for the month of February, 1966. Show all debits and credits to each account and the ending account balances. Include any supporting schedules or computations that may be necessary. Assume that a perpetual inventory system is used.

8. The Nicklausse Corporation produces liquid soap in a single, continuous process. A process cost accounting system and absorption costing are employed. All inventories are costed under the FIFO assumption. At February 28, 1966, the corporation had an inventory of 600 gallons of soap in process. All materials required for these 600 gallons were already

in process, and the inventory was estimated to be half complete with respect to labor and overhead. The costs in this inventory were as follows:

Materials	$1,020
Labor	270
Overhead	144

During March, 1966, 12,000 gallons of soap were completed and transferred to the finished stock warehouse. On March 31, 800 gallons remained in process. They were complete with respect to materials but only one-fourth complete with respect to labor and overhead. Charges to Work in Process during the month of March were as follows:

Materials	$21,350
Labor	10,710
Overhead	5,950

Required:

1. Compute the equivalent units produced during the month of March, 1966.
2. Compute the unit costs of production for the month of March.
3. Compute the costs of the soap completed during March and the cost of the inventory of Work in Process at March 31.

9. The Hoffman Manufacturing Company produces a single product in one continuous production operation. A process cost accounting system and the FIFO cost flow assumption are used. Both variable and fixed overhead are charged to production at normal rates per direct labor hour of $.40 and $.60 respectively. Physical production for April, 1966 is summarized below.

Work in Process, April 1—5,000 units, complete with respect to materials and 40% complete with respect to labor and overhead.

Started into process during April—55,000 units.

Work in Process, April 30—12,000 units, complete with respect to materials and one-third complete with respect to labor and overhead.

No units are lost or spoiled in the production process.

Production costs in the beginning inventory of Work in Process totaled $32,000. Current manufacturing costs incurred included the following:

Materials issued to factory—$264,000
Direct labor—60,000 hours @ $2.25
Actual overhead:
Variable—$25,000
Fixed—$33,000

Required:

1. Compute the equivalent units of production for the month of April, 1966.
2. Compute the unit production costs for April.

3. Compute the costs of the production completed during April and of the inventory of unfinished production at the end of the month.

10. The Crespel Company manufactures an antiseptic powder in two successive production processes, compounding and packaging. A process cost accounting system is employed. Inventories are costed in accordance with absorption costing and the first-in, first-out method.

At December 31, 1965, the company's inventory balances were as follows:

Raw Materials	$ 56,000
Work in Process—compounding	85,000
Work in Process—packaging	18,000
Finished Product (22,000 lbs.)	165,000

In the compounding department, the first production process, the inventory above consisted of 30,000 pounds of product, two-thirds complete with respect to materials and half complete with respect to labor and overhead.

During 1966, raw materials purchases totaled $1,500,000. Raw materials were issued to the two production departments in the following amounts:

Compounding	$1,025,000
Packaging	380,000

Direct labor costs in the two departments were as follows:

Compounding	160,000 hours @ $2.50
Packaging	150,000 hours @ $2.00

Overhead costs incurred in each department during 1966 were as follows:

	Compounding	*Packaging*
Fixed:		
Supervision	$ 52,000	$ 24,000
Repairs and maintenance	48,000	21,000
Depreciation	220,000	45,000
Variable:		
Factory supplies	72,000	40,000
Indirect labor	160,000	148,000
Power	28,000	22,000

Overhead is applied to production at the following rates per direct labor hour:

	Compounding	*Packaging*
Variable	$1.70	$1.34
Fixed	2.05	.66

During 1966, a total of 390,000 pounds of product were completed in the compounding department and transferred to packaging. At the end of the year, 50,000 pounds remained in process in compounding. This inventory was 80% completed with respect to materials and 50% complete as to labor and overhead. In the packaging department, a total of 380,000 pounds of product were completed and transferred to the warehouse for Finished Product. The total unit cost of these units finished in 1966 was $7.70. (This includes the accumulated costs of the compounding and packaging processes.)

During 1966, 375,000 pounds of product were sold.

Required:

1. Prepare general journal entries to record all of the operations for 1966. Include all necessary supporting schedules and computations.
2. Prepare a statement of the cost of goods manufactured and sold for the year ended December 31, 1966. Any net under- or overapplied overhead should be added or subtracted at the end of this statement.

11. The Miracle Shortening Corporation produces a liquid cooking oil in two successive production processes, blending and bottling. Only variable manufacturing costs are charged to products in the company's process cost system. Inventories are costed by the FIFO assumption. The following cost data are taken from the records of the two production processes for the month of August, 1965:

	Blending	*Bottling*
Direct materials used	$18,000	$7,500
Direct labor	14,400	6,000
Variable overhead incurred	6,500	4,200
Fixed overhead incurred	7,200	8,400
Variable overhead applied	6,400	4,350

Production statistics (in gallons) for the two processes are as follows:

	Blending	*Bottling*
Inventory, August 1	6,000	0
Completed during August	33,000	33,000
Inventory, August 31	3,000	0

Both the beginning and the ending inventory in the blending process were complete with respect to direct materials and one-third complete with respect to conversion costs. The balance in Work in Process—Blending at August 1 was $5,200.

The inventory of Finished Product on August 1 included 25,000 gallons with a cost of $1.78 per gallon. During August, 30,000 gallons were sold at a net selling price of $3 each. Variable selling expenses average $.25 per gallon. Fixed selling and administrative expenses totaled $4,400 for the month. The applicable federal income tax rate is 48%.

Required:

1. Prepare a production report for the blending process for August, 1965. The report should include computations of equivalent units of product, unit production costs, and total costs of completed production and ending inventory.

2. Prepare an income statement and a supporting statement of cost of goods manufactured and sold for the month of August.

12. The Darnay Company uses the absorption costing method. During 1965, 60,000 units were produced; and 54,000 units were sold. The following data were extracted from the company's adjusted trial balance at December 31, 1965:

	Debit	*Credit*
Sales		$365,000
Cost of goods sold	$248,000	
Variable overhead control	53,000	
Fixed overhead control	88,000	
Variable selling expenses	33,000	
Fixed selling expenses	41,000	
Fixed administrative expenses	30,000	
Variable overhead applied		54,000
Fixed overhead applied		90,000
Federal income tax	7,200	

The inventory of Finished Product on January 1, 1965, was comprised of 6,000 units of product. The same normal overhead rates used in 1965 were used in prior years.

Required:

1. Compute the net income of the company for 1965 under absorption costing. A formal income statement is not necessary.
2. Compute the net income of the company for 1965 under variable costing. A formal income statement is not necessary. (The income tax will be unaffected by the change in costing methods.)
3. Reconcile the incomes under absorption and variable costing if they are different.

13. Following is the income statement of the Carton Products Company for 1966:

CARTON PRODUCTS COMPANY
Income Statement
For year ended Dec. 31, 1966

Sales		$675,000
Cost of Goods Sold:		
Finished product, Jan. 1 (8,000 units)	$ 50,400	
Cost of goods manufactured (70,000 units)	441,000	
	491,400	
Finished product, Dec. 31 (3,000 units)	18,900	
	472,500	
Less overapplied fixed overhead	6,000	466,500
Gross margin		208,500
Selling and administrative expenses		144,000
Net operating income		64,500
Federal income tax		31,000
Net income		$ 33,500

Sidney Carton, the company's president, is disappointed at this report; for it reflects a decline in income from the previous year despite the fact that 1966 sales volume reached an all-time high.

A study of the cost records shows that variable overhead has been applied at a rate of $1.00 per unit of product and that fixed overhead has been applied at a rate of $1.20 per unit. Variable selling and administrative expenses average $.80 per unit sold. All of these rates have been in effect since the company was founded.

Required:

1. Prepare an income statement for Carton Products Company for 1966 in accordance with the variable costing method. This method will not be accepted for income tax purposes.
2. Explain with appropriate computations and comments any difference between the reported net income of $33,500 and the net income determined under variable costing.

14. Jerome Cruncher started manufacturing operations in a small plant early in 1965. At the end of his first year of operations, Cruncher's accountant prepared the following income statement:

CRUNCHER CRACKER COMPANY
Income Statement
For year ended Dec. 31, 1965

Sales (90,000 units)		$54,000
Variable costs:		
Variable cost of goods sold	$27,000	
Distribution expenses	10,800	37,800
Variable profit		16,200
Fixed costs:		
Manufacturing expenses	$10,500	
General administrative expenses	6,700	17,200
Net loss		$(1,000)

As the company is unincorporated, income taxes need not be considered in its financial statements.

Cruncher was very discouraged with the results of his first year's operations. A friend suggested that his mistake was adopting the variable costing approach to income reporting. He contended that conversion to absorption costing would be a profitable move for Cruncher.

Total output for 1965 was 175,000 units of product.

Required:

1. Evaluate the friend's contention. Compute the company's 1965 income under absorption costing. Does this computation prove the friend correct? Explain.
2. Assuming that Cruncher again produces 175,000 units in 1966 but sells 250,000 units and assuming that all costs and expenses follow the same patterns as in 1965, which method will result in the higher

reported income in 1966—variable costing or absorption costing? Why? Support your answer with appropriate computations.

15. A. Manette & Co., Inc., commenced operations on January 2, 1965. Following is a summary of its operations during the first three years of the company's existence:

	1965	*1966*	*1967*
Physical volume (units):			
Sales	25,000	30,000	22,000
Production	30,000	35,000	15,000
Selling price per unit	$20	$20	$20
Variable costs per unit:			
Production	$10	$10	$10
Distribution	$ 3	$ 3	$ 3
Fixed costs per year:			
Production	$120,000	$120,000	$120,000
Distribution	$ 60,000	$ 60,000	$ 60,000

Under the absorption costing alternative, fixed overhead would be applied to production at a normal rate of $4 per unit of product in each of these three years.

Required:

1. Prepare comparative income statements under absorption costing and variable costing for the first three years of the company's operations.
2. Explain any differences in incomes under the alternative costing methods for the individual years and for the aggregate three-year period.
3. Which alternative do you feel presents the more useful picture of the company's income over these three years? Why?

16. The Two-Cities Steel Company maintains its ledger and prepares all internal reports in conformity to the variable costing method. For its annual report to stockholders, however, the company's independent auditor requires the use of absorption costing. The conversion from variable to absorption costing is made by debiting or crediting (as appropriate) an account titled "Fixed Overhead in Inventory" in an adjusting entry made at the end of each year. No other entries are ever made to this account. This account is then included with Work in Process and Finished Product, which are still carried at variable production costs only, in the balance sheet. Any under- or overapplied fixed overhead which appears in the conversion to absorption costing is debited or credited to "Under-/Overapplied Overhead."

The following pertinent data are taken from the internal reports for the first three years of the company's operations:

	1964	*1965*	*1966*
Tons of steel:			
Sold	800,000	1,400,000	2,000,000
Actual output	1,000,000	1,500,000	1,800,000
Budgeted output	1,000,000	1,500,000	2,000,000
Fixed overhead:			
Actual	$4,000,000	$4,400,000	$4,800,000
Budgeted	$4,000,000	$4,500,000	$5,000,000

The company's inventories are costed under the first-in, first-out cost flow assumption.

Required:

Prepare the necessary entry at the end of each of these three years to adjust the company's accounts from the variable costing method to absorption costing. Include schedules of supporting computations for the adjusting entries.

Part II
COSTS FOR PLANNING AND CONTROL

Chapter 5

STANDARDS AND STANDARD COSTS

DISCUSSIONS IN the preceding two chapters have dealt with various aspects of accounting for costs that have actually been incurred. The principal questions raised have concerned the classifying, recording, and reporting of actual cost data. Cost bookkeeping involves the measurement of costs but not the critical appraisal of the amounts so measured. Cost planning and control involve the analysis and evaluation of costs. Planning and control are managerial functions dependent largely upon accounting information and procedures. These functions are concerned with what costs have actually been in the past, but with an eye to the future. With respect to the future, management is interested not merely in what costs may reasonably be expected to be but also in what costs ought to be. Knowledge of what costs should be provides a basis for intelligent planning and effective control. This chapter and the succeeding several are concerned with cost planning and control. The principal tools of planning and controlling costs are standards and budgets. Standards are discussed in the present chapter. Budgets will be considered in detail in Chapters 6 through 9.

STANDARDS

In general, *standards* may be defined as measured quantities which should be attained in connection with some particular operation or activity. The amount which "should be" attained is determined by management in accordance with its best judgment. Standards are not determined according to unquestioned and immutable natural laws. They are set by human judgment and, consequently, are subject to the same fallibility which attends all human activity. In the paragraphs that follow, we shall consider some of the quantities for which standards are frequently established in manufacturing enterprises and also the degree of excellence or precision implicit in standards.

Price Standards

Materials Price Standards. In most manufacturing operations, one of the most important cost elements is the cost of purchased raw materials. Management is interested in keeping this cost as low as possible, consistent with the need to maintain product quality. Part of the control of materials cost depends upon efficient purchasing and obtaining the most favorable possible price for the materials needed. A *materials price standard* is the price which should be paid for a particular raw material under the most favorable possible conditions. "The most favorable possible conditions" must be interpreted in light of the individual firm. The best price for one firm for a particular material may be either lower or higher than the best price for another firm for the identical item. In most cases, materials price standards can be set only for the firm, not for the industry as a whole.

Included in the standard materials price are all components of the amount which must be expended in order to acquire a particular material. Different suppliers may sell the same materials at different list prices. Assuming no differences in the qualities of the goods or in the services rendered by the various suppliers, the supplier offering the lowest price would be selected; and the materials price standard would be established on that basis. Differences in quality or in service may justify the selection of a higher price supplier, however. Thus, a supplier who cannot be relied upon to deliver materials when needed ought not be chosen simply because he sells materials at lower prices than his more dependable competitors. To the extent that his lower prices are reflected in unsatisfactory service, they are false savings to the buyer.

Freight charges are part of the purchase cost of materials, and they normally vary with the distance between the supplier and the purchaser. Thus, in setting materials price standards, a firm should look to the closest reliable sources of supply (presuming that all other factors are equal). Where materials are purchased from foreign suppliers, there may be import duties involved. These should be included as part of acquisition costs and incorporated in price standards.

Where discounts are available to the purchaser of materials, they should be included in the determination of price standards. *Quantity discounts* are granted for purchases of materials in relatively large lots. For example, the price per unit of an item may be lower when it is purchased in carloads than when it is purchased in smaller quantities. To the extent that quantity discounts are reasonable in the circumstances of the individual purchaser, they should be included in the calculation of the standard materials price. Obviously, it would be unreasonable for a firm to set materials price standards on the basis of carload discounts when carload quantities would represent supplies for excessively long periods of time and would involve undue storage and handling costs. *Cash discounts* are granted for prompt payment of invoices, typically within ten or fifteen days. For example, the terms "2/10,n/30" on an invoice mean that the purchaser may deduct a 2% discount from the billed price if he pays within ten days and that, in any event, the amount billed is due within thirty days. Historically, the materials cost in such an instance was regarded as the gross amount billed; and the 2% discount, if taken by the purchaser, was treated as miscellaneous revenue. More recently, accountants have come to view the actual price of such materials as the net invoice price after deduction of the discount. This would be 98% of the gross amount billed in the example above. This view assumes that all cash discounts will be taken by a profit motivated firm. Any discounts not taken (accounts not paid within the allowed discount period) are then regarded as financial costs attributable to a lack of proper planning of cash resources and not to improper purchasing practices. In our discussion, we shall accept this latter view of cash discounts and shall incorporate them in the price standards established.

Let us now consider a simple illustration of the setting of a materials price standard. The Rackstraw Marine Corporation has investigated alternative sources of supply and has determined that the Bobstay Company is the most advantageous supplier of red lead. Rackstraw's usage of red lead is such that it is practical for it to purchase this item in carload lots. Bobstay's list price for red lead is $6 per gallon, f.o.b. shipping point (i.e., the purchaser bears the freight charges). For carload lots, Bobstay offers a 5% quantity discount on list price; and all orders are billed at terms of 1/15,n/30. The freight charge to Rackstraw's plant for one carload, containing 3,000 gallons of red lead, is $120. Rackstraw's computation of the standard price for one gallon of red lead is as follows:

List price..................................		$6.000
Add: Freight charge per gallon		
($120 ÷ 3,000 gals.)...............		.040
		6.040
Deduct: Quantity discount		
(.05 × $6.00)..................	$.300	
Cash discount		
(.01 × $5.70)..................	.057	.357
Standard price per gallon..............		$5.683

While the quantity discount is based upon the list price, the cash discount is based upon the actual price billed (i.e., the list price minus the quantity discount). In the case of carload purchases, the price billed is $5.70 per gallon. The standard price of $5.683 per gallon affords a basis for planning future materials costs and also for controlling current costs by providing a criterion against which actual materials prices may be compared.

Labor Rate Standards. The price paid for labor is usually stated as a wage rate per hour or per piece of production or as a weekly or monthly salary. While it is possible to conceive of a standard weekly or monthly salary, such labor costs are normally not stated in terms of standards. Salaries are typically controlled by means of budgets rather than standards. Thus, labor price standards may be thought of as *wage rate standards* only. The rate may be either an hourly rate or a piece rate.

Wage rate standards are normally either a matter of company policy or the result of negotiations between management and a union. In either case, the accountant simply incorporates the rate established, however it may have been determined, in his work as appropriate. Deviations from established wage rates are unlikely to occur without foreknowledge on the part of management. A contractual wage increase due to a rise in the consumer price level, for example, may be predicted and planned for by observation of the trend of behavior of the Consumer Price Index.

In most manufacturing firms there will be several different wage rates. Rates will vary depending upon the degree of skill necessary for a particular job, the element of danger (if any) involved in a specific task, and the seniority within the company of the various workers. Both hourly rates and piece rates may be paid in the same plant. Thus, there is typically a series of standard wage rates rather than a single rate. In most of the illustrations in this text, however, a single rate will be assumed. This is done for the sake of simplicity and brevity of the illustrations, and it in no way detracts from the validity of the discussions. For the understanding of the development and handling of one standard wage rate can be extended very readily to any number of rates.

Quantity Standards

Materials Usage Standards. The cost of materials used by a manufacturer is a function of two factors, the price paid for the materials and the quantity of the materials used. Materials price standards have already been discussed. The quantity of materials used for the production of a particular product can also be subjected to standardization. Of course, there will be different quantity standards for different materials; and different standards will apply to the usage of a single material in different products. *Materials quantity standards,* or *materials usage standards,* are established on the basis of necessary input-output relationships between materials and products and also upon observations of actual experience. For example, it may be a simple fact that a two-pound hammerhead requires two pounds of steel. It may also be a fact that the firm's experience shows that a two-pound hammerhead can be manufactured only by using slightly more than two pounds of steel in order to allow for weight losses due to scraping and smoothing. Both of these facts should be incorporated in the materials usage standard for hammerheads. These standards do not represent the minimum possible use of materials in production but the minimum efficient use after due allowances for materials shrinkage and loss. Any time that a liquid is boiled, for example, there will be some quantity loss due to evaporation. It would be clearly unrealistic and useless in such a case to set a materials quantity standard that did not allow for the evaporation loss.

The Rackstraw Marine Corporation makes, among other products, a 36-foot, self-bailing motor lifeboat. Painting the hull of this boat requires a bare minimum of 6 gallons of red lead, and this amount requires that every ounce of paint actually adheres to the hull. The spray-painting process employed is not so perfect, however; and experience has shown that approximately 10% more red lead than the bare minimum is needed to paint one boat. This additional quantity should be incorporated in the materials usage standard thus:

Minimum quantity requirement	6.0 gal.
Normal allowance for loss	.6 gal.
Standard materials usage per boat	6.6 gal.

This standard does not and should not include a provision for spillage due to clumsy handling of the paint. This is the type of loss which the standard is intended to help eliminate.

Labor Time Standards. Labor quantities are measured in units of time, generally units of time required to complete a particular operation. Thus, *labor time standards,* or *labor efficiency standards,* are the amounts of time which particular productive operations should take. The labor time standard for a product is the sum of the time standards for all operations necessary to the completion of the product. Labor time standards are normally established on the basis of observations of actual operations and a critical evaluation of whether or not those operations are being performed as efficiently as is feasible. Labor time standards typically include provisions for a reasonable amount of time lost simply because human beings are not mechanical devices and cannot utilize every second on the job for actual production. However, labor efficiency standards ought not provide for prolonged periods of idleness or for incompetence. If such time losses were incorporated in them, the standards would be of little value to management for purposes of cost control.

The setting of a labor time standard may be illustrated for a product which is manufactured in three successive processes, or operations. Operation 1 requires a minimum of three man-hours to complete; Operation 2, one and one-half man-hours; and Operation 3, two man-hours. These are absolute minimums under perfect conditions. The company's experience shows that it is reasonable to expect these minimums to be exceeded by approximately 5% in each operation, even by the most efficient workers. The labor time standard for this product is then determined as follows:

		Hours
Operation 1:		
Minimum time	3.000	
Normal excess time	.150	3.150
Operation 2:		
Minimum time	1.500	
Normal excess time	.075	1.575
Operation 3:		
Minimum time	2.000	
Normal excess time	.100	2.100
Total standard time		6.825

While the time standard might be expressed in terms of hours, minutes, and seconds (6 hours, 49 minutes, and 30 seconds in this illustration), it is common business practice to express minutes and seconds as fractions of an hour. This facilitates further computations, such as the multiplication of time by an hourly wage rate.

Degree of Precision in Standards

The discussion of quantity standards in the preceding paragraphs has suggested that these standards be set in light of reasonable circumstances and not in accordance with some determination of perfect performance. Most standards, in practice, do provide for reasonable amounts of excess quantities. Such standards are described as *current attainable standards.* They reflect quantities which can reasonably be attained under current conditions. They provide for lost time and materials due to circumstances which cannot reasonably be corrected. This does not mean that they are based simply upon what is actually done presently, but rather, upon what can be done by efficient performance of tasks. For example, a labor time standard may be set according to the conclusions drawn from a time and motion study as to the length of time required for a competent and experienced worker to perform an operation, with due allowances for normal lost time. If the firm has several inexperienced workers performing this operation at a particular time, it is highly improbable that the time standard will be met. This does not invalidate the standard, nor does it necessarily mean that these workers' performance is bad. The workers' inexperience serves to explain a temporary deviation from the standard. It may be expected that these deviations will diminish and ultimately disappear as the workers reach the "standard" level of experience.

The principal alternatives to current attainable standards are *perfection standards,* which allow only those quantities of materials or time which are absolutely essential to the accomplishment of a job. For example, it may be mathematically possible to obtain 324 brass disks of a 2-inch diameter from 1 square yard of sheet brass. The shortcomings of both humans and machines are such, however, that it is extremely unlikely that so many could actually be obtained. Nevertheless, a perfection standard would ignore this fact and would be based upon the maximum possible yield of disks. A current attainable standard, on the other hand, would allow for additional lost materials in light of what can be ascertained to be reasonable. The perfection standard, it should be observed, does allow for materials loss in this illustration, but only that loss which is technologically unavoidable. Obviously, not all of the brass in a sheet can actually be used in the cutting out of round pieces.

Some businessmen have contended that perfection standards are preferable to attainable standards because they provide a stimulus, or incentive, to workers to achieve the best possible performance. While this may prove true in some instances, it is more likely that a perfection standard, never attained, will result only in discouragement and resentment on the part of workers and, thus, defeat its own avowed purpose. A better incentive may be provided by an attainable standard which is set as "tight" as appears to be reasonable. Thus, while it may not be met often, it at least offers the workers a goal which they feel can be reached. Urging a runner to a four-minute mile may stimulate his competitive spirit; urging him to a three-minute mile may only frustrate him.

Review and Revision of Standards

A standard set at one moment of time may be reasonably attainable and may be a suitable criterion for the evaluation of actual performance at that moment. At some later time, however, the standard may no longer be attainable; or it may be so easily bettered that it is useless for purposes of planning and control. As market conditions change, prices change. A materials usage standard and/or a labor time standard may be rendered obsolete by technological innovations. Hence, standards must not be regarded as static quantities. As conditions change, relevant standards must change with them in order to remain useful. This means that all standards must be re-examined frequently and, when necessary, altered to conform to new circumstances. It is not necessary that standards be altered every time there is some slight change in the factors which bear upon them. If this were attempted, a company might find that its principal products were standards and that a technique originally adopted to control costs had become excessively costly itself. While minor changes in conditions do invalidate standards slightly, such minor changes can be compensated for in management's evaluation of actual performance against standards. Temporary changes in conditions, even if material in their effects, should not cause changes in standards. For example, a temporary shortage of a particular commodity may increase its price subsantially, but not permanently. Many firms which employ standards adhere to a practice of frequent (perhaps monthly) review of standards but revision of standards only as of the beginning of a new fiscal year, except where a substantial and permanent change in circumstances makes earlier revision appear desirable.

STANDARD COSTS

Materials and Labor

In line with our discussion of standards, *standard costs* may be defined as costs which reasonably should be incurred in the performance of specific business operations. The standard costs of a product for direct materials and for direct labor are based upon price and quantity standards. They are the products of price standards multiplied by quantity standards. This relationship should be understood clearly. The standard costs depend upon the standards, but the two concepts are not identical. Given price and quantity standards, materials and labor standard costs are easily determined. An example of such determination is presented below:

One of the products of the Excelsior Products Company is product M.

It is manufactured in two successive production processes and requires three different raw materials. The materials used and their standard prices are as follows:

Material A	$2.50 per pound
Material B	$6.00 per gallon
Material C	$ .75 per ounce

Current attainable quantity standards call for the use of 2 pounds of material A, ½ gallon of material B, and 8 ounces of material C for each unit of product M. All direct laborers in the company's plant receive a standard hourly wage rate of $2.40. Operation 1 requires two man-hours and Operation 2, three-quarters of an hour to complete one unit of this product. The standard materials and labor costs of product M are computed as follows:

Materials		
A—2 lbs. @ $2.50	$5.00	
B—½ gal. @ $6.00	3.00	
C—8 oz. @ $ .75	6.00	$14.00
Labor:		
Operation 1—2 hrs. @ $2.40	4.80	
Operation 2—¾ hr. @ $2.40	1.80	6.60
		$20.60

Overhead

The standard costs of a product for materials and for labor are based upon price and quantity standards. This is possible because there is a functional relationship between the number of units of the product produced and the quantities of materials and labor required and because each material has its standard price and each worker, his standard wage rate. No such functional relationship exists between the units produced and total overhead cost, however. Even that portion of overhead which varies with the volume of production cannot be closely related thereto as can direct materials and labor. As a consequence, standard costs for overhead are based upon budgets, not upon standards. Again, a proper understanding of the distinction between standards and standard costs is important. The latter can exist without the former, and they do in connection with overhead.

Variable overhead costs are budgeted per unit of output on the basis of the firm's past experience, adjusted for observed and projected changes in conditions. The standard variable overhead cost per unit is then that budgeted cost per unit. Standard fixed overhead costs are employed only under absorption costing. Under variable costing, the total fixed costs incurred are treated simply as period costs. In absorption costing, however, standard fixed overhead costs are determined on the basis of budgeted fixed cost, in total, and budgeted volume. For example, if fixed costs are budgeted at $600,000 per year and annual output is budgeted at 250,000 units, the standard fixed overhead cost per unit will be set at $2.40. Standard costs for materials and labor are predicated upon the validity of the underlying standards. A standard variable overhead cost per unit is based on the validity of the budgeted unit costs. A standard fixed overhead cost is predicated upon the validity of both the budgeted total fixed cost and the budgeted output.

Where many products are produced in the same facilities, it is quite likely that the unit of product will not be a suitable base, or common denominator, for the application of overhead costs to production. In such a case, some other measure, such as direct labor hours, may be used for this purpose. If overhead is applied to production in proportion to labor hours, then standard overhead costs are expressed initially in terms of rates per labor hour. The standard costs per unit of product are then computed by multiplying the standard hourly rates by the standard number of hours required for the production of one unit. This will be illustrated below in a continuation of the example in the previous section.

The Excelsior Products Company budgets overhead costs by processes, or operations, and sets standard rates per labor hour for each operation. In Operation 1, variable costs are budgeted at $1.20 per labor hour and total fixed costs are budgeted at $450,000 for one year. Annual volume is budgeted at 300,000 labor hours for Operation 1. In Operation 2, variable costs are budgeted at $2.00 per hour and total fixed costs, at $345,000 per year. Annual volume in Operation 2 is expected to be 115,000 labor hours. From this budget information, standard overhead rates can be computed. The computation below, including a fixed overhead rate, assumes the use of absorption costing. This assumption is employed here simply because absorption costing is the more inclusive alternative. Its technique includes the procedure for variable costing, that is, the calculation of a variable overhead rate alone. Standard overhead rates per hour for the Excelsior Products Company are computed below:

Operation 1:

Variable overhead rate	$1.20
Fixed overhead rate ($450,000 ÷ 300,000 hrs.)	$1.50

Operation 2:

Variable overhead rate	$2.00
Fixed overhead rate ($345,000 ÷ 115,000 hrs.)	$3.00

From the preceding section, we know that the standard labor times necessary to produce one unit of product M are two hours in Operation 1 and three-quarters of an hour in Operation 2. The standard overhead cost of one unit of product M is then the sum of the several standard overhead rates multiplied by the respective standard labor hours, as follows:

Operation 1:	
Standard variable cost (2 hrs. @ $1.20)	$2.40
Standard fixed cost (2 hrs. @ $1.50)	3.00
Operation 2:	
Standard variable cost ($\frac{3}{4}$ hr. @ $2.00)	1.50
Standard fixed cost ($\frac{3}{4}$ hr. @ $3.00)	2.25
Total standard overhead cost per unit of product M	$9.15

The total standard cost of $29.75 per unit of product M is the sum of the $20.60 for materials and labor (computed in the preceding section) and this $9.15 unit overhead cost.

The total standard cost of product M may also be subclassified into its variable and fixed components. The total variable standard cost is $24.50 ($20.60 + $2.40 + $1.50). The total fixed standard cost per unit is $5.25 ($3.00 + $2.25). It is extremely important that the student understand that this fixed cost per unit is valid only in light of the budgeted volume data upon which the standard fixed overhead rates are based. Fixed costs can be expressed per unit of product only when an assumed volume of production is given. If the assumed volume is changed, the unit fixed-cost figure changes also. Variable costs begin as costs per unit. Fixed costs begin as total amounts and can be expressed in terms of units only with respect to a given volume.

In the example of product M, the standard cost of the product was stated as the cost for one unit. Especially where each unit is small and inexpensive, standard product costs may be expressed in terms of a group of units—one gross, one hundred, one thousand, etc. For example, the standard cost of one clothespin may be so small and so many pins may be produced in one period that it is more practical to state standard costs in terms of lots of one thousand. Also, the budgeting of overhead costs in this illustration is presented in an extremely simple fashion. A more refined and more useful technique for budgeting overhead costs will be explained in Chapter 9.

Nonmanufacturing Operations

Historically, standards and standard costs have been related almost exclusively to manufacturing. In recent years, considerable interest has been demonstrated in methods of setting and using standards for nonmanufacturing operations. Obviously, standards can be established only for routine, repetitive situations. Certain nonmanufacturing activities do not lend themselves to standardization. It would be impossible to establish a useful standard cost for the retail sale of one automobile, for example. No two customers and, hence, no two sales are exactly the same. It may not be impossible to set standards for certain automobile servicing functions, however, or for the routine processing of customers' accounts. Conceivably, certain nonmanufacturing supplies may be controllable by the use of price and quantity standards, much in the same way as are materials. Some administrative work may lend itself to the establishment of wage rate and labor time standards. More often, however, administrative employees receive weekly or monthly salaries that do not vary with the amount of work done. Thus, while some standard costs for nonmanufacturing operations may be feasible on the basis of price and quantity standards, most commonly such standard costs are based upon budgets in a manner similar to the setting of standard overhead costs. A more expansive treatment of this subject will be deferred until Chapter 12. The reader should be aware, however, that standards and standard costs are not necessarily restricted to manufacturing costs, even though the vast majority of their applications has been in that area.

VARIANCES

Insofar as cost control is concerned, the most important concepts in the use of standard costs are *variances,* the differences between actual costs and standard costs. Variances are dollar amounts. They are favorable when actual costs are less than standard costs, and they are unfavorable when actual costs exceed standard costs. The terms favorable and unfavorable are used here in a limited, technical sense and should not be interpreted in the ordinary sense. Thus, all excesses of actual cost over standard cost are not necessarily adverse to the enterprise's economic welfare. For example, a wage rate increase may be more than justified by improvements in productivity and completely agreeable to management; but, until it is reflected in a revised labor rate standard, it will cause an unfavorable variance. Likewise, not all favorable variances represent actual benefits to the firm. For example, if actual materials cost is lower than the standard cost because a low-grade substitute material is temporarily being used in the manufacture of the product, the adverse implications of the lower product quality may greatly outweigh the apparent cost saving. The terms favorable and unfavorable, when applied to variances, should be interpreted only as indicating the directions of variances from standard costs and not as suggesting good and bad results.

Management by Exception

Variances are particularly useful tools in the implementation of the concept of *management by exception.* This concept is founded on the very simple and logical premises that the limited time of business executives should be employed as profitably as possible and that their time may most profitably be spent in seeking ways to correct conditions which are not as they should be. In other words, the basic rule of management by exception is to concentrate on those operations and segments of an enterprise which appear to be unsatisfactory rather than to spend a lot of time reviewing satisfactory performance. Variances indicate instances where actual costs have failed to meet established standards. As suggested in the previous paragraph, favorable variances may call for correction just as well as the unfavorable ones; and not all unfavorable variances require corrective action.

Variances are just as useful to management in the implementation of its cost control objective as the standards from which they stem are valid. If standards are current and attainable quantities, then variances may be regarded as useful bases for the evaluation of actual performance. If standards are out-of-date, the usefulness of the resultant variances will be impaired. Where perfection standards are employed, there is little point in management's attempting to eliminate all variances; for the standards cannot reasonably be expected to be met. In this case, management must be able to distinguish between that portion of a variance which is potentially controllable and that portion which is to be expected. Thus, perfection standards must be accompanied by standard variances, that is deviations from standard amounts that are regarded as unavoidable. These standard variances would, in effect, convert the perfection standards to attainable standards. And only reasonably attainable standards are useful to management as bases for cost control.

Analysis of Variances

The key to effective use of standard costs for control purposes lies in the careful analysis of variances. Any extensive consideration of variance analysis must await further examination of related topics. More detailed knowledge of budgeting and of the incorporation of standard costs in a cost accounting system is necessary. However, certain fundamental ideas should be observed at this point.

Variances can be traced to the basic components underlying standard costs. Materials standard costs are based upon price and quantity standards. Hence, the total difference between actual and standard materials costs can be traced to price and quantity causes; and two separate variances can be computed—the *materials price variance* and the *materials usage variance.* Labor standard costs are also based upon price and quantity standards. The total variance of actual labor cost from standard cost can be broken down into a *labor rate variance* and a *labor time (efficiency) variance.* Standard overhead costs are based upon budgeted amounts rather than standards. As described above, standard overhead rates are set on the bases of budgeted costs and budgeted volume. The total difference between actual and standard overhead costs may be separated into a component which reflects actual spending for overhead items being different from budgeted spending—the *overhead spending variance*—and a component that results from a difference between actual and budgeted volume—the *overhead volume variance.* The spending variance may be related separately to variable and fixed costs. The volume variance relates only to fixed costs, for only in connection with fixed costs is an estimate of volume necessary in order to set a standard rate.

The mere identification of the source of a variance is not sufficient for purposes of control, of course. The really important facet of variance analysis is not discovering where the variance arose but learning why it arose and what, if anything, can be done about it. It is always possible that nothing can be done about a particular variance except to alter the standards or budgets which underlie it. The need for revision of standards is always a possible conclusion of the analysis of variances.

STANDARDS AS TOOLS OF PLANNING AND CONTROL

Throughout this chapter, frequent references have been made to the use of standards and standard costs for purposes of cost control. Standards provide bases for the evaluation of actual data. The differences between actual and standard costs may be analyzed by management in an effort to eliminate such differences in the future. Standards are also very useful in planning future operations. If standard costs for materials and for labor and a standard variable overhead rate are available, an estimate of volume in the future can be converted to an estimated of future variable manufacturing costs by simple multiplication. Materials usage standards, along with volume estimates, can provide the bases for purchase planning. Hiring policies can be better formulated if volume estimates can be coupled with labor efficiency standards.

As a final note, it is often argued that standards and standard costs are pertinent only to large firms, that a small firm cannot afford the added costs of implementing a standard cost system. There is some truth in this point, but it should not be taken as conclusive proof that small companies cannot use standards. A small organization may be able to make effective use of very limited standards at a proportionately limited cost. Thus, only materials price standards might be used in a particular case; or, perhaps, materials price and usage standards might be feasible for a given firm. An extensive and integrated standard system is not necessary in all cases. Standards and standard costs are, primarily, tools of management. As such, they should be used to the extent they are economical and useful—no more and no less. In the areas of cost planning and control, as in so many other contexts, something is infinitely better than nothing.

QUESTIONS FOR DISCUSSION

1. Explain the difference between a standard and a standard cost.
2. What factors should be considered in setting a materials price standard? A materials usage standard?
3. There is a very fundamental difference between standard costs for materials and labor and standard costs for overhead. What is the nature of this difference? What is the cause of it?
4. How do standards and standard costs facilitate managerial planning and control?
5. "If standard costs are to be useful techniques for improving cost performance and tightening cost control, they must be based upon perfection standards. Anything less will only encourage inefficiency." Do you agree or disagree with this statement? Why?
6. The basic notion underlying the concept of management by exception is applicable to much of human activity, both in business and in nonbusiness affairs. How does the concept of management by exception apply to each of the following situations: (1) a purchasing agent reviewing purchase orders before approving them; (2) a football coach viewing films of last Saturday's victory; (3) a housewife caring for her baby; and (4) a foreman studying labor time reports for his department? How do standards and standard costs relate to the concept of management by exception?
7. "Sometimes, from the point of view of management, unfavorable variances from standard costs are preferable to favorable variances." Comment on this statement.
8. "So long as standards are reasonably attainable and are set on the basis of a careful interpretation of all pertinent facts and circumstances, there should never be a need to change them." Do you agree or disagree with this statement? Why? If you disagree, indicate how often standards should be changed.

9. In a large manufacturing firm, who would you expect to be responsible for setting price and quantity standards for materials and labor?
10. The following cost data were reported by the Brownlee Manufacturing Company for the month of August, 1965:

	Standard	*Actual*
Direct materials	$360,000	$375,000
Direct labor	280,000	288,000
Variable overhead	135,000	132,000
Fixed overhead	240,000	196,000

Suggest as many possible reasons as you can why each of these cost items may have differed from its respective standard cost.

PROBLEMS

1. The Tucker Paint Company manufactures a paint thinner from a single raw material. This material is regularly purchased in half-carload lots of 400 barrels. Each barrel contains 40 gallons. The most advantageous supplier's list price for this material is $2.50 per gallon. He allows a discount of 2% for payment of invoices within 15 days. In addition, the buyer is billed $8 for each barrel shipped; this is a deposit on the barrel itself. The buyer receives full credit of $8 for each barrel returned to the supplier. On the basis of past experience, it is reasonable to expect that 10% of the barrels received will unavoidably not be returned for credit. No discount is allowed on barrel deposits forfeited. The freight charge for a half-carload is $960.

   The paint thinner is manufactured in standard lots of 120 gallons. Experience has shown that 4% of the materials put into the production process are unavoidably lost through evaporation.

Required:

Compute (1) the standard price per gallon of raw material; (2) the standard usage of materials per 120-gallon lot of production; and (3) the standard materials cost per gallon of finished product.

2. The Merrill Manufacturing Corporation produces product Z from an input of two raw materials, A and B. Material A is purchased in 100 pound sacks at a list price of $360 per sack. This price is subject to a 2½% state sales tax. The supplier sells material A on terms of 1/15,n/30. Freight charges average $2,700 per truckload of 250 sacks. Material B is imported from South America. Its list price is $44 per gallon. Import duties of $3.25 per gallon must be paid. The average freight cost for a shipment of 1,500 gallons is $675.

   Product Z is manufactured in standard batches of one gross of pint jars each. Jars are purchased in cases of 250 at a standard price of $9 per case. Ten percent of the jars received are broken before they can be filled; this breakage is regarded as normal. The price of the jars is subject to the 2½% sales tax. For each batch of product Z produced, 8 pounds of material A and 16 gallons of material B are required.

Required:

Compute the standard materials cost per pint of finished product.

3. A new product of Elise Toiletries, Inc., is Lano-Lov Skin Lotion, to be sold in 4-ounce bottles at a suggested retail price of $1. Cost and production studies show the following anticipated costs:

Raw Materials

Container:

Item	*Cost*	*Comments*
4-oz. bottle	$5.50 per gross	Allow additional 2% for breakage
Label	$3.30 per 1,000	Allow additional 3% for waste

Ingredients:

Item	*Cost*	*Quantity Used per 125-gal. Batch*
Compound 34A	$40 per 100 lbs.	70.0 lbs.
Alcohol and glycerine	$40 per 100 lbs.	76.0 lbs.
Perfume oil	(see below)	3.5 lbs.

Perfume oil is produced in 90-pound batches by the company; the standard cost of one such batch is as follows:

Materials	$2,170.00
Labor (4.4 hrs. @ $2.25)	9.90
Variable overhead (4.4 hrs. @ $1.95)	8.58
Fixed overhead	7.52
	$2,196.00

An allowance for lost ingredients due to overfilling, waste, and bottle breakage is made in the amount of 4% of total ingredients cost before loss.

Direct Labor per Gross

Compounding	.12 hrs. @ $1.90
Filling and packing	1.00 hrs. @ $1.60

Overhead

Variable:

Compounding	$3.00 per standard labor hour
Filling and packing	$1.50 per standard labor hour

Fixed:

Compounding	$1.50 per gross
Filling and packing	$1.25 per gross

Required:

Prepare a standard cost sheet for one gross of 4-ounce bottles of Lano-Lov Skin Lotion.

(Adapted from CPA Examination)

4. The Warren Company produces a liquid sweetener in three successive production departments, blending, cooking, and bottling. The operations of each department have been studied and time study reports reveal the following time data for the completion of a 100-gallon batch of the sweetener:

	Blending	*Cooking*	*Bottling*
Minimum possible time	2.00 hrs.	4.00 hrs.	.50 hrs.
Normal time by adequately trained and experienced personnel	2.10 hrs.	4.05 hrs.	.52 hrs.
Average time currently	2.25 hrs.	4.10 hrs.	.55 hrs.
Standard hourly wage rate	$2.80	$1.80	$2.50

On the basis of past experience and an evaluation of future production requirements, it is estimated that overtime work will be required in each department. Normal overtime will average 10% of straight time. Each hour of overtime work is paid at one and one-half times the regular standard hourly wage rate.

Required:

Compute the total standard labor cost of one gallon of the liquid sweetener.

5. The Anthony Office Furniture Company manufactures five-shelf steel bookcases in four successive production operations. These operations and their respective labor time and wage rate standards are as follows:

Frame forming	$\frac{1}{3}$ hr. per frame at $2.25 per hour
Shelf cutting	$\frac{1}{10}$ hr. per shelf at $2.10 per hour
Assembling	$\frac{1}{4}$ hr. per bookcase at $2.00 per hour
Painting	2 hrs. per rack at $1.60 per hour

In the assembling process, 5 shelves are welded to a frame. The completed bookcase is then hung on a rack. When 20 bookcases have been placed on a rack, the rack is wheeled into the paint shop where all of the bookcases on it are spray-painted and baked dry. The finished bookcases are then transferred to the warehouse pending shipment to customers.

Required:

Compute the standard direct labor cost per finished bookcase.

6. The Cassel Tool Corporation manufactures hammers in three production processes. Each finished hammer consists of a steel head weighing exactly one pound and a wooden handle.

The standard purchase prices of the raw materials used are as follows:

Steel	$180 per ton
Lumber	$ .20 per board-foot

In the process of cleaning the molded hammerheads, approximately .05 pounds of steel are necessarily scraped away. Eight handles are cut from 1 board-foot of lumber, and 10% of the handles cut are broken or otherwise spoiled before they are finished. This loss is considered unavoidable.

The direct labor times and rates in the three production processes are as follows:

	Time	Hourly Rate
Head molding:		
Mold pouring	.08 hrs. per head	$1.75
Mold cleaning	.25 hrs. per head	2.20
Handle forming:		
Cutting	.05 hrs. per handle	2.40
Finishing	.15 hrs. per handle	2.00
Assembly	.04 hrs. per hammer	1.75

Both variable and fixed overhead costs are charged to production at standard rates per direct labor hour. The budgeted overhead costs and labor hours, by departments, are as follows:

	Head Molding	Handle Forming	Assembly
Variable overhead per hour	$1.00	$.80	$1.20
Fixed overhead per year	$60,000	$32,000	$40,000
Labor hours per year	60,000	40,000	8,000

Required:

Prepare a complete standard cost sheet for one hammer.

7. The Steven Make-Up Company produces a mild astringent for cosmetic use. It is sold to distributors in cases of four dozen 5-ounce bottles. The company uses variable costing in its production accounting system.

The only raw material is a special chemical purchased in 50-gallon drums. The supplier's list price is $4.25 per gallon. There is a state sales tax of 4%. The supplier allows a 2% discount on the list price for payment of invoices within ten days. Freight charges average $5 per drum.

The astringent is manufactured in 60-gallon batches. One-sixteenth of the material put into process is lost due to normal evaporation and spillage. Direct labor costs are incurred as follows:

Distilling—6 man-hours @ $2.25 per 60-gallon batch

Bottling—½ man-hour @ $1.95 per case

Budgeted overhead costs are as follows:

Distilling—$1.60 per labor hour plus $18,000 per month

Bottling—$1.10 per labor hour plus $27,500 per month

Direct labor hours were budgeted at 4,500 per month in distilling and at 12,000 per month in bottling.

Required:

Compute the standard cost per case of finished product.

Chapter 6

BUDGETS: TOOLS OF PLANNING AND CONTROL

DISCUSSIONS IN Chapters 3 and 5 explained how normal and standard fixed overhead rates are based upon budgeted cost data. This is only one special application of budget data, however. In their broadest contexts, budgets relate to every activity and every segment of a business enterprise. Properly understood and implemented, they can be extremely useful tools of management in the planning and controlling of business operations and in the efficient allocation of capital resources.

Definition of a Budget

In a business enterprise, a budget is a comprehensive and coordinated plan, expressed in financial terms, for the operations and resources of an enterprise for some specified period in the future.[1] It is not suggested that the student memorize this definition verbatim but that he understand the essential elements of it. These elements are discussed in some detail below.

Comprehensive. A budget is comprehensive in that it takes into account all of the many facets and activities of the enterprise. It is a plan for the firm as a whole rather than for only one segment of the firm. It is true that we very commonly encounter such things as departmental budgets and advertising budgets. This terminology is perfectly correct, but implicit in it is the assumption that a departmental or advertising budget is but one component of a total budget for the firm. Clearly, one segment of a company cannot have any significant plan of its own unless that plan is a part of a master plan for the entire enterprise. The total plan will be referred to here as the *master budget;* the component budgets, as *budget schedules.*

---

[1] For governmental units and for certain nonprofit institutions this definition would not be suitable. In such organizations, budgets commonly represent authorizations of and limitations on the conduct of the operations of the organization; they are much more than plans—they are mandates.

Coordinated. If a comprehensive plan for an even moderately complex organization is to be useful, it must consider all segments of that organization and recognize the situation and problems of each segment. The plans for the various segments of the firm must be prepared jointly and in harmony with one another. If these component plans are not coordinated logically and practically, the whole will not be equal to the sum of the parts; and the master plan will evoke only confusion.

Plan. In the foregoing paragraphs, the word "plan" has been used without amplification. While it is a word the meaning of which is commonly understood, it has some very specific connotations when used in connection with budgeting. A housewife plans a menu, something which is totally within her discretion. She also plans for winter, the occurrence of which is completely beyond her control. Planning the menu is a matter of active intent; planning for winter is one of passive expectation. A business budget normally is somewhere between these two notions of planning. Some of the factors which will determine a firm's future operations are entirely within its own discretion and control—such as promotional programs, manufacturing processes, and executives' bonuses. Other determinants of future activities are wholly beyond the control of the firm—general business conditions, governmental regulatory policies, and shifts in population age groups, for examples. Thus, a business budget is an expression partly of what the firm's management expects will happen and partly of what management intends to make happen. This does not suggest that mere wishing can make something come true, but careful planning and preparation can bring about a result that would not otherwise be obtained. In other words, good budgeting can not only suggest what will happen but can also make things happen.

Financial Terms. Business budgets are stated in terms of the monetary unit (the dollar in the United States). This is essential if a budget is to be comprehensive, for the monetary unit serves as the common denominator of business activities. A materials budget, for example, may deal with tons of steel; and a labor budget will involve men and man-hours. But tons and man-hours cannot be summed to any significant quantity. Similarly, the advertising budget may deal with such quantities as hours of network television time, pages of national magazine space, and thousands of direct mail brochures; but some common denominator is needed to express a total amount of planned advertising effort. A wide variety of quantities are likely to be involved in the basic development of a budget, but the final budget must express business plans in terms of money.

Operations. One of the fundamental objectives of a budget is the quantification of the revenues that will be realized and the expenses that will be incurred in the future. This information must be provided in detail. Revenues should be related to particular products sold or services rendered. Expenses should be identified with specific goods and services employed in the production of those revenues. The development of budgets for operations is discussed in detail in Chapter 7.

Resources. It is not sufficient simply to plan revenues and expenses for the future. The enterprise must also plan the resources necessary for the operating plans to be realized. Basically, the planning of financial resources involves planning for the various types of assets (cash, inventory, plant property, etc.) in the proper amounts for the efficient operation of the firm and planning the sources of the capital to be invested in these assets. Various aspects of planning for capital resources will be discussed in Chapter 8.

Specified Future Period. A budget is meaningless unless it is related to a particular period of time. It is not helpful for management to know that $10,000,000 of sales will be made unless it also knows *when* these sales will be made. It is, of course, entirely appropriate for business management to formulate general plans for resources and operations in the indefinite future. The expanding function of research in business firms is based primarily upon the premise that new products and new techniques will be developed and will benefit the company in some presently undeterminable future period. But such planning, however important it may be, is not budgeting. (Of course, a firm can and should budget the costs of its research activities in the immediate future even though the ultimate benefits therefrom, if any, will be derived in the indefinite future.)

Purposes of Budgets

As the title of this chapter implies, budgets are intended to facilitate the managerial functions of planning and control. Good managers do not enter into new periods blindly. They plan, as carefully as possible, the normal operations of the period, as well as the unusual occurrences to the extent that these can be foreseen. Good budgets compel management to plan in a comprehensive and coherent manner and to plan specifics, not vague generalities. Planning improved profits is of no value unless the planning involves the specific production, distribution, and financial programs necessary to yield higher profits.

The control implications of budgeting are inextricably linked with the planning aspects. For example, to plan delivery costs of $60,000 during the first quarter of the next year when such costs are viewed as reasonable and consistent with planned sales is to afford, simultaneously, a basis for evaluating the propriety of actual delivery costs. Of course, changes in sales as compared with the budget may reasonably necessitate changes in delivery costs. Perhaps a more useful approach to the budeting of delivery costs would be to plan them in relation to units of sales volume so that changes in delivery costs may be anticipated and handled efficiently as actual sales volume is seen to deviate from the budgeted volume. This latter approach to the budgeting of costs and expenses is commonly referred to as *flexible budgeting* and will be discussed in detail in Chapter 9.

As a tool of control, the budget gives the responsible manager a guide to the conduct of operations and a basis for evaluating actual results. Actual revenues and expenses can be adjudged satisfactory or unsatisfactory in light of the relevant budgeted data and also in light of changes in conditions since the budget was prepared. The last portion of the preceding sentence is very important. The budget should not be regarded as a rigid requirement of performance. As already observed, many of the factors upon which a budget must be based are beyond the control of the firm's management; and all of them are subject to some degree of uncertainty. The budget is a plan, not an immutable commitment to performance; it is a means of control, but not a straitjacket on operations. Blind compliance with a budget may be worse than having no budget at all.

Another important aspect of budgetary planning and control is the efficient (i.e., profitable) allocation of the capital available to the enterprise. All expenditures require capital, in one form or another; and capital is invariably limited. Not unusually, the sum of all desirable expenditures exceeds the total amount of available capital. Where such is the case, there must be some procedure and some person in the budget system to weigh the alternative uses of capital and to select those uses which offer the greatest profit potential for the firm. Thus, one of the functions of the budget is to plan the most efficient possible allocation of the capital resources of the firm.

As a final note here, it is important to remember that a budget is a tool of management to be employed appropriately in the pursuit of management's basic objective, the optimum long-run profit of the firm. Like all tools, budgets are costly; and the more detailed and carefully prepared a budget is, the more it will cost. In any firm, the cost of the budget should be justified in terms of the additional revenues and/or cost savings it produces. Not the same degree of budget sophistication is appropriate for all firms. The discussions of budgeting in this text assume a relatively large company which finds it economically expedient to employ a complete and carefully detailed budget. The concepts illustrated here, however, may be adapted with more or less modification to suit the needs and means of a firm of any size.

FRAMEWORK FOR BUDGETING

The Budget Period

In order to be operationally meaningful, a budget must be related to a specific time period, called the budget period. A detailed budget for all segments and activities of an enterprise is normally prepared for relatively short periods of time only, typically no longer than one year. A fully detailed budget would include all expected revenues, expenses, receipts, disbursements, and other financial activities for each segment (e.g., division) of the firm for each significant time interval (e.g., a month) in the budget period. For example, an operating budget for one year may include a complete breakdown of revenues and expenses for each of the twelve months of the year. Alternatively, it might provide monthly detail for the first half of the year only, with the budgeted data for the second six months given by quarters or in total only. Long-range plans looking further than one year into the future may be developed for those segments of the business in which they are considered useful. Detailed long-range planning for the enterprise as a whole is seldom practicable. However, in certain segments of the firm it is highly desirable, if not necessary. As examples, long-range planning is almost essential in the areas of product development, equipment replacement, plant expansion, and the procurement of long-term capital.

In a fully developed budget system, there may be two or more budget periods planned simultaneously, the differences among such periods being the relative amounts of detail in which they are planned. Following is a description of such a budget system for a hypothetical corporation: By December 15, 1965, the operating budget for 1966 is finalized. This budget is fully detailed, by months, for all phases of operations for the first half of 1966. It includes details of budgeted revenues, expenses, receipts, and disbursements by divisions of the corporation and by product lines. For the second half of 1966, estimated data for the entire company are summarized by quarters only. No detail is given for the several divisions or for the individual product lines. By June 15, 1966, a new budget will be prepared. This will provide full details for the second half of 1966 and summarized quarterly estimates for the first half of 1967. This procedure is repeated every six months. Thus, the budget system is constantly moving forward into the future but is able to build its short-range detailed budget partly upon the basis of an earlier semidetailed plan. In addition to this formalized annual budget, the corporation prepares annually an intermediate-range sales forecast for the next three years. Finally, long-term capital procurement and investment needs are planned in general terms five years ahead.[2]

Thus, there are three different time periods in the future for which financial plans are formulated. Each of these might be regarded as a unique budget period. Within the framework of the definition of a budget posited earlier, however, only the operating plan for the next year would qualify as a true budget. Even within that year, there are two subperiods of differing budget detail. While the terminology of budgeting is not so standardized that definitive conclusions can be stated here, there is a useful distinction to be made between budgeting, as such, and long-range planning. For purposes of discussion in this text, we shall regard any plans that are not comprehensive and coordinated for the entire enterprise and that extend further into the future than the normal detailed budget period as falling into the category of long-range planning. This distinction is adopted here only for purposes of simplifying discussion. Many businessmen and writers today are making very specific distinctions between intermediate and long-range planning. Such distinctions are beyond the scope of this text, however.

Environmental Factors

Once the budget period has been established, the persons responsible for preparation of the budget must attempt to determine the nature of the environmental conditions that will obtain during that period. By environment here we mean all factors and circumstances outside the firm that will influence the operations of the firm but will not be subject to any direct control by the firm's management. These environmental factors may be classified as social, economic, and political. Actually, these separate classifications are useful only for explanatory purposes. Obviously, all political and economic factors have social implications. Similarly, any social or political condition influencing a business enterprise is, thereby, of economic significance. Hence, the factors discussed below will be categorized as social, economic, or political according to popular notions of these terms.

---

[2] Long-range planning is not limited to five years in the future, of course. It may be carried forward as far as is considered practical in the individual firm. Generally speaking, however, the longer the planning period the less certain the plans will be.

Social Factors. Any aspect of the way people act and think is a social factor of potential importance to business operations. Some examples will be considered along with their possible implications for business planning. Mass population movements out of urban and into suburban areas might reasonably be expected to have major impacts upon patterns of demand for consumer products. More recreational equipment and garden tools may be demanded. Automobiles may be operated over more miles and, thus, the demand for gasoline may rise. An increase in the proportion of the total population in one particular age group (e.g., over 65 or under 18) will have implications for product demand. A reduction in the average family size will have obvious implications for housing demand. Fads and styles have important effects upon certain industries, notably women's clothing. It is important to attempt to plan for these styles and fads but, at the same time, difficult to do so; for they typically influence demand for relatively short periods of time and are notoriously unpredictable. The reader can readily add further examples to this list of social factors which have business implications.

Business managers must be aware of these varied social developments and must attempt to determine their impacts upon individual firms' operations. Changing patterns of population composition and movement are reflected in statistics compiled and published by the U.S. government. Changes in styles and tastes are reflected in specific markets. Competent managers should be able to trace the implications of shifts in demand in other markets to the markets for their own products. For example, an increased demand for small automobiles relative to that for standard-size cars will have implications for the demand for basic steel. In some instances, advertising and other promotional programs may be able to cause or to restrict certain types of social change; but, for the most part, these changes are beyond the direct control of the firm. They are part of the environment in which the firm must operate, and the firm must adapt to them rather than they being adapted to suit the firm.

Economic Factors. As already mentioned, anything that affects a business enterprise may be thought of as an economic factor bearing upon the firm's operations. However, there are certain types of circumstances which, in common parlance, are generally referred to as economic conditions. Seasonal patterns of demand and/or supply affect many business enterprises. Budgets must take these seasonal factors into consideration. If the entire demand for a particular product (e.g., snow removal equipment) occurs during one season of the year, the manufacturer of that product must realize that substantially all of his sales will be made during or just prior to that season and that his production and financing must be planned accordingly. He may plan production in a number of ways. One possibility is to produce only during the season of peak demand and to leave facilities idle during the remainder of the year. Another approach would be to manufacture the product at approximately the same quantity throughout the year and to plan an inventory buildup prior to the peak sales season and an inventory reduction during that season. A third alternative would be to diversify and produce other products with different seasonal patterns (e.g., lawn and garden equipment).

Cyclical fluctuations in economic activity, or business cycles, have tended to recur in more or less regular patterns. Some fluctuations, such as the boom of the 1920s followed by the great depression of the 1930s, are of great magnitude. Others, such as the recession and recovery in the period 1961–62, are comparatively slight. Cyclical fluctuations affect individual firms differently. Historically, producers of heavy equipment have usually experienced substantial and direct impacts from cyclical changes in demand. Food producers, on the other hand, typically experience relatively mild effects as the cycle ebbs and floods. While one might expect a direct effect of business cycles on sales and production—that is, sales and production to decline during the period of recession and to rise during the period of recovery—this is not always so. A manufacturer engaged almost exclusively with government contracts for defense materials might find that his sales demand varies inversely with the business cycle. As a part of its overall countercyclical effort, the federal government may increase purchases of defense items during the period of recession in order to bolster industrial production and employment and then reduce such purchasing to normal levels when the upturn occurs. While business cycles may be attributed to the aggregate behavior of all enterprises in the economy, the individual enterprise may regard them as entirely beyond its own control. Budget preparation should always incorporate consideration of the stage of the business cycle expected to obtain during the budget period and of the influence that this stage will have upon the firm's operations.

Long-term and apparently permanent shifts in demand or supply are referred to as secular trends in economic activity. These secular trends frequently relate to basic social changes and are likely to be irreversible. If a firm finds that there is a permanently decreasing demand for its product, it must either shrink with that demand or add new products to its line. If, on the other hand, the secular trend is upward and demand for a product can be expected to expand at an increasing rate, the manufacturer should plan to expand his productive facilities in order to maintain his relative share of this market.

Political Factors. The line between political and economic factors is impossible to draw. For example, countercyclical monetary and fiscal policies employed by the federal government stimulate politically designed economic conditions. There are certain types of conditions, however, whose origins are quite distinctly political. Perhaps the extreme political circumstance is war. The impact of World War II on the American economy and on individual business firms was enormous. Even without actual war, a period of international tension (cold war) necessitating a continually improving defense posture has major economic implications. The sudden termination of such a period would entail very serious consequences for individual firms. Examples of other political factors that might influence the planning for an enterprise include new directions in antitrust legislation, more aggressive enforcement of existing antitrust laws, direct or indirect price and wage controls, and changes in the income tax law.

The combination of social, economic, and political conditions make up the environment within which business budgets must be developed. To some extent, these conditions are predictable and fairly easily incorporated in the budget. There remain a great many unpredictable environmental factors, however, which make even the most carefully worked out budget tenuous and subject to substantial deviations from actual operating results.

Company Policies

In addition to the environmental factors, there are many internal conditions and policies that must be taken into account in the preparation of a budget. For example, a firm may have the policy of limiting itself to the production of a high quality, high-priced commodity. If such a policy is to be continued, then a number of additional avenues for distribution of the product must be regarded as closed. A family corporation may adhere to a policy of operating only within one region of the country because expansion into the national market would not permit the family to maintain effective control over the corporation. While management may believe that entry into the national market would be highly profitable, it must exclude any such profits from its planning because of the policy imposed by the family owners of the firm. At this point we need not be concerned with whether such policies are wise. We merely note that they frequently exist and form a part of the framework within which the budget must be developed.

PERSONNEL IMPLICATIONS OF BUDGETING

Thus far, we have discussed budgeting in an impersonal manner and have used the term management as an impersonal singular noun. But management is an aggregation of people, and these people must prepare and implement the budget. Insofar as the actual workings of a budget are concerned, the most important aspects are the effects of people upon the budget and, conversely, the effects of the budget upon people.

Personnel Involved in Budget Preparation

There is no standardized organization of people for budget preparation. Different firms use different procedures, but there are certain basic concepts which are applicable in all cases and should be given proper recognition. These basic concepts may be stated as follows:

1. The budget must be prepared in such a way that it will best serve the needs of the enterprise as a whole, not the needs of specific segments to the detriment of the total entity.
2. The budget must coordinate all segments and functions of the enterprise logically and efficiently.
3. The budget must be understood and accepted by those who will actually have to work with it and under it.

The Budget Director. Every firm should have one executive who is responsible for the coordination, timing, and final presentation of the budget. He does not prepare the budget himself so much as he supervises its preparation. The ideal budget director would be a man with no other functional responsibilities, who reports directly to the top management (executive vice-president or higher). Such a person would be as independent of special interest as any corporate executive could be. Being responsible for no functional operations and having a minimal staff working under him, he would have no personal motive for favoring one segment of the firm to the prejudice of others. Rather, he would be able to seek the best allocation of corporate resources for the enterprise as a whole.

If the vice-president for manufacturing were also the budget director, no matter how hard he might try to avoid doing so, he would inevitably tend to favor his own division of the company in the allocation of scarce capital resources. This tendency would not indicate any dishonesty on his part but would be a perfectly natural consequence of his specialized knowledge of manufacturing problems and needs. In many firms, the chief budget officer is the controller. While he typically has no functional responsibilities, the controller may have a very large staff under him and may be responsible for a large number of staff services. Faced with a choice between the purchase of new production equipment or of an electronic computer, the controller, in his capacity as budget director may almost unconsciously favor the computer purchase because of his greater appreciation of the benefits to be derived from the use of the computer. His bias may be unintentional, but it is nonetheless real. Not all firms may be large enough to be able to afford a budget director with no other responsibilities. In such instance, the job might best be assigned to the executive vice-president. While he is not free of functional responsibility, he has the next best qualification for unbiased judgment. He has responsibility for *all* functions of the business.

The Budget Committee. In order to ensure that all segments of the firm are properly coordinated in the final budget, all major segments should be represented on a committee of executives that prepares the budget in its final form. This committee would be chaired by the budget director and would include representatives of all major functional divisions of the firm—including manufacturing, distribution, finance, research, and any other distinct functions recognized in the firm's organization. The controller would also be a member of this committee. The composition of the budget committee would differ among firms, but the purpose would be the same in all cases—effective coordination of planning for the firm. The budget committee should not prepare the budget from the start but should prepare it in its final form, after satisfactorily reconciling all initial conflicts in the various components.

Primary Budget Preparation. The initial development of budget data should come from those persons who will be responsible for performance under the budget. The preparation of the budget should be a "bottom-up" operation. Budget data should originate at the lowest level of operating management and should be refined and coordinated at higher levels. Thus, the initial budget of operating costs in a production department should be made by that department's supervisor. The initial sales plan for a particular territory should come from the sales manager in that territory, and he, in turn, should build his forecast on sales estimates provided him by his salesmen. These initial budget schedules may be revised considerably before the final budget is approved by top management, but it is essential that they start at the bottom.

The persons primarily responsible for operations within the budget or for explaining why such operations are impossible or undesirable are the lowest operating executives—the department foremen, for example. If these persons are not sympathetic with the budget, it will be of little practical value to the firm. Their sympathy or acceptance may be obtained, in part, by adequate education in the objectives of the budget. But it will be won principally by their own participation in the development of the budget. If they plan their own performances, they will be much more interested in striving to meet or better those performance levels. This approach might well be described as "before-the-fact responsibility accounting."

The manager of a single department cannot initiate his own budget schedule entirely by himself, of course. If he is a production department supervisor, there is no point in his attempting to plan his department's output for the coming year until he is given an indication of the expected sales demand for the product of his department. Thus, he must be provided with certain basic constraints before he can intelligently plan his own operations. It is highly unlikely that the initial budget schedule for a department will be identical to the final one. When all production departments' schedules are compiled and compared by the factory manager, he may find that they are not compatible. Similarly, when all divisions' budgets have been submitted to the budget committee, inconsistencies among them may well appear. The sum of the capital expenditure plans, for example, may exceed the available capital resources for the period. Some paring down of individual plans must be made, or else additional sources of capital must be located. Any changes made in initial budget estimates should be made first by the lowest responsible executive, however. The preliminary budget should be sent back to the bottom for revision and a second ascent through the several echelons of management to the budget committee. Perhaps this process will have to be repeated several more times. The goal of this repeated "bottom-up" budget development is complete acceptance of the budget at all levels of management. And this complete acceptance will be attained only if each manager really feels that the budget against which his performance will be evaluated is truly *his* budget.

The Final Budget. Once all internal inconsistences and conflicts have been resolved and the various operating managers have submitted budget schedules which are in harmony with each other, with the goals of the enterprise, and with the realities of the environment of the budget period, a final master budget is prepared by the budget director with the assistance of the budget committee. This budget is submitted to top management, the president and/or the board of directors, for final approval. Once approved at this level, the budget is disseminated among all managers responsible for performance under it. As a final caution, we should remember that, even in this final form, the budget is still only a plan, not a hard and fast requirement. The budget is only an aid to intelligent thinking and discretion, not a substitute therefor.

Budgets and Human Behavior

The author is not a psychologist and this does not purport to be a text on industrial psychology. Hence, the discussion in this section will be both brief and nontechnical. However, it is important for the student to have at least a general appreciation of the potential impacts of budgets on human behavior. If a budget is prepared realistically by a department supervisor and revised with his aid and approval, it may evoke a favorable response from him and serve as a stimulus to his efficient and profitable performance. If it is prepared by someone else without his aid or approval, it may generate hostility and act as a deterrent to his own intelligent thinking and, ultimately, may reduce efficiency and profits. However the budget is prepared, people will react to it. Their reactions will be either positive or negative, depending upon whether they feel the budget is reasonable and whether they were involved in its preparation. (Totally neutral reaction to a budget is conceivable but highly unlikely.) Thus, the budget is as much a tool of good human relations as of financial planning and control. The latter objectives will not be well served if the former is not carefully incorporated in the preparation and implementation of the budget.

Budget systems may include rewards and punishments for good and bad performances under the budget. Rewards might take the form of additional monetary compensation, faster advancement within the firm, public recognition, and/or other means. Punishment might involve simply the loss of additional compensation, promotion, or recognition; or it might take the form of positive unfavorable action such as demotion or dismissal. Where rewards and/or punishments are involved in a budget, it is extremely important that they be meted out in light of actual conditions during the budget period and not be based wholly upon the predetermined budget data. The rewards should be so conceived as to be given for performance which is in the overall best interests of the firm. A department supervisor may be able to minimize his operating costs and, hence, maximize his own reward by employing operating procedures that do not serve the best interests of the entire firm. Punishment for failure to meet reasonable budgeted achievement should be designed in such a way as to avoid fear and the blunting of initiative on the parts of responsible supervisors. Slavish adherence to budgets should not be the aim of budget reward and punishment schemes. Budgets must walk a narrow line between encouragement and discouragement, between motivation and fear. Specifically how this is to be accomplished is beyond the scope of this volume, but it is of critical importance to the success of a budget system.[3]

BUDGETARY REVIEW

Once the budget period has begun, the budget process must not cease to function until it is time to prepare the next period's budget. If the budget is to be an effective tool of control and an aid to dynamic planning, it must be reviewed periodically with views to both the past and the future. As regards the past, budgetary review is concerned with a comparison of actual operating performance with budgeted performance for a given period of time. As regards the future, budgetary review provides a basis for revising and/or extending future plans.

Budgetary review is commonly accomplished by preparation of periodic reports and holding periodic meetings of the budget committee to evaluate actual performance and to reappraise future plans. While there is no standard frequency for these formal reports and meetings, monthly review is found in many business firms. Probably budgetary review should be undertaken in a formal manner at least quarterly. Waiting until the end of a budget period before a careful comparison of actual and budgeted performance is made leaves no room for corrective action during that period. Only the next budget period can benefit from such review.

The comparison of actual and budget data is designed to afford a basis for controlling current and future operations. It is always possible that the conclusion from the comparison of actual and budgeted operating data will be that the budget was unrealistic to begin with or that actual conditions during the budget period are so different from those anticipated that the budget data are no longer valid. In any event, the causes of deviations of actual performance from the budget should be sought and, where appropriate, corrected. The mere fact that actual operating data differ from the budget and are so reported is only the prelude to managerial control. Identification of causes and corrective action are the essence of control.

In addition to evaluating past performance in light of the budget, the budget committee should review and reappraise the budget data for the

[3] The results of an empirical study concerned with budgetary motivation, rewards, and penalties are reported in Andrew Stedry, *Budget Control and Cost Behavior* (Englewood Cliffs, N.J.: Prentice-Hall, Inc., 1960).

remainder of the current budget period. Changes in actual conditions from those originally expected normally require parallel changes in operating plans. When such changes in the budget are deemed appropriate, they should be made and approved by all responsible managers. This revised budget, brought up-to-date by a discriminate budgetary review policy, then becomes the formal statement of operating plans for the remaining portion of the budget period. Further, in this process of reviewing conditions and prospects for the current budget period are the seeds of the budget for the subsequent period. Thus, budgeting can and should be a continuous, dynamic process.

CONSTRUCTION OF THE BUDGET

The mechanics of budget preparation are the topics of the following two chapters. At this point, however, it is appropriate to consider two general aspects of budget preparation.

Limiting Factor on Operations

In every enterprise, there is some factor which effectively restricts the total magnitude of operating activity during a given period. In the majority of industrial firms in the United States, this limiting factor is sales demand. Most of these firms find that the reasonably expected sales of their products determine the overall scope and size of their operations. In other firms, notably those engaged in gold mining and agriculture, production is usually the limiting factor on operations. A firm mining gold in the United States faces an unlimited demand at a fixed price set by Congress. In such instance, the amount of gold which the company can produce determines its sales for any period. Substantially the same situation obtains in agriculture,[4] although here the prices of commodities are not necessarily fixed. In some firms, the limiting factor is working capital. No matter how great the demand for its product and irrespective of available production facilities, a firm must have working capital in order to operate. Firms with a history of financial difficulties not infrequently find they are unable to obtain the necessary funds to produce and sell at a volume that would cure their financial ills.

Whatever the limiting factor for a firm may be, it is the element which determines the size of total operations and, hence, the point at which the planning process should begin. There is no sense in planning production greatly in excess of forecasted sales unless some profitable use

[4] It is probably true that few farmers undertake any formal, comprehensive budgeting; but they must make some plans stated in financial terms.

of the resultant inventory accumulation can be foreseen in the more distant future. It may happen that, as a budget is developed from one limiting factor, a different one is discovered. For example, the preparation of a budget may begin with a sales forecast on the assumption that sales demand is the limiting factor on operations; but the planning may reveal production limitations which cannot be exceeded and which require a reduction in the planned sales volume. Alternatively, it may be found that additional working capital would be needed to operate at the level called for in the sales forecast and that none is available.

Setting Budget Allowances

There is no one way in which the appropriate quantity for a particular budget item is determined. All budget data are, of course, estimates; but they are influenced strongly by past experience. After all, the only basis management has for judging the future is the past. This does not mean that budgeting simply presumes that what happened in the past will happen again. Changes in future conditions must be taken into account in applying the lessons of the past to the future. But even expectations of changes are necessarily conditioned by experience. Nevertheless, planning is essentially a future-looking activity. Actual data of the past are useful in budgeting only to the extent that they help to develop estimates of future data. Budget data must be drawn primarily from studies of the future.

One possible way to estimate future data is to extend the actual data of the past by means of an average rate of growth or decline in a particular quantity that has persisted over some significant period of time. Seasonal variations in historical data should also be considered. Thus, March of 1965 may be a useful basis for planning for March of 1966. Further, the relationship between March of 1965 and the fourth quarter of 1964 may be of some help in estimating data for March of 1966 when the data for the fourth quarter of 1965 are known.

For many items, standards may be used to set budget allowances. However, we must remember that standards indicate what should be achieved; budgets indicate what is expected to be achieved. The two are not necessarily identical. Management may be aware of certain circumstances during the budget period which will make it impossible to meet particular standards. For example, if management knows that an unusually large number of trainees will be on the job during a particular period, it may reasonably anticipate that the labor time standards will not be met but may decide that no change in those standards is necessary. In such a case, a variance from standard should be budgeted. Such variance must then be taken into account in using the labor time standard for control purposes during the budget period. All budget allowances must be evaluated against a criterion of reasonableness. An unreasonable budget is not only not useful to management but may even be dangerous.

QUESTIONS FOR DISCUSSION

1. "Budgets may actually be detrimental to effective managerial control. They provide preconceived plans as the criteria for evaluating actual operations. Thus, any errors in the planning process may be compounded in the control process." Comment on this criticism of budgets.
2. What are the essential elements of good budgeting?
3. "The establishment of a formal budget period imposes arbitrary and potentially harmful limitations upon management's planning function." Do you agree or disagree with this assertion? Why?
4. In a company that uses both standards and budgets, should the control function be based upon budgeted data or standard data when the two are not the same (i.e., when variances from standards are budgeted)? If control should be based upon one of these alternatives, what is the proper role or significance of the other?
5. What social, economic, and political conditions existing at the present time and/or expected within the coming year would you expect to have the most significant identifiable impacts upon the operations of a residential construction contractor? A manufacturer of guided missile components? A tobacco grower?
6. You have recently been hired as budget director and systems analyst for a medium-sized manufacturer. The company has been in operation for many years and has a history of steady progress and work force stability. The president has asked you to design and install a budget system as soon as practicable. He has called a meeting of all middle managers and supervisory personnel. Your task at his meeting will be to explain the objectives and goals of the new budget system and to outline how the system will work. Write the first hundred words (more or less) of your talk at this meeting.
7. "Inasmuch as the plant accountant has direct and regular contact with all production cost data and has a broad perspective of the entire plant's operations, he is the most logical person to draft the expense budgets for the plant's several manufacturing departments." Discuss this statement.
8. The Blackwood Company employs a merit system in compensating its supervisory personnel. In addition to his basic salary, each department foreman receives a bonus which is based upon the relationship between his department's actual performance and its budget. The following specific comparisons are used in this merit system: actual and budgeted output, actual and budgeted materials usage, actual and budgeted labor time, and actual and budgeted maintenance expenses. An excess of actual data over

the budget results in negative points for the foreman. An excess of budgeted data over actual results in positive points. The foreman's bonus is then computed by multiplying the algebraic sum of the points accumulated in his department by an established budget rate. Net negative bonuses are ignored. Evaluate this bonus system.

9. What benefits ought to be derived from the periodic meetings of a budget committee?
10. "Realistically, sales demand is the only limiting factor on the size of a firm's operations. Sales demand will invariably generate the necessary productive capacity and attract the required capital to meet that demand." Discuss this statement.
11. What is the proper relationship between past experience and future planning in a dynamic economy?
12. "Do you know," said the president of the Culbert Corporation, with a satisfied puff on his cigar, "our new budget system has saved us $250,000 in the first two years it has been in operation." How would you expect such a financial saving to have been determined? Do you believe it really can be measured in a meaningful way? Discuss.
13. How might statistical analysis be used to advantage in a budget system?

Chapter 7

PROFIT PLANNING: THE OPERATING BUDGET

IN AN overall sense, it is impossible to plan the operations of a business firm on a piecemeal basis; for all segments and activities of the firm interact with each other. Nor is it possible to divorce the planning of profits from the planning of financial resources; for the two are interdependent. Profits cannot be obtained without capital resources, and, conversely, resources cannot be maintained indefinitely without profits (excepting in nonprofit institutions dependent upon contributions for their capital). Thus, the separate discussions of profit and resource planning in this and the following chapter are employed only to simplify the introduction of the problems involved. The interdependence will be evident.

A single, extended illustration of budgeting will be developed in this and the succeeding chapter. This illustration will depict the preparation of the master budget of Shadbolt Products, Inc., for the year 1966. Shadbolt Products manufactures light industrial equipment and has two distinct product lines, industrial pumps and chain saws. Industrial pumps are sold principally to industrial users, although a substantial number are also sold to dealers. Most chain saws are sold to dealers, but some are sold directly to users, particularly in foreign countries. For purposes of efficient distribution, the corporation has three sales divisions, the Western Division, the Eastern Division, and the International Division. All production is accomplished in the company's two plants located in Oakland and in Indianapolis. As the various component budgets are discussed in the pages that follow, they will be illustrated for Shadbolt Products, Inc.

THE SALES FORECAST

As mentioned in the preceding chapter, every firm faces some factor which effectively limits the magnitude of its total operations. In most industrial companies, this limiting factor is the demand for its product. While sales demand is not always the limiting factor with which the budget process must begin, it frequently is and will be regarded as such in the discussion and illustration in this chapter.

Factors Determining Sales

The Environment. The importance of the various social, economic, and political factors that go to make up the environment within which a business firm operates was discussed in the preceding chapter. In no respect are these environmental factors more important than in the preparation of the sales forecast. Sales represent one of the principal points of contact between a firm and its environment. Insofar as sales are concerned, the environment may be identified with the market (or markets) for a firm's products. In order for a firm to plan its sales for a coming period, it must be able to understand and evaluate the market for its products. Markets are enormously complex; they defy precise definition. Yet, management must not only arrive at an operational definition of its market but must also anticipate the behavior in that market during a particular future period. One of the best available indications of a market's behavior in the future is its behavior in the past. This is always a tenuous indicator, at best, however; for the future is always somewhat different from the past. It has been said that the only thing that is certain, in addition to death and taxes, is change. Thus, future market behavior must be predicted on the basis of past experience as adjusted for anticipated changes in behavioral patterns. The task of making such a prediction is difficult, and the cost of making a bad prediction may be very high, as witnessed by the large number of business failures in the United States each year.

For purposes of the Shadbolt Products, Inc., illustration, we shall presume that the American economy during 1965 has been recovering from a minor recession and that the year 1966 is expected to be one of general prosperity and probable record highs in the national economic indicators (e.g., gross national product, personal income, business investment, and corporate profits). This prosperity will be reflected in most foreign markets as well. No unusual political or social changes are expected to have any significant impact, favorable or adverse, upon sales during 1966. On the basis of past years' experience and economic forecasts for 1966, the company's economist has estimated that the total sales of industrial pumps in the United States during 1966 will amount to $300,000,000 and sales of chain saws, to $300,000,000 also. An appraisal of environmental factors can ordinarily lead no further than a forecast of total demand for a product. What portion of that total demand may be expected to be filled by an individual firm can be predicted in most cases only after additional information is obtained.

Competition. Each firm's share of a market is determined, primarily, by competition among firms. Any time that two or more firms offer to sell the same product in the same market, there will be some degree of competition among them. Such firms may, of course, agree among themselves to restrict competitive activities in a manner that is designed to benefit all of them. Where such an agreement completely eliminated competition, the combination of the noncompeting firms (a cartel) would, in effect, be a monopoly. In the United States, such agreements to lessen competition are ordinarily illegal under the provisions of the antitrust laws. Even a monopolist is not wholly immune to competition, however. He must recognize the possibility of future competition from new firms entering his market and also of competition from substitute products in other markets (e.g., aluminum for steel, tea for coffee, etc.).

In economic theory, competition simply describes a situation in which there are many sellers of a product in a market. In common parlance, competition is used to denote rivalry. In this latter sense, competition among firms may take many forms; but all of these may be reduced to three basic forms, competition as to price, product, and promotion. Customer services are included in the area of product competition. Whatever form it may take, competition entails the possibility of shifts in market shares among competing companies. Like the environmental factors discussed above, competitive forces are subject to much uncertainty and are difficult to predict. Nevertheless, these forces must be taken into account in preparing a sales forecast for an individual firm. The responsible executive must evaluate the effect of his own firm's and competing firms' various efforts to increase their respective market shares on the sales of his firm's products during the budget period. Pricing and promotional policies, as well as product changes, may be contemplated by the firm during the budget period. Such policies are obviously relevant to the sales forecast and must be incorporated therein. At this point it might be appropriate to note that not all competitive efforts are aggressive and intended to increase a firm's market share at the expense of other firms. Much competitive effort is almost entirely defensive, designed simply to maintain an existing market share.

Shadbolt Products, Inc., enjoys a well-established position in the market for industrial pumps. This is a fairly stable market, insofar as relative shares are concerned. For several years Shadbolt's share of the market has amounted to approximately 15% of total domestic sales, and it is expected that this same proportion of the market will be obtained in 1966. In the market for chain saws, Shadbolt is fairly new and the sales manager believes the company's share of that market will continue to increase. In 1965, Shadbolt accounted for approximately 6% of the domestic sales of chain saws. The sales manager feels it is reasonable to expect this share to be increased to 8% in 1966. For both product lines, the company is unable to ascertain its percentage share of the foreign market. Statistics as to total foreign sales are difficult to obtain and unreliable. There are many very unpredictable factors, political and economic, which render foreign sales highly uncertain. However, the company's top management believes that its continued success in foreign markets is a reasonable expectation and that its export sales of chain saws, particularly to the developing nations, will continue to increase.

Company Policies. The sales of a company's products are obviously dependent largely upon a wide variety of company policies including pricing, product development, and promotion. These policies must be stated in order for the responsible executives to plan sales realistically. Further, these policies interact with those of other firms in a competitive market, as described above. The ultimate consequences in terms of sales revenue of environmental conditions, competitive forces, and managerial actions cannot be predetermined with certainty. But a careful evaluation of these various factors can result in the avoidance of certain pitfalls in the budgeting process.

Developing the Sales Forecast in Detail

Personnel Involved. As discussed in the preceding chapter, the budget should be developed initially by the persons who will be responsible for performance under it. Thus, the sales forecast should originate with salesmen. Initial sales estimates will most likely have to be revised by higher management in light of factors which are not known to salesmen in the field and also adjusted for tendencies on the parts of particular men to over- or underestimate their territories' sales potential. In large firms, a number of staff specialists such as economists and market research analysts may be involved in the planning of sales. They must not wholly supplant the salesmen in the planning process, however. If a salesman is handed a sales quota derived from a forecast in the development of which he was not consulted, his reaction is almost certain to be unfavorable. He may contrive to meet a quota which he honestly believes to be excessive by offering unwarranted concessions to buyers or by other practices which are not in the best interests of the firm as a whole.

Breakdown of the Forecast by Segments. Given an estimate of total sales of a product in the market and the expected percentage share of a firm in that market, the anticipated sales of that firm might be computed by simple multiplication. For example, total domestic sales of industrial pumps for 1966 was estimated at $300,000,000; and Shadbolt Products' share of this market was estimated at 15%. These two data would yield planned domestic sales of industrial pumps by Shadbolt of $45,000,000. But this is an end figure, not an appropriate beginning for the sales forecast. A single total is not enough. The company must know which specific pumps will be sold, when, where, and how. In other words, the sales forecast must be built up by the various segments of the business in as much detail as is believed relevant in the individual firm.

Generally speaking, the sales forecast should always include detail as to the timing of expected sales. The forecast should indicate planned sales on a monthly basis, not merely totals for the entire budget period (typically one year). Sales data might be broken down further by product lines, by operating divisions, by sales territories, by channels of distribution, by sizes of customers, or by any other scheme of classification which suits the needs of management. In the Shadbolt illustration, the sales forecast for the year 1966 is subdivided according to months, sales divisions, product lines, and channels of distribution. These subdivisions are merely illustrative and do not purport to be applicable to all industrial firms; they would, however, be suitable in a large number of firms.

In addition to a detailed breakdown of the sales forecast, it is common practice for the actual and budgeted data for the previous year to be included in the formal sales budget schedule. This comparative information affords management some frame of reference for appraising the new forecast. This is not to say that the past is always a valid basis for evaluating the future, but it often is the most readily available basis. Showing both actual and budgeted data for the previous year further affords some basis for appraising the efficiency of the budgeting process. In some instances it might be felt desirable to include actual and/or budgeted data for two or more previous years. Within certain limitations, the more comparative data available, the better can the new budget be evaluated. However, the reader of the budget must not be misled into thinking that the sales forecast for the coming period is nothing more than a statistical extension of actual data for several prior periods.

Tables 7–1 through 7–4 illustrate the several stages of the sales forecast for Shadbolt Products, Inc., for the fiscal year 1966. Each successive exhibit illustrates a different scheme of subclassification of the sales budget; and, with the exception of Table 7–4, each represents a different level of responsibility.

Table 7–1 is the summary sales forecast for the entire corporation for

TABLE 7–1

SHADBOLT PRODUCTS, INC.
Summary Sales Forecast
For Fiscal Year 1966
(thousands of dollars)

	1966				*1965*	
	Western Division	*Eastern Division*	*International Division*	*Total Company*	*Actual Total*	*Budget Total*
January	$ 3,410	$ 1,532	$ 865	$ 5,807	$ 5,187	$ 5,218
February	2,780	1,402	889	5,071	5,230	5,136
March	2,510	1,329	916	4,755	5,016	4,825
April	2,659	1,168	1,074	4,901	4,721	4,640
May	2,367	1,117	1,008	4,492	4,181	4,076
June	2,585	1,223	920	4,728	4,363	4,537
July	2,415	1,425	1,143	4,983	4,869	5,162
August	2,995	1,540	994	5,529	5,381	5,375
September	3,629	1,829	881	6,339	5,759	5,828
October	4,338	2,085	1,068	7,491	6,389	6,018
November	4,745	2,148	1,101	7,994	6,780	6,598
December	3,337	1,522	1,051	5,910	5,599*	5,087
	$37,770	$18,320	$11,910	$68,000	$63,475	$62,500

* Estimate.

the budget period. The forecast is stated in terms of dollars of sales revenue only, and the only breakdown of the firm is by sales divisions. Budgeted sales are indicated for each month of the budget period. Comparative data are provided in the form of the actual sales and the budgeted sales for 1965. Notice that the actual sales figure for December, 1965 is an estimate. As the 1966 budget must be completed prior to the end of 1965 (by December 15, 1965, in the case of Shadbolt Products), the final actual sales figure for December will not be available when the 1966 budget is completed. The monthly breakdown of sales must be based principally upon previous experience with seasonal variations in demand. Notice that approximately the same seasonal pattern obtains for the two domestic sales divisions. In the case of the International Division, however, no seasonal pattern is readily apparent. This situation follows from the fact that different parts of the world experience different seasonal changes. As a final caution, the rate of deviation of actual 1965 sales from that year's budget must not be taken as any indication of 1966 performance. Insofar as it is possible to predict, the sales forecast as prepared should be taken as the best estimate of the coming year's sales.

Table 7–2 takes a closer and more detailed look at the first sales

TABLE 7–2

SHADBOLT PRODUCTS, INC.
Sales Forecast—Western Division
For Fiscal Year 1966
(thousands of dollars)

	Industrial Pumps			*Chain Saws*			*Division Total*
	P-115	*P-85*	*Total*	*C-7*	*C-3*	*Total*	
January	$ 1,920	$ 1,050	$ 2,970	$ 240	$ 200	$ 440	$ 3,410
February	1,440	875	2,315	240	225	465	2,780
March	1,200	700	1,900	360	250	610	2,510
April	1,200	700	1,900	384	375	759	2,659
May	960	525	1,485	432	450	882	2,367
June	960	525	1,485	600	500	1,100	2,585
July	960	525	1,485	480	450	930	2,415
August	1,440	700	2,140	480	375	855	2,995
September	1,920	1,050	2,970	384	275	659	3,629
October	2,400	1,400	3,800	288	250	538	4,338
November	2,880	1,400	4,280	240	225	465	4,745
December	1,920	1,050	2,970	192	175	367	3,337
	$19,200	$10,500	$29,700	$4,320	$3,750	$8,070	$37,770

forecast column of Table 7–1. It depicts the detailed sales forecast for the Western Division only. A similar forecast would be prepared for the Eastern Division. The same type might also be prepared for the International Division; however, in this instance, a somewhat different form is used for that division.[1] In Table 7–2, sales are still expressed in terms of dollar revenue only. Monthly breakdowns are again given. Divisional sales are now detailed by product lines and these product lines are further subclassified. As may be seen in Table 7–2, two different types of industrial pumps are produced and sold by the company. Model P-115 is larger and has a higher selling price than model P-85. Similarly, chain saws are available in two models, the C-7 and the C-3, the former being larger and higher-priced. Notice in this illustration that the seasonal sales pattern of the division is dominated by that of the industrial pump line but that the seasonal pattern of demand for chain saws tends to offset that for pumps. Where seasonal sales patterns exist, there are numerous advantages of having two or more product lines whose

[1] Cf., Table 7–4.

seasonal patterns tend to counterbalance so that the total sales are fairly uniform throughout the year.

Table 7–3 goes one step further in the detailed development of the

TABLE 7–3

SHADBOLT PRODUCTS, INC.
Sales Forecast—Industrial Pumps—Western Division
For Fiscal Year 1966

(units)

	P-115			P-85		
	Industrial Users	*Dealers*	*Total*	*Industrial Users*	*Dealers*	*Total*
January	3,000	1,000	4,000	2,250	750	3,000
February	2,200	800	3,000	1,900	600	2,500
March	1,900	600	2,500	1,500	500	2,000
April	1,900	600	2,500	1,500	500	2,000
May	1,600	400	2,000	1,180	320	1,500
June	1,500	500	2,000	1,180	320	1,500
July	1,400	600	2,000	1,100	400	1,500
August	2,200	800	3,000	1,500	500	2,000
September	3,000	1,000	4,000	2,250	750	3,000
October	3,700	1,300	5,000	3,000	1,000	4,000
November	4,800	1,200	6,000	3,200	800	4,000
December	3,000	1,000	4,000	2,300	700	3,000
Total units	30,200	9,800	40,000	22,860	7,140	30,000
Unit price	$480	$480	$480	$350	$350	$350
Total sales (000s)	$14,496	$4,704	$19,200	$ 8,001	$2,499	$10,500

sales forecast. It shows the budgeted sales of the Western Division for one product line by channels of distribution. In this illustration, there are only two such channels, sales to industrial users and to dealers. Monthly detail is again given. In this forecast, sales data are given in terms of units of product and are converted to dollars of revenue only in total for the year. This schedule is a further breakdown of the first three columns of Table 7–2, and the relationship between the two exhibits should be clear. Note that no column is included in Table 7–3 for total units sold. Such a total would be irrelevant, for the two models of pumps are not the same. Total dollar sales, of course, are relevant. Similar forecasts would be prepared for industrial pumps in the other divisions and for chain saws in all three divisions.

The three budget schedules illustrated and discussed above would be particularly relevant to different levels of responsibility within the firm. Table 7–1, the overall summary of expected sales, would likely be the only sales forecast used by top management (i.e., the board of directors, president, and executive vice-president). Table 7–2 would be more pertinent to the interests of the vice-president for marketing and the sales manager of the Western Division. Finally, Table 7–3 would probably be used only within the Western Division by the division sales manager and his subordinates. These relationships between levels of managerial responsibility and the budget schedules illustrated are intended to suggest the types of detail in a sales forecast which the various levels of management are likely to want and not to indicate standardized budget forms for the several management echelons cited.

For some purposes, specialized budget forms may be found appropriate. Thus, in Shadbolt Products, experience has led the vice-president for marketing to employ a different form of divisional sales forecast for the International Division than that employed for the other two sales divisions. Specifically, he has found that an initial breakdown of foreign sales by country or region is more useful than that by product lines. The International Division sales forecast is presented as Table 7–4. This

TABLE 7–4

SHADBOLT PRODUCTS, INC.
Sales Forecast—International Division
For Fiscal Year 1966
(thousands of dollars)

	Canada	*Latin America*	*Western Europe*	*Other**	*Total*
January	$ 315	$ 119	$ 346	$ 85	$ 865
February	325	120	355	89	889
March	328	130	366	92	916
April	386	154	429	105	1,074
May	362	144	403	99	1,008
June	330	128	368	94	920
July	408	166	457	112	1,143
August	360	139	397	98	994
September	318	121	352	90	881
October	394	143	427	104	1,068
November	401	150	440	110	1,101
December	388	141	420	102	1,051
	$4,315	$1,655	$4,760	$1,180	$11,910

* Principally sales to Australia, Japan, and certain African nations.

forecast is prepared in terms of sales revenue, by countries or regions, and on a monthly basis. The last column in Table 7–4 is identical to the third column in Table 7–1. Details of expected foreign sales by product lines would be developed in budget schedules similar to those in Tables 7–2 and 7–3.

Budgeting Sales in Total Only

In the foregoing section, the sales forecast was developed by estimating unit sales volume for each product in each sales division and then multiplying those units by the selling prices to obtain budgeted sales revenue. This approach is feasible for Shadbolt Products, Inc., because it has only four different products and four selling prices. For many firms, this approach would be extremely difficult and time consuming, if not wholly impossible. It is difficult to imagine this approach being efficient for a firm selling several thousand different items at different prices, particularly where new products frequently are being added and old ones dropped from the line. A large department store, a mail-order house, or a drug wholesaler would find that sales forecasting based upon expected unit sales and selling prices was a practical impossibility. In such cases, the sales forecast may be developed from the start in terms of dollars of sales revenue. Breakdowns by sales divisions, by departments, by channels of distribution, and by sizes of customers may be feasible; but any complete breakdown by products is unlikely. Such an approach to the sales forecast is based almost entirely upon the firm's past experience, with adjustment for changes in the aggregate demand for the company's products which may reasonably be anticipated and/or price changes. While this approach may appear to be less precise than the other, it is not necessarily so. A sales forecast prepared by this method may be every bit as reliable and useful for purposes of planning and control as one prepared initially from expected unit sales.

Long-Range Sales Planning

The sales forecast described in the preceding pages is normally adequate for purposes of budget preparation. Any attempt at long-range sales forecasting would be beyond the requirements of the immediate budget period. However, the studies and analyses upon which the short-run sales forecast is predicated should also provide some indication of sales demand in the more distant future. A long-range sales forecast is typically expressed in round totals for the company, with a minimum of detail. It is most probably subject to considerably more error than the short-run forecast. Nevertheless, it is helpful to management in planning future plant capacity and future capital requirements.

Shadbolt Products, Inc., follows the practice of preparing a long-range sales forecast at the same time as its formal forecast for the coming budget period. This long-range plan is stated in terms of expected total revenues in each of the next five years, including the immediate budget period and the following four years. The only breakdown made is between domestic and foreign sales. Such a plan is illustrated in Table 7–5. Notice that this illustration shows a continually rising pattern of

TABLE 7–5

SHADBOLT PRODUCTS, INC.
Long-Range Sales Forecast
For the Period 1966–70

(thousands of dollars)

	Domestic Sales	*Foreign Sales*	*Total Sales*
1966	$56,990	$11,910	$68,000
1967	57,500	12,500	70,000
1968	61,000	13,000	74,000
1969	65,000	14,000	79,000
1970	68,000	15,000	83,000

sales. This is, in part, because no period of recession in general business activity has been anticipated in preparing the long-range forecast. The firm's management does not, thereby, express its belief that no recession will occur during the next five years. It merely demonstrates its belief that the timing of business fluctuations is too unpredictable to incorporate in a plan of this nature. Because this long-range sales forecast is quite tenuous and not relevant to normal operations in the coming period, it is circulated only among the top echelon of the company's management.

PRODUCTION BUDGETS

Factors Determining Production

Sales. In most cases, the volume of production is determined principally by the anticipated volume of sales. With comparatively few exceptions, most companies' current output is designed principally to fill current sales demand. The timing of sales, as well as the total sales for the period, is important in planning output during the budget period. Production must flow from the factory according to a schedule that enables the firm to fill sales orders as they are received. Where there is a significant degree of seasonal variation in sales demand during a period, production may be scheduled either to vary with the fluctuations in sales or to ignore them. In the first instance, where output is scheduled to vary with sales, the firm must plan to expand its overall operating activities, including its work force probably, during or immediately prior to periods of peak demand and to reduce its operations and lay off workers during the slack seasons. In the second instance, where output is stabilized despite seasonal fluctuations in demand, the company must plan to build up its inventory of finished product during the slack period and to reduce these stocks during the peak sales season. Of course, there is also the opposite situation, in which production is subject to seasonal fluctuations but sales are not. Certain canning companies experience such conditions. In these cases, there is little alternative to periods of peak and low (if, indeed, any) production and inventory buildups and reductions.

Inventory Plans. While production normally is determined chiefly by budgeted sales, it should be planned with inventory requirements in mind also. For example, if a firm anticipates that future sales demand will continue to rise, it may decide that its inventory of finished product as of the end of the budget period should be greater than that at the start of the period. Obviously, if the inventory at the end of the period is planned to be greater than at the beginning of the period, production volume during that period must exceed planned sales volume. On the other hand, an enterprise may believe that it has been carrying too much inventory of finished product and may wish to reduce this balance as of the end of the budget period as compared with the beginning. In such case, planned output will be lower than the forecasted sales volume. Of course, it is not always easy to determine long in advance the level of inventory that will be needed at the end of a period; and the impact of inventory plans on production is unlikely to be nearly so significant as that of sales demand. Nevertheless, some plan for ending inventory should be incorporated in the production budget.

Capacity. Finally, production is necessarily limited by the productive capacity of the enterprise. Capacity, however, does not admit of any simple practical definition. It is not merely a matter of plant size. Capacity may be expanded by adding work shifts, by working the regular shift overtime, by working six or seven days a week, and by other schemes to increase the output of existing plant facilities. Such schemes increase operating costs, of course. Night shifts, overtime work, and weekend work command higher wages than those paid for regular straight-time work. Thus, insofar as practical operations are concerned, capacity is established by managerial decisions as well as by physical facilities. However defined, capacity places an upper limit on output. That limit may be somewhat flexible, but it cannot be stretched indefinitely.

Summary of Production Budget

While total budgeted production costs will be reported to top management in summary form, the first line of cost control is at the level of the operating department supervisors. Hence, the costs of production must be budgeted on departmental bases so that the individual responsible managers can plan and evaluate their own performances and so that their performances may be reviewed by their superiors within the proper framework of responsibility. These departmental budget schedules accumulate to make up the overall production budget for the firm.

Table 7–6 is a summary production budget for one of the two plants

TABLE 7–6

SHADBOLT PRODUCTS, INC.
Production Cost Budget—Oakland Plant
For Fiscal Year 1966

(thousands of dollars)

	Materials	*Labor*	*Variable Overhead*	*Total Variable Costs*	*Fixed Overhead*	*Total Costs*
January	$ 1,116	$ 904	$ 283	$ 2,303	$ 460	$ 2,763
February	1,116	904	283	2,303	460	2,763
March	1,118	904	283	2,305	460	2,765
April	1,123	906	285	2,314	460	2,774
May	1,127	905	286	2,318	460	2,778
June	1,118	905	283	2,306	460	2,766
July	1,116	904	283	2,303	460	2,763
August	1,112	904	282	2,298	460	2,758
September	1,109	905	281	2,295	460	2,755
October	1,109	904	281	2,294	460	2,754
November	1,116	904	283	2,303	460	2,763
December	1,116	904	283	2,303	460	2,763
	$13,396	$10,853	$3,396	$27,645	$5,520	$33,165

of Shadbolt Products, Inc. A similar budget schedule would be prepared for the other plant, and a further summarization might be made for the entire company. The budget schedule in Table 7–6 would be directed principally to the manager of the Oakland plant and higher levels of authority within the manufacturing division of the corporation. Budgeted production costs are reported here as variable and fixed in order to facilitate management's appraisal of the effects of any changes in budgeted volume. The variable cost data were obtained by multiplying the budgeted unit output of the several products by their respective standard costs for materials, for labor, and for variable overhead. For the sake of simplicity, it is assumed here that no variances from these standard costs need be budgeted. The total planned fixed costs for the year were simply divided by twelve to obtain the monthly budget allowances. A comparison of this production cost schedule with the summary sales forecast in Table 7–1 reveals that the seasonal variation in sales is not reflected in the budget of output for the Oakland plant. (The output of the Oakland plant fills all sales orders for the Western Division and most of the orders for the International Division.) Thus, the inventory of the finished product at the Oakland plant is increased during the spring and summer and reduced during the peak sales period in the autumn and winter.

Production must also be budgeted in terms of units of output, of course. Table 7–7 is an example of a schedule of production for one

TABLE 7–7

SHADBOLT PRODUCTS, INC.
Unit Production Budget—Industrial Pumps—Oakland Plant
For Fiscal Year 1966
(units)

	P-115			P-85		
	Units Produced	*Units Shipped*	*Ending Inventory*	*Units Produced*	*Units Shipped*	*Ending Inventory*
Inventory, January 1			9,500			6,000
January	4,850	5,300	9,050	3,850	4,400	5,450
February	4,850	4,100	9,800	3,850	3,600	5,700
March	4,850	3,500	11,150	3,800	2,900	6,600
April	4,800	3,400	12,550	3,800	2,900	7,500
May	4,700	3,000	14,250	3,750	2,200	9,050
June	4,850	2,600	16,500	3,800	2,200	10,650
July	4,850	2,800	18,550	3,850	2,200	12,300
August	4,900	4,100	19,350	3,900	2,900	13,300
September	4,900	5,400	18,850	4,000	4,400	12,900
October	4,950	6,800	17,000	3,900	5,800	11,000
November	4,850	7,900	13,950	3,850	5,800	9,050
December	4,850	5,800	13,000	3,850	4,400	8,500
	58,200	54,700		46,200	43,700	

product line, industrial pumps, in the Oakland plant of Shadbolt Products. Similar schedules would be developed for the chain saw line and for the Indianapolis plant. The particular usefulness of this schedule lies in its comparison of the planned output of the plant with the budgeted shipments (sales) from it on a monthly basis. This comparison shows the month-by-month development of the inventory of finished pumps.

Labor Budget

Where the maximum practical output of a plant is not required to meet current sales demand, there is a degree of flexibility as to the scheduling of production. Within this range of flexibility, production may be planned so as to minimize the total costs of manufacturing. This end may be accomplished in different ways in different firms. However, in many firms it can best be achieved by making maximum use of a stabilized work force. In the Shadbolt Products' Oakland plant, for example, it apparently was determined to be better to level production throughout the year rather than to vary production with sales demand. More and more, the practical problems related to labor costs dictate as much stabilization of operations as is possible.

Traditionally, labor cost has been regarded as variable. Often, however, direct labor is a variable cost only by definition. When workers are not actually producing units of product, their wages are not accounted for as direct labor cost; but they are not necessarily stopped. Wages paid to workers during idle periods are accounted for as overhead, but they are still paid. The accounting treatment of labor costs cannot make them truly variable in an ultimate sense. For a variety of reasons labor costs have tended to become more nearly fixed than variable in large segments of American industry. This tendency is due largely to the efforts of labor uions, but it has not developed in business firms wholly as a result of external pressures. A stable work force with a minimum of turnover is likely to enhance employees' morale and efficiency and also to minimize training costs and operating inefficiencies during training periods. Where labor is substantially a fixed cost, total labor cost can usually be minimized by utilizing the work force in production on a level basis. If there are significant seasonal variations in sales, stable production will entail inventory buildups during periods of slack demand. The costs of financing, handling, and storing these inventories tend to offset some of the costs saved by stabilizing the labor force. In any particular company, the production schedule selected will be based upon the lowest total budgeted costs. As labor moves more toward becoming a fixed cost, level output during the period is more likely to result in the lowest total cost.

The labor budget for the Oakland plant of Shadbolt Products, Inc., is illustrated in Table 7–8. This is simply a summary of man-hours expected to be employed in each production department in the plant during the budget period. The man-hours are then extended at the standard wage rates in those departments to arrive at the total budgeted labor cost for the year. This illustration is deliberately simplified in that there is only one type of laborer in each department. Where there are two or more classes of workers in one department, each class receiving a different hourly wage rate, a departmental budget schedule subclassified

TABLE 7–8

SHADBOLT PRODUCTS, INC.
Direct Labor Budget—Oakland Plant
For Fiscal Year 1966
(man-hours)

	Frame Forming Dept.	*Pump Assembly Dept.*	*Saw Assembly Dept.*	*Total Man-Hours*
January	102,975	222,500	56,800	382,275
February	102,975	222,500	56,800	382,275
March	102,425	221,500	58,300	382,225
April	101,800	220,000	60,800	382,600
May	100,000	216,000	65,800	381,800
June	102,425	221,500	58,300	382,225
July	102,975	222,500	56,800	382,275
August	104,150	225,000	53,300	382,450
September	105,250	227,000	50,900	383,150
October	104,775	226,500	51,200	382,475
November	102,975	222,500	56,800	382,275
December	102,975	222,500	56,800	382,275
Total hours	1,235,700	2,670,000	682,600	4,588,300
Standard wage rate	$2.00	$2.50	$2.50	
Total cost	$2,471,400	$6,675,000	$1,706,500	$10,852,900

by types of workers might be appropriate. Alternatively, a weighted average wage rate for the department could be computed and used. The total labor cost in Table 7–8 is the same as the total cost in the labor column of Table 7–6, except for an immaterial difference due to rounding.

Materials Budget

As in the case of direct labor, raw materials cost has traditionally been regarded as a variable cost of production. Unlike labor, materials cost has, in most instances, remained very nearly perfectly variable. The principal reason for this is that materials can be stored by themselves and used only as needed in production. Most materials cannot be stored indefinitely, of course. Some raw materials, notably in the food-processing industry, must be used quite promptly after their acquisition. Others can be stored for considerable periods of time, but very few are wholly immune to the value-erosive influences of physical deterioration and obsolescence. Because of the capacity of most raw materials to be stored for some period of time, materials cost typically is quite readily adaptable to variations in the level of output, whereas labor cost is comparatively inflexible in most industrial companies.

Purchase Planning. The fact that the usage of raw materials is quite flexible does not necessarily mean that they may be purchased in a manner dictated simply by fluctuations in production. There are many factors which bear upon materials purchasing policies. In an ideal situation, materials would be purchased just prior to their being required for use in production. In this way, the amount of capital tied up in materials inventory would always be at a minimum. There may be many cogent reasons for purchasing more than will be needed in production in the immediate future, however. Some examples are purchasing in larger quantities than immediately needed in order to take advantage of quantity discounts, purchasing materials in advance of announced or anticipated price increases, and building stocks as a hedge against expected strikes in suppliers' plants.

In any case, there are certain general rules pertaining to the scheduling of materials purchases. The schedule for purchases of a particular material should be keyed to the schedules of production of the products in which that material is used. Purchasing policies should give proper recognition to normal time lags (order lead time) between placement of orders and the receipt of materials from suppliers. Generally speaking, it is safer to overestimate the lengths of these time lags than to attempt to plan purchases so that materials will arrive just when they are needed for production; stock-outs are far too disruptive and costly. Purchasing should be planned in such a way as to minimize the total cost of materials to the firm. One technique for the accomplishment of this objective is the determination of the most economical (i.e., the least costly) lot size in which to purchase materials.

Economical Lot Size Buying. There are certain factors which bear upon purchasing policies that favor purchases in large lots. Quantity discounts are frequently available for purchases of large quantities. Purchasing large quantities means fewer purchases and, consequently, costs saved by processing fewer purchase orders and related documents. Other factors tend to favor purchases in small quantities. Small purchases involve lower investments in inventory and, hence, lower interest costs. Small purchase quantities avoid the need for large and costly materials storage facilities. Purchasing in small lots leaves the firm in a more flexible position with regard to future operations. For example, a firm might more quickly discontinue an unprofitable product line if it did not have on hand a large stock of a material that can be used only in that line.

Several formulas have been developed to facilitate identification of the optimum lot size, or economic order quantity, in which materials should be purchased. One such formula is as follows:

$$Q = \sqrt{\frac{2CS}{UI + A}}$$

where Q = number of units in optimum purchase lot.
C = cost of placing an order for materials.
S = number of units required for use each year.
U = cost of one unit of the material.
I = interest rate which firm must pay for capital.
A = cost of carrying one unit in inventory for a year.[2]

However precise this and similar formulas may appear, they involve a number of approximations. The cost of placing an order for materials is very difficult to measure. It should include only the avoidable costs of processing one order; the fixed costs of order placing are not relevant to any single order. The annual requirements for a particular material can usually be estimated fairly closely, given the budget of production. The unit cost of the material is also usually determinable with reasonable confidence. The interest rate which the firm must pay for its capital, however, is commonly subject to a great deal of uncertainty.[3] Finally, the annual carrying cost of materials inventory is difficult to allocate among the individual materials carried. Thus, economical lot size formulas should be interpreted as reasonable indicators of optimum purchase quantities; but they cannot be taken as infallible guides to efficient purchasing.

The introduction of high-speed computers in business firms has been of considerable assistance in the planning of purchases. These machines can perform complex mathematical computations quickly and accurately. A great deal of information can be fed into and processed by them, and they are capable of printing solutions to the problems introduced into them. A manufacturer can put into a computer information concerning the purchasing and usage of materials, related costs, and an initial inventory balance. The computer can then store this information, keep it up-to-date as further transactions occur, and recall and print a current summary of the information whenever desired. The computer

---

[2] Adapted from Robert I. Dickey (ed.), *Accountants' Cost Handbook* (2d ed.; New York: The Ronald Press Company, 1960), p. 5 · 16.

[3] The problems of measuring the interest cost of capital will be considered at greater length in Chapter 8.

can be programmed to advise the firm when the stock of a particular material has been reduced to a previously established reorder point. But the computer does not establish that reorder point; this must be done by the responsible manager. Computers have been proved to be great aids to management, but they have not replaced people as managers.

Materials Purchase Schedule. As a part of the overall production budget, there should be a schedule for the purchases of each raw material used in a company. This schedule should identify the material, its principal uses in the firm's production, the principal suppliers, and planned purchases, usage, and inventory balances by months. Table 7–9

TABLE 7–9

SHADBOLT PRODUCTS, INC.
Materials Purchase Schedule
For Fiscal Year 1966

Item #310 gage — Suppliers Norton Gauges, Inc.
Uses all industrial pumps — Lewellyn, Brown & Co.

(units)

	Orders	*Receipts*	*Usage*	*Ending Inventory*
December 31, 1965				25,640
January	24,000		11,220	14,420
February		24,000	11,220	27,200
March	22,000		11,170	16,030
April		22,000	11,120	26,910
May	24,000		10,965	15,945
June		24,000	11,170	28,775
July	22,000		11,220	17,555
August		22,000	11,320	28,235
September	22,000		11,425	16,810
October		22,000	11,375	27,435
November	24,000		11,225	16,210
December		24,000	11,220	28,990
	138,000	138,000	134,650	

is an illustration of such a schedule. It covers purchases of a particular gage for both plants, as Shadbolt Products' purchasing is centralized in the home office. The schedule is based upon the following facts and policies: There is a normal delay of approximately thirty days between the date of sending an order and the date of receiving shipment on that order. The company has found that the most economical lot size for the purchase of this gage is between 20,000 and 25,000 units. Thus, it has established the policy of ordering this item bimonthly, each order being sufficient to cover approximately two months' usage. Orders are planned not only with regard to current production but also with a view toward specific inventory plans. The company's policy is never to permit the inventory of a material to fall below 125% of the budgeted production requirements for that item for the following month. Further, in this instance, the company, anticipating increased production in 1967, plans that the inventory of gages at the end of the budget period will be greater than at the start of the period. Usage of the gage is based upon budgeted production of all industrial pumps in both plants plus a standard breakage allowance of 2%. Notice in Table 7–9 that only the receipts and usage affect the balance on hand at the end of each month; orders are not received in stock until the month following that in which they were placed.

Departmental Overhead Budgets

Where manufacturing operations are departmentalized, overhead costs should be budgeted by departments. These departmental overhead budgets are the bases for planning and controlling those costs during the budget period and also the bases for establishing normal or standard overhead rates. Because of differences among departments as to the types of overhead costs incurred and the behavior of those costs with respect to fluctuations in production volume, departmental budgets are practically mandatory. The departmental overhead budget schedule should detail the various cost items and should distinguish between the variable and the fixed items. The distinction between variable and fixed overhead costs permits the budget to be adjusted to conform to changing levels of production volume. The budgeting of overhead is discussed at length in Chapter 9.

BUDGETS OF NONMANUFACTURING COSTS

Budgets for distribution, administrative, and research costs are typically prepared in essentially the same way as are budgets for factory overhead. They are prepared on departmental bases as appropriate in the particular firm. To the extent feasible, they should be subclassified to identify variable and fixed costs. The basis for cost variability in a nonmanufacturing department will be quite different from that in a manufacturing department, of course. For example, in a shipping department the most suitable measure of volume might be the number of items or the number of separate shipments handled. In a billing department, the number of bills prepared or, possibly, the number of items on bills prepared would be a likely indicator of activity and cost behavior. For certain types of activities there may be no readily identifiable measure of activity nor any observed causal factor for cost fluctuations. This might be true of certain research operations. In such a case, the departmental budget would not include any volume measure nor would it be subclassified into variable and fixed costs. In effect, all costs would be budgeted as though they were fixed costs for the period, probably in the maximum amount approved by management for spending in that department during the budget period.

BUDGETED INCOME STATEMENT

The operating budget is ordinarily summarized in the form of a budgeted income statement for the budget period. This is prepared in the same format as the actual income statement, except that the data in it represent the enterprise's profit plan for the coming period, not its actual profit. Table 7–10 is Shadbolt Products' budgeted income statement for

TABLE 7–10

SHADBOLT PRODUCTS, INC.
Budgeted Income Statement
For Fiscal Year 1966
(thousands of dollars)

	First Quarter	*Second Quarter*	*Third Quarter*	*Fourth Quarter*	*Year*
Gross sales	$15,633	$14,121	$16,851	$21,395	$68,000
Sales discounts and allowances	313	282	337	428	1,360
Net sales	15,320	13,389	16,514	20,967	66,640
Variable expenses:					
Cost of Goods Sold					
Materials	3,898	3,377	4,030	5,670	16,975
Labor	3,212	2,626	3,228	4,754	13,820
Overhead	986	856	1,024	1,434	4,300
	8,096	6,859	8,282	11,858	35,095
Distribution	782	706	842	1,070	3,400
Administrative	313	282	337	428	1,360
Total	9,191	7,847	9,461	13,356	39,855
Variable profit	6,129	5,992	7,053	7,611	26,785
Fixed expenses:					
Overhead	1,550	1,550	1,550	1,550	6,200
Distribution	1,800	1,800	1,800	1,800	7,200
Administrative	2,250	2,250	2,250	2,250	9,000
Research	150	150	150	150	600
Total	5,750	5,750	5,750	5,750	23,000
Net operating profit	379	242	1,303	1,861	3,785
Interest expense	75	85	106	91	357
Net income before tax	304	157	1,197	1,770	3,428
Federal income tax	143	73	562	833	1,611
Net income	$ 161	$ 84	$ 635	$ 937	$ 1,817

1966. It is presented in the variable costing form illustrated in Table 3–5 in Chapter 3. For external financial reports to stockholders and others, generally accepted accounting principles have customarily been interpreted as requiring the income statement to be prepared in accordance with absorption costing. But the budgeted income statement is prepared only for managerial use, and the firm may elect any form of presentation which its management finds most useful. Shadbolt Products, Inc., has decided to use the variable costing approach in its profit planning, as it uses this approach in its internally distributed interim reports. Since Shadbolt Products regularly prepares actual financial statements quarterly, the budgeted income statement is detailed by quarters also. Monthly detail would also be possible, but the company's management has not felt that the additional refinement would be particularly significant.

Budgeted sales revenues for the year and for each quarter are obtained from the company's summary sales forecast (Table 7–1). The variable cost of goods sold is computed by applying the standard costs for materials, labor, and variable overhead to the budgeted unit sales of the various products. The variable cost of goods sold is here broken down by manufacturing cost elements because there is no supporting schedule of budgeted costs of goods manufactured and sold. All fixed costs of the budget period are reduced to a quarterly basis simply by dividing the expected annual total costs by four. Federal income taxes are apportioned among the quarters simply by applying the corporate tax rate (assumed here to be a flat 47%) to the before-tax incomes of the several quarters. The interest expense consists of 6% interest on long-term bonds outstanding in the amount of $5,000,000 plus, in the last three quarters, interest on short-term bank borrowing. This short-term borrowing is discussed in the following chapter in connection with the cash budget.

QUESTIONS FOR DISCUSSION

1. Given the budgeted sales volume for a period and the plan respecting inventory at the end of the period, with which cost element would you begin the preparation of the production cost budget—materials, labor, or overhead? Why?
2. If you were the budget director of a large manufacturing company with sales outlets in fifteen states and several hundred salesmen, how would you go about preparing the initial draft of the sales forecast?
3. List all of the factors you would take into consideration in preparing a materials purchase schedule, and list them in what you believe to be the order of their relative importance.

4. What would be the implications for production planning if direct labor were, substantially, a fixed cost?
5. "Where standard production costs are used, the preparation of the production cost budget is virtually automatic once physical production volume has been established." Comment on this statement.
6. In this chapter, it was suggested that the planned level of inventory of finished product at the end of the budget period should be a partial determinant of the physical production volume budgeted for that period. How might management decide what the level of ending inventory should be?
7. Some companies determine the compensation of their salesmen partly on the basis of sales in excess of predetermined sales quotas. Should these sales quotas be equal, in total, to budgeted sales? If so, why? If not, what should be the relationship between the sales budget and the quotas?
8. What alternatives with respect to the timing of production are available to a firm which experiences significant seasonal variations in the level of sales volume? Discuss some of the advantages and disadvantages of each of these alternatives.
9. Discuss some of the problems one might expect to encounter in budgeting each of the following expenses:
   a. Packing and shipping goods to customers.
   b. Repair and maintenance of equipment.
   c. Advertising.
   d. Executives' salaries.

PROBLEMS

1. The Crawford Boat Corporation manufactures fiber glass boat hulls. Actual sales data for the year 1965 are summarized below:

First quarter	$ 3,000,000
Second quarter	6,500,000
Third quarter	5,000,000
Fourth quarter	3,500,000
	$18,000,000

The seasonal sales pattern experienced in 1965 is typical of the company's operations. For the past several years, the corporation has had a secular growth in sales volume of 4% per year. This growth rate is expected to continue through 1966. In response to generally rising costs, the company plans to increase all selling prices by 5% effective January 1, 1966. It is not anticipated that this price increase will alter the growth in sales volume.

Required:

1. Prepare a sales forecast by quarters for 1966.
2. If a recession were expected in the latter half of 1966, how would this sales forecast be altered?

2. The Martti Machine Tool Company manufactures precision instruments in its San Jose plant. There is no notable seasonal pattern to the sales of these instruments. The total production time for the products averages one and one-half months from start to completion. On December 31, 1965, there was an inventory of 15,000 finished units on hand. Unit sales for 1966 have been forecast as follows:

January	9,000	July	12,000
February	9,600	August	12,600
March	10,000	September	13,000
April	10,500	October	13,500
May	11,000	November	14,000
June	11,500	December	14,400

The plants productive capacity during 1966 is 15,000 units of product per month.

Required:

Prepare a monthly production schedule, in units, for precision instruments for 1966. This schedule should show units produced, units shipped to customers, and finished units in stock at the end of the month. Explain the amount of inventory planned for December 31, 1966.

3. The Hansen Company produces a single product. The revised sales forecast for this product, by weeks, for the fourth quarter of 1966 is as follows:

Week	*Unit Sales*	*Week*	*Unit Sales*
1	1,500	8	600
2	1,200	9	800
3	1,000	10	1,000
4	800	11	1,200
5	600	12	1,500
6	400	13	1,800
7	600		

The inventory of finished product at September 30, 1966, contains 1,000 units; the company wishes to have the same quantity in inventory at December 31, 1966.

The present work force (i.e., at October 1, 1966) consists of 150 hourly employees. The standard hourly wage rate is $2. Standard production time is 6 man-hours per unit of product. (You may assume that both the wage rate and the labor time standards will be met at all times.) The wage premium for overtime work is 50% of the standard hourly wage rate. The administrative cost of hiring one new worker is $20; no training period is required. Each employee dropped from the payroll receives severance pay equal to one 40-hour week's wages. If an employee is laid off temporarily but retained on the payroll, he is paid $.50 per hour for all such lay-off time up to a total of twenty-six 40-hour weeks.

The cost of storing finished product is $1 per unit per week. This cost is measured weekly by the number of units in storage at the end of the week.

Required:

Prepare a production schedule and a budget of labor costs and storage costs, by weeks, for the fourth quarter of 1966. The production schedule selected should be such as to minimize total labor and storage costs for the quarter. (Assume that each work week in the fourth quarter will consist of 40 hours of straight-time work. Any excess must be paid at the overtime rate.)

4. The McClary Steel Corporation converts scrap steel into usable ingots. This conversion process requires one working day. For every ton of scrap put into process there is a yield of .8 tons of usable steel. In carload lots of 3,000 tons, scrap steel is purchased for $25 per ton. Freight charges on a carload average $2,700. In lots smaller than a carload, the price of scrap steel is $33 per ton. Freight charges on odd lots average $1.50 per ton.

Ordinarily, orders for scrap steel must be placed one month in advance of the date on which the materials are needed. The company's storage facilities can accomodate a maximum of 20,000 tons at one time. At December 31, 1965, the inventory of scrap steel consisted of 16,000 tons. No materials were on order as of that date.

The sales forecast for the year 1966 is as follows:

Month	*Ingot Tons*	*Month*	*Ingot Tons*
January	11,000	July	10,000
February	14,000	August	12,000
March	15,000	September	14,000
April	15,000	October	14,000
May	12,000	November	15,000
June	12,000	December	13,000

Preliminary estimates indicate that 12,000 ingot tons will be sold in January, 1967. The company plans no net increase or decrease in its inventory of finished ingots as of the end of 1966.

It is a company policy that all orders for scrap steel are placed on the first day of a month. Hence, all shipments may be expected to arrive on the first day of the following month. It is also a company policy that the inventory of scrap steel will never be permitted to fall below 1,000 tons.

Required:

Prepare a schedule, by months, of scrap steel orders, purchases (i.e., receipts), usage, inventory balances, and total purchase costs. This schedule should meet production requirements and should minimize total materials costs for the year.

5. The Boggs Corporation wishes to purchase its raw materials in the most economical lot sizes. In order to achieve this objective, it applies the economic lot size formula illustrated in this chapter to each of the various raw materials it uses. This formula is as follows:

$$Q = \sqrt{\frac{2CS}{UI + A}}$$

For one of the company's raw materials, the cost of placing an order (C) is estimated to be \$57.80. The annual usage of this material (S) is approximately 600,000 units. The unit cost of the Material (U) is \$25. The company's interest cost of capital (I) is 8%. The annual cost of carrying one unit in inventory (A) averages \$4.

Required:

1. Compute the economic order quantity (Q) in which this material should be purchased.
2. How would you expect each of the five variables under the radical in this formula to be measured? Which would you expect to be the most difficult to measure?
3. What additional factors, if any, not included in the formula might be considered in determining the lot size in which material should be ordered?
4. Can you draw any generalizations as to the utility of this economic lot size formula?

6. The assembly department of the Frumer Toy Truck Company assembles each of the company's five models. The standard man-hours per toy in the assembly department and the budgeted output of each for the month of March, 1966 are given below.

Model	*Standard Man-Hours*	*Budgeted Unit Output*
Moving van	.36	3,000
Bulldozer	.20	4,000
Cement mixer	.25	3,200
Trench digger	.40	2,500
Dump truck	.33	4,000

The budgeted variable overhead in the assembly department is \$.75 per man-hour. The budgeted fixed overhead for the year 1966 is \$132,000. Budgeted volume for 1966 in the assembly department is 66,000 man-hours. All of these budget data are regarded as reasonable forecasts of the comparable actual data.

Required:

1. Compute the budgeted variable and fixed overhead costs, in total, for the assembly department for the month of March, 1966.
2. Does this budget include any budgeted over- or underapplied overhead? Explain.

7. The Casper Machine Company sells light machinery to manufacturers. Sales orders are obtained in two ways. Most are obtained by the company's salesmen when they call on customers. Others, called catalog orders, are placed directly with the company by customers. The salesmen leave catalogs with all customers for this purpose. Salesmen receive commissions of 5% of the sales they obtain personally and 2% of the catalog sales orders received from their territories.

Budgeted sales for 1966 are as follows:

Quarter	*Total Sales*	*Salesmen's Orders*	*Catalog Orders*
First	$3,000,000	85%	15%
Second	5,000,000	75%	25%
Third	6,000,000	70%	30%
Fourth	4,000,000	85%	15%

Shipping and billing costs average $.025 per sales dollar regardless of the source of the order. Fixed selling expenses for the year 1966 have been budgeted as follows:

Sales salaries	$220,000
Advertising	800,000
Travel	200,000

Sales salaries and travel expenses are paid out in a regular flow throughout the year. Advertising expenditures, however, will be made at irregular intervals.

Required:

1. Prepare a budget schedule, by quarters, of selling expenses for 1966.
2. Explain your allocations of fixed selling expenses to the several quarters.
3. It has been suggested that a 50% increase in budgeted advertising expenses would increase budgeted sales in each quarter by 5%, double the proportion of catalog sales to total sales, and reduce budgeted travel expenses by 50%. Would operations under this suggested plan be more profitable than operations now budgeted? Support your answer with appropriate computations.

8. The Ives Corporation manufactures two products, Bon and Bet. As of January 1, 1966, the estimated inventory of finished product will include 25,000 units of Bon and 30,000 units of Bet. The sales forecast in units for 1966 is as follows:

Quarter	*Bon*	*Bet*
First	60,000	40,000
Second	45,000	45,000
Third	40,000	55,000
Fourth	70,000	60,000

The unit selling prices of Bon and Bet are, respectively, $6.95 and $9.75.

Both products are manufactured from a single raw material, the standard price of which is $.50 per pound. Standard usage per unit of Bon is 3 pounds and per unit of Bet is 4 pounds. At January 1, 1966, it is estimated that the inventory of raw materials will contain 140,000 pounds and that an additional 250,000 pounds will be on order. Delivery of materials is routinely obtained about one month after placing an order. Present storage facilities will hold no more than 400,000 pounds of raw material. The minimum stock of raw material considered necessary at any time is 100,000 pounds. All purchases must be in lots of 10,000 pounds.

The standard wage rate per hour in the factory is $1.80. The standard production time for Bon is one man-hour and for Bet, two man-hours. The standard variable overhead rate has been set at $.60 per man-hour. The maximum productive capacity of the factory is 150,000 man-hours per quarter. This cannot be increased during 1966.

Variable selling expenses average 10% of selling prices. Budgeted fixed expenses for 1966 are as follows:

Manufacturing	$360,000
Selling	125,000
Administration	110,000

The applicable federal income tax rate is 40%.

Planned inventory balances at December 31, 1966, have been set as follows:

Raw material	150,000 pounds
Bon	30,000 units
Bet	20,000 units

The finished product warehouse will accommodate a maximum of 75,000 units of product—Bon and/or Bet. Any inventory in excess of that amount at the end of a quarter must be stored in public warehouses at a cost of $1.50 per unit. The company's production process is such that there is never any significant quantity of work in process at the end of a day.

Required:

Prepare the following budget schedules for the Ives Corporation for the year 1966:

1. Unit production schedule by products.
2. Production cost budget.
3. Materials purchases schedule.
4. Budgeted income statement in accordance with variable costing.

Each of these schedules should show details by quarters. Where alternatives appear feasible, select that one that will tend to minimize the corporation's costs for the year.

Chapter 8

RESOURCE PLANNING: FINANCIAL BUDGETS

As STATED in Chapter 6, all budgets are expressed in financial terms, that is, in terms of money. There are, however, certain budgets which are concerned specifically with the financial function of the business enterprise. As is evident in the preceding chapter, the operating budget is concerned primarily with the functions of manufacturing, distribution, administration, and (where significant) research and development. The budgets discussed in this chapter involve the planning of the capital, both long-term and short-term, required in order for the budgeted operations to be carried on effectively. Hence, they are financial budgets in the narrow sense of relating to the planning of capital resources normally associated with the special area of responsibility of financial executives, such as the treasurer. If a firm is thought of as a complex operating machine, long-term capital may be thought of as the machine itself and short-term capital, as the lubricant without which the machine cannot operate. The distinction between long- and short-term capital is not always readily identifiable, of course; but it is a useful one for purposes of discussion.

PLANNING SHORT-TERM CAPITAL

Short-term capital consists of those financial resources which flow into and out of a business in connection with the day-to-day operations of the firm and usually are provided by sources other than permanent or long-term investments by stockholders and creditors. This is not really a satisfactory definition, for it leaves many questions unanswered. If the proceeds of the sale of common stock are used to meet a current payroll, are those proceeds short-term or long-term capital? What is the status of the proceeds of a two-year bank loan? While such questions are interesting, they need not be answered in order that we may have a workable concept of short-term capital. For practical purposes, we shall consider short-term capital to be synonymous with working capital, that is, the excess of current assets over current liabilities.[1] Whatever theoretical shortcomings this definition may have, it has the considerable practical advantage of ready measurability. In budgeting working capital, one current asset is of such great importance to the firm that considerable attention is given to it alone; and it is budgeted in great detail and with great care. This asset is, of course, cash.

Cash Budget

Cash is a critical asset in any firm, and its planning requires great care. Almost paradoxically, both too little and too much cash are undesirable from the viewpoint of good management. A certain amount of cash is necessary in order for a firm to carry on its day-to-day operations. Payrolls and other current obligations must be met on time. But cash is not an earning asset. No revenue derives from holding cash itself, whereas revenue does derive from such other assets as inventory, plant, and investments in securities. Thus, too little cash endangers the liquidity of a company and too much cash tends to restrict profitability. The basic objective of the cash budget is to plan cash profitably, that is, to plan for sufficient cash at all times to meet the needs of current operations and of such long-term projects as will require cash during the budget period but for no more cash than is reasonably necessary for these purposes. Unfortunately, cash planning, like all budgeting, is subject to a great deal of uncertainty. Hence, the cash budget normally calls for more than the minimum amount of cash required in order to allow some margin for error in planning. Further, management should always be prepared to obtain additional cash in the event that the normal sources fail to provide the amount needed for current operations. The sources and uses of cash in a business enterprise are commonly distinguished according to whether they relate to the ordinary operations of the firm or to other activities.

Operating Sources and Uses of Cash. In most firms, the principal source of cash is the sales of the company's products and/or services. In the case of cash sales, receipt of cash occurs at the time of sale. In the case of credit sales, receipt of cash occurs sometime after the sale. The average time required for cash to be received on credit sales is referred to as the average collection period for receivables. Obviously, this period must be taken into account in preparing a cash budget. For most firms, the amount of credit sales will exceed the amount of cash that may be

[1] Working capital can, of course, be a negative amount when current liabilities exceed current assets.

expected to be received as a result of those sales. Sales discounts, returns and allowances, and uncollectible accounts all reduce the amount of cash potentially collectible from credit customers.

Operating outlays of cash typically include payments to employees at regular payroll dates, remittances to the government and to others of amounts withheld from employees' wages and salaries, payments to suppliers for materials and supplies, payments for purchased services such as electricity and water, insurance premiums, property tax payments, and an almost endless variety of other items. Within quite restricted limits, and timing of cash outlays for current operations is subject to the control of management. Nevertheless, these outlays often must be made regardless of the timing of cash receipts from operations. Thus, the operating sources of cash during any given period may or may not be adequate to cover the operating outlays of that period. Where operating outlays are expected to exceed operating receipts during a period, the excess must be met either from a previously accumulated cash balance or from nonoperating sources.

Nonoperating Sources and Uses of Cash. The principal nonoperating sources of cash are sales of long-lived assets and sales of securities. Assets sold may be either operating assets, such as plant and machinery, or nonoperating assets, such as stocks and bonds held as investments. It is important to remember that the sale of assets at a loss (i.e., at less than their book values), while reflected unfavorably on the income statement, still provides cash to the enterprise. Sales of securities should be interpreted broadly to include sales of stock (equity financing) and sales of all types of debt instruments, including bonds, commercial paper, and short-term notes (debt financing). Here again we see that the distinction between short-term and long-term capital is not a sharp one. Cash, the most liquid current asset, may be provided by either a thirty-day note or a thirty-year bond issue.

Nonoperating uses of cash include such transactions as purchases of long-lived assets, repayments of debt, retirements of stock, payments of dividends, payments of interest, and payments of income taxes. Even though an asset purchased is an operating asset (e.g., a production machine), the outlay for it is considered a nonoperating cash disbursement in the period of payment; for the asset will benefit the operations of several periods. Although interest and dividend payments may be normal and recurrent, they are generally not regarded as part of the operations of a business but, rather, as costs of obtaining the capital with which to conduct operations. Assuming continuous profitable operation, income taxes also are recurrent; but they are not costs of operations in the ordinary sense.

The Cash Budget Illustrated. Table 8–1 is the cash budget schedule of Shadbolt Products, Inc., for the year 1966. It is prepared on a monthly basis. It is not sufficient to say that total cash receipts for the year will exceed cash disbursements. The sequence of the receipts and disbursements in relation to each other is extremely important so that temporary cash excesses or shortages may be foreseen and appropriate plans made. As a matter of fact, operational cash budgeting must be on a day-to-day basis. The fact that the net cash flow for a month is expected to be satisfactory is no assurance that a cash shortage will not develop sometime during that month. It would be impractical to construct a formal cash budget schedule for each working day of the year, but financial management's planning of cash must assure that the firm's cash position will be adequate each day. In many firms, a weekly cash budget is prepared for a total period of less than one year—often for one quarter at a time. In Table 8–1, budgeted cash receipts from and outlays for operations are reported first and the net cash provided by operations is shown. Then nonoperating sources and uses are added and deducted, respectively. The resultant figure at this point is the net cash generated by the firm during the period. Adding to this the cash balance at the beginning of the period yields the ending balance for the period. Cash provided by short-term borrowing is included in the body of Table 8–1. The need for this borrowing was first determined by preparing the cash budget without it and observing the timing and amounts of cash deficiencies which would have to be covered by borrowing.

Profitable Cash Management. As indicated in the preceding paragraph, the cash budget is used to determine the timing and amounts of short-term borrowings required to maintain liquidity in the enterprise. It should also be used to determine when excess cash is expected to be on hand so that financial management may plan to employ that cash productively. Where excess cash balances will be available temporarily, it is common business practice to invest such balances in short-term marketable securities. Among the most popular securities for this purpose are ninety-day U.S. Treasury bills, certificates of deposit, and short-term commercial paper issued by large finance companies. Any security, however, including common stock, may be purchased and held as a short-term investment of temporarily idle cash. The advantage of converting idle cash into securities is obvious. The securities yield a return in the form of interest and/or dividends; cash, in itself, generates no

TABLE 8–1

SHADBOLT PRODUCTS, INC.
Cash Budget, for Fiscal Year 1966
(thousands of dollars)

	January	*February*	*March*	*April*	*May*	*June*	*July*	*August*	*September*	*October*	*November*	*December*	*Year's Summary*
Operating receipts:													
Cash sales	$ 625	$ 600	$ 560	$ 500	$ 450	$ 450	$ 500	$ 600	$ 675	$ 750	$ 750	$ 650	$ 7,110
Collections on account	4,756	4,709	4,321	4,092	4,051	3,971	4,068	4,330	4,778	5,503	6,314	6,285	57,178
	5,381	5,309	4,881	4,592	4,501	4,421	4,568	4,930	5,453	6,253	7,064	6,935	64,288
Operating outlays:													
Payrolls	2,264	2,263	2,265	2,264	2,262	2,265	2,265	2,264	2,263	2,266	2,264	2,264	27,169
Payments to suppliers	1,475	1,481	1,486	1,488	1,487	1,485	1,491	1,487	1,488	1,485	1,489	1,485	17,827
Factory overhead	711	710	711	712	710	711	710	712	712	712	710	710	8,531
Distribution expenses	342	341	340	340	341	340	341	342	343	343	345	342	4,100
Administrative expenses	125	125	125	125	125	125	125	125	125	125	125	125	1,500
Research expenses	66	67	67	66	67	67	66	67	67	66	67	67	800
	4,983	4,987	4,994	4,995	4,992	4,993	4,998	4,997	4,998	4,997	5,000	4,993	59,927
Net cash from operations	398	322	(113)	(403)	(491)	(572)	(430)	(67)	455	1,256	2,064	1,942	4,361
Nonoperating receipts:													
Sale of land		145											145
Short-term borrowing					394	1,182	394	493	1,379				3,842
		145			394	1,182	394	493	1,379				3,987
Gross cash provided	398	467	(113)	(403)	(97)	610	(36)	426	1,834	1,256	2,064	1,942	8,348
Nonoperating outlays:													
Interest				150						150			300
Dividends	100			100			100			100			400
Income taxes			350			400			400			400	1,550
Repayment of short-term loans								400	1,200	400	500	1,400	3,900
	100		350	250		400	100	400	1,600	650	500	1,800	6,150
Net cash provided	298	467	(463)	(653)	(97)	210	(136)	26	234	606	1,564	142	2,198
Beginning cash balance	821	1,119	1,586	1,123	470	373	583	447	473	707	1,313	2,877	821
Ending cash balance	$1,119	$1,586	$1,123	$ 470	$ 373	$ 583	$ 447	$ 473	$ 707	$1,313	$2,877	$3,019	$ 3,019

earnings. Securities are, of course, subject to market fluctuations. Thus, their yields may be enhanced by gains when they are sold if the market has risen or offset by losses if the market has declined. Maximizing the total yield on these investments is the responsibility of financial management. Assuming that the management of Shadbolt Products believes that $750,000 is the maximum cash balance which it ever needs to carry, the cash budget in Table 8–1 indicates that excess cash balances could be turned to short-term investments during the first and fourth quarters of 1966. Conversely, assuming that the minimum acceptable cash balance is believed to be $400,000, short-term borrowing would be necessary during the second and third quarters. Even then, the cash balance would dip slightly below the minimum desired balance at the end of May; presumably, this minor deviation from the usual policy is here regarded as tolerable. Seasonal variations in cash flows and cash requirements are quite common.

Working Capital Budget

In addition to the cash budget, a firm may want a formal budget of total working capital, by months or quarters, for the budget period. This budget would include cash as indicated in the cash budget and short-term marketable securities, the purchase and resale of which would be suggested by the cash budget. In addition, the working capital budget would present expected balances of receivables, inventories, prepaid expenses, and miscellaneous current assets. The receivables, in most instances, would derive chiefly from planned sales to credit customers. There might also be receivables from employees, representing salary advances or outright loans, from affiliated companies, and from anyone else to whom the firm might extend credit for one reason or another. Budgeted inventories of materials, work in process, and finished product would be derived from budgeted production and, in the case of finished product, from the sales forecast also. Budgeted prepaid expenses would be determined on the basis of company policies, such as the use of a postage meter, and also on the basis of contractual commitments, such as insurance premium prepayments.

Current liabilities typically include such items as trade accounts payable, notes payable, and accrued expenses. Trade accounts arise principally from purchases of materials and/or supplies, and these are planned as part of the production budget. Notes payable would include the firm's own notes discounted at the bank; these obligations would be planned as part of the cash budget as explained in the preceding section. Among the commonest accrued expenses are accrued wages and salaries, which arise simply because the regular payroll dates do not always coincide with the dates on which financial statements are prepared. Inasmuch as working capital items will be included in the budgeted balance sheet (Table 8–2), no budget of these items alone will be illustrated here.

Lest the discussion in the foregoing paragraphs be interpreted as suggesting that the working capital budget is prepared quite mechanically and is of little significance, we must observe that a firm's working capital position is of great importance to it as an indicator of its credit standing. Rightly or wrongly, institutions (notably banks) which grant short-term credit to business enterprises typically place considerable emphasis upon the existence and maintenance of a satisfactory working capital position, commonly measured by the current ratio (the ratio of current assets to current liabilities). Hence, planning working capital may be viewed as one facet of planning short-term borrowing.

LONG-TERM CAPITAL PLANNING

Budgeting cash and working capital is almost invariably restricted to the immediate budget period, usually no more than one year in the future. Continuous operation at a profit demands more extensive planning for future resources, however. There is no limit on the number of future periods for which capital resources should be planned. A good general rule is that capital planning should be extended as far into the future as is practicable and meaningful. For some industrial firms, this may be no more than five years. For other enterprises, public utilities being likely examples, such planning may reasonably be projected as many as twenty-five or more years into the future. For purposes of discussion here, we shall consider first the sources from which long-term capital may be expected to be obtained and then what the firm plans to do with it. Actually, the sources and uses of capital are inextricably interrelated. Often capital is obtained for a specific purpose, and it might be unobtainable for other purposes. In such case, the source is wholly dependent upon the planned use.

Sources of Long-Term Capital

Debt Financing. Long-term capital sources are commonly classified as either debt or equity financing. Debt financing for long periods is usually accomplished by the sale of bonds, by mortgages, or by bank term loans. While considered as long-term borrowing, term loans are seldom of as long maturities as bonds or mortgages. There are, of course, differences among these various sources of debt capital; there are several different types of bonds alone. These differences are not of particular significance to the present discussion, however. All debt financing has certain common features which are relevant to long-term capital planning. To begin with, all debts have maturity dates at which they must be repaid. Even though a firm may plan to repay one long-term obligation with the proceeds of a new one, it must still make such a plan and arrange for the new borrowing. Perhaps the most important single aspect of debt financing is the interest charge which accompanies it. Interest payments must be made in stipulated amounts and at specified times, regardless of the profitability of operations or of the cash position of the firm. Failure to meet interest payments normally means that the principal amount of the debt becomes due immediately, and it may well precipitate the liquidation of the enterprise. Thus, a decision to obtain long-term capital by borrowing involves a concomitant commitment to fixed cash disbursements at regular intervals with the attendant threat of serious consequences should those disbursements not be made on schedule.

Long-term borrowing may impose additional restrictions upon a firm. Bond indentures frequently contain provisions designed to protect the bondholders by limiting further financial activities of the bond issuer. Examples of such restrictions are limitations upon dividend payments, prohibitions against additional borrowing, and requirements of minimum working capital balances. Each of these restrictions narrows the scope of management's discretion as to operations for as long as the debt is outstanding. A requirement of a particular working capital position, typically measured by the current ratio, may prevent management from taking advantage of a potentially profitable opportunity because such action would temporarily reduce the current ratio below the required minimum.

Equity Financing. Long-term capital provided by the owners of an enterprise is generally referred to as equity capital. It may be provided directly by them through investments of their personal wealth in the enterprise, or it may be provided indirectly by the reinvestment of enterprise earnings in the business. In a corporation, direct investments by owners are effected by sales of the corporation's stock. Indirect investments are usually measured by the amount of retained earnings in the corporation. Equity capital is normally regarded as permanently invested in the firm. With certain exceptions, such as the issuance of redeemable preferred stock, it is not contemplated that amounts paid for stock will ever be repaid to the stockholders by the corporation. This does not mean that equity capital is not subject to reduction. Just as retained earnings increase the stockholders' investment, accumulated losses may reduce their investment. In fact, continuous losses may completely eliminate the stockholders' capital investment and may erode capital provided by debt financing as well. (Such would be the case where total liabilities exceeded total assets.)

To the extent that future profits may be predicted, long-range capital planning may be predicated in part upon the expectation of the reinvestment of enterprise earnings. In an expanding company, however, it is likely that reinvested earnings will not be sufficient to meet all future capital needs. Further, stockholders' desires for dividends place a practical limitation on the amount of income that may be retained in the business. Thus, most successful firms find that they must periodically obtain additional long-term capital by selling additional shares of stock or by borrowing. Some of the considerations which should precede a decision to borrow were discussed in the preceding section. While stock does not command a regular fixed dividend amount comparable to the interest on bonds, the practical exigencies of good stockholder relations demand that reasonable dividends be paid more or less regularly. In a closely held corporation, such as a family business, sale of stock to outsiders may endanger the close control enjoyed by the present stockholders. Loss of control may be prevented by the sale of nonvoting stock. Most nonvoting stock is preferred stock, which normally carries a cumulative preference as to dividends. For a number of reasons, there is little market for nonvoting common stock.[2]

The Cost of Capital. One of the principal factors to be considered in any business decision is the cost to be incurred as a result. This is no less true of a decision among alternative sources of capital than of any other decision. All capital has a cost, but not necessarily the same cost. Different firms are likely to be faced with different costs of capital. Different sources of capital usually entail different costs. Further, capital costs are not static. They change with time to reflect changes in supply and demand in the capital markets. Thus, the cost of capital to an individual firm at a particular time is not easily measured.

Unfortunately, the difficulties involved in measuring it do not obviate the necessity for determining some operational measure of the cost of capital to a firm. If a decision is to be made to commit capital to some long-term investment project, that decision must be supported by some indication that the yield from the investment will at least equal and hopefully exceed the cost of obtaining the capital invested. In Chapters

[2] The New York Stock Exchange will not even list nonvoting common stock.

15 and 16, we shall analyze capital investment decisions by means of techniques that require a quantitative statement of the firm's cost of capital. There we shall assume that the cost of capital is known, without examining the manner in which it was determined. Any really useful discussion of the determination of capital costs would be beyond the scope of this book, but it is certainly within the scope of responsibility of financial managers.

Long-Term Capital Investments

Resource Allocation. The problems and procedures associated with the planning of long-term capital investments are popularly referred to as *capital budgeting.* The basic problem of capital budgeting is ascertaining the most profitable uses of the scarce capital available to the firm. In most firms, the various opportunities for investment exceed the available capital. Thus, the capital budgeting process must strive to identify the most profitable of the alternative investment opportunities in order that the scarce capital of the enterprise will be employed most effectively. Profitability, it must be remembered, is a long-run objective; and the maximum long-run profit is never determinable in advance with certainty. Thus, management must weigh a variety of factors relative to each alternative investment opportunity; and not all of these factors are readily translatable into rates of profit. Despite the difficulties involved in estimating the profit potentials of alternative investments, it is very important that management be able to forecast investment profitability and to do so with a high degree of success. Long-term capital investments, by definition, commit the enterprise's capital to particular projects and/or assets for long periods of time. Just as the profits from such investments are expected to continue for a long time, losses resulting from them are likely to persist also. And the abandonment of unprofitable long-term projects or long-lived assets is likely to entail the loss of a substantial portion, if not all, of the capital invested therein.

Chapter 16 will discuss quantitative techniques for evaluating the relative profit potentials of alternative investment opportunities. Before considering these techniques, however, we must examine the relevance of particular types of costs in specific decision-making situations. At this point it is appropriate only to make one observation concerning these techniques. While the mathematical methodologies of the techniques are precise, so long as the data to which the techniques are applied are estimates the conclusions drawn from the techniques are estimates also.

Project Planning. Long-term capital investments may take many forms. They may involve the acquisition of long-lived tangible assets, such as buildings and machinery. They may involve purchases of intangible assets such as franchises, leaseholds, and patents. Major advertising and other promotional programs frequently entail long-term commitments of substantial amounts of capital. An investment in a going concern—the acquisition of a subsidiary corporation, for example—is likely to include all of the foregoing types of investments. Whatever the nature of the particular investment, it should be defined and measured carefully. Most investments involve some initial outlay of capital, but this outlay may not be the full measure of the investment. The construction of a factory, for example, commits the firm not only to the purchase price of the building and equipment but also to many years' operating and maintenance costs. Both the sum and the timing of these several outlays are very important to effective capital budgeting. Outlays must be compared with receipts expected to be derived from the investment over its useful life in order to evaluate its profit potential. Commonly, the profit potential of long-term investment projects is stated as a rate of return on the amount invested.

Typically, the need for or desirability of a particular long-term investment is first determined by the responsible executive who would be most concerned with it. The sales manager is likely to originate the idea for a major promotional program; a department supervisor will probably first suggest the replacement of a piece of machinery or the purchase of additional machines; and the controller may propose the acquisition of an electronic computer. The executive requests that corporate funds be allocated to the particular project. It is not at all unusual for the sum of such requests to exceed the amount of available capital. Thus, priorities must be assigned by top management. These priorities are based upon an analysis of the relative profit potentials of the several projects. The responsible executives prepare estimates of total outlays required for their respective projects, along with the timing thereof, and estimates of the revenues to be derived from them. Each executive requesting an allocation of capital must justify it in terms of the long-run objectives of the entire firm. Top management then coordinates the various requests for capital expenditures with the expected amount of available long-term capital and determines which projects will be undertaken and in what sequence.

Effective control over capital expenditures requires that actual spending be consistent with planned outlays for approved projects. Often, of course, it proves necessary to spend more or less for a particular project than was originally anticipated. Any excess spending should be specifically justified and approved. It must be observed here, however, that it may be difficult to avoid additional expenditures once a project has been started and capital committed to it. For example, a building may be planned at a total cost of $8,000,000. After construction has begun and several millions of dollars have been spent, it may be determined that the total cost will actually be $12,000,000. Despite the fact that this represents a 50% increase over the amount originally budgeted, management may feel that it has no alternative to spending the additional $4,000,000. At this point, the choice may be between spending the additional money for a completed building which can be used to produce revenue or abandoning the construction project and any hope of revenue from it. In a situation such as this, if the expected revenues from use of the building are adequate to justify the *future* outlays necessary to complete the structure, the amount already expended is not relevant. It cannot be recovered if the building is left unfinished. Even if only a portion of it can be recovered by completion of the building, such completion would be financially advantageous. The future costs are the relevant ones for decision making.

THE BUDGETED BALANCE SHEET

In current accounting practice, the financial resources of a firm are summarized periodically in the form of a balance sheet, or statement of financial position. As a part of the master budget, a budgeted balance sheet is sometimes included to indicate the anticipated financial position of the firm at the close of the budget period and, perhaps, at selected dates during the period. Just as the actual balance sheet has come to be regarded by many as less important than the income statement, the budgeted balance sheet is likely to be viewed as less useful to management than the budgeted income statement and related component operating budget schedules. One study of budget practices showed that only 56% of the firms observed prepared budgeted balance sheets, whereas 98% of them prepared budgeted income statements.[3] Nevertheless, a budgeted balance sheet should be of some use in identifying the anticipated consequences of budgeted operations for a period. Table 8–2 is the budgeted balance sheet of Shadbolt Products, Inc., for 1966. Consistent with the budgeted income statement (Table 7–10), balance sheet data are estimated for the end of each quarter of the budget period. The development of most of these data should be obvious. Cash, of

[3] Burnard H. Sord and Glenn A. Welsch, *Business Budgeting: A Survey of Management Planning and Control Practices* (New York: Controllership Foundation, Inc., 1958), pp. 277 and 280.

TABLE 8–2

SHADBOLT PRODUCTS, INC.
Budgeted Balance Sheet
(thousands of dollars)

	March 31, 1966	*June 30, 1966*	*Sept. 30 1966*	*Dec. 31, 1966*
Current assets:				
Cash	$ 750	$ 583	$ 707	$ 750
Short-term marketable securities	373			2,269
Accounts receivable (net)	3,830	3,804	4,950	5,131
Inventories	10,167	14,046	15,532	12,137
Prepaid expenses	45	36	28	35
	15,165	18,469	21,217	20,322
Current liabilities:				
Bank notes payable		1,600	2,300	
Accounts payable	2,188	3,453	4,446	3,716
Accrued expenses	1,865	1,970	2,140	3,088
Dividends payable	100	100	100	100
	4,153	7,123	8,986	6,904
Working capital	11,012	11,346	12,231	13,418
Fixed assets:				
Land	2,450	2,450	2,450	2,450
Plant and equipment	22,600	22,600	22,600	22,600
Less: Accumulated depreciation	(8,400)	(8,650)	(8,900)	(9,150)
	16,650	16,400	16,150	15,900
	27,662	27,746	28,381	29,318
Long-term debt:				
6% bonds payable	5,000	5,000	5,000	5,000
Net assets	22,662	22,746	23,381	24,318
Stockholders' equity:				
Common stock	15,000	15,000	15,000	15,000
Paid-in capital	5,000	5,000	5,000	5,000
Retained earnings	2,662	2,746	3,381	4,318
Net worth	22,662	22,746	23,381	24,318

course, is obtained directly from the cash budget (Table 8–1). Short-term marketable securities are determined by the information in the cash budget and the company's policy of investing cash balances in excess of $750,000. Receivables are determined by reference to the sales forecast and to the average collection period; adjustment must be made for cash sales and for discounts, allowances, and uncollectible accounts. Inventory balances are developed from purchase plans, production schedules, and the sales forecast. Accounts payable balances are derived from purchase plans and the firm's policy regarding the timing of payments to suppliers. Bank notes payable are derived from the cash budget. The other balances reported are derived from existing balances adjusted for specific plans for and/or experience with particular items.

BUDGET REVIEW REPORTS

The importance of budgetary review in the managerial control process was mentioned in Chapter 6. At the periodic meetings of the budget committee, budget review reports comparing actual and budgeted performances are studied and discussed. In order that these discussions may be pointed and fruitful, the reports should be prepared and disseminated in sufficient time before the meeting that the responsible executives may study them, pursue any material variations of actual data from the budget, and attempt to identify the causes thereof.

Shadbolt Products, Inc., holds its monthly budget review meeting on the 10th of each month to consider performance of the previous month and of the year to date. Table 8–3 is an example of a budget review

TABLE 8–3
SHADBOLT PRODUCTS, INC.
Sales Report—Western Division
For the month ended October 31, 1966
(thousands of dollars)

	October			*Year to Date*		
	Actual	*Budget*	*Variance*	*Actual*	*Budget*	*Variance*
Industrial pumps:						
P-115	$2,520	$2,400	$120	$15,504	$14,400	$1,104
P-85	1,435	1,400	35	7,770	8,050	(280)
Total	3,955	3,800	155	23,274	22,450	824
Chain saws:						
C-7	258	288	(30)	3,672	3,888	(216)
C-3	248	250	(2)	3,250	3,350	(100)
Total	506	538	(32)	6,922	7,238	(316)
Total sales	$4,461	$4,338	$123	$30,196	$29,688	$ 508

report. It is a sales report for the Western Division and is broken down by products. Actual data for the last month and for the year to date are compared with the pertinent budgeted sales data. The budgeted sales figures are taken from the sales forecast for the Western Division (Table 7–2). This report indicates that sales of industrial pumps have been exceeding budgeted volume. While both models of pumps sold more than the budgeted amounts for the month of October, the sales of the P-

85 pump for the first ten months of the year (in total) have been below budgeted volume. A substantial excess of actual over budgeted sales of the P-115 model has more than compensated for the reduced sales of the P-85, however. For both the month and the year to date, sales of both models of chain saws have lagged behind budgeted volume. It will be recalled that the company planned sales of chain saws for 1966 on the assumption that its share of the total market for these products would increase from 6% to 8%. Evidently this assumption has not been validated by actual sales.

Knowing the amounts of deviations of actual data from the budget is only the beginning of the control process, of course. The really important step is the next one, attempting to determine why these deviations occurred. Causes of favorable deviations are just as important as causes of unfavorable ones. If the company is able to identify the reasons for the increased demand for the P-115 model pump, it may be able to direct its efforts toward those reasons to reinforce and extend them. On the other hand, the causes of the lower demand for the company's chain saws should be sought out and, if possible, corrected. If the company has failed to obtain the percentage of the chain saw market that it forecast, it should attempt to learn the reason. Perhaps the price is too high and/or the product quality is too low relative to competing saws. Perhaps promotion of the chain saw line is inadequate. And perhaps the sales goal, which represented a one-third increase in the company's share of the market, was unrealistic to begin with. Whatever the reason, the essence of control is finding that reason and taking such action as is appropriate to correct the situation.

Similar budget review reports would be prepared for all segments of the firm and for all aspects of operations. Expense reports with comparative budget data will be illustrated in the following chapter.

QUESTIONS FOR DISCUSSION

1. Distinguish between short-term and long-term business capital. Of what significance to management is this distinction?
2. What are the basic rules to be observed in effective cash planning?
3. Cash budgeting is sometimes described as the process of reconciling conflicting objectives with respect to cash in the most satisfactory compromise. To what does this description refer? Does cash planning really involve conflicting objectives?
4. Of what value is a working capital budget in a firm which already has prepared a cash budget?

5. How might alternative accounting principles affect a budget of working capital? How might they affect a budgeted balance sheet?
6. If the cost of capital is common to all business activities, can it safely be ignored in making a specific decision relative to one segment of an enterprise? Why or why not?
7. What are the essential problems of capital budgeting?
8. "In the implementation of any long-term investment project, there is always some 'point of no return' beyond which it is not possible to abandon the project, regardless of the additional cost of completing it." Assuming for the moment that this statement is true, how would one identify this "point of no return"? Now, is the statement necessarily true? Under what circumstances, if any, would it be untrue?
9. Why do you think more business firms prepare budgeted income statements than prepare budgeted balance sheets? Do you feel the reason(s) is (are) valid?
10. Study the budget review report in Table 8–3 in this chapter. How might this report be improved to make it more useful to management?
11. "The operating budget must be prepared before the financial budgets, for the latter are dependent upon the former, particularly as regards cash and working capital generated from operations. The operating budget, however, can be completed without regard to the financial budgets." Discuss the validity of these two statements.

PROBLEMS

1. The Ransford Corporation's operating budget for 1966 includes the following revenues and expenses involving cash receipts and disbursements:

	First Quarter	*Second Quarter*	*Third Quarter*	*Fourth Quarter*
Sales on account	$800,000	$750,000	$680,000	$950,000
Purchases of materials on account	175,000	175,000	200,000	200,000
Payroll	330,000	315,000	340,000	350,000
Miscellaneous expenses	150,000	150,000	150,000	150,000

The company's experience indicates that 50% of accounts receivable are collected in the quarter in which the sales are made; 40% is collected in the following quarter; 8% is collected in the second following quarter; and 2% is uncollectible. Sales in the third and fourth quarters of 1965 were $600,000 and $800,000 respectively.

Purchases are paid for in the following quarter. Purchases in the fourth quarter of 1965 amounted to $180,000. All payrolls and other expenses are paid in the quarter in which incurred.

Nonoperating cash outlays call for dividend payments of $20,000 on the last day of each quarter. In addition, serial bonds in the amount of $250,000 mature on June 30, 1966, and must be paid from the regular cash account.

Interest on bonds in the amount of $15,000 is also payable on June 30. On December 31, bond interest of $7,500 must be paid.

The cash balance at January 1, 1966, will be $50,000. The minimum cash balance considered necessary is $25,000.

Required:

Prepare a cash budget, by quarters, for 1966. If borrowing is necessary at any time during the year, include it in the budget. Assume that all borrowing will be for a period of 90 days and will bear interest at 6%.

2. The Optimal Company has completed its operating budget schedules for 1966 and has prepared the following monthly analysis of budgeted cash provided by (or consumed in) operations:

January	$ 80,000	July	$ 50,000
February	40,000	August	70,000
March	(20,000)	September	100,000
April	(60,000)	October	(10,000)
May	(75,000)	November	(80,000)
June	(20,000)	December	(90,000)

The cash balance at January 1, 1966, is expected to be $35,000.

The company adheres to a strict policy of cash management, designed to provide adequate cash balances at all times and to avoid excessive balances. If the company's cash balance is between $25,000 and $50,000, the cash position is regarded as satsifactory and no specific action is taken. If the balance falls below $25,000, short-term borrowing is used to maintain the minimum balance. All borrowing will be in even multiples of $1,000 and will bear interest at 6%, payable when the debt is repaid. If the cash balance exceeds $50,000, the excess is invested in short-term marketable securities. These securities will be purchased and, when necessary, resold in even multiples of $1,000. They will earn interest at a rate of 4%, collectible when the securities are resold. For budgeting purposes, it is assumed that these marketable securities will be resold at neither a gain nor a loss.

Required:

Prepare a schedule, by months, showing (1) total cash balances expected; (2) amounts to be invested in short-term securities; (3) sales of short-term securities; (4) short-term borrowing; and (5) repayments of short-term borrowing. For simplicity, assume that all cash transactions in each month occur on the last day of the month. Apply a first-in, first-out assumption when marketable securities are resold.

3. The Appliance Store plans to begin operations on January 1, 1967. Estimated sales, in units, for the first six months of that year are as follows:

January	100
February	160
March	180
April	220
May	380
June	360

Each appliance will be sold at a list price of $200. It is anticipated that 25% of sales will be for cash and the remainder, on instalment contracts. The instalment contract will require a down payment of 10% of the price and 10 monthly payments of $20 each, including all finance charges.

The store will purchase appliances for $125 each. Purchases will be financed by paying 20% down and giving a noninterest bearing note for the balance. This balance must be paid at the end of the month in which the appliance is sold. An average inventory of 200 units is to be kept in stock.

The store plans to use the instalment contracts as collateral for bank loans equal to 60% of the unpaid balance on all new instalment contracts obtained each month. These loans must be repaid monthly in an amount equal to 60% of the instalment collections for the month. The interest charge on these bank loans will be 6% per annum on the balance of loans outstanding at the end of the preceding month. Interest will be paid monthly.

Salesmen will receive a commission of $20 on each appliance sold. The commission is payable in the month of sale. Other variable out-of-pocket expenses will be $30 per unit sold. Fixed out-of-pocket expenses are expected to average $1,200 per month.

Receipt of the bank loans and repayments thereof will be effected on the last day of the month.

Required:

Prepare a cash budget, by months, for the first half of 1967. Include any appropriate supporting schedules. It will be the company's policy to maintain a minimum cash balance of $5,000. Any deficiency of cash provided from the business will be made up by additional investments by the owner of the store.

(Adapted from CPA Examination)

4. The Forward Corporation is in the midst of a major expansion program. Its new plant building is scheduled for completion by September 30, 1966. Construction contract payments must be made as the work progresses, according to the following established schedule:

February 1, 1966	$100,000
April 1, 1966	100,000
June 1, 1966	150,000
August 1, 1966	200,000
September 30, 1966	350,000
Total contract price	$900,000

As of January 1, 1966, the corporation has a sinking fund for plant expansion consisting of marketable securities with a total market value of $500,000. Their market value is not expected to change during the first nine months of 1966. The cash balance at January 1, 1966, is $20,000. Cash provided by (or consumed in) operations during 1966 is budgeted as follows:

January	$ 10,000	July	$40,000
February	30,000	August	50,000
March	50,000	September	30,000
April	(20,000)	October	20,000
May	(40,000)	November	20,000
June	10,000	December	10,000

A cash balance of $40,000 is desired as of December 31, 1966. During the year, however, a minimum cash balance of $30,000 is considered both necessary and adequate. Temporary excess cash balances will not be invested.

Any construction payments which cannot be met from operating sources or from liquidation of sinking fund securities will be financed by borrowing on a 6% bank loan. The corporation will be able to repay this loan as it chooses, except that it must repay at least 10% of the principal in each of the quarters following the quarter in which the loan is drawn.

The sinking fund securities yield 4% per annum. As of December 31, 1965, all sinking fund earnings had already been collected. Earnings in 1966 will be collected as the securities are sold.

Required:

Prepare a schedule, by months, showing (1) cash from operations; (2) cash realized on sales of sinking fund securities; (3) cash borrowed from the bank; (4) construction contract payments; (5) bank loan repayments; and (6) cash balances. Assume that securities will be sold and that the bank loan will be drawn and repaid in even multiples of $1,000 only.

5. The Dorian Doll Company makes and sells five dolls. All sales are to retailers and toy wholesalers at the same prices. The budgeted sales volume and the list prices for the month of December, 1965 are as follows:

Doll	*Budgeted Unit Sales*	*List Price*
Dancing Dottie	5,000	$5.75
Raggy Ruth	11,000	1.10
Sleepy Susie	4,500	4.80
Sophisticated Sophie	3,800	7.50
Talking Tessie	6,600	6.00

Actual sales, in units and in dollars, for December were reported as follows:

	Actual Sales	
Doll	*Units*	*Dollars*
Dancing Dottie	7,000	$ 37,800
Raggy Ruth	6,500	6,500
Sleepy Susie	3,000	13,500
Sophisticated Sophie	4,200	33,600
Talking Tessie	6,900	41,400
		$132,800

Required:

1. Prepare a sales report for the month of December to compare actual and planned sales in whatever manner you feel would be most useful to management.
2. What differences between actual and budgeted sales would you consider worthy of special attention and action by management?
3. What additional information might be helpful to management in evaluating the sales report for December, 1965?

6. The Double-Bubble Beverage Company plans to introduce a new soft drink, called Fruit-Fizz, in 1967. Expected sales volume, in cases, for the company's several sales territories during 1967 is as follows:

Month	*East*	*South*	*Midwest*	*West*	*Overseas*
January	6,000	3,000	5,000	6,000	1,000
February	6,000	3,000	5,200	7,500	1,000
March	6,500	3,300	6,000	7,500	1,000
April	7,000	3,500	6,000	8,000	1,000
May	7,500	5,000	6,800	8,000	1,000
June	8,000	5,500	7,500	9,000	1,000
July	9,500	6,000	8,500	10,000	1,000
August	10,000	6,600	9,000	10,000	1,000
September	9,000	6,500	8,000	10,000	1,000
October	8,000	6,000	6,500	9,500	1,000
November	7,000	5,500	6,000	9,000	1,000
December	7,000	5,500	6,000	9,000	1,000

Actual sales data for the first seven months of 1967 show the following numbers of cases sold in the various sales territories:

Month	*East*	*South*	*Midwest*	*West*	*Overseas*
January	6,184	3,212	4,384	8,300	265
February	6,072	3,180	4,880	8,118	484
March	5,900	3,302	4,910	8,240	920
April	6,885	3,633	5,845	8,418	762
May	7,249	4,750	6,920	8,006	1,314
June	8,110	5,118	7,778	7,870	1,180
July	9,875	5,424	8,180	7,644	835

All sales were made at the standard list price of $1.60 per case.

Required:

1. Prepare a budget review report of sales for the month of July 1967.
2. What facts disclosed in this report would you expect to be of chief concern to the company's sales manager?
3. What generalization as to the validity of the seasonal pattern of sales shown in the budget can be drawn from this report?

Chapter 9

FLEXIBLE EXPENSE BUDGETS

WE HAVE already seen that the operating budget for an enterprise includes budget schedules of operating costs and expenses in all of the various departments within the firm. Among manufacturing costs, those that are directly traceable to the product and that vary in direct proportion to the volume of production—direct materials and labor costs—are relatively easy to budget. They are direct functions of the volume of production. If the actual volume of production deviates from the planned volume, planned materials and labor costs can be adjusted quite readily to conform to the new volume. For indirect manufacturing costs, however, this direct functional relationship does not obtain. Overhead costs are, of course, incurred because of and for the sake of production; but the direct input-output relationship existing between materials and labor costs and production volume is lacking. Even those overhead costs which vary with the volume of production typically do so in a vaguely defined manner. For example, experience may indicate that indirect materials cost varies quite nearly in direct proportion to output; but it may be impossible to identify any specific indirect materials input per unit of output. Fixed manufacturing costs, of course, are incurred in amounts unrelated to variations in output.

What is true of overhead in this context is largely true of nonmanufacturing costs also. These latter costs usually vary, in part, with the volume of sales (or, in some cases, with the volume of production); but, as in the case of overhead, there is usually no direct relationship between individual nonmanufacturing cost items and units of sales. (Sales commissions are the classic exception here.) Certain nonmanufacturing costs are fixed in amount, regardless of the volume of sales or production. In summary, then, there is some degree of variation of overhead and of most nonmanufacturing costs with appropriate measures of volume; but the variation is partial and the total costs cannot readily be expressed as a certain amount per unit of output or of sales.

If indirect costs are budgeted simply at a given amount for the budget period, with no indication as to how those costs would behave if volume were to deviate from the planned level, such a budget would be of limited usefulness to management. If, however, the budget schedule is developed in some way that indicates what the overhead or nonmanufacturing costs may be expected to be at various levels of volume, its utility for purposes of cost planning and control is greatly enhanced. Budgets of indirect costs at a single volume only, with no basis for determining the impact of a change in volume on the budgeted costs, are called *fixed budgets* or *static budgets.* Budgets which do provide a basis for determining the costs anticipated at various levels of operating activity are referred to as *flexible budgets, variable budgets,* or *sliding budgets.* The first term seems most descriptive of the essential character of these budgets and will be used consistently throughout this book.

CONSTRUCTION OF FLEXIBLE BUDGET

Departmentalization of Costs

In any firm large enough to have significant departmental distinctions for operating purposes, flexible budgets should be prepared individually for the indirect costs of each department, whether it be a manufacturing, administrative, selling, or other type of department. The development and construction of flexible budgets are the same, whether they pertain to manufacturing or nonmanufacturing operations. Flexible budgets for indirect manufacturing costs may have more uses than nonmanufacturing cost budgets, however. For example, a flexible budget for overhead is ordinarily used to establish a normal or a standard overhead cost of the product. Since nonmanufacturing costs are treated as period costs rather than as product costs in current accounting practice, this particular application would not be pertinent to a flexible budget for a nonmanufacturing department. The remainder of the discussion in this chapter will have reference to flexible budgets for overhead costs only. This limitation is solely for the sake of uniformity and clarity in the presentation. The same concepts are applicable to nonmanufacturing cost budgets. Nonmanufacturing costs will be given specific attention in Chapter 12.

An illustration of a flexible overhead budget is presented in Table 9–1. This budget is for the light machinery department of the M-G Stanley Corporation. Similar schedules would be prepared for the other manufacturing departments and for the various nonmanufacturing departments. Because the M-G Stanley Corporation prepares monthly operating reports for its management and wishes to analyze and evaluate its operating costs monthly, the budgeted overhead data in this illustra-

TABLE 9–1

M-G STANLEY CORPORATION

Monthly Expense Budget

Department Light machinery | Approved 12/10/65

Supervisor W. S. Gilbert

	Variable Rate per Hour	*Fixed Cost per Month*				
Measure of volume Direct labor hours			15,000	18,000	21,000	24,000
Controllable costs:						
Indirect labor	$ .90		$13,500	$16,200	$18,900	$21,600
Labor-related costs	.20	$ 800	3,800	4,400	5,000	5,600
Indirect materials	.50		7,500	9,000	10,500	12,000
Fuel and power	.08	2,000	3,200	3,440	3,680	3,920
Repairs and maintenance	.10	4,000	5,500	5,800	6,100	6,400
			33,500	38,840	44,180	49,520
Noncontrollable costs:						
Supervision		3,200	3,200	3,200	3,200	3,200
Taxes and insurance		800	800	800	800	800
Depreciation		25,000	25,000	25,000	25,000	25,000
			29,000	29,000	29,000	29,000
Total costs	$1.78	$35,800	$62,500	$67,840	$73,180	$78,520
Normal rates per labor hour:						
Variable rate			$1.7800	$1.7800	$1.7800	$1.7800
Fixed rate			2.3867	1.9889	1.7048	1.4917
Total rate			$4.1667	$3.7689	$3.4848	$3.2717

tion are for one month. Obviously, the data in the flexible budget can be expressed in terms of any period of time—a month, a quarter, a year. As a practical matter, the flexible budget would rarely, if ever, apply to more than one year.

The Measure of Volume

The essence of a flexible budget is the presentation of estimated cost data in such a manner that permits their determination at various levels of volume. As a practical matter, this means that all costs must be identified as to how they behave with changes in volume—whether they vary or remain fixed. In order to identify the behavior of the various cost items in a department, it is necessary first to define volume in the most meaningful way. For a department which is engaged in the production of several substantially different products (e.g., refrigerators, clothes dryers, and ranges), units of output would not be an appropriate measure of volume; for the various units are not alike. In such a case, volume is typically expressed in terms of some unit of input, such as direct labor hours, direct labor cost, or machine hours. The volume measure selected for any given department should be that quantity which displays the greatest degree of correlation with those costs of the department that do vary with the level of operating activity. The various cost items may be tested by appropriate statistical methods against two or more alternative measures of volume. That measure which shows the highest degree of correlation with the variable costs would then be chosen as the volume indicator for the department.[1]

Different departments are likely to use different measures of volume. The light machinery department in Table 9–1 uses direct labor hours as its volume measure, presumably because observations and studies have shown that the variable cost items tend to vary more nearly in proportion to the labor hours worked in the department than to any other possible indicator of departmental activity. In the same firm's heavy machinery department, it might be found that machine hours afford the best indication of cost behavior. There is no reason why the same volume measure should be used in all departments within a single firm. One might even raise the question as to whether it is necessary that only one measure be employed in each department. Correlation analyses might show that some costs in a department vary in proportion to labor hours, while others vary in proportion to machine hours. Should both measures of volume be used for the department, or should only one be selected? In theory, there would be no objection to two or more volume indicators being used in a single department. In practice, this would require two or more flexible budgets for the department and as many departmental overhead rates. Whether the additional precision would be worth the additional clerical cost involved in such a plan is dubious. In the discussion in this chapter, a single measure of volume for each department will be assumed.

Budget Cost Allowances

Cost Variability. Once the measure of volume has been selected, the next step in the development of the flexible budget is the determination of the behavior of each cost item with respect to that volume indicator. In the illustration in Table 9–1, this means that each cost item had to be studied in conjunction with direct labor hours to determine how it behaved as the hours increased and decreased. The first two money columns in this budget schedule depict the behavior of each cost item

---

[1] The student is referred to any basic statistics text for the specific technique to be employed for this correlation analysis.

with respect to labor hours worked in the department. Fixed costs are budgeted as total amounts. Variable costs are budgeted as amounts per labor hour. Some of the cost items—labor-related costs, fuel and power, and repairs and maintenance—comprise both variable and fixed components. In total, therefore, these are semivariable costs. For reasons to be explained shortly, semivariable costs restrict the usefulness of the flexible budget. Hence, in practice, they are most frequently treated as either wholly variable, totally fixed, or some combination of the two.

These first two columns, showing the variability and/or fixedness of the departmental cost items, are the essence of the flexible budget. In fact, if we were not interested in the individual cost items but only in the total departmental costs, the final figures in these two columns would be all we would need. The entire flexible budget could be reduced to a simple statement that variable costs in the department are incurred at the rate of $1.78 per direct labor hour and fixed costs are $35,800 per month. With this information we could estimate total departmental cost at any volume. Even where the details of the several cost items are of interest, the first two columns provide an adequate statement of the flexible budget. With the information in these columns, we can provide budget estimates for any volume. To demonstrate this, the student should use the data in those first two columns to calculate the budget cost allowances for 16,000 and for 19,245 hours.

Cost Controllability. As a part of the overall plan of cost control, the flexible budget is commonly developed in such a way as to distinguish between those costs which are regarded as controllable by the department supervisor and those which are not. The noncontrollable costs in Table 9–1 include the supervisor's own salary and those of the assistant foremen in the department, for these are set by the plant manager. Taxes, insurance, and depreciation on departmental equipment are also regarded as beyond the control of the supervisor, as they derive from decisions made at higher levels of management. It must be understood that the noncontrollable costs in Table 9–1 are such only at the level of responsibility of the departmental supervisor. At some higher level of responsibility, they also would be controllable. All costs in a firm should be controllable at some level of responsibility.

Cost controllability must always be evaluated critically and cautiously. Not all of the items listed as controllable costs are necessarily completely subject to the discretion of the department supervisor. A certain amount of maintenance cost, for example, is inevitably incurred as a consequence of the decision to acquire and use equipment. If this decision is not made by the department supervisor, it is doubtful that this basic maintenance cost can be said to be truly controllable by him. Nevertheless, the identification of controllable and noncontrollable costs at the several levels of responsibility is so important to effective cost control that a practical distinction between the two is needed. That distinction must then be interpreted reasonably.

Normal Overhead Rates

Given budgeted overhead costs and budgeted volume, normal overhead rates can be computed from either a fixed or a flexible budget. The important difference is that only one set of rates can be computed from a fixed budget, whereas rates for any level of volume can be calculated from a flexible budget. The normal variable overhead rate is the same at any volume, as illustrated at the bottom of Table 9–1. The normal fixed overhead rate, however, is a function of a constant total cost and budgeted volume. Thus, the normal fixed rate is lower at higher volumes, as can be seen in Table 9–1. It is extremely important that the student understand the nature of a normal fixed overhead rate. Fixed overhead can be expressed as a rate per unit of volume only at a given volume. At any other volume, that rate is not really valid. What has been said here for normal overhead rates is basically applicable to standard overhead rates as well, except that the volume at which the standard fixed overhead rate is determined is not necessarily the budgeted volume for the period. Standard overhead rates are discussed in the next chapter.

ESTABLISHING BUDGET ALLOWANCES

As with so many things in life, the most important step in the development of a flexible budget is the most difficult. A flexible budget is only as good as the cost allowances included in it and the separation of these costs into variable and fixed components. At the outset, we must recognize that no flexible budget can be perfect, because the composite budgeted cost allowances cannot be perfect. In a practical situation, it is unlikely that there will be any perfectly variable costs, those which vary in direct proportion to volume over the full range of possible operating volumes. Likewise, there will probably be few absolutely fixed costs that do not change at all over the entire range of possible operations. Nevertheless, the concepts of variable and fixed costs are so essential to effective planning and control that it is better to make a reasonable assumption regarding the variability or fixedness of a cost than to throw up one's hands in frustration at a fruitless search for perfection.

Variable Costs

Despite the fact that there may be no costs which are perfectly variable over all ranges of volume, there may be a substantial number of cost items which come fairly close to being so. In addition, there may be cost items which approach perfect variability over the relevant range of volume, that is, the range within which the department is almost certain to operate. For example, if a particular department regularly operates between 60% and 90% of capacity, there is little merit in the accountant's being concerned with the behavior of departmental costs at 20% or 30% of capacity. In such a case, the flexible budget may be entirely valid over the range of activity which may reasonably be expected. The fact that it is not valid at some operating level which would be obtained only under highly unusual circumstances—such as a strike—is then of little practical consequence. Thus, many cost items which do not meet the strict definition of a variable cost are commonly treated as variable costs for purposes of establishing flexible budget allowances and for subsequent analyses. The attendant degree of imprecision is greatly outweighed by the utility of the flexible budget to management.

Fixed Costs

Certain costs in most enterprises are likely to meet the strict definition of a fixed cost. For example, if a factory building is owned at all, whether used currently for production or not, it must be insured and it will be subject to property taxes. The insurance premium and the property tax bill are fixed in amount for the term covered, most commonly one year. These costs are fixed by their nature as far as the enterprise is concerned. Other cost items may be equally fixed in amount, but fixed by policy rather than by their natures. For example, depreciation is most often treated as a fixed cost as a matter of company policy. Under any depreciation method which relates the expiration of the cost of long-lived assets to the passage of time, depreciation will be a fixed cost in each period. This is true of the straight-line method and also of the so-called accelerated depreciation methods, such as the declining balance and sum-of-years' digits methods. Under the accelerated depreciation methods, the depreciation charge is fixed for one period even though it is different in each successive period. Where depreciation is determined in proportion to the use of an asset—the units-of-output method or the productive hours method—it is a variable cost, again by company policy. Such methods are employed relatively infrequently, however.

Many other cost items remain constant over substantial ranges of possible volume but do increase as volume reaches certain critical levels. This may be the case of supervision cost, for example. A single supervisor may be able to direct operations within a department up to 30% of capacity. Above 30%, a second supervisor becomes necessary. At 60%, a third is added; and a fourth is employed when production exceeds 90% of capacity. Obviously, supervision cost in this case does not qualify as a true fixed cost. However, if the department's operations are almost certain to fall somewhere between 60% and 90% of capacity, supervision may validly be treated as a fixed cost. Changes in the cost outside the relevant range of operations are irrelevant. As in the case of variable costs, utility is a much more significant criterion than perfection.

Semivariable Costs

Unfortunately, not all costs are so nearly variable or fixed that they may be treated as one or the other without further study. Many cost items do vary with volume even within fairly small ranges but do not do so in a manner even close to direct proportionality. One possible method of dealing with such costs is to budget them at each of the several levels of volume which are to be tabulated in the formal flexible budget schedule without reference to how they might behave at nontabulated levels. This method is usually described as *step budgeting.* While this solution to the problem would permit the preparation of a formal budget schedule, it would limit the flexibility of the budget. It would not permit management to determine the expected cost at some volume not tabulated. As may readily be imagined, the likelihood of actual volume falling precisely at a tabulated level is small; yet, it is important that management be able to determine the budgeted cost for the volume actually achieved. The alternative to step budgeting is to eliminate semivariable costs from the budget by treating them as either variable or fixed or as both.

Classification by Dominant Characteristics. The simplest and, unfortunately, the least precise method of disposing of semivariable cost items is to treat them as either variable or fixed according to their dominant characteristics. Thus, if observation shows that a particular semivariable cost is closer to being variable than fixed, it is treated as variable and an average rate of variability is established on the basis of past experience, as adjusted for expected changes in conditions. If inspection indicates that the item is closer to being fixed, it is treated as such in an amount which would be expected to be incurred at the most likely level of operations. Obviously, this solution to the problem of semivariable costs introduces a considerable degree of imprecision into subsequent analyses based upon the flexible budget allowances. In a study of practices in fifty-eight firms, the National Association of Accountants found that identification of variable and fixed costs on the basis of their dominant characteristics was a common, if not the commonest practice.[2]

High-Low Method. This method is based on the presumption that a semivariable cost can be separated into a fixed and a variable component. The separation is based upon the firm's actual experience at a high and at a low volume, again with adjustments for changes in conditions as appropriate. For example, assume that a department incurred the maintenance costs indicated below during the year just ended and that volume in the department is measured by machine hours.

	Machine Hours	*Maintenance Costs*
January	72,000	$44,000
February	71,300	43,600
March	68,400	42,180
April	64,200	39,900
May	61,000	38,500
June	59,500	38,000
July	58,000	37,240
August	60,100	38,270
September	64,500	40,300
October	69,000	42,630
November	73,800	44,980
December	75,000	45,400

The high volume in this range of experience is 75,000 machine hours in December; the low volume is 58,000 hours in July. The cost incurred at the high volume was $45,400 and at the low, $37,240. These are all of the actual data needed to separate maintenance cost into a variable and a fixed component by the high-low method. If we may assume that there will be no change in maintenance cost during the budget period, except that caused by volume changes, we can proceed immediately to the separation computations. If, on the other hand, maintenance costs are expected to change because of factors other than volume, the actual data of the past period should first be adjusted to reflect this anticipated change. For example, if maintenance costs are expected to increase by 5% in the budget period, we would have to increase the costs incurred at the high and low volumes by 5% and then proceed with the separation.

For this illustration, let us assume that no adjustment to the previous

[2] "Separating and Using Costs as Fixed and Variable," *N.A.A. Bulletin,* Accounting Practice Report No. 10, Vol. XLI (June, 1960), sec. 3, p. 15.

year's data is believed necessary. The first step in the separation process is the calculation of a variable rate per machine hour. This is accomplished by the following computations:

	Machine Hours	*Maintenance Costs*
High volume	75,000	$45,400
Low volume	58,000	37,240
Difference	17,000	$ 8,160

This calculation shows that, as volume changed by 17,000 machine hours, the total semivariable cost changed by $8,160. Logically, the portion of a semivariable cost that changes with volume is the variable portion. Hence, the variable rate in maintenance cost is the ratio of the change in cost to the change in volume.

$$\$8{,}160 \div 17{,}000 \text{ hours} = \$.48 \text{ per hour}$$

With this variable cost rate, we can compute the fixed cost component at either the high or the low volume or at both (*but not at any other volume*).

	High	*Low*
Total cost	$45,400	$37,240
Variable portion ($.48 × machine hours)		
$.48 × 75,000 hours	36,000	
$.48 × 58,000 hours		27,840
Fixed portion	$ 9,400	$ 9,400

Thus, maintenance cost has been reduced to a variable rate of $.48 per machine hour and a fixed amount of $9,400. It should be remembered that the high-low method is a technique for approximating variable and fixed components in a semivariable cost. The variable and fixed costs determined by this method are estimates based upon the relationships between cost and volume at the high and low volumes only. At some other volume, the exact same relationship may not obtain. It is useful, however, to assume that same relationship at all volumes.

Graphic Method. In the study by the National Association of Accountants referred to earlier, it was found that most of the firms whose practices were observed and which did separate semivariable costs into variable and fixed components did so by means of a graphic analysis of the relationship between cost and volume.[3] This graphic analysis

[3] *Ibid.*, p. 11.

involves the plotting of the cost experience of the past, as adjusted for expected changes in the future, on a chart and then fitting a least squares regression line to the plot of experienced data. This regression line then shows the estimated behavior of the cost item with respect to changes in volume. The graphic method differs from the high-low method principally in that it is based upon the cost-volume relationships at many instead of at only two levels of experienced volume. Figure 9–1 depicts the graphic analysis of the maintenance costs used in the illustration in the preceding section. Costs are measured on the vertical axis of the graph and volume for each month, on the horizontal axis. The actual cost data are then plotted on the graph, and a least squares regression line is fitted to the plot. This line indicates the estimated total cost at any level of volume.[4] This analysis does not show directly a variable cost rate and a fixed cost amount, but it does permit the determination of the total

---

[4] Following are the computations for the least squares regression line in Figure 9–1. The student who is unfamiliar with this statistical technique is referred to any standard textbook on statistics.

	X *Machine Hours*	Y *Maintenance Cost*	x $X - \frac{\Sigma X}{N}$	xY	x^2
January	72,000	$ 44,000	5,600	246,400,000	31,360,000
February	71,300	43,600	4,900	213,640,000	24,010,000
March	68,400	42,180	2,000	84,360,000	4,000,000
April	64,200	39,900	−2,200	− 87,780,000	4,840,000
May	61,000	38,500	−5,400	−207,900,000	29,160,000
June	59,500	38,000	−6,900	−262,200,000	47,610,000
July	58,000	37,240	−8,400	−312,816,000	70,560,000
August	60,100	38,270	−6,300	−241,101,000	39,690,000
September	64,500	40,300	−1,900	76,570,000	3,610,000
October	69,000	42,630	2,600	110,838,000	6,760,000
November	73,800	44,980	7,400	332,852,000	54,760,000
December	75,000	45,400	8,600	390,440,000	73,960,000
	796,800	$495,000		190,163,000	390,320,000

$$Y_c = a + bx$$

$$a = \frac{\Sigma Y}{N} = \frac{\$495,000}{12} = \$41,250$$

$$b = \frac{\Sigma xY}{\Sigma x^2} = \frac{190,163,000}{390,320,000} = .4872$$

Cost allowances at three selected volumes are determined as follows:

$$Y_{58,000} = \$41,250 + .4872(-8,400) = \$37,157.52$$
$$Y_{68,400} = \$41,250 + .4872(+2,000) = \$42,224.40$$
$$Y_{75,000} = \$41,250 + .4872(+8,600) = \$45,439.92$$

FIGURE 9–1

GRAPHIC ANALYSIS OF SEMIVARIABLE COST

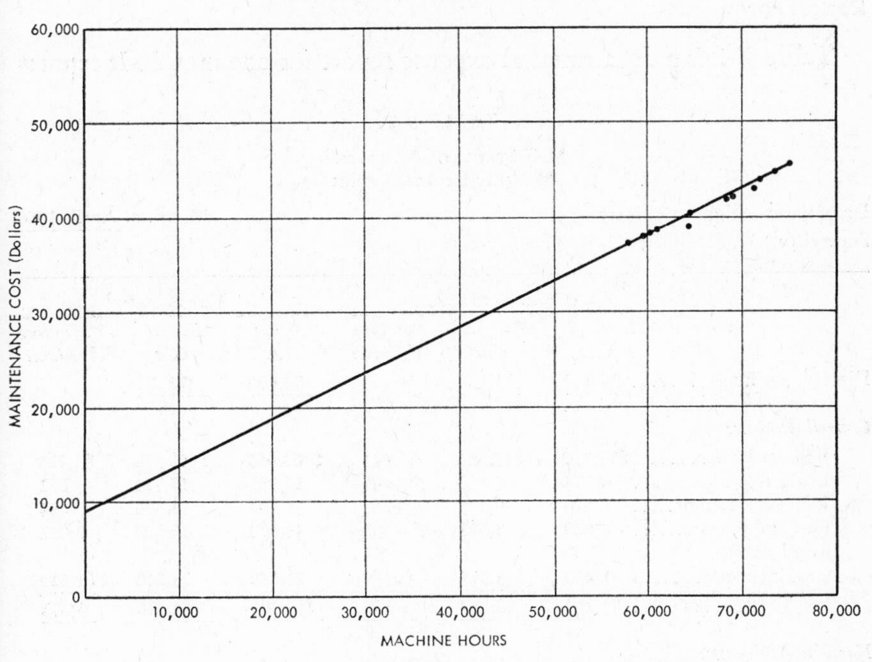

maintenance cost at any level of operations; and this latter result is the basic aim of all techniques for eliminating semivariable costs, as such, from the flexible budget. On the graph, the monthly fixed cost is measured on the vertical axis at the point of intersection of that axis with the regression line. The variable rate is, in effect, measured by the slope of the regression line.

Because it employs all of the cost data collected from past experience rather than the data from two levels of volume only, the graphic method is a somewhat better technique for eliminating semivariable costs from the flexible budget than is the high-low method. The reader must not be mesmerized or deceived by the mathematical precision of this method, however. The mathematical manipulations are precise, but they are applied in the development of an estimate of cost behavior. Regardless of methodological precision, the graphic method, like the high-low method, separates semivariable costs into variable and fixed elements because such separation is useful to management, not because it is intrinsically valid.

DEPARTMENTAL EXPENSE REPORTS

Report Form

Table 9–2 is a departmental expense report for one month. It reports

TABLE 9–2

M-G STANLEY CORPORATION
Monthly Expense Report

Department Light machinery — Month of April, 1966
Supervisor W. S. Gilbert

	Current Month			*Year to Date*		
	Actual Cost	*Budgeted Cost*	*Spending Variance*	*Actual Cost*	*Budgeted Cost*	*Spending Variance*
Direct labor hours	19,150	19,150		72,600	72,600	
Controllable costs:						
Indirect labor	$17,880	$17,235	$ 645	$ 68,465	$ 65,340	$3,125
Labor related costs	4,675	4,630	45	17,982	17,720	262
Indirect materials	9,318	9,575	(257)	36,394	36,300	94
Fuel and power	4,120	3,532	588	15,820	13,808	2,012
Repairs and maintenance	5,200	5,915	(715)	21,640	23,260	(1,620)
Total	41,193	40,887	306	160,301	156,428	3,873
Noncontrollable costs:						
Supervision	3,360	3,200	160	13,120	12,800	320
Taxes and insurance	800	800		3,200	3,200	
Depreciation	26,500	25,000	1,500	101,500	100,000	1,500
Total	30,660	29,000	1,660	117,820	116,000	1,820
Total costs	$71,853	$69,887	$1,966	$278,121	$272,428	$5,693
Budgeted cost for actual labor hours		$69,887			$272,428	
Budgeted cost for budgeted labor hours		67,840			271,360	
Volume variance		$ 2,047			$ 1,068	

the actual expenses incurred in the light machinery department of the M-G Stanley Corporation for the month of April, 1966. Actual expenses are compared with the budgeted expenses as presented in the departmental flexible budget, Table 9–1 in this chapter. Differences between the actual and budgeted cost data are identified as variances and provide the focal point from which the process of cost control proceeds. Table 9–2 is not offered as a standard report form, but it is representative of the type of information usually contained in such expense reports. Inclusion of data for the year to date as well as for the month just ended is not essential to the basic nature of the report, but it does afford management a basis for appraising the department's cost performance over a series of months and for evaluating the effectiveness of cost control efforts suggested by prior months' reports. The various components of this report will be discussed in the paragraphs that follow.

Adjusting the Budget to Actual Volume

If the M-G Stanley Corporation used fixed departmental budgets instead of flexible budgets, there would be only one level of budgeted costs against which actual costs could be compared. Assume that the corporation estimated that operating volume in the light machinery department would be approximately 18,000 direct labor hours per month during the budget period under consideration. A fixed budget would present only the costs budgeted for that volume, with no indication of cost variability or fixedness. While this would afford some basis for evaluating actual costs, it would not permit management to distinguish between those variances which arise because actual operating volume has differed from that originally anticipated and those variances attributable to spending more or less than the budget calls for. A flexible budget enables management to distinguish between these two types of variances, for it allows the determination of budgeted costs at any volume.

In order to appraise departmental spending during a given period, management wishes to compare actual costs with the costs which the budget indicates should have been incurred at the operating volume actually achieved during the period. Thus, the budgeted costs tabulated in Table 9–2 are budgeted costs for 19,150 direct labor hours, the actual volume for April. To the extent that costs are variable (cf., Table 9–1), budget allowances for the actual volume are simply the products of 19,150 hours times the several variable cost rates per hour. To the extent that costs are fixed, they are the same dollar amount at any volume. Repairs and maintenance costs, for example, are budgeted at 19,150 hours by multiplying 19,150 by $.10, the variable rate per hour, and then by adding $4,000, the fixed amount per month. Similar computations are made to determine budgeted costs for the actual volume of the year to date. In this instance, the actual labor hours used (72,600) are the total actual hours worked in the department during the first four months of 1966.

Variances from the Budget

Spending Variance. The difference between actual costs and budgeted costs for the actual volume is described as the *spending variance.* This is not the ideal term, for not all of the cost items in a department necessarily involve current spending. Depreciation, for example, shows a spending variance in Table 9–2, although we know that depreciation does not involve current cash outlays. The term is fairly widely used, however, and will suit the purpose so long as we understand what it means. Insofar as cost control is concerned, this is probably the more important variance to management. It is the variance more likely to be subject to control by the department supervisor.

Volume Variance. The *volume variance* is the difference between the budgeted costs for the actual volume and the budgeted costs for the volume originally expected when the complete operating budget was prepared. In the illustration at hand, the volume variance for April is the difference between the costs budgeted at 19,150 direct labor hours and those budgeted at 18,000 hours. The volume variance for the year to date is the difference between the costs budgeted at the actual total direct labor hours of 72,600 and the costs budgeted at the originally planned labor hours, 72,000. This variance is only as controllable as the reason for the difference between actual volume and that originally planned. It does, however, complete an explanation of the difference between actual departmental costs and those planned in the operating budget.

As a final note, it is well to observe carefully that the variances discussed here are variances from budgeted overhead costs. In the next chapter we will consider variances from standard overhead cost. While a standard overhead cost is developed from budget data, it is quite different from a budgeted cost itself. Consequently, variances from standard are very different from those variances illustrated here. The variances here have been computed and identified without regard to any standard or normal overhead rates. They are derived from a comparison of actual costs and budgeted costs only.

QUESTIONS FOR DISCUSSION

1. Why is a flexible budget for overhead a better technique for planning and controlling costs than a static budget?
2. "If the separation of overhead into variable and fixed components is inexact, the resultant flexible budget will be inexact. And any consequent efforts at cost control are likely to result in confusion, ill feelings, and inappropriate managerial action." Comment on this allegation.
3. The flexible budget illustrated in Table 9–1 and the expense report illustrated in Table 9–2 in this chapter could both have been completed without identification of cost items as controllable and noncontrollable. Why, then, should controllable and noncontrollable costs be distinguished in these exhibits?

4. Discuss the advantages and disadvantages of step budgeting of semivariable costs. What are the principal alternatives to step budgeting?
5. Both the high-low method and the least squares regression method of resolving semivariable costs into variable and fixed components entail an element of artificiality and, hence, imprecision. In view of this fact, would it not always be better to use the high-low method, which is easier and faster than the least squares method?
6. What is the significance of the spending variance from budgeted costs? What is the significance of the volume variance? Which is more important to management in evaluating the operating performance of a departmental supervisor? Explain.
7. The controller of the Ex-Ray Corporation is impressed with the success experienced in using flexible overhead budgets in the firm's production departments. He would like to use them also in the departments under his direct supervision—payroll, billing, and bookkeeping. What are the prerequisites to the establishment of useful flexible budgets for nonproduction departments such as these?
8. Flexible budgets involve, fundamentally, the distinction between variable and fixed costs. Are they, then, as useful in variable costing systems, where only variable costs are charged to production, as they are in absorption costing systems? Explain.
9. Discuss the potential applicability of flexible budgets to the planning and control of (*a*) direct materials cost; (*b*) executives' salaries and bonuses; and (*c*) advertising expenses.
10. Normal variable and fixed overhead rates may be computed from either a static or a flexible budget. Would the normal rates computed from a flexible budget be better than those derived from a static budget? Explain.

PROBLEMS

1. The Huntsford Frozen Food Company packages all of its products in its packing department. The budgeted costs in this department for 1966 have been set as follows:

Variable costs:	
Raw materials	$1,240,000
Direct labor	640,000
Packing supplies	48,000
Indirect labor	128,000
Labor-related costs	38,400
	2,094,400
Fixed costs:	
Maintenance	46,000
Heat, light, and power	35,000
Taxes and insurance	14,000
Depreciation	65,000
	160,000
Total budgeted departmental costs	$2,254,400

Management wishes to have flexible budgets prepared for all operating departments. Operating volume in the packing department may best be measured in direct labor hours. Direct labor cost in the department is budgeted at the standard rate of $2 per hour.

Required:

1. Prepare, in its most elementary form, a flexible budget of overhead for one year in the packing department.
2. Compute the normal overhead rates for the department for 1966.

2. The following overhead costs may reasonably be expected to be incurred in the assembly department of the Braithwaite Office Furniture Company:

Indirect materials	$.12 per labor hour
Indirect labor	$6,500 per month plus $.30 per labor hour
Supervision	$18,200 per month
Repairs and maintenance	$3,350 per month
Depreciation	$8,400 per month
Cleaning supplies	$.06 per labor hour
Heat, light, and power	$1,600 per month plus $.18 per labor hour
Insurance and taxes	$950 per month

All of these cost items, excepting supervision, depreciation, and insurance and taxes, are regarded as controllable at the level of the departmental foreman.

Required:

1. Prepare a tabular flexible budget for overhead in the assembly department at each of the following monthly levels of production volume: 44,000; 48,000; 52,000; and 56,000 labor hours.
2. Assuming that the company uses absorption costing and that it expects production to average 52,000 labor hours per month, compute the normal overhead rates to be used in charging assembly department overhead to production.

3. You have recently been appointed budget director of the Blackmoor Machine Corporation. One of your objectives is to establish flexible overhead budgets for all production departments. For this purpose, you asked each department supervisor to submit a report of his normal monthly costs. The following report was received from Fred Snoot, supervisor of the stamping department:

"My biggest cost item, of course, is labor. There are six machines in the department. Each one needs an operator, a materials handler, and an assistant. Operators get $3 an hour; handlers, $2 an hour; and assistants, $1.60 an hour. Then I have one relief operator. He relieves the regular operators when they take their breaks and any other time they need relief. He gets only $2.40 an hour. Then there is the janitor; he gets $350 a month. My own salary is $950 a month. When the machines are operating the full eight-hour day, our monthly maintenance charges run about $15,000. Even when we were shut down for three months during the strike last year, though, routine maintenance cost about $4,440 each month. Power is metered at each machine, and each one uses about 60 kilowatt-hours for each hour it is in use. Supplies seem to depend on how much the machines are being used. For a full eight-hour day, we use about $96 worth of supplies. If the machines are working less, the supplies go down accordingly. I know there are other costs charged to the department on the monthly reports, but I don't know how they are arrived at."

Further investigation reveals that the monthly depreciation on the machinery in the stamping department is $15,000. Insurance and taxes on the machinery are $36,000 a year. The rate paid by the corporation for electric power is $.05 per kilowatt-hour. From the payroll department, you learn that fringe benefits average 10% of the gross wages and salaries.

Each month may be assumed to consist of 22 eight-hour working days.

Required:

1. What measure of operating volume would you use for the stamping department's flexible overhead budget? Why?
2. Prepare a flexible budget schedule for overhead in the stamping department for one month. Show budget allowances for 75% and 100% of full operating capacity.

4. The Warrick Corporation is developing flexible expense budgets for the first time. It appears that the indirect labor in the light machinery department is a true semivariable cost. Further, it is believed reasonable to forecast indirect labor in 1966 on the basis of the actual costs incurred in 1965. The actual indirect labor costs in the light machinery department in 1965 were as follows:

Month	*Indirect Labor*	*Labor Hours*
January	$40,075	38,750
February	38,860	36,880
March	36,710	33,445
April	35,464	31,610
May	34,115	29,600
June	34,733	30,550
July	36,380	32,875
August	38,945	36,950
September	40,500	39,200
October	41,338	40,680
November	42,422	42,380
December	41,530	41,000

Labor hours will be used as the measure of volume in the department. Semivariable cost items will be budgeted as partly variable and partly fixed.

Required:

Resolve the indirect labor cost of the light machinery department into a variable and a fixed component by means of the high-low method.

5. The Marshman Electric Company wishes to set flexible budgets for each of its operating departments. A separate maintenance department performs all routine and major repair work on the company's equipment and fa-

cilities. It has been determined that maintenance costs is primarily a function of machine hours worked in the various production departments. The actual machine hours worked and maintenance costs incurred during 1965 are as follows:

Month	*Machine Hours*	*Maintenance Costs*
January	118,500	$134,000
February	121,000	135,000
March	116,000	132,000
April	109,500	127,000
May	106,400	124,000
June	101,000	120,000
July	110,000	128,000
August	117,500	133,000
September	122,000	134,000
October	33,000	92,000
November	124,000	130,000
December	136,000	148,000

The company's plant was closed by a strike for three-and-a-half weeks during October, 1965.

Required:

1. Assuming that maintenance costs in 1966 are expected to be 5% higher than in the preceding year because of rising prices, compute the variable maintenance cost per machine hour and the fixed maintenance cost per month by the high-low method.
2. If the company wishes to charge maintenance costs to the several production departments in which machinery and equipment is used and wishes to do so by means of a normal rate, how would that rate be computed? Explain the procedures to be used in setting the normal rate. How would you suggest any difference between actual maintenance costs incurred and maintenance costs charged out at the normal rate be accounted for?

6. The cost of heat, light, and power in the Berkshire Value Company tends to vary with the volume of direct labor hours worked in the factory, but not in direct proportion thereto. Actual heat, light, and power cost in 1965, by quarters, was as follows:

Quarter	*Cost*	*Labor Hours*
First	$18,000	30,000
Second	20,000	36,000
Third	24,000	45,000
Fourth	23,800	35,000

The rate paid for heat, light, and power was increased by 10%, effective at the beginning of the fourth quarter of 1965. The new rate is expected to continue throughout 1966.

Required:

1. By means of the least squares regression method, compute budgeted heat, light, and power cost allowance at volumes of 30,000, 40,000, and 50,000 direct labor hours per quarter for 1966.
2. Plot the indicated relationship between heat, light, and power cost and direct labor hours on a graph.

7. The Devon Plastics Company is preparing a flexible overhead budget for its stamping and pressing department. Volume in the department is measured in machine hours. The actual power costs incurred in 1965 are regarded as valid indicators of the budgeted power costs for 1966. Actual data for 1965 are as follows:

Month	*Machine Hours*	*Power Costs*
January	8,000	$4,600
February	9,000	4,800
March	10,000	5,000
April	10,000	5,100
May	11,000	5,500
June	10,000	5,000
July	9,000	4,700
August	11,000	5,600
September	10,000	5,100
October	12,000	6,100
November	11,000	5,400
December	9,000	4,900

Required:

1. Construct a graph of the relationship between machine hours and power costs in 1965.
2. By the least squares regression method, compute the budgeted power cost allowances at 8,000 and 12,000 machine hours.
3. If the actual volume in the month of January, 1966 proved to be 9,800 machine hours, how would the budgeted power cost for that actual volume be determined?

8. The Pitdown Company is attempting to establish a flexible budget allowance for indirect labor in its plant and wishes to know what is the most appropriate measure of volume for this purpose. Volume may be measured in three ways: pounds of output, direct labor hours, and machine hours. Actual indirect labor costs and the three measures of volume for the last half of 1965 were as follows:

Month	*Indirect Labor*	*Pounds of Output*	*Labor Hours*	*Machine Hours*
July	$20,000	40,000	9,800	1,200
August	20,000	42,000	10,000	1,500
September	30,000	65,000	22,600	1,800
October	40,000	80,000	35,400	2,000
November	60,000	100,000	59,700	2,400
December	70,000	105,000	72,500	2,500

Required:

Which of the three alternatives would be the best measure of volume insofar as indirect labor cost is concerned? Explain your answer and show any computations used to arrive at it.

9. The monthly flexible overhead budget for department 201 of the Cranert Manufacturing Company is as follows:

Cost Item	*Variable Rate per Hour*	*Fixed Costs*	*90,000 Labor Hours*	*110,000 Labor Hours*	*130,000 Labor Hours*
Indirect labor	$.38	$ 18,840	$ 53,040	$ 60,640	$ 68,240
Supervision		32,350	32,350	32,350	32,350
Labor-related costs	.15	440	13,940	16,940	19,940
Indirect materials	.12		10,800	13,200	15,600
Power and light	.07	6,100	12,400	13,800	15,200
Maintenance		9,770	9,770	9,770	9,770
Depreciation		35,600	35,600	35,600	35,600
General expenses		12,400	12,400	12,400	12,400
	$.72	$115,500	$180,300	$194,700	$209,100

The volume of operations in department 201 was expected to average 110,000 labor hours per month. During May, 1966, actual operations in the department totaled 114,800 labor hours. The actual overhead cost incurred during May were as follows:

Indirect labor	$ 63,215
Supervision	33,820
Labor-related costs	18,044
Indirect materials	13,436
Power and light	14,887
Maintenance	7,455
Depreciation	37,400
General expenses	12,400
	$200,657

Required:

1. Draft an expense report for department 201 for May, 1966. Show the variances of actual costs from budgeted costs in as much detail as you believe relevant to management.
2. What would the normal variable and fixed overhead rates be in department 201 for 1966?

10. The flexible overhead budget for the packing department of the Brown-Ferguson Drug Company allows $39,500 per month plus $.95 per man-hour worked in the department. Actual costs data for the first quarter of 1966 are summarized below.

Month	*Variable Costs*	*Fixed Costs*	*Man-Hours*
January	$39,350	$40,300	41,400
February	42,760	40,600	46,200
March	38,120	39,600	38,800

Operating volume in the department for 1966 has been budgeted at 40,000 man-hours per month.

Required:

1. Prepare a report showing the spending and volume variances from the budget for each month and for the quarter in total.
2. What inferences may be drawn from an examination of the variances in this report? What are the implications of these inferences for cost control in the department?

11. Following is the flexible overhead budget for the shearing department of the Buttercup Swimsuit Company for one month:

Direct labor hours	6,000	8,000	10,000	12,000
Indirect labor	$2,200	$2,700	$ 3,200	$ 3,700
Supplies	1,800	2,400	3,000	3,600
Space occupancy	4,100	4,100	4,100	4,100
	$8,100	$9,200	$10,300	$11,400

Volume for 1966 has been budgeted at 10,000 direct labor hours. During July, 1966, the department worked a total of 8,500 direct labor hours; and the following overhead costs were incurred:

Indirect labor	$2,700
Supplies	2,610
Space occupancy	4,250
	$9,560

Required:

1. Identify the behavior of each cost item in this budget as variable, fixed, or semivariable.
2. By some valid method, reduce this budget to a single variable rate per direct labor hour and a single fixed cost per month.
3. Prepare a brief expense report for the month of July, 1966. Show variances between actual and budgeted costs.

12. You have been engaged as a management consultant to the Eggers Manufacturing Company. The firm is not large, and its entire factory is treated as a single cost center for purposes of charging overhead costs to production. The company manufactures three products, Dese, Dem, and Dose. Standard production times for these products are, respectively, 2 labor hours, 1 labor hour, and 6 labor hours.

You learn that budgeted output for 1965 called for production of 20,000 units of Dese, 40,000 units of Dem, and 10,000 units of Dose. Factory overhead for the year was budgeted at $350,000 for variable costs and $490,000 for fixed costs. Variable overhead is known to vary in proportion to direct labor hours. You are satisfied that the budgeted cost allowances were reasonable and that the classifications of costs as fixed and variable are proper.

The company's chief accountant established normal overhead rates per unit of product by means of the average labor time per unit of budgeted output. This average labor time was computed as follows:

Product	*Budgeted Units*	*Labor Hours per Unit*	*Total Labor Hours*
Dese	20,000	2	40,000
Dem	40,000	1	40,000
Dose	10,000	6	60,000
	70,000		140,000

Average labor time per unit of output = 140,000 hours ÷ 70,000 units = 2 hours per unit.

The normal overhead rates used to cost production were then determined thus:

	Total Cost	÷	*Total Hours*	=	*Normal Rate per Hour*	×	*Average Hours per Unit*	=	*Normal Rate per Unit*
Variable cost	$350,000		140,000		$2.50		2		$ 5.00
Fixed cost	490,000		140,000		3.50		2		7.00
Total	$840,000				$6.00				$12.00

Actual output for 1965 consisted of 20,000 units of Dese, 25,000 units of Dem, and 25,000 units of Dose. Standard production times for the several products were met exactly throughout the year. Actual variable overhead cost for the year totaled $520,000 and actual fixed overhead, $500,000. The chief accountant submitted the following analysis of underapplied overhead to the factory manager in support of the income statement:

Actual overhead costs incurred	$1,020,000
Overhead applied to production (70,000 units produced × $12)	840,000
Underapplied overhead	$ 180,000

The factory manager is surprised and disappointed at this report. He states that the actual operations in the plant for 1965 were well above the original plans, and he cannot understand how almost 18% of total overhead could have been unabsorbed by production. He asks you to review the cost and production records and submit a report to him.

Required:

1. Evaluate the overhead costing procedure used by the company's chief accountant.
2. Prepare for the factory manager a report showing what you believe to be the most useful comparison of actual and planned overhead costs for 1965.
3. The company's inventory of finished product at December 31, 1965, consists of 2,000 units of Dese, 3,000 units of Dem, and 2,500 units of Dose. There is no inventory of work in process at the end of the year. Finished

product is costed by the first-in, first-out cost flow assumption. As a consequence of the cost procedures used by the chief accountant, are the Finished Product and Cost of Goods Sold accounts correctly stated at December 31, 1965? If not, what adjusting entry or entries should be made to correct them? Support any adjustments with computations. (Assume that the inventory of finished product at the beginning of 1965 was costed correctly.)

Chapter 10

ACCOUNTING FOR STANDARD MANUFACTURING COSTS

STANDARD COSTS were introduced to the reader in Chapter 5. At that point, however, we were concerned only with the basic nature of standard costs and the manner of their determination. We then saw in Chapter 7 that standard costs are useful in the development of the operating budget, particularly in the budgeting of materials and labor costs. In Chapter 9 we saw that flexible budgets are employed in the development of standard overhead costs. In this chapter we shall consider some of the technical aspects of accounting for standard costs and the related variances of actual costs from standard. The control applications of standard costs will be discussed in the following chapter. While management is concerned primarily with the control aspects of standard costs, the technical aspects are important to managers as well as to cost accountants. A manager cannot make effective use of a control device which he does not understand.

USES OF STANDARD MANUFACTURING COSTS

The principal purpose of standard manufacturing costs in a business enterprise is to facilitate control of actual manufacturing costs. Standard costs provide criteria against which actual costs may be compared and evaluated. Where actual costs deviate materially from standard, appropriate managerial action should be taken. If standard costs were used only for cost control, they might be employed in budgets and in operating reports without ever affecting the cost accounting system directly. Business experience has shown, however, that standard costs are useful in the accounting system itself. Quite commonly, they are used in lieu of actual costs as the basis for costing manufacturing inventories. When inventories are valued at standard costs, the cost of goods sold will be measured in terms of standard costs also. Thus, standard costs quite regularly find their way into the balance sheet and the income statement of the manufacturing enterprise.

The incorporation of standard costs in the accounting system is likely to save clerical time and effort and, consequently, to reduce the cost of operating the accounting system. For example, if an inventory of finished product is valued at standard cost, the inventory records may be maintained in terms of physical quantities only. For the cost of the inventory may be determined at any time simply by multiplying the quantity on hand by the standard cost per unit. This use of standard costs in inventory accounts avoids the necessity of employing some inventory cost flow assumption such as FIFO, LIFO, or average cost, except when the standard cost for the particular inventory is changed. So long as the standard costs in use are current and reasonably attainable, they are acceptable bases for reporting inventories and cost of goods sold in financial statements prepared for stockholders, creditors, and other interested parties. In other words, standard costs are included in the current framework of generally accepted accounting principles.

From one point of view, the valuation of inventories at standard costs may be regarded as not only acceptable but actually preferable to valuation at actual costs. If standard costs represent the costs which should be incurred in the manufacture of a product, one might argue that only they should be charged to that product. Any excess of actual costs over standard costs, then, would be regarded as costs of inefficiency of one sort or another rather than as costs of production. This argument may appear less reasonable in the opposite case, where actual costs are less than standard costs. However, in such case, one might view the cost difference as cost savings attributable to unusual efficiency in operations rather than to production itself.

VARIANCE COMPUTATION

Differences between actual costs and standard costs are called variances. Where actual cost is greater than standard cost, the variance is unfavorable. Where actual cost is less than standard, the variance is favorable. These terms are used in a specialized sense here to denote the direction of the variance from standard cost. A qualitative evaluation of variances as good or bad can be made only after the variances have been studied and their underlying causes identified. In this text, variances are computed by subtracting actual costs from standard costs, so that favorable variances will appear as positive amounts and unfavorable variances, as negative amounts. Obviously, the opposite arithmetic approach could be taken to arrive at exactly the same variances. The approach used here has been selected simply because there seems to be an intuitive logic in variances identified as favorable appearing as positive figures and those identified as unfavorable appearing as negative figures.

Variance computation, discussed in the following sections, is the mathematical technique for determining the amount of a variance. Variance analysis, discussed in the next chapter, is the investigative process of ascertaining the causes of variances. Obviously, the latter is the more important procedure insofar as management is concerned; but computation of variances ordinarily must precede their analysis. Variance computation may be learned by committing to memory a series of variance formulas. Such an approach to learning, however, cannot relate the mathematical technique to the ultimate managerial objective. Hence, the discussion of each variance in the paragraphs that follow will begin with a description of the fundamental meaning of variance. If one understands what a variance is intended to depict and understands the natures of the standard and actual quantities from which the variance is derived, the variance formula should follow logically.

Materials Variances

The cost of materials in a manufactured product is determined by two basic factors, the price paid for materials and the quantity of materials used in production. Since the time of purchase and the time of usage are not ordinarily the same, a single net materials variance comprising both price and usage elements usually cannot be computed. Materials may be purchased in one period and used in a subsequent period. To the extent that a materials cost variance arises from purchasing, it should be associated with the period in which the purchase was made. To the extent that it arises from usage, it should be associated with the period in which the materials were used in production.

Materials Price Variance. When materials are purchased, they may be bought either at the established standard price or at some price other than standard. In the latter instance, a variance will arise because of the price differential from standard. This is the *materials price variance.* While this variance is not necessarily attributable to good or bad purchasing practices, it does arise at the time of purchase and, logically, should be identified at that point. Obviously, the total amount of the variance will be greater the more units of materials are bought. Thus, the materials price variance is a function of the difference between the standard and actual prices per unit of material and the quantity of material purchased. The formula then follows logically:

The materials price variance is equal to the difference between the standard price and the actual price per unit of material multiplied by the quantity of materials purchased.

or

(1) $$MPV = (SP - AP) \times Q$$

This variance, as well as the others discussed in this chapter, will be illustrated for a hypothetical manufacturing company with a highly simplified manufacturing cost structure. The Rapa Nui Company makes imitation Polynesian statues. It uses a single raw material in the production process. This material, a chemically treated clay substance, has a standard price of $10 per pound.[1] During the month of October, 1966, the company purchased 14,000 pounds of this material at a price of $9.96 per pound. The materials price variance for the month is computed as follows:

$$MPV = (\$10.00 - \$9.96) \times 14{,}000 = \$.04 \times 14{,}000 = \$560.$$

As the actual price in this instance is lower than the standard price, the variance is favorable and, hence, a positive number.

Materials Usage Variance. The *materials usage variance* (or *materials quantity variance*) seeks to identify the difference between actual and standard materials costs attributable to the use of more or less materials in production than the standard quantity. The actual usage of materials is determined from a summary of materials issue reports during the period under study. For the Rapa Nui Company, this summary shows total actual usage of 12,500 pounds in October, 1966. The standard quantity of materials in production depends upon two factors, the standard quantity of materials required for each unit of product and the number of units produced during the period. The standard cost card of the Rapa Nui Company calls for an input of 8 pounds of material for each statue produced. During the month of October, 1966, 1,560 statues were completed and there was neither a beginning nor an ending inventory of work in process. Where there is a beginning or an ending inventory of work in process or both, the degree of completion of such inventories must be determined; and the units produced during that period must be expressed in terms of equivalent units of production.[2] For

[1] Refer to Chapter 5 for the manner of establishing price and quantity standards for both materials and direct labor.

[2] Refer to Chapter 4 for the method of computing equivalent units of production.

the Rapa Nui Company, the standard quantity of material in production for October, 1966 is 12,480 pounds (1,560 units produced, each requiring 8 pounds of material).

If the materials usage variance is to do what it is intended to do, namely, to measure the cost variance attributable to usage of materials, it must abstract from the problem of price differences. As the difference between actual and standard price (if any) is determined at the time of purchase of materials, the usage variance ignores such difference and translates physical quantities to costs by means of the standard price only. Thus, the materials usage variance is a function of the difference between the standard and actual materials input quantities and the standard materials price. The formula is as follows:

The materials usage variance is equal to the difference between the standard quantity of materials in production and the actual quantity used multiplied by the standard materials price.

or

(2) $$MUV = (SQ - AQ) \times SP$$

For October, 1966, the materials usage variance of the Rapa Nui Company is computed thus:

$$MUV = (12{,}480 - 12{,}500) \times \$10 = (20) \times \$10 = (\$200).$$

In this and in subsequent illustrations, negative amounts are shown in parentheses. As here, where the actual usage exceeds the standard quantity in production, a negative variance is unfavorable.

Labor Variances

Unlike materials, labor cannot be stored. Hence, the purchase and usage of labor may be viewed as simultaneous. Actually, payment for labor services is usually made at regular paydays after the work has been performed. Wages and salaries accrue as work is done, however, so that the purchase and usage of labor services are effectively simultaneous. Hence, a single net labor variance for a given period can be computed. It is the difference between the actual and standard labor costs of the period. It is, however, both feasible and useful to break this net variance down into components attributable to price and quantity differences. Unlike the two materials variances described above, these two labor variances do sum to a single significant variance.

Labor Rate Variance. The difference between standard and actual labor costs attributable to a difference between the standard and actual hourly wage rates is identified as the *labor rate variance* (or *wage rate variance*). (As mentioned in Chapter 5, weekly or monthly salaries are controlled by budgets and are not expressed as standard rates.) In order to isolate the effect of wage rate differentials, the labor rate variance ignores the question of whether the number of labor hours worked during the period was above or below the standard number that should have been worked. It is concerned only with the number of hours that actually were worked and, hence, that were paid at the actual wage rate and should have been paid at the standard rate. The labor rate variance, thus, is a function of the difference between the standard and actual wage rates and the actual labor hours worked. The formula is as follows:

The labor rate variance is equal to the difference between the standard wage rate per hour and the actual wage rate multiplied by the actual number of hours worked.

or

$$LRV = (SR - AR) \times AH \tag{3}$$

The Rapa Nui Company has only one class of direct laborers; their standard wage rate is $2 per hour. During October, 1966, the actual payroll shows 31,100 hours worked at an actual wage rate of $2.03 per hour. Computation of the company's labor rate variance for the month is as follows:

$$LRV = (\$2.00 - \$2.03) \times 31{,}100 = (\$.03) \times 31{,}100 = (\$933).$$

As the actual hourly rate is higher than the standard rate, the variance is unfavorable.

Labor Efficiency Variance. The quantity of labor used in a period is measured in units of time (usually man-hours). The time required for production is commonly thought of as an indication of the efficiency of the labor force. Hence, the variance which seeks to identify the impact of working more or less hours than the standard hours in production is called the *labor efficiency variance* (or *labor time variance*). It abstracts from problems of rate differences, which are identified in the labor rate variance, and is concerned only with the standard wage rate. The actual hours worked are determined from payroll summary sheets. The standard hours in production are determined by the established standard hours required for the production of one unit of product and the number of units produced during the period under study. Again, where there are partially completed inventories of work in process at the beginnning and/or end of the period, production must be stated in terms of equivalent units. Thus, the labor efficiency variance is a function of the difference between standard and actual labor hours worked and the standard wage rate. The formula is as follows:

The labor efficiency variance is equal to the difference between the standard and the actual labor hours worked during a period multiplied by the standard wage rate per hour.

or

$$LEV = (SH - AH) \times SR \quad (4)$$

The standard cost card of the Rapa Nui Company calls for 20 man-hours of work for each statue manufactured. Actual production for the month of October, 1966 totaled 1,560 statues. Standard hours in production, then, total 31,200 (1,560 units × 20 hours). The labor efficiency variance for the month is computed as follows:

$$LEV = (31{,}200 - 31{,}100) \times \$2 = 100 \times \$2 = \$200.$$

Since the actual hours worked are less than the standard hours in production, the variance is favorable.

Overhead—Measures of Volume

As explained in Chapter 5, standard overhead costs are based upon budgets and, typically, upon flexible budgets such as the one illustrated in Table 9–1 in Chapter 9. Standard variable overhead costs are determined independently of the level of volume planned, but standard fixed overhead costs can be determined only at some specified level of volume. An understanding of standard overhead costs and overhead variances requires a prior understanding of several concepts of production volume.

Normal Volume. A standard fixed overhead cost per unit of volume must be set at one given level of volume which is considered representative of the company's operations. The volume level most commonly selected for this purpose is normal volume. *Normal volume* is usually defined as that volume which reflects the average level of production activity over the period of a complete business cycle (including periods of prosperity, decline, depression, and recovery). This is often a difficult concept to quantify, particularly in growing firms where there is a rising secular trend in production in addition to cyclical fluctuations. The concept may be somewhat clearer if contrasted with the budgeted volume expected for a particular year. Anticipated conditions in any one year may be such that unusually high or low production is planned; the operating budget for such a year would be predicated upon the volume actually expected. Normal volume, on the other hand, ignores unusually high or low levels of activity in individual periods and seeks to identify the average level of activity over several periods. Normal volume may be stated in terms of either units of output or units of input.

Actual Output Volume. Where production volume is measured in units of output, *actual output volume* is simply the number of units of product actually produced during a given period. Output measures the results of production. These may be regarded as good or bad, satisfactory or unsatisfactory, according to established plans for output. There is no such concept as "standard output volume," however, as the term standard is used here. In this context, "standard" refers only to inputs, such as materials, labor hours, and machine hours. In October, 1966, the actual output of the Rapa Nui Company totaled 1,560 units of product. Although the company uses input rather than output in measuring production for purposes of charging overhead costs to products, actual output is necessary to determine the standard materials usage and standard labor hours in production.

Standard Input Volume. Where production volume is measured in units of input, it measures the productive efforts of the firm rather than the results of production. The input quantity used as a measure of production volume in the illustration in this chapter is direct labor hours. *Standard input volume* is the total quantity of labor hours (or some other input quantity) that the labor time standard indicates is necessary to produce the actual output of a period. Thus, standard input volume and actual output volume, although stated in different quantities, are equivalent measures of the results of operations. The standard input volume for the Rapa Nui Company in the month of October, 1966 is simply the 31,200 standard direct labor hours in production. This total is determined by multiplying the 1,560 units of output (i.e., completed statues) by the labor time standard of 20 man-hours per statue. Standard input volume is always a direct function of the actual output and the relevant standard (labor time, in this case) per unit of output.

Actual Input Volume. Where volume is measured in labor hours, *actual input volume* is simply the actual labor hours worked during a period. This may be greater than standard input volume by the amount of excess, or wasted, hours worked or less than standard by the amount of hours saved. Actual input volume measures the firm's total productive effort during a period, whether that effort was fruitful in terms of output or not. For October, 1966, the actual input volume of the Rapa Nui Company was 31,100 labor hours. This amount includes the 31,200 standard labor hours minus the 100 hours saved.

Overhead Variances in General

As in the case of direct labor, a single variance for overhead is significant. This is the net difference between the standard overhead cost of production for a period and the actual overhead costs incurred in the period. Where volume is measured in units of output, standard overhead cost is computed by multiplying the actual units produced by the standard variable and fixed overhead costs per unit of product. Where volume is measured in units of input, standard overhead cost is computed by multiplying the standard input volume by the standard variable and fixed overhead rates per unit of input. If input is stated in labor hours, these are standard rates per hour. A variable overhead rate is simply the budgeted amount per unit by which variable overhead costs are expected to change in response to changes in volume. It is used in both variable and absorption costing. A fixed overhead rate is determined by dividing total budgeted fixed overhead costs for a period by the normal volume for that period. The fixed rate, of course, is used only in absorption costing. As absorption costing is the more inclusive alternative, we shall discuss standard overhead costs here within that framework.

The flexible overhead budget of the Rapa Nui Company allows total variable overhead costs of $1.20 per direct labor hour plus total fixed costs of $51,200 per month. (The entire company is treated here as a single cost center having a single flexible budget. This is done merely to keep the size of the illustration easily manageable.) Normal volume has been established as 32,000 labor hours per month. Thus, the standard fixed overhead rate is $1.60 per labor hour ($51,200 ÷ 32,000 hours). The total standard overhead cost in production for the month of October is computed by multiplying the 31,200 standard direct labor hours in production by the variable and the fixed rates per hour, thus:

Standard variable overhead (31,200 × $1.20)	$37,440
Standard fixed overhead (31,200 × $1.60)	49,920
Total standard overhead cost for month	$87,360

The actual overhead costs incurred during October totaled $89,000, including $37,650 of variable costs and $51,350 of fixed costs. The net overhead variance, then, is the difference between standard and actual overhead costs:

Total standard overhead cost	$87,360
Total actual overhead cost	89,000
Net overhead variance	($ 1,640)

As the actual costs are greater than the standard cost, the net overhead variable is unfavorable.

Overhead Variances—Three-Variance Plan

Where volume is measured in units of input, the net overhead variance can be further broken down into three component variances.

Overhead Spending Variance. The *overhead spending variance* seeks to identify and isolate that portion of the net overhead variance that is attributable to differences between actual and budgeted spending on overhead cost items. It ignores any differences that may exist between actual and standard input volumes or between standard input volume and normal volume. It accepts actual input volume at face value and measures the difference between the budgeted overhead spending for the actual input volume and the actual overhead costs incurred. Flexible overhead budgets are essential for the computation of this variance, for the budget must be adjusted from whatever volume was originally planned to the actual input volume of the period. The formula for this variance is as follows:

> The overhead spending variance is equal to the difference between the budgeted overhead costs for the actual input volume and the actual overhead costs incurred.

or

$$OSV = BCAIV - AC \tag{5}$$

For the month of October, 1966, the actual input volume of the Rapa Nui Company was 31,100 direct labor hours. The flexible budget allows $1.20 per labor hour plus $51,200 per month. The actual overhead costs were given in the preceding section. The company's spending variance for October is computed as follows:

Budgeted costs for actual input volume:		
Variable costs (31,100 hours × $1.20)..........		$37,320
Fixed costs..................................		51,200
		88,520
Actual costs:		
Variable costs................................	$37,650	
Fixed costs..................................	51,350	89,000
		($ 480)

As the actual costs exceed the budgeted costs, the variance is unfavorable. Separate spending variances for variable and fixed overhead could be computed easily from the data above. In this illustration, both would be unfavorable variances—$330 for variable overhead and $150 for fixed overhead.

The spending variance computed in the preceding paragraph includes both variable and fixed overhead cost items, for the Rapa Nui Company uses absorption costing. The question arises as to whether both variable and fixed overhead would be included in the determination of the spending variance in a company using variable costing. If the variance is to conform to the definition of product cost under variable costing, fixed overhead would be excluded from it. Thus, it might be referred to as the variable overhead spending variance. This approach would be consistent with the exclusion of any fixed overhead from standard production cost under variable costing. On the other hand, just because fixed overhead is not charged to production, its control cannot be ignored. Costs must be controlled regardless of how they are accounted for. Thus, for cost control purposes, a total overhead spending variance, including both variable and fixed costs, would still seem more appropriate. Perhaps the simplest solution to this question would be to compute separate spending variances for variable and fixed overhead, recognize only the variable cost variance in the accounts, but use both for control purposes.

For effective cost control, the spending variance should be determined separately for each item of overhead cost, as was done in Table 9–2 in Chapter 9. The causes of the total overhead spending variance may be quite varied. The variance may be caused, in part, by differences between the actual prices paid for goods and services included in overhead and the prices assumed in the development of the budget. It may also be caused, partly, by differences in the actual usage of such goods and services as compared with the usage planned in the budget. For example, assume that the flexible budget includes a variable allowance of $.10 for indirect materials. This allowance may be based upon a price of $.05 per pound and an expected rate of consumption of 2 pounds per direct labor hour. If the actual price is more than $.05 per pound and the actual consumption rate is greater than 2 pounds per hour, the actual cost of indirect materials will be higher than the budgeted indirect materials cost for the actual input volume. That higher cost will be caused by both price and usage factors. Other overhead items may involve either more or less spending than the budget calls for. If a depreciation rate on factory equipment is changed after the flexible budget is established, actual and budgeted depreciation will differ; and this difference will appear in the overhead spending variance.

Overhead Efficiency Variance. This variance exists only where volume is measured in units of input. The *overhead efficiency variance* measures the excess cost incurred or the cost saving due to the fact that actual input volume is more or less, respectively, than standard input volume. Logically, this variance relates only to variable overhead costs; for only variable costs are affected by variations in volume. The formula for the efficiency variance is as follows:

The overhead efficiency variance is equal to the difference between the standard input volume and the actual input volume multiplied by the standard variable overhead rate per unit of volume.

or

$$OEV = (SIV - AIV) \times SVOR \tag{6}$$

Where labor hours are the input quantity used to measure volume, the overhead efficiency variance is caused directly by labor efficiency. Thus, some have argued that the overhead efficiency variance should be regarded as part of the labor efficiency variance. Certainly, they have a common cause; but there is no objection to these two efficiency variances being stated separately.

For the Rapa Nui Company in October, 1966, the standard input volume is 31,200 direct labor hours. The actual input volume is 31,100 hours, and the standard variable overhead rate is $1.20 per hour. The variance is then computed thus:

$$OEV = (31{,}200 - 31{,}100) \times \$1.20 = 100 \times \$1.20 = \$120.$$

Since the actual input volume is less than the standard input volume, variable overhead costs should have been saved; and the variance is favorable. Whenever volume is measured in labor hours, the labor efficiency variance and the overhead efficiency variance will always both be favorable or both be unfavorable.

Overhead Volume Variance. The *overhead volume variance* is attributable to differences between the standard input volume and normal volume. Specifically, it arises because a standard fixed overhead rate is computed at normal volume and applied to production at standard input volume. Strictly, a fixed overhead rate per unit of volume is valid only at the volume at which the rate is computed. This is so because fixed overhead costs are constant in total and, hence, are different per unit at each different level of volume. Nevertheless, in a standard cost system, a fixed overhead rate computed at normal volume is charged to production at a different volume, standard input volume. This practice necessarily produces a variance. The standard fixed overhead rate is strictly conceived to absorb total budgeted fixed overhead only at normal volume. If used at any other volume, the fixed overhead rate will result in either more or less than the total budgeted fixed overhead being absorbed by production. As fixed overhead is charged to production only in absorption costing, the volume variance can exist only in that method. The formula for the overhead volume variance is as follows:

The overhead volume variance is equal to the difference between the standard fixed overhead cost charged to production and the budgeted fixed overhead cost.[3]

or

$$OVV = SFOC - BFOC \quad (7)$$

For the Rapa Nui Company, the standard fixed overhead charged to production during October, 1966 was $49,920 (31,200 standard hours × $1.60 per hour). The budgeted fixed overhead is given as $51,200 per month. The volume variance, then, is computed thus:

$$OVV = \$49{,}920 - \$51{,}200 = (\$1{,}280).$$

The variance is unfavorable because the standard input volume is not sufficient to absorb all of the budgeted fixed overhead costs at the standard fixed overhead rate of $1.60 per hour. Any time that a fixed overhead rate is applied at a volume lower than the normal volume at which it was computed (as is the case here), the standard fixed overhead cost will be less than the budgeted fixed cost; and the volume variance will be unfavorable. Conversely, if a fixed overhead rate is applied at a volume higher than normal volume, the volume variance will invariably be favorable.

Summary of Three-Variance Plan. We have observed the determination of three separate overhead variances. Their algebraic sum should be equal to the net overhead variance of $1,640 computed earlier. That this is, in fact, so may be demonstrated simply.

Overhead spending variance	($ 480)
Overhead efficiency variance	120
Overhead volume variance	(1,280)
Net overhead variance	($1,640)

The spending variance relates to both variable and fixed overhead cost items; the efficiency variance relates exclusively to variable cost items; and the volume variance relates exclusively to fixed overhead.

[3] An alternative method of calculating the overhead volume variance is to multiply the difference between the standard input volume and the normal volume by the standard fixed overhead rate. Actually, this is not a different formula but a different arrangement of the same formula.

Overhead Variances—Two-Variance Plan

Where production volume is measured in units of output rather than input, only two separate overhead variances can be computed. As the Rapa Nui Company uses an input measure of volume, we must construct a different illustration for the two-variance plan. Assume that the following budgeted and actual data are taken from the records of the Easterland Company for the month of June, 1966:

Normal volume	15,000 units of output
Budgeted variable overhead	\$.60 per unit of output
Budgeted fixed overhead	\$13,500 per month
Actual output	15,800 units of product
Actual overhead costs:	
Variable	\$9,500
Fixed	\$13,900

The standard fixed overhead rate is \$.90 per unit (\$13,500 ÷ 15,000 units at normal volume). The net overhead variance is then computed as follows:

Standard overhead cost for month:		
Variable cost (15,800 units × \$.60)		\$ 9,480
Fixed cost (15,800 units × \$.90)		14,220
		23,700
Actual overhead cost for month:		
Variable cost	\$ 9,500	
Fixed cost	13,900	23,400
Net overhead variance		\$ 300

The net variance here is favorable.

Overhead Budget Variance. Where overhead is charged to production on the basis of output rather than input, there is no basis for measuring overhead efficiency and, hence, no overhead efficiency variance. Thus, the two-variance plan identifies overhead variances attributable to spending and volume differences only. The *overhead budget variance* in the two-variance plan is fundamentally similar to the spending variance in the three-variance plan. The use of a different name for the variance in the two-variance plan is common practice and is helpful in distinguishing the two plans. Further, the budget variance is not identical to the spending variance. Even though overhead efficiency is not measurable separately in the two-variance plan, it may still exist. If it does, the budget variance includes both spending and efficiency factors; whereas the spending variance in the three-variance plan specifically excludes the efficiency factor. The budget variance is the difference between the actual costs incurred and the costs which the flexible budget indicates should be incurred at the actual output volume achieved. The formula is as follows:

The overhead budget variance is equal to the difference between the budgeted overhead cost for the actual output volume and the actual overhead cost incurred.

or

$$OBV = BCAOV - AC \quad (8)$$

For cost control purposes, the budget variance should be determined separately for each distinct overhead cost item.

For the Easterland Company for the month of June, 1966, the overhead budget variance is the difference between the budgeted costs for the actual output volume of 15,800 units of product and the actual costs incurred in June. It is computed as follows:

Budgeted cost for actual output volume:		
Variable (15,800 units × $.60)		$ 9,480
Fixed		13,500
		22,980
Actual cost:		
Variable	$ 9,500	
Fixed	13,900	23,400
		($ 420)

As the actual costs exceed the budget allowances for the actual volume, the variance is unfavorable.

The budget variance can be employed in firms which use an input measure of volume also. In such firms, it is simply the algebraic sum of the spending and efficiency variances in the three-variance plan. It is computed as the difference between the budgeted cost for the standard input volume and the actual cost. Because of the basically different sources of the spending and efficiency variances, however, the three-variance plan is normally more useful to management where it can be used.

Overhead Volume Variance. The volume variance is identical under both the two-variance plan and the three-variance plan. It is the difference between the standard fixed overhead cost charged to production and the budgeted fixed overhead cost. Where volume was measured in units of input, standard fixed overhead cost was computed by multiplying the standard fixed rate by the standard input volume. Where volume is stated in units of output, standard fixed overhead cost is determined by multiplying the standard fixed rate by the actual output volume. But standard input volume and actual output volume, it should be recalled, are equivalent concepts. Both measure the results of production. For the Easterland Company, the volume variance for June, 1966 is computed thus:

Standard fixed overhead cost (15,800 units × $.90 standard fixed rate per unit)	$14,220
Budgeted fixed overhead cost per month	13,500
	$ 720

The variance is favorable because actual output volume is greater than normal volume.

Summary of Two-Variance Plan. The algebraic sum of the overhead budget and volume variances computed for the Easterland Company should be equal to the net overhead variance of $300, computed earlier. That this is so is shown below:

Overhead budget variance	($420)
Overhead volume variance	720
Net overhead variance	$300

The budget variance deals with both variable and fixed costs, while the volume variance relates exclusively to fixed costs.

Summary of Variance Formulas

For the sake of ease in studying and reviewing variances, the formulas for the eight variances discussed in the foregoing pages are summarized below. In each case, the formula is so stated that a positive variance is favorable and a negative variance, unfavorable.

(1) Materials price variance = (standard price per unit of material − actual price) × quantity of materials actually purchased.

(2) Materials usage variance = (standard quantity of materials in production − actual quantity used) × standard price per unit.

(3) Labor rate variance = (standard wage rate per hour − actual wage rate) × actual labor hours worked.

(4) Labor efficiency variance = (standard labor hours in production − actual hours worked) × standard wage rate per hour.

Overhead—Three-Variance Plan:

(5) Overhead spending variance = budgeted overhead costs for actual input volume − actual overhead costs.

(6) Overhead efficiency variance = (standard input volume − actual input volume) × standard variable overhead rate.

(7) Overhead volume variance = standard fixed overhead cost in production − budgeted fixed overhead cost.

Overhead—Two-Variance Plan:

(8) Overhead budget variance = budgeted overhead cost for actual output volume − actual overhead cost.

(7) Overhead volume variance—same as under three-variance plan.

RECORDING STANDARD MANUFACTURING COSTS

There is no uniform system of accounting by which standard costs are incorporated in the recording process of the cost accounting cycle. There are at least three basic types of standard cost systems, and there are variations in the techniques used under each system. All of these differences are methodological, however, and not conceptual. The same variances would be computed under any of these systems,[4] although they might be recorded differently in the accounts. In this chapter we shall illustrate the so-called *single plan* of standard cost accounting, wherein all manufacturing inventory accounts are charged only for standard costs. Differences between standard and actual costs are charged or credited to variance accounts. Favorable variances appear as credit balances, for they represent cost savings (or offsets against cost) as compared with standard costs. Unfavorable variances appear as debit balances, for they are additional costs in excess of standard amounts.

The cost accounting cycle for the Rapa Nui Company for October, 1966 will be illustrated here. Fundamentally, the entries here are the same as those illustrated in Chapter 3 for an actual cost system. The variances recorded in the entries below are those computed in the foregoing sections and will not be explained further.

1. *Purchase of Materials.* Fourteen thousand pounds of raw materials were purchased at a price of $9.96 per pound. The standard price is $10.00 per pound.

Account	Debit	Credit
Materials Inventory	140,000	
Materials Price Variance		560
Vouchers Payable		139,440

The inventory account is charged for the standard price of the units

[4] There is one exception to this statement. Under one variation of any of the basic standard cost systems, the materials price variance is computed for the units used only, rather than for the total number of units purchased. From the standpoint of managerial control, this approach to the materials price variance seems to be less useful than the one employed in this chapter; hence, it will not be discussed or illustrated.

purchased. The liability to the supplier, of course, is recorded at the actual price; for this is the amount that will have to be paid to him.

2. *Usage of Materials.* Twelve thousand five hundred pounds of materials were actually used. The standard input is 8 pounds per statue produced. As 1,560 statues were manufactured during the month, standard materials usage amounts to 12,480 pounds.

Work in Process	124,800	
Materials Usage Variance	200	
Materials Inventory		125,000

Work in Process is charged for the standard quantity of materials at the standard price. Materials Inventory must be credited for the actual quantity used at the standard price.

3. *Manufacturing Payroll.* The actual hours worked by direct laborers totaled 31,100 for the month. The standard hours in production amounted to 31,200. The actual wage rate paid was $2.03 per hour, as compared with the standard rate of $2.00 per hour.

Work in Process	62,400	
Labor Rate Variance	933	
Labor Efficiency Variance		200
Payroll Summary		63,133

Work in Process is charged for the standard hours in production at the standard wage rate. The Payroll Summary is credited for the actual direct labor cost of the month (the actual hours at the actual rate). This entry is deliberately simplified to focus attention on the basic labor cost accounting procedures. Actually, it is likely that some amount of indirect labor would be included in the payroll; this would be charged to an overhead control account, of course. The entry for payment of the payroll is no different from the same entry under an actual cost system. The payroll department is concerned with actual labor cost data only. Standards do not affect the amounts paid to workers and withheld for subsequent remittance to the government or some other third party.

4. *Actual Overhead Cost Incurrence.* The actual overhead costs incurred are recorded in the same way under a standard cost system as in an actual cost system. The $89,000 of actual overhead costs incurred were comprised of $37,650 of variable costs and $51,350 of fixed costs.

Variable Overhead Control	37,650	
Fixed Overhead Control	51,350	
Various accounts		89,000

5. *Application of Overhead Cost to Production.* Work in Process is charged for the standard overhead cost of the units produced during the month. Under absorption costing, this will be the sum of the standard variable cost rate ($1.20 per labor hour) and the standard fixed cost rate ($1.60 per labor hour), each multiplied by the standard labor hours in production for the month (31,200 hours).

Work in Process	87,360	
Variable Overhead Applied		37,440
Fixed Overhead Applied		49,920

Under variable costing, only variable overhead would be charged to the product. The fixed Overhead Control account would be closed directly to Revenue and Expense Summary.

6. *Recording Overhead Variances.* The entries illustrated in paragraphs 4 and 5 above do not show the overhead variances directly. Rather, they leave the net overhead variance as the difference between the debit balances in the Overhead Control accounts and the credit balances in the Overhead Applied accounts. This may be an entirely satisfactory method of accounting for these variances. If, however, management wishes to have them recorded in individual accounts as are the materials and labor variances, the Overhead Control and Applied accounts may be closed and the desired variance accounts set up. This procedure will be illustrated below for the absorption costing method only and for the three-variance plan only. Similar entries for variable costing and/or for the two-variance plan should be obvious.

Variable Overhead Applied	37,440	
Fixed Overhead Applied	49,920	
Overhead Spending Variance	480	
Overhead Volume Variance	1,280	
Overhead Efficiency Variance		120
Variable Overhead Control		37,650
Fixed Overhead Control		51,350

7. *Completion of Production.* The standard cost sheet (or standard cost card) for the product of the Rapa Nui Company under the absorption costing method is as follows:

Materials (8 lbs. @ $10.00)		$ 80.00
Labor (20 hours @ $2.00)		40.00
Overhead:		
Variable (20 hours @ $1.20)	$24.00	
Fixed (20 hours @ $1.60)	32.00	56.00
		$176.00

Thus, the total standard cost of one statue is $176. Under variable costing, it would be $144 per statue, the $32 of fixed overhead being omitted. Since Work in Process has been charged only for the standard cost of goods put into production, logically it will be the standard cost of completed units that will be transferred from that account to Finished Product. The entry for this transfer, under absorption costing, is as follows:

Finished Product................................	274,560	
Work in Process.........................		274,560

The standard cost of 1,560 finished statues is $274,560 (1,560 @ $176). Under variable costing, the standard cost of the finished production would be less, totaling only $224,640 (1,560 statues @ $144).

8. *Sales.* During October, 1966, the Rapa Nui Company sold 1,500 statues at a unit price of $240. The entry to record the sales revenue is, of course, unaffected by the costing method employed by the firm.

Accounts Receivable..............................	360,000	
Sales..................................		360,000

The cost of sales depends upon the costing method used, however. Under absorption costing, the cost of goods sold would be the product of the 1,500 statues sold multiplied by the standard unit cost of $176.

Cost of Goods Sold..............................	264,000	
Finished Product.........................		264,000

Under variable costing, the cost of sales would be equal to 1,500 statues sold at a standard variable cost of $144 per statue.

DISPOSITION OF VARIANCES

Charge or Credit to Current Period's Income

Once the variances have been computed and have been charged or credited to individual variance accounts,[5] the question arises as to what should be their final disposition. In most cases, as a practical matter, variance accounts are charged (unfavorable variances) or credited (favorable variances) to the income of the current period. This may be accomplished by closing the variance accounts either to Revenue and Expense Summary or to Cost of Goods Sold. Net income, of course,

[5] The same effect can be achieved by charging or crediting all variances to a single Variance Summary account.

would be the same under either alternative; only the manner of reporting the variances would differ. If the variances are closed directly to Revenue and Expense Summary, they are probably reported among the nonoperating items (miscellaneous gains and losses) on the income statement. Cost of Goods Sold would thus remain stated at standard cost. In view of the fact that manufacturing inventory accounts are carried at standard costs on the balance sheet, this result would appear to be consistent. Further, the total amount of all variances is not likely to be attributable wholly to goods sold; some portion is probably applicable to unsold and to unfinished production. On the other hand, if the variances are closed to Cost of Goods Sold, they will be reported as part of that cost on the income statement and will be associated, quite properly, with the costs of manufacturing. A useful compromise here would be to close the variance accounts to Revenue and Expense Summary and to report them in the income statement as a net addition to (net unfavorable variance) or deduction from (net favorable variance) Cost of Goods Sold, which would still be reported initially at standard cost.[6] Showing in detail the amount of each individual variance would seem unnecessary in a summary report such as the income statement, but it certainly would not be objectionable.

So long as standards are current and attainable and so long as flexible budgets for overhead are based upon reasonable current cost estimates, charging or crediting manufacturing variances to current income appears to be a theoretically sound and practically satisfactory method of disposing of them—with one possible exception to be noted shortly. If, on the other hand, standards and budgets are not current and attainable, standard cost is not a satisfactory measure of current production costs; and, hence, the variances are not valid indicators of departures from cost levels that should have been attained. In such instance, it would be better to dispose of the variances by adjusting the several manufacturing cost accounts from the invalid standard cost to the actual cost of the period.

Deferral of Volume Variance. Even where standards and budgets are current and reasonably attainable, it is questionable whether the volume variance ought to be closed to current income. The volume variance is a function of the difference between normal volume and the actual output volume achieved during a particular period. If normal volume is defined as the average level of activity expected over the course

---

[6] This is essentially the same method of reporting as suggested in Chapter 3 for net under- or overapplied overhead.

of a complete business cycle, a volume variance may reasonably be expected in any one period; for the business cycle usually spans several accounting periods. Thus, in theory, it would be more accurate to treat the volume variance as a deferred charge or deferred credit in each period on the assumption that the volume variances of several periods (i.e., a complete business cycle) will net out at zero. As a matter of practical expediency, the volume variance is generally charged or credited to current income along with the other variances. So long as the amounts of successive volume variances are not material in relation to net income, there should be no serious objections to this practice.

Allocation of Variances to Manufacturing Cost Accounts

If standards and budgets do not reflect current attainable cost levels, charging or crediting variances to income may result in an overstatement or understatment of inventories and cost of goods sold. In such a case, it is better to adjust the inventory and cost of goods sold accounts to actual costs by allocating the manufacturing variances among them. Variances would be allocated among the several accounts to which the standard manufacturting costs had been charged—Work in Process, Finished Product, and Cost of Goods Sold. The amount allocated to each of these accounts would be determined by the amount of the relevant standard cost in each account as of the end of the period relative to the total amount of that standard cost charged to production during the period. For example, labor variances would be allocated on the basis of standard labor cost of the period. Assume that a total of $600,000 of standard labor cost had been charged to Work in Process during a given period. Of that total, $540,000 had been transferred to Finished Product and $420,000 had been further transferred from Finished Product to Cost of Goods Sold. At the end of the period, the standard labor cost of the period in each of these accounts would be as follows:

Work in Process	$ 60,000
Finished Product	120,000
Cost of Goods Sold	420,000
	$600,000

The net labor variance would then be allocated as follows: one-tenth to Work in Process, two-tenths to Finished Product, and seven-tenths to Cost of Goods Sold. Allocation of materials and overhead variances would be accomplished in a similar manner, standard materials cost and standard overhead cost, respectively, being used as the bases for allocations. It should be noted that the materials price variance would likely be allocated partly to Materials Inventory as well as to the three accounts listed above.

QUESTIONS FOR DISCUSSION

1. "Inasmuch as standard costs reflect costs that should have been incurred rather than costs that actually were incurred, they are useful only for purpose of cost analysis and control. They may not be used in the valuation of inventories or in the measurement of income. If standard costs are used for the latter purposes, the balance sheet and the income statement will show, in part, the operating goals of the firm rather than its operating results." Comment on this statement.
2. Explain the essential nature of each of the following variances. From what conditions or circumstances do they derive?
   a. Materials price variance.
   b. Labor rate variance.
   c. Materials usage variance.
   d. Labor efficiency variance.
   e. Overhead spending variance.
   f. Overhead efficiency variance.
   g. Overhead volume variance.
3. Which of the variances listed in Question No. 2 above would be different in variable costing than in absorption costing? Explain the reasons for these differences.
4. Can any of the variances listed in Question No. 2 above be computed without knowledge of the volume of output during a period? If so, which one(s) and why?
5. Define each of the following terms: (*a*) normal volume; (*b*) actual output volume; (*c*) standard input volume; and (*d*) actual input volume. What is the role of each of these four concepts of volume in the determination of three overhead variances for a company that charges overhead to production on the basis of direct labor hours?
6. Why is it generally invalid to sum algebraically the materials price and usage variances and to describe the total as the "net materials variance"?
7. The labor rate variance computed in this chapter is the difference between the standard and actual wage rates per hour multiplied by the total actual hours worked. This might be further broken down into two subvariances: the excess wage rate multiplied by the standard labor hours in production and the excess wage rate multiplied by the excess (or saved) hours above (or below) the standard hours. Do you believe this further refinement of the labor rate variance would be useful to management for purposes of cost control? Why or why not?
8. What are the basic differences between the two-variance plan and the three-variance plan for analyzing overhead costs? Under what circumstances

may only one of these plans be used? Under what circumstances may either be used? When either may be used, which is preferable? Why?

9. How may variances be disposed of in the accounts and reported in the financial statements? If there are alternatives, which is the most appropriate? Why?
10. The Amtek Corporation has approximately 800 standard materials used in its various products. It wishes daily reports of materials usage and the usage variance but does not feel it is practicable to make a detailed analysis of the usage of each raw material every day. Can you suggest a procedure that would yield reasonably dependable *and complete* materials usage variance reports daily without the necessity of analyzing each individual material daily?
11. What criteria might be established by management for determining whether a variance is significant and requires specific corrective action?

PROBLEMS

1. The Browning Corporation manufactures ceramic ashtrays. A standard cost system is used to account for production. The standard cost sheet for one ashtray is as follows:

Raw materials:	
Clay—2 lbs. @ $.12½	$ .25
Pigment—3 oz. @ $.84	2.52
Direct labor—¾ hr. @ $2.40	1.80
Overhead:	
Variable	.38
Fixed	.75
	$5.70

During the month of October, 1966, the actual production totaled 18,000 ashtrays. Actual operating statistics for that month are summarized below:

Materials purchases—40,000 lbs. of clay @ $.12 and 55,000 oz. of pigment @ $.82
Materials usage—36,850 lbs. of clay and 53,200 oz. of pigment
Direct labor—13,150 hrs. @ $2.48
Variable overhead—$6,910
Fixed overhead—$13,660

There were no beginning or ending inventories of work in process for the month. Sales for October amounted to 17,200 ashtrays.

Required:

Compute the following quantities and show all computations:

1. Standard materials, labor, and overhead costs in production for October.
2. Standard cost of finished production.

3. Standard cost of goods sold.
4. Materials price and usage variances.
5. Labor rate and efficiency variances.

2. The Single Product Company manufactures widgets and employs a standard cost accounting system. The standard cost of one widget is as follows:

Materials—12 units @ $.60		$ 7.20
Labor—½ hour @ $3.00		1.50
Overhead:		
Variable—½ hour @ $1.70	$.85	
Fixed—½ hour @ $1.60	.80	1.65
		$10.35

During the year 1965, actual output included 100,000 finished widgets. The inventory of work in process at January 1 consisted of 30,000 widgets, complete with respect to materials and half complete with respect to labor and overhead. At December 31, 40,000 widgets were in process, complete with respect to materials and half complete with respect to conversion costs.

Materials purchases for the year totaled 1,500,000 units at a price of $.58 each. The total materials usage for the year was 1,360,000 units. The factory payrolls for the year included a total of 53,200 direct labor hours at an average rate of $3.08 per hour.

Required:

Compute the materials price and usage variances and the labor rate and efficiency variances. Show all computations.

3. The Puerile Company manufactures a variety of children's clothing. All products require some work in the stitching department. Normal production volume in that department is 21,000 direct labor hours per month. The budgeted monthly overhead cost for the stitching department is $29,400 plus $1.60 per direct labor hour. The company uses absorption costing.

During June, 1966, the stitching department recorded a total of 22,600 labor hours, 900 of which were in excess of the standard hours allowed for the department's production in that month. Actual overhead costs for the month included $30,000 of fixed costs and $34,300 of variable costs.

Required:

Compute three variances from standard overhead cost for the month of June, 1966. Show all computations.

4. Following is the flexible overhead budget for the Ditmer Company for one month:

Percent of capacity	70	80	90	100
Standard machine hours	3,500	4,000	4,500	5,000
Variable costs	$21,000	$24,000	$27,000	$30,000
Semivariable costs	$ 8,000	$ 8,600	$ 9,200	$ 9,800
Fixed costs	$72,000	$72,000	$72,000	$72,000

It is believed that the range of volume tabulated in this budget encompasses any volume that might reasonably be expected to occur. Normal volume has been set at 80% of capacity. Both variable and fixed overhead costs, including variable and fixed components of the semivariable costs, are charged to production at standard rates per machine hour.

Actual operating data for the month of April, 1966 are as follows:

Actual machine hours	4,400
Standard machine hours	4,250
Variable overhead costs	$26,100
Semivariable overhead costs	$ 9,000
Fixed overhead costs	$72,000

Required:

1. Resolve the semivariable costs in the budget into variable and fixed components by means of the high-low method. Then compute standard variable and fixed overhead rates per machine hour.
2. Calculate three variances from standard overhead cost for the month of April, 1966.
3. Explain briefly the essential meaning of each of these three variances.

5. The Dountourth Products Company uses a standard cost system and variable costing. Overhead is applied to production on the basis of direct labor cost (i.e., dollars of standard direct labor cost). The flexible budget for the company's overhead allows $40,000 per month plus $.60 per direct labor dollar. Budgeted direct labor costs for the month of October, 1966 are $80,000. Actual operations for October are summarized below:

Actual direct labor cost	$78,000
Standard direct labor cost	75,000
Actual variable overhead	48,000
Actual fixed overhead	41,200

Required:

1. Compute the standard overhead cost of production for the month of October, 1966.
2. Compute as many variances from standard overhead for October as you can.

6. The Thanatops Company produces a single product. Both variable and fixed overhead costs are charged to production at standard rates per unit of product. The flexible budget for overhead allows $1.60 per unit of product plus $36,000 per month. Normal volume is 24,000 units per month. During the month of July, 1966, a total of 27,500 units were produced. Actual variable overhead totaled $42,200 and actual fixed overhead, $37,800.

Required:

1. Compute the standard overhead cost of production for July, 1966.
2. Compute as many variances from standard overhead cost as you can.

7. The Wanzer Manufacturing Company processes its three products in three separate production departments. Product A is processed in department 10. Overhead is charged to production in this department at standard rates per unit of product A. The standard variable overhead rate is $.35; the standard fixed overhead rate is $.85. Normal production volume is 600,000 units of product A annually.

At January 1, 1966, 20,000 units of product A were in process in department 10. They were complete as to materials and half complete as to conversion costs. A total of 550,000 units of product A were finished during the year, and 50,000 units remained in process at December 31, 1966. These unfinished units were 80% complete with respect to materials and 40% complete with respect to conversion costs. Actual overhead for 1966 included variable costs of $185,000 and fixed costs of $525,000.

Required:

Compute as many variances from standard overhead cost in department 10 during 1966 as you can.

8. The Bakersfield Corporation manufactures a single product line. Production is costed at standard variable cost. The standard cost sheet for one unit of product is as follows:

Materials—6 pieces @ $1.25	$7.50
Labor—½ hour @ $3.00	1.50
Overhead—½ hour @ $1.80	.90
	$9.90

The flexible budget for overhead allows $1.80 per direct labor hour plus $176,000 per year.

Actual operating data for 1966 are summarized below:

Unit output—175,000 units of product
Materials purchases—900,000 pieces @ $1.19
Materials usage—1,100,000 pieces
Direct labor hours—86,000
Direct labor cost—$266,600
Variable overhead—$150,000
Fixed overhead—$185,000

Required:

Compute as many variances from standard cost for 1966 as you can.

9. The Togo Toga Company manufactures women's clothing. Work in Process is charged with standard manufacturing costs, including both variable and fixed factory overhead. The Kismet nightgown is the sole product of the sheer department and is produced in standard lots of 100 units. The relevant standards and budget data are as follows:

Raw materials:
Silk—360 yards per lot at $2.20 per yard
Lace—300 yards per lot at $.40 per yard
Direct labor—25 man-hours per lot at $1.60 per hour

Flexible overhead budget for sheer department for one month:

Labor hours	800	900	1,000	1,100
Variable costs	$960	$1,080	$1,200	$1,320
Fixed costs	$800	$ 800	$ 800	$ 800

Normal volume is 40 lots of production per month.

The actual operations of the sheer department for the month of December, 1966 are summarized below:

Purchases of materials:
Silk—25,000 yards at $2.10 per yard
Lace—30,000 yards at $.42 per yard

Usage of materials:
Silk—12,740 yards
Lace—10,200 yards
Direct labor—880 man-hours at $1.65 per hour

Overhead:
Variable—$1,180
Fixed—$800
Output—3,400 Kismet nightgowns

Required:

Compute as many variances from standard cost for the month of December as you can.

10. The Starbuck Company uses the single plan of standard cost accounting and absorption costing in its production records. The standard cost card for one of its principal products is as follows:

Product S

Materials:		
3 pieces of material B @ $1.00		$3.00
Labor:		
½ hour @ $1.50		.75
Overhead:		
Variable—½ hour @ $.80	$.40	
Fixed—½ hour @ $1.20	.60	1.00
		$4.75

Normal production volume of product S has been set at 3,000 labor hours per month.

Actual operations for the month of April, 1966 are summarized below:

a. Purchased 16,000 pieces of material B at $1.05 each.
b. Used 20,000 pieces of material B in production.
c. The total actual payroll included 3,000 hours of work on product S at an average rate of $1.60 per hour.
d. Actual overhead applicable to product S included variable costs of $2,600 and fixed costs of $3,720.

e. During April, 6,100 units of product S were completed and transferred to finish stock. On April 1, 600 units had been in process; these were complete with respect to materials and half complete with respect to labor and overhead. At the end of April, 800 units remained in process, complete as to materials and half complete as to labor and overhead.

Required:

1. Prepare a schedule showing all postings to Work in Process—Product S for the month of April, 1966, including the opening and closing balances in the account.
2. Compute as many variances from standard production cost for April as you can.

11. The Beckman Products Company produces a single product. Absorption costing and the single plan of standard cost accounting are used in the valuation of inventories and in the measurement of periodic income. The standard cost sheet for the company's product appears as follows:

Materials—2 lbs. @ $.50	$1.00
Direct labor—$\frac{1}{3}$ hr. @ $1.80	.60
Overhead	.50
	$2.10

The flexible budget for overhead allows $.25 per unit of product. Normal production volume has been set at 7,500 units of product monthly.

Transactions for the month of January, 1966, the first month of operations, are as follows:

Materials purchased—16,000 pounds @ $.56
Materials used—12,750 pounds
Direct labor—2,150 hours @ $1.90
Variable overhead—$1,500
Fixed overhead—$2,025
Completed production—5,600 units
Ending inventory of work in process—500 units complete with respect to materials and half complete with respect to conversion costs

Required:

Compute as many variances from standard cost for January, 1966 as you can.

12. The Rackstraw Marine Corporation produces a single product. Absorption costing and standard cost accounting are employed. The standard direct production costs of one unit of product are as follows:

Materials—15 lbs. @ $.60	$ 9
Labor—4 hrs. @ $2.50	10

The flexible budget for overhead allows variable costs of $.80 per direct labor hour and fixed costs of $1.20 per labor hour, based upon a normal volume of 25,000 direct labor hours per year.

Actual operations during 1966 were as follows:

a. 4000 units of product were completed. 2000 units were in process at the end of the year; they were complete as to materials and half complete as to labor time. There was no work in process at the start of the year.

b. 100,000 pounds of raw material were purchased at an average price of $66 per pound.

c. 88,000 pounds of material were used in production.

d. The factory payroll included 21,200 direct labor hours at an average wage rate of $2.35 per hour.

e. Variable overhead costs totaled $13,600; fixed overhead amounted to $29,800.

f. 3,500 units of product were sold at a price of $42 per unit.

Required:

1. Compute as many variances from standard cost as you can.
2. Prepare general journal entries to record the operations of 1966.

13. The Meridian Washer Company manufactures rubber washers and employs a standard cost system with absorption costing. Standards have been set for production of lots of 1,000 washers. Materials standards call for 12 pounds of rubber per lot at a standard price of $.08 per pound. Labor standards call for $1\frac{1}{2}$ hours at a standard wage rate of $2 per hour. The flexible budget for overhead for one month is as follows:

Output (in lots)	12,000	18,000	24,000
Machine hours	18,000	27,000	36,000
Variable costs	$13,500	$20,250	$27,000
Fixed costs	$33,750	$33,750	$33,750

Overhead is applied to production on the basis of machine hours. Normal production volume has been set at 18,000 lots.

Operations for October, 1966 are summarized below:

Purchases—200,000 pounds of rubber at $.0875 per pound
Materials usage—244,000 pounds of rubber
Direct labor—28,500 hours at $2.10 per hour
Variable overhead—$24,150
Fixed overhead—$34,850
Machine hours worked—31,000
Output—20,000 lots
Sales—22,000 lots

Required:

Prepare general journal entries to record the operating transactions for the month of October, 1966.

14. Electric Products, Inc., manufactures condensers in department 101. Standard costing and absorption costing are employed in accounting for production. The standard cost card for one condenser is as follows:

Materials:	
Part #98736—1 piece @ $.50	$.50
Part #98742—2 pieces @ $.20	.40
Labor—.8 hour @ $1.75	1.40
Overhead:	
Variable—.8 hour @ $.45	.36
Fixed—.8 hour @ $.60	.48
	$3.14

The flexible budget for department 101 allows variable overhead of $.45 per labor hour and fixed overhead of $48,000 per year. Normal volume is 80,000 hours per year.

During 1965, 80,000 condensers were produced. The average actual prices paid for parts #98736 and #98742 were $.55 and $.18, respectively. Eighty-five thousand pieces of part #98736 and 160,000 pieces of part #98742 were purchased. The total direct labor cost in department 101 during 1965 was $117,500; total labor time was 62,500 hours. A summary of materials requisitions show that 82,000 pieces of part #98736 and 163,800 pieces of part #98742 were used during the year. Variable overhead for the year totaled $26,875; fixed overhead totaled $47,200. During 1965, 75,000 condensers were sold at an average price of $4.80.

Required:

Prepare general journal entries to record the operations of 1965 and to close all variance accounts to Revenue and Expense Summary at the end of the year.

15. The Amundsen Corporation manufactures turnbuckles in lots of 200. A single plan standard cost accounting system is used. The standard cost of one lot of production is as follows:

Materials—250 lbs. @ $.30		$ 75
Labor—10 hrs. @ $2.00		20
Overhead:		
Variable—10 hrs. @ $1.20	$12	
Fixed—10 hrs. @ $1.30	13	25
		$120

Normal production volume has been established at 20,000 direct labor hours per month.

Actual operating data for the month of February, 1966 are summarized below:

Output—1,800 lots
Materials purchases—400,000 lbs. @ $.33
Materials usage—460,000 lbs.
Labor—17,600 hrs. @ $2.12

Overhead:
Variable—$22,000
Fixed—$26,800
Sales—350,000 turnbuckles @ $1.18

Selling and administrative expenses:
Variable—$70,000
Fixed—$53,000

The applicable income tax rate is 25%.

Required:

1. Compute as many variances from standard cost as you can.
2. Prepare general journal entries to record the operating transactions for the month of February.
3. Prepare an income statement for February, 1966.

16. The Scott Engine Company produces engine blocks in its forging department. Blocks are charged with the standard variable costs incurred in production. The standard cost sheet for one engine block is as follows:

Materials—60 lbs. @ $.75	$45.00
Direct labor:	
Machine operators—¾ hr. @ $2.40	1.80
Handlers—½ hr. @ $1.60	.80
Variable overhead—2 machine hrs. @ $3.20	6.40
	$54.00

The output of the forging department is budgeted at 8,000 units annually. Fixed overhead in this department is budgeted at $96,000 per year.

During 1966, the actual output of the forging department was 5,000 engine blocks. Three hundred and thirty thousand pounds of materials were purchased at an average price of $.72 per pound. Materials usage reports show that a total of 318,000 pounds were used during 1966. The cost accounting department's records show that machine operators worked 3,800 hours at an actual wage rate of $2.52 and that handlers worked a total of 2,300 hours at a wage rate of $1.75. Forging department's cost records show that total variable overhead was $36,000 and total fixed overhead was $88,000. Total actual machine hours worked during 1966 amounted to 10,400.

Required:

Prepare general journal entries to record the operations of the forging department during 1966 and to close nominal accounts at the end of the year.

17. The Shackleton Company assembles power drills in two successive production departments. Actual assembly work is done in department 10; the drills are then tested and boxed in department 20. The company uses variable costing and a single plan standard cost system. The standard cost sheet for one drill is as follows:

Materials:		
Drill housing—1 @ $2.85	$2.85	
Electric motor—1 @ $4.75	4.75	
Cord (with plug)—1 @ $.69	.69	
Box—1 @ $.06	.06	$ 8.35
Labor:		
Department 10—¼ hr. @ $2.20	$ .55	
Department 20—⅓ hr. @ $1.80	.60	1.15
Variable overhead:		
Department 10—¼ hr. @ $1.60	$ .40	
Department 20—⅓ hr. @ $2.40	.80	1.20
		$10.70

The same standard cost has been in effect for several years.

During 1966, a total of 300,000 power drills were assembled in department 10. There was no inventory in process in this department at either the beginning or the end of the year. In department 20, there was an inventory of 8,000 units in process at January 1, 1966; it was one-fourth complete with respect to conversion costs and, of course, fully complete with respect to the costs of department 10. During the year, 296,000 drills were boxed and transferred to the finished stock room. At the end of the year, 12,000 drills remained in process in department 20; they were half complete with respect to conversion costs. Drills are boxed only after testing has been completed and they are ready to be transferred to finished stock.

Actual materials purchases in 1966 were as follows:

Drill housings—305,000 @ $2.98
Electric motors—280,000 @ $4.90
Cords—300,000 @ $.65
Boxes—360,000 @ $.04

Actual materials usage is summarized below.

In department 10:

Drill housings—302,000
Electric motors—300,480
Cords—301,700

In department 20:

Boxes—310,000

The payroll for 1966 shows the following summary charges to the two production departments:

Department 10—72,000 hrs. @ $2.15
Department 20—101,800 hrs. @ $1.90

Actual overhead costs incurred during 1966 were as follows:

In department 10:
Variable—$127,000
Fixed—$80,000

In department 20:
Variable—$216,500
Fixed—$48,000

Required:

1. Compute as many variances from standard cost as you can.
2. Prepare an analysis showing all debits and credits to the accounts Work in Process—Department 10 and Work in Process—Department 20. Include opening and closing balances, if any.

18. The Excelsior Paper Company began operations in 1965. During that year, it completed production of 115,000 reams of paper. Materials standards called for 5 pounds of pulp per ream at a price of $.12 per pound. Actual materials usage in 1965 totaled 800,000 pounds of pulp. A total of 1,000,-000 pounds were purchased at an average price of $.18 per pound. At the end of the year, the inventory of work in process consisted of 10,000 reams of paper, half complete with respect to all cost elements. The ending inventory of finished product contained 20,000 reams of paper.

The company's auditors have stated that they regard the materials price and usage variances as excessive because the relevant standards were not realistic. Accordingly, management has agreed to adjust the affected accounts to reflect the average actual cost of raw materials. The single plan of standard cost accounting has been employed.

Required:

1. Prepare a schedule showing the allocations of the materials price and usage variances to the affected accounts so that they will reflect approximate average actual materials cost.
2. Prepare the general journal entry (or entries) to adjust the accounts.

19. The Earnshaw Manufacturing Company produces a single product. The standard costs for materials and labor total $15.60 per unit of product. The flexible budget allows $1.80 per machine hour for variable overhead and $900,000 per year for fixed overhead. Normal volume is 300,000 machine hours per year. During 1966, the company was shut down by a strike for five months. Actual cost and production data for 1966 are as follows:

Actual output volume—60,000 units of product
Standard input volume—180,000 machine hours
Actual input volume—190,000 machine hours
Actual variable overhead—$350,000
Actual fixed overhead—$900,000
Sales—50,000 units of product @ $50
Variable nonmanufacturing expenses—$300,000
Fixed nonmanufacturing expenses—$500,000

There are no materials or labor variances for 1966. Ignore income taxes.

Required:

1. Compute as many overhead variances as you can, under the assumption that the company uses absorption costing.
2. Prepare an income statement for 1966 in the absorption costing format.
3. Assuming now that the company consistently employs variable costing, prepare an income statement for 1966 in that format.

20. The Frangipani Drug Company produces a patented cough syrup in its Muncie plant. The standard cost sheet for one case of twenty-four 4-ounce bottles is as follows:

Raw materials:		
Glycerine—60 ounces @ $.06	$3.60	
Alcohol—8 ounces @ $.15	1.20	
Cherry flavoring—32 ounces @ $.05	1.60	
Bottles—25 @ $.03	.75	$ 7.15
Direct labor:		
Blending department—⅛ hr. @ $1.60	$ .20	
Bottling department—½ hr. @ $2.10	1.05	1.25
Overhead:		
Blending department:		
Variable—⅛ hr. @ $.72	$.09	
Fixed—⅛ hr. @ $1.84	.23	
Bottling Department:		
Variable—½ hr. @ $.96	.48	
Fixed—½ hr. @ $1.60	.80	1.60
		$10.00

Normal volume in the blending department is 2,000 labor hours per month and in the bottling department, 8,000 labor hours per month.

The glycerine, alcohol, and flavoring are mixed together in 25-gallon batches in the blending department and then transferred to the bottling department. In the latter department, the mixture is placed by machine into 4-ounce bottles and then is packed in cases of 24 and transferred to the warehouse to await shipment to customers.

During August, 1966, a total of 18,000 cases of cough syrup was prepared and bottled. There were no inventories in process in either department at the beginning or end of the month. Purchases of raw materials during August are summarized as follows:

Glycerine—9,000 gallons @ $7.50
Alcohol—1,250 gallons @ $20
Cherry flavoring—4,800 gallons @ $6.40
Bottles—4,000 gross @ $4.10

Actual materials usage during August was as follows:

Glycerine—8,100 gallons
Alcohol—1,250 gallons
Cherry flavoring—4,800 gallons
Bottles—3,250 gross

The actual payroll included 2,400 hours in the blending department at an average wage rate of $1.68 and 8,500 hours in the bottling department at an average wage rate of $2.22. The actual overhead costs incurred were as follows:

Blending department:
Variable—$1,800
Fixed—$3,900

Bottling Department:
Variable—$8,500
Fixed—$13,000

During August, 16,000 cases of cough syrup were sold at an average price of $28 per case. Variable selling expenses amounted to 10% of sales revenue. Fixed administrative expenses totaled $175,000. The applicable income tax rate is 40%.

Required:

1. Compute as many variances from standard cost for August, 1966 as possible.
2. Prepare general journal entries to record the operating transactions for August.
3. Prepare an income statement for August, 1966.

Chapter 11

COST CONTROL THROUGH VARIANCE ANALYSIS

VARIANCE computation answers the comparatively simple question of by how much actual costs differed from established standard costs. This answer is of significance to management, but only as a starting point from which to pursue the objective of cost control. The more crucial questions remain to be answered. Why did actual costs differ from standard? Was the difference favorable or adverse to the enterprise in view of its basic objective of long-run profit maximization? Who was responsible for the difference? What, if anything, can or should be done about it? These questions cannot be answered by simple mathematical formulas, although mathematical analyses may be useful in answering some of them. Nor are the answers to be found directly in accounting data, although the accounting system may be so structured as to facilitate finding the answers. In this chapter we shall consider some of the problems associated with management's attempts to answer these questions. In doing so, we shall encounter more problems than solutions; but solutions can never be attained until problems have been identified.

CAUSAL ANALYSIS OF VARIANCES

In Chapter 10 we saw that variances may be resolved into components, or elements. The net difference between actual and standard labor costs, for example, may be subdivided into a price component and a quantity component. Merely knowing that the actual price paid for labor services during a particular period exceeded the standard price, however, does not explain why it did. Computing specific variances identifies areas of information for further investigation, but it does not pinpoint reasons for cost differences. In the paragraphs that follow, we shall consider briefly each of the variances computed in Chapter 10 and attempt to suggest some of the types of reasons why they may arise. Specific reasons, however, can be determined only in specific cases.

Materials Price Variance

The materials price variance is simply the difference between the actual price and the standard price paid for raw materials purchased. As it arises at the point of purchase, one might be inclined to take it as an indicator of the efficiency or inefficiency of the purchasing function in a firm. Such a conclusion would be tenuous at best, however, and might prove to be completely erroneous. For example, if the actual price exceeded the standard price because of a marked shift in market conditions, whether temporary or permanent, the resulting price variance might be wholly beyond the control of the purchasing department or, for that matter, of anyone in the firm. If the market price for a particular material has increased by 5% from the level implicit in the firm's price standard and the firm's price variance for the period is 4% in excess of standard, the situation might reflect unusually efficient purchasing practices. Here a nominally unfavorable variance would be traceable ultimately to a combination of uncontrollable circumstances and exceptionally good performance. On the other hand, an unfavorable price variance may reflect the purchasing department's negligence in failing to seek the most advantageous sources of supply. A favorable price variance might be achieved by purchasing from an unreliable supplier, but consequent delivery delays may precipitate a partial shutdown of production facilities and delays in filling customers' orders, if not the actual loss of orders. Such a favorable variance, obviously, is favorable in name only; it is clearly adverse in effect.

A particular price variance or some portion thereof may be attributable to a department other than purchasing. For example, if the foreman of a production department fails to notify purchasing of a shortage of materials on hand, an emergency order may become necessary at a price above standard—perhaps because special handling and airfreight charges must be incurred in order to obtain delivery in time to avert a production stoppage. In this example, a price variance is caused by inefficiency in a materials using department.

In an actual situation, it is likely that several different causes will combine to produce a net price variance. To begin with, variances of different directions and various causes may occur in connection with purchases of different raw materials. Different types of variances may be encountered in connection with successive purchases of a single material. In such a case, the net materials price variance may not be very useful to management. A net variance of $800, for example, may appear negligible when compared with total purchases of $4,000,000. But that net variance may be the algebraic sum of very substantial offsetting favorable and unfavorable variances. Obviously, the apparently negligible net variance here masks significant component variances; and the latter are important to effective cost control.

Materials Usage Variance

A materials usage variance may be traced to a great variety of causes. Excessive usage may be caused by careless handling of materials by production personnel, by inefficient or poorly adjusted machinery, by pilferage, by a tightening of quality control requirements, or by an almost endless list of other possible circumstances and events. Changes in product specifications may cause either favorable or unfavorable usage variances, for which the only solution may be to alter materials usage standards. Purchasing of substandard materials may result in excessive materials consumption. This may or may not be desirable, depending upon the net impact on total cost. For example, a firm's price and usage standards for copper tubing may be based upon purchases of precut pieces of uniform length. The purchasing department may learn that it can effect substantial savings by buying random mill lengths instead, but use of these random length pieces will result in greater amounts of scrap in the factory. The consequent unfavorable materials usage variance may be more than offset by a favorable price variance. If so, the unfavorable usage variance is actually a reflection of a profitable change in policy and will ultimately be eliminated by a change in the materials usage standard to conform to the new policy.

Separate materials usage variances should be determined for each type of material used and for each job order or each production center. Tracing variances to cost centers is at least the beginning of an answer to the question, "Who is responsible for the variances?" Responsibility must be determined before control can be effected.

Labor Rate Variance

A difference between the actual and standard wage rates may be attributed simply to a negotiated wage increase not yet reflected in the standard wage rate. While management may not be pleased about the wage increase, the resultant wage rate variance, as such, is a normal and proper consequence of the change in the rate. Of course, the net labor rate variance should be analyzed according to different classes of laborers. A wage increase may not be uniform among all classes of workers, and variances in different classes may have significantly different causes.

Part of a labor rate variance may be caused by the assignment of higher paid workers to jobs regularly performed by lower paid employees. Such practice is not desirable but sometimes is unavoidable. For example, a temporary reassignment of highly paid workers may be necessary to reduce a production bottleneck. During a period of reduced demand and output, the company may prefer to lay off the lower paid employees and reassign the higher paid ones in order to retain the more highly skilled and, hence, more highly paid members of its work force.

Of the variances considered here, the labor rate variance is probably the least susceptible to direct control by management. This does not mean that its causes are of no interest, however. Knowing the causes of variances assists management in planning future costs as well as in controlling current costs.

Labor Efficiency Variance

It is not unlikely that there are as many possible causes of a labor efficiency variance as there are laborers. A worker's efficiency may be affected by his health, family problems, financial worries, a fellow employee's grievance against management, the World Series, and an almost limitless number of other factors and circumstances. This is not to say, of course, that all labor efficiency variances are caused by changes in workers' operating effectiveness, whether for the better or for the worse. The variance may be caused by the fact that a worker is a trainee on the job; in this case, the variance is really a cost of training rather than of production. The variance may be caused by the introduction of new machinery or tools into the production process. An improved machine may cause a favorable labor efficiency variance until such time as a new time standard can be set. Here, the cost saving is presumably a planned consequence of the purchase of the new machine. Substandard materials, unusual amounts of rework time on units rejected by a production inspector, improper processing in a prior production department, and inadequate supervision may all cause unfavorable efficiency variances. While idle time is usually charged to overhead rather than to direct labor, it is not always possible to account for every minute of idle time correctly. Thus, some of it may show up in the labor efficiency variance.

It would be possible to continue listing potential causes of excess or saved labor time almost indefinitely. A few basic ideas of general validity are more practicable, however. The existence of a labor efficiency variance does not necessarily indicate good or bad performance by workers. Poor planning by management may cause the variance. Also, labor timekeeping, however carefully it may be devised, cannot be perfect. Finally, labor time standards are usually averages set on the basis of test observations of the performances of competent workers. But the "average man" implicit in the resultant standards does not really exist.

Overhead Spending Variance

The flexible budget, upon which the standard overhead rates are based, presumes a particular amount of cost for each item in the budget. For the variable cost items, this amount is expressed as a cost per unit of the relevant measure of volume. For the fixed-cost items, it is a total dollar amount per time period. In either case, if the actual cost incurred differs from the amount presumed in the budget, the difference will be reflected in the spending variance. If, for example, indirect materials cost is greater than budgeted, the excess will appear in the spending variance. That excess may be caused by an increase in the price paid for indirect materials or by an increase in the rate of use thereof or by some combination of the two. Price and usage differences may be traced to the same types of causes as mentioned earlier in connection with direct materials. Similarly, indirect labor cost may differ from the budgeted amount because of rate and/or time differences, which, in turn, may be attributed to any of the causes discussed in connection with direct labor. Power costs may be affected by rate changes and by a difference in the rate of power consumption per unit of volume from the consumption rate assumed in the establishment of the budget. Property tax rates may change from those initially estimated and/or the assessed valuation of the firm's taxable property may be changed.

A change in the depreciation charged to production will be included in the spending variance. Depreciation changes may be caused by changes in the estimated useful lives of depreciable assets or by acquisitions and/or dispositions of depreciable assets. Whatever the cause, it seems questionable to describe a change in depreciation as a *spending* variance; for depreciation is usually considered the classic example of a noncash expense. In pursuing its objective of cost control, management is certain to be aided by a separation of that portion of the overhead spending variance due to a change in the depreciation rate on machinery from the portion due to such causes as excessive usage of indirect materials.

Overhead Efficiency Variance

This variance is concerned exclusively with variable costs, and it abstracts from the question of their deviation from budgeted amounts. It seeks to identify solely the impact upon total variable overhead costs of a difference between the actual and standard input volumes. As mentioned in Chapter 10, this variance can exist only where volume is measured in terms of some input quantity and, consequently, there can be some measurable concept of efficiency. If volume is measured in labor hours, the causes of the overhead efficiency variance will be the same as those of the labor efficiency variance. If, on the other hand, machine hours are used as the volume measure, the causes of the overhead efficiency variance must be sought independently. In a real sense, given its operating capacity, machinery cannot be efficient or inefficient of itself. If a machine is running slower than its normal operating speed, the reason must be human at its ultimate source. The machine operator may be unskilled or unfamiliar with the particular piece of equipment. The plant foreman may be negligent in his observance of the prescribed maintenance schedule. In any event, the overhead efficiency variance is caused not by changes in overhead costs as such but, rather, by changes in the volume of activity requiring the incurrence of overhead costs.

Overhead Budget Variance

The budget variance of the two-variance plan is basically comparable to the spending variance in the three-variance plan. Hence, the discussion of the spending variance above is applicable to the budget variance also. Even where volume is measured in units of output, overhead costs may be influenced somewhat by labor efficiency or inefficiency. Hence, some of the causes of the overhead efficiency variance described in the preceding section may be present in the budget variance.

Overhead Volume Variance

The volume variance is unique among variances from standard cost in that it is caused, in a real sense, by the mechanics of the cost accounting system itself. Since the volume variance relates exclusively to fixed costs, it is encountered only where the absorption costing method is employed. Under variable costing, no fixed overhead would be charged to production at all; hence, there could be no such quantity as standard fixed overhead cost and no variance therefrom. In absorption costing, however, fixed overhead is charged to production. Differences between the actual and budgeted amounts of fixed overhead will appear in the spending (or budget) variance. The volume variance is attributable solely to the fact that a standard fixed overhead rate is computed at a normal volume and is then applied to production at some actual volume which is unlikely ever to be exactly equal to the normal level. For example, if fixed overhead is budgeted at $480,000 and normal volume is set at 150,000 direct labor hours, the standard fixed overhead rate will be $3.20. If the standard input volume for a given period totals 160,000 hours, the standard fixed overhead cost will total $512,000. Thus, there will be a $32,000 volume variance. This variance is simply the consequence of applying a standard rate of $3.20 to 10,000 more hours than were presumed when that rate was established. In this case, had the standard fixed overhead rate been set at 160,000 labor hours, it would be $3.00 per hour and there would be no volume variance. In effect, the $3.20 rate is too high in light of the greater than normal volume. The total budgeted fixed costs could be spread over the higher volume of production at a lower rate per unit of volume.

Lest the foregoing discussion suggest that management need not be concerned at all with the volume variance, we should hasten to point out that the cause of the difference between actual and normal volumes may require investigation. If normal volume is an average level of operations over a complete business cycle, management may reasonably expect that it will not be achieved in any one period. Here the real question is why actual volume differed from that planned for the particular period. Volume changes may be attributable to shifts in demand, to labor disputes, to materials shortages, to shortages of working capital, to ineffective marketing practices, to poor product quality, or to any one or combination of a number of other factors. As may be seen quite readily, some of these causes may be within the control of management and some may not be. Some businessmen make the mistake of regarding volume as inherently uncontrollable. Actually, the difference between a successful and an unsuccessful businessman may be their relative abilities to influence their operating volumes.

Problems of Finding Causes of Variances

In the foregoing paragraphs we have mentioned some of the possible causes of variances of actual cost from standard. Identifying actual causes in actual instances may be extremely difficult, if not impossible. Some causes are fairly easily identified—such as machinery breakdowns, wage increases, and usage of substandard materials. Others may be too elusive to be determined specifically. This should not be taken as grounds for despair, of course. It simply means that cost control can never be complete. But some control is infinitely better than none.

REPORTING VARIANCES BY RESPONSIBILITY

Determining the cause of a variance will usually entail the fixing of responsibility for it at the same time. Additionally, in many cases, it is possible to fix responsibility without ascertaining the precise cause of a variance. For example, a labor efficiency variance may be traced to a particular production department fairly readily if cost data are departmentalized. Fixing responsibility for the variance upon an individual department supervisor does not, of course, assure effective control; but it does set the problem at the level at which it may be controllable. Hence, one of the most important facets of a standard cost system is the variance reporting mechanism. This mechanism must be so structured as to get the right information to the appropriate people at the proper time and in the most useful manner.

Reports are expensive. There are costs involved in their preparation, their transmittal, their reading, and their storage. These costs, like all costs in a business enterprise, should be justifiable in terms of profit improvement. Too many reports can be just as bad as too few. It might be possible to report daily all manufacturing variances to all supervisory personnel in a plant. If this were done, however, it is quite likely that the surfeit of information would only confuse the readers of the reports and obscure the truly relevant facts. A much more practicable and useful practice might be to report daily *some* variances to *some* supervisors. Other variances might be reported less frequently and only to selected persons.

Timing of Reports

In some companies it may be both feasible and useful to prepare daily variance reports covering certain variances. Probably these would be relatively large companies, but daily reports might be equally useful in some small organizations. Daily reports are most useful in connection with those variances which may arise and, hence, may be controlled from day to day. This is likely to be particularly true of the materials usage and the labor efficiency variances. It may be equally true of the overhead spending variance, at least as regards some components of it. The latter is such a conglomerate variance, however, that day-to-day control might be prohibitively expensive. Where overhead is applied to production on the basis of labor hours, control of the overhead efficiency variance should be regarded as part of the control of labor efficiency. Even if some materials are purchased each day, it is unlikely that the same materials would be purchased daily. Hence, daily reports of the materials price variance would not appear to be desirable. In some industries, however, daily purchases of the same materials may be common; if so, daily price variance reports may be very useful. The labor rate variance is not likely to lend itself to day-to-day control efforts and, consequently, seems an unlikely candidate for daily reporting. Finally, daily reports of the overhead volume variance would almost certainly be both useless and meaningless. For those variances where daily reporting and control are inapplicable, monthly reports may be adequate. It is not possible to state general rules for the frequency of reporting specific variances. It is pertinent to observe, however, that, once a frequency has been established, reports should be disseminated as promptly as possible. Late reports are of as little value as last week's newspaper.

Addressees of Reports

As a general rule, variance reports should be directed only to those persons in the organization who may reasonably be held responsible for the variances. Thus, a departmental foreman should probably receive reports of materials usage and labor efficiency. If materials prices and labor rates are beyond his scope of authority, there would seem to be little value in reporting price and rate variances to him. While his conduct may on occasion be the cause of price variances (as when he delays requesting a reorder of materials until the stock is so low that an emergency purchase must be made at an unfavorable price), his responsibility in such instance can be fixed without furnishing him copies of all price variance reports. The plant manager should receive reports of all manufacturing variances, with the possible exception of the volume variance, for which he is not likely to be responsible. Reports to him would usually be less detailed than those submitted to the department foremen; the only breakdown may be by departments. If an individual is not responsible for a variance, the only valid reason for reporting it to him would be to broaden his perspective of the enterprise's operating problems. In such case, the report would seem to be a training rather than an operating practice. Variance reports to top corporate management are typically submitted in summary form on a monthly basis. Even if certain variances are reported to immediate supervisors daily, it is unlikely that they would be made available to top management so frequently.

Format of Reports

It is not possible to formulate a standard variance report which might be used by any firm. However, certain fundamental ideas should be considered. Where variances are analyzed by causes in the report, some effort should be made to distinguish between amounts which are and which are not controllable at the level of responsibility to which the report is directed. Controllability is quite often a very difficult concept to identify operationally, but some effort in that direction is likely to be beneficial to management. Comparison of current variances with those of some prior period and/or with those of the year to date is often helpful in establishing a frame of reference within which the current data can be appraised. Variances may be stated as percentages of standard costs, particularly where comparative data are presented. Percentages often afford a more meaningful basis for comparison than do absolute figures. Materials usage and labor efficiency variances may be reported to departmental foremen in terms of physical quantities only. If a foreman knows that his time is excessive on certain operations, it is questionable whether his capacity to control the excess would be improved by his knowing the dollar impact of the excess time on production costs. Finally, variance reports may be more useful in graphic form than in tabular form.[1] If so, the graphic form should be adopted. The ups and downs of a curve of labor efficiency may be easier to understand than a comparative list of excess and saved hours. The variance report is, after all, a means of communicating information; it should be prepared in whatever form best facilitates communication.

VARIANCES FROM BUDGETED COSTS

Thus far in this chapter and in the preceding one, we have been concerned with computing, accounting for, and analyzing variances from standard costs. While such variances are generally useful in the managerial process of cost control, they are not necessarily the most significant bases for control. Often, particular variances will be expected during a future period and will be incorporated into the operating budget for that period. For example, a materials price variance may be budgeted in the anticipation of a temporary market shortage of raw materials. If an unusually large number of trainees will be on the job during a budget period, it would be reasonable to budget an unfavorable labor efficiency variance. And as long as fixed overhead is charged to production (under absorption costing) at a rate established at normal volume, it is quite likely that a volume variance may be budgeted each year; for no one year is likely to be the average year implicit in the concept of normal volume.

Where variances are included in the budgeted manufacturing costs for a period, it would seem that the more significant variances are those not budgeted, that is, those which reflect deviations of actual costs from budgeted levels. For example, a substantial favorable volume variance

[1] See Figure 19–1 in Chapter 19.

may be budgeted in a period of peak business activity. If the actual volume variance is favorable, as compared with standard cost, but is not as great as the budgeted variance, the indication is that actual volume, while still above the normal level, was not as high as originally planned for the period. Thus, there may be an unfavorable variance from the budget included in a favorable variance from standard. (Remember that the terms favorable and unfavorable are used in this context to indicate the direction of a variance, not a qualitative evaluation of it.) Once variances have been included in the formal operating plan for the year, management will be better served by concentrating upon any additional, unplanned variances. A budgeted variance is a part of the operating plan rather than a deviation therefrom. Of course, changing conditions during the budget period may require adjustments to any of the budgeted data, including budgeted variances. As long as the budget is considered a valid basis for planning and control, however, budgeted variances should be considered as parts of the base from which operating deviations are measured rather than as parts of the deviations.

QUESTIONS FOR DISCUSSION

1. The production manager of a manufacturing firm notices that the usage of a particular raw material has consistently exceeded the standard for several weeks. A review of production techniques and product quality control practices indicates that the materials quantity standard for this item is still reasonable and attainable. How might the production manager go about determining the specific cause of this materials usage variance and identifying the person(s) responsible for it?
2. If a labor rate variance can be traced directly to a negotiated increase in wage rates and, accordingly, is regarded as uncontrollable, is there any useful purpose served in reporting it to management? Explain.
3. The price of some commodities are established in well-organized markets and, not infrequently, fluctuate from day to day. An example of such a commodity is wheat. Are materials price standards and price variances practicable techniques for cost control in firms which use such commodities as raw materials? Explain.
4. Where a standard cost system is employed, is "variance control" the same thing as "cost control"? Can management effectively control costs by focusing its attention exclusively upon variances and their control? Discuss.
5. What is the difference between variances from standard costs and variances from budgets? In a firm in which both budgets and standard costs are used, might there be differences between budgeted costs and standard costs for the same items? If so, which variances would be more useful to management for purposes of cost control—variances from the budget or variances from standard costs? Explain.

6. Is the overhead volume variance controllable? If so, by whom? If not, why not?
7. The management of a manufacturing company notices that the variable cost portion of its overhead spending variance is almost invariably favorable when production volume exceeds normal and unfavorable when operations fall below normal volume. Conversely, the fixed cost portion of the spending variance is favorable when operations are below normal volume and unfavorable at volumes above normal. Without further information, what conditions(s) might this situation suggest?
8. Is there any relationship between the analysis of variances from standard production cost and the evaluation of the results of product quality control tests? Is it possible that the results of these two procedures would indicate that a single cause had produced favorable variances and unfavorable product quality or vice versa? If so, illustrate such causes.
9. The Breeden Manufacturing Company, which experiences significant seasonal variations in sales and output, has established the following schedule for reporting variances from standard cost:

   Daily:
   - Materials usage variance
   - Labor efficiency variance

   Monthly:
   - Materials price variance
   - Labor rate variance
   - Overhead spending variance

   Annually:
   - Overhead efficiency variance
   - Overhead volume variance

   Overhead is applied to production on the basis of direct labor hours. Do you feel that the frequency of reporting each of these variances here is appropriate? Explain your answer.
10. Is fixing the responsibility for a variance equivalent to ascertaining its cause? Explain.
11. "In general, materials usage control can be tighter under a job order cost system than under a process cost system." Do you agree or disagree with this statement?
12. Where variable costing is used, should fixed overhead be included in the computation of the overhead spending variance? Explain the reasons for your position.

PROBLEMS

1. The net labor efficiency variance for the stamping department of the Auto-Rite Lamp Corporation for the month of November, 1966 was computed thus:

Standard labor hours	18,200
Actual labor hours	19,400
Excess hours	(1,200)
Standard wage rate per hour	$ 2.50
Unfavorable variance	$(3,000)

The factory superintendent is responsible for all production operations. He asked the stamping department foreman to explain the reasons for the excess labor hours worked in his department. The foreman submitted the following analysis of excess labor time for November:

Standard hours in production		18,200
Excess hours:		
Trainee operating machine	26	
Experienced operator assisting trainee	14	
Rework time on units rejected by inspector	160	
Rework time on job #319: original specifications in error	60	
Raw material received from storeroom too thick	42	
Work done on obsolete standby equipment; regular equipment overloaded	330	
Partial lot run on job #336	10	
Extra set-up time after machine breakdown	8	
Idle time; no production scheduled	450	
Unexplained	320	1,420
		19,620
Hours saved:		
New tools used; more efficient	150	
Consecutive jobs run for same product; no regular set-up time required for second job	30	
Assistant foreman assigned to machine operation for one week	40	220
Actual hours worked		19,400

Required:

Prepare a report analyzing the various causes of this labor efficiency variance. Classify the causes as controllable by the department foreman, controllable by the factory superintendent, or uncontrollable at the factory level. Identify those causes which you believe should be pursued further by management. Suggest remedies for unfavorable controllable variances. Discuss any further action that might be taken in connection with uncontrollable variances.

2. Die casting in the North Bend Tool & Die Co. is performed in three separate but basically identical departments. The company's management believes that its total volume is too great to be handled efficiently in a single department. Monthly materials usage reports are prepared to compare the three departments. These reports detail standard usage, actual usage, and the variance for the current month and for the year to date. A tabular summary of the data reported in the first half of 1966 is presented as follows:

	Tons of Metal		
	Standard Usage	*Actual Usage*	*Variance*
Department 1:			
January	11,000	10,800	200
February	11,400	11,400	
March	11,800	11,900	(100)
April	12,000	12,250	(250)
May	11,500	11,800	(300)
June	12,300	12,750	(450)
Department 2:			
January	11,600	12,700	(1,100)
February	11,500	12,200	(700)
March	11,900	12,600	(700)
April	12,200	12,500	(300)
May	12,500	12,600	(100)
June	12,500	12,300	200
Department 3:			
January	12,000	12,200	(200)
February	12,700	12,800	(100)
March	11,800	11,500	300
April	11,400	11,600	(200)
May	12,000	11,800	200
June	12,400	12,500	(100)

Required:

Draft a report in what you believe to be the best form for purposes of a comparative analysis of the operating efficiencies of the three departments with respect to materials usage during the first half of 1966.

3. Refer to Problem 11 in Chapter 10. Discuss the significance of each of the variances computed in that problem in the light of the information available. Identify any special circumstances that should be taken into consideration by management in evaluating these variances.

4. Refer to Problem 16 in Chapter 10. The output of the forging department of the Scott Engine Company in that problem is substantially below the budgeted annual output. Can the effects of this reduced volume on costs be measured within the framework of the standard cost system employed by the company? Explain.

5. Refer to Problem 19 in Chapter 10. Discuss alternative presentations of the overhead volume variance computed in that problem under absorption costing. Which alternative would be most useful to management in this situation? Are similar alternatives available under variable costing? Discuss.

Chapter 12

CONTROL OF NONMANUFACTURING COSTS

THE DISCUSSIONS in the preceding three chapters have been concerned almost exclusively with procedures for effective planning and control of manufacturing costs. This relative emphasis upon production costs reflects typical business practice. American industry has long been production oriented, and the most notable efforts toward efficiency and cost control have been directed at manufacturing operations. Recently, there has been increasing interest in extending these efforts into nonmanufacturing areas. The costs of distributing goods and services, of administering large and complex organizations, and of conducting significant research comprise a large and generally increasing portion of the total costs of business enterprises and of our gross national product. That portion is too great to ignore or to dismiss with glib generalities as to the impossibility of precise controls. In general, the same types of control procedures applicable to manufacturing costs are pertinent to nonmanufacturing operations, with more or less adaptation. It is, of course, true that nonmanufacturing costs present certain problems quite different from those encountered in manufacturing operations. It is equally true that the manufacture of furniture on job orders differs considerably from the refining of oil, normally accounted for by a process cost system. Nevertheless, the same basic cost accounting and control techniques are employed in both of these production operations. The same fundamental techniques may be adapted to meet the particular problems of nonmanufacturing activities. The different problems do not invalidate the basic methods of handling them.

PECULIAR PROBLEMS OF NONMANUFACTURING COSTS

The relatively high degree of controllability of manufacturing costs is typically ascribed to the routine and repetitive nature of manufacturing operations. The Industrial Revolution largely ended the individual work of the artisan and replaced it with mass production. Manufacturing operations became standardized and, hence, manufacturing costs lent themselves to standardization. As a rule, nonmanufacturing operations have been considered to be nonstandard; and their costs, consequently, have been treated as immune to the control techniques applied to production costs. To be sure, there are many nonmanufacturing activities which most probably can never be routinized. The conduct of directors' meetings and the retail sale of women's hats, for example, are probably inherently nonstandard; no two may ever be the same. There are, however, a great many nonproduction operations which are routine and repetitive. Also, there are many nonroutine operations which appear to be quite susceptible to control.

We shall consider briefly some of the problems peculiar to costs of distribution, administration, and research and development. Financial costs are chiefly interest costs and, as such, are controlled as part of the firm's decisions to obtain and invest capital. They will not be considered at this point.[1]

Distribution Costs

Distribution encompasses a wide range of activities, and there is no clearly defined and generally accepted distinction between distribution and other functions. For example, are credit losses (bad debts) distribution or financial costs? Are sales-training programs distribution or administrative costs? Perplexing though these questions may be, it is not necessary that they be answered in order for management to control the costs involved. For purposes of discussion here, we shall classify distribution costs in three categories, direct selling, promotion, and customer servicing. The boundaries between these three categories are admittedly vague, but also unimportant to our basic purpose in the discussion.

Direct Selling Costs. Direct selling costs include those incurred in the course of actually making sales (or attempting to make sales) to customers. They would include such things as salesmen's commissions and salaries, salesmen's travel expenses, and the costs of operating sales and display facilities. In the long run, of course, such costs must be related to and justifiable in terms of results, that is, sales. For purposes of short-run control, however, these costs may be more effectively related to effort than to accomplishment. Travel expenses, for example, may vary greatly among salesmen and among time periods in relation to sales

---

[1] Capital costs will be considered in Chapter 16.

volume, whether measured in units or in dollars. However, they may bear readily definable and logical relationships to calls made and miles traveled. In the long run, of course, calls made must be translatable into sales revenue if the calls are to be justified. In the short run, however, the frequency and duration of calls are usually established as a matter of policy. Given such a policy, travel expenses should be largely controllable in terms of calls and mileage. For purposes of long-run control, the policy itself must be evaluated in light of actual and anticipated sales.

Promotional Costs. Costs of promotion are intended to stimulate demand for the company's products and/or services. Hopefully, this demand will then be translated into actual sales. Promotion includes such things as advertising, premium offers, contests, and catalogs. It is very difficult to relate these costs to actual sales, because they are intended to stimulate future sales. Even after the fact, it is seldom possible to trace specific amounts of sales to particular promotional projects. Hence, the costs of such projects are unlikely to be controllable in terms of any measure of sales volume. Advertising costs may be related to measures of coverage, such as the number of readers or viewers reached per dollar of advertising expenditure. Such measures are useful for purposes of evaluation and comparison of alternatives, but they are not readily convertible into measures of sales volume.

While promotional costs may not be easily controllable against some volume criterion, they may well be reasonably controllable in total. In one sense, such costs are wholly discretionary; management decides what promotion will be done and, consequently, what it will cost. Realistically, of course, factors of competition necessitate a great deal of promotional expenditures. Much advertising, for example, is regarded as chiefly defensive, intended to retain present customers more than to attract new ones. Thus, in a practical sense, not all promotional efforts may properly be considered discretionary. Nevertheless, management must decide how promotion costs are to be incurred and in what amounts. These decisions should be justifiable in terms of some financial analysis as well as on the grounds of competition. To the extent that promotional campaigns are expected to enhance sales of two or more future periods, they should be evaluated as long-term capital investment projects.[2]

Customer Servicing Costs. Customer servicing is used here to include all functions attendant upon sales, such as billing, shipping, credit analysis, handling customers' claims and complaints, etc. Many of these operations, notably billing, may be very routine and repetitive and may

[2] See Chapter 16.

lend themselves to the same types of cost control techniques applied to production activities. These customer servicing functions are likely to be departmentalized and, therefore, may be fairly readily controlled by means of departmental budgets.

A number of other costs usually associated with the distribution function in a firm are actually administrative costs. This would be true of such items as the salaries of the vice-president for marketing, the sales manager, and others in top management positions. These types of costs are regarded here as elements of administration and will be discussed in the following section.

Administrative Costs

The twentieth century has witnessed a significant increase in the number of white-collar, or administrative workers relative to blue-collar, or production workers. Since most administrative personnel are on weekly or monthly salaries and typically are laid off only in unusual circumstances, the total labor cost of most American enterprises has become increasingly fixed in amount. Guaranteed annual wages and other wage continuation plans for production workers have accentuated this movement from variable to fixed labor costs. Many nonlabor administrative costs, such as the costs of occupying office space, are also fixed. Thus, the greater portion of total administrative cost in any given firm is likely to be insensitive to fluctuations in either production or sales volume and, hence, uncontrollable in relation to volume. This does not mean that fixed administrative costs are inherently uncontrollable. The overall amount of such costs should be justified in terms of efficient and profitable operations. To the extent that administrative costs are fixed and continuing in amount, they may be evaluated as capital investment decisions. This approach is particularly appropriate in view of the fact that experience shows administrative organizations commonly continue to expand but seldom shrink.

Not all administrative costs are fixed, however. Some vary in proportion to the volume of administrative work done. For example, the payroll department may be considered as part of the administrative organization. Part of the cost of preparing and distributing periodic payrolls varies with the number of payroll checks prepared. Even where the number of checks prepared is constant (reflecting a highly stable labor force), the volume of checks may afford a useful basis for evaluating and controlling payroll department costs. Stenographic costs may be controllable, at least partly, on the basis of the number of letters, reports, memoranda, and other documents prepared.

Research and Development Costs

Research costs are among the most difficult to trace to any specific measures of accomplishment; yet they may be among the most important costs in some firms, notably in the drug industry. True research efforts, by definition, can benefit only the future revenues of the firm. Even scientifically fruitful research may have no immediately identifiable implications for enterprise profit. To the extent that product development efforts are concerned with future developments and new products, they may be regarded in the same way as research. On the other hand, product development that relates only to the testing and improvement of currently marketed products should be traceable to current revenues and revenues of the very short-term future.

Many business firms are now wrestling with the problem of how much to spend on research and development. Unfortunately, the best answer to that question lies in the unknowable future. Efforts to base research and development outlays upon indicators of current operations may be dangerous. Some firms, for example, have sought to budget research and development spending as a percentage of sales. Logically, this appears to be a somewhat backward approach to the problem. One would expect sales to be determined, partially, by research and development efforts; basing the latter upon the former seems to suggest just the opposite relationship. Actually, sales are probably selected as the basis for research and development outlays on the grounds that they indicate the firm's ability to make such expenditures. But research should be a function of need as well as of ability to spend. Perhaps the company with declining sales has the greatest need for rising research and development outlays. To some degree, the need for expenditures to improve future operations may vary inversely with the ability to make them. Obviously, the ability to spend and the availability of capital cannot be ignored in planning research and development programs; but these must not be the only determining factors. In practice, research and development costs are probably best predicated upon a combination of such factors as future product needs, industrial trends, competitors' actions, and available resources. None of these factors, incidentally, is subject to precise measurement—particularly the first one, which is probably the most important.

A Note on Accounting for Research and Development Costs. Most firms making significant and recurring expenditures for research and development today account for those outlays as current expenses. Where such expenditures are fairly uniform from year to year, this practice has been defended on the grounds of consistency and simplicity. If the benefits from research programs flow to the firm in a fairly constant stream, this accounting practice would appear conceptually valid. Actually, however, the fruits of research efforts are more likely to appear sporadically. Five years' cost and effort may go into a program that ultimately results in a new product. The generally accepted accounting principle of matching related revenues and costs would require that those research costs be deferred (in an asset account) until such time as revenues are realized from sales of the new product. Then the research costs should be amortized (i.e., transferred from the asset to an expense account) over the market life of the new product. Not all research efforts bear fruit, of course. Some may be continued over several years and ultimately abandoned. The costs of such projects should be deferred until they have been identified as nonbeneficial; then they should be written off as nonoperating losses. The accounting procedures recommended here involve greater problems of estimation and classification than the practical expedient of expensing all research and development costs in the period incurred, but they also offer the promise of more meaningful cost analyses and financial statements.

FLEXIBLE BUDGETS FOR NONMANUFACTURING COSTS

Measures of Volume

For certain nonmanufacturing operations, it is entirely reasonable that cost control can be effected by means of departmental flexible budgets, much in the manner of factory overhead costs. In order for flexible budgets to be operative, it is essential that the operations of the department be expressible in terms of some measure of volume that bears a significant relationship to the costs incurred in the department. A significant amount of the total departmental cost must vary in reasonably direct proportion to the volume measure selected. A flexible budget comprising only fixed costs would be no more useful than a static budget and would provide little basis for short-term cost control. Some selling expenses are likely to vary in proportion to sales volume. This is, of course, true of salesmen's commissions. It may also be true, although not so closely, of such expenses as credit losses and packaging and shipping. Other nonmanufacturing costs, such as billing and stenographic costs, may exhibit considerable degrees of variability with respect to some specialized concept of volume applicable only to the particular operation. Such volume measures are frequently called *work units.* Examples are bills prepared, invoices typed, lines on invoices typed, and letters typed. Conceptually, the number of lines in letters typed might be a more precise measure of stenographic volume; but the time consumed in actually measuring volume—counting lines—would probably invalidate the additional precision. The number of lines (items) on invoices typed, on the other hand, must be checked anyway and would be a feasible measure of volume if the number of invoices were considered too imprecise.

Cost Behavior

Once a relevant volume measure is selected for a particular department, all departmental costs are then stated in terms of that measure. Variable costs are stated as rates per unit of volume and fixed costs, as total dollar amounts. Semivariable costs are resolved into variable and fixed components by one of the methods described in Chapter 9 in connection with overhead.

Table 12–1 is an illustration of a flexible budget for the packing and

TABLE 12–1

REGAL PRODUCTS CORPORATION

Monthly Expense Budget

Department Packing and shipping — Approved 12/16/65

Supervisor Rex Edipos

	Variable Rate per Cwt.	*Fixed Cost per Month*				
Measure of volume Hundredweight handled			1,400	1,500	1,600	1,700
Controllable costs:						
Cartons	$1.10		$ 1,540	$ 1,650	$ 1,760	$ 1,870
Packing supplies	.30		420	450	480	510
Packing labor	1.20		1,680	1,800	1,920	2,040
Shipping labor	.65	$ 400	1,310	1,375	1,440	1,505
Clerical labor	.35	360	850	885	920	955
Freight charges	3.60		5,040	5,400	5,760	6,120
			10,840	11,560	12,280	13,000
Noncontrollable costs:						
Supervision		1,600	1,600	1,600	1,600	1,600
Heat, light, and power		800	800	800	800	800
Janitorial services and maintenance		650	650	650	650	650
Space occupancy		750	750	750	750	750
			3,800	3,800	3,800	3,800
Total costs	$7.20	$4,560	$14,640	$15,360	$16,080	$16,800

shipping department of the Regal Products Corporation. Volume is measured in hundredweights shipped. This measure was selected because there are significant differences in the weights of the company's several products, and these differences are reflected in the time and effort required to pack and ship them. If all products were substantially similar, units shipped might be used as the volume measure. The departmental cost items are classified as controllable and noncontrollable at the level of the department supervisor. Most of the items in this budget are self-explanatory and require no special comment. The fact that packing labor is treated as a wholly variable costs suggests that personnel who do packing work are reassigned to other jobs when there is a slack in the packing and shipping department. An alternative possibility would be that they are sent home when the orders for the day have been packed, regardless of the time. Evidently some portions of the shipping and the clerical labor are not so flexible, for these items are partly fixed. Space occupancy includes taxes, insurance, depreciation, and maintenance on the portion of the corporation's building occupied by the department. Like any flexible expense budget, this one may be reduced to its basic terms and stated simply as a budgeted cost of $4,560 per month plus $7.20 per hundredweight handled.

Departmental Expense Reports

Where flexible budgets are used for nonmanufacturing operations, periodic expense reports for those operations may be prepared and compared with the budget as a basis for managerial appraisal and control. Such a report is illustrated in Table 12–2 for the packing and shipping department of Regal Products Corporation. This report is for the month of January, 1966. Actual volume for the month was 1,440 hundredweight. The budgeted monthly volume for 1966 was 1,600 hundredweight. The actual costs incurred during January are compared with the budgeted costs for the actual volume. The differences make up the spending variance, developed on an item by item basis. The total budgeted cost for the actual volume is then compared with the budgeted cost for the budgeted volume; this difference is the volume variance. These are variances of actual costs from budgeted costs, not from standard costs. Hence, the variances in this report are equivalent to those developed in Table 9–2 in Chapter 9, not to those explained and illustrated in Chapter 10. Since this is the first month of the year, no data are given for the year to date. Other comparative data might be presented, of course. January, 1966 might be compared to January, 1965 or any other period for which comparison is believed relevant.

TABLE 12–2

REGAL PRODUCTS CORPORATION
Monthly Expense Report

Department Packing and shipping — Month of January, 1966

Supervisor Rex Edipos

	Actual Cost	*Budgeted Cost*	*Spending Variance*
Hundredweight handled	1,440	1,440	
Controllable costs:			
Cartons	$ 1,675	$ 1,584	$ 91
Packing supplies	445	432	13
Packing labor	1,704	1,728	(24)
Shipping labor	1,412	1,336	76
Clerical labor	900	864	36
Freight charges	5,046	5,184	(138)
Total	$11,182	$11,128	$ 54
Noncontrollable costs:			
Supervision	$ 1,600	$ 1,600	
Heat, light, and power	820	800	$ 20
Janitorial services and maintenance	675	650	25
Space occupancy	750	750	
Total	$ 3,845	$ 3,800	$ 45
Total costs	$15,027	$14,928	$ 99
Budgeted cost for actual volume (1,440 cwt.)		$14,928	
Budgeted cost for budgeted volume (1,600 cwt.)		16,080	
Volume variance		$(1,152)	

STANDARD NONMANUFACTURING COSTS

Only infrequently have standard costs been used to control nonmanufacturing costs. There seem to be two reasons for this. First, standard costs have generally been considered as bases for inventory valuation as well as devices for cost control; and nonmanufacturing costs are not charged to inventory accounts. Second, and probably more important, standard costs are applicable only to routine and repetitive operations. Rightly or wrongly, businessmen have generally concluded that nonproduction operations are not sufficiently standardized themselves to admit of useful standard costs. Actually, there is probably a great deal of standardization in nonmanufacturing activities; and standard costs are feasible for many such activities. The unpopularity of standard costs in this area is probably attributable largely to the fact that business management has found that satisfactory cost control can be achieved by means of budgets. Despite the infrequent use of nonmanufacturing standard costs in current business practice, it will be useful to consider briefly how such standard costs might be developed and applied.

Price and Quantity Standards

As explained in Chapter 5, standard costs for direct materials and labor are derived from price and quantity input standards. This method of derivation assumes a direct functional relationship between units of output and quantities of input. Expressed another way, it means that materials and labor costs are variable in direct proportion to output. In order for standards to be useful in the area of nonmanufacturing costs, there would have to be some significant amount of such costs which varied in proportion to some readily identifiable measure of volume. For example, it might be reasonable and practical to establish wage rate and time standards for a shipping clerk or for a deliveryman. Shipping and packing materials may readily admit of price and usage standards.

For a great many nonmanufacturing operations, input standards could not be established. This is true of any fixed cost and of any cost which cannot readily be related to some measurable concept of volume. For example, a company's experience may show that much of the accounting department's cost varies in reasonable direct proportion to dollar sales volume. This fact may be useful in budgeting accounting costs, but it does not suggest some functional relationship between sales dollars and accounting department cost that is expressible as an input standard. The utility of nonmanufacturing standards will differ among companies and among industries, depending upon the amount of routine, repetitive work done and upon the ease of measuring that work in terms of standard units of output.

Standard Costs and Flexible Budgets

Overhead standard costs are based upon flexible budgets rather than upon price and quantity standards. Technically, there is no reason why similar standard costs cannot be determined for any operation for which a flexible budget can be prepared. For example, standard shipping and packing rates per hundredweight handled could be computed very easily from Table 12–1. If normal volume were set at 1,600 hundredweight per month, the standard fixed rate would be $2.85 per hundredweight ($4,560 ÷ 1,600). The standard variable rate would be $7.20 regardless of volume. From the viewpoint of management, the important question is whether such standard costs are more useful than the flexible budgets alone, not whether their calculation is feasible. It is very doubtful that variances from standard packing and shipping costs in this instance would be more beneficial to cost control efforts that the variances from the budget computed in Table 12–2. Unless there is some definite advantage in recording standard costs for nonmanufacturing operations—and, as suggested in the preceeding section, this seems unlikely—flexible budgets themselves seem to be sufficient techniques for cost control.

DISTRIBUTION COST ANALYSIS

Cost control necessarily presumes some prior causal analysis of costs. If a particular cost is deemed to be excessive, management must attack the problem at its source. That source must be identified very specifically. We shall consider here some examples of source analysis of distribution costs. Similar analyses may be performed for administrative and for research and development costs.

Distribution cost analysis requires that the distribution function of the enterprise be subclassified into categories or types of operations to which distribution costs may be traceable logically and practically. The following are illustrations of such subclassifications:

1. Product lines.
2. Sales territories.
3. Channels of distribution.
4. Sizes of customers' orders.

The particular categories selected in one firm depend, of course, upon the nature and problems of its operations. The four categories listed above, it should be noted, are not mutually exclusive. Each classification will encompass all distribution activities. Some distribution costs are directly traceable to a particular classification. Others are only indirectly associated with that classification, but they may be directly traceable to some other category. Thus, these classifications are used here as costing units to identify direct and indirect costs. Direct costs with respect to one costing unit may be indirect with respect to other units. The distinction between direct and indirect costs in this context is very important to effective cost control. In the paragraphs that follow, we shall discuss a few specific distribution cost items in relation to the four classifications of sales listed above.

At one extreme in the spectrum of cost traceability, or directness, are salesmen's commissions. These are determined directly by sales, and, hence, they are directly traceable to any classification of sales. If sales can be identified by product lines, by territories, by channels of distribution, and by sizes of customers' orders, so can commissions. If salesmen are paid straight salaries, however, this universal traceability disappears. If each salesman is assigned to a single territory, then sales salaries may be related to and controlled by territories. Assuming that customers placing orders of varying sizes buy all of the firm's products through various channels of distribution in each territory, salesmen's salaries would be indirect costs in relation to each of the other three classifications under consideration here.

Advertising costs may be direct or indirect with respect to almost any of the sales categories listed. Costs of advertisements for individual products are directly traceable to product lines. Some advertising costs may be traceable directly to particular channels of distribution. As an illustration, assume that a manufacturing company sells its products to wholesalers, to retailers, and directly to consumers. Catalogs sent only to wholesalers and advertising in wholesaling periodicals appear logically traceable to the first channel of distribution. Advertising directed toward ultimate consumers, on the other hand, cannot be traced to any one channel. Increased consumer demand may reasonably be expected to stimulate sales through all three channels of distribution, but the effects upon specific channels probably could not be quantified.

Costs of certain routine operations of servicing customers may be expressed as budgeted rates per volume of activity, as explained earlier in this chapter. By means of such rates, these costs may be traced to sales territories, to channels of distribution, and/or to customers by order size. The last-mentioned possibility may be particularly useful to management in evaluating the relative costs of serving customers who place large and small orders. While these costs may be uniform per order, they may be much less per sales dollar for large orders than for small ones. Such information may be useful not only in seeking to optimize company profit but also in allowing quantity discounts to customers who place large orders.[3]

The discussions in the foregoing paragraphs, obviously, are intended to be illustrative rather than exhaustive. They suggest the types of relationships which may be determined to exist between subclassifications of operating functions and specific cost items. Merely tracing a cost to some particular segment of the firm, however, does not mean that the cost is thereby controlled or even controllable. Tracing salesmen's salaries to sales territories, for example, does not, of itself, provide any basis for saying whether the cost is appropriate or excessive; nor does it answer the question of how excessive salaries may be reduced. But it does

---

[3] The importance of cost in this connection will be discussed in Chapter 17.

direct management's attention to the area in which the problem exists. Conversely, the fact that a cost cannot be traced to any subclassification of the distribution function—as is likely in the cases of the general sales manager's salary and of institutional advertising—does not mean that the cost is inherently uncontrollable. The type of analysis presented here is only one approach to cost control.

PROSPECTS FOR IMPROVED CONTROL

Manufacturing cost controls are fully matured business practices. They have been included in management's bag of profit control tools for many years. Rarely have they been extended into the area of nonmanufacturing costs, however; and even the present movement in that direction is a slow one. The slowness of this movement may be attributed partly to the admitted difficulties of measuring nonmanufacturing volume and correlating costs thereto. It seems inevitable that a sense of urgency in this connection must arise, however. Business organizations have gone through periods of special concern for particular facets of enterprise operations—finance, production, and, most recently, organizational and administrative theory. Certainly, none of these areas of managerial concern will disappear or even greatly diminish in the future. There are, however, indications of an increasing awareness of and concern for problems of distribution. As distribution occupies more and more of management's time and efforts, effective methods for planning and controlling its costs will be demanded. The demand will be met. New measures of volume and of cost-volume relationships, once thought too difficult to determine, may be selected and analyzed quickly and accurately by the use of computers. Automation, currently considered primarily as a manufacturing phenomenon, will spread to many facets of the distribution and administration processes. With it, necessarily, will come greater routinization and control of these processes. The demand for improved control of nonmanufacturing operations and costs is inevitable. Accountants must prepare to assume their share of the responsibility for meeting this demand.

QUESTIONS FOR DISCUSSION

1. Discuss the problems associated with the establishment of useful standard costs for nonmanufacturing operations.
2. "Direct selling costs are wholly uncontrollable, as they are incurred as a direct and inescapable consequence of sales. Promotional costs, on the other hand,

are wholly controllable; for they are incurred at the discretion of management." Comment on these assertions.

3. Suggest some useful criteria for the planning and control of research and development costs in a manufacturing corporation. Rank these criteria in what you believe to be their order of importance. Justify your selection of the most important criterion.
4. How would you go about establishing a flexible expense budget for the cost accounting department of a manufacturing corporation? Compare this process with that of establishing a similar budget for one of the corporation's production departments.
5. "As a general rule, the controllability of a cost is a function of its directness and its variability. Thus, a direct cost is more controllable than an indirect cost; and a variable cost is more controllable than a fixed cost." Do you agree with this statement? Explain your position.
6. Suggest work units that might be practical measures of the operating volumes in the nonmanufacturing departments listed below. Briefly explain why each work unit suggested was chosen. If you believe no practical measure of departmental volume is available, explain your reasons.
   a. Customer billing department.
   b. Stenographic pool.
   c. Maintenance department.
   d. Plant first-aid station.
   e. Company-owned electric power plant.
7. Indicate whether you would expect each of the costs listed below to be direct or indirect with respect to each of the following classifications of distribution costs: (1) product lines; (2) sales territories; (3) channels of distribution; and (4) sizes of customers' orders.
   a. Salesmen's travel expenses.
   b. Accounts receivable posting.
   c. Shipping and postage charges on merchandise sold.
   d. Printing and distribution of price lists and catalogs.
   e. Bad debts.
8. For purposes of further discussion, accept the following statement as a valid proposition: "Costs are controllable at three stages of business planning. (1) Virtually automatic control of some costs is provided by the volume of operations. (2) Some costs are controllable by management decisions within relatively short spans of time (e.g., less than a year). (3) Finally, some costs are controllable only at long and irregular intervals; these are costs incurred as a direct consequence of long-term investment decisions." Within the context of this proposition, what would be the stage of controllability of each of the following costs:
   a. Advertising materials.
   b. Office supplies.
   c. Insurance on office building and equipment.
   d. Sales commissions.
   e. Depreciation on salesmen's automobiles.
   f. Research costs.

If you believe any of these costs is controllable at two or more stages of planning, so indicate. Be prepared to justify your answers.

9. "Technical advances in business information systems and data processing will ultimately provide the same degree of control over nonmanufacturing costs as over manufacturing costs." Do you agree or disagree with this prediction? Why?

PROBLEMS

1. The Maniplex Corporation's management believes that its planning and control of nonmanufacturing costs are far less efficient than its procedures for production costs. Accordingly, it is seeking to establish departmental budgets and standards for nonmanufacturing operations. The facts outlined below are developed from a study of the costs incurred in the purchasing department.

The purchasing department's supervisor receives a monthly salary of $1,800. His secretary receives $360 per month. Three purchasing clerks are paid monthly salaries of $500 each. Typists are paid $1.50 per hour. The standard six-part purchase order form used costs $.06 per set; one set is used for each purchase order issued. On the basis of past experience, it is estimated that approximately 10% of the sets started are spoiled and have to be torn up and thrown away. Typing supplies are estimated to cost $.18 per hour of typing time. Rent on the office space occupied by the purchasing department is charged on the basis of floor space; this charge amounts to $280 per month. Property taxes on this portion of the building are $360 per year. Labor related costs average 7% of hourly wages and 10% of monthly salaries. During a normal month, approximately 400 purchase orders are issued. The average purchase order contains 12 lines. The typists can type approximately 60 lines per hour. When not working in the purchasing office, these typists are reassigned to the stenographic pool.

Required:

1. Prepare a flexible expense budget for the purchasing department for one month. Include cost allowances for normal volume and for both 80% and 120% of normal volume.
2. Compute the standard purchasing cost per unit of volume.

2. A study of the costs of the payroll department of the Amplifile Company for 1965 shows the following statistics:

Month	*Pay Checks*	*Cost*
January	14,800	$6,480
February	15,100	6,520
March	15,250	6,550
April	15,700	6,800
May	15,900	6,810
June	17,200	7,040
July	18,000	7,200
August	18,400	7,380
September	16,400	7,000
October	15,900	6,880
November	15,500	6,760
December	15,100	6,690

Approximately the same level of payroll department costs is expected to recur in 1966.

Required:

1. By use of the high-low method, compute flexible budget cost allowances for the payroll department for 1966.
2. Budgeted volume for January, 1966 is 15,500 checks. Actual volume is 14,600 checks. Actual payroll department costs for the month total $6,700. Compute the spending and volume variances *from the budget* for the month of January, 1966.

3. The following flexible expense budget has been set up for the billing department of the Colortone Television Corporation:

	Cost per Customer	*Cost per Month*
Billing clerks	$.20	$1,600
Office supplies	.08	240
Supervision		750
Heat and light		85
Labor-related costs	.02	25
Rent		130
Depreciation on equipment		90
Taxes and insurance		40
Postage	.10	
	$.40	$2,960

Each customer is billed once a month. The billings are prepared and mailed to customers on an alphabetically staggered schedule throughout the month. A total of 3,150 customers were billed during the month of September, 1966. The actual billing costs were recorded as follows:

Billing clerks	$2,260
Office supplies	700
Supervision	750
Heat and light	60
Labor-related costs	91
Rent	130
Depreciation on equipment	105
Taxes and insurance	40
Postage	474
	$4,610

Beginning in September, the company initiated the policy of inserting promotional brochures in the monthly billing envelopes. These brochures weigh 1 ounce each and cost $.06 each for printing; this printing cost is included in the September charge for office supplies.

Required:

Prepare an expense report for the billing department for the month of September, 1966. Analyze any variances from the budgeted costs in whatever manner you feel will be most useful to management.

4. The Research Division of Amalgamated Petrochemicals, Inc., has recently been reorganized and expanded. It is directed by a vice-president for research and development. The chief of research is Dr. Erhardt Schlotz. He is assisted by a research staff of four graduate scientists. In addition, there are twenty laboratory technicians on the staff. The personnel complement of the division is completed by secretaries, maintenance men, watchmen, and janitors. The division occupies its own building in Tulsa.

   The work of the research division is carried on in a series of distinct research projects of widely varying lives. Each project is assigned to the immediate supervision and control of one of the four staff scientists. Each of these men is normally responsible for two or more projects at any one time. Dr. Schlotz, of course, has general responsibility for all research projects. The vice-president in charge of the division is concerned with the administrative aspects of its operation.

   Most projects involve the testing of various materials for desired properties and efforts to develop new materials with the desired characteristics. Some projects require the use of special equipment, which is then sold for scrap when the project is completed. All equipment and materials used in the research division are procured by the company's central purchasing office in Dallas.

   When a project culminates in the development of a new and valuable material, a patent is obtained and the new product is produced and marketed. Many projects, however, result in no useful achievement at all and must be abandoned.

   For the past several years, all costs incurred in the research division have been charged to current expense as they were incurred. As the total costs of research and development have grown rapidly, management has become concerned that this practice may be obscuring the true financial implications of this division. You have been engaged as a management consultant to study the situation and make recommendations.

Required:

   In a report to be submitted to the company's president, outline a plan for the recording and analysis of research costs in this firm. In this report, consider the individual cost items, not merely the total cost. Suggest what you feel to be the best methods of reporting these costs to management and to the readers of the company's published annual financial statements.

5. The Brandex Company has established standard costs for its packing and shipping operation. The standard time allowed for packing and shipping one case of merchandise is .3 man-hour. The costs of packing and shipping are budgeted at $.80 per man-hour plus $4,400 per month. Normal operating volume has been set at 8,000 cases packed and shipped per month. During June, 1966, a total of 6,500 cases were packed and shipped. Labor time records for the month show that 2,120 man-hours were worked. Actual variable costs for the month amounted to $1,750 and actual fixed costs, to $4,550.

Required:

   Compute as many variances from standard packing and shipping cost for June, 1966 as you can.

6. Timespan, Inc., has established standard costs for its invoicing department. The standard costs are set as follows:

Variable cost per invoice prepared	$.35
Variable cost per invoice line typed	.04
Fixed cost per invoice prepared	.25

In a normal year, it is estimated that 32,000 invoices will be prepared. During 1965, 36,000 invoices were prepared. A random sample of 600 invoices showed that the average number of lines typed on an invoice was 7.5. The total fixed cost incurred for invoicing during 1965 was $8,800. The total variable cost was $25,000.

Required:

Compute as many variances from standard invoicing cost in 1965 as you can.

Part III
COSTS FOR DECISION MAKING

Chapter 13

COST-VOLUME-PROFIT RELATIONSHIPS

AS THE title of Part III suggests, the chapters in this part of the book will be concerned with the analysis and application of cost data in specific business decision-making situations. This must not be interpreted to mean that the costs and procedures discussed in the previous parts of the book have no impact upon business decisions. A budget, for example, is a decision in itself; and budgeted costs are integral components of that total decision. Cost control, however effected, requires that specific decisions be made; these decisions must be based primarily upon accumulated cost data, including actual, planned, and standard costs. The same fundamental types of costs are involved in decision-making analysis, but here they are classified and analyzed in accordance with their relationships to the specific facts of the decision at hand. A great many business decisions affect directly the revenues, the costs, and/or the operating volume of the enterprise. Thus, at the outset, it will be useful to examine the relationships among these quantities and the implications thereof for the firm's ultimate objective—profit. At this point, before proceeding, the reader may wish to review the discussion of cost behavior in relation to volume in Chapter 2.[1] Much of the material in this and in the following chapters assumes a full understanding of the natures of variable and fixed costs, as well as of the practical difficulties involved in attempting to identify specific costs as variable or fixed.

Costs identified as variable are assumed to vary in direct proportion to volume, however volume may be measured. Fixed costs are assumed to be absolutely fixed over all significant ranges of volume. So long as these basic assumptions are reasonably valid, the behavior of an enterprise's costs with respect to changes in the volume of its operations can be predicted and analyzed quite accurately. The existence of truly semivariable costs, however, clouds the cost-volume picture. The effective elimination of such costs by one of the methods described in connection with the development of flexible budgets[2] simplifies the analysis but

---

[1] Pages 23 to 27.

[2] Cf., Chapter 9.

also renders it that much less precise. Nevertheless, the usefulness of cost-volume analysis to management justifies this simplification and overrides the degree of imprecision created thereby.

Revenues, like variable costs, are assumed to vary in direct proportion to the volume of units sold. Where sales volume is expressed in terms of sales dollars, it is definitionally equal to revenues (excluding from consideration here such nonoperating revenues as interest, dividends, and rent). As both revenues and variable costs vary directly with volume, the net difference between them—variable profit—must also vary in proportion to volume. Thus, the effects of changes in operating volume may be analyzed simply in terms of a variable profit which varies, in total, in direct proportion to changes in volume (and, hence, is constant per unit of volume) and fixed costs which are constant in total regardless of volume fluctuations. Such analysis is quite simple, but there may be some fairly complicated problems underlying it. The most appropriate measure of volume is not always obvious. In a single product firm, volume may be measured quite readily in terms of units of product. In a multiproduct firm, however, it is more likely that sales volume will be measured in terms of dollar sales and production volume, in terms of some measure of input (e.g., labor hours). Further, the volumes of sales and production are not necessarily equal. Thus, no one volume measure may be a suitable common denominator for total operations. This problem will be discussed further in a subsequent section. Finally, as observed in Chapter 2, the concepts of variable and fixed costs are simple and definite; the task of classifying actual costs as one or the other may be quite difficult, however. The discussions in this and the following chapter will assume that these practical problems have been resolved satisfactorily and will be concerned only with the basic analysis.

BREAK-EVEN ANALYSIS

The most familiar form of cost-volume profit analysis is break-even analysis. In fact, many businessmen and accountants regard these two ideas as synonymous. More precisely, though, the latter is a specific type of the former. Break-even analysis involves the study of revenues and costs in relation to volume and, specifically, the determination of that volume at which the firm's revenues and expenses will be exactly equal. The *break-even point* may be defined as that level of operations at which total revenue is equal to total expense and, hence, net income is equal to zero.

Determining the Break-Even Point

In Units of Product. For a single product firm, the break-even point may be computed very conveniently in terms of units of product. The break-even volume for a given period is the number of units of product that must be sold in order to create enough revenue just to cover all expenses, both variable and fixed. Each unit sold will cover its own variable costs and leave a remainder, the variable profit per unit, to contribute to covering fixed costs. When enough units have been sold so that the total variable profit is equal to the total fixed expenses, the break-even point has been reached. Thus, the break-even volume in units may be expressed algebraically as follows:

$$\text{Break-even volume} = \frac{\text{total fixed costs}}{\text{variable profit per unit}}$$

Assume that a small manufacturing company produces a single product. The selling price is $8 per unit and the variable costs are $5 per unit. These variable costs include all items that vary in proportion to volume—both manufacturing and nonmanufacturing costs. The company's annual fixed costs total $150,000. In order to break even, the company must sell 50,000 units of product annually. This volume is computed as follows:[3]

$$\text{BE} = \frac{\$150{,}000}{\$3} = 50{,}000 \text{ units.}$$

That the company's net income is equal to zero at a volume of 50,000 units may be demonstrated quite easily.

Revenues (50,000 units @ $8)	$400,000
Variable costs (50,000 units @ $5)	250,000
Variable profit	150,000
Fixed costs	150,000
Net income	$ 0

In Dollar Sales Volume. There are few single product companies in our modern industrial society, and most multiproduct firms are not able to measure volume in terms of any common unit of product. Such firms typically express sales volume in terms of total dollar sales. The basic requirement of the break-even point is unchanged, however; total revenue must just cover total expense. In this situation, variable costs

[3] Here and in subsequent illustrations, the abbreviation "BE" is used to represent the break-even volume.

and variable profits are expressed as amounts per dollar of sales or, more simply, as percentages of sales. The break-even volume is then computed by equating total variable profit to total fixed costs, as before. Since the variable profit is a known ratio, or percentage, of total sales revenue, the sales volume necessary to generate sufficient variable profit just to cover fixed costs may be computed thus:

$$\text{Break-even volume} = \frac{\text{total fixed costs}}{\text{variable profit ratio}}$$

Assume that a medium-sized multiproduct manufacturing corporation compiles the following budgeted operating data:

Budgeted sales for one year	$20,000,000
Budgeted variable costs for one year	14,400,000
Budgeted fixed costs for one year	3,920,000

The variable costs can be seen to be equal to 72% of sales; hence, the variable profit is 28% of sales. The break-even volume is then computed as follows:

$$\text{BE} = \frac{\$3{,}920{,}000}{.28} = \$14{,}000{,}000.$$

Proof of this break-even computation is as follows:

Revenues	$14,000,000
Variable costs (72% of $14,000,000)	10,080,000
Variable profit	3,920,000
Fixed costs	3,920,000
Net income	$ 0

As a Percentage of Full Capacity. Many business managers are accustomed to thinking of their firm's operations in terms of percentages of full productive capacity. Full capacity is usually defined as the greatest volume presently attainable, given the firm's production facilities, operating policies, and practices; this concept is sometimes termed *practical capacity.* It is not necessarily the maximum possible volume. Unusual amounts of overtime by both men and machines may stretch a firm's capacity considerably, but ordinarily only for fairly short periods of time. Whatever volume is selected as full capacity, it is established as 100% of capacity. While the break-even point as a percentage of full capacity cannot be determined by direct computation, it may easily be determined indirectly. If the operating volume at full capacity is known in terms of units or dollar sales and the break-even point has been determined in comparable terms, the latter may be stated as a percentage of the former y simply. In the illustration of the single product company above, ume that full capacity is 100,000 units of product. The break-even int, 50,000 units, is reached at 50% of capacity. If full capacity for multiproduct corporation illustrated in the preceding paragraph is at an annual sales volume of $21,000,000 and the break-even sales lume is $14,000,000 the break-even point is achieved at 67% (two-rds) of full capacity.

ak-Even Graphs

Break-even analysis is very commonly presented in graphic form. eak-even graphs can depict the profit-volume position of the firm arly and simply. The traditional break-even graph is illustrated in ure 13–1. This is a graphic depiction of the break-even point

FIGURE 13–1

BREAK-EVEN GRAPH

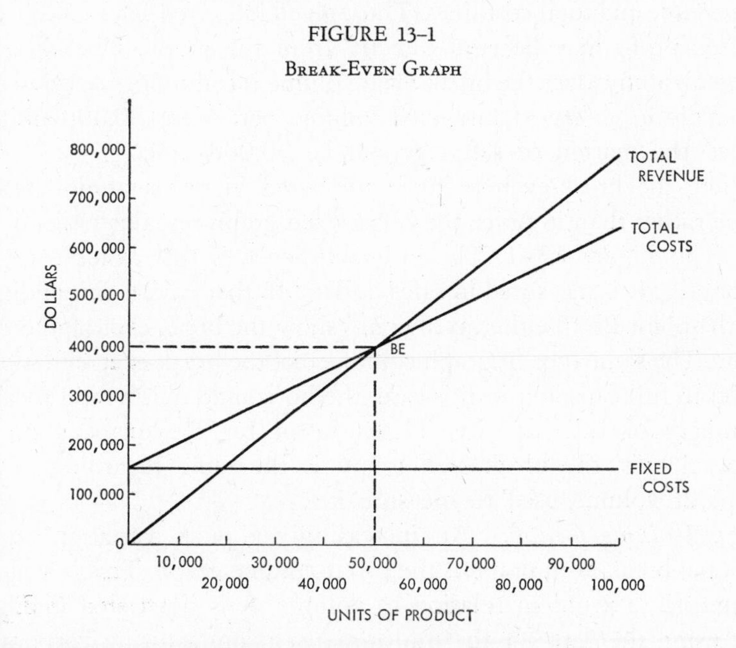

nputed in units of product for the single product firm in the preceding tion. Units of product are measured on the horizontal axis and dollars oth revenues and costs), on the vertical axis. Fixed costs are shown as onstant amount, $150,000, at all levels of operation. Variable costs then plotted over and above total fixed costs. The resultant line is the al cost line, including both variable and fixed costs. There is no iable cost line in the graph; variable costs are depicted as the vertical tance between the fixed-cost and the total cost lines. The total cost at y point is the sum of the $150,000 fixed costs plus the $5 variable cost

per unit of product multiplied by the number of units sold at that poi
Total revenue at any point is the product of the unit price of $8 and t
number of units sold at that point. The upper limits of the graph a
determined on the basis of the firm's full capacity, 100,000 units
product in this illustration. The break-even point (BE) occurs at t
intersection of the total revenue and total cost lines. Dropping
perpendicular from the point BE to the horizontal axis shows the brea
even point in units of product. Dropping a perpendicular from BE to t
vertical axis shows the break-even point in dollar sales volume. Bel
(to the left of) point BE, total costs are higher than total revenue a
operations are unprofitable. Above (to the right of) BE, total reven
exceeds total costs and operations are profitable. The amount of t
profit or loss at any volume is simply the vertical distance between t
total revenue and total cost lines. Thus, given budgeted sales volume, t
budgeted profit may be read directly from the graph. The excess
budgeted volume over the break-even volume is commonly referred to
the *margin of safety.* If budgeted volume here were 80,000 units
product, the margin of safety would be 30,000 units.

Where the break-even point is measured in terms of dollar sa
volume rather than in units, the break-even graph remains basically t
same as in Figure 13–1. The only difference is that volume on t
horizontal axis is measured in sales dollars. In that case, a perpendicu
from the point BE to either axis would show the break-even dollar sa
volume. The same type of graph could depict the break-even situation
relation to full capacity; in this case, the horizontal axis would measu
percentages of full capacity. Thus, except for the quantity on t
horizontal axis, the break-even graph is the same regardless of t
concept of volume used to measure it.

Profit-Volume Graph. An increasingly popular variation on t
traditional break-even graph is the profit-volume graph. This is a plot
an enterprise's profit in relation to volume. It is illustrated in Figu
13–2, using the data for the multiproduct manufacturing corporati
whose break-even point was computed in dollar sales volume earli
Total profit or loss is measured on the vertical axis—profit above t
horizontal axis and loss below it. Volume is measured on the horizon
axis, which is drawn at the point of zero profit (i.e., the break-ev
point). Volume may be expressed in whatever terms desired by manag
ment. Here, it is stated in terms of percentages of full capacity. T
maximum loss, which occurs at a volume of zero, is simply the total fix
costs of the enterprise. As volume increases, a proportionate variab
profit (a negative total profit until the break-even point is reache

appears and increases with it. The operating loss declines and ultimately disappears at that volume at which the total variable profit is equal to total fixed costs—the break-even volume. Beyond this point, there is a positive net income. On this graph, the break-even point is measured on the horizontal axis at the point where that axis is intersected by the profit line.

In Figure 13–2, the total fixed costs and, hence, the maximum loss are $3,920,000. The variable profit rate is 28% of sales. As already demonstrated, this company breaks even at a sales volume of $14,000,000, or two-thirds of the firm's capacity. The graph shows the amount of profit or loss which may be expected at any level of

FIGURE 13–2

PROFIT-VOLUME GRAPH

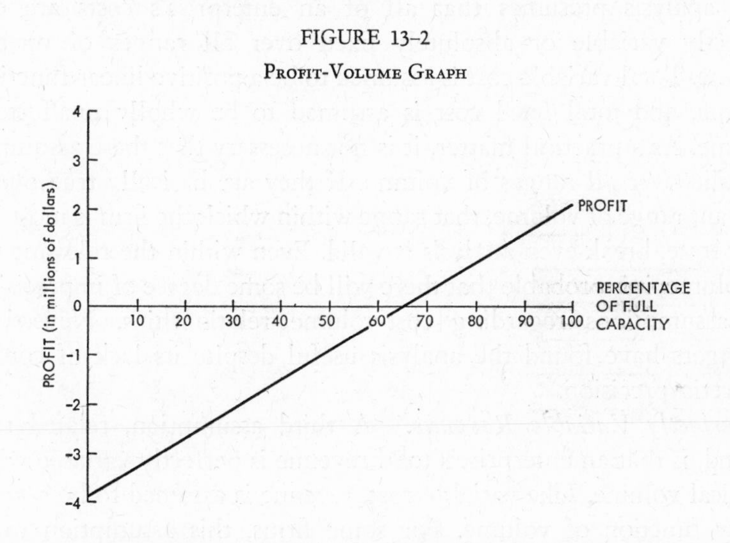

operations. At full capacity, for example, the budgeted profit would be just below $2,000,000 ($1,960,000 to be precise). This profit may be read from the profit-volume graph or computed by applying the variable profit rate (28%) to all sales in excess of the break-even volume. (Sales at full capacity here exceed break-even sales volume by $7,000,000.)

Assumptions Underlying Break-Even Analysis

The validity of the break-even analyses explained and illustrated above is based upon several assumptions. Effective use of break-even analysis demands an appreciation of the significance of each of these assumptions.

Uniform Prices. The assumption that all financial data are comparable underlies all of accounting, not merely break-even analysis. If dollar amounts are to be compared in any meaningful way, the dollars involved should have the same real value (i.e., the same purchasing power). In break-even analysis, the dollars of revenue and the dollars of cost should be uniform in terms of their purchasing powers. Dollars of depreciation on assets acquired in past periods should be adjusted to conform to the current price level before a break-even point is determined. Unfortunately, price-level adjustments are only infrequently made in present business practice. Hence, a great many break-even computations violate the uniform price assumption without even specifically recognizing it.

Completely Predictable Cost Behavior. As is evident in both the formulas and the graphs in the preceding sections, conventional break-even analysis presumes that all of an enterprise's costs are either perfectly variable or absolutely fixed over all ranges of operating volume. Total variable cost is assumed to be a positive linear function of volume, and total fixed cost is assumed to be wholly unaffected by volume. As a practical matter, it is not necessary that these assumptions be valid over all ranges of volume. If they are basically true over the relevant range of volume, that range within which the firm is most likely to operate, break-even analysis is valid. Even within the relevant range of volume, it is probable that there will be some degree of imprecision in the assumptions regarding cost-volume relationships. Nevertheless, managers have found the analysis useful despite its lack of complete theoretic precision.

Perfectly Variable Revenue. A third assumption, related to the second, is that an enterprise's total revenue is perfectly variable with its physical volume. Like variable cost, revenue is assumed to be a positive linear function of volume. For some firms, this assumption may be completely valid; selling prices per unit may be the same at all volumes. For others, however, it is not valid. The same products may be sold to large customers at lower prices per unit than to small customers. Price reductions may be necessary in order to attain high levels of sales volume. Once again, however, the assumption is generally useful and not so unrealistic as to impair the analysis seriously.

Effect of Imperfect Cost or Revenue Behavior. If revenue and/or variable costs are not perfectly variable with physical volume—that is, if they are nonlinear functions of volume—and/or if fixed costs are not absolutely fixed, the revenue and/or cost lines in the break-even graph (Figure 13–1) will not be straight. If one or more of these lines is curved or kinked, it is possible that the total revenue and total cost lines will intersect at two or more points. Such a situation would imply multiple break-even points. These might be caused by a nonlinear revenue function, a nonlinear variable cost function, a fixed-cost line that is other than perfectly horizontal, or by any combination of these circumstances. Figure 13–3 illustrates a graph of multiple break-even points in which each of the three possible circumstances is present. (Notice the similarity between the cost lines in this exhibit and those in Figure 2–2 in Chapter 2.)

The existence of multiple break-even points in Figure 13–3 is caused by three circumstances. First, total revenue is not a perfectly linear function of volume. At 67% of full capacity, the total revenue line is kinked. This reflects the fact that the average net selling price is expected

FIGURE 13–3

ILLUSTRATION OF MULTIPLE BREAK-EVEN POINTS

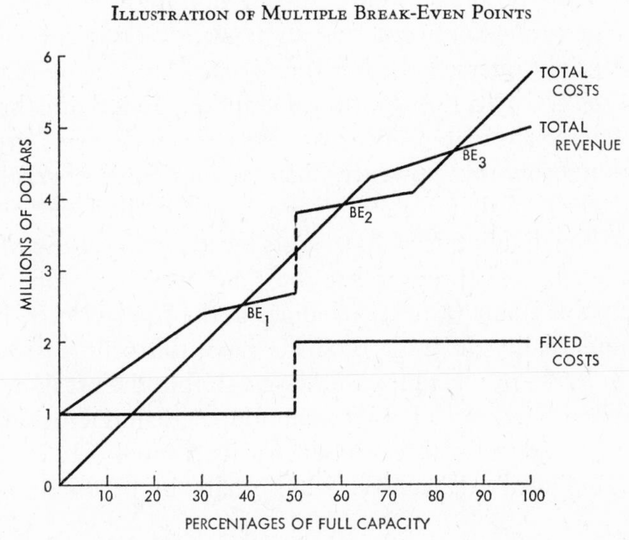

to decrease beyond that level of sales volume. Second, variable costs are not a perfectly linear function of volume either. At 30% of capacity, the rate of variable costs decreases; and at 75% of capacity, this rate increases again. Thus, the total cost line is kinked at both 30% and 75% of capacity. Third, total fixed costs are increased in a single step at 50% of capacity. As a consequence, both the fixed-cost line and the total cost line are discontinuous at that point. Both are pushed upward by the amount of the increase in fixed costs. As a result of these three circumstances and their relationships to each other, there are three break-even points. The first is reached, much as in Figure 13–1, when total revenue is sufficient to cover total costs; this is at point BE_1. Above BE_1, operations are profitable until the firm reaches the volume at which the fixed costs are increased. Between that point and BE_2 operations are again unprofitable. Between BE_2 and BE_3 profits are once more realized. Finally, beyond BE_3 operations are unprofitable because of a decline in revenue per unit of volume and an increase in unit variable cost. Such a graph would be enormously useful to management if cost behavior could be budgeted so precisely. Even apart from the existence of multiple break-even points, knowledge of alterations in cost behavior at critical levels of volume would be extremely useful. As a practical matter, business managers have found that break-even analysis is more feasible and still useful where the conventional assumptions about cost and revenue relationships to volume are employed.

The profit-volume graph (Figure 13–2) would be affected in much the same way as the break-even graph by nonlinear revenue and cost functions. The profit line would not be straight; it might be discontinuous; and it might intersect the horizontal axis at two or more points.

Stable Product Mix. A fourth assumption underlying break-even analysis relates only to multiproduct firms. As such firms are characteristic of our economy, however, this assumption is generally applicable. We have seen that, for a multiproduct firm, the break-even point is determined by dividing total fixed costs by an average ratio of variable profit to sales. If each product has the same variable profit ratio, the break-even point is unaffected by changes in the product mix. However, if, as is more likely, different products have different variable profit ratios, a shift in the product mix can cause a shift in the break-even point. This is illustrated in the following example: A manufacturing corporation produces and sells three products; its annual fixed costs total $420,000. Budgeted sales and variable profits, by products, are as follows:

Product	*Budgeted Sales*	*Variable Profit*	*Variable Profit Ratio*
X.	$ 600,000	$120,000	20%
Y.	900,000	315,000	35%
Z.	500,000	125,000	25%
	$2,000,000	$560,000	

The average variable profit ratio in this budget is 28% ($560,000 ÷ $2,000,000). The break-even sales volume, then, is $1,500,000 ($420,000 ÷ .28). This break-even point is based upon a weighted average variable profit ratio computed from the budgeted product mix. If the product mix is altered, the average variable profit ratio and the break-even point may be changed also. Assume, for example, that the actual sales and variable profit data for the budget period turn out to be as follows:

Product	Actual Sales	Variable Profit	Variable Profit Ratio
X	$1,000,000	$200,000	20%
Y	200,000	70,000	35%
Z	800,000	200,000	25%
	$2,000,000	$470,000	

The average variable profit ratio is now 23.5% ($470,000 ÷ $2,000,000), and the break-even volume is $1,787,235 ($420,000 ÷ .235). The raising of the break-even point is caused by a shift in the product mix, with no change whatever in total sales volume. In comparison with the budget, there has been an increase in the sales of products with low variable profit ratios and a decrease in the sales of the product with the high ratio. The impact of this change in product mix on income before taxes is substantial. Budgeted income was $140,000; actual income is $50,000.

Equality of Sales Volume and Production Volume. A final assumption underlying conventional break-even analysis is that the volume of sales and the volume of production are equal. Everything produced is sold; there is no significant change in the level of inventory of goods on hand. This assumption is necessary because the analysis matches total costs and total revenues for the period and relates them jointly to a single measure of volume. It is, of course, very possible that some of the costs of one period will be incurred in the production of goods to be sold in a subsequent period. This is quite a normal business occurrence, but it tends to complicate the calculation of a break-even point for one period. Where this assumption is clearly invalid (i.e., where sales and production volumes are significantly different), the break-even point may still be computed as shown above if the sales value of production is substituted for current revenue in the computation. In effect, this alternative assumes that goods produced for inventory will eventually be sold at the current selling price.

Utility of Break-Even Analysis

Probably the best summary evaluation of break-even analysis is to say that it is a useful tool of managerial planning and decision making but not a sharp tool. Because of the several restrictive assumptions underlying the analysis, the computation of a break-even volume should be regarded as an approximation rather than as a precise measurement. Nevertheless, even if the analysis yields only an approximate break-even operating volume, this estimate is much superior to no such information at all. The break-even point is of special interest to management, for it identifies that level of operations below which the objective of profit would be missed altogether. A corollary of the profit motive is the desire to avoid losses. Some managers may feel a stronger desire to avoid a loss of a given amount than to obtain a profit of the same amount. If management places a proportionately higher value upon a situation that involves some profit (and avoids any loss) than upon one that involves an increase in an existing level of profit, then the break-even point represents the operating volume at which management's scale of values changes. As such, it is of unique significance.

Even if the break-even point is not considered uniquely useful, the analysis underlying it may be. Often management is more interested in the general pattern of the relationships among volume, costs, and profit than in the break-even point itself. The popularity of the profit-volume graph (Figure 13–2) attests to this interest, for that graph focuses attention upon expected profits at all levels of operations.

ANALYSIS OF CHANGES IN PRICES, COSTS, AND VOLUME

One of the most useful and simplest applications of cost-volume-profit relationships is the analysis of changes in one or more of the basic elements—revenue, cost, and volume. This type of analysis can be employed to answer questions such as the following: What would be the impact upon profits of a price increase if that increase caused volume to decline? Can profits be improved by increasing the advertising budget and thereby boosting volume? Can prices be raised to offset the impact on profits of a wage increase? What sales volume must be achieved in order to attain some target profit? The analysis of problems of these types will be illustrated in the following paragraphs.

Effect of Price Increase

If a price increase has no effect upon volume, the effect upon profit will be very simple. Profit before taxes will rise by the amount of the price increase multiplied by the present volume. Net income after taxes will be increased by the before-tax profit rise multiplied by the complement of the applicable income tax rate (i.e., 100% minus the tax rate). As a matter of fact, however, it is likely that volume will decline in response to a price increase. The extent of the volume decline depends upon the degree of competition in the market and upon the price elasticity of demand for the product (i.e., the extent to which buyers' demand for it is influenced by its price). Assume that a manufacturer is contemplating a 5% price increase on all of its products in 1967. Its sales in 1966 totaled $6,000,000 and its variable costs, $4,800,000. The

5% price increase would raise total revenue by $300,000. However, the company expects that the sales volume of all products will be 8% lower in 1967 because of the higher prices. Since volume affects both revenue and variable costs proportionately, the impact of the volume reduction may be computed directly in terms of the variable profit. Without a change in volume, variable profit in 1967 would be $1,500,000 ($6,300,000 − $4,800,000). The volume decline, however, means that the variable profit will be 8% lower than this amount, or 92% of it. Thus, the budgeted variable profit would be $1,380,000. This is still better than the 1966 variable profit of $1,200,000. If the applicable income tax rate is 47%, the after-tax increase in profit is $95,400 (53% of $180,000, the increase in variable profit). The company's fixed costs may be ignored in this analysis, for they will be unaffected by the proposed change.

Effect of Increase in Fixed Costs

An increase in the total annual fixed costs of an enterprise may be caused either by external circumstances (e.g., an increase in property taxes) or by a managerial decision (e.g., an increase in executives' salaries). In either event, the effect is to raise the break-even point of the firm, assuming no change in the variable profit. Any increase in price or decrease in variable costs would tend to offset this effect, for either would increase the variable profit ratio. Of course, an increase in fixed costs might cause an increase in volume; while not affecting the variable profit ratio, this could increase the total variable profit. For example, assume that a small company producing and selling a single product sold 25,000 units during 1966 at a price of $80. Variable costs per unit are $60 and fixed costs total $400,000, including $50,000 of advertising costs. The company's management is dissatisfied with the present rate of income on sales volume. The market research firm engaged to study the problem suggests that a 20% increase in the advertising budget would boost sales volume by 6%. Would such a move be profitable? The question can be restated as follows: Will the additional variable profit generated by the higher volume cover the increase in fixed costs? The variable profit of $20 per unit would be obtained on an additional 1,500 units (6% of 25,000); in total, then, variable profit would be increased by $30,000. This would be three times the amount of the increase in fixed advertising cost—$10,000 (20% of $50,000). After income tax at a rate of 47%, net profit would be greater than in 1966 by $10,600 (53% of $20,000).

This profit-volume analysis must be employed carefully; it is not always appropriate. A very different type of situation is presented by the firm that finds it is unable to meet the demand for its products because of limited production facilities. It is considering doubling its productive capacity by building a new plant. Such a move would increase annual fixed costs by $7,500,000. Present sales volume is $72,000,000 annually; annual variable costs total $48,000,000. It is expected that the additional capacity would result in a 25% increase in sales volume during the first year of operations in the new plant. This would mean a 25% increase in the current variable profit, or an increase of $6,000,000. Obviously, this additional profit does not justify a $7,500,000 increase in fixed costs. But, just as obviously, it is not valid to seek to justify an increase in productive capacity in terms of one year's sales increase alone. The new plant will last for many years, and it must be justified or defeated in light of the expected impact upon variable profit over all of those years. For reasons to be explained in Chapter 16, simple profit-volume analysis is inadequate for an evaluation of effects that will occur over a period of several years. Unlike the increase in the advertising budget, the construction of a new plant commits the enterprise's resources to a specific use for a long period of time. Its profitability, thus, must be evaluated by means of long-term investment analysis, not by any short-run profit measurement.

Effect of Wage and Price Increases

A great deal has been written in recent years about the so-called wage-price spiral, in which wage increases trigger price increases which, in turn, cause further wage and price rises ad infinitum. If given credence at all, this spiral is usually thought of as a phenomenon of the economy as a whole. For the individual firm, the wage-price problem is unlikely to be so clear or so nearly automatic. A firm may wish to raise prices to offset the decline in profits attendant upon a wage increase. As we have already observed, however, a price increase may result in a volume decline, which tends to reduce profits also. As an example, assume that a firm prepares the following budgeted income statement in the variable costing form:

Sales	$50,000,000
Variable costs	30,000,000
Variable profit	20,000,000
Fixed costs	15,000,000
Net profit before tax	5,000,000
Income tax (47%)	2,350,000
Net income	$ 2,650,000

Shortly after the preparation of this forecast, it is learned that a wage increase will cause variable costs to be 4% higher than originally budgeted. With no change in price or volume, this would reduce variable profit and profit before tax by $1,200,000. The firm wishes to raise its prices to compensate for this wage boost. Market research indicates that a 3% price increase would result in a volume decline of 1½%. If a 3% price rise were adopted, the budgeted income statement would appear as follows:

Sales	$50,727,500
Variable costs	30,732,000
Variable profit	19,995,500
Fixed costs	15,000,000
Net profit before tax	4,995,500
Income tax (47%)	2,347,885
Net income	$ 2,647,615

This revised budget reflects the impact of only one combination of price increase and volume decrease. Similar computations might be made for other percentage price rises and volume declines. If the ratio between the price increase and the volume decrease is constant (e.g., 2 to 1, as suggested above), the necessary price increase to achieve any desired effect upon income can be computed by fairly elementary algebra. Such computation, of course, does not mean that the requisite price increase is feasible; factors of competition must also be considered before any price decision can be made.

Volume Needed to Attain Target Profit

The basic mechanics of break-even analysis may be adapted very easily to determine the operating volume necessary for a firm to attain a specific target profit. Assume, for example, that a corporation seeks a minimum rate of return on invested capital of 8% after taxes. For a given budget period, this objective requires a net income of $2,120,000. The company's variable costs average 60% of selling prices; fixed costs total $18,000,000 per year; and the applicable income tax rate is 47%. The volume here must be sufficient to produce a total variable profit that will cover fixed costs plus the target profit. Since fixed costs are a before-tax quantity, the profit employed in the analysis must also be measured before taxes. The target profit before taxes here is $4,000,000 ($2,120,000 ÷ .53). Thus, sales volume must be sufficient so that 40% of it—the variable profit—will be $22,000,000, the sum of the fixed costs and the target profit before tax. This volume is computed thus:

$$\text{Target volume} = \frac{\$22{,}000{,}000}{.40} = \$55{,}000{,}000.$$

This and the other analyses illustrated in the foregoing paragraphs are but examples of the types of situations and problems that may be analyzed in terms of the relationships among revenue, cost, and volume.

ADVANTAGE OF VARIABLE COSTING

Throughout the discussion in this chapter, the importance of an effective separation of variable and fixed costs and of the variable profit as a unique figure has been obvious. The distinction between variable and fixed costs and the identification of the variable profit are essential to the variable costing method and to variable costing reports. While the same data may be derived from absorption costing records, they are incidental to rather than inherent in that method. In practice, it has been observed that firms using absorption costing usually do not separate variable and fixed costs in the accounting records. Consequently, when such cost data are required for special analyses, they must be developed in a manner not characteristic of the cost accounting system in use and, hence, at extra cost. Under variable costing, on the other hand, separate reporting of variable and fixed costs is basic to the system. Hence, the distinction is always available for analysis. Further, the variable costing income statement shows directly the variable profit. Thus, without additional information, management can make analyses of the anticipated impacts of volume, price, and/or cost changes. Such analyses are ordinarily not possible from absorption costing income statements without supplementary information. Thus, variable costing appears to be clearly superior insofar as the utility of the income statement for profit-volume analysis is concerned. This does not mean, of course, that variable costing is preferable to absorption costing as a general rule; but it certainly is a notable point in favor of the former approach.

QUESTIONS FOR DISCUSSION

1. Describe in detail the effects on company profit of a change in sales volume when all other pertinent factors remain unchanged. What are the effects on profit of a change in production volume only?
2. "Since business firms seldom operate at their break-even points for any prolonged period of time, break-even analysis is of very limited value to management." Evaluate this statement.
3. What would be the impact on a firm's break-even point if there were a general increase in the price level, that is, an increase of the same proportion in all prices? Consider the case of a firm which holds a sufficient inventory of merchandise to meet all anticipated sales demand during the coming fiscal period. Effective on the first day of that period, all prices are doubled as a consequence of a devaluation of the currency. In that coming period, when would this firm break even, when revenues equalled the original dollar costs of the merchandise or when revenues equalled the current market value of the merchandise? (Ignore any costs other than costs of merchandise sold in answering the latter part of this question.)

4. Does the choice between absorption costing and variable costing have any implication for the break-even point of a firm? Explain.
5. Is it a fair generalization to say that the product with the highest variable profit ratio is the most profitable product in a company's line? Explain.
6. If a firm's management believed that its anticipated break-even sales volume for a particular budget period were too high, what action(s) might management take to lower that break-even volume?
7. Will a firm that plans to liquidate previously accumulated inventory during a period break even at a different volume than if it were planning to build up its inventory during that period? Explain.
8. If, as is customarily assumed in economic analysis, there is an inverse relationship between sales volume and selling price, what is the effect on profit of an increase in price when costs remain unchanged? Does the assumption of a linear relationship between volume and total revenue in break-even analysis conflict with the customary assumption that volume and selling price vary inversely with each other? Explain.
9. How might a profit-volume graph be used by management in the process of developing a comprehensive operating budget?
10. How should income taxes be considered in break-even computations?

PROBLEMS

1. The manufacturer of a single product reports the following summarized data:

Unit selling price	$6.50
Unit variable costs	$4.55
Annual fixed costs	$733,200
Annual operating capacity	700,000 units

Required:

Compute the break-even point of this company in terms of (1) unit sales, (2) dollar sales volume, and (3) a percentage of operating capacity.

2. The income statement of the Ascot Cravat Company for 1966 appeared as follows:

ASCOT CRAVAT COMPANY

Income Statement
For year ended December 31, 1966

Sales		$860,000
Variable cost of sales	$415,000	
Variable distribution expenses	58,000	473,000
Variable profit		$387,000
Fixed production expenses	$125,000	
Fixed administrative expenses	80,000	205,000
Income before taxes		$182,000
Federal and state income taxes		94,000
Net Income		$ 88,000

Required:

1. Assuming that the operating data for 1966 are representative of future periods, what is the break-even point for this company?
2. Draft a break-even graph for this company and label all important components of it.

3. The Pacific Products Co. is considering purchasing an old lumber mill in Coos Bay, Oregon, to manufacture widgets. The mill would cost $2,480,000, and an additional $2,200,000 would have to be spent to convert it to an efficient widget factory. The converted plant would have an estimated useful life of twenty years and an expected salvage value of $750,000. It would have a productive capacity of 17,500 widgets per month.

Widgets sell for $11 apiece. Variable costs for one widget are as follows:

Materials	$2.20
Labor	3.20
Overhead	1.10
Distribution	1.20
Franchise fee	.30

The annual fixed out-of-pocket operating costs of the factory would amount to $178,500.

Required:

1. Compute the annual break-even point for the widget factory in terms of units and dollar sales volume.
2. Draft a properly labeled break-even graph for this company.

4. The graph below depicts the conventional break-even analysis. Physical units of product are measured on the y axis. Budgeted physical sales volume for the period in question is depicted by the line 0-i.

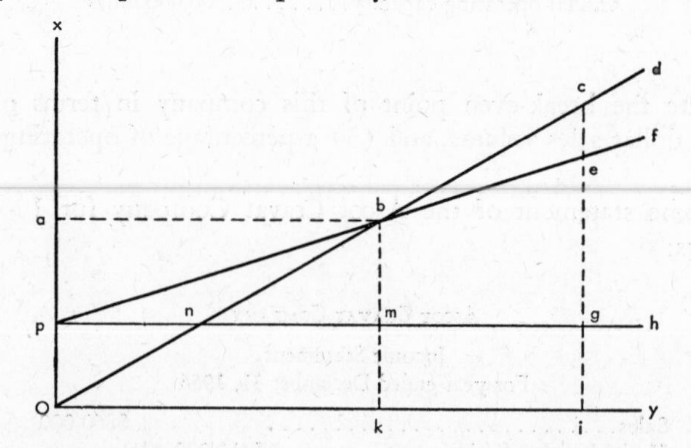

Required:

By use of the letters in the graph above, identify the point, line, or area on the graph which represents each of the following items or quantities:

1. Total revenue at any volume
2. Total variable cost at maximum volume
3. Fixed costs
4. Break-even point in dollar sales

5. Break-even point in unit sales
6. Margin of safety
7. Total budgeted revenue
8. Total budgeted variable cost
9. Total budgeted fixed cost
10. Budgeted operating profit
11. Maximum possible total loss

5. The Ahab Corporation manufactures a variety of hand tools. The following summary data are taken from the operating budget for 1967:

Sales	$3,200,000
Variable expenses	2,080,000
Fixed expenses	700,000

Required:

1. Compute the break-even point.
2. Draft a profit-volume graph for the Ahab Corporation. Indicate on it the budgeted profits for sales volumes of $1,600,000 and $2,800,000. (Ignore income taxes.)
3. What sales volume would have to be achieved to produce a net income after taxes of $100,000. The applicable income tax rate is 47 per cent.
4. List some of the assumptions underlying the break-even computation in part 1 above.

6. The budgeted income statement, by product lines, of the Mantika Corporation for 1966 is as follows:

	Product A	*Product B*	*Product C*	*Total*
Sales	$700,000	$800,000	$500,000	$2,000,000
Cost of goods sold	455,000	640,000	300,000	1,395,000
Gross profit	245,000	160,000	200,000	605,000
Selling expenses	140,000	160,000	100,000	400,000
Administrative expenses	22,400	25,600	16,000	64,000
	162,400	185,600	116,000	464,000
Operating profit	82,600	(25,600)	84,000	141,000
Income tax	33,040	(10,240)	33,600	56,400
Net Income	$ 49,560	$(15,360)	$ 50,400	$ 84,600

Further investigation discloses that, on all products, fixed overhead is charged at a rate of 20 per cent of sales and variable selling expenses are equal to 15 per cent of sales. All administrative expenses are fixed. Sales volume and production volume are expected to be equal. Income tax is levied at a rate of 40 per cent of all operating income.

Required:

1. Compute the budgeted break-even point of the corporation from the data given.
2. What would be the effect on budgeted income if half of the budgeted sales volume of Product B could be shifted to Products A and C in

equal dollar amounts and in such a way that the total budgeted sales volume would remain unchanged?

3. What would be the effect of the shift in product mix suggested in part 2 on budgeted break-even volume?

7. The budgeted sales of the Donnybrook Company for 1966 amount to $120,-000,000. Variable costs are expected to average 65% of sales. Fixed costs are budgeted at $28,000,000 for the year.

Required:

1. What is the break-even point for the company for 1966?
2. What sales volume would be necessary in order to increase budgeted profit before tax by 50%?
3. Would it be profitable for the company to increase the budgeted sales volume by 25%, without changing prices, by increasing variable costs by 10% of sales?

8. The Kirchnet Company manufactures a single product in one continuous process. The standard cost sheet for the product is as follows:

Raw materials	$16.00
Direct labor—10 hrs. @ $2.10	21.00
Variable overhead—10 hrs. @ $.80	8.00
Fixed overhead—10 hrs. @ $1.80	18.00
	$63.00

Normal production volume is 45,000 units of product per year. Sales and output for 1966 have been budgeted at 50,000 units. The product is sold at a price of $125 per unit. Variable selling expenses average 12 per cent of selling price. Fixed selling, administrative, and research and development costs are estimated at $490,000 per year.

Required:

1. What is the break-even point for the company for 1966?
2. Would the break-even point be lower if volume were budgeted at 40,000 units instead of 50,000 units? Explain.
3. Would it be profitable for the company to raise its selling price to $160 if such a move would result in a loss of sales of 15,000 units? What effect, if any, would such a move have on the break-even point?

9. The income statement of the Rastex Corporation for the year 1966 appeared as follows:

RASTEX CORPORATION
Income Statement
For year ended Dec. 31, 1966

Sales		$84,500,000
Cost of goods sold (at standard cost)	$53,400,000	
Add: Overhead volume variance	4,800,000	58,200,000
Gross margin		$26,300,000
Selling and administrative expenses		24,500,000
Income before tax		$ 1,800,000
Federal income tax		900,000
Net Income		$ 900,000

The corporation's president is very dissatisfied with the year's operating results. He considers income far too low in relation to sales volume, and he is concerned that operations for the year were scarcely above three fourths of capacity.

Further study of the cost records shows that fixed overhead of $15,200,000 was included in the standard cost of goods sold to customers during 1966. Twelve million dollars of fixed selling and administrative expenses were incurred during the year. Production and sales volumes for 1966 were equal. The applicable income tax rate is 50 per cent on all income.

Required:

The president believes that the company should realize an income after tax of at least 10 per cent of sales. What sales volume would be necessary to achieve this minimum income objective? In light of the information available, do you believe this objective is presently feasible?

10. The KLM Company manufactures and distributes industrial machinery in two sales territories. Budgeted income statements for these territories and the company as a whole for the year 1967 are presented below.

	Northwest Territory	*Southwest Territory*	*Company Totals*
Sales	$1,200,000	$900,000	$2,100,000
Variable expenses:			
Materials	300,000	225,000	525,000
Direct labor	160,000	120,000	280,000
Overhead	240,000	180,000	420,000
Selling	180,000	135,000	315,000
Fixed expenses:			
Overhead	50,000	50,000	100,000
Selling	40,000	30,000	70,000
Administrative	80,000	60,000	140,000
Total expenses	1,050,000	800,000	1,850,000
Income before tax	150,000	100,000	250,000
Income tax (40%)	60,000	40,000	100,000
Net Income	$ 90,000	$ 60,000	$ 150,000

All of the fixed expenses, excepting overhead, are incurred in the home office and are allocated to the two territories on the basis of their expected sales volumes. Fixed overhead is actually traceable to the individual territories.

The manager of the Southwest Territory has argued that his sales volume could be increased by 10 per cent with no change in price if he were permitted to spend $40,000 on sales promotion in his territory. The vice-president for sales feels that a price reduction of 5 per cent in both territories would increase sales volume in both by 20 per cent. The manager of the Northwest Territory contends that sales efforts should be concentrated in his territory, which he believes to be the more profitable one. He points out that the Southwest Territory anticipates sales equal to three fourths of his but a profit equal to only two thirds of his. Thus, he argues, every dollar of sales in the Northwest Territory will be more profitable than a dollar of sales in the Southwest.

Required:

1. Accepting the validity of the underlying assumptions, determine the effects on company income of the suggestions made by the manager of the Southwest Territory and by the vice-president for sales.
2. Evaluate the argument of the manager of the Northwest Territory.

11. The Janus Corporation plans to introduce a new product in 1967. The variable costs to produce and sell one unit will total $20. The annual fixed costs incurred directly because of this new product will be $100,000. Market research studies indicate that 5,000 units could be sold at a price of $40 per unit and that sales volume will decline by 10 units as price is increased by $1 beyond $40. The company has established a policy that all products must yield, over and above the variable and fixed costs directly traceable to them, a profit margin equal to 20% of the total sales revenue from them.

Required:

What price, if any, will yield the profit margin called for by the company's policy on this new product?

12. Sales of the Rantour Company's product have been declining over the past several years. In 1966, 60,000 units were sold. For 1967, sales volume has been budgeted initially at 50,000 units, which is only half the company's productive capacity. Several plans have been proposed to reverse this downward sales trend.

The sales manager recommends reducing the price of the product by 10%. This, he contends, will result in a 25% increase in sales volume over the amount initially budgeted for 1967.

The production engineer argues that the difficulty lies with product quality. He asserts that an additional 20,000 units over the initial 1967 sales budget could be sold if a higher quality raw material were used in the product. Use of this new material would increase materials cost by 15% and variable overhead cost by 8%.

A market consultant recommended that the production engineer's proposal be coupled with a 10% price increase. This, he believes, would increase budgeted sales volume for 1967 by 12%.

In any event, the company's direct labor cost will be increased by 8% in 1967 as compared with 1966.

Income for 1966 was reported as follows:

Sales		$4,500,000
Raw materials cost	$1,200,000	
Direct labor	900,000	
Variable overhead	300,000	
Fixed overhead	500,000	
Variable selling expenses	240,000	
Fixed selling expenses	400,000	
Fixed administrative expenses	600,000	4,140,000
Income before tax		$ 360,000

Required:

Analyze the impact of each of the plans proposed for 1967 and indicate which would result in the highest budgeted profit before tax. Unless something to the contrary is indicated, it may be assumed that all operating data for 1966 will continue in 1967.

13. Flear Company has a maximum productive capacity of 210,000 units per year. Normal capacity is regarded as 180,000 units per year. Standard variable manufacturing costs are $11 per unit. Fixed factory overhead is $360,000 per year. Variable selling expenses are $3 per unit and fixed selling expenses are $252,000 per year. The unit sales price is $20.

The operating results for 1966 are summarized as follows:

Sales	150,000 units
Production	160,000 units
Beginning inventory	10,000 units

There was a net unfavorable variance from standard variable manufacturing costs of $40,000. All variances are disposed of as additions to or deductions from the standard cost of goods sold.

Required:

For parts 1, 2, and 3 assume no variances from standard manufacturing costs.

1. What is the break-even point in dollar sales?
2. How many units must be sold to earn a net income of $60,000 per year before taxes?
3. How many units must be sold to earn a net income before taxes of 10 per cent of sales?
4. Prepare formal income statements for 1966 under (a) absorption costing and (b) variable costing.
5. Account for the difference in net income between the two income statements in part 4.

(Adapted from CPA Examination)

14. The Specialties Co., Inc., is engaged in manufacturing and wholesaling two principal products. As their management consultant, you have been asked to advise management on sales policy for the coming year. Two different plans are being considered by management, either of which plans, management believes, will (1) increase the volume of sales, (2) reduce the ratio of selling expense to sales, and (3) decrease unit production costs as compared with the preceding year. These two plans are as follows:

Plan 1—Premium Stamp Books

Each package of Product A will contain 8 premium stamps, and each package of Product B, 4 premium stamps. Premium stamp books will be distributed to consumers, and when a book is filled with 100 stamps it will be redeemed by the award of a cash prize, the amount of which is indicated under an unbroken seal attached to the book at the time of distribution.

Every 10,000 books distributed will provide for prizes in accordance with the following schedule:

Number of Books	*Prize per Book*	*Total Prizes*
1	$150.00	$ 150
5	50.00	250
14	20.00	280
50	10.00	500
160	5.00	800
1,020	1.00	1,020
8,750	.40	3,500
10,000		$6,500

The cost of this plan will be as follows:

Books, including distribution..........$15 per 1,000 books
Stamps..............................$1 per 1,000 stamps
Prizes..............................see above

This plan will take the place of all previous advertising; the previous selling prices will be maintained.

Plan 2—Reduced Selling Prices

The selling price of Product A will be reduced by $8\frac{1}{3}\%$ and that of Product B, by 5%. Advertising expenditures will be increased by 25% over the rate of advertising cost incurred in the preceding year.

The two plans are mutually exclusive alternatives. In addition to the information above, management has provided you the following data concerning operations of the preceding year and expected changes under the alternative plans:

	Product A	*Product B*
Preceding year's operations:		
Units sold	200,000	600,000
Production cost per unit	$.40	$.30
Selling price per unit	$.60	$.40
Selling expenses (one-third of which was advertising)	18% of sales	18% of sales
Administrative expenses	5% of sales	5% of sales
Expected changes:		
Increase in unit sales volume:		
Plan 1	50%	50%
Plan 2	40%	25%
Decrease in unit production cost:		
Plan 1	5%	10%
Plan 2	$7\frac{1}{2}\%$	$6\frac{2}{3}\%$
Administrative expenses:		
Plan 1	4% of sales	4% of sales
Plan 2	same total dollar amount as last year for both products	

Selling expenses other than advertising will be incurred at the same rate as last year under either plan.

Required:

1. Prepare for management a schedule comparing the operations of the preceding year with those proposed for the coming year under both of the alternative plans.
2. Is management right in its expectations of the three specific operating improvements mentioned in the first paragraph of the problem?

(Adapted from CPA Examination)

Chapter 14

INCREMENTAL PROFIT ANALYSIS FOR DECISION MAKING

AT ONE time, accounting data were accumulated in business firms almost solely for the purpose of reporting the results of operations after they had occurred. Accounting, consequently, was regarded primarily as a backward-looking function. Accounting reports were required for investors but were of limited use to management. Recent years have witnessed a marked departure from this point of view. The importance of reports to investors has not diminished, but the uses of accounting data by management have grown to the point that they are often regarded as more important than reports to investors. Actually, accounting reports are equally important to both groups, but often in quite different ways. The types of data required by management and the manner of their presentation frequently differ greatly from the data in and form of conventional reports to investors. Investors' reports continue to emphasize historical data; this emphasis may be debated, but it remains a fact of "generally accepted accounting principles." Management, on the other hand, is not bound by the constraint of general acceptance. Managers are concerned chiefly with data pertinent to the future, and they are not satisfied with historical reports as indicators of future operations. Managers want to know very specifically what costs and profits can be and should be, not just what they were. Further, management must be concerned with the details of operating problems and prospects for individual segments or components of the enterprise. Investors, on the other hand, are ordinarily interested in the operations of the enterprise as a whole only. The accounting system should be designed so as to meet the needs of both management and investors as completely as possible.

Accounting data are generally recognized to be indispensable tools of management in the making of business decisions. These financial data alone do not make decisions, but they are essential elements to be considered in the process of deciding. For purposes of discussion in this book, business decisions will be classified as two general types, short-term operating decisions and long-term investment decisions. The distinction between these two types is one of time. Short-term decisions may be implemented and, if desired, reversed within a short period of time. (As a practical expedient, a "short period of time" is often considered as one year or less.) Long-term investment decisions affect the operating position of a firm for a sufficiently long period of time that their financial consequences must be evaluated in light of the impact of time upon them. Investment decisions involve the commitment of capital resources to some asset (e.g., a building) and/or to some project (e.g., a new product line) for an anticipated long period of time. Abandonment of the asset or project before the end of its expected economic life may entail a substantial loss of capital. Short-term decisions, on the other hand, do not involve long-term capital commitments. If a short-term decision proves to be unwise, it may be reversed promptly without significant loss of capital. Hence, the element of time may be ignored in the decision-making analysis. Short-term decisions will be discussed in this chapter. Long-term investment decisions will be considered in Chapter 16.

RELEVANT COSTS FOR DECISION MAKING

Differential Costs

For purposes of inventory valuation and profit reporting, the distinction between manufacturing and nonmanufacturing costs is an important one. In profit-volume analysis, the distinction between variable and fixed costs is most important. For purposes of making a specific decision among alternative possible courses of action, however, these distinctions are merely incidental. The essential distinction for decision making is between relevant and irrelevant costs. Any costs that will be affected by a particular decision—whether they will be increased or decreased—are relevant to that decision. Such costs are termed *differential costs,* as they will be different depending upon the decision made. Costs that will be the same regardless of the decision made in a particular situation are obviously irrelevant to the decision. These are commonly called *sunk costs* or *common costs;* they are inherent in the situation no matter what decision is reached.[1] There are no generally applicable rules for distinguishing between differential and sunk costs. These can be determined only in light of the circumstances attendant upon a particular decision. Some decisions are fairly simple to identify—whether to accept or reject

[1] See Chapter 2, pages 28 through 32 for further discussion of cost classifications for purposes of decision making.

a single proposed course of action. Others are more complex—which of several alternatives to select. The ease or difficulty in identifying a decision is, of course, quite a different matter from the ease or difficulty of deciding.

Variable Costs. It is not possible to say that all variable costs are differential costs, although any costs that vary with volume will be affected by decisions that will cause changes in volume. Some decisions, however, may relate to variable costs without affecting their amount. For example, a decision among alternative methods of handling and storing raw materials will have no effect upon the cost of the materials; yet, materials cost is almost always regarded as variable with the level of production volume. Differential costs can be identified only in light of the specific decision at hand. However, by their very nature, variable costs are highly susceptible to change. Hence, it is probably a fair generalization to say that variable costs should always be scrutinized to determine whether or not they will be affected by a decision.

Differential Fixed Costs. For purposes of short-term decision making, fixed costs may be classified as differential and common. *Differential fixed costs* are those that are wholly traceable to a specific decision. That is, the particular fixed cost will be incurred only if a particular decision is made. For example, the decision to open a new sales territory would likely entail the salary of a new sales manager for that area. His salary would be a fixed cost if it were to be incurred, but it would be incurred only if the decision to open the territory were made. A common fixed cost, on the other hand, will be the same regardless of the decision made. The salary of the vice-president for marketing, for example, would probably be unaffected by the decision with respect to a new sales territory. It would most likely be incurred in the same amount whether the territory is opened or not; hence, it would be irrelevant to the decision. In summary then, differential fixed costs are, by definition, relevant costs; common fixed costs are irrelevant costs. It is not necessary, of course, that differential fixed costs be present in every decision situation; but the possibility of their existence should always be investigated.

Interest. In strict theory, the interest cost of an enterprise is a factor independent of individual decisions. It is the cost of obtaining capital and, as such, is not affected by decisions as to the utilization of that capital. In practice, however, sources and uses of business capital are often viewed as interdependent, particularly in connection with short-term decisions. One of the alternatives under consideration in a given case may necessitate short-term borrowing, while the other(s) do not. In such case, the interest on that borrowing may be considered a relevant cost in the decision-making process. If all of the alternative courses of action would require equal short-term borrowing, of course, the interest would be common to all of the possible choices and would amount to a sunk cost. Inclusion of short-term interest among the differential costs of a particular alternative is appropriate only if the short-term borrowing would be undertaken if and only if that course of action were adopted.

In theory, the firm is thought of as faced with a wide range of possible uses of capital, whether short-term or long-term, not all of which alternatives would be related to one specific decision. Thus, short-term borrowing would be entered into in any event so long as there were some profitable use for the capital. As a practical matter, however, business managers usually are unable to evaluate all possible uses of short-term capital in so broad a perspective. Business decisions are often made within the framework of a single problem or program. In such cases, it would be quite reasonable to regard short-term borrowing and the interest thereon as peculiar to one possible decision. This could be true only for short-term interest, however. In the long-run, a broad overview of all possible investment opportunities must be adopted.

Depreciation. Depreciation is the periodic amortization of the cost of a long-lived asset acquired at some time in the past. As such, it necessarily derives from a long-term investment decision. Once the investment decision has been implemented and the asset purchased, the subsequent depreciation expense is determined in light of the asset's expected useful life and in accordance with one of a number of alternative depreciation methods available at the option of management. Thus, depreciation is inherently related to what we have described as a long-term decision. To include depreciation as a differential cost in any short-term decision-making situation may be seriously misleading. If a particular decision would have the effect of increasing periodic depreciation, the increase could be attributed to an investment in a new asset, to a shortening of the life of an old asset, or to a change in the depreciation method used. Either of the first two causes would entail an investment decision which would have to be analyzed in relation to the relatively long period of time involved. The third possible cause would involve no substantive financial implications, except in the event that the step-up of depreciation charges were acceptable for income tax purposes. Any reduction in depreciation attendant upon the disposition of a long-lived asset would also be a consequence of a long-term investment decision. Actually, in this case, it would be a disinvestment decision. Thus, as a practical matter, depreciation may be ignored in short-term decision-making situations. If depreciation cannot be ignored, then the decision cannot be analyzed by the procedure to be described in this chapter.

Incremental Profit

A full analysis of the expected accounting implications of a specific decision, including both costs and revenues relevant to it, will yield the amount of profit which that decision would contribute to the enterprise as a whole. This amount is referred to as the *incremental profit* from the decision. The incremental profit is that portion of the total income of the firm which can be traced directly to a particular decision. It may be either positive or negative. It may be the net difference between incremental revenues and incremental costs generated by the decision; as such, it would be either positive or negative depending upon whether the revenues or the costs, respectively, were greater. Revenues need not be involved, of course. The incremental profit may be simply the amount of a cost reduction (positive incremental profit) or of a cost increase (negative incremental profit). A change in the method of handling materials, for example, would not be likely to affect revenues; but it could reduce or increase the materials handling costs.

It should be noted here that all business decisions need not produce positive incremental profits. In order for a decision to be profitable in the short run, the incremental profit must be positive. But short-run profits may be sacrificed in the anticipation of improved long-run profits, however vague the expectation may be. A negative incremental profit is certainly an adverse feature of a possible course of action, but it does not necessarily mean that the decision must go against that course. Financial data are indispensable parts of the decision-making process, but they do not make the decision by themselves.

Determination of the incremental profit in a given situation begins with an identification of the differential costs and the incremental revenues that would obtain if a particular decision were made. The incremental profit may be computed as follows:

Additional revenues		xxx
Plus: Cost savings		xxx
		xxx
Less: Lost revenues	xxx	
Cost increases	xxx	xxx
Incremental profit		xxx

Any one or all but one of the items in this computation might be equal to zero, of course. If all of them were zero, the decision would appear to have no direct financial implications. Such a decision might be illustrated by the choice of a new production manager. The choice made may well have very substantial long-run and/or short-run profit implications, but it is highly unlikely that they could be quantified in advance.

SHORT-TERM DECISION-MAKING PROBLEMS

In the paragraphs that follow, we shall examine and analyze several short-term decision-making situations in terms of their incremental profits. Some of the nonfinancial considerations which would be pertinent to the decisions will also be noted briefly. The nature and purposes of this text demand that the financial data be emphasized in these illustrations, but they are still only parts of the total decision-making process, albeit essential parts.

Extent of Processing a Product

The Facts. The Blaine Corporation manufactures a single product which it sells to other manufacturers who process it further for ultimate sales to clothing manufacturers. The normal monthly operating volume for the corporation is 100,000 units of product produced and sold. The unit selling price and unit costs under the present operations are shown below:

Selling price		$6.50
Costs:		
Direct materials	$1.20	
Direct labor	1.75	
Variable overhead	1.10	
Fixed overhead	.85	
Variable selling expense	.90	
Fixed selling expense	.30	6.10
Unit profit before tax		$ .40

The corporation's management is considering the possibility of performing the further processing necessary for the corporation itself to sell directly to clothing manufacturers. A study has shown that this further processing would require no added investment in productive facilities. After further processing, the product could be sold to clothing makers for $8.00 per unit. The additional costs of the further processing are estimated as follows:

Direct labor	$.65 per unit
Variable overhead	$.25 per unit
Variable selling expense	$.10 per unit
Fixed overhead	$15,000 per month
Fixed selling expense	$10,000 per month

The decision at hand is whether to process the product further or to continue selling it as is now done.

Incremental Profit Analysis. Before commencing an analysis of the alternative choices here, it is well to observe the way in which fixed costs have been presented above. The current fixed costs are stated as amounts per unit of product. By definition, fixed costs can be expressed per unit only at one given volume. Here, that volume is 100,000 units per month. Thus, the present fixed overhead amounts to $85,000 per month and fixed selling expense, to $30,000 per month; and this is how fixed costs should be stated. In this particular case, no change in volume is contemplated in connection with the decision; but the practice of stating fixed costs per unit of volume is potentially misleading and should be avoided.

The analysis of the financial data in this situation may be made by preparing comparative budgeted income statements for the two alternatives which may be selected. Such statements, in the variable costing form, are presented below.

	Present Processing	*Further Processing*
Sales revenue	$650,000	$800,000
Variable costs:		
Direct materials	120,000	120,000
Direct labor	175,000	240,000
Overhead	110,000	135,000
Selling expense	90,000	100,000
	$495,000	$595,000
Variable profit	$155,000	$205,000
Fixed costs:		
Overhead	85,000	100,000
Selling expense	30,000	40,000
	$115,000	$140,000
Income before tax	40,000	65,000
Federal income tax (47%)	18,800	30,550
Net income	$ 21,200	$ 34,450

So long as the income tax rate is less than 100%, inclusion of the tax in the analysis only reduces the absolute amount by which further processing would increase profits; but the relative advantage of further processing remains. Nevertheless, it is good practice always to include income taxes in decision-making analyses. In some cases, tax implications may be controlling factors in the decisions.

The same result as developed above can be obtained from a much shorter analysis, dealing only with the incremental revenues and costs associated with the decision to engage in further processing.

Incremental revenue per unit	$1.50
Incremental variable cost per unit	1.00
Incremental variable profit per unit	.50
Monthly volume in units	100,000
Incremental variable profit per month	$ 50,000
Incremental fixed cost per month	25,000
Monthly incremental profit before tax	$ 25,000
Federal income tax (47%)	11,750
Incremental profit	$ 13,250

Inasmuch as the incremental profit is positive, the decision to undertake further processing would be more profitable in the short-run than continuing the present operating policy.

Other Considerations. The facts in this illustration indicate that a decision to engage in further processing would not require additional capital investment. This is a very important factor. If further capital investment were necessary, the decision would have to be evaluated as an investment proposal; incremental profit analysis as illustrated above would not be adequate. The analysis above also presumes that additional laborers could be obtained and laid off on short notice. Even if hiring new workers presents no problem, laying them off might; periodic hirings and layoffs are discouraged by the provisions of many union labor agreements. The Blaine Corporation must also question whether its production personnel have the technical knowledge and skill to perform the further processing efficiently. The decision to process further entails the marketing of the company's product in an unfamiliar channel of distribution. Establishing effective working agreements with clothing manufacturers may make new demands on the abilities of the sales force and it may take some little time. Not all of these considerations lend themselves to precise financial measurement, but they must not be ignored. Thus, the monthly incremental profit of $13,250 is an important factor in the decision-making process; but it is not the final answer in itself.

Make or Buy

The Facts. The Bonham Radio Company manufactures a variety of electronics equipment, including a large number of pieces for sale to the Department of Defense. Several of the items produced contain one or more units of a small capacitor, part no. 63812 in the company's list of standard materials. This capacitor is manufactured by the company in its own parts plant. The standard cost for one capacitor is as follows:

Materials	$3.20
Direct labor	2.40
Variable overhead	1.10
Fixed overhead	1.40
	$8.10

All of these are current attainable standards. Monthly usage of this part averages 60,000 units. At a budget meeting, the purchasing agent suggested that the company might save money by purchasing this part from an independent supplier. He stated that he knew it could be purchased in the quantity used by the Bonham Company for $7.00 per unit. Buying the part would increase clerical purchasing costs by approximately $1,000 per month. The supervisor of the stores department estimated that the additional costs of storing and handling the part, if purchased, would be about $.25 per unit. No additional facilities would be needed to store the part, nor would any production facilities be abandoned if its production were discontinued. The parts plant manager reported that the manufacture of this capacitor is not so significant a portion of his total operation that its discontinuance would have any impact upon the plant's fixed overhead.

Incremental Profit Analysis. A cursory glance at the facts in this situation might suggest that a decision to buy the capacitor would indeed be a cost saving. Eighty-five cents per unit ($8.10 — $7.25) would appear to be saved, and this amounts to $51,000 per month for 60,000 units. Even after the additional clerical cost of $1,000 per month, there appears to be a $50,000 monthly cost saving (before taxes, of course). The saving is purely illusory in this case, however. Part of the standard cost of $8.10 for this part is fixed overhead. For inventory costing purposes, it is perfectly correct to assign $1.40 of the parts plant's fixed overhead to this capacitor, assuming that the absorption costing method is employed and that a valid cost allocation scheme is applied. However, discontinuing the manufacture of this part will not affect the parts plant's fixed overhead at all. The fixed cost now charged to part no. 63812 would either be reallocated to other parts or be charged to the volume variance. In either event, the plant's fixed overhead would not be reduced. Thus, fixed overhead is a sunk cost in respect to the decision to make or buy part no. 63812. Only the variable production costs—materials, direct labor, and variable overhead—are relevant to the decision. The variable costs to manufacture total $6.70. Thus, there is an incremental cost of $.55 per unit ($7.25 — $6.70) inherent in the decision to purchase this part. At a monthly usage of 60,000 units, the decision to purchase the capacitor would be analyzed as follows:

Monthly purchase cost (60,000 units @ $7.25)........	$435,000
Plus: Differential monthly clerical cost...............	1,000
	436,000
Differential manufacturing costs per month (60,000 units @ $6.70)...............................	402,000
Incremental cost to purchase (before taxes)...........	34,000
Federal income tax (47%).........................	15,980
Incremental cost per month to purchase part no. 63812..	$ 18,020

Thus, an apparent incremental cost saving is actually an incremental cost. The incremental profit of the suggested change in policy is a negative $18,020 per month.

Other Considerations. If a decision to make a part would require an investment in new production facilities or if a decision to buy a part would permit the disposal of existing facilities, the alternatives would have to be evaluated as long-term investment decisions. The situation described here suggests that any decision made may be reappraised and reversed at least within one month. Other factors must also be considered. If the part were purchased, could the capacity of the parts plant thus idled be employed in some other profitable manner? The analysis above implies that the answer to this question is "No," but the question was not really raised. It should be. Would there be any difference in the quality or technical characteristics of the purchased capacitor as compared with the present part no. 63812? Would an independent supplier be as reliable as the company's own parts plant? Even if the differential costs of purchasing the part were lower, the danger of a costly stock-out due to an unreliable source of supply might outweigh the computed cost saving. Finally, the incremental profit analysis in the preceding paragraph presumed that direct laborers could be laid off if the production of the capacitor were discontinued. Even if such a layoff were feasible, it might create long-run labor relations problems which would offset the short-run cost saving. The impact of a decision on labor relations can seldom be quantified, but it should never be ignored.

Profitability of Product Lines

The Facts. The Turandot Products Company produces and markets three products. It has prepared the following income statement in the absorption costing form:[2]

[2] The distinction between variable and fixed costs is not ordinarily made in absorption costing statements, but it is included here to facilitate subsequent analysis. If not included in the income statement, it could be derived from the cost records.

	Ping	*Pang*	*Pong*	*Total*
Sales	$600,000	$450,000	$150,000	$1,200,000
Cost of goods sold:				
Variable	360,000	270,000	105,000	735,000
Fixed	120,000	90,000	30,000	240,000
	480,000	360,000	135,000	975,000
Gross margin	120,000	90,000	15,000	225,000
Selling expenses:				
Variable	40,000	30,000	15,000	85,000
Fixed	30,000	22,500	7,500	60,000
	70,000	52,500	22,500	145,000
Net income before tax	50,000	37,500	(7,500)	80,000
Income tax (47%)	23,500	17,625	(3,525)	37,600
Net income	$ 26,500	19,875	(3,975)	42,400

The company's management is considering dropping Pong from the line of products because it has consistently shown a loss.

Incremental Profit Analysis. A useful starting point in this analysis is to recast the income statement presented in the variable costing form and to eliminate the allocation of common fixed costs among the products. However valid such an allocation may be for purposes of inventory costing and income measurement, it is not relevant to the question of the profitability of the individual products. Here we shall assume that all of the company's fixed costs are common to the three products. We also assume that the sales and production volumes for the year were equal, so that the same total amount of fixed manufacturing costs will be charged to revenue under variable costing as under absorption costing.[3] The report of profits by product lines in the variable costing form and under the assumptions postulated is as follows:

	Ping	*Pang*	*Pong*	*Total*
Sales	$600,000	$450,000	$150,000	$1,200,000
Variable costs:				
Production	360,000	270,000	105,000	735,000
Selling	40,000	30,000	15,000	85,000
	400,000	300,000	120,000	820,000
Variable profit	$200,000	$150,000	$ 30,000	380,000
Fixed costs:				
Production				240,000
Selling				60,000
				300,000
Net income before tax				80,000
Income tax (47%)				37,600
Net income				$ 42,400

[3] See Chapter 4, pages 97 to 100, for a discussion of the impact of differences between sales and production volumes on reported incomes under these alternative costing methods.

Now it is clear that each product has a positive variable profit. So long as there are no differential fixed costs, each product also has a positive incremental profit. Here Pong's contribution to the total profit of the firm (before taxes) is $30,000. The apparent loss from its continued sale can be seen to be attributable to the allocation of a portion of the common fixed costs of the company to it. Even if differential fixed costs were present in the analysis, Pong would have a positive incremental profit as long as its differential fixed costs were less than $30,000. Whenever a decision is to be made on the basis of the relative profitabilities of several product lines, their respective profits should be measured by their incremental profits. Allocations of common fixed costs are irrelevant and misleading.

On the basis of the information given, the incremental profit of a decision to discontinue production and distribution of Pong would be a negative $15,900 ($30,000 × .53). This may be proved by subtracting all data relevant to Pong from the totals for the company in the income statement above and then recomputing the income tax accordingly.

Other Considerations. Any decision concerning the continuation of one product in a company's line must take into account a wide range of possible implications. Product income statements can be very misleading; they may show only the apparent profitability of each product. For example, if one product is dropped from the line, there may be adverse effects on the sales of other products. If two or more products are complementary, discontinuing one is almost certain to result in reduced sales of the other(s). As an illustration, a manufacturer of machinery could reasonably expect to sell fewer machines if he stopped making and selling spare parts for the machinery. Buyers may place orders with a particular seller because they can obtain a complete line of merchandise from him. If he reduces that line, the buyers may look elsewhere for suppliers from whom they can purchase the complete line. Thus, in the case analyzed above, discontinuance of Pong might involve a negative incremental profit of more than the amount computed because of reduced sales of Ping and/or Pang. Unfortunately, such inter-product demand relationships usually cannot be measured precisely; but they can be extremely important.

The discontinuance of a product line was illustrated here as a very simple situation. Ignored was the very pertinent question of what might be done to fill the void left by the abandoned product. If a company discontinues making and selling one product, there will be some amount of idle capacity in both production facilities and the sales force. This idle capacity may be diverted to production and sales of a new product or of one or more of the other products already in the line. For example, the decision to discontinue Pong would take on new and significant dimensions if we knew that the capacity thus idled could be diverted to additional output and sales of Ping and/or Pang. Suppose that the loss of all Pong sales could be replaced with an equal dollar volume of some combination of Ping and Pang sales. The latter two products both have a variable profit ratio of one-third of sales, as compared with Pong's variable profit ratio of 20%. Thus, additional sales of either or both of these products in the amount of $150,000 would add $50,000 to total variable profit. The incremental profit of the decision to discontinue Pong would then be positive, as shown below.

Increase in variable profit from Ping/Pang	$50,000
Less: Loss of variable profit from Pong	30,000
Incremental profit before taxes	$20,000
Incremental profit after tax ($20,000 × .53)	$10,600

Finally, there are other factors which may not lend themselves to short-run financial analysis. What will be the impact of the discontinuance of a product line on the overall company image? What will be the impact of the decision on the company's employees—specifically, their job security? What psychological effect, if any, might this decision have upon the salesmen in their subsequent promotion of the other products? Regrettably, the fact that these questions may be unanswerable does not mean that they must not be asked.

COMMON PRODUCTION COSTS

In some manufacturing enterprises, two or more different products emerge from a single, common production process and a single raw material. A familiar example is the variety of petroleum products derived from the refining of crude oil. Such products present some peculiar and important problems to cost accountants and to managers charged with the responsibility of making decisions regarding them. They are identifiable as separate products only at the conclusion of the common processing. This point of separation is commonly referred to as the *split-off point.* The costs incurred up to the split-off point are true common costs; they cannot be traced to the separate products in any direct or logical manner. For inventory costing purposes, however, it is necessary that all production costs be charged to products and, more particularly here, to separate products. For purposes of managerial analysis, of course, costs need not be identified with individual products unless it is both meaningful and useful that such identification be made.

Thus, common production costs must be allocated among the products manufactured jointly in order that inventory values and income may be determined in accordance with generally accepted accounting principles. In certain decision-making situations, however, such allocation may not only be unnecessary but may be invalid. Both the inventory costing and the decision-making implications of common costs will be considered in the sections that follow.

Allocation of Common Production Costs

Coproducts. Where two or more products are derived from a common production process and each is regarded as a major product of the company, they are usually referred to as *coproducts,* or *joint products.* For purposes of inventory valuation and income determination, the common costs of producing coproducts are allocated among them according to some reasonable scheme. The most widely accepted basis for this allocation is the relative sales values of the several coproducts at the split-off point. This may be illustrated by a simple example. Products A, B, and C are obtained from a single raw material. Each product is salable as it comes from the common processing; that is, each has a readily determinable market value at the split-off point. The common production costs—including raw materials, direct labor, and all overhead—total $600,000 for a given period. The unit output and market value of each product is indicated below, along with the allocation of the common production costs in proportion to the relative market values of the products at the split-off point.

Product	*Unit Output*	*Market Value at Split-off*	*Allocation of Common Cost*
A.	20,000	$ 600,000	$300,000
B.	25,000	200,000	100,000
C.	15,000	400,000	200,000
	60,000	$1,200,000	$600,000

This illustration assumes the absorption costing approach. Under variable costing, fixed overhead would be excluded from the cost of the coproducts; but the same allocation problem would remain for the common variable costs.

It has sometimes been suggested that the common costs be allocated among coproducts in proportion to the number of units produced. If such an allocation scheme were applied to the three products above, their respective costs would be as follows:

Product A	$200,000
Product B	250,000
Produc tC	150,000

Since the cost allocated to product B under this scheme is greater than its sales value, product B would appear to be unprofitable. Of course, its lack of profitability in that case could be traced directly to the cost allocation method employed. Hence, the common cost allocation is usually made on the basis of relative sales values. This is a neutral method insofar as individual product profitability is concerned. Allocation by relative sales values assures that each product will have the same gross margin ratio at the split-off point. In the illustration above, each product has a gross margin ratio of 50% of sales value.

If a product is not readily salable at the split-off point, its market value at that point may be approximated by subtracting from its ultimate sales value the further costs of processing it separately. Thus, if product C above could be sold at a final price of $500,000 but only after further processing costs of $80,000, its market value at the split-off point would be estimated to be $420,000. Obviously, such an approach assumes that no profit attaches to the product beyond the split-off point; value added beyond that point is presumed to be exactly equal to the separate processing costs. Despite the logical invalidity of this assumption, the approach is quite widely used. Where separate processing costs are not substantial in relation to the common costs, this method would not appear to be seriously objectionable. If the separate costs are substantial and, particularly, if they differ significantly among the several coproducts, sales value at the split-off point may be estimated in a slightly different manner to allow for a portion of the profit to be associated with the separate processing. The ratio of the total gross margin on all products to total production costs, both common and separate, would be computed. Given this ratio, it would then be assumed that the same percentage gross margin attaches to each dollar of production cost. Sales at the split-off point would then be approximated by subtracting both the separate processing costs and the gross margin assumed to attach thereto from the final sales value of each product.

By-Products. If one of the products emerging from a common production process is regarded as relatively unimportant in the overall product line of the company, it is described as a *by-product.* A by-product is usually regarded as produced incidentally to the manufacture of a principal product, or main product. Generally speaking, a by-product is identified as such if its revenue is not considered a significant portion of total revenue and if little special effort is required in its manufacture and distribution. No portion of the common production costs is allocated to a by-product. Rather, all of the common costs are charged to the principal product(s). The net realizable value (final sales value minus any separate costs of processing and selling) of the by-product is then credited to the total cost of manufacturing the principal product(s). This may be illustrated by a very simple example. A corporation produces two products, Mapo and Bypo; the former is the principal product and the latter, a by-product. Output, cost, and sales data for a year are as follows:

	Mapo	*Bypo*
Units produced	100,000	8,000
Unit selling price	$5.00	$.40
Common production costs	$300,000	
Separate costs	$ 60,000	$1,200

The cost of the principal product would then be determined thus:

Common costs		$300,000
Separate costs		60,000
		360,000
Less: Net realizable value of Bypo		
Sales value	$3,200	
Less: Separate costs	1,200	2,000
Total cost of Mapo		$358,000
Units produced		100,000
Unit cost		$3.58

If all of the by-product is sold in the period in which it is produced, its full net realizable value is realized; there is no inventory of by-product. If there remains an inventory of by-product, it must be valued at its net realizable value in order that the full amount of net realizable value of by-product produced during a period may be credited to the cost of the principal product manufactured in the same period. This deviation from the customary practice of valuing inventories at cost is generally accepted and, in view of the relative insignificance of by-products, is not likely to have a material effect upon total asset valuation or upon reported income.

There are no set rules for distinguishing between coproducts and by-products. The distinction is a matter of judgment to be made in each individual situation. Similarly, the distinction between by-products and scrap is a question of judgment. Salable scrap is ordinarily accounted for in substantially the same way as by-products. Unsalable scrap, of course, requires no accounting, except to the extent that costs are incurred in order to dispose of it.

Common Production Costs in Decision Making

When a decision concerning the production of an entire group of coproducts or of principal product(s) and by-product(s) is under consideration, the common production costs are relevant to the decision to the extent that they would be avoided if the entire product group were abandoned. The relevant common costs in such a case would be materials, labor, and variable overhead and might include some differential fixed costs. If the decision at hand involves only one product in the group, however, the common production costs are not relevant to it. Abandonment of only one of a group of coproducts (or of a by-product) would not reduce the common costs at all. The incremental profit of the entire group is measured by the difference between the revenue obtained from all of the products and the total costs, both common and separate, directly traceable to the group. The incremental profit of an individual product in the group, however, is measured by the excess of its own revenue over its own separate costs. Any allocation of common cost to one product is irrelevant to its incremental profit. Common cost allocations can be dangerously misleading for decision-making purposes, particularly if the allocations are made on some basis other than relative market values.

It may seem somewhat bothersome that the incremental profits of two coproducts can be determined without regard to the very significant common costs of making those products. But incremental profit is not the same thing as profit. Incremental profit is the amount which an individual product (or a decision) contributes to total enterprise profit, recognizing that the sum of all incremental profits from the several products (or other segments) of the enterprise must be greater than the common costs if a net profit for the firm as a whole is to be realized. The relationship of the profit contributed by one segment of an enterprise to the total enterprise profit will be amplified in Chapter 18.

Incremental Profits of Coproducts. The preceding paragraphs suggested that the incremental profit of an individual coproduct is simply the difference between its sales value and its separate costs. This is true if "separate costs" are properly defined and measured. The relevant separate costs of a product are those which are directly traceable to it and would be avoided if the product were discontinued. Thus, if the cost accounting system allocates a portion of general factory administrative cost and other general factory overhead to all operations in the plant, that portion of the separate processing costs which represents such allocations is irrelevant to the incremental profit of an individual product. The same is true of fixed selling and administrative expenses which may be allocated among the various products for some reporting purpose (not inventory valuation, of course). Only those selling and administrative expenses directly traceable to the individual product may be included in the determination of the product's incremental profit.

Everything said above concerning coproducts is equally true of by-products. In the case of a principal product (as distinguished from a by-product), on the other hand, it would seem that the revenue from the sales of that main product should normally be adequate to cover not only its own separate costs but also the production costs common to it and the by-product. There are instances where this is not so and where the overall profitability of the combination of principal product and by-product is assured only by sales of the by-product. In such instance, it would appear that the by-product is such only by arbitrary definition; in a very real sense, it is a coproduct.

Extent of Processing a Coproduct or By-Product. Sometimes a firm has an alternative with respect to the disposition of a particular coproduct or by-product. It may sell the item in its stage of completion at the split-off point or may subject it to further processing and sell it in a more advanced stage of completion at a higher price. Such an alternative should be evaluated as any other decision concerning the extent of processing a product. The analysis for such a decision was illustrated earlier in this chapter. The incremental profit from a decision to process the item further would be equal to the additional revenue realized from selling the product at the advanced stage of completion over that revenue realizable from sale at the split-off point minus the further processing and other costs directly traceable to the product. If that incremental profit is positive, the decision to process further would be advantageous from the point of view of short-run profit maximization. As in all decisions, there may be other considerations which cannot be quantified or reduced to financial consequences but which are, nevertheless, critical to the decision. And, of course, if the decision to engage in further processing would require the purchase or construction of additional productive facilities, the proposal would have to be analyzed as a long-term investment decision. Simple incremental profit analysis would not be appropriate.

QUESTIONS FOR DISCUSSION

1. For purposes of decision making, what are relevant costs?
2. Is the incremental profit from a decision the same as the variable profit from the decision? Explain.
3. Distinguish clearly among the following three concepts: differential cost, direct cost, and variable cost. Distinguish among these concepts: fixed cost, indirect cost, and sunk cost.
4. Suggest an operational distinction between short-term and long-term de-

cisions. Into which classification would you expect each of the following decisions to fall:

a. Decision to purchase a new building.
b. Decision to rent a new building.
c. Decision to sell products in markets not previously served.
d. Decision to establish a long-term planning committee of the board of directors.

5. "Since fixed costs are unaffected by a change in the volume of operations, they are always irrelevant to any business decision short of a decision to discontinue operations altogether." Evaluate this statement.
6. Do you believe incremental profit analysis is pertinent to decision making in nonprofit institutions such as schools and hospitals? Discuss.
7. The uses of cost data in income measurement and inventory valuation are not always consistent with the uses of cost data for decision making. How can a single cost accounting system provide data for both of these purposes? Would such a system include all of the cost data necessary for financial accounting purposes? Would it include all of the cost data necessary for decision making?
8. Describe the procedures that the management of a manufacturing firm might employ to identify and measure all of the costs relevant to a decision as to whether to make or to buy a part used in the manufacture of a particular product.
9. This chapter suggests that the common costs of producing two or more coproducts are relevant to the valuation of inventories of the individual products but irrelevant to a decision respecting any one of the coproducts. This appears to be inconsistent. If a cost is irrelevant to whether a product is produced or not, how can such a cost reasonably be included in the cost of an inventory of that product? In this connection, would it make a significant difference whether absorption or variable costing were used?
10. "Unlike the common costs of coproducts, the costs associated with by-products are handled in essentially the same way for financial accounting purposes as for purposes of decision making." Do you agree or disagree with this statement? Explain.
11. A lumber company is planning to build a new mill. It has two basic alternatives with regard to the disposition of sawdust. The sawdust can be swept up, placed in sacks, and sold or it can be burned in a large incinerator. Assuming that the incinerator will be needed for other refuse regardless of the decision respecting sawdust, what factors would be relevant to the decision as to the disposition of the sawdust? Would the situation be changed materially if the incinerator would not be needed if the sawdust were not to be burned?
12. How should the lumber company in the preceding question determine whether sawdust is to be accounted for as a coproduct, a by-product, or salable scrap, if the decision is made to sell the sawdust?
13. If depreciation on manufacturing equipment is computed by the productive hours method and the company is considering adding a second production

shift, is depreciation on the equipment a relevant cost in connection with the decision regarding the second shift? Why or why not?

14. Are income taxes differential costs with respect to decisions that are anticipated to have the effect of increasing or decreasing taxable income? Could income tax considerations ever be the deciding factors in such decisions? Explain.

PROBLEMS

1. The Wroth Radio Company produces most of its own parts. The standard labor cost in the Parts Department is $2.00 per hour. Variable overhead is applied at a rate of $.50 per labor hour, and fixed overhead at a rate of $1.50 per labor hour.

For its 1966 output, the company will need a new part never before used. This part could be made in the Parts Department without any expansion of the existing facilities. It is estimated that the labor time for the new part would be one-half hour per unit. Materials cost has been estimated at $2.75 per unit. Alternatively, the part could be purchased from independent suppliers for $4.40 per unit delivered. The company estimates that its annual usage of this new part will be 50,000 units.

Required:

In the short run, would it be more profitable to make or to purchase the new part? Support your answer with appropriate financial analysis.

2. The Gargery Forge Company produces a single product in its New Haven plant. This product is manufactured in three successive production processes, each organized as a separate operating department. Following are the budgeted annual variable production costs for an output of 40,000 units, which is regarded as normal volume:

	Dept. A	*Dept. B*	*Dept. C*
Direct materials	$48,000	$ 5,500	
Direct labor	12,000	15,000	$9,000
Variable overhead	8,000	11,000	5,500

Fixed overhead is applied to production at a plant-wide rate of 150 percent of direct labor cost. None of the fixed overhead is considered to be directly traceable to individual departments.

Recently, the company has learned that is can purchase a semi-finished product, ready for work in Department B, from a Providence manufacturer at a unit price of $1.80 delivered. If this semi-finished product were purchased, Department A could be closed.

Required:

1. On the basis of short-run profitability, would it be advantageous for the company to purchase the semi-finished product and close Department A?
2. What additional factors should the company's management consider before making the decision in this situation?

3. The Rawlins Engine Company produces most of its engine parts in its own plant. Recently, it has been considering the merits of purchasing finished parts instead of manufacturing them. At present, it is weighing the advantages of purchasing Part No. 1402 from an outside supplier for $5.00 per unit. If this were done, monthly purchasing costs would be increased by $500.

Part No. 1402 is now manufactured in the Stamping Department along with several other parts. The department would continue operations on a somewhat reduced basis if Part No. 1402 were no longer produced. The average monthly usage of Part No. 1402 is 12,000 units. The direct costs of producing the part include $1.20 per unit for materials and 2 labor hours per unit at a wage rate of $1.50 per hour. Overhead is applied to production in the Stamping Department on the basis of direct labor hours. The monthly overhead budget for this department is as follows:

Direct labor hours	150,000	180,000	210,000
Variable costs	$ 60,000	$ 72,000	$ 84,000
Semi-variable costs	45,000	48,000	51,000
Fixed costs	60,000	60,000	60,000
	$165,000	$180,000	$195,000

Normal production volume in the Stamping Department has been set at 180,000 labor hours per month.

Required:

Would it be more profitable for the company to continue making Part No. 1402 or to purchase it?

4. At present, the Baum Corporation owns and operates its own fleet of 100 automobiles for the use of its sales force. The president has asked for a report on the relative advantages of three alternatives: (1) continuing to *own* cars, (2) arranging to *lease* 100 cars annually, and (3) agreeing to *reimburse* 100 salesmen for the use of their own cars at the rate of $.08 per mile (business mileage only, of course). The traffic manager has recommended leasing and has presented the following analysis in support of his position:

	Cost per mile per car to:		
	Own	*Lease*	*Reimburse*
Gasoline	$.0200	$.0200	
Grease and oil	.0015	.0015	
Tires	.0040	.0040	
Maintenance	.0300		
Depreciation	.0260		
Insurance	.0030		
Taxes and license	.0015		
Rental		.0500	
Reimbursement			$.08
	$.0860	$.0755	$.08

He states that these figures are based on the following information:

1) Each car is operated, on the average, 60,000 miles per year.

2) Gasoline cost may reasonably be expected to vary directly with mileage.

3) The cars are greased and the oil is changed every 4,000 miles; no oil is added between changes.

4) Four new tires, at a net cost of $100, are put on each car every 25,000 miles.

5) Company-performed maintenance is done in the company's service garage, which is operated at a monthly cost of $20,000 plus supplies and parts. This garage must be maintained to service trucks and warehouse vehicles as well as automobiles. However, if no cars were serviced, the basic monthly cost of operating the garage could be reduced by $8,000. Maintenance supplies and parts average $50 per car every 10,000 miles.

6) The original cost of each car is $2,600. Each car is assumed to have a useful life of 100,000 miles and a salvage value of $400 at the end of this life.

7) Insurance is $180 annually per car.

8) Taxes and license fees total $90 per year per car.

9) The rental charge per car is $50 per month plus $.04 per mile. This charge includes maintenance, insurance, and taxes and license fees.

Because of the expanding sales territories covered by the firm, it is estimated that each car will be operated, on the average, 100,000 miles per year in the future.

Required:

The president has asked you, the controller, to review the traffic manager's report and add your own recommendation to his. Prepare a report to comply with the president's request.

5. The Prynne Lettering Co. produces Product A. The product sells for $18 per unit. Variable costs to make and sell the product are $5 per unit, and fixed costs $7 per unit at a normal output of 100,000 units per year. Sales volume in recent years has been equal to normal output.

Rearbuck Stores, Inc., has offered the Prynne Co. a contract for 50,000 units of Product A each year at a price of $14. As these units would be distributed under Rearbuck's private brand name, there would be no adverse effect upon sales of the product under the Prynne brand name and Prynne could avoid $.60 of variable selling expenses per unit. Fixed production costs would have to be increased by $200,000 annually in order to increase production volume to 150,000 units.

The production engineer has recommended a plan to improve product quality and, thereby, increase sales volume. His proposal would increase variable production costs by $2 and fixed costs by $160,000 per year. Sales volume would be increased by 50,000 units annually with no change in the selling price.

The sales manager has suggested still another plan to boost volume. He would reduce the selling price by 5 percent. This price reduction would increase sales volume by 40 percent. The additional output could be achieved by an increase in fixed costs of $250,000 per year.

None of the three proposed changes in operations would necessitate any new capital expenditures. In each case, the additional output would be obtained by more intensive use of existing facilities.

Required:

Accepting the assumptions underlying each of the proposals for change in operations, evaluate the profitability of each alternative course of action and indicate which would be most profitable in the short run.

6. The Sweetmaid Bakery sells two specialty cakes, a butter cream delight and a German chocolate cake. Both are baked in one oven, which will accommodate six cakes at a time and can be operated for fifty-four hours a week. The demand for both cakes is so great that the bakery could sell the entire output of the oven in any combination of the two cakes, including only one or the other. The only variable costs of making the cakes are their respective ingredients costs. A comparison of the prices, costs, and oven times of the two cakes is as follows:

	Butter Cream Delight	*German Chocolate*
Price	$1.60	$1.20
Ingredients cost	$ .80	$ .72
Oven time	27 min.	15 min.

Required:

What would be the most profitable sales mix of these two cakes? Support your answer with appropriate financial analysis.

7. The Gold Coast Products Corporation manufactures component parts for hydraulic equipment. Two of these products, the Type C Valve and the Type K Elbow Joint, are currently suffering greatly reduced sales volume because of competition from lower priced substitute products. Data pertinent to these two items are as follows:

	Type C Valve	*Type K Elbow Joint*
Selling price	$11.75	$5.60
Units currently sold annually	10,000	24,000
Unit production costs:		
Materials	$ 3.25	$ .85
Labor	2.80	1.10
Variable overhead	1.45	1.40
Fixed overhead	1.35	.75
	$ 8.85	$4.10

Unabsorbed fixed overhead currently is $13,500 per year.

The sales manager has suggested that selling prices of $10.50 for the Type C Valve and $4.95 for the Type K Elbow Joint would restore the company's normal market shares of these items, 15,000 units per year of the Type C Valve and 33,000 units per year of the Type K Elbow Joint.

The purchasing agent has pointed out that identical items could be purchased from Japanese manufacturers below the corporation's own cost and resold to the corporation's customers. Such an arrangement, he claims, would partially mitigate the impact of the suggested price reduction. Type C Valves could be purchased from Japanese suppliers for $7.95 each and Type K Elbow Joints, for $3.75. Both of these prices include all freight and duties.

The volume of production of the two items in question here is not so great that any decision affecting them would have a significant impact upon investments in factory, sales, and administrative facilities. All selling and administrative costs are regarded as fixed; they currently average 20 percent of manufacturing cost.

Required:

Submit a report showing the relative profitabilities of the alternative selling prices suggested for the two products in question. Show also the relative profitabilities of buying the items from Japanese manufacturers and continuing production of them.

8. You are the independent auditor for the Scoopa Company. When you had completed your audit for the preceding year, management asked your assistance in arriving at a decision whether to continue manufacturing a part or to buy it from an outside supplier. The part, which is named Faktron, is a component used in some of the finished products of the company.

From your audit working papers and from further investigation, you develop the following data relative to the company's operations:

1. The annual requirement for Faktrons is 5,000 units. The lowest price quotation from a supplier was $8 per unit.

2. Faktrons have been manufactured in the Precision Machinery Department. Following are the total costs of this department during the preceding year, when 5,000 Faktrons were produced:

Materials	$67,500
Direct labor	50,000
Indirect labor	20,000
Light and heat	5,500
Power	3,000
Depreciation	10,000
Property taxes and insurance	8,000
Payroll taxes and other fringe benefits	9,800
Miscellaneous	5,000

Discontinuing production of Faktrons would reduce the operating volume of the Precision Machinery Department but would not permit the disposal of any of the department's assets.

3. The following proportions of the variable costs in the Precision Machinery Department are directly traceable to Faktrons:

Materials	30%
Direct labor	40%
Indirect labor	30%
Power	10%

4. If Faktrons are purchased from an outside supplier, shipping charges would average $.50 per unit and indirect labor in the Precision Machinery

Department would be increased by $5,000 for receiving, inspecting, and handling.

Required:

1. Prepare a schedule showing the relative costs of making and buying Faktrons to assist management in reaching a decision.
2. Discuss the consideration in addition to costs that you would bring to the attention of management in helping them make a decision in this situation.

(Adapted from CPA Examination)

9. The Marcia Company has asked your assistance in determining an economical sales and production mix of their products for 1967. The company manufactures a line of dolls and a doll dress sewing kit.

The company's sales department provides the following data:

Product	*Estimated Demand in 1967 (units)*	*Established Net Price per Unit*
Laurie doll	50,000	$5.20
Debbie doll	42,000	2.40
Sarah doll	35,000	8.50
Kathy doll	40,000	4.00
Sewing kit	325,000	3.00

To promote sales of the sewing kit, there is a 15 percent reduction in the established net price for a kit purchased at the same time as a Marcia Company doll. The company anticipates that sewing kits will be sold in conjunction with 80 percent of the sales of each of the four dolls.

From the accounting records, you have developed the following data:

1. Standard direct production costs per unit:

Product	*Material*	*Labor*
Laurie	$1.40	$ .80
Debbie	.70	.50
Sarah	2.69	1.40
Kathy	1.00	1.00
Sewing kit	.60	.40

2. The standard labor rate of $2 per hour is expected to continue without change in 1967. The plant has an effective capacity of 130,000 labor hours per year on a single shift basis. Present equipment can produce all of the products.

3. Variable overhead will amount to $1 per direct labor hour. Total fixed costs for 1967 will be $100,000.

4. No inventory is available to meet the sales demand of 1967.

Required:

1. Prepare a schedule showing the incremental profit per unit of each product.

2. Prepare a schedule showing the incremental profit of each product per direct labor hour.
3. Is the present effective capacity on a single shift basis adequate to meet estimated sales demand in 1967? If it is not, how would you recommend the company alter its budgeted product mix to keep production within the limits of single shift capacity?
4. Irrespective of your answer in part 3, assume now that capacity is not sufficient to meet sales demand in 1967. How might the company expand its capacity to meet that demand? Under what conditions would each of these methods of expanding capacity be profitable in 1967?

(Adapted from CPA Examination)

10. Following is the income statement of the Doan Production Co. for the month ended March 31, 1966:

	Product X	*Product Y*	*Product Z*	*Total*
Sales	$80,000	$45,000	$63,000	$188,000
Cost of goods sold:				
Materials	17,500	5,000	16,500	39,000
Labor	19,000	6,000	15,000	40,000
Variable overhead	4,500	2,000	7,000	13,500
Fixed overhead	12,500	14,000	4,800	31,300
	53,500	27,000	43,300	123,800
Gross margin	26,500	18,000	19,700	64,200
Selling and administrative expenses:				
Variable	9,000	7,000	6,500	22,500
Fixed	12,500	12,000	4,200	28,700
	21,500	19,000	10,700	51,200
Net income before tax	5,000	(1,000)	9,000	13,000
Income tax (20%)	1,000	(200)	1,800	2,600
Net income	$ 4,000	$(800)	$ 7,200	$ 10,400
Units produced and sold	1,000	1,000	1,500	

The plant was operated at full capacity during March. It takes half again as long to complete one unit of Product X as it does to complete one unit of either Product Y or Product Z. (In other words, during a given period of time, two units of Product X can be manufactured for every three units of Product Y or Product Z.) All fixed costs are common to the company as a whole.

Required:

1. Rank the three products in the order of their contributions to company profit per unit of factory time.
2. Assume that the company decides to discontinue production of the least profitable product, as shown by the ranking in part 1 above, and to produce equal quantities of the remaining two products.

Operations would continue at full capacity. Which two products would be manufactured and how many of each?

3. Assuming unlimited flexibility of the product mix (including production of only one of the three products), determine the lowest possible break-even point for the company as a percentage of full capacity.

11. The management of the Southern Cottonseed Company has engaged you to assist in the development of information to be used for managerial decisions. The company has the capacity to process 20,000 tons of cottonseed per year. The yield of a ton of cottonseed is as follows:

Product	*Average Yield per Ton of Cottonseed*	*Average Selling Price per Trade Unit*
Oil	300 lbs.	$00.15 per lb.
Meal	600 lbs.	$50 per ton
Hulls	800 lbs.	$20 per ton
Lint	100 lbs.	$ 3 per cwt.
Waste	200 lbs.	

A special marketing study revealed that the company can expect to sell its entire output for the coming year at the average selling prices listed above. You have determined the company's costs to be at follows:

Processing costs:
Variable—$9 per ton of cottonseed put into process
Fixed—$108,000 per year
Marketing costs (all variable): $20 per ton sold
Administrative costs (all fixed): $90,000 per year

From the above information, you prepared and submitted to management a detailed report on the company's break-even point. In view of conditions in the cottonseed market, management has told you that they would also like to know the average maximum amount that the company can afford to pay for a ton of cottonseed. Management defines this average maximum price per ton as the amount that would result in the company's having losses no greater when operating than when closed down. You are told that all fixed costs would be incurred even if operations were to be shut down.

Required:

1. Compute the average maximum amount that the company can afford to pay for a ton of cottonseed.
2. The stockholders consider the minimum satisfactory return on their equity in the firm to be 25 percent before income taxes. The stockholders' equity in the company is $968,000. Compute the maximum average price that the company can pay for a ton of cottonseed and still realize the minimum satisfactory return on the stockholders' equity.

(Adapted from CPA Examination)

12. Natchez Hosiery Mills, Inc., manufactures and sells women's stockings. Productive capacity is three million pairs per year. All pairs produced are carefully inspected. Twenty percent of the output is flawed and marked as "seconds." The remaining 80 percent of output is sold under the brand name "Natchez Maids" for $1.65 per pair. "Natchez Seconds" are sold for $1.10 per pair. Budgeted sales volume for 1966 is as follows:

Natchez Maids	2,000,000 pairs
Natchez Seconds	500,000 pairs

Budgeted costs for 1966 include the following items:

Variable production costs	$.48 per pair
Fixed production costs	$360,000
Variable selling expenses	$.07 per pair
Fixed selling and administrative expenses	$200,000

A marketing consultant engaged by the firm has advised management that the sales of the seconds under the Natchez brand name injure sales of the "Natchez Maids." He estimates that sales volume of "Natchez Maids" could be increased by 25 percent in 1966 if the sales of the seconds under the company's brand name were discontinued.

The sales manager has learned that the entire output of seconds, without brand name identification, could be sold to a chain of discount stores for $.78 per pair. The normal variable selling expenses on these sales could be avoided. Additional annual selling and billing costs of $25,000 would be incurred, however.

There is no significant inventory of seconds in stock as of December 31, 1965. The company wishes to maintain the same inventory of "Natchez Maids" at the end of 1966 as is on hand at the start of the year.

Required:

Assuming the validity of the marketing consultant's estimates, what would be the most profitable course of action with respect to the disposition of "seconds" in 1966? Present a report to the company's management in support of your conclusion.

13. The Biograph Theater has shown the motion picture, "Silverthumb," for the past two weeks. It has been one of the most successful films that has played at the theater in several years. Because of the daring costuming in the picture and the compromising situations in which the hero repeatedly finds himself, the manager of the theater has scrupulously restricted admission to adults only. The manager is convinced that attendance will continue to be above normal for another two weeks if the run of "Silverthumb" is extended. Another movie, "Tiny Tots in Toyland," is booked for the next two weeks, however. Even if "Silverthumb" is extended, the theater will have to pay the regular rental on "Tiny Tots in Toyland" as well.

Normal attendance at the Biograph Theater is 1,800 patrons per week. Approximately one third of these are children under the age of 12. Attendance for "Silverthumb" has been twice the normal total, despite (or perhaps because of) the "adults only" policy. The manager believes that this would taper off in the second two weeks. He estimates that attendance would be 25 percent below that of the first two weeks during a third week and 50 percent lower during a fourth week. Attendance for "Tiny Tots in Toyland" would be expected to be normal throughout its run, regardless of the length of that run.

All features at the theater are shown at the regular prices of $1.25 for adults and $.65 for children under 12. The weekly rental charge for "Silverthumb" is $450. For "Tiny Tots in Toyland," it is $375. All other operating costs are fixed in the amount of $1,500 per week, except the cost of popcorn and candy which is 60 percent of the selling price. Sales of popcorn and candy regularly average $.15 per patron, regardless of age.

Required:

The manager of the Biograph Theater has three courses of action open to him for the next two weeks. He can extend the run of "Silverthumb" either for two weeks or for one week, or he can halt its run and show "Tiny Tots in Toyland" for the full two weeks. Which alternative would be most profitable?

14. The Carroll Corporation manufactures two coproducts, Dum and Dee. Under present operations, raw materials are processed in Department A and the two products are separated at the end of this process. For every unit of Dum, two units of Dee are obtained. Dum is then finished in Department B and Dee, in Department C. Actual operating data for 1965 are as follows:

	Dept. A	*Dept. B*	*Dept. C*	*Total*
Units produced:				
Dum	25,000	25,000		25,000
Dee	50,000		50,000	50,000
Costs incurred:				
Raw materials	$90,000			$ 90,000
Direct labor	50,000	$45,000	$45,000	140,000
Variable overhead	30,000	30,000	30,000	90,000
Differential fixed overhead	10,000	5,000	15,000	30,000
Common fixed overhead (allocated by engineering formula)	30,000	15,000	15,000	60,000

At present, Dum is sold for $10 per unit and Dee, for $5.50 per unit. Both products are readily marketable at the split-off point also—Dum for $6 per unit and Dee for $4 per unit. Department B and/or Department C could be shut down completely if Dum and/or Dee, respectively, were sold at the split-off point.

Required:

1. Under an absorption costing system, what was the unit cost of Dum and the unit cost of Dee during 1965? Show all computations. Take the allocation of common fixed overhead as given.
2. From the point of view of short-run profit maximization, when should each product be sold—after final completion or at the split-off point? Show computations to support your answers.

15. The Lewis Corporation manufactures three different products from a single raw material. A summary of operating data for 1966 is presented below.

	Product A	*Product B*	*Product C*	*Total*
Output in pounds	60,000	150,000	90,000	300,000
Selling price per pound	$ .75	$ .80	$ 1.50	
Production costs:				
Materials				$ 80,000
Direct labor	$ 2,000	$ 10,000	$18,000	55,000
Variable overhead	1,000	5,000	9,000	30,000
Fixed overhead	15,000	20,000	20,000	95,000

No allocation of the common production costs incurred up to the split-off point has been made in the foregoing cost figures. All of the output of 1966 was sold. The company uses absorption costing.

Required:

1. Allocate the production costs incurred prior to the split-off point among the three products in some reasonable manner.
2. If the products were to be sold at the split-off point, what would be the minimum selling price necessary for each in order that the company realize the same gross profit earned in 1966? Present appropriate support for your answer.

16. The Franklin Packing Company prepares and packs a variety of meat products. Bones are cleaned of all usable meat and then are ground into meal, which is packed in 50-pound sacks and sold to fertilizer manufacturers. The company's output and sales in 1966 were as follows:

	Meat	*Bone Meal*
Production (in pounds)	400,000	30,000
Sales (in pounds)	380,000	20,000
Sales revenue	$300,000	$ 4,800

Total operating costs for 1966 were as follows:

Raw materials used	$89,800
Direct labor	36,000
Variable overhead applied	18,000
Fixed overhead applied	41,400
Selling and administrative expenses	50,000
Underapplied overhead	6,700

Variable overhead is applied to production at a normal rate of $.50 per dollar of direct labor cost. Fixed overhead is applied at a rate of $1.15 per direct labor dollar. The direct labor cost of grinding and bagging the bones was $1,800 in 1966. This work was done in facilities and with equipment used in the production of meat products. No fixed overhead or nonmanufacturing costs could be avoided by simply scrapping the bones. The company accounts for bone meal as a by-product.

Inventories are accounted for by the average cost method. The inventory of Finished Product at Dec. 31, 1965, consisted of 10,000 pounds of meat at an average cost of $.42 per pound. Production costs were incurred at the same level throughout 1966. There was no inventory of unsold bone meal at Dec. 31, 1965. There were no inventories of Work in Process at the beginning or at the end of 1966. The applicable income tax rate is 30 percent.

Required:

Prepare an income statement and a supporting schedule of cost of goods manufactured and sold for the year 1966.

17. The basic processing of raw materials in the Dryer Chemical Corporation's plant yields three semi-finished products, Worlon, Nantron, and Kortex. The budgeted cost of the basic processing for 1966 is $1,959,000. Production, price, and cost data for the three products are as follows:

	Worlon	*Nantron*	*Kortex*
Output in units	250,000	150,000	15,000
Selling price per unit	$ 12	$ 10	$ 4
Separate processing costs:			
Variable per unit	$ 3	$ 1.80	$ 2.20
Fixed	$150,000	$ 85,000	$15,000

Worlon and Nantron are accounted for as coproducts. Kortex is treated as a by-product.

Required:

1. Assuming that all budgeted data are actually realized, compute the final unit cost of each of the coproducts for 1966.
2. By increasing the basic processing cost by $50,000, the product mix could be altered to yield one-fifth more units of Worlon and one-third more units of Kortex with no change in the total number of units of all products produced. Would such a change in the production plans be profitable in 1966?
3. By increasing the basic processing cost by $75,000, all production of Kortex could be converted to equal quantities of Worlon and Nantron. Would such a change in the production process be profitable in 1966?

Chapter 15

RATE OF RETURN ON INVESTED CAPITAL

INVESTORS are invariably interested in knowing how profitable their investments are. There are many ways in which the profitability of an investment may be measured, but the most popular is the rate of return on the investment. The *rate of return,* or *yield,* on an investment is the ratio of the income from the investment to the amount invested. Income here is defined as the excess of all values received from the investment over the amount invested. Obviously, an "investment" which returns nothing more than the amount initially "invested" has no yield at all and cannot properly be described as an investment. A bank demand deposit, for example, by law can offer no yield to the depositor; hence, it is not an investment in the sense intended here. Investors wish to know the rates of return on their investments both in prospect and in retrospect. The anticipated rate of return on a proposed investment may be the most important single factor in deciding whether or not the investment should be made. The actual rate of return realized on an investment made earlier may be the best indicator of the quality of that investment.

Managers, as well as stockholders and creditors, are investors, although they typically invest other persons' capital rather than their own. Nevertheless, they too are concerned with the profitability of investments, both before and after the fact. The discussions in this chapter will include the computation and the evaluation of the rate of return on an investment, both in prospect and in retrospect. The discussions will be facilitated if we consider first the rate of return on an investment made in the past and then the rate of return on proposed investments.

RATE OF RETURN OF A BUSINESS ENTERPRISE

In retrospect, the rate of return for any type of investment may be computed by the same basic approach, whether it is an investment in a single share of stock, in a single residence leased to tenants, or in a complex business enterprise. In keeping with the overall point of view of this book, we shall illustrate here the rate of return on a business concern only.

Objectives and Assumptions

For many purposes, the total capital invested in a business enterprise may be regarded as a single investment with a single rate of return. The actual rate of return for a firm is typically determined periodically, most often annually. The annual rate of return of a business may be used as a measure of the efficiency of the operation of the firm during a year and, hence, as a technique of appraising the performance of management during the year. This performance should be of concern to everyone with a financial interest in the firm, including management itself. The annual rate of return may also be used by the owners of the enterprise to evaluate the profitability of their investment in the firm. As we shall see shortly, a single measure of the rate of return may not be appropriate for both of these purposes.

For either purpose mentioned above—determining management's operating efficiency or measuring the profitability of stockholders' investment—the rate of return on investment is presumed to be a valid criterion for making a judgment. Necessarily, it is a relative criterion. What is a good rate of return on a particular investment depends upon rates of return on alternative investments. Whether a given rate of return on the stockholders' investment in a corporation is satisfactory or not depends upon the rate which might have been realized on an investment in some other business activity of comparable safety and stability. The safety of the principal invested must not be overlooked in evaluating rates of return on alternative investments. Similarly, whether management's overall operating performance for the year has been good or bad depends upon how it compares with performances by the managements of comparable firms in the same year. Unfortunately, establishing comparability among business enterprises can be extremely difficult. To begin with, no two enterprises are identical. Factors of geography, timing, and varying levels of managerial training and skill all tend to impair comparability. To make matters worse, the impacts of a fluctuating price level and of diverse accounting methods impede comparison of firms which appear structurally and operationally similar. As general rule, businessmen and investors assume that comparisons of firms within the same industry are valid, although, even here, significant differences of circumstances and methods may exist.

If a rate of return is to be a useful basis for business decisions, it should e comparable within a firm from year to year. This may not always be ossible. Substantial changes in the structure and/or operations of a firm ıay impair inter-period comparability. The operations and profitability f an enterprise may reasonably be expected to be different after an nportant merger or a major product change. It is not uncommon for a rm to change its methods of accounting from time to time. However alid the reasons for such changes, the changes do impair comparisons ver time. Finally, computing an annual rate of return for an enterprise ssumes that both the investment in and income of that enterprise may e measured for a year with some degree of precision and reliability. uch measurements are not always as obvious as one might wish.

ate of Return on Stockholders' Equity

Computing the rate of return on stockholders' investment in a orporation is designed to show the profitability of that investment for a iven period of time. Where there are both preferred and common stock ssues outstanding, the rate of return is normally computed on the ommon stockholders' equity only. The return to preferred shareholders s usually limited to the amount of the stated dividend preference.[1] Thus, he rate of return (r) would be computed as follows:

$$r = \frac{\text{net income after taxes} - \text{preferred dividends}}{\text{common stockholders' equity}}$$

he component parts of this computation may be complicated by a great nany factors, including the various legal rights and preferences of the referred stockholders. Probably the most difficult measurement probem is the determination of net income, in view of the many alternative ccounting procedures which may be employed and which affect the mount of income. The impact of price-level changes must also be onsidered. In current accounting practice, the effects of inflation or leflation on financial statements are ignored. Thus, stockholders' equity s stated in terms of the dollars at the time of original issue of the stock nd at the various times at which earnings were retained and reinvested n the firm. In order for this rate of return to be wholly valid, both ncome and stockholders' equity would have to be stated in terms of lollars of the same purchasing power. Unfortunately, only in rare nstances are corporate financial statements adjusted to a "common dolar."

---

[1] If the preferred stock is fully participating in dividends with common stock, determiıation of the rate of return for total stockholders' equity (common and preferred) would e appropriate. Participating preferred stock is quite rare, however.

The amount of common stockholders' equity for purposes of this rate of return calculation is usually that reported in the firm's balance sheet at the end of the year. If there have been significant changes in that equity (e.g., substantial sales or retirements of common stock), the equity figure used as the base in the computation should be the average equity balance for the year. Earnings of the current year, less current dividends, are included in common stockholders' equity at the end of the year. Thus, they are included in both the numerator and denominator of the rate of return fraction. Where their inclusion in common equity has a material effect upon the rate of return, some adjustment to an average equity may be necessary. As a practical matter, this is usually ignored.

The rate of return on stockholders' equity shown above is computed from the point of view of the enterprise rather than that of the stockholder. The income used is that available to the common shareholders, but not necessarily that distributed to them. The investment base used is the equity of the common stockholders as carried on the company's books. To an individual stockholder, a more significant measure of his own rate of return might be the ratio of the dividends he receives to the cost of his own investment (again with any necessary adjustment for price-level changes) or to the market value of his investment (his opportunity cost of holding the stock).

Rate of Return on Total Assets

In appraising the performance of management, there is fairly general agreement that the appropriate rate of return is that on the total investment in assets of the enterprise, regardless of the source of their financing. Unfortunately, there is still some disagreement as to what items should be included in income for this purpose and as to how total assets should be measured. We shall consider some of these questions in the sections that follow, but, at this point, we shall simply explain the basic methodology of the computation. The basic computation of the rate of return on total assets is as follows:

$$r = \frac{\text{income}}{\text{total assets}}$$

Frequently, the same end result is achieved by means of a two-step calculation. First the rate of income to sales is computed.

$$\text{rate of return on sales} = \frac{\text{income}}{\text{sales}}$$

Then, the ratio of sales to total assets is calculated; this is called the asset turnover.

$$\text{asset turnover} = \frac{\text{sales}}{\text{total assets}}$$

'he rate of return on assets is then the product of these two intermediate mounts.

$$r = \text{rate of return on sales} \times \text{asset turnover}$$

The two-step approach to the rate of return on total assets is often onsidered preferable for two reasons. It brings into the analysis the very nportant quantity of sales volume and it facilitates comparisons beween firms of unequal sizes. The latter advantage can best be seen in a mple illustration. Consider the following data for two firms in the same ndustry but of very different sizes:

	Company A	*Company B*
(*a*) Total assets	$30,000,000	$2,000,000
(*b*) Income	$ 3,600,000	$ 240,000
(*c*) Rate of return on total assets: (*b*) ÷ (*a*)	.12	.12
(*d*) Sales	$24,000,000	$4,800,000
(*e*) Rate of return on sales: (*b*) ÷ (*d*)	.15	.05
(*f*) Asset turnover: (*d*) ÷ (*a*)	.8	2.4
(*g*) Rate of return on total assets: (*e*) × (*f*)	.12	.12

f only assets and income are considered, the operating performances of ne two companies' managements appear equally good (or bad). By ncluding the sales data, however, it is apparent that company A earns nree times the income per sales dollar as company B and that company B obtains three times as much sales volume as company A per dollar nvested in assets. There may be many reasons for these differences, and hese reasons must be identified and examined carefully. Mere determiation of different rates of return on sales and/or asset turnovers does ot entail any qualitative evaluation of managerial performance, but it nay lead to such an evaluation.

'roblems of Measuring Investment in Assets

Some of the difficulties that might be encountered in measuring ommon stockholders' equity (i.e., net assets) correctly were discussed arlier and will not be considered further here. We shall now consider ome of the problems and controversies in the area of measuring assets or the computation of rate of return on total assets.

Book Value or Market Value? In computing rate of return, should ssets be stated at their book values (i.e., cost less accumulated depreciaion or amortization) or at their current fair market values (or replacement costs)? Certainly, the former is more easily obtained; it may b taken directly from published financial statements. On the other hand the latter may be more meaningful. Book value ignores the effects c general price-level changes and also of specific price changes for specifi assets. Also, book value may be influenced by the depreciation metho used. If an accelerated depreciation method is used, the book value c plant property will decline faster than under straight-line depreciation This fast reduction may or may not be offset by increases in other assets If book value is used, any comparison between firms which acquire their respective assets at significantly different price levels will be im paired. If the rate of return on total assets is a valid indicator of the effi ciency of one firm's management relative to others, it should be state in terms that facilitate comparison among firms. The most significan basis of valuation for an investment in assets, in light of alternatives, i its opportunity cost; and current market value normally is the best avail able measure of opportunity cost. The conceptual advantage of marke value over cost in the computation of rate of return on total assets i somewhat offset by the greater difficulty of measuring market value This measurement may be particularly difficult for long-lived assets fo which there is no active market.

Capital Available or Capital Employed? A few firms have adopte the practice of computing a rate of return only on assets productivel employed, any excess or idle assets being excluded from the base for th computation. This approach distinguishes between capital employe (productive assets) and capital available (all assets, including those no actually in use). Such an approach to the rate of return seems illogical however. The exclusion of idle assets from the base seems to conflic with the purported objective of the computation, namely, measuring th efficiency of management. Excess or idle assets suggest manageria inefficiency, and to omit them from consideration when management' performance is being appraised would appear to defeat the purpose o the evaluation before it is begun. In this context, it would appear that th only legitimate reason for separate identification of idle assets would b to document managerial inefficiency.

Operating and Nonoperating Assets. Even among the assets produc tively employed by a firm, there may be some significant differences Operating assets are those employed in the principal business activities o the enterprise. Nonoperating assets are those intended to generat revenue from sources other than the firm's principal operations; they ar usually classified as "investments" in the enterprise's balance sheet. Th tes of return on operating and nonoperating assets may be quite fferent. If so, the rate of return on total assets would be a weighted erage of the two. Calculation of all three rates of return—on total sets, on operating assets, and on nonoperating assets—would seem esirable in such a case. A basically favorable rate of return on total ssets might mask a very unsatisfactory rate on nonoperating assets and, ence, an inefficient utilization of some of the firm's resources. Even here separate rates of return are determined for operating and nonoperating assets, however, the rate of return on total assets is still the basic ndicator of management performance.

roblems of Measuring Income

The measurement of periodic income always involves problems. The ccrual basis of accounting requires estimates of certain expenses, such as epreciation and credit losses, in any case. Revenues recognized in a articular period may require some estimation also, as, for example, hen goods are sold under long-term instalment contracts. These types f problems are not peculiar to the rate of return calculation, however, nd will not be amplified here. There are certain items which do present eculiar problems for this calculation, and these will be discussed briefly n the following paragraphs.

Depreciation. For purposes of measuring an enterprise's rate of eturn in retrospect, depreciation is an appropriate deduction in the etermination of income. But how much depreciation is appropriate? f a firm employs one of the accelerated depreciation methods, its epreciation expense will be higher and its income lower in the early ears of the life of an asset; and the opposite will be true in the later ears. Even where accelerated depreciation is used, annual depreciation xpense may be fairly constant if many assets are owned and some are eing purchased and others retired each year. Nevertheless, the possibility exists that the rate of return for any one year will be significantly ffected by the depreciation method used.

Of all the expenses in the income statement, depreciation is the most ikely to be affected materially by price-level changes. Current revenues nd out-of-pocket expenses are stated in terms of current dollars as a natter of course. Depreciation, however, is stated in terms of the dollars f the year in which the depreciable asset was acquired. If, as recommended above, assets are included in the rate of return calculation at heir current market values, it is only logical that depreciation on market values be used also.

Interest. It is a matter of both accounting practice and income tax law that interest is deductible in the computation of income. Interest, of course, is the cost of borrowed capital. There is general agreement that capital costs should not be included in the computation of the rate of return on total assets. Thus, interest expense should be added back to net income before computing the rate of return. If interest is not added back the rate of return will be influenced by the source of capital as well as the use thereof. If this rate is a meaningful measure of managerial efficiency it should consider only the employment of capital resources without regard to their sources. Inclusion of the interest deduction in the computation tends to penalize managements which borrow capital, even though borrowing may be a profitable policy.

Income Taxes. In computing the rate of return on common stockholders' equity, it is clear that income taxes should be deducted from income. The matter is not so clear in the computation of the rate of return on total assets, however. To omit income taxes is to omit one of the most significant charges on most corporate income statements. Under present tax laws in this country, corporate income taxes roughly halve earnings before tax. Can this be ignored in computing the rate of return? Planning for taxes and planning to minimize them should be a characteristic of good management. If the rate of return calculation were to include income before taxes, one element of managerial efficiency would be excluded from the data employed to measure it. On the other hand, generally accepted accounting principles regarding the amount of income tax which should be reported in the income statement are complex; and the amount so reported may be more or less than the amount management has contrived to pay for the year. Also, the income tax liability may be affected by significant adjustments arising from events of previous years. Hence, as a matter of expediency, some firms use income before taxes in the rate of return computation. Ideally, income after taxes should be used. A useful compromise might be to compute both, recognizing always that income after taxes in any one period may be substantially affected by factors beyond the scope of management's discretion or control, at least in the current year.

Nonoperating Revenues. Obviously, the assets and income used in the rate of return calculation should be consistent with each other. If separate rates are computed for operating and nonoperating assets, nonoperating revenues such as rents, dividends, and interest must be identified separately from normal operating revenues also. Further, if income after taxes is used in the computation, the taxes applicable to operating and nonoperating income must also be distinguished.

Summary Evaluation

Any overall judgment as to the usefulness of rates of return as ıdicators of operating performance and profitability is difficult. Cerıinly, a rate of return is useful only as a comparative device. Compariɔns may be made between similar enterprises and within the same nterprise over two or more periods of time. Obviously, where compariɔns are made, the mechanics of computing the several rates to be ɔmpared must be consistent. Consistency is a prerequisite to comparaility. As with any quantitative tool of managerial analysis, any evalution of a rate of return must be tempered with judgment. The very ıct that the quantitative measure is available, however, usually means ıat a better basis for the exercise of judgment exists.

ATE OF RETURN ON A CAPITAL INVESTMENT PROPOSAL

If the actual rate of return on investments already made is of interest ɔ management, the forecasted rate of return on proposed investments hould be even more a matter of concern. The planned rate of return on n investment proposal can be compared with the cost of capital to etermine whether the investment would be profitable. It can also be ɔmpared with anticipated rates of return on alternative investment pportunities to determined that the best possible use is made of the nterprise's resources. A critical evaluation of the rate of return as a basis ɔr evaluating proposed investments will be deferred until the next hapter where an alternative analytical technique will also be explained nd appraised. The methods of computing the rate of return in prospect vill be considered here.

inancial Statement Method

Of the two common methods of computing the rate of return for a ɔroposed investment, the easier and, regrettably, less precise method is ısually referred to as the *financial statement method,* or the *simple nethod.* This rate of return is computed from the same type of data used n the typical computation of the rate of return for an enterprise in etrospect, that is, data that appear in the balance sheet and the income tatement. The simple rate of return on an investment proposal is the atio of the budgeted average net income from the investment to the ımount of the investment itself. There is some diversity of practice in neasuring the amount of the investment here. Some firms compute his rate of return on the initial amount invested; others, on the average ımount invested over the life of the investment. The initial investment is simply the amount of the cash outlay necessary at the outset in order t make the investment. The average investment is the unamortized por tion of that outlay after half of the investment's life has elapsed assuming straight-line amortization. The average investment may b computed either by dividing the sum of the initial investment and th terminal salvage value of the investment by two or by subtracting half c the total straight-line amortization that will be recognized over th investment's life from the amount of the initial investment. The averag annual income from an investment is determined by the usual proce dures for measuring periodic net income. It is the difference between th budgeted revenues and the budgeted expenses, including depreciation directly traceable to the investment. Cost reductions are equivalent t revenues for this purpose.

The financial statement method of computing rates of return on both the initial and the average investment is illustrated below. Two investments are considered. In several important respects—initial invest ment, life, and total net cash inflows over the life of th investment—they are identical. They differ, however, in the timing o their respective cash flows and in their terminal salvage values. Th relevant data for each investment are as follows:

	Investment A	*Investment B*
(*a*) Initial investment	$75,000	$75,000
(*b*) Life	10 years	10 years
(*c*) Terminal salvage value	0	$10,000
(*d*) Average investment: [(*a*) + (*c*)] ÷ 2	$37,500	$42,500
(*e*) *Annual net cash inflow:*		
All ten years	$12,000	
First five years		$14,000
Second five years		$10,000
(*f*) Average annual net cash inflow	$12,000	$12,000
(*g*) Annual straight-line amortization: [(*a*) − (*c*)] ÷ (*b*)	$7,500	$6,500
(*h*) Average annual net income: (*f*) − (*g*)	$4,500	$5,500

The net cash inflows may be the difference between cash revenues and cash-operating expenses or they may simply be reductions in cash expenses. Although the timing (first five years relative to second five years) of the annual cash inflows of the two investments differs, the annual average is the same because the total cash inflows over ten years are the same for both investments. The average net incomes differ, therefore, only because the one investment has a salvage value, which reduces the base of that investment subject to periodic amortization. The rates of return on the initial investments are computed as follows:

$$\text{Investment A}: r = \frac{\$4{,}500}{\$75{,}000} = 6.00\%$$

$$\text{Investment B}: r = \frac{\$5{,}500}{\$75{,}000} = 7.33\%$$

he rates of return on the average investments are as follows:

$$\text{Investment A}: r = \frac{\$4{,}500}{\$37{,}500} = 12.00\%$$

$$\text{Investment B}: r = \frac{\$5{,}500}{\$42{,}500} = 12.94\%$$

As may be seen from these computations, where there is no salvage alue, the simple rate of return on the average investment is just twice hat on the initial investment; for the average investment is just half the itial investment. As the existence of a salvage value increases the verage investment, the rate of return on average investment where here is a salvage value is less than double that on the initial investment.

Shortcomings of the Financial Statement Method. The rate of return n initial investment ignores the fact that the amount originally invested ay be recovered serially over the investment's life; the rate of return on verage investment assumes this. As serial recovery is typical of most nvestments, particularly those in depreciable assets, use of the average nvestment in the rate of return calculation is usually more appropriate. ince an average net income is used, neither method of computing the mple rate of return takes into account the timing of cash flows from an nvestment. If investment B above had no salvage value, its rate of eturn on both the initial and the average investment would be identical o that for investment A. Yet, if only intuitively, there seems to be omething preferable about a larger cash inflow in the early years of an nvestment's life. Thus, the financial statement method ignores the iming of cash inflows and, in doing so, ignores the fact that money has ime value. The significance of this time value will be explained shortly.

Despite its conceptual shortcomings, the financial statement method f computing the rate of return on a proposed investment is quite widely sed. Its usage is probably due largely to its simplicity. As the more recise methods of evaluating investment proposals become more familar, it is likely that the use of the financial statement method will liminish.

Payback Period

The *payback period* of a proposed investment is the length of time required for the net cash inflows from the investment to equal, in total the amount of the initial outlay. More simply, it is the time required for the investment to pay for itself. Although not a rate of return, the payback period is fairly widely used as an indicator of the financial desirability of an investment. The logic of such usage is that, other things being equal, an investment that will pay for itself quickly is better than one that will require a long time before the initial outlay is recovered. The payback period is stated in units of time, typically years. The usual formula for its computation is as follows:

$$\text{payback period} = \frac{\text{initial investment}}{\text{average annual net cash inflow}}$$

By this formula, the payback periods for both investment A and investment B above are determined to be 6.25 years ($75,000 ÷ $12,000). This formula obviously ignores the timing of the cash flows from the respective investments. For investment A, the payback period actually is 6.25 years; for the average annual cash inflow is also the expected inflow for each year. In the case of investment B however, the cash inflows in the first five years are expected to be $14,000 annually. Thus, $70,000 will have been recovered at the end of five years. As the annual cash inflow for the remaining five years is $10,000, the balance of the initial outlay will be recovered in another half year. Thus, the payback period of investment B is actually 5.5 years if the timing of the cash flows is incorporated in the computation. The average annual cash inflow should be used here only if the deviations of budgeted inflows for the individual years from the average inflow are negligible.

Discounted Cash Flow Method

The principal shortcoming of the financial statement method of computing rate of return is that it ignores the fact that money has time value. The same nominal amount of money is more valuable today than one year from today. If available today, it can be invested to yield a return. Assuming that money can be invested to yield a 5% return at the end of each year, $100 today can be increased to $105 a year later. Thus a claim to receive $100 one year from today is not financially equivalent to $100 today. One hundred dollars one year from today are presently worth $95.24, for this amount invested at 5% would grow to $100 in one year. Thus, the present value of future cash flows, both receipts and payments, is less than their face value; and the present value is increasgly lower the further in the future the cash flows will occur. The nancial statement method ignores this very fundamental fact. It treats e cash flows of the last year of an investment's life exactly the same as ose of the first year, even though their respective present values are ery different. The process of adjusting the face value of future cash ows to their present value by means of the interest rate which may be btained on money invested today is called *discounting.* The rate of turn calculation that takes into consideration the time value of money called the *discounted cash flow method* or, sometimes, the *scientific ethod.* The resultant rate is referred to as the *discounted rate of return,* *effective yield,* of an investment. Conceptually, this rate of return is ecidedly superior to the simple rate computed by the financial statement ethod.

The discounted rate of return is that interest rate which, when used to iscount all future cash flows related to an investment, will equate the resent values of the cash outlays for and the cash inflows from the ivestment. Referring to investment A in the section above dealing with e financial statement method, the discounted rate of return is that iterest rate which will make the present value of the budgeted cash iflow of $12,000 annually for ten years equal to $75,000, the present alue of the outlay. In this case, the present value of the outlay is the ame as its face value; for the outlay occurs at the present. The discounted rate of return involves considerations of the life of the investment and the timing of the cash flows associated with it. The discounted ate of return on investment B would be different from that on investment A because the former involves annual cash flows of a larger mount during the early years of the investment's life as compared vith the later years and also because it has a final cash inflow after ten ears in the form of a salvage value.

Rate of Return from Compound Interest Tables.[2] The discounting of uture cash flows is based upon compound interest principles. Compound nterest formulas can be very cumbersome and tedious to work with. ortunately, the troublesome computations have been made for a great nany situations and the results published in tables such as the tables of resent values in Appendix B. These tables can usually be employed to etermine the discounted rate of return on an investment proposal with nore or less effort, depending upon the complexity of the cash flows elated to the investment. For fairly simple situations, such as that in nvestment A, this rate of return may be found from the tables quite asily. If the investment is more complicated, however, the finding of its

[2] The reader not already familiar with the use of compound interest tables should study he explanatory material and the illustrations in Appendix B before continuing at this point.

rate of return from the tables is correspondingly complicated. F
Investment A, there is a single initial outlay followed by ten annual cas
receipts of $12,000 each. A series of equal annual amounts to b
received or paid for a stipulated period of time in the future is an annuit
In investment A, as in many business investments, the annual cas
inflows are received not in a lump sum once a year but in a regul
stream over the entire year. The present value of an annuity received
paid in a uniform stream for a given number of years may be found i
Table B-1 in Appendix B.

The discounted rate of return on investment A may be determine
readily from Table B-1. The present value of the outlay, $75,000,
already known. Thus, we have but to find that interest rate in the tabl
which will equate an annuity of $12,000 for ten years to $75,000. Sinc
the table available is for an annuity of $1, both the annuity and th
present value must be divided by 12,000. The same rate of return tha
will equate $12,000 annually for ten years to $75,000 will equate $
annually for ten years to $6.25 ($75,000 ÷ 12,000). We can now ent
Table B-1 at the line for ten-year annuities and look for a present valu
of 6.25. At an interest rate of 10%, the present value of $1 annually fo
ten years is 6.3213 (or $6.32); at 11%, it is 6.0649. The know
present value of 6.25 falls somewhere between 10% and 11%, there
fore. For many purposes, this may be sufficiently precise. If desired,
more precise rate of 10.28% may be determined by interpolatio
between the two tabulated figures for 10% and 11%. Many business
men would question the significance of this additional precision, particu
larly in view of the fact that the future cash flows being discounted her
are estimated amounts.

Determining the discounted rate of return for investment A is ver
simple because the only cash outlay is an immediate one and has
present value equal to its face value. Also, the cash inflows are in th
form of a level annuity, the present value of which may be found b
reference to one line in Table B-1. Investment B is somewhat mor
complex, however. The present value of the outlay is still equal to it
face value, but the cash inflows are not expected to be the same each
year. For each of the first five years, $14,000 will be received in a uni
form stream; for each of the last five years, the annuity will be $10,000
And there will be a terminal lump-sum receipt of $10,000 at the end o
ten years. The present values of the two annuities ($14,000 and
$10,000) may still be found in Table B-1, but separately. The presen
value of the salvage value must be found in Table B-3. Thus, we need
two different tables and must enter one of them at two different places
in order to find the discounted rate of return on investment B. Here we

need an interest rate to begin with in order to enter the tables. Thus, we must begin by guessing at the discounted rate of return on investment B and then discounting all cash flows at that guessed rate. If the present value of all inflows proves to be equal to the present value of the outlays, we have been fortunate enough to guess the correct rate. Most likely, however, several guesses will have to be made until we have interest rates on either side of the correct rate, which may then be found by interpolation. This trial and error approach can be very tedious and quite discouraging if the initial guess is far off. This method will be illustrated below for investment B. We will cheat a bit by estimating first 12% and then 13%. As it happens, these rates straddle the correct rate and do so very closely. The present value of an annuity of $1 for the first five future years can be found directly in Table B-1. The present value of an annuity of $1 for the second five years is obtained by subtracting the present value factor for the first five years from the factor for the first ten years.

The present value of all cash inflows from investment B, discounted at 12% (our first guess) is determined as follows:

	Face Amount	×	*Present Value Factor at 12%* *Table*	*Factor*	=	*Present Value*
Annual cash inflow, first five years	$14,000		B–1	3.7599		$52,639
Annual cash inflow, second five years	10,000		B–1	2.0639		20,639
Terminal salvage value	10,000		B–3	.3012		3,012
						$76,290

As the present value of the inflows here is greater than that of the outlay ($75,000), the 12% rate must be too low. The same computations are then repeated for a guess of 13%.

	Face Amount	×	*Present Value Factor at 13%* *Table*	*Factor*	=	*Present Value*
Annual cash inflow, first five years	$14,000		B–1	3.6765		$51,471
Annual cash inflow, second five years	10,000		B–1	1.9193		19,193
Terminal salvage value	10,000		B–3	.2725		2,725
						$73,389

As the present value of the inflows now is less than $75,000, 13% must be too high. Since the correct present value figure of $75,000 falls roughly halfway between the two amounts computed, the correct discounted rate of return is approximately 12½%. For most practical purposes, this rough type of interpolation is satisfactory. (By mathematica interpolation, the rate is 12.44%.)

Shortcut Estimates of Discounted Rate of Return. As is evident from the analysis of investment B above, the computation of the discounted rate of return by means of compound interest tables may become quite tedious if the cash flows relative to an investment are fairly complex There are some methods for approximating the discounted rate of return by fairly simple formulas. Even if these formulas do not give satisfactory rates by themselves, they may be useful in selecting a rate at which to begin the trial and error process illustrated in the preceding paragraph If the life of an investment is at least twice the length of the payback period and particularly if the payback period is very short, the discounted rate of return may be approximated fairly closely by finding the recipro cal of the payback period, thus:

$$r = \frac{1}{p}$$

where r = discounted rate of return and
p = payback period.

This formula does not work very well for either of the investment illustrated earlier, for in both of those cases the payback period is longe than half the life of the investment. The reciprocal of the payback period for investment A is .16; this suggests a rate of return of 16%, wherea the actual discounted rate of return is 10.28%. If the annual cash inflow of $12,000 from investment A were expected to continue for twenty years instead of ten and the initial outlay were not changed, the discounted rate of return from Table B-1 would be approximatel 15.75%. As the payback period would still be 6.25 years, its reciproca would still be .16; this is now very close to the actual rate of return.

More complex formulas may yield somewhat better results. One such formula involves only the life and the payback period of the investment It does not work well if the payback period is shorter than three years or if the life of the investment is less than one year longer than the payback period. It is as follows:[3]

$$r = \frac{n^2 - p^2}{p(n^2) - p(n - p)}$$

where r = rate of return,
n = life of the investment, and
p = payback period.

For investments A and B, respectively, this formula yields rates of return of 10.3% and 13.3%. These are quite close to the actual rates o

[3] The author is indebted to Prof. Ray H. McClary for the development of this formula

10.28% and 12.5%, respectively. This formula works less satisfactorily where the annual cash inflows vary greatly from year to year and where there is a very substantial salvage value.

QUESTIONS FOR DISCUSSION

1. Of what use to management and/or to stockholders is the actual rate of return on investment in a business enterprise for a period in the past?
2. The chapter suggests that any rate of return is useful only in comparison to other rates of return. Assuming the validity of this point of view, what other rate(s) of return would you expect the management of a firm to use in comparing the rate of return on its own assets? What other rate(s) would you expect stockholders to use for comparative purposes?
3. Discuss some of the problems that management might encounter in attempting to obtain a truly meaningful and comparable rate of return on investment in assets. Would these problems be basically the same or significantly different for stockholders attempting to determine the rate of return on their equity? Explain.
4. Discuss the merits and shortcomings of computing the actual rate of return on investment in assets on each of the following bases:
   a. Book value.
   b. Original cost adjusted for changes in the general price level.
   c. Current fair market value (replacement cost).
   d. Only the assets productively employed (at any valuation).
   e. Only assets employed in normal operations (at any valuation).
5. Of what value are the computations of a rate of return on sales and the turnover of assets in the evaluation of the rate of return on a company's investment in assets?
6. How does the computation of the prospective rate of return on an investment proposal differ from the computation of the actual rate of return on assets invested in a firm?
7. Why is the discounted rate of return preferable to the simple rate of return on an investment proposal? Under what conditions, if any, is the simple rate of return equally satisfactory (not merely by coincidence)?
8. If a manager knows the correct discounted rate of return on an investment proposal, does he have all of the financial data necessary for making a decision regarding that investment? Explain.
9. Is it a safe generalization to say that any investment having a payback period shorter than its life is profitable? Why or why not?
10. Your neighbor is planning to start his own business. He will purchase a store building, display counters, other furnishings, and inventory. In talking with you about his plans, he mentions that he is fortunate in not having to worry about interest; for all of the money he invests in the business will be his own savings, now on deposit in his bank checking account. How would you react to this comment?
11. How might the principles of probability theory be used to improve the financial analysis of a proposed investment?

PROBLEMS

1. The Mercury Seating Company's comparative financial statements for the preceding two years are as follows:

MERCURY SEATING COMPANY
Comparative Balance Sheet
Dec. 31,

	1966	1965
Current assets:		
Cash	$ 300,000	$ 300,000
Accounts receivable	600,000	500,000
Inventory	1,200,000	700,000
	2,100,000	1,500,000
Fixed assets:		
Investments	200,000	500,000
Plant property and equipment	5,500,000	3,400,000
Accumulated depreciation	(1,650,000)	(1,400,000)
Intangible assets	350,000	400,000
	4,400,000	2,900,000
Total assets	$ 6,500,000	$ 4,400,000
Current liabilities:		
Trade accounts payable	$ 400,000	$ 400,000
Accrued income taxes	300,000	200,000
	700,000	600,000
Long-term liabilities:		
6% debentures, due 12/31/90	2,000,000	
Stockholders' equity:		
Common stock, $25 par value	2,500,000	2,500,000
Paid-in capital in excess of par value	800,000	800,000
Retained income	500,000	500,000
	3,800,000	3,800,000
Total liabilities and stockholders' equity	$ 6,500,000	$ 4,400,000

MERCURY SEATING COMPANY
Comparative Income Statement
For year ended Dec. 31,

	1966	1965
Sales	$16,500,000	$14,200,000
Cost of goods sold	11,700,000	10,100,000
Gross margin	4,800,000	4,100,000
Nonmanufacturing expenses	3,380,000	3,220,000
Income from operations	1,420,000	880,000
Interest expense	120,000	
Income before tax	1,300,000	880,000
Income tax (40%)	520,000	352,000
Net income	$ 780,000	$ 528,000

Required:

1. Compute the rate of return on investment in total assets and the rate of return on stockholders' equity for 1966 and for 1965.
2. Explain any significant change in the relationship between these two rates of return in the successive years 1965 and 1966.

2. Following are comparative trial balances for the Triton Corporation as of the ends of the fiscal years 1965 and 1966:

	1966	*1965*
Current assets	$ 2,500,000	$ 1,900,000
Fixed assets (net)	12,400,000	9,600,000
Cost of goods sold	14,000,000	17,600,000
Administrative expenses	1,900,000	1,800,000
Selling expenses	4,200,000	4,500,000
Federal income tax	1,360,000	1,180,000
	$36,360,000	$36,580,000
Current liabilities	$ 1,300,000	$ 1,000,000
Capital stock	10,000,000	8,000,000
Retained earnings	1,860,000	1,180,000
Sales	23,200,000	26,400,000
	$36,360,000	$36,580,000

Required:

1. Compute (*a*) the rate of return on sales, (*b*) the asset turnover, and (*c*) the rate of return on total assets for each year.
2. What circumstances or changes in operations might account for changes in the foregoing ratios between 1965 and 1966?

3. Following are the financial statements of the Pandora Corporation for the year ended June 30, 1966:

PANDORA CORPORATION
Balance Sheet
June 30, 1966

Current assets	$ 290,000	Current liabilities	$ 80,000
Investments	200,000	Long-term debt	250,000
Plant and equipment	1,060,000	Capital stock	750,000
Accumulated depreciation	(350,000)	Retained earnings	120,000
	$1,200,000		$1,200,000

PANDORA CORPORATION
Income Statement
For year ended June 30, 1966

Sales		$3,600,000
Cost of goods sold		2,100,000
Gross margin		1,500,000
Selling and administrative expenses		1,205,000
Operating income		295,000
Nonoperating revenue and expense:		
Investment revenue	$ 8,000	
Interest expense	(15,000)	(7,000)
Income before tax		288,000
Income tax (50%)		144,000
Net income		$ 144,000

Required:

1. Compute the rate of return on stockholders' equity for 1966.
2. Compute the rate of return on total assets for 1966. Include computations of the rate of return on sales and the asset turnover.
3. Compute separate rates of return on operating assets and investments.

4. What additional information would you want in order to make these rate of return computations more meaningful?

4. The total assets of the Diana Diaper Company at Dec. 31, 1965, amount to $6,400,000 at book values. Included in this total are plant assets carried at a net book value of $4,000,000. Of this amount, $600,000 is the cost of land purchased on July 1, 1950. The balance is the undepreciated cost of a factory constructed on the land and put into service on Jan. 2, 1951. This factory cost $8,500,000 originally and is being depreciated by the straight-line method over a useful life of twenty-five years; no salvage value is anticipated. At Dec. 31, 1965, the replacement cost of the land is $1,000,000 and the replacement cost of the factory, in its present condition, is $5,000,000. Net income after taxes for the year ended Dec. 31, 1965, is $704,000.

Required:

Compute the rate of return on total assets of the Diana Diaper Company (1) when assets are valued at book value and (2) when assets are valued at replacement cost. (For income tax purposes, depreciation may be deducted at historical cost only, not at replacement cost.)

5. The balance sheet of the Neptune Canning Corporation at Sept. 30, 1966, and the income statement for the year then ended appear as follows:

NEPTUNE CANNING CORPORATION
Balance Sheet
Sept. 30, 1966

Cash	$ 80,000	Accounts payable	$ 120,000
Receivables	160,000	Accrued expenses	300,000
Inventories	750,000	6% mortgage notes	1,500,000
Land	100,000	Deferred income tax payable	300,000
Building	3,600,000	Common stock, $50 par value	2,500,000
Accumulated depreciation—Building	(1,200,000)	Retained earnings	1,980,000
Equipment	1,500,000		
Accumulated depreciation—Equipment	(450,000)		
Investments in securities	1,660,000		
Goodwill	500,000		
	$6,700,000		$ 6,700,000

NEPTUNE CANNING CORPORATION
Income Statement
For year ended Sept. 30, 1966

Sales	$20,500,000
Cost of goods sold	12,537,000
Gross profit	7,963,000
Nonmanufacturing expenses	6,450,000
Operating profit	1,513,000
Dividend and interest revenue	83,000
	1,596,000
Interest expense	96,000
Net profit before tax	1,500,000
Federal income tax (40%)	600,000
Net profit	$ 900,000

You have been engaged as a consultant to the Neptune Canning Corporation and have been asked to submit to management an analysis of the company's rate of return on invested capital. In the course of your examination of the accounting records and other available information, you obtain the following pertinent data:

1. Equipment costing $450,000 with accumulated depreciation to Sept. 30, 1966, of $50,000 is not used except when operations exceed normal capacity. This has not occurred since 1962. No depreciation is recorded on this equipment when it is not in use.

2. Land has a current fair market value of $800,000. The building's current market value is $3,000,000. Equipment regularly used has a fair market value of $800,000. The idle equipment has a market value of $250,000. The aggregate market value of the securities held on Sept. 30, 1966, is $2,075,000. All other assets have market values substantially identical to their book values, with the exception of the goodwill which has no ascertainable market value by itself.

3. The cost of goods sold includes depreciation of $120,000 on the building and $105,000 on the equipment.

Required:

Prepare an analysis of the rate of return on invested capital of the Neptune Canning Corporation for the fiscal year ended Sept. 30, 1966. Include as much detail as you feel is appropriate in the situation and as many different rates of return as you feel may be useful to management.

6. The Nike Pencil Company was founded in 1945. All of the common stock was sold on Dec. 31, 1945, for $110 per share. On the next day, the plant property was purchased at a total cost of $4,000,000. This price included $400,000 for land; the balance was for building and equipment which has an expected useful life of thirty years. At Dec. 31, 1965, the condensed balance sheet of the company appears as follows:

NIKE PENCIL COMPANY
Balance Sheet
Dec. 31, 1965

Current assets	$ 900,000	Current liabilities	$ 300,000
Plant property (net)	1,600,000	Common stock	2,000,000
		Premium on common stock	200,000
	$2,500,000		$2,500,000

Net income for 1965 was $250,000. Examination of the general price index shows the index was 100 at Dec. 31, 1945, and is 200 twenty years later.

Required:

Compute rates of return on total assets and on stockholders' equity based upon book values and also based upon book values adjusted for the increase in the general price level. (Assume that all working capital accounts, revenues, and out-of-pocket expenses are already stated in terms of the current price level.)

7. Certain critical financial data for the Orfeo Electronics Corporation for the preceding ten years are given below. All of these data are expressed in millions of dollars:

Year	*Sales*	*Total Assets*	*Income*
1956	$21	$10.50	$3.78
1957	19	9.50	2.85
1958	22	12.22	3.74
1959	24	12.63	3.84
1960	21	13.12	2.94
1961	24	16.00	3.84
1962	25	16.67	3.75
1963	27	22.50	4.05
1964	29	20.70	4.64
1965	30	27.27	5.40

The following industrial averages are obtained from trade publications for the segment of the electronics industry in which Orfeo competes:

Year	*Rate of Return on Sales*	*Asset Turnover*	*Rate of Return on Assets*
1956	14%	1.8	25.2%
1957	11%	1.5	16.5%
1958	13%	1.9	24.7%
1959	15%	2.0	30.0%
1960	12%	1.8	21.6%
1961	13%	2.1	27.3%
1962	15%	2.2	33.0%
1963	14%	2.1	29.4%
1964	12%	2.2	26.4%
1965	14%	2.0	28.0%

Required:

1. Prepare a graphic comparison of the operating results of the Orfeo Electronics Corporation with the industry averages for the preceding ten years.
2. Point out in brief narrative comments accompanying the graph any significant discrepancies between the corporation's operations and the industry averages.

8. The Poseidon Tractor Company is contemplating the establishment of a subsidiary in Australia. Component parts would be shipped from the United States to an assembly plant in Sydney. The assembled products would then be distributed through sales branches in Sydney, Melbourne, and Perth. Construction of the assembly plant would require an expenditure of $5,400,000. Building and outfitting each of the sales branches would cost approximately $600,000. The budgeted annual operating statement for the Australian subsidiary, after conversion from pounds to dollars, is as follows:

Sales		$12,500,000
Assembly costs:		
Materials	$4,800,000	
Shipping costs	240,000	
Direct labor	2,160,000	
Indirect labor	330,000	
Power and light	140,000	
Maintenance, insurance, and property taxes	270,000	
Depreciation	260,000	8,200,000
Manufacturing margin		4,300,000
Selling expenses:		
Sales salaries	$1,250,000	
Advertising	600,000	
Maintenance, insurance, and property taxes	60,000	
Depreciation	90,000	
Administrative expenses:		
Salaries	1,400,000	
Supplies	60,000	3,460,000
Operating margin		840,000
Australian income tax (25%)		210,000
Net income		$ 630,000

The Australian income before tax is also subject to the U.S. federal income tax at the rate of 40 percent. The Australian tax paid is allowed as a tax credit against (i.e., is deducted from) the U.S. tax so computed, however.

Required:

1. By the financial statement method, compute the rate of return on the initial investment and the rate of return on the average investment in the Australian subsidiary.
2. The current rate of exchange for one Australian pound is $2.80. Operating costs in Australia are incurred and revenues are realized in pounds. If the exchange rate were to increase to $3.60 after the construction of the assembly plant and sales branches but before operations began, what would be the impact upon the subsidiary's rates of return computed in part (1)? A new rate of return need not be computed here. Simply indicate the direction of the change, if any, in the rate of return and briefly explain why it occurs.

9. The Thor Hammer Company is considering the purchase of a stamping machine to perform an operation now done by hand on forges. The machine would cost $240,000. It would have a useful life of 15 years and a terminal salvage value of $30,000. A comparison of budgeted out-of-pocket operating costs with the machine in operation and under the present production method is presented below.

	Machine	*Forges*
Raw materials	$126,000	$120,000
Direct labor	22,000	68,000
Indirect labor	28,000	12,000
Indirect materials	8,000	8,000
Repairs and maintenance	6,000	2,000
Property tax and insurance	1,800	600
Labor-related costs	3,000	4,800
Tools	3,000	18,000
	$197,800	$233,400

The forges have been in service for many years and are fully depreciated. Minor maintenance keeps them serviceable, however.

Required:

1. By means of the financial statement method, compute (*a*) the rate of return on the initial investment in the stamping machine and (*b*) the rate of return on the average investment in the machine.
2. Compute the payback period of the stamping machine.

10. What is the discounted rate of return on an investment that promises to yield $15,000 annually for twenty years and requires an initial outlay of $121,260?

11. If one's cost of capital were 8 percent, what is the maximum amount he could afford to pay for a ten-year mortgage note that would yield monthly payments of $1,050 (including both principal and interest)?

12. Mike Juno has an opportunity to purchase a large cruiser harbored at Key West and used commercially as a party fishing boat. The boat has a remaining useful life of twelve years. The cost of the boat would be $650,000, and it would have terminal salvage value of $50,000. The annual receipts from passengers are expected to average $1,100,000. Annual out-of-pocket operating costs are estimated at $950,000.

Required:

1. Compute the payback period of the proposed investment in the boat.
2. Compute the rate of return on the investment by means of the financial statement method (*a*) on the initial investment in the boat and (*b*) on the average investment.
3. Compute the discounted rate of return on the investment. Show all computations.

13. The Olympic Manufacturing Corporation has been offered the opportunity to buy a patent on a revolutionary new electric potato peeler. The price asked by the patent holder is $260,000. While the legal life of the patent is seventeen years, the corporation's management believes it would have an economic life of only ten years. If the patent is purchased, the Olympic Corporation would not manufacture the potato peeler itself. Rather, it would grant manufacturing rights to other firms and would receive royalties on all units produced. The budgeted royalties for the economic life of the patent are as follows:

First year	$20,000
Second year	40,000
Third year	60,000
Fourth year	60,000
Fifth year	60,000
Sixth year	60,000
Seventh year	50,000
Eighth year	50,000
Ninth year	30,000
Tenth year	10,000

Required:

1. Compute the simple rate of return on the initial investment in the patent.
2. Compute the simple rate of return on the average investment.
3. Compute the discounted rate of return on the investment.
4. If the Olympic Corporation's cost of capital were 15 percent, would the purchase of the patent be profitable?
5. Discuss the relative merits of the three rates of return computed above and explain the reasons for any significant differences among them.

14. A. B. Rose has an opportunity to purchase a lease on a service station for $86,000. The purchase would be financed by a cash payment of $36,000 and a twelve-year note payable for the balance. Monthly payments of $500 would be required under the terms of the note. The lease has a remaining term of twelve years and is not renewable. All property rights revert to the lessor at the termination of the lease. Monthly receipts from the operation of the station are estimated at $5,000 and monthly out-of-pocket operating costs, at $4,070.

Required:

1. Compute the simple rate of return on the average investment.
2. Compute the payback period of the investment.
3. Compute the discounted rate of return on the investment.
4. What is the effective (i.e., discounted) rate of interest on the twelve-year note payable?

15. The data below pertain to three independent investment opportunities, *A*, *B*, and *C*.

	A	*B*	*C*
Initial outlay	$1,000,000	$6,400,000	$3,600,000
Life in years	10	25	12
Annual cash proceeds:			
Entire life	$ 150,000		$ 500,000
First 15 years		$ 400,000	
Last 10 years		$ 200,000	
Terminal salvage value	$ 200,000	$1,500,000	

Required:

For each of these three investment opportunities, compute the discounted rate of return first by one of the short-cut formulas illustrated in the chapter and then by use of the tables in Appendix B.

16. The Ariadne Realty Company is contemplating the purchase of an old apartment building on the Chicago lakefront. The purchase price would be $2,200,000. Extensive renovation would be required at an estimated cost of $600,000. The renovated building would have a remaining economic life of fifteen years, at the end of which time the property would have a residual value of $75,000. At full occupancy, which may reasonably be expected, the

annual rents collected from tenants would total $520,000. Regular operating and maintenance expenditures would average $240,000 per year.

Required:

What would be the discounted rate of return on the proposed investment?

Chapter 16

CAPITAL BUDGETING: ANALYSIS OF INVESTMENT DECISIONS

LONG-TERM investment decisions, often called capital budgeting decisions, involve commitments of capital to specific assets and/or projects for long periods of time. Once made and implemented, such decisions ordinarily cannot be reversed easily without significant loss of the invested capital. This does not mean, of course, that capital budgeting decisions are irreversible; but it does mean that their implications are more extensive than those of the short-run decisions discussed in Chapter 14. Investment decisions typically require fairly long periods of time for their financial justification. A decision to purchase parts rather than to make them may be justified by cost savings almost at once; cumulative cost savings over a long period are not necessary in order that the decision be proved a good one. A decision to purchase a building, on the other hand, ordinarily can be justified financially only over a period of many years. The purchase is made in contemplation of continued economic benefits from the building throughout a long useful life.

The time factor is the crucial element in investment decisions; it is the factor which necessitates analysis by techniques different from those explained in Chapter 14. The time factor requires financial planning into the fairly distant future, and it necessitates capital outlays that can be recovered only over a period of many years. Because of this element of time, capital budgeting decisions are subject to a higher degree of risk and uncertainty than most short-term decisions. Thus, investment decisions must be founded upon very good budgeting procedures. The factor of time also injects the element of interest into investment decisions. If a decision is to be made on the basis of expected cash receipts in the future, it would be foolish to ignore the fact that those future receipts have a present value significantly lower than their face values. Thus, the simple incremental profit analysis used for short-term decision making is inadequate. Capital budgeting decisions should be evaluated in terms of discounted cash flows.

BASIC OBJECTIVE AND APPROACH

Optimum Allocation of Scarce Capital

The basic aim of a long-term investment decision is to maximize the enterprise's long-run profit. Specifically, the investment decision must select the most profitable employment of the capital available to the enterprise. Management typically is faced with a variety of alternative possible investments, many of which appear profitable. Frequently, the potentially profitable investment opportunities exceed the capital available for investment. Thus, management must select those investments which are *most* profitable. It is not sufficient to identify investment opportunities as profitable; they must be ranked according to their relative profit potentials. This need for ranking suggests that capital is rationed to a firm, that not all profitable investment opportunities may be accepted because of the scarcity of capital. Capital, of course, is a scarce resource; and, as such, it has a cost.[1] Thus, only those investments which promise to yield a rate of return in excess of the cost of capital are potentially profitable. In theory, a firm should be able to obtain capital so long as it can invest that capital to yield more than its cost. In practice, however, most firms regard their available capital as more limited than this. The desire to maintain control of a corporation within a small group may preclude obtaining additional capital by the sale of stock. Managerial caution and/or restrictions imposed by existing contracts (e.g., bond indentures) may prevent a firm from borrowing additional capital even though potentially profitable uses of such capital are available. Reinvestment of earnings in the firm is limited by stockholders' desires for dividends. Capital budgeting, then, is the analytical process of allocating the scarce capital available to a firm to the most profitable possible uses.

Types of Investments

Before analyzing them, management must understand the natures of the various investment opportunities available and any relationships among them. Some investments are complementary; making one investment either necessitates or, at least, suggests another. For example, a decision to invest in a fleet of company-owned automobiles may suggest a decision to invest in a company-owned garage for the repair and maintenance of the fleet. Other investments are mutually exclusive; acceptance of one necessarily involves rejection of the other(s). If, for example, either of two machines would perform a particular manufac-

[1] See Chapter 8, pages 192 and 193, for a discussion of the cost of capital.

turing operation more efficiently than it is performed presently, the purchase of either might be a profitable investment. Only one such machine can be used, however. Thus, a decision to buy one machine automatically involves a decision to reject the other. Finally, some investments are basically independent. The decision to purchase an electronic computer, for example, would be unlikely to have any direct relationship to the decision to purchase a patent, except to the extent that the scarcity of capital would preclude both purchases. Either or both decisions might be made or rejected independently of the other.

Importance of Cash Flows

If investment decisions are to be analyzed in terms of discounted future cash flows, the relevant cash flows must be identified and budgeted as accurately as possible. Both the amounts and the timing of expected cash flows are important to the analysis for the investment decision. The relevant cash flows, of course, are the differential flows, those cash receipts and disbursements which will occur if and only if the particular investment decision is implemented. The natures of these future cash flows vary. A decision to purchase new production machinery may generate cash receipts only in the negative way of reducing out-of-pocket operating costs. A decision to undertake a long-range promotional program is usually expected to generate cash in the form of increased variable profit, the net result of increased sales less the variable costs of such sales. It is important to identify clearly those cash flows which are directly traceable to a specific investment decision. Some increase in revenue and, hence, variable profit may be anticipated as a normal consequence of a secular rise in demand. Such additional variable profit should be separated from that attributable to a specific investment, such as a promotional program.

Cash Flows and Income Taxation. For a business enterprise, most cash receipts and disbursements must be analyzed after consideration of their income tax implications. Assuming an income tax rate of 47% on all ordinary business income, ordinary operating receipts and payments are measured after taxes at 53% of their face amounts before taxes. Some receipts are specifically excluded from taxation, however; and some expenditures are specifically nondeductible in the determination of taxable income. Thus, it is important that management be advised as to the full tax implications of all pending decisions.

Depreciation is a noncash expense and, as such, would not be relevant to capital budgeting decisions. However, depreciation is also a deductible expense in the computation of taxable income. Thus, although it has no before-tax cash implications, it generates cash inflows (or negative cash outflows) in the form of lower income tax payments. Different depreciation methods involve different patterns of after-tax cash flows. The accelerated depreciation methods call for higher depreciation deductions in the early years of an asset's useful life. The after-tax cash inflow from the depreciation deduction is thus accelerated as well. Because of the time value of money, accelerated depreciation methods can involve permanent cash advantages relative to the straight-line depreciation method and not merely temporary advantages. So long as the tax rate is not expected to rise and taxable earnings are expected in all future periods, the accelerated depreciation methods are financially advantageous to the taxpayer. Thus, the method of depreciation to be used should be considered by management as part of the asset investment decision. It is a matter of direct concern to management and not simply a technical accounting question.

The federal income tax law of the United States is very complex. It provides for numerous special situations which may be pertinent to a particular investment decision. Certain gains, for example, are identified as long-term capital gains and currently are taxed at a rate below the rate applicable to ordinary income. The after-tax cash inflows from capital gains, thus, are higher than those from ordinary profits of the same amount before taxes. Operating losses of one period may be carried over to subsequent periods and offset against operating profits. Thus, tax implications are not always bounded by the limits of a single year. If, for example, a proposed investment in a subsidiary corporation is not expected to be profitable for several years, the tax savings from the early years' losses are not lost but deferred to the subsequent profitable years. For purposes of the discussions, illustrations, and problems in this book, no technical knowledge of the income tax law is required. Tax rates will be stated and any special tax treatments explained as appropriate in connection with each illustration or problem. To ignore tax implications in these illustrations would be unrealistic. Tax planning is fundamental to good management accounting.

TECHNIQUES OF INVESTMENT ANALYSIS

The mechanical process of analyzing the budgeted data relevant to a particular investment proposal is only part of the total investment decision-making process, but it is an important part. The assumptions and limitations underlying these analytical techniques, as well as their mechanics, should be clearly understood by management. Two techniques of investment analysis were introduced in the preceding chapter—the discounted rate of return and the payback period. A critical evaluation of these techniques will be made after we have observed the workings of a third analytical device, the *net present value method.* This is the method which we shall employ in subsequent illustrations of capital investment decisions.

Net Present Value Method

The net present value of an investment is the difference between the discounted present values of the budgeted cash inflows and the budgeted cash outflows directly traceable to the investment. If the net present value is positive (i.e., the present value of the inflows exceeds that of the outflows), the investment is profitable; if the net present value is negative, the investment is unprofitable. Future cash flows are discounted to their present values at the time of making a decision by an interest rate equal to the enterprise's cost of capital. The cost of capital is the logical rate to use for this discounting, for it is the break-even rate for long-term investments. The yield from an investment must be higher than the cost of the invested capital in order that the investment be profitable. If the net present value of all cash flows associated with an investment is positive, the yield of the investment must be greater than the capital cost. For an investment that only breaks even—one for which the yield and the cost of capital are equal—the net present value is zero.

The mechanics of computing the net present value are much the same as those explained in the preceding chapter for computing the discounted rate of return by the use of compound interest tables. The trial and error calculations used to find the discounted rate of return on investment B in the previous chapter [2] are, in effect, the net present value computations. The cash inflows there were discounted at estimated rates to determine whether they were equal to, higher than, or lower than the already known present value of the outflows. If the present value of the outflows (equal, in the case of investment B, to the face amount of the original expenditure) were subtracted from the discounted present value of the inflows, the remainder would be the net present value of the investment at the discount rate chosen. The principal difference under the net present value method is that the discount rate is known in advance. It is the company's cost of capital, and only one set of discounting computations is necessary to determine the net present

---

[2] See pages 368 and 369.

value. If the cost of capital were 10%, the net present value of investment B would be computed as follows:[3]

	Face Amount	Present Value Factor at 10% Table	Present Value Factor at 10% Factor	Present Value
Cash inflows:				
Annual cash inflow, first five years	$14,000	B–1	3.9347	$55,086
Annual cash inflow, second five years	10,000	B–1	2.3866	23,866
Terminal salvage value	10,000	B–3	.3679	3,679
				82,631
Cash outflows:				
Initial investment	75,000			75,000
Net present value				$ 7,631

Since the net present value of the investment is positive at a cost of capital of 10%, the investment would be profitable. This agrees with what we already know about the investment, namely, that it has a discounted rate of return of approximately 12½%, clearly higher than the capital cost assumed here.

A somewhat more complex illustration of the net present value method is presented in Table 16–1. Here consideration is given to the

TABLE 16–1

ANALYSIS OF PROPOSED INVESTMENT IN MACHINE

	Cash Flow before Tax	Tax Effect	Cash Flow after Tax	Present Value Factor at 6% Table	Present Value Factor at 6% Factor	Present Value
Cash inflows:						
Annual labor cost saving	$ 22,000	$(10,340)	$ 11,660	B–1	6.3536	$ 74,083
Depreciation tax deduction						
First four years		6,580	6,580	B–1	3.5562	23,400
Second four years		8,460	8,460	B–1	2.7974	23,666
Terminal salvage value	8,000		8,000	B–3	.6188	4,950
						126,099
Cash outflows:						
Original cost of machine	(120,000)		(120,000)			(120,000)
Cost to replace motor	(16,000)		(16,000)	B–3	.7866	(12,586)
						(132,586)
Net present value						$(6,487)

income tax implications of the future cash flows, and the cash outflows are not simply a single initial payment. The investment decision ana-

[3] For the basic data of this illustration, refer to page 364 in the preceding chapter.

lyzed in Table 16–1 is whether to purchase a machine to do work now done by manual labor. The pertinent facts are as follows: The machine would be purchased for $120,000 cash; it would have a useful life of eight years and a salvage value at the end of that time of $8,000. After four years of use, the machine's motor would have to be replaced at a cost of $16,000; for tax purposes, this replacement expenditure would be capitalized (i.e., charged to the cost of the machine) and recovered by depreciation. It is expected that the use of this machine would result in annual labor cost savings of $22,000 for the full eight-year life of the asset. The company would use the straight-line depreciation method for the machine. The applicable income tax rate is 47%, and it is expected that this rate will remain unchanged for the ensuing eight years. The enterprise's cost of capital is estimated to be 6% after taxes.[4]

The analysis in Table 16–1 includes each of the several cash flows associated with the proposed investment; negative flows are shown in parentheses. The primary cash inflow from the investment in this machine is in the form of reduced labor costs as compared with the present method of operations. The reduction in costs will, of course, involve a corresponding reduction in the tax deduction for labor; the tax implication of the cost saving is adverse, therefore. The annual cash inflow from lower costs is reduced by 47%; the net cash saving annually, thus, is $11,660 (53% of $22,000) after taxes. This amount constitutes an 8-year annuity, which is discounted at 6% by the appropriate factor from Table B–1 in Appendix B. Depreciation is not a cash item at all before taxes. However, as it is deductible in the computation of taxable income, it has a favorable tax effect on cash flows. Cash outflows to the government for taxes are reduced by 47% of the annual depreciation charge. Thus, depreciation is an after-tax cash inflow in that amount. Because of the additional capital outlay at the end of the fourth year of the machine's life, the annual depreciation charge and the corresponding tax saving are increased for the last four years. Thus, depreciation after taxes involves two different annuities, one for the first four years and one for the last four years. Both are discounted by present value factors from Table B–1 in Appendix B. The factor for the first four years is taken directly from the table; the factor for the second four years is the difference between those for the first eight and the first four years. As the terminal salvage value is a lump-sum receipt, it is discounted by the appropriate factor from Table B–3. Since the expected salvage value

[4] The cost of capital must be determined after taxes, for one capital cost—interest—is a deductible expense in the determination of taxable income. Nominal interest of 8%, for example, is effective interest of 4.24% (53% of 8%) after taxes at 47%.

is simply the unrecovered cost of the machine at the end of its useful life, it has no tax implications; there is no planned taxable gain or deductible loss at the time of the disposition of the machine. The outlay for the machine itself and the subsequent expenditure for the replacement motor also have no direct tax effects; the cash outflows, thus, are the same after taxes as before. Both of these expenditures give rise to after tax inflows in the form of depreciation deductions, of course. As the original cost of the machine must be paid out at once, its present value is equal to its face value. The cost of the replacement motor four years in the future, however, must be discounted by the appropriate factor from Table B-3.

As the present value of the total cash outflows for this investment proposal exceeds the present value of the total inflows from it, the net present value is negative and the investment is not profitable under the conditions described. If the cost of capital were lower, the investment might be profitable. If any of the cash flows could be altered, the result might be different also. One cash inflow in this illustration is subject to some manipulation by the management of the firm. If depreciation were computed for tax purposes by one of the accelerated depreciation methods, the net present value of the investment would be higher (the negative amount lower). In this case, the net present value would still be negative but by less than half the amount reported in Table 16–1. The depreciation method to be used is not a neutral factor of no consequence to management. The earlier that depreciation may be deducted, the greater will be the total present value of the after-tax cash inflow attributable to it; for the earlier cash flows have higher present values per dollar than the later ones.

Critical Appraisal of Analytical Techniques

We have now discussed and illustrated three different techniques for the analysis of investment proposals—the net present value method, the discounted rate of return, and the payback period. The first two of these may be thought of as complete analytical devices. They both indicate the profitability of the investment in light of the enterprise's cost of capital. If the net present value of an investment is positive, the investment is profitable; for the present value of the cash inflows exceeds that of the cash outflows, all cash flows having been discounted at the capital cost rate. The discounted rate of return is compared to the cost of capital; if the rate of return is greater than the capital cost, the investment is profitable. The payback period, on the other hand, is only a partial analytical technique. The payback period may be compared to the life of the investment, but such comparison does not necessarily reflect the investment's profitability. Obviously, if the payback period is longer than the life, the investment cannot be profitable. However, the mere fact that the payback period is shorter than the life does not necessarily mean that the investment is profitable. Thus, the payback period should be used only as a supplementary analytical device in conjunction with other methods of analysis. Basing an investment decision upon an evaluation of the payback period alone would be dubious management practice at best.

Both the net present value method and the discounted rate of return method give recognition to the time value of money, although they do so in slightly different ways. Both discount the budgeted cash flows relative to an investment to their present values, but at different interest rates. The discounting mechanics of both methods involve implicit assumptions as to the reinvestment of cash inflows from the investment being analyzed. The net present value method assumes that all cash inflows are immediately reinvested to yield a rate of return equal to the cost of capital. The discounted rate of return method assumes that all cash inflows are at once reinvested to yield a rate equal to the rate of return on the investment under analysis. Refer again to investment B, examined in the preceding chapter and earlier in the present one. The computation of its net present value at a capital cost of 10%[5] involves the assumption that all cash proceeds will be promptly reinvested in some project(s) that will yield a rate of return of 10%. Similarly, the computation of its rate of return at 12½%[6] presumes that cash inflows will be reinvested so that they also will yield 12½%. If it appears clear that one or the other of these alternative reinvestment assumptions is more realistic, there is a logical argument for using that analytical method which involves the better reinvestment assumption. Unfortunately, it is all too often the case that no specific reinvestment plans are formulated in advance of actual receipt of the cash inflows; in such case, a reinvestment assumption is likely to be ignored altogether. Reinvestment plans are admittedly tenuous in most cases, but they should be incorporated in a firm's total long-range planning.

On a very pragmatic plane, the net present value method has an advantage of simplicity as compared to the discounted rate of return procedure. Where the cash flows associated with an investment are fairly complicated, the computation of the rate of return may require several trials before the correct rate is determined. Each of these trials involves

[5] Cf., page 386 above.

[6] Cf., pages 368 and 369 in Chapter 15.

the discounting of the cash flows related to the investment at a different interest rate. The net present value method, on the other hand, requires only one discounting of the cash flows. The simplicity of the computation of the net present value is offset somewhat by the relative unfamiliarity of the concept. Interest rates are familiar to businessmen and investors generally. If a corporation president is informed that the proposed investment in a foreign subsidiary will yield a rate of return of 10%, he can immediately grasp the significance of this measure. He has but to look at the financial section of his morning paper to see the yields obtainable in the bond markets expressed as percentages. The net present value, on the other hand, is a relatively new concept and has not yet achieved the status of familiarity which interest rates enjoy. This is simply a problem of education, of course. In time, the concept of net present value will become more familiar to business executives and probably will be much more widely employed. (It is always possible, of course, that new developments in the future will render all presently employed analytical techniques obsolete.)

Finally, the discounted rate of return suffers one technical deficiency which does not afflict the net present value method. The net cash flow associated with an investment in any one period is either positive (net inflow) or negative (net outflow). In a simple situation, the net cash flow is negative only at the present moment, the moment of the initial outlay. Subsequently, the net cash inflow is consistently positive, even though it may fluctuate somewhat in face amount. In this simple case, the algebraic sign of the net cash flows changes only once; it is negative at the outset and then positive in all future periods. If the signs of the net cash flows in successive periods change more than once, the discounted rate of return may not be determinate. Two or more different rates may be computed, each of which rates equates the present value of the total cash inflows with that of the total cash outflows. Obviously, such a solution to the analysis of the investment proposal is unsatisfactory. As the net present value does not involve multiple solutions in any instance, it is clearly the preferable method where the signs of the net cash flows change more than once.

Conclusions. Both the net present value and the discounted rate of return methods are fundamentally valid and complete techniques of investment analysis. Although the discounted rate of return is stated as a more familiar quantity, an interest rate, it suffers some fairly significant drawbacks when the cash flows associated with an investment are complex. Thus, the net present value method is here advocated as a consistent and comparatively simple method of investment analysis. The student working the problems at the end of this chapter will find most of them most easily solved by use of the net present value method. The payback period is an incomplete and imprecise technique. All other things being equal, the investment which will recover its initial outlay fastest is most attractive. All other things are so seldom equal, however, that the payback period cannot generally be relied upon as a useful indicator of the most profitable investment opportunities.

FURTHER PROBLEMS OF CAPITAL BUDGETING

The discussions of investment decision making above have been restricted to situations involving only one investment proposal and full knowledge of the amounts and timing of all related cash flows. Typically, management is confronted with alternative investment opportunities, not all of which may be selected at the present time. Further, there is almost invariably a considerable degree of uncertainty regarding the future cash flows pertinent to an investment. Some of these problems and some proposals for coping with them are discussed in the sections that follow.

Ranking of Alternative Investments

Early in this chapter, we observed that some investments are complementary, some are mutually exclusive, and some are independent. These traits must be identified before the various investment opportunities available can be evaluated as alternatives. If two or more investments are regarded as complementary (particularly if the full benefit from one cannot be realized unless the other is undertaken also), they should be combined and analyzed as a single proposal in competition with alternative independent investments. If two or more investments are mutually exclusive, a selection should be made between them before they are considered as alternatives to other independent investments. Once complementary investments are paired and mutually exclusive alternatives eliminated, management is faced with an array of independent alternatives. All those not potentially profitable may be discarded without further analysis. Each of the remaining profitable investments presumably will be undertaken if sufficient capital is available. If the available capital is insufficient to permit the enterprise to make all of the possible investments, then only the most profitable ones should be selected.

It would be very convenient if the alternative investments could be ranked according to their relative profitabilities. Management could then go down the list and select investments in declining order of profitability until the available capital were exhausted. Such a ranking might seem feasible, for each investment has a positive net present value and a discounted rate of return. These measures are not necessarily valid bases for ranking, however. The net present value of an investment calling for a large initial outlay may be substantially greater than that of an investment with a small initial outlay. This is to be expected, of course, and does not demonstrate that the former is more profitable than the latter. Thus, any ranking according to net present values would unduly favor large investments. The same is not true of the discounted rate of return, but other factors may operate so that an investment with a lower rate of return may be more profitable in the long run than one with a higher yield. Changes in interest rates, price-level changes, uncertainty as to future cash flows, and differences in the sizes of investments all tend to cloud the capital budgeting picture and to invalidate simple rankings.

Changes in Interest Rates

As we have seen, both the net present value and the discounted rate of return methods make assumptions about the yields on the reinvestment of cash inflows. These assumptions necessarily involve a further assumption that future interest rates are predictable. Capital markets, which determine interest rates, are subject to substantial fluctuations, however; and these fluctuations can seldom be forecast with any high degree of confidence except in the very short-term future. Nevertheless, some consideration of future interest rates is essential. Suppose, for example, that a firm is faced with alternative investments X and Y. Both involve initial outlays of $100,000. X has a rate of return of 12% and a life of 3 years. Y has a rate of return of 10% and a life of 6 years. A simple ranking by their rates of return would clearly favor X, and X would have the higher net present value at any assumed cost of capital. Assume now, however, that the market interest rate which may be expected to be earned on future investments is no higher than 7%. In that case, Y would offer a slightly more attractive total rate of return or net present value over a six-year period than would a combination of X and some subsequent investment made in three years at a yield of 7%.[7] An investment with a long life may be more profitable in the long run than one with a short life if interest rates are expected to decline, even though the latter may have a higher rate of return by itself than the former. The

[7] This assumes that the entire $100,000 will be reinvested at the end of the third future year to yield 7% for another three-year period.

investment opportunities at the end of the shorter life are important to the present decision. One obvious conclusion from this discussion is that it is difficult to compare and rank investments of different lives.

Changes in the Price Level

Even after discounting, dollars received in the future may not be directly comparable to dollars received or paid at the present. Inflation and/or deflation alter the real value of cash flows. If inflation or deflation can be predicted, future cash flows can be adjusted for it by means of the predicted index of the general price level. If, for example, it is expected that the general price level will continue to increase at an annual rate of 2% in the indefinite future, future cash flows can be restated first in terms of constant dollars (i.e., price-adjusted dollars) and then in terms of present values. An annuity of $1,000 per year for 5 years has a present value of $4,121 at 8%, assuming constant prices. If prices are expected to rise at an annual rate of 2%, starting from an index of 100 (or 1.00) in the first year, the present value of this annuity could be computed as follows:

Year	*Face Amount*	*Price Index*	*Constant Dollars*	*Present Value*[8] *Factor at 8%*	*Present Value*
1	$1,000	1.000	$1,000	.9610	$ 961
2	1,000	1.020	980	.8872	869
3	1,000	1.040	962	.8189	788
4	1,000	1.061	943	.7560	713
5	1,000	1.082	924	.6979	645
					$3,976

In this illustration, the factor of inflation reduces the present value of the annuity from $4,121 under conditions of price-level stability to $3,976. If the required investment outlay to obtain this particular annuity were $4,000, the factor of inflation would make the difference between its being a profitable or unprofitable investment.

Uncertainty and Probability

In our discussions thus far, we have tacitly assumed that the future cash flow relative to an investment can be budgeted accurately. Any budget, of course, is subject to some degree of uncertainty; the budgeted cash flows reasonably to be expected from an investment may actually be better described as a range of possible amounts. Uncertainty cannot be eliminated from capital budgeting, but it may be possible to quantify certainty and uncertainty to some extent and, thus, incorporate them in

[8] From Table B-2 in Appendix B.

the analysis. Specifically, it may be possible to assign probabilities to alternative possible cash flows. The actual cash flow may fall anywhere within a broad range of possibilities, but some simplification of the possibilities is necessary if the investment proposal is to be analyzed effectively. It may be feasible to budget three alternative patterns of cash flows for an investment proposal—a high (optimistic) pattern, a median pattern, and a low (pessimistic) pattern. Each of these alternatives would then be evaluated to determine the probability of its occurrence. A certainty has a probability of 1. An uncertain event has a probability somewhere between 0 and 1. Each alternative cash flow would be a separate uncertain event having a probability expressed as a positive quantity less than 1. The sum of the probabilities of the individual alternatives would be 1.

To illustrate the use of probabilities in evaluating investment proposals, consider a proposed product promotion campaign which will involve an initial outlay of $600,000. Market research indicates that the increased sales generated by this campaign, after deducting the additional variable costs, will increase variable profit by $250,000 per year for 3 years. The applicable income tax rate is 47%, and the entire amount of the promotional outlay will be deductible for tax purposes in the year in which it is spent. The firm's cost of capital is 8%. A simple analysis of this proposal appears in Part A of Table 16–2. Here, only one possible

TABLE 16–2

USE OF PROBABILITIES IN CAPITAL BUDGETING ANALYSIS

PART A

	Before Tax	*After Tax*	*Present Value Factor at 8%*	*Present Value*
Cash inflow	$250,000	$132,500	2.6671	$353,391
Cash outflow	(600,000)	(318,000)		(318,000)
Net present value				$ 35,391

PART B

	Before Tax	*After Tax*	*Proba-bility*	*Weighted Amount*	*Present Value Factor at 8%*	*Present Value*
Cash inflows:						
High	$350,000	$185,000	.2	$ 37,100		
Medium	250,000	132,500	.5	66,250		
Low	150,000	79,500	.3	23,850		
				$127,200	2.6671	$329,255
Cash outflow	(600,000)	(318,000)				(318,000)
Net present value						$ 11,255

pattern of cash flows is considered. Assume now that the market research done indicates that the promotional campaign may increase variable profit by as much as $350,000 or as little as $150,000 and that $250,000 is a median estimate. Further, the research indicates that the probability of realizing the high estimate of variable profit is .2 (two chances in ten). The probability of achieving the median estimate is .5 (one chance in two), and that of realizing only the low estimate is .3 (three chances in ten). Incorporation of these probabilities into the capital budgeting analysis is illustrated in Part B of Table 16–2. The high, median, and low incremental variable profit estimates after taxes are weighted (i.e., multiplied) by their respective probabilities. The sum of these weighted amounts is then taken as the face amount of the estimated annual cash inflow from the investment. Its present value is computed in the usual way, as is the net present value. In this illustration, the net present value of the investment is lower when probabilities are included in the analysis because the probability of the low estimate being realized is greater than that of the high estimate.

The foregoing is a very brief and simplified presentation of the relevance of probability to the capital budgeting decision. We have abstracted from some very practical problems. How were the three probabilities measured? What, if any, is the probability of an annual cash inflow of some other amount (say $280,000)? Nevertheless, the fundamental point should be clear. Capital budgeting involves estimates of future cash flows. If these estimates can be improved by a consideration of the relative probabilities of alternative patterns of cash flow, the ultimate decision can be that much better.

Investments of Different Amounts

Management must be very careful in comparing and deciding among investments of different sizes (i.e., different amounts of initial outlays). Here the net present value method must be employed with caution. Suppose a firm has available $100,000 for long-term investment and is faced with the following six independent alternative investment opportunities, each having the same useful life as the others and the pattern of cash flows indicated:

Investment	*Present Value of Cash Inflows*	*Initial Outlay*	*Net Present Value*
L	$116,200	$100,000	$16,200
M	59,600	50,000	9,600
N	34,500	30,000	4,500
O	23,300	20,000	3,300
P	23,200	20,000	3,200
Q	11,400	10,000	1,400

Although the alternatives are listed in order of their net present values, they are not thereby ranked in the order of their profitabilities. It should not be surprising that investment L has the largest net present value, for it requires an initial outlay twice the amount of the next largest one. It is not directly comparable by means of net present values to the other investment proposals. In fact, the only two alternatives directly comparable in terms of net present values are O and P. The real decision here is between L and some combination of the others which totals $100,000. There are three such combinations, MNO, MNP, and MOPQ; any other combination would total more or less than $100,000. From the viewpoint of total enterprise profit, it would be inefficient for the firm to invest less than the full $100,000 so long as individually profitable investment opportunities remain. Assuming that the six proposals listed are the only potential uses of the available $100,000, the investments (or combinations thereof) which might be undertaken are ranked in order of profitability as follows:

	Total Net Present Value
MOPQ ($9,600 + $3,300 + $3,200 + $1,400)	$17,500
MNO ($9,600 + $4,500 + $3,300)	17,400
MNP ($9,600 + $4,500 + $3,200)	17,300
L	16,200

A device for adapting the net present value method to rank alternative investments of differing amounts according to their relative profitabilities has been suggested. It is called the *net present value index* and is the ratio of the present value of cash inflows from an investment to the present value of cash outflows for it. The net present value index (*NPVI*) is computed as follows:

$$NPVI = \frac{\text{present value of cash inflows}}{\text{present value of cash outflows}}$$

The index for any profitable investment will be greater than 1; for an unprofitable investment, it will be less than 1. The initial outlays for the

Investment	*Present Value of Cash Inflow*	*Present Value of Cash Outflow*	*NPVI*
M	$ 59,600	$ 50,000	1.192
O	23,300	20,000	1.165
L	116,200	100,000	1.162
P	23,200	20,000	1.160
N	34,500	30,000	1.150
Q	11,400	10,000	1.140

six investments listed in the preceding paragraph are the only cash outlays involved and, hence, are equal to the present values of the outlays. The six investments are ranked in the order of their net present value indexes in the table at the bottom of the preceding page. Although the net present value index does indicate the individual investments' relative profitabilities, it results in a ranking which still may not indicate the most advantageous total investment program. Obviously, if the two investments with the highest net present value indexes above are selected, the investment with the third highest index cannot be chosen also. If L is ignored, the three investments with the highest indexes are M, O, and P. If these three are selected, the next ranked investment, N, cannot be made because it would exceed the limits of the available capital. Thus, the most profitable investment program would be MOPQ, the first, second, fourth, and sixth ranked investments in order of net present value indexes.

EQUIPMENT REPLACEMENT DECISIONS

A fairly common illustration of a capital budgeting decision is the equipment replacement decision. Business managers frequently must consider the possibility of replacing equipment presently in service with more modern and efficient equipment, even though the old units' useful lives have not yet expired. Obviously, if the old equipment is no longer useful, the replacement decision takes on a very different character; it is then a decision to replace or to discontinue the operations for which the equipment has been used. Assuming that the operations can be carried on with either the present or the new equipment, the replacement decision will depend upon which alternative is more profitable. The profitability of replacement may be indicated by the net present value of a decision to invest in the new equipment. For purposes of this decision, whether the old equipment is fully depreciated or is only one year old is irrelevant. The original cost incurred for the old equipment is now a sunk cost; it has no direct effect upon the decision. As a matter of fact, a loss on the disposition of the old equipment has a favorable implication for the replacement decision if that loss is deductible for income tax purposes. The basic factors bearing upon the decision are the difference between the out-of-pocket costs (after taxes) of operating the alternative pieces of equipment, the outlay required to obtain the new equipment, and the current salvage value of the old asset. The analysis of an equipment replacement decision by the net present value method is illustrated in Table 16–3.

TABLE 16–3

ANALYSIS OF EQUIPMENT REPLACEMENT DECISION

	Cash Flow before Tax	*Tax Effect*	*Cash Flow after Tax*	*Present Value Factor at 7% Table*	*Factor*	*Present Value*
Cash inflows:						
Annual operating cost saving	$ 30,000	$(14,100)	$ 15,900	B–1	4.8993	$ 77,899
Depreciation tax deduction (*see* Schedule 1 below)						
First year		24,283	24,283	B–2	.9658	23,453
Second year		14,883	14,883	B–2	.9005	13,402
Third year		7,817	7,817	B–2	.8396	6,563
Fourth year		4,439	4,439	B–2	.7829	3,475
Fifth year		1,655	1,655	B–2	.7299	1,208
Sixth year		174	174	B–2	.6806	118
Terminal salvage value of new machine	15,000		15,000	B–3	.6570	9,855
						135,973
Cash outflows:						
Net cash price of new machine	(125,000)		(125,000)			(125,000)
Terminal salvage value of old machine	(5,000)		(5,000)	B–3	.6570	(3,285)
						(128,285)
Net present value						$ 7,688

Schedule 1.—Tax Deduction Due to Greater Depreciation Charge

Year	*Declining Balance Depreciation on New Machine*	*Straight-Line Depreciation on Old Machine*	*Difference*	*Tax Rate*	*Tax Deduction*
1	$ 60,000	$8,333	$51,667	47%	$24,283
2	40,000	8,333	31,667	47%	14,883
3	26,667	8,333	18,334	47%	7,817
4	17,778	8,333	9,445	47%	4,439
5	11,852	8,333	3,519	47%	1,655
6	8,703	8,333	370	47%	174
	$165,000				

The data for this illustration are as follows: A corporation is now performing certain manufacturing operations on a machine purchased 3 years ago at a cost of $80,000. At the time of purchase, it was estimated that the machine had a useful life of 9 years and a terminal salvage value of $5,000. Depreciation has been computed on the straight-line basis for both financial reporting and income tax purposes. A new machine has been developed to perform the same operations at a lower cost. The new machine has a cost of $160,000, a useful life of 6 years, and a terminal salvage value of $15,000. The company would be granted a trade-in allowance of $35,000 for the old machine. Thus, the actual cash outlay to acquire the new machine would be only $125,000. A comparison of the annual operating costs under the alternative machines is as follows:

	Old Machine	*New Machine*
Direct labor	$120,000	$ 85,000
Repairs and maintenance	7,000	10,000
Taxes and insurance	3,000	5,000
	$130,000	$100,000

It would be a mistake to include depreciation on either machine in this annual cost comparison. We are interested here in out-of-pocket costs only. The applicable income tax rate is 47% and the company's cost of capital, 7%.

The principal sources of cash inflows from a decision to replace the equipment would be the $30,000 annual operating cost saving for the next 6 years and the additional depreciation deductions for the same period. The lower operating cost would be reflected in higher income and, consequently, higher income tax payments at the 47% rate. Thus, the after-tax cash inflow from the cost saving is only $15,900 (53% of $30,000) annually. Depreciation is deductible for income tax purposes and, thus, reduces the annual tax payment. The annual tax saving here is equal to 47% of the difference between depreciation on the new machine and that on the old one. The company will elect to deduct depreciation on the new machine, if purchased, by the double declining balance method, one of the accelerated depreciation techniques allowed for federal income tax purposes.[9] As this method produces high depreciation charges in the early years of the asset's life and low charges in the later years, the annual depreciation deductions will decline. Conse-

[9] Under the double declining balance method, a depreciation rate equal to twice the straight-line rate for the useful life of the asset is used. For an asset with a life of 6 years, the straight-line rate is 16⅔; twice this is 33⅓. This double rate is then applied to the book value (original cost less accumulated depreciation) of the asset. Thus, the depreciable base of the asset declines each year. Total depreciation charged by this method cannot exceed the original cost less the salvage value ($15,000 in this illustration) of the asset. The taxpayer may elect to change from the double declining balance method to the straight-line method for the remaining book value and life of the asset whenever he wishes. Here, the taxpayer plans to do this only in the last year of the asset's life. In that last year, then, the depreciation charge is simply the remaining book value of the new machine less the $15,000 salvage value.

quently, the difference between double declining balance depreciation on the new machine and straight-line depreciation on the old one will decline. The tax saving from depreciation, thus, is not in the form of a level annuity; and each individual year's tax saving must be discounted separately. The computation of each year's tax saving due to depreciation is shown in Schedule 1 of Table 16–3.

If the old machine is traded in, there will be a loss on its disposition amounting to $20,000. This is the difference between its book value of $55,000 ($80,000 cost minus $25,000 accumulated depreciation for 3 years) and the trade-in allowance of $35,000. Under current federal income tax law, this loss is not deductible in the year in which the old asset is disposed of but is added to the cost of the new asset and deducted over the latter's useful life in the form of depreciation. Thus, the depreciable cost of the new asset would be $180,000 ($160,000 price plus the $20,000 loss). Total depreciation cannot exceed $165,000, the tax base of the asset less its estimated terminal salvage value.

The basic cash outflow for this investment is the net cash price of $125,000 for the new machine. A minor outflow is the terminal salvage value of the old machine of $5,000, which must be foregone if the new one is to be purchased. This amount might also have been offset against the inflow from the salvage value of the new machine, for both amounts would be received at the end of six years. Either way, the net present value of the replacement decision is the same.

In this illustration, the total useful life of the new machine is equal to the remaining life of the old one. This fact simplifies the analysis, for both alternatives, replacing or keeping the old machine, involve the same time period. If the new machine had a useful life of longer than six years, the decision-making analysis would have to give consideration to the possible replacement opportunities six years hence when the old machine would have to be replaced in any event. Such opportunities might be difficult to define at this point.

Importance of Depreciation Method

In the equipment replacement decision analyzed in Table 16–3, the company's management decided that depreciation on the new machine would be charged, for income tax purposes, according to the double declining balance method. The selection of this depreciation method is an extremely important element in the total decision respecting the purchase of the new machine. Because the double declining balance method allows larger depreciation deductions in the early years of an asset's life than the straight-line method, it offers a permanent advantage to the taxpayer, not merely a temporary one. The face amount of the total taxes paid over the life of the machine is the same regardless of the depreciation method used, so long as the tax rate remains unchanged. The present value of the taxes paid is lower under the double declining balance method, however; for lower taxes are paid in the early years and more in the later years. The present value of the dollars paid out in the later years is lower than that of the same number of dollars paid out in the early years.

The present value of the decision to adopt double declining balance depreciation instead of straight-line depreciation is computed as follows:

Year	*Double Declining Balance Depreciation*	*Straight-Line Depreciation*	*Difference*	*Present[10] Value Factor at 7%*	*Present Value*
1	$ 60,000	$ 27,500	$ 32,500	.9658	$ 31,389
2	40,000	27,500	12,500	.9005	11,256
3	26,667	27,500	(833)	.8396	(699)
4	17,778	27,500	(9,722)	.7829	(7,611)
5	11,852	27,500	(15,648)	.7299	(11,421)
6	8,703	27,500	(18,797)	.6806	(12,793)
	$165,000	$165,000	$ 0		

Present value of double declining balance method before income tax	10,121
Federal income tax rate	.47
Present value of double declining balance method after taxes	$ 4,757

Notice that the total depreciation deducted over the six years is the same under both methods. Only the timing of the deductions differs. Yet the present value of the decision to elect the double declining balance method is $4,757 after taxes. This is the amount by which the net present value of the decision to purchase the new machine would be reduced if the straight-line depreciation method were to be elected. Inasmuch as the net present value of this equipment replacement decision is only $7,688 (cf., Table 16–3), the selection of the depreciation method is obviously a material factor in the total decision. Clearly, then, the selection of a depreciation method for tax purposes is an important managerial decision in most situations.

QUESTIONS FOR DISCUSSION

1. What are the distinctive characteristics of an investment decision as opposed to a short-term decision (discussed in Chapter 14)?

[10] From Table B–2 in Appendix B.

2. This chapter is concerned primarily with the financial analysis of long-term investment decisions confronting business managers. While financial analysis is indispensable to an intelligent decision, it is not the sum and substance of the decision-making process. What other factors might be relevant to the decision? Have these other factors any financial implications? If so, why are they not incorporated in the formal financial analysis? If not, how are they relevant to the decision?
3. What implications for capital budgeting are involved in an assumption that the capital available to a firm is rationed to an amount less than the sum of all profitable investment opportunities? How would the capital budgeting process be altered if the capital rationing assumption were eliminated?
4. Discuss the relevance of each of the following expenses commonly appearing in corporate income statements to the financial analysis for an investment decision:
   a. Depreciation
   b. Interest
   c. Income taxes
5. Define the net present value of an investment in a way that should be clear to the reasonably informed layman (i.e., one who is not an accountant nor an expert in financial matters).
6. The controller of a large corporation wishes to establish a standard procedure for the evaluation of proposed capital investments. He has asked your assistance in the development of such a procedure. What data should be utilized in the evaluation of an individual investment proposal? Who should provide these data? How should they be analyzed in the decision-making process?
7. Of what use is the payback period in capital investment analysis?
8. Discuss some of the principal problems involved in an attempt to rank several alternative investment proposals in the order of their profitability.
9. Assume that the general price level in the economy will rise at an annual rate of 3 percent. How should this inflation factor be incorporated in a decision to invest $100,000 (*a*) in public utility bonds and (*b*) in a retail grocery store?
10. Weighing alternative possible outcomes of prospective investments by their respective probabilities of occurrence affords some basis for dealing with the problem of uncertainty in capital budgeting. The results of the capital budgeting analysis, of course, are no better than the data employed in the analysis. How might a firm go about determining the respective probabilities of two or more alternative patterns of cash flow from a single investment proposal?
11. "The discounted rate of return is a common denominator of investments, regardless of the initial amount invested. The net present value, however, is not; it tends to vary directly with the size of the initial investment. The net present value index, on the other hand, is an appropriate common denominator of investments." Discuss this statement.
12. A small manufacturing corporation has two machines of the same basic type. One was purchased twenty years ago and is now fully depreciated,

although still in service. The other was purchased one year ago and is being depreciated by the straight-line method over a useful life of twenty years. A revolutionary new machine has been developed and put on the market. It makes the old type machine obsolete, although still physically usable. Both of the old type machines the corporation is presently using could be sold at the same low scrap value. Management is planning to scrap the machine purchased twenty years ago and replace it with one of the new type. The machine purchased a year ago, however, will be retained; for management feels it would be unprofitable to bear so heavy a loss on its disposition. Evaluate this pair of decisions respecting the two machines presently in use.

13. "Because of the time value of money, it is always advantageous for a business enterprise to use one of the accelerated depreciation methods for income tax purposes rather than the straight-line method." Discuss the validity of this assertion.
14. Do you believe the principles of capital budgeting discussed in this chapter are relevant to governmental and other nonprofit institutions, such as schools and hospitals? Explain.
15. Your rich uncle has an opportunity to purchase for $100,000 a small retail store that will produce an annual net income after taxes of $10,000. He intends to accept this offer, as it will yield a 10 percent rate of return on his investment and, in his own words, "that beats government bonds." Criticize your uncle's analysis of this investment opportunity.

PROBLEMS

1. Compute the net present value of each of the following independent investment proposals:

   Investment A:
   - Initial outlay—$250,000
   - Annual cash inflow—$50,000
   - Life—10 years
   - Cost of capital—12 percent

   Investment B:
   - Initial outlay—$300,000
   - Annual cash inflow—$25,000
   - Life—15 years
   - Terminal salvage value—$30,000
   - Cost of capital—7 percent

   Investment C:
   - Initial outlay—$500,000
   - Annual cash inflows:
     - First 5 years—$80,000
     - Second 5 years—$40,000
     - Last 5 years—$10,000
   - Life—15 years

Terminal salvage value—$25,000
Cost of capital—10 percent

Investment D:
Initial outlay—$200,000
Subsequent outlays:
At end of 8 years—$100,000
At end of 16 years—$50,000
Annual cash inflows:
First 5 years—$20,000
Next 10 years—$40,000
Last 10 years—$20,000
Life—25 years
Terminal salvage value—$10,000
Cost of capital—8 percent

Investment E:
Initial cash inflow—$140,000
Annual cash outflow—$25,000
Life—7 years
Cost of capital—9 percent

2. Following is a summary of the important financial data relative to five independent investment proposals:

Investment	*Initial Outlay*	*Annual Cash Proceeds*	*Life in Years*
A.	$ 60,000	$ 8,000	15
B.	88,000	15,000	22
C.	2,150	1,000	3
D.	20,500	3,000	10
E.	425,000	150,000	20

The applicable cost of capital is 6 percent.

Required:

Rank these five investment proposals according to each of the following criteria:

1. Simple rate of return on average investment.
2. Pay-back period.
3. Discounted rate of return.
4. Net present value index.

3. The Consolidated Paper Products Corporation is considering the construction of a new plant to produce facial tissue. The cost of the plant would be $3,000,000. It would have a useful life of fourteen years and a terminal salvage value of $200,000. Depreciation on the plant would be deducted for tax purposes by the straight-line method. Annual cash revenues from the sale of the plant's output are budgeted at $5,000,000 and annual out-of-pocket

operating costs for the plant, at $4,300,000. The corporate income tax rate is 40 percent. The corporation's cost of capital is 9 percent.

Required:

Would the proposed investment in the new plant be profitable over its expected useful life? Support your answer with some organized and appropriately labeled computations.

4. Anthony Wayne, 50 years of age, has received an inheritance of $150,000 from his mother. He is currently employed as store manager of a large metropolitan haberdashery. His salary is $18,000 per year, and he does not anticipate that it will change if he remains in the position to retirement at age 65. He is considering two alternative employments of his inheritance. The first plan would be to continue in his present employment and to invest the $150,000 in 15-year term bonds yielding 8 percent interest. The second plan would be to purchase and operate his own store. He knows of a haberdashery that is for sale at a price of $140,000, including $45,000 for merchandise and the balance for building and fixtures. If he purchases the store, an additional $10,000 will have to be invested for working capital needs. The expected annual receipts of this store are $360,000. Annual out-of-pocket operating costs are estimated at $325,000. Annual depreciation of $5,000 would be deductible for tax purposes. As Wayne would manage his own store, he would have to leave his present employment. At the end of fifteen years, when he wishes to retire in any event, he estimates the store could be sold for $20,000. The applicable personal income tax rate is 25 percent.

Required:

Which course of action would be more profitable for Wayne? Assume that the two plans described above are the only alternatives available to him.

5. The Home-Maid Products Company has developed a new kitchen appliance that it plans to introduce in the coming year. It is estimated that this product will have a market life of ten years. An initial expenditure of $150,000 for equipment to manufacture the product will be necessary. After two years, additional equipment costing $270,000 will have to be purchased. The original equipment will have no significant salvage value at the end of the product's market life. The equipment purchased two years later will be sold for approximately $30,000 at the end of the market life of the appliance. Depreciation on all equipment will be deducted by the straight-line method.

Projected sales volumes of this new appliance during its market life are as follows:

1st year	$ 300,000
2nd year	600,000
3rd—7th years	1,000,000
8th—10th years	400,000

Variable out-of-pocket costs to manufacture and distribute the product will average 50 percent of the selling price. Fixed out-of-pocket operating costs will average $100,000 annually. In addition, a special sales promotion campaign is planned. Its annual costs will be as follows:

1st year	$200,000
2nd year	150,000
3rd—10th years	75,000

The relevant income tax rate is 40 percent. It should be assumed that the company, as a whole, will have taxable income in every year, regardless of profit or loss in any one product line. The company's cost of capital has been estimated at 10 percent after consideration of tax implications.

Required:

What is the net present value of the proposed investment for this new product? Will it be profitable for the company to market the product?

6. Eighteenth Century Lion is planning a super-spectacular motion picture entitled "Custer's Last Stand." Production is scheduled to begin at once and is expected to take two years to complete. Operating cash outlays, including actors' salaries (except as noted below), are expected to total $6,000,000 each year during this production period. In addition, the producers will have to make an immediate payment of $250,000 to the government for the exclusive right to use Custer Battlefield National Monument for outdoor scenes.

To enhance the artistic image and international appeal of the picture, the producers have decided to engage the distinguished Latin American actor, Pancho deLeon, to play the role of Sitting Bull. Señor deLeon has agreed to accept either a salary of $250,000 to be paid in weekly installments over the two-year production period or 5 percent of the gross receipts from the film for the first two years it is in release. The latter alternative would call for two payments, one at the end of each of the first two years that the picture is exhibited; each of these payments would be equal to 5 percent of the gross receipts for the year just ended. No salary or percentage for Señor deLeon is included in the $6,000,000 annual outlay mentioned above.

The producers have estimated that the gross cash receipts from the film would be $3,000,000 during the first year it is in release, $4,000,000 during the second year, $2,000,000 during each of the next five years, and $1,000,000 during each of the last three years. They believe that any receipts after ten years would be negligible in amount if the picture were further exhibited in theaters. Television rights to the film could be sold at that time for $1,000,000, however. The picture will be released as soon as production is completed.

The production company estimates its cost of capital at 12 percent after taxes. The applicable income tax rate is 30 percent.

Required:

1. Assuming that the picture will be made, should the producers pay Pancho deLeon the $250,000 salary or 5 percent of the first two years' gross?

2. Ian Frugal, a major stockholder in the production company, questions the advisability of undertaking this picture at all. He believes that it would be an unprofitable venture and that, in any event, Custer was a scoundrel and ought not to be glorified in wide-screen color. Is Mr. Frugal right on either or both points?

7. The Gercken Corporation sells computer services to its clients. The company completed a feasibility study and decided to obtain an additional computer on Jan. 1, 1967. Information regarding the new computer is as follows:

1. The purchase price of the computer is $230,000. Maintenance, property taxes, and insurance will be $20,000 annually. If the computer is rented, the annual rent will be $85,000 plus 5 percent of annual billings to clients. The rental includes maintenance, taxes, and insurance.

2. Due to competitive conditions, the company feels it will be necessary to replace the new computer at the end of three years with one that is larger and more advanced. It is estimated that the computer will have a resale value of $110,000 at the end of three years. The computer will, if purchased, be depreciated on a straight-line basis for both financial reporting and income tax purposes.

3. The corporate income tax rate is 40 percent.

4. The estimated annual billing for the services of the new computer will be $220,000 during the first year and $260,000 during each of the second and third years. The estimated annual expense of operating the computer is $80,000 in addition to the expenses mentioned above. Also, $10,000 of start-up costs will be incurred at the beginning of the first year.

5. If it decides to purchase the computer, the company will pay cash for it. If the computer is rented, the $230,000 can be otherwise invested at a 15 percent rate of return after taxes.

Required:

1. Prepare a schedule comparing the estimated annual net incomes from the new computer under the purchase and the rental alternatives.
2. Prepare a schedule showing the annual cash flows under the purchase and rental alternatives and comparing the net present values of these alternative cash flows.
3. How should the new computer be acquired, by purchase or by lease?

(Adapted from CPA Examination)

8. The Sentinel Corporation has developed a revolutionary new remote control device for television sets. It can be installed easily and inexpensively on any set. The corporation plans to build a new factory for the production of this device. The initial cost of the factory will be $8,000,000. Its useful life is estimated at twenty years and its terminal salvage value, at $600,000.

The device is to be sold for $12 per unit. The variable out-of-pocket costs to make and sell it will be $5 per unit. In addition, there will be annual fixed factory expenses of $770,000, including salaries, taxes, insurance, maintenance expenditures, and straight-line depreciation on the factory.

An initial sales promotion campaign is planned. It calls for an immediate expenditure of $150,000 and outlays throughout the first three years of the product's market life in the following total amounts:

First year	$ 60,000
Second year	100,000
Third year	50,000

After the third year, promotion of this device will be accomplished through the company's regular promotional program at no additional cost. Regular promotional outlays average $250,000 annually.

Forecasted annual sales volumes for the device are as follows:

First year	100,000 units
Second year	150,000 units
Third year	200,000 units
Fourth through twentieth years	250,000 units

The applicable income tax rate is 40 percent. The company estimates its cost of capital at 12 percent after taxes.

Required:

Prepare a report showing the budgeted profitability of the proposed investment in the new factory.

9. The Wabash River Transport Co. is contemplating expanding its fleet of barges by purchasing eight new barges having a freight capacity of 200 tons each. Maximum operating capacity for a barge is 480,000 ton-miles per month. Each barge would cost $225,000 and would have an estimated service life of fifteen years. Depreciation would be computed by the straight-line method for income tax reports.

The company's standard freight rate is $.04 per ton-mile. Variable out-of-pocket operating costs average $.02 per ton-mile. Fixed monthly out-of-pocket costs are $3,500 per barge. The income tax rate is 25 percent, and the company's cost of capital is 9 percent.

Management has estimated that the chances are 6 in 10 that the new barges will be utilized at 75 percent of their operating capacity. (Routes and schedules would make it impossible for the company to purchase and operate six barges at 100 percent of capacity in lieu of eight barges at 75 percent of capacity.) The actual operating rate may be affected by the outcomes of pending events, however. One of the company's chief competitors is the Lafayette & Southern Railway, which is presently discussing a merger with the Midcontinent Railroad. If this merger is approved—and the chances are 3 in 10 that it will be—Lafayette & Southern's operating position will be strengthened. It could then attract freight now handled on the rivers, and the utilization of the new barges would be only 50 percent of operating capacity. On the other hand, if the rail merger is not approved, there is 1 chance in 10 that Lafayette & Southern would be forced to discontinue operations entirely. In this event, the barges would be utilized to their maximum operating capacity.

Required:

On the basis of the available information, would it be profitable for the Wabash River Transport Co. to invest in eight new barges?

10. The Flanders Flinders Bar Company is considering three alternative plans for the development and promotion of its product. High, medium, and low forecasts of revenues under each plan have been formulated and their respective probabilities of occurrence have been estimated. These budgeted revenues and probabilities, along with related cost data, are summarized below.

	Plan A	*Plan B*	*Plan C*
Budgeted revenue (probability of occurrence):			
High	$3,000,000 (.3)	$2,400,000 (.2)	$5,000,000 (.2)
Medium	2,000,000 (.3)	2,000,000 (.7)	2,500,000 (.5)
Low	500,000 (.4)	1,500,000 (.1)	0 (.3)
Variable costs as percentages of sales revenue	60%	75%	70%
Initial investment	$1,500,000	$2,000,000	$1,500,000
Life in years	5	8	6

It may be assumed that the foregoing alternative estimates of revenue are exhaustive. No other level of revenue might occur under any of the plans.

The company's cost of capital is 10 percent. Income taxes may be ignored in this case.

Required:

1. Compute the net present values of the three alternative plans. Which plan is the most profitable?
2. Which plan would result in the lowest maximum loss, in the event the worst happened?
3. What factors are present in this situation, in addition to the problem of uncertainty, that impair comparison of the three plans?

11. The Porcelain Products Company has a total of up to $5,000,000 available for investment. The cost of capital, estimated to be 5 percent after taxes, is incurred only on capital actually invested. The company has five independent investment opportunities available to it. The basic financial data relative to these investments are outlined below.

Investment	*Initial Outlay*	*Annual Cash Receipts*	*Annual Cash Outlays*	*Life in Years*
A	$2,500,000	$3,000,000	$2,300,000	10
B	1,500,000	2,150,000	1,800,000	12
C	1,000,000	850,000	660,000	15
D	2,000,000	2,500,000	2,000,000	12
E	2,000,000	1,860,000	1,220,000	8

The applicable income tax rate is 40 percent. Initial outlays may be amortized, for tax purposes, over the lives of the investments.

Required:

1. Rank these five independent investments by their net present value indexes.
2. In the situation as described above, what would be the most profitable total capital investment program for the company?
3. Assume now that the entire $5,000,000 of capital available is in the company's possession and entails the 5 percent capital cost whether invested or not. Assume also that the only other possible investment of capital is in savings deposits yielding 4 percent interest per annum. Would your answer to part 2 be different under these conditions? Explain.

12. The Zam B-Z Corporation manufactures small electronic components largely by hand labor. Recently, a machine has been developed to automate part of this work. The machine would cost $1,220,000 delivered and installed and would have a useful life of twelve years. Its salvage value at the end of twelve years is estimated at $20,000. Use of the machine would render useless a number of work benches now in use. These benches originally cost $30,000 eighteen years ago and are being depreciated over a useful life of thirty years, with no assumed salvage value. The benches could now be sold for about $2,000. Any loss on the sale of the benches would be tax-deductible in the year of the sale.

A comparison of annual operating costs under the present hand-labor method and with the machine in use is as follows:

	Hand Labor	*Machine*
Raw materials	$ 400,000	$420,000
Direct labor	650,000	300,000
Indirect labor	40,000	75,000
Heat, light, and power	40,000	60,000
Depreciation	1,000	100,000
Taxes and insurance	5,000	40,000
	$1,136,000	$995,000

The corporation will use straight-line depreciation for both financial reporting and income tax returns. The pertinent income tax rate is 30 percent. The corporation's cost of capital is 10 percent after taxes.

Required:

Would it be profitable for the corporation to purchase the machine? Support your answer with appropriate financial analysis.

13. The Hanover Printing Company is considering replacing its present press with a new one that would double present capacity and improve the quality of the work done. The new press would cost $80,000 and would have a useful life of ten years and an expected terminal salvage value of about $7,000. The old press has a book value (i.e., cost less accumulated depreciation) of

$18,000. It can be traded in for a $3,000 allowance on the price of the new press. Thus, any loss on disposition of the old press would be added to the cost of the new one and recovered through depreciation deductions for income tax purposes. If held for ten more years until the end of its useful life, the old press would have a terminal salvage value of $1,000.

Annual operating costs under each press at the present volume of work are compared below.

	Old Press	*New Press*
Variable expenses:		
Materials and supplies	$60,000	$75,000
Labor	40,000	55,000
Fixed expenses:		
Miscellaneous out-of-pocket expenses	10,000	25,000

While the new press will double capacity, the company anticipates that actual volume will increase by only 50 percent. The company bills all jobs at variable cost plus 40 percent thereof. This practice would be continued if the new press is purchased, and the improved quality of the work would permit the consequent increase in prices.

The income tax rate is 40 percent. The company's estimated after-tax cost of capital is 6 percent.

Required:

Prepare an analysis to assist management in deciding whether or not to replace the old press with the new one.

14. The Umpqua Dredge and Dock Corporation is currently using a harbor dredge purchased two years ago at a cost of $775,000. This dredge was estimated to have a useful life of ten years and a terminal salvage value of $50,000. A substantially improved dredge is now available at a cost of $1,200,000. It operates faster than the one presently in service and would increase the corporation's total revenue by an estimated $750,000 annually. It would also increase annual operating costs by approximately $500,000, exclusive of depreciation.

    The new dredge would have a useful life of eight years and an expected terminal salvage value of $60,000. If the new one is purchased, the company will have no further use for the old dredge, which can be sold currently for about $250,000.

    The corporation's cost of capital is 9 percent. The income tax rate is 40 percent. For tax purposes, the corporation uses straight-line depreciation on all assets. Losses on sales of assets are tax-deductible in the year of the sale.

Required:

Prepare an analysis of the available data and make a recommendation as to whether the corporation should replace the dredge now in service with the new one.

15. The Compton Company is contemplating the acquisition of several new

machines at a total cost of $600,000. These machines would have useful lives of ten years and no significant terminal salvage values. If they are purchased and put into use, out-of-pocket operating costs of $106,000 would be saved each year.

The company would have two alternatives for deducting depreciation on these machines for income tax purposes. One would be to use straight-line depreciation over the entire ten-year life. The other would be to use double declining balance depreciation for the first five years and straight-line depreciation for the second five years. The latter alternative would work thus: For each of the first five years, depreciation would be deducted by applying twice the straight-line rate for a ten-year life to the book value of the machines (i.e., their original cost less the accumulated depreciation of prior years). For each of the second five years, depreciation would be computed by applying the straight-line rate for a five-year useful life to the book value of the machines as of the beginning of the sixth year (i.e., the original cost less accumulated depreciation by the declining balance method for the first five years).

The income tax rate is 30 percent. The company's cost of capital is 10 percent.

Required:

1. Prepare a report comparing the cash flows from the new machines under the alternative depreciation schemes. Should the machines be purchased? If so, which depreciation plan should be used?
2. Under other circumstances, might the depreciation plan *not* recommended in part 1 be preferable financially? If so, indicate what these circumstances might be.

16. Bingham purchased an apartment building thirty years ago at a cost of $900,000. It has a remaining economic life of fifteen years. His annual income statement for the operation of this building is as follows:

Rent		$135,000
Expenses:		
Out-of-pocket	$60,000	
Depreciation	20,000	80,000
Income before tax		55,000
Income tax at 40%		22,000
Income		$ 33,000

Ryder has expressed a desire to buy this building "if the price is right." It may be assumed that the rents and out-of-pocket expenses will continue as shown above for the remaining useful life of the building. Ryder is in the same income tax bracket as Bingham.

Both men have a cost of capital after taxes of 6 percent.

Required:

What is the least Bingham can afford to take for the building? What is the most Ryder can afford to pay for it?

Chapter 17

THE ROLE OF COSTS IN PRICING DECISIONS

PROBABLY THE most important single decision which the management of a business enterprise must make is the setting of the price for the firm's product or service. In a multiproduct firm, many pricing decisions must be made. The pricing decision is critical not only at the outset, but it must be reappraised and, possibly, remade regularly. The pricing decision affects the entire enterprise and must be made with this fact in mind. It is not simply a marketing or a financial decision. It is the genesis of the revenues which the firm realizes. If those revenues persistently fail to cover the costs of the firm, the enterprise as a whole will ultimately fail. The accountant, as a compiler, planner, and analyst of financial data, is importantly involved in the price-setting decision. Financial data and, more specifically, cost data are fundamental elements in the price-setting process; but they are only part of that process. Their relevance to the pricing decision must be neither exaggerated nor underestimated; either error could be financially fatal. This chapter is concerned only with the proper role of cost data in price-setting decisions. It does not purport to offer a comprehensive analysis of pricing.

ECONOMIC THEORY OF PRICE DETERMINATION

It is not the purpose of this section to expound or to summarize price theory as commonly developed in the discipline of economics. A few basic notions will be reviewed, however, to establish a general framework for the ensuing discussion of the pertinence of costs to pricing decisions.

Supply and Demand

The basic factors determining price in economic theory are the supply of a product (or service) and the demand for it. If there is an actual market for a product, there must be some price at which the physical volume of product that suppliers are willing to sell is equal to that volume which customers (i.e., "demanders") are willing to buy. That is the price at which the product is traded. This relationship between supply and demand is commonly depicted graphically by a positively sloped supply curve and a negatively sloped demand curve, as illustrated in Figure 17–1. The price of the product (*p* in Figure 17–1) is deter-

FIGURE 17–1

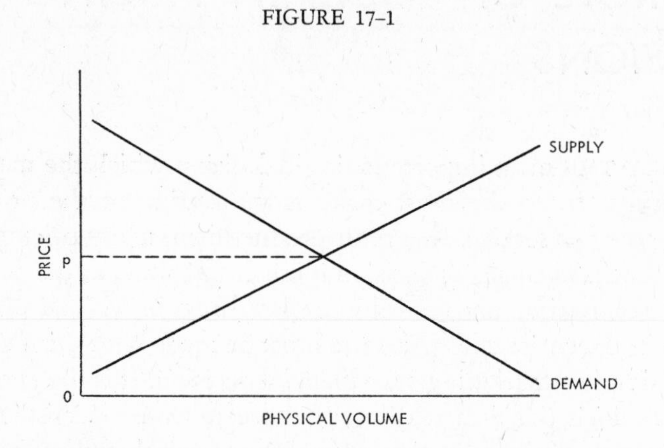

mined at the point of intersection of the supply and demand curves. The conceptual validity of this analysis is readily apparent. Its practical applicability, however, is not always so apparent. Managers do not have access to neat supply and demand curves such as those in Figure 17–1. They may be able to estimate the general patterns of supply and demand for their products, but these estimates are subject to varying and indeterminate degrees of error.

Elasticity of Demand. One of the most critical characteristics of the demand for a product is its price elasticity, that is, the relative degree to which changes in the price of the product cause changes in the volume of sales of that product. Obviously, knowledge of the elasticity of demand for a product is crucial to any price change decision. Yet, the elasticity of demand for most products is subject to a considerable degree of uncertainty. The demand for certain products, such as salt, is usually agreed to be highly inelastic. A substantial increase in the price of a pound of salt may have no appreciable impact upon consumers' purchases of it. Other products, however, have definitely elastic demand schedules. Substantially more units will be purchased at low prices than at high prices. (The demand curve in Figure 17–1 obviously is elastic.) Observing that the demand for a product is generally elastic or inelastic is one thing.

Measuring its elasticity—determining the impact upon physical sales volume of a specific price change—is quite another. Yet, it is just this determination that is important to the business manager contemplating a change in the price of his product.

His problems are further complicated by the factor of cross-elasticity of demand. This is the relative degree to which the sales of one product are affected by changes in the price of a substitute product (e.g., the impact on the sales of steel of a reduction in the price of aluminum). The problem of measuring cross-elasticity is further clouded by the prior problem of identifying substitute products.

A review of the discussions in the preceding three paragraphs suggests that management cannot measure accurately the most basic factors underlying the price-setting decision. Nevertheless, these economic factors cannot be ignored. Subsequent discussions of the role of costs in pricing decisions will not deal extensively with the factors of supply and demand, but these factors will always be present as the basic constraints within which the pricing decision must be made.

Competition

Price-setting decisions must be weighed and evaluated with adequate consideration of the impact of competition upon the decision and the impact of the decision upon competition. In the "pure competition" of economic theory, the individual seller is, in effect, the captive of competition. He has no price-setting discretion at all. One of the requisites of pure competition is homogeneity of product; all sellers' products must be identical. If there exists an element of product differentiation among sellers, the market is described as imperfectly competitive. In an imperfect market, the individual seller has some range of discretion within which he may set his price. The extreme of price-setting discretion is the monopolist. He is the only one selling his particular product and, therefore, is limited in his pricing decisions only by the factors of supply and demand. However, as in the case of public utilities, the government may step in and impose additional constraints on the monopolist's pricing policies.

Subsequent discussions of pricing decisions in this chapter will assume some degree of imperfect competition in the market for the product whose price is in question. The seller will always be assumed to have some range of discretion in setting his price. This assumption is generally valid in respect to the operations of most American manufacturers and distributors.

PRICING STANDARD PRODUCTS

Not all pricing decisions have the same dimensions. There may be great differences between a decision as to the price of one of a company's standard products and a decision regarding the pricing of a special order. The former type of decision will be considered here. Pricing special orders will be discussed in a later section. Standard products here include all items regularly produced and sold by the company, whether they are produced continuously for inventory or on individual customers' orders only.

Cost-Plus Pricing

Cost Plus Normal Markup. One of the simplest approaches to price-setting decisions is to set the price at an amount equal to the standard or budgeted cost of production (or purchasing, in the case of a merchandising enterprise) plus a normal markup. This normal markup is a target gross profit, intended to cover nonmanufacturing costs and leave a remainder for net profit before taxes. The normal markup is customarily stated as a percentage, either of selling price or of cost. Normal markups are fairly widely employed in retailing, where they are regularly expressed as percentages of selling prices. Thus, in a retail store, a markup of 30% for an item with a cost of $3.50 means a selling price of $5.00. Whenever one encounters a normal markup percentage, he should be careful that he understands whether selling price or cost is the base of that percentage.

The simplicity of pricing at cost plus a normal markup is matched by its lack of economic logic or general validity. This approach to pricing assumes, first of all, that it is possible to trace all manufacturing costs to individual products. This assumption is clearly invalid for the great majority of firms. The presence of common costs in most firms is obvious. Although these common costs may be allocated among the several products of a firm for inventory valuation and income determination purposes, the same allocations are likely to be invalid for decision-making purposes. And pricing is very definitely a decision-making situation. Further, adding a normal markup to production cost and establishing the total as the selling price presumes either that there is no competition or that the resultant selling price is competitive. A manufacturer may find that his production cost plus a normal markup results in a price that is either too high or too low for the existing market. As long as buyers recognize some difference between his product and substitute products in the market, they will accept a commensurate difference in price. The range of the individual seller's price-setting discretion in such a case varies with the degree of substitution among the several sellers' products. The closer the degree of substitution, the narrower is the individual seller's range of pricing discretion.

In a dynamic market, characterized by change and uncertainty, pricing at cost plus a normal markup is not a generally valid or sustainable policy. It may be a useful starting point for the pricing decision, but the seller must be prepared to deviate from such a target price and, perhaps, to deviate greatly from it. What is basically unsound in this approach is not its recognition of the need to cover costs but its insistence upon a normal margin.

Cost Plus Fixed Fee. In a cost-plus-fixed-fee sales contract, the selling price is agreed to be the costs of producing and delivering an item plus a fixed dollar profit margin. This has been a very popular method of pricing goods sold to the federal government, particularly in cases of defense contracts for special items. In government contracting, the costs which may be included in the contract price are carefully specified in advance; and actual costs billed are subject to government audit. In recent years, the government has evidenced a desire to get away from cost-plus-fixed-fee contracts and has favored contracts which reward the seller for cost minimization and/or penalize him for excessive costs. One of the inherent shortcomings of cost-plus-fixed-fee pricing is that it tends to dull the seller's interest in cost control. As long as the buyer agrees to bear certain costs incurred by the seller and assure him of a fixed dollar profit, the seller is likely to exert little effort to minimize those costs. Cost-plus-fixed-fee pricing has little if any merit in the pricing of standard products. On special orders for the manufacture of new items with which the seller has had no production experience, it does have some merit; for the costs of such orders are likely to be very difficult to estimate in advance. The fixed fee, or profit margin, presumably is the result of negotiations between buyer and seller.

Relevant Costs for Pricing Decisions

Direct Costs. In a single product firm, all of the costs incurred may be regarded as traceable to the one product. Hence, all costs are direct costs with respect to the product. In setting a price for such a product, management would properly expect it to cover all of the company's costs and provide a profit margin. In a multiproduct firm, however, not all costs are directly traceable to individual products. Some are true common costs; any assignment of these to individual products is purely arbitrary. What costs in the multiproduct firm, then, are relevant for pricing decisions? When a decision is to be made regarding the price of an individual product, only those costs directly traceable to that product, those costs which could be avoided by discontinuing production and sale of the product, should be considered directly. In other words, this type of pricing decision should be approached by means of the incremental profit analysis described in Chapter 14. In the incremental profit approach, the selling price must cover all direct costs—both manufacturing and nonmanufacturing, both variable and fixed—that are attributable to a product. The price should also contribute to the covering of common costs and the realization of a profit. The common costs are not ignored in this approach; they are provided for by the excess of the selling price over the direct costs. Common costs are not assigned to the individual products for the simple reason that they bear no direct relationship to those products.

For a short period of time it is tolerable for the price of a product to do no more than cover its direct costs or even, possibly, only the direct variable costs. This may be the case, for example, when a new product is introduced. The initial direct promotional costs may be unusually high relative to sales volume, and special price concessions may be granted in connection with introductory offers. In this case, the negligible contribution to common costs in the short run is accepted in anticipation of long-run profits. In other cases, a very low contribution from one or more products may be accepted for want of a more profitable alternative. A low contribution is better than none at all.

In the long run, of course, the aggregate revenues from all products must cover the common costs as well as the direct costs. Ideally, each product should make a significant contribution to common costs; but it is not possible to state any general rule for determining satisfactory and unsatisfactory contributions. If factors of demand and/or competition prevent a firm from setting a price for one of its products that will cover direct costs, there may be no alternative to discontinuation of that product. If a competitive price does cover direct costs and yields some contribution to common costs, however, how high must that contribution be to justify long-run continuance of the product in the company's line? This question can be answered only in light of the available alternatives. If the product is discontinued, are there others which may be substituted for it and which will yield a higher contribution to common costs? What effect will discontinuance of this product have upon the demand for other products in the line? The elimination of one product from the line may cause the loss of sales of other, complementary products.[1] Product-pricing decisions should be made with a view toward maximum company profit in the long run. This objective should be regarded as a total company accomplishment, not a piecemeal result of several independent decisions.

Full Cost Pricing. Pricing decisions should be made in recognition of the need for the firm to cover all costs, at least in the long run. A fairly popular extension of this recognition is the practice of "full cost pricing," wherein all costs or, at least, all manufacturing costs are assigned to individual products. This extension, however, is not valid. It seeks to establish specific cost-product relationships in cases of common costs where no such relationships actually exist. If only manufacturing costs are assigned to individual products, "full cost pricing" ignores the fact that some nonmanufacturing costs may be directly traceable to products. Under the incremental profit approach, each product's price must cover its own direct costs, whether manufacturing or nonmanufacturing. Once this requirement is met, then all products' incremental profits must cover common costs. The responsibility for covering common costs should be associated with the aggregate pricing policies of the firm, not with individual product-pricing decisions.

At this point, the reader may raise the question of how common costs can be assured to be covered if individual prices are set in consideration of direct costs only. To begin with, the covering of direct costs is only a starting point in the pricing decision. Factors of supply and demand and competition may permit prices which will yield very substantial contributions to common costs. Nevertheless, a low contribution from a single product does not necessarily mean that the price is too low or that the product ought to be discontinued. If the economic determinants of price are such that the combined prices for all of a company's products are insufficient to cover common costs in the long run, the conclusion is not that the individual prices are wrong but, rather, that the firm is economically inefficient. Such a firm must either improve its operating efficiency or cease operations and liquidate.

Pricing a New Product

The introduction of a new product in a company's line may entail some additional problems. If it is significantly different from any product already available, there is no established market for it. Until its introduction, there has been no supply of the product and, hence, no demonstrated demand for it. The company may believe firmly that the demand

[1] See page 335 in Chapter 14.

will be substantial, but this has yet to be proved in the market. In all likelihood, there are some near-substitute products currently on the market; but their actual degree of substitution is as yet unknown. Thus, the competitive influence on the price of the new product can only be estimated. Further, the firm may have no reliable estimate of the direct costs of manufacturing and marketing the new product. Its cost patterns are likely to change as the firm obtains experience with the product and as its sales volume increases. In summary, then, pricing decisions for new products involve essentially the same considerations as those discussed earlier for established products. These considerations are subject to considerably greater uncertainty, however.

Test Marketing. One fairly popular technique employed to obtain valuable experience with a new product is test marketing. The product is introduced in selected areas only, often at different prices in different areas. Such tests afford the firm's management some idea as to the amount and elasticity of the demand for the product, the competition it will encounter, and the contribution to common costs and profit it may be expected to yield at various prices and volumes. Test marketing, of course, is not a perfect simulation of full-scale production and distribution. It may, however, provide very useful information for better planning of the full-scale marketing effort. It also permits initial pricing mistakes to be made in miniature rather than on a large scale.

Pricing for a Target Rate of Return. In most cases, the introduction of a new product involves some capital investment outlays and should be evaluated, in part at least, as a long-term investment decision. The price set for the product should be sufficient to yield at least the minimum acceptable rate of return on investment required by the firm. In other words, the price must be high enough that the net present value of the investment is positive. In capital investment analysis, management is concerned with the net cash inflow to be derived from a decision. For a new product, the net cash inflow is a function of both price and volume. If volume were a fixed quantity, the required price could be determined quite easily by means of discounted cash flow analysis. However, as long as there is some elasticity of demand for the product, the price and volume will vary inversely with each other. The pattern of this variation may be determined from test marketing or estimated from experience with near-substitute products.

To illustrate the relevance of capital investment analysis to pricing decisions, assume that a company is introducing a new product for which it feels it has considerable latitude in setting price. The product has been test marketed in three areas at three different prices. As a result of these tests, the firm estimates that the three alternative prices will yield the annual sales volumes indicated in Table 17–1. (For the sake of

TABLE 17–1

	Test Area 1	*Test Area 2*	*Test Area 3*
Test selling price per unit	$ 6.00	$ 7.50	$ 9.00
Direct costs per unit	4.00	4.00	4.00
Incremental profit per unit	$ 2.00	$ 3.50	$ 5.00
Budgeted unit sales volume	100,000	80,000	30,000
Total incremental profit before tax considerations	$200,000	$280,000	$150,000
Income tax (47%)	94,000	131,600	70,500
	$106,000	$148,400	$ 79,500
Tax deduction for depreciation of investment in equipment, etc. ($420,000 × ⅓ × 47%)	65,800	65,800	65,800
Annual cash inflow after tax	$171,800	$214,200	$145,300
Present value factor for 3 years at 12% (from Table B–1)	2.5194	2.5194	2.5194
Present value of cash inflows	$432,833	$539,655	$366,069
Present value of cash outflow	420,000	420,000	420,000
Net present value	$ 12,833	$119,655	$(53,931)

simplicity in the illustration, we shall assume that no other price is possible. Obviously, this assumption would hardly be valid in a real situation. Adding further price alternatives would only expand the illustration, however, not change it.) The direct costs of this product, all of which costs are variable, amount to $4 per unit. The units test marketed were produced on existing equipment. The investment in equipment to produce the product in volume and in initial promotion totals $420,000. This investment is expected to have an economic life of three years. The applicable income tax rate is 47%. The company's cost of capital is 12% after taxes. The analysis in Table 17–1 shows that the highest price, $9.00, will not generate sufficient sales volume to afford a positive net present value at 12%. At that price, the rate of return would be less than the capital cost. Either the $6.00 or the $7.50 price would yield a satisfactory rate of return, but the latter is obviously preferable, given the facts and circumstances as stated.

The foregoing illustration is highly simplified. It assumes only three possible alternative prices. It assumes that the direct costs of the new product are perfectly variable with sales volume. Actually, efficiencies of large volume might well cause these costs per unit to decline as volume increases. Different volumes might also require different levels of capital investment. More equipment and/or promotional effort might be necessary to achieve the higher volumes. A constant sales volume is assumed during the first three years of the product's market life. Actually, it is probable that sales volume would start low and grow during those early years. Any shifting of sales in the illustration from the first year to later years would, of course, have the effect of reducing the present value of the cash inflows and, hence, the net present value of the investment. Further, sales potential and additional capital outlays beyond the first three years are not considered at all. Finally, the pricing decision, viewed as an investment decision, is subject to all of the same imprecisions and uncertainties that characterize capital budgeting decisions in general.[2] The element of uncertainty is probably greater in this case. Many firms attempt to compensate for this additional uncertainty by requiring a higher than usual rate of return on investments in new products. Although conceptually valid, this approach still demands some practical decision as to how much additional return is needed to compensate for the greater risk.

PRICING SPECIAL ORDERS

For purposes of the present discussion, special order pricing decisions include only nonrecurring, or "onetime," decisions. These will be classified according to two general types, orders for special products and orders for standard products at special prices. The first type of special order is for a custom-made product, designed and manufactured to a single customer's specifications, by a firm that does not regularly handle such orders. If a firm routinely produces special items to customers' orders, it should view the price of each such order as part of a general pricing policy. In this type of business more than in any other, pricing at cost plus a normal markup has some merit. The second type of special order involves a special, lower than usual, price for a standard product. Such orders are most often placed by large buyers. The important distinguishing characteristic of both of these types of special pricing decisions is that they pertain to individual sales only. They are not intended to influence the regular prices of the seller's standard products.

Orders for Special Products

Incremental Profit Analysis. The decision as to the price of an order for a custom-made item should be made in consideration of the alternatives. If such an order is received when a firm is producing at full

[2] See pages 391 to 397 in Chapter 16.

capacity, acceptance of it would necessitate either a reduction in the output of standard products or overtime. If the order is taken at the cost of regular production, its price must be adequate to yield an incremental profit at least equal to that foregone on the standard products which cannot be produced because of the special order. In order to determine their respective incremental profits, management must know the direct costs of both the special order and the standard products. These will include variable costs and, possibly, direct fixed costs. Special setup and training costs incurred in connection with the special order must be assigned to it, even though they may derive from sources normally included in general plant overhead. For example, indirect labor for machinery setup and maintenance is commonly a part of overhead, charged to standard products at a normal or standard rate. If the special order requires setup and maintenance costs in excess of those that would routinely be incurred for production of standard items, that *excess* is a direct cost of the special order.

If an order for a custom-made product is received at a time when the firm is operating below capacity and its acceptance would involve simply the utilization of otherwise idle facilities, the price of such order need cover its own direct costs only. Here the alternative to the special order is no output at all. If the order yields any incremental profit at all, the firm's net income will be increased. The alternative of sales of regular products does not exist.

Capital Investment Analysis. Acceptance of an order for a custom-made product was discussed above as a short-run decision. Implicit in this analysis is the assumption that the order could be produced without additional capital investment in production facilities. If new investments were necessary in order for the firm to accept the order, either the price of the order would have to cover the full amount of such investments or the firm would have to have reasonable expectations of further profitable employment of the new facilities. In the latter instance, those other profitable opportunities should be quantified; and the proposal should be evaluated as any capital investment decision.

Other Considerations. Handling special orders occasionally may afford a company the opportunity of examining the possibilities of entering new markets without committing itself thereto. On the other hand, a firm's unfamiliarity with a special product may present peculiar difficulties. The costs of processing the order may be increased beyond the planned amount because of unexpected overruns on time and/or expenses. If the order is priced in advance on the basis of budgeted costs (as would often be the case), any significant cost overrun could convert a planned profit to a loss. With this possibility in mind, management may accept orders for new and unfamiliar items only if the buyer agrees to bear any reasonable and unforeseen additional costs. Finally, if special orders are processed at the sacrifice of production of standard products, there may be a danger of losing customers for standard items not just at the present but permanently.

Orders for Standard Products at Special Prices

Incremental Profit Analysis. Not uncommonly, manufacturers are asked to supply large quantities of standard products to individual customers at prices below regular list prices. If such an order is received when a manufacturer is operating at full capacity, it will almost certainly be rejected. Why should a firm cut prices when it can sell the same quantity at regular list prices? If, however, the manufacturer is producing below capacity, the special order affords an opportunity to employ idle facilities in the production of the company's standard products. In this situation, any price that yields some incremental profit will increase net income in the short run. From the viewpoint of incremental profit analysis, the only costs relevant to the decision are those direct costs that would be avoided if the order were not accepted. Ordinarily, these will be the variable production and delivery costs.

As an example, assume that a company operating at 70% of normal capacity is asked to produce 25,000 units of one of its regular products for a large drugstore chain at the special price of $1.65 per unit. The regular selling price is $2.25 per unit. The standard production cost of the item is as follows:

Raw materials	$ .48
Direct labor	.65
Variable overhead	.29
Fixed overhead	.38
	$1.80

Acceptance of the order would place no strain whatever on production facilities and would not affect output of items for sale at regular prices. The incremental administrative cost of handling this order is estimated to be $900. At first glance, the order might appear unprofitable; for the proposed selling price is less than the standard cost of the product. However, it must be remembered that the fixed overhead will be incurred in any event. Whether it is charged to production or charged to the volume variance, it is incurred. The proposed price of $1.65 does exceed the variable production costs (raw materials, direct labor, and variable overhead) by $.23 per unit. Thus, the total variable profit on the order would be $5,750 (25,000 units × $.23). After deducting the direct fixed administrative cost of $900, the incremental profit before tax would be $4,850.

Capital Investment Analysis. The illustration in the preceding paragraph involved a special order for a large quantity of a standard product at a lower price only once. However, a manufacturer might be offered a similar proposition on a continuing basis. The distributor might offer to purchase annually a minimum quantity of a particular product at a reduced price. Such an offer would involve a long-term commitment of resources to one sales contract. Hence, it would have to be evaluated as an investment opportunity. If the only alternative to acceptance of this order were employment of the same resources to produce the same product for sale at the regular price, a decision to reject the offer could be made without resort to discounted cash flow analysis. However, if the alternative is idle capacity, the decision may be very different. The unusable idle facilities could probably be disposed of, at least in part, for their current salvage value. The special order would be profitable, then, if the present value of the after-tax cash inflow from it exceeded the current salvage value (after consideration of the tax impact of the disposition) of the idle facilities. A third alternative might be to construct new plant facilities specifically to handle the special order. Such an investment should be analyzed as any capital investment proposal. Management should bear in mind, however, that the implications of the decision upon cash flows may extend beyond the special order itself.

Other Considerations. Before any decision is made to sell a regular product at a special low price, consideration should be given to the possible repercussion upon sales of that product at the regular price. If other customers learn that the item has been sold at a reduced price, they may demand a similar price or they may even threaten to cancel their orders. If it becomes common knowledge that a product is being sold at a "cut-rate" price, the image of the product's quality may be impaired. If the buyer at the low price is a private brand distributor, however, the manufacturer's name might never be associated with the item when resold below the usual selling price. Thus, if the special sale can be kept secret, the dangers suggested above might not arise. If the manufacturer enters into a long-term contract to supply a private brand seller with a product, knowledge of the arrangement is likely to spread. To some extent, this depends upon the nature of the product. If the product is a radio, minor changes in the exterior of the cabinet might effectively mask the manufacturer's identity. If it is an automobile tire, however, the tread design might reveal the manufacturer despite the presence of the distributor's private brand name on the casing. As a manufacturer's sales volume is obtained increasingly from one or a few large buyers, his bargaining position with them deteriorates. Ultimately, his continued solvency may depend upon their will. Obviously, this possibility should be considered before entering into sales contracts of the type described here. As a final consideration, the offering of standard products to individual buyers at reduced prices might be in violation of the federal antitrust law.

ROBINSON-PATMAN ACT

In 1936 the Congress passed and Pres. Franklin D. Roosevelt approved the Robinson-Patman Act. This law amended the Clayton Act of 1914 and added to the federal government's arsenal of antitrust legislation. Specifically, the Robinson-Patman Act deals with price discrimination, situations in which a seller offers the same product to different buyers at different prices. Section 2(a) of this act provides that it is unlawful for a seller to discriminate in price between different purchasers of goods of like grade and quality if such discrimination would tend to lessen competition or to create a monopoly.[3] However, the seller who so discriminates may justify price differentials by showing that they are attributable to actual cost differences. This cost defense provision of the law reads as follows:

> *Provided,* That nothing herein contained shall prevent differentials which make only due allowance for differences in the cost of manufacture, sale, or delivery resulting from the differing methods or quantities in which such commodities are to such purchasers sold or delivered.[4]

The Robinson-Patman Act is enforced, and the cost defense interpreted, by the Federal Trade Commission. The following paragraphs do not purport to contain an exhaustive discussion of the act or of the cost defense alone. They simply attempt to indicate the role of cost accounting in one important area of antitrust legislation.[5]

The cost defense has not played a major role in formal proceedings of the Federal Trade Commission in cases of alleged price discrimination. It

---

[3] 49 Stat. 1526 (1936).

[4] *Ibid.*

[5] For more expansive treatments of this act and the cost defense in particular, see Corwin D. Edwards, *The Price Discrimination Law* (Washington, D.C.: The Brookings Institution, 1959), ch. 18 on the cost defense; and Wright Patman, *Complete Guide to the Robinson-Patman Act* (Englewood Cliffs, N.J.: Prentice-Hall, Inc., 1963), pp. 70–83 on the cost defense.

has, however, been of considerable importance in many of the commission's investigations which have terminated without formal complaints.[6] Thus, managers responsible for price-setting decisions should be cognizant of the relevance of the antitrust law to their work and of the particular pertinence of cost data to the legality of price differentials. As the Robinson-Patman Act deals with price discrimination between different buyers of the same product, it is relevant only to pricing decisions respecting standard products. The pricing of custom-made products does not come within the scope of the act.

Although the cost defense includes within its scope both manufacturing and nonmanufacturing costs, there is no question that distribution costs are the most important ones in establishing an effective cost defense. Some cost differentials are easy to show; lower freight charges on carlot shipments are examples. Other cost differentials may be more difficult to demonstrate. For example, it is generally agreed that the costs of order taking, invoicing, and billing are lower per sales dollar on large orders than on small orders. If the seller's cost accounting system is not set up so as to develop these costs as amounts per sales dollar, however, he may have difficulty in establishing an acceptable cost defense on such basis.

Earlier in this chapter, the prime importance of direct costs in pricing decisions was emphasized. For purposes of the cost defense in the Robinson-Patman Act, however, both direct and indirect costs are relevant. The Federal Trade Commission will not accept the assignment of only the direct costs of a product or of a particular method of distribution to that product or method in a cost defense. A reasonable allocation of common costs to all products or to all business activities of the firm is required.[7] In determining what is a reasonable cost allocation scheme, the commission has shown a general inclination to accept widely employed cost accounting practices. If a seller wishes prior approval of his cost allocation practices, he may submit them to the commission's accounting staff for review. The commission may then indicate approval or suggest modifications. In order to avoid future difficulties, the seller probably will conform to the commission's suggestions. In this way, a cost defense is established before the fact. As costs and other operating conditions change, of course, cost differences justifying price differentials are likely to change also. In other words, a cost defense, once established, is not immutable; it must be kept current.

---

[6] Edwards, *op. cit.*, pp. 587–89, and Patman, *op. cit.*, pp. 75–76.

[7] Edwards, *op. cit.*, p. 586.

The cost defense provision in the Robinson-Patman Act offers a challenge to the cost accountant. It requires him to develop and defend detailed cost analyses that may go beyond the ordinary requirements of product costing or of managerial analysis. It demands more detailed analysis of distribution costs than most firms have yet developed. Finally, it imposes upon the accountant the professional responsibility for developing cost accounting systems that entail the most appropriate and reasonable cost classifications and allocations. To some extent, the reasonableness and equity with which the price discrimination law is administered depend upon accountants' acceptance of this responsibility.

QUESTIONS FOR DISCUSSION

1. The suggestion that an individual seller's costs have some pertinence to his pricing decisions implies that he has some degree of pricing discretion. How is this implication consistent with the generally accepted notion that prices are determined by forces of demand and supply in the market?
2. The sales manager of a medium-sized manufacturing corporation makes the following statement at a meeting of the firm's policy committee: "When we get around to setting prices, every cost we incur had better be charged to one or another of our products if we expect to make any money. I don't care how or why a cost is incurred, if it's there it has to be covered by some product's price. Anybody who thinks differently just doesn't understand the realities of business." How would you, as the corporation's controller and a member of the policy committee, respond to this statement?
3. Under what circumstances, if any, is pricing at cost plus a fixed fee a valid and useful approach to the pricing decision?
4. What are the relevant costs in a decision regarding the price of one of a company's regular products?
5. "Although conceptually valid, the practice of pricing new products so that they will yield a specified rate of return on the investments in such products is usually extremely difficult, if not impossible." Do you agree or disagree with this statement? Explain.
6. Which costs are relevant to the pricing of a special order for a custom-made product? Why?
7. Which costs are relevant to the pricing of a special order for a standard product at a reduced price, if the special order will not affect other output for sale at the regular price? Why?
8. Your company is introducing a new product in the home appliance market. It performs work now done by hand or by less efficient appliances. Initial market research indicates that demand for this product will be sufficient to justify the ultimate expansion of the company's factory facilities. Expected sales in the first year or two of the product's market life could be met by production in existing facilities, however. Outline the factors that you

believe should be considered by management in setting a price for this product. What factors should be considered in the decision regarding the timing of expansion of factory facilities?

9. Your company has been approached by a large drugstore chain with an offer to purchase a minimum quantity of electric hair dryers at a price 20 percent below your normal selling price to distributors. This minimum quantity represents 25 percent of your current annual production of hair dryers. The additional units could be produced in existing factory facilities. What costs would be relevant to the decision whether to accept this offer? What factors other than costs should be considered in evaluating the potential profitability of the offer?

10. Assume that your company has accepted the offer outlined in the preceding question. Another of your customers, who has paid the regular price for the hair dryer, has learned of the lower price paid by the drugstore chain. He has filed a complaint with the Federal Trade Commission, alleging price discrimination by your company. How would you go about establishing a cost defense in connection with this allegation? Would your procedure here be different from the cost analysis undertaken to support the decision to accept the drug chain's offer originally? Explain.

PROBLEMS

1. Napa Supreme Wineries, Inc., produces and sells a wide variety of wines. Among the company's products is a cocktail wine called Krystal Brite. This wine has been on the market for three years. When it first appeared, it was the only wine of its kind in its general price range; and initial sales exceeeded expectations. In the past year, however, other producers have introduced their own low-priced cocktail wines; and sales of Krystal Brite have declined substantially.

   Krystal Brite was originally introduced at a retail price of $1.49 per bottle. Napa Supreme Wineries, Inc., sold it to retailers for $12.75 per case of twelve bottles. The competing wines that have appeared in the past year sell at $1.00 per bottle in retail stores. Retailers pay $9.75 per case of twelve bottles for these other wines. Napa Supreme has received numerous complaints from retailers who indicated that many customers still called for Krystal Brite but bought a competing brand because of the significant price difference. Some retailers have cut the price of Krystal Brite to as little as $1.19 per bottle, but they contend that they cannot make a profit on it at that price. In recent months, Napa Supreme has begun cutting its price per case to retailers.

   Summary sales data for Krystal Brite during its three years on the market are as follows:

Year	*Cases Sold*	*Average Price per Case*
1	16,000	$12.75
2	24,000	12.75
3	18,000	12.25

Variable production and distribution costs average $5.85 per case. Fixed overhead is assigned to all wines at a normal rate of $1.10 per case. Fixed selling and administrative costs are allocated among products at a rate of 20 percent of total sales. Production facilities are common to all wines. The only fixed distribution costs directly traceable to Krystal Brite are advertising and promotion expenses budgeted at $36,000 per year. The company's management regards these expenses as necessary if any significant sales volumes of the product is to be achieved.

A survey of retailers and consumers suggests that Krystal Brite does have a superior product image in the cocktail wine market, but that it is not great enough to warrant the existing retail price differential. Retailers who sold Krystal Brite in the price range between $1.19 and $1.29 reported that their sales of the product were not materially affected by the introduction of the competing wines. Napa Supreme Wineries has a generally acknowledged reputation for higher quality products than the producers of the competing cocktail wines. The president is concerned that reducing the price of Krystal Brite in the face of low-price competition might undercut that reputation. He agrees, however, that further declines in Krystal Brite sales may be expected in the coming year unless some positive action is taken to reverse the trend.

Required:

Prepare an analysis of this situation. Indicate the factors that Napa Supreme Wineries, Inc., should take into consideration in setting a price for Krystal Brite. What price per case would you recommend the company set for the coming year? Why? What would be the lowest price the company could set if sales volume were expected to be 24,000 cases? If $1.25 per bottle were regarded as a price effectively competitive with the lower price of the other cocktail wines, what would be the highest competitive price per case the company could set?

2. The following budgeted and standard data are planned for the Blackwell Manufacturing Co. for the year 1967:

	Products			
	A	*B*	*Y*	*Z*
Budgeted sales volume in units	800,000	250,000	500,000	75,000
Budgeted selling price	$9	$20	$12	$24
Standard cost per unit:				
Raw materials	$2.20	$4.10	$1.90	$8.80
Direct labor	1.50	4.50	3.00	6.00
Variable overhead	.80	2.40	1.60	3.20
Fixed overhead	1.20	3.60	2.40	4.80
Standard labor hours per unit	1	3	2	4

Variable selling expenses are budgeted at 5 percent of sales. Fixed selling expenses are budgeted at 10 percent of sales. Administrative costs are planned at $800,000 for the year. Research and development expenditures have been budgeted at $2\frac{1}{2}$ percent of sales. The only budgeted variance from standard cost is an unfavorable $180,000 overhead volume variance. A study of the company's costs shows that none of the fixed costs are directly traceable to any one product.

The company has prepared the following budgeted income statement for 1967. Amounts shown are thousands of dollars.

	Products				*Company*
	A	B	Y	Z	*Totals*
Sales	$7,200	$5,000	$6,000	$1,800	$20,000
Standard cost of goods sold	4,560	3,650	4,450	1,710	14,370
Gross profit	2,640	1,350	1,550	90	5,630
Selling expenses	1,080	750	900	270	3,000
Administrative expenses	200	200	200	200	800
Research and development expenses	180	125	150	45	500
	1,460	1,075	1,250	515	4,300
Profit by products	$1,180	$ 275	$ 300	$ (425)	$ 1,330
Volume variance					180
Income before tax					1,150
Income tax (40%)					460
Net income					$ 690

Fixed selling and research and development expenses have been allocated among the products above in proportion to sales volumes. Administrative expenses are charged equally to the four products, for management believes that its total efforts are evenly divided among the products, despite the differences in their sales volumes.

Required:

1. Reconstruct the budgeted income statement so that it will present the data in a manner consistent with the aims of effective product pricing.
2. Would it be profitable for the company to increase the price of Product Z by 25 percent if this would cause a reduction in sales volume of the product of 33⅓ percent?
3. Would it be advantageous for the company to discontinue Product Z altogether if the productive time now planned for it could be used to produce additional units of Product B for sale at the budgeted selling price?

3. The Wabash Corporation plans to introduce a new product in 1967. Sales volumes, consistent selling prices per unit, and direct costs per unit have been estimated as follows:

Volume in Units	*Price*	*Direct Cost*
10,000	$6.00	$4.80
20,000	5.60	4.50
30,000	5.25	4.25
40,000	5.00	4.10
50,000	4.80	4.00
60,000	4.50	3.95
70,000	4.20	3.90
80,000	4.00	3.88

The volumes listed are limits for their respective prices and direct costs. That is, any sales above the volume listed would have to be made at the next lower listed price and direct cost.

Indirect costs are expected to total $10,000 at any volume up to and including 40,000 units. At any volume in excess of 40,000 units, indirect costs will be $12,000.

Required:

At what price should the company introduce its new product?

4. Panhandle Products, Inc., has recently developed a new electric bottling machine. While operating on the same principle as machines currently on the market, it is faster and results in less spillage and bottle breakage. The company's management is seeking the best price at which to introduce this machine and has requested your assistance in making this pricing decision.

To assist you in your work, management has provided you the following information:

1. There are four basically competitive bottling machines on the market at present. Their prices are indicated below.

Sooner Bottler	$25,750
Beaver Automatic Bottling Machine	26,200
Buckeye Bottling Machine	25,800
Tarheel Bottle Filler No. 3100	24,950

Management is convinced that the new machine will save users operating costs as compared with competing equipment and, hence, believes a higher price will be justified.

2. Cost estimates for producing and selling the new machine have been developed. Variable production costs per unit have been budgeted as follows:

Materials	$9,200
Direct labor	6,800
Overhead	1,700

Fixed overhead is applied to all products at a normal rate of 75 percent of direct labor cost. Variable distribution costs are expected to average $2,200 per machine. Fixed nonmanufacturing expenses are usually allocated among products in proportion to total revenues. In recent years, this allocation has averaged 8 percent of sales revenues.

3. Additional equipment costing about $250,000 will be needed to manufacture the new bottling machine. Otherwise, existing facilities and staff are believed adequate to meet the expanding operations of the company.

4. The company's products currently yield an average profit margin before taxes of 15 percent of sales, after deductions for both direct costs and indirect cost allocations.

Required:

1. Prepare for management a preliminary report summarizing your analysis of the factors that should be considered in setting a price for the new product.

2. Indicate what additional information you would want to have before making a specific price recommendation.

5. The Limberlost Specialties Corporation has developed a golfers' "cart-bag," replete with novel gadgets. If the clubs are stored in the bag in proper order, the desired club is extended automatically at the touch of a button. There is a built-in ball washer, an eighteen-hole score keeper, and a retractable umbrella for sudden showers. The cart-bag has its own wheels and handle and, because of its size and weight, is self-propelled by a small battery-powered motor.

The corporation's management has decided to "skim the cream" off the market for several years before introducing the cart-bag to the mass market at a price within the means of the average golfer. Consequently, initial production facilities will be limited to produce an output below expected initial demand. The early promotional efforts will be directed at the high-income golfer. Because of this very selective distribution plan, management feels it has wide latitude in setting its price. There is no effectively competitive product on the market.

The cost of the production facilities required to manufacture the cart-bag initially will be $750,000. The annual output of these facilities will be 1,600 units. They will have an economic life of five years and no significant terminal salvage value. Promotional outlays are planned at $90,000 during each of the first five years. The variable costs of producing the cart-bag and distributing it will average $175 per unit. Additional fixed operating costs incurred for this new product are budgeted at $30,000 per year.

It is the company's objective to earn a rate of return after taxes of 10 percent on investments in new products. Income taxes are levied at a rate of 40 percent. Straight-line depreciation is used for tax reports.

Required:

1. What initial selling price is necessary to obtain the desired rate of return on the investment in the cart-bag?
2. If, after several months, management decided to increase output of the cart-bag and seek a greater penetration of the market than originally planned, the pricing decision would probably have to be reviewed. What factors bearing upon this new pricing decision would you expect to be different from the factors analyzed in the pricing decision in part 1?

6. The Merrimack Company plans to introduce a new product in 1967. Initial tests and studies indicate that the product might be sold at any one of four prices. Pertinent data for each of these prices are summarized below.

Price	$ 3.00	$ 4.40	$ 5.50	$ 7.50
Direct costs per unit	$ 1.20	$ 1.50	$ 1.80	$ 2.00
Annual unit sales volume	600,000	400,000	250,000	120,000
Annual promotion costs	$ 500,000	$ 750,000	$ 500,000	$ 350,000
Investment required to produce annual sales volume	$4,000,000	$3,000,000	$2,000,000	$1,500,000

All capital investments will be amortized by the straight-line method over a useful life of ten years. The applicable income tax rate is 40 percent. The company's cost of capital is 8 percent.

A total of $200,000 has already been invested in the preliminary tests and studies related to the development of the new product.

Required:

1. Prepare an analysis of the alternative prices indicated in the information provided. Which price would produce the greatest profit? Which price(s) would be unprofitable?
2. Justify your treatment of the $200,000 already expended for tests and studies.

7. The Ozark Manufacturing Company produces a variety of precision instruments and components. Most are sold to manufacturers of electronics equipment and to laboratories. The company's policy is to price all of its products at 150 percent of direct variable costs to produce and sell.

Recently the Department of Defense has requested bids on a special fire-control panel for use in submarines. The company's president is interested in the possibility of the firm entering the government market as a primary contractor and has asked the controller to prepare a cost estimate for this fire-control panel from the specifications provided by the Department of Defense. The controller has prepared the following estimate, based upon a total output of 600 panels, as called for in the specifications:

Raw materials	$ 72,000
Direct labor	45,000
Variable overhead	27,000
Fixed overhead (120% of direct labor)	54,000
Production set-up costs	14,000
Cost of special tools and dies	1,500
Clerical costs to process government documents and reports	500
Total cost	$214,000
Cost per panel	$ 356.67

The specifications require delivery of all 600 panels within the next eight months. In order to meet this schedule, the Ozark Manufacturing Company would have to forego orders for its other products in a total amount of $240,000.

Required:

What would be the lowest price at which the company could bid for the fire-control panel without sacrificing short-run profit?

8. In late 1965, the Allegheny Corporation invited the Monongahela Company to submit a design for, and to bid on the production of, twenty-five new fork-lift trucks to meet the peculiar needs of the former's storage facilities. A similar invitation was sent to three other firms.

The Monongahela Company has suffered from considerable excess capacity for several years and has seen little hope of remedying the situation. Con sequently, it accepted the Allegheny Corporation's invitation and has spent a total of $60,000 in design and cost study work in connection with it. As a result of this work, a bid of $14,400 per truck has been submitted. In support of this bid, the controller of Monongahela Company prepared the following budgeted income statement for the Allegheny order:

Revenue (25 units @ $14,400)		$360,000
Costs to produce and ship:		
Materials (25 @ $4,000)	$100,000	
Direct labor (25 @ $3,600)	90,000	
Variable overhead (25 @ $720)	18,000	
Fixed overhead (25 @ $2,000)	50,000	
Shipping expense (25 @ $240)	6,000	
Design costs	60,000	324,000
Profit before tax		$ 36,000

The Allegheny Corporation has indicated that it likes the Monongahela design better than any other but that the bid price of $14,400 is excessive. Allegheny will award the contract to Monongahela, however, at a price of $10,000 per truck.

Required:

Should Monongahela Company accept the Allegheny contract at the offered price of $10,000 per truck?

9. The Baum Manufacturing Company produces a wide variety of valves and pipe fittings. One of its products is the 38J valve, the standard cost of which is as follows:

Materials	$2.50
Labor	1.50
Variable overhead	1.00
Fixed overhead	2.00
	$7.00

The 38J valve is produced in a series of departments, all of which also work on the company's other products. The 38J valve is sold to wholesalers and industrial users for $11.50. Variable selling expenses average $.80 per valve. Fixed selling expenses are budgeted at 10 percent of budgeted sales revenue.

The Baum Company has been approached by a large manufacturer of boilers with an offer to buy 10,000 38J valves annually at a special price of $8.50. This offer, if accepted, would increase Baum's output significantly and would necessitate an increase in annual fixed manufacturing costs of $17,000. No increase in capital investment would be required, however.

Required:

1. On the basis of short-run profitability only, would you recommend acceptance of the offer in this case?
2. Are there any other considerations that might influence your decision in this case? If so, identify them.

10. The Nasswan Corporation is currently operating at an annual production volume of 750,000 direct labor hours. Its annual operating capacity, which cannot be exceeded, is 1,000,000 labor hours. Recently, a private-brand distributor has offered to buy 100,000 units of Product Y at a special price of $10.50 per unit. The regular selling price is $12.90 per unit. The standard cost sheet for one unit of Product Y appears as follows:

Materials: 6 lbs. @ $.40		$ 2.40
Direct labor: 2 hrs. @ $2.50		5.00
Overhead:		
Variable—2 hrs. @ $.75	$1.50	
Fixed—2 hrs. @ $1.20	2.40	3.90
		$11.30

Required:

1. In the short run, would it be profitable to accept the private-brand distributor's offer? Support your answer with appropriate financial analysis.
2. Would your answer to part 1 be different if the offer called for 250,000 units of Product Y instead of 100,000 units? Why?

11. The Ravenswood Company manufactures a portable electric knife sharpener. The standard cost sheet for one sharpener is as follows:

Materials	$3.25
Labor	1.85
Variable overhead	.90
Fixed overhead	1.60
	$7.60

Variable selling costs of $.50 per unit are incurred when the sharpener is sold under the Ravenswood brand name. The regular selling price is $12.50 per unit. Annual fixed selling and administrative expenses total $120,000.

The productive capacity of the company is 360,000 units per year. Budgeted sales and output for 1966 are both 240,000 units. Normal volume is 300,000 units per year.

The company has received three offers for special purchases of the knife sharpener at reduced prices. These three offers, none of which has been included in the budgeted data above, are outlined below.

Offer A: The prospective buyer would take 75,000 units during 1966 at a price of $7.25 per unit. This buyer would sell the sharpener under the Ravenswood brand name.

Offer B: The prospective buyer would take 100,000 units during 1966 at a price of $6.25. These units would be sold under the buyer's brand name and in housings slightly different from the regular ones.

Offer C: The prospective buyer would take 200,000 units during 1966 at a price of $8.00. These units would be sold under the buyer's private brand name and in modified housings.

The modifications of the sharpener housing required in Offers B and C would not affect the production costs per unit, nor would they require any new equipment.

Required:

Evaluate each of the three offers outlined above. Show the impact of accepting each on budgeted net income for 1966. Mention any other factors that might be relevant to the decision regarding the acceptance or rejection of each offer.

12. The San Joaquin Fruit Products Company produces and bottles four types of fruit juices. Most of its output has been sold to grocery wholesalers. Sales of one product, lime juice, have never come up to the company's expectations when the product was added to the company's line. Sales, in cases of twelve 6-ounce bottles, during 1966 were as follows:

Product	*Cases*	*Case Price*
Prune juice	125,000	$9.60
Apple juice	90,000	$7.50
Lemon juice	50,000	$8.75
Lime juice	15,000	$8.40

Operating costs in 1966 are summarized below.

	Cost per Case	*Cost per Year*
Raw materials:		
Prunes	$3.50	
Apples	1.60	
Lemons	2.80	
Limes	3.25	
Direct labor	.85	
Overhead	.30	$210,000
Direct selling	.20	65,000
Advertising		156,000
Administration		240,000

A chain of "cut-rate" liquor stores has offered to purchase 25,000 cases of lime juice annually at a price of $4.80 per case. These sales would not involve any variable direct selling costs. In addition, because of the substantial increase in output of lime juice, materials cost per case would be reduced to $3.00.

Required:

1. Would it be profitable for the company to accept the liquor chain's offer?
2. Irrespective of your answer in part 1, assume that the company did accept the liquor chain's offer and that a wholesale grocery customer has filed a complaint alleging price discrimination on the part of the San Joaquin Fruit Products Company. Can an effective cost defense, as provided for in the Robinson-Patman Act, be established in this case? Support your answer with some appropriate cost analysis.

Chapter 18

DIVISIONAL PROFIT ANALYSIS

As BUSINESS enterprises grow larger and more complex in structure, increased attention typically is directed toward the operations of segments of such enterprises. Most large business corporations are subdivided into several divisions. These divisions operate with varying degrees of autonomy, but they ordinarily represent unique centers of activity and responsibility. It is only natural that top management should be concerned with the profitability of each such division and with the operating performance of each division's management. The segments of an enterprise for which profit information is sought need not be established formally as divisions. They may be departments, sales territories, product lines, channels of distribution, classes of customers, or any other subdivisions of the firm which are regarded by management as having significance as unique entities. Thus, as the term is used in this chapter, a division may be any segment of a business enterprise for which financial data are separately accumulated and analyzed.

Before proceeding with a discussion of divisional profit analysis, the reader should divest himself of a notion that, although quite natural, can seriously impede his understanding of the subject. The mathematical axiom that the sum of the parts is equal to the whole is not necessarily applicable in the determination of divisional profits. Each division of a firm may be profitable individually, and, yet, the firm as a whole may be operating at a loss. Divisional profit is measured and analyzed as a unique concept, separate and distinct from company profit. This does not mean that company profit is no longer the basic objective of the firm's plans and operations. It means simply that company profit and divisional profit are not measured in the same way. Company profit is determined in accordance with generally accepted accounting principles. It requires a matching of all of the revenues of a period with all of the expenses incurred by the firm in obtaining those revenues. Divisional profit, on the other hand, is determined in accordance with the needs and objectives of management. It requires only an identification of the effect which a single division's operations have upon profits. The distinction between company profit and divisional profit will be explained more specifically in the paragraphs that follow.

DIVISIONAL RESPONSIBILITY AND PROFIT

The importance of divisional profit analysis tends to vary with the degree of responsibility and discretion allowed divisional managers. At one extreme, the division is a purely arbitrary subclassification of the firm's total operations. Its activities are planned, directed, and controlled by central management. The divisional manager is simply the agent of that central management. In such a case, divisional profit is of no more significance than the division itself. It is meaningful only to the extent that the division is a valid and useful subclassification of the total responsibility of the central management. At the opposite extreme, the division is virtually an independent firm in itself. The division manager has full range of discretion in planning and controlling division operations. He may make decisions without consulting central management. He may actually compete with other divisions of the firm, and he need trade with them only to the extent that it is profitable to his own division to do so. In most firms, divisional organization falls somewhere between these two extremes. Thus, in most cases, divisional profit analysis is useful not only as a partial analysis of total operations but also as an indicator of the efficiency of semi-autonomous divisional managers.

Where divisional managers have maximum freedom in conducting the operations of their own divisions, it is possible that the objectives of maximum divisional profit and maximum company profit may not be wholly compatible, at least in the short run. For example, assume that a corporation has two operating divisions, both operated independently by managers who have full freedom to act in such a way as to maximize their own profits. Division A has regularly purchased one of its principal raw materials from division B at a price of $12 per unit. Division A now finds that it can purchase the same material from an outside supplier at a price of $10 per unit. If division A does change its source of supply, division B will be unable to make up for the consequent loss in its own sales volume and will experience substantial idle capacity. So long as the outside purchase price is lower than division B's price, division A's profit will be increased by making the change. Its incremental profit would be $2 per unit of the raw material used.

Current cost per unit purchased from division B	$12
Cost per unit purchased from outside supplier	10
Incremental profit (cost saving) per unit of material by changing suppliers	$ 2

From the viewpoint of the company as a whole, however, the desirability of division A changing its source of supply depends upon a net cost saving to the company, not just to one division. Total company cost will be reduced only if the outside purchase price is lower than the avoidable cost of producing the material in division B. This avoidable cost here is assumed to be wholly variable in the amount of $9 per unit of material. For the company as a whole, the alternative is whether to make or buy the material. The decision may be analyzed as follows:

Cost to purchase one unit from outside supplier	$10
Avoidable cost to make one unit in division B	9
Incremental profit (cost saving) per unit of material by manufacturing in division B	$ 1

Thus, a decision by the manager of division A to purchase from an independent supplier will, in the short run, maximize his own division's profit only at the expense of total company profit. It is possible, of course, that loss of division A's orders will stimulate the manager of division B to improve his operating efficiency and to reduce his costs and his price. If this does happen, the end result of the situation may be improved long-run company profits.

The basic conclusion to be drawn from the foregoing illustration is that company profit must remain the principal aim of management. As this is a long-run objective, however, its planning is subject to a great deal of uncertainty. In the short run, management must make such decisions as the available information suggests will maximize long-run profit. If long-run profit subsequently appears good in light of the normal criteria for judging it, the decisions will appear to have been good ones. The real wisdom of these decisions may never be known with certainty; for the long-run profit that would have resulted from some alternative decision cannot be measured.

MEASURING THE PROFIT OF PART OF A FIRM

Any segment or division of an enterprise for which separate profit determination is made may be referred to as a *profit center*. Profit centers need not be organizational components of the firm, such as divisions or departments. They may be product lines, channels of distribution, or any other logical subentities. There are two basic criteria for the establishment of a profit center. First, the segment so established should have separate and distinct operating significance within the firm. Its separate analysis should be meaningful and useful to management in planning and controlling the overall activities and profit of the firm. Second, revenues and/or costs must be traceable to the segment selected for treatment as a profit center.

Incremental Profit Analysis

Traditional divisional profit computations in most business enterprises involved allocations of common costs among the several divisions according to some reasonable scheme. A fairly substantial portion of cost accountants' time was devoted to the development and refinement of cost allocation systems. Recent developments in the field of managerial accounting have emphasized the tracing of costs to those segments of the firm responsible for their incurrence and the acceptance of common costs as such, not allocable to segments. Refined procedures and systems of cost analysis may permit the identification of more costs with divisions than was formerly possible. To the extent that direct identification of costs with divisions is not possible, however, the common character of such costs must be recognized and no effort made to assign them to individual segments of the enterprise. In this modern approach, the profit of a division is its incremental profit. As such, the sum of the profits of all divisions separately is not necessarily equal to the total company profit. The difference, of course, is the company's common costs.

The incremental profit approach to divisional profit analysis is illustrated in Table 18–1. The Race Manufacturing Company operates three divisions. Each has its own sales force and production facilities. All revenues are directly traceable to specific divisions. For brevity in the illustration, the direct costs of the three divisions are not further subclassified, except as to their behavior with respect to changes in sales volume. They include, of course, the usual manufacturing and nonmanufacturing cost items. The company's common costs include the administrative costs of the central corporate office and companywide advertising and promotional costs. All common costs here are fixed costs. This is not always the case, of course; but typically most common costs are fixed. The analysis in Table 18–1 is substantially the same as that in Chapter 14 where the relative profitability of product lines was analyzed.[1] Indeed,

[1] Pages 333–36.

TABLE 18–1

RACE MANUFACTURING COMPANY
Divisional Profit Statement
For Month of June 1966

	Western Division	*Eastern Division*	*International Division*	*Company Totals*
Sales	$600,000	$400,000	$250,000	$1,250,000
Direct costs:				
Variable	360,000	240,000	150,000	750,000
Fixed	100,000	60,000	40,000	200,000
	460,000	300,000	190,000	950,000
Divisional profit	$140,000	$100,000	$ 60,000	300,000
Common fixed costs				200,000
Profit before tax				100,000
Income tax (47%)				47,000
Net income				$ 53,000

the latter illustration is also an example of divisional profit analysis, there product lines being the "divisions" under study.

The corporate income tax in Table 18–1 is treated, in effect, as a common cost. Actually, assuming the validity of the divisional revenues and direct costs, the income tax may be assigned to the individual divisions. This would result in divisional profits after tax. So long as the same tax rates and the same measures of taxable income apply to all divisions (and this may not be true of an international division), charging income taxes to the divisions would only reduce their respective profits by a uniform percentage. Even if the several divisions are subject to differing tax regulations, their respective income taxes may be assigned to them. In either case, divisional income taxes would exceed the total corporate income tax because of the deductibility of the unallocated common costs. If divisional income taxes are included in the report, a companywide tax reduction equal to the common costs multiplied by the tax rate would have to be included under the company totals. Such a presentation of the income tax is valid but is seldom encountered.

The key to effective divisional profit measurement is accurate identification of revenues and costs with segments of the firm. This is not always as easy as may be inferred from Table 18–1. If profit is to be measured by product lines, for example, interactions between sales of different products may complicate the determination of profit truly attributable to one product. An apparently minimally profitable (or, perhaps, even unprofitable) spare parts product line may stimulate many sales of basic equipment for which those parts are required. Perhaps the best solution to this particular problem would be to combine the equipment and spare parts into a single product line, or profit center. Such a solution illustrates the previously expressed criterion that profit centers be logical entities of significance and utility to management.

Profit Centers and Cost Centers

Some segments of an enterprise do not lend themselves to profit analysis in the same way as the operating divisions illustrated in the preceding section. Manufacturing departments, maintenance departments, power plants, and computer installations may have no revenues of their own in the ordinary sense of the term. If a manufacturing department transfers its finished production to inventory for subsequent sale or to another department for further processing, it has no sales revenues uniquely attributable to it. Ultimate sales of the product must be attributable at least partly to the further processing and/or to marketing efforts. Maintenance departments, power plants, and computer facilities are commonly regarded as service departments, operated for the benefit of other departments and with no expectations of direct revenues. Can such subentities be regarded as profit centers? Many firms have answered this question in the negative and treat such segments simply as *cost centers.* Only costs are traced to these centers. Their efficiency is measured by comparisons of their actual costs with standard costs and/or budgets.

It may be possible and useful to management to convert apparent cost centers to profit centers by appropriate use of opportunity cost data. The opportunity cost of the services rendered by a power plant to the other operating departments of a factory is the fair market value of those services. This market value is best measured by the price which the firm would have to pay an outside power company to provide the same services. If the outside company's price were \$.025 per kilowatt-hour, this would be taken as the measure of the company-owned power plant's "revenue." This is a comparatively simple illustration, for the power plant's service has a readily determinable market value. Such may not be the case of a maintenance department. Although outside firms may offer factory maintenance services on a contract basis, these services may not be identical to those rendered by a company-operated maintenance staff. It is difficult to assign financial values to differences in services and, therefore, to measure the real opportunity cost of operating a maintenance department. In the case of a company-owned computer, determination of opportunity cost may be extremely complex. Many of the computer services provided by the company's own installation might alternatively be obtained from an independent computer center at established hourly rates. This might be particularly true of such services as payroll preparation and inventory control. Other analyses might not be obtained from the outside source, however. Special market studies of products in the development stage, engineering studies of new equipment, and experimental budget models might be run on a company-owned computer at a negligible incremental cost. They might not be done at all if they had to be paid for at the regular hourly rate charged by an independent data-processing center. The long-range benefits to the firm from such special analyses represent their opportunity costs. Yet, in the short run, these benefits are probably immeasurable.

Responsibility Profit Analysis

If divisional profit analysis is to be used as a measure of the operating efficiency of managers in charge of divisions, departments, or other organizational components of a firm, care must be exercised to ensure that the revenues and costs employed in the analysis are consistent with the various managers' levels of responsibility. Assume, for example, that the data below are a further breakdown of those in Table 18–1 depicting the operating results of the Western Division of the Race Manufacturing Company for June, 1966.

Sales		$600,000
Direct costs:		
Variable		
Materials	$110,000	
Labor	120,000	
Overhead	60,000	
Selling	70,000	
	360,000	
Fixed		
Supervisory salaries	25,000	
Depreciation, taxes, and insurance on building and equipment	40,000	
Depreciation, taxes, and insurance on salesmen's automobiles	20,000	
General administration	15,000	
	100,000	460,000
Divisional profit		$140,000

The division manager is responsible for all phases of his division's operations, except that central management appoints all division supervisory personnel and determines their salaries and that all buildings and machinery are acquired and retained in accordance with a capital budget developed and implemented by central management.

Table 18–2 is a profit report for the Western Division which emphasizes the distinction between costs controllable by the division manager and those controllable by central management. The division

TABLE 18–2

RACE MANUFACTURING COMPANY
Divisional Profit Report—Western Division
For Month of June, 1966

Sales		$600,000
Costs controllable by division manager:		
Variable costs		
Materials	$110,000	
Labor	120,000	
Overhead	60,000	
Selling	70,000	360,000
Variable profit		240,000
Fixed costs		
Depreciation, taxes, and insurance on salesmen's automobiles	$ 20,000	
General administration	15,000	35,000
Division manager's contribution to profit		205,000
Company-controlled fixed costs:		
Supervisory salaries	25,000	
Depreciation, taxes, and insurance on building and machinery	40,000	65,000
Divisional profit		$140,000

manager's contribution to profit might be called the "responsibility profit," as distinct from the total divisional profit. In effect, the division is controlled by two different levels of management; and Table 18–2 classifies division costs according to those two levels. For purposes of determining the profitability of the division as a complete entity, all direct division costs are relevant. For purposes of appraising the division manager's performance, however, only those costs subject to his control are relevant. The divisional profit and the division manager's responsibility profit are not necessarily identical. Inclusion of the division's variable profit in the report is actually incidental to the question of control, but it will facilitate further analyses such as divisional break-even computation.

DIVISIONAL BREAK-EVEN ANALYSIS

In Chapter 13 we saw that the break-even point of an enterprise is that sales volume at which total revenues just cover total costs. It is computed by dividing the total fixed costs by the firm's variable profit.[2]

[2] See pages 301 and 302 in Chapter 13.

The break-even point of a division is that volume of divisional sales at which the revenues of the division just cover the direct costs traceable to it. It is computed by dividing the direct fixed costs of the division by the variable profit for the division. Referring again to the data in Table 18–1, we shall compute the break-even point for each of the three divisions of the Race Manufacturing Company in terms of dollar sales volume. The variable profit ratios of the three divisions are computed as follows:

Division	*(a) Revenues*	*(b) Direct Variable Costs*	*(c) Variable Profit*	*(d) Variable Profit Ratio (c) ÷ (a)*
Western	$600,000	$360,000	$240,000	.40
Eastern	400,000	240,000	160,000	.40
International	250,000	150,000	100,000	.40

The three divisional break-even points are then computed thus:

Division	*Direct Fixed Costs*	*Variable Profit Ratio*	*Divisional Break-Even Sales Volume*
Western	$100,000	.40	$250,000
Eastern	60,000	.40	150,000
International	40,000	.40	100,000

As all three divisions have the same variable profit ratio, it is possible to compute the break-even sales volume for the company as a whole without making any specific assumption as to the sales mix among the divisions. Total company fixed costs, both direct and common, are $400,000. Dividing this total by the variable profit ratio of 40% yields a company break-even sales volume of $1,000,000. The sum of the break-even volumes of the individual divisions is only $500,000. Thus, the divisions individually can break even in terms of divisional or incremental profits with an aggregate sales volume only half that necessary for the entire enterprise to break even in terms of net income.

The results of the break-even analyses in the preceding paragraph should not be startling. As stated at the beginning of this chapter, in analyzing the profitability of segments of a firm the sum of the parts need not always equal the whole. Yet, one may ask whether it is reasonable to assert that all divisions can break even at an aggregate volume at which the company as a whole operates at a substantial loss. The answer here is simply that the alternative, allocating common costs among the divisions, is clearly unreasonable. There is no way of determining reasonably and practically how much of the common costs must be covered by a single division before that division may be said to break even. As long as common costs would be unaffected by the closing of a division, none of them can reasonably be assigned to it.

To illustrate one decision-making application of divisional break-even analysis, assume that a firm produces a product that is sold to other manufacturers for further processing. It is now considering the possibility of expanding its own operations to include this further processing. After the additional processing, the product sells in the market for $6.50 per unit. The company now sells its semifinished product for $4.75 per unit. Cost studies indicate that the variable costs of further processing would be $1.25 per unit and the additional fixed costs, $250,000. Management wishes to know what annual sales volume of the finished product would be required in order for the additional processing operation to break even. This divisional break-even point, in units, is determined as follows:

The relevant variable profit is computed thus:

Price after further processing	$6.50
Present price of semifinished product	4.75
Incremental revenue per unit	1.75
Incremental variable cost per unit	1.25
Incremental variable profit per unit	$ .50

The units required to break even in the further processing are then computed thus:

$$BE = \frac{\text{Incremental direct fixed costs}}{\text{Incremental unit variable profit}} = \frac{\$250{,}000}{\$.50} = 500{,}000 \text{ units.}$$

Management now knows that annual volume must exceed 500,000 units if further processing of the product is to increase total company profit. If, as is probable, the decision to engage in additional processing requires new capital investment, the decision-making analysis should include a determination of the projected net present value or discounted rate of return of the investment.

DIVISIONAL RATE OF RETURN

Chapter 15 discussed the employment of a rate of return on investment in assets as a measure of the operating efficiency of a firm's management. Similar rates of return may be used to appraise the performance of a division manager.[3] Determination of the rate of return for a segment of an enterprise requires prior measurement of the segment's incremental profit and of the investment in assets in that segment. Only the assets directly committed to the operations of a division should be employed in this rate of return calculation. Divisional rates of return are independent of the company's rate of return. There may well be assets used by the company which are not traceable to any one division. There may also be some nondivisional income, although any such amounts are likely to be very small. Once again, the company in total may amount to more than a simple sum of the divisions.

For divisions with very small investments in assets, rates of return may be extremely high. Such rates cannot be compared with rates for a company as a whole. They must be evaluated in terms of the peculiar circumstances and operations of the individual divisions. Further, great care must be exercised in comparing rates of return of different divisions. A new division might be expected to have a lower rate of return than others. If so, any comparison of its rate with those of other divisions is likely to result only in misunderstanding and possibly even inappropriate action.

INTERDIVISIONAL PRICING

Among the numerous complex and largely unresolved problems of accounting is the question of the price to be set for goods transferred from one division of a firm to another. In the normal sense, no sale has occurred. There has merely been an intracompany transfer. Nevertheless, if the division making the transfer is to be evaluated as a profit center, some measure of the sales value of its product must be established. Interdivisional pricing involves questions of company profit measurement, divisional profit measurement, and a variety of special problems that may arise in individual firms. A single price may not be appropriate for all of these purposes. Each of the aforementioned aspects of interdivisional pricing is considered in the sections that follow.

Pricing at Full Cost

For purposes of enterprise profit determination, income arises only from transactions with outside customers. No profit may be recognized on transfers between divisions of a company. Thus, the appropriate price at which one division should transfer goods to another is the full cost of

[3] Rate of return on stockholders' equity, also discussed in Chapter 15, is not relevant to analyses of segments of a corporation.

the transferring division, including any costs which it may have incurred in connection with a transfer into it from some prior division. In this way, the full cost of the company's products follows them through the various divisions.[4] Profit arises only at the point of ultimate sale. "Full cost" here includes those production costs normally charged to products in accordance with the company's cost accounting system. If absorption costing is employed, full cost includes the fixed costs of manufacturing. If variable costing is used, only variable production costs are included in this concept of "full cost." In either case, the basic objective of the interdivisional pricing scheme is conformity to the conventional technique for measuring company income. (It should be noted again that variable costing does not conform to current generally accepted accounting principles. Thus, even though internal pricing at variable costs may be consistent with management's practices of internal profit reporting, adjustment to the absorption costing basis will probably be necessary for purposes of external financial statements.)

If a company, for some reason, followed the practice of pricing interdivisional transfers at a price in excess of actual costs, some adjustment would most likely be necessary in order to measure company profit correctly. If all goods transferred internally during a period were also sold to outside customers in the same period, no adjustment would be required. However, if some of the goods transferred between divisions remained in inventory at the end of the period, that inventory would include an element of unrealized profit which is not properly recognized until the goods are sold. Assume, for example, that division S transfers to division T 100,000 units of a product which has a unit cost in division S of $5. The transfer is recorded at a price of $7 per unit. Division T sells 80,000 of these units and holds 20,000 in inventory at the close of the year. Unless an adjustment is made, the company's net profit for the year will be overstated by $40,000 (20,000 units in inventory × $2 unrealized profit per unit). The adjustment would be made by debiting whatever account had been credited for the unrealized profit when the transfer between divisions was recorded and crediting the inventory account.

Although correct for purposes of company profit measurement, pricing intracompany transfers at full cost has shortcomings insofar as managerial analysis is concerned. It does not permit any measurement of divisional profits, nor does it afford an indication of the efficiency of

---

[4] Refer to pages 93 through 95 in Chapter 4 for an illustration of the flow of production costs through a company from department to department.

divisional operations other than by a comparison of actual and planned costs. And it may not be a useful basis for decision making.

Pricing at Market Value

For purposes of measuring the profit of a division as a separate entity, the appropriate interdivisional transfer price is market value or net realizable value. Market value here is the price at which the transferring division could sell its product to outside buyers. Net realizable value is this price less the costs of selling the product which are avoided in the internal transfer. (Note that such cost items as packing and shipping may be incurred in intracompany transfers as well as in outside sales.) The market value or net realizable value, whichever is appropriate in the particular circumstances, represents the opportunity cost of the interdivisional transfer. Use of market value for internal pricing purposes permits the analysis of the transferring division as a profit center.

To the division receiving goods on intracompany transfers, the opportunity cost of such goods is the market price which the division would have to pay for them if they were to be purchased from outside suppliers. Use of this price is appropriate where the receiving division's manager does not have discretion to purchase either from other divisions or from independent suppliers, for it establishes a fair value for his purchases, over which he has no control. In this way, the receiving division may be evaluated more nearly as an independent entity, operating in such a way as to maximize its own profit. If the division manager has full discretion as to where he buys his materials, of course, his actual purchase costs will reflect his operating efficiency. Ordinarily, the market selling price of the transferring division and the market purchase price of the receiving division would be expected to be the same. There may be situations in which this is not the case, however. For example, the transferring division might be able to sell its product to distributors at a higher price than the receiving division, as a manufacturer, would have to pay for it. In such a situation, use of the two different prices would be consistent with the aims of individual division profit determination. Of course, in this case, the company's central management ought to consider the effect on long-run profit of altering its operations so that these two divisions do trade with outside customers and suppliers, as is indicated to be possible.

In many instances, firms will find that there is no ready market for semifinished products transferred between divisions. In these cases, pricing at market value may not be feasible. The market value of a semifinished product may sometimes be approximated by subtracting from the market value of the finished product the costs of the finishing processes and of selling. As this approach implicitly assumes that no profit accrues as a result of the subsequent processing and the sales efforts, it may be modified to include a further deduction to allow for such profit.[5] Since this modification involves an arbitrary allocation of total profit among the several divisions and activities of the company, it deviates from the goal of an objectively and independently measured divisional profit. If no reasonably objective basis for determining divisional profit is available, the attempt to do so should be abandoned and the division should be analyzed simply as a cost center. Arbitrary measurements designed to create a profit center will introduce the same type of irrelevance and potential bias as arbitrary allocations of common costs.

The fact that a market value—or any other amount different from full product cost—is used as the price of interdivisional transfers for some purposes does not mean that it must be recorded in the company's journals and ledgers. As these records are the basis for external financial statements, it may be considered preferable to maintain them according to principles applicable to such statements. Market values can be used in reports submitted internally to management without their being used in formal journal entries and postings. This procedure serves the needs of both internal and external reporting without requiring adjustments such as that explained in the preceding section.

Cost-Plus Pricing

Some firms have adopted a practice of pricing interdivisional product transfers at some arbitrarily determined price above full cost. This, in effect, assures the transferring division of a specified gross margin. Such a margin is of no real significance in measuring either company profit or divisional profit, however. This practice is sometimes supported on the grounds that it keeps total company profit a secret from the managers of the final selling division. This is a dubious objective at best, and it may ultimately create serious personnel problems for the firm. In summary, then, the practice of pricing intracompany transfers at arbitrary prices has nothing to recommend it except, possibly, clerical simplicity.

[5] Refer to page 338 in Chapter 14 where this approach is explained in connection with the valuation of coproducts at their split-off point.

Conclusion

As stated at the outset, interdivisional pricing is a complex and controversial problem. The preceding discussion is neither a complete analysis of the problem nor a comprehensive solution to it. It should, however, make clear that different measures of intracompany prices may be appropriate for different purposes. And it should demonstrate that interdivisional transfer pricing is not a purely technical question devoid of significance for management.

QUESTIONS FOR DISCUSSION

1. Are the conceps of divisional profit and company profit compatible? If so, how? If not, why not?
2. "Divisional profit analysis, as discussed in this text, is simply a particular application of incremental profit analysis." Do you agree or disagree with this statement? Explain.
3. What is meant by "responsibility profit" in a business enterprise? Of what value to management is this concept of profit?
4. Each of the departments listed below is found in many business firms. Each normally generates no revenues directly. For each of these departments, indicate whether you believe it might reasonably be evaluated as a profit center. If you believe it might be so treated, indicate the data that would be used to measure its profit. Alternatively, explain your reasons for believing it could not be treated as a profit center.

   a. Payroll Department
   b. Advertising Department
   c. Motor Vehicle Pool
   d. Receiving Department

5. It has been asserted here that no truly common costs are relevant to a determination of the profit of one segment of a firm. An example of a truly common cost is the administrative expense of the head office of a multi-division corporation. Yet, many successful and generally progressive firms do allocate such head office costs among their divisions and require that the several divisions cover the common costs allocated to them as well as their own direct costs. Are the firms that do this acting irrationally, or is there some valid reason for the practice? Discuss.
6. As the principal objective of a business enterprise is company profit, of what significance to management is the break-even point of a division when each division may operate above its own break-even point while the company as a whole is operating below its break-even level?
7. Discuss the various objectives of intra-company transfer pricing and the various prices which best serve those objectives.
8. "If an operating division that does not sell its output to outside customers but simply transfers it to another division within the same firm is to be

evaluated as a profit center, its intra-company transfers must be priced above its costs. Hence, cost-plus pricing is the most logical method of accounting for these intra-company transfers." Comment on this statement.

PROBLEMS

1. The Sinex Manufacturing Company produces and distributes three products. All three are manufactured in the same plant and distributed by the same sales organization. In the factory, Department 200 assembles all three products. Department 110 performs the basic processing on Product A; Department 120, on Product B; and Department 130, on Product C. Production for 1966 is planned so that the level of inventories of finished products at the end of the year will be the same as at the start of the year.

Budgeted operating data for 1966 are as follows:

	Products		
	A	*B*	*C*
Unit selling price	$3.50	$12.50	$40.00
Unit raw material cost	$ .80	$ 2.20	$ 8.00
Direct labor hours per unit:			
Department 110	$\frac{1}{2}$		
Department 120		1	
Department 130			3
Department 200	$\frac{1}{4}$	$\frac{1}{2}$	1
Sales volume in units	400,000	200,000	60,000

Departmental labor and overhead cost data are outlined below.

	Production Departments			
	110	*120*	*130*	*200*
Hourly wage rate	$1.80	$1.50	$2.00	$2.40
Overhead rates per labor hour:				
Variable	$ .30	$ .25	$ .40	$ .80
Fixed	$ .75	$1.20	$ .50	$ .80
Normal volume in labor hours	200,000	250,000	225,000	300,000

A summary of budgeted nonmanufacturing costs is as follows:

Sales commissions	5% of sales
Miscellaneous selling expenses	$200,000 per year
Advertising:	
General	$250,000 per year
Product A	$70,000 per year
Product B	$25,000 per year
Product C	$30,000 per year
Research and development	$200,000 per year
General administration	$500,000 per year
Income taxes	40%

Required:

Prepare a budgeted income statement for 1966. Show the divisional profits of the three products and the company profit in total.

2. The Petra Electric Company manufactures automatic washing machines in three organizationally distinct divisions. The Motor Division in Topeka produces the sealed electric motors for the machines. The Steel Division in St. Louis makes the housings, including all component structural parts. Both of these divisions then ship their products to the Assembly Division in Kansas City, where the finished washers are assembled and shipped to customers.

Actual product costs and production data for the three divisions for the first year of the company's operations are as follows:

	Motor Division	*Steel Division*	*Assembly Division*
Variable cost per unit	$ 22	$ 15	$ 12*
Fixed cost per year	$3,000,000	$4,800,000	$2,700,000*
Unit of output	motor	housing	washer
Units produced	250,000	240,000	180,000
Units shipped	240,000	200,000	175,000

* Cost incurred in the prior divisions are not included in the cost data for the Assembly Division.

There were no inventories of work in process in any of the divisions at the end of the year. The company uses a strict actual cost system; neither standard costs nor normal overhead rates are used.

The company has learned that it could purchase electric motors from an independent supplier for $30 each. It has also learned that the output of the Steel Division could be sold to other washer manufacturers for $44 per housing, with only minor modifications in design that would have no significant impact on the division's costs. The finished washers are sold to customers for $150 each.

Required:

1. If each division is regarded as an independent entity, what is the divisional profit of each for the first year of operations?
2. What is the gross profit for the company as a whole for the first year of operations?
3. Would it be profitable for the company to purchase electric motors from an independent supplier for $30 each? Discuss.
4. Would it be profitable for the company to have the Steel Division sell its output to other washer manufacturers for $44 per housing? Discuss.

3. The power plant of the Gibson Company produced a total of 6,000,000 kilowatt hours in 1966. The variable operating costs of the power plant were $120,000 for the year, and the fixed costs directly traceable to it were $90,000. Additional fixed costs of $36,000 were allocated to the power plant as its share of general corporate expenses. The rate for electricity from the local power and light company is $.04 per kilowatt hour.

Traditionally, the company has evaluated the performance of the power plant by comparing its actual costs with its budgeted costs. The new chairman of the board, however, wants all operating segments of the company set up and evaluated as profit centers.

Required:

1. How can the power plant be evaluated as a profit center? Illustrate the method you recommend by determining the power plant's profit for 1966.
2. Using the same approach as recommended in part 1, compute the power plant's annual break-even volume.

4. The Transportation Department of the Pico Distributing Corporation maintains a fleet of five automobiles for use by authorized company personnel. The department budget allows $.08 per mile that the cars are operated plus $6,000 per year for general maintenance. During 1967, the five cars were operated a total of 300,000 miles. Total Transportation Department cost was $33,000. The rental cost of similar cars would be $.12 per mile.

Required:

1. Evaluate the operations of the Transportation Department in 1967 if it is regarded as a cost center.
2. Evaluate the operations of the Transportation Department in 1967 if it is regarded as a profit center.
3. In 1967, was it more profitable to own cars than to lease them? At what volume, if any, would it be more profitable to lease the cars? (Ignore capital investment considerations in answering this part of the question.)

5. The Central Products Company manufactures two products jointly in its Refining Plant. They are accounted for as coproducts. For every 10 pounds of raw materials put into the refining process, 5 pounds of Product W and 3 pounds of Product Z are obtained. Both products presently are sold immediately after the refining process, Product W for $3 per pound and Product Z for $6 per pound. It would also be possible to sell Product Z after further processing for $8.50 per pound. This further processing would cost $1.80 per pound plus $28,000 per year.

During 1966, 100,000 pounds of raw materials were used in the Refining Plant. Total costs in the plant were $198,000. The company uses absorption costing in valuing inventories of manufactured products.

Required:

1. What were the unit production costs of Products W and Z in 1966 for purposes of inventory valuation?
2. At what point, if ever, would it be more profitable for the company to process Product Z further?

6. The White River Plant of the Martinsville Manufacturing Company produces control panels used on most of the company's final products. This plant and all of the equipment in it are leased; the lease is cancellable by the company without penalty on thirty days notice. Budgeted production and cost data for this plant for 1967 are as follows:

Output of control panels	25,000
Materials cost	$1,000,000
Direct labor	700,000
Variable plant overhead	300,000
Fixed plant overhead, including rent	500,000
Variable shipping expense	50,000
Fixed plant administrative expenses	250,000
Plant's share of general corporate expenses	400,000
Total costs	$3,200,000
Unit cost ($3,200,000/25,000 units)	$ 128

The output of the White River Plant is planned to meet the production needs of the company's main manufacturing plants. Recently, the company has learned that it could purchase the same control panel from an independent supplier in any quantity at a price of $122 per panel, delivered.

Required:

1. In 1967, would it be more profitable to purchase the control panel or to continue to manufacture it?
2. Is there any point at which the opposite policy from the one suggested in part 1 would be more profitable? If so, at what point would this change in policy be profitable?

7. The Arena Distributing Corporation is organized into two operating divisions, Domestic Wholesale and Export-Import. Both divisions are controlled through the Head Office in Seattle. A summarized income statement for 1966 is as follows:

Sales:		
Domestic Wholesale		$11,600,000
Export-Import		10,460,000
		22,060,000
Expenses:		
Domestic Wholesale	$9,400,000	
Export-Import	8,220,000	
Head Office	2,440,000	
Income taxes (40%)	800,000	20,860,000
Net income		$ 1,200,000

The book values of the corporation's assets, classified by the divisions in which they are used, are as follows:

Domestic Wholesale	$ 8,800,000
Export-Import	4,800,000
Head Office	3,400,000
	$17,000,000

Published industry statistics indicate that the average rates of return on investments in assets for certain distributing companies are as follows:

Domestic wholesalers	12%
Export-import dealers	20%
Foreign and domestic wholesalers	10%

Required:

Compute the rates of return on investments in assets for each division and for the corporation as a whole in 1966. Evaluate these rates of return in light of the available industry averages.

8. The Jewell Plumbing Supplies Company has three sales territories. Each territory has its own sales force and distribution facilities. All products are manufactured in the company's plant in Cleveland. They are charged to the several sales territories at standard production costs, including standard fixed overhead.

The Northeast Sales Territory is the oldest of the three and still has the largest annual sales volume. Physical facilities in this territory were acquired at an original cost of $5,000,000. Depreciation of $3,000,000 has been accumulated on these facilities as of Dec. 31, 1967. At this same date, these facilities have an aggregate fair market value of $4,000,000.

The North-Central Sales Territory was opened shortly after World War II. Its physical facilities originally cost $7,000,000. They currently have a book value of $4,500,000 and a fair market value of $4,800,000.

The Southeast Sales Territory was opened just two years ago. Facilities in that territory have an original cost of $4,000,000, a book value of $3,600,-000, and a fair market value of $3,000,000.

The company's income statement for 1967, by sales territories, is shown below. Dollar amounts are in thousands of dollars.

	Company Total	*North-east*	*North-Central*	*South-east*
Sales	$36,000	$19,000	$12,000	$5,000
Standard cost of goods sold	21,600	11,400	7,200	3,000
Gross margin	14,400	7,600	4,800	2,000
Nonmanufacturing expenses:				
Variable selling expenses	3,600	1,900	1,200	500
Fixed selling expenses	1,800	950	600	250
Head office expenses	4,320	2,280	1,440	600
Product research expenses	2,880	1,520	960	400
Interest expense	540	285	180	75
	13,140	6,935	4,380	1,825
Profit by territories	1,260	$ 665	$ 420	$ 175
Manufacturing variance	648			
Income before tax	612			
Income tax (25%)	153			
Net income	$ 459			

Selling expenses are charged directly to the sales territories in which they are incurred. All other nonmanufacturing expenses are allocated on the basis of dollar sales volume. Standard fixed overhead is 20 percent of total standard production costs.

The factory, testing laboratory, and office facilities in Cleveland have a total original cost of $15,000,000 and accumulated depreciation of $8,000,-000. Their current fair market value is $10,000,000.

Required:

1. Compute the divisional profit of each sales territory.
2. Compute the rates of return on investments in assets in each territory and for the company in total.

9. The product of the Sunset Manufacturing Co. is processed sequentially through three departments before being placed into the Finished Product storeroom. The output of each department is priced at standard cost in that department plus 25 percent thereof and is transferred to the next department at that price. Standard costs in the subsequent departments include the full transfer price(s) of the prior department(s). The objective of this pricing system is to establish a normal profit margin in each production department. An actual profit margin greater or less than normal then reflects efficiency or inefficiency in the operation of the department.

The outputs of the three departments (listed in the sequence of the production process) at their respective transfer prices were as follows during 1966:

Department E	$ 600,000
Department F	1,200,000
Department G	2,500,000

The inventory of Finished Product at the beginning of 1966 was carried at a total of $325,000. The ending inventory of Finished Product was carried at a total of $700,000. There have been no changes in standard costs or in the internal pricing system since the company was founded.

Sales in 1966 amounted to $3,300,000. Nonmanufacturing expenses totaled $800,000. Net variances from standard costs in the three production departments were as follows:

Department E	$75,000 favorable
Department F	2,000 unfavorable
Department G	84,000 unfavorable

Required:

1. Evaluate the interdepartmental pricing systems used by the Sunset Manufacturing Co.
2. Compute the correct income before taxes for the company in 1966.

10. The Hillcrest Athletic Equipment Co. manufactures trampolines in two plants. The Casting Plant makes tubular aluminum frames, which are then shipped to the Assembly Plant. The Assembly Plant affixes the canvas nets to the frames and stores the finished trampolines until they are shipped out on customers' orders.

The company uses absorption costing in charging costs to products. The materials cost per frame in the Casting Plant is $14.20. Three man-hours at a rate of $2.10 per hour are required for the completion of each frame. The flexible budget for overhead in the Casting Plant for one year is as follows:

Man-hours	150,000	200,000	250,000
Variable costs	$180,000	$240,000	$300,000
Semivariable costs	60,000	75,000	90,000
Fixed costs	385,000	385,000	385,000

Normal volume in the Casting Plant is 200,000 man-hours per year. Trampoline frames account for 30 percent of production at normal volume.

Comparable frames could be purchased from independent manufacturers for $27.50 each. Finished trampolines are sold for $55 each. Selling and shipping costs amount to $6 per unit.

Required:

1. At what price should frames be transferred from the Casting Plant to the Assembly Plant? Why?
2. Would it be advantageous for the company to buy frames from independent manufacturers rather than to make them in the Casting Plant? Explain.
3. Would your answer to part 2 be different if the Casting Plant did nothing but make trampoline frames? Why?

Chapter 19

EFFECTIVE REPORTS TO MANAGEMENT

THE END product of much of the work of accountants is a report. The end results of the financial accounting cycle are the familiar financial statements, the balance sheet, the income statement, the statement of funds or cash flow, and the statement of retained earnings. The conclusion of the tax accountant's work is usually the preparation of a tax return. In management accounting, too, reports represent the culmination of much of the accountant's effort. The present chapter offers some basic guides for the preparation of reports to management. External financial reports, such as balance sheets and income statements, are not discussed specifically; but many of the rules applicable to management reports are equally pertinent to external reports.

COMMUNICATION THROUGH ACCOUNTING

Accounting is fundamentally a means of communicating financial information. Accountants accumulate and process financial data so that others may use them in making decisions. Seldom do the users of these data gather them for themselves. The users with whom we are concerned here are business managers. Financial information is recorded and classified by accountants for use by management. Accounting reports serve as the bridge between the accumulation and the utilization of financial information. The effectiveness of managerial decisions depends to a considerable extent, therefore, upon the effectiveness of accounting reports. Reporting efficiency involves, basically, getting the right information to the right persons at the right time.

Identification of the right information for business planning, control, and decision making is the essence of management accounting. It is the basic theme of most of this book. Managers know (or should know) what they wish to accomplish and what information they need in order to accomplish it. Accountants know (or should know) what information is available, how it may be analyzed, and the cost of processing it as desired. Cost-conscious management must never forget that data processing and reporting activities involve significant costs. The supply of and demand for financial information must be harmonized in a meaningful and a reasonable manner. Managers, who need information, must work jointly with accountants, who accumulate information, to develop and implement the best possible data-processing and reporting system at the lowest possible cost. This objective requires that managers be familiar with the potentialities and the limitations of accounting and that accountants be conversant with the aims and the problems of management.

For example, management may be considering reclaiming and using production waste now sold as scrap. In order to evaluate the profitability of such a proposal, management should know its opportunity cost. The real opportunity cost of such a proposal, of course, is a future quantity which cannot be predicted with certainty. Nevertheless, that future cost information can be approximated from actual cost data accumulated and analyzed from the past. The accountant must be able to prepare a report containing the correct information for this purpose, and that report must communicate such information to management in the most meaningful and comprehensible manner. The remainder of this chapter is concerned with some general rules for the development of meaningful and comprehensible reports for management.

BASIC RULES OF GOOD MANAGEMENT REPORTING

Accountants would do well to keep something akin to Kipling's "six honest serving-men"[1] as rules for report writing. As Kipling was a storyteller rather than a report writer, his particular servingmen may not be directly applicable to accountants' reports; but the basic notion most certainly is. Six rules of report writing are suggested in the sections that follow. They are timeliness, clarity, conciseness, written reports, responsibility reporting, and reporting exceptions.

Timeliness

If a report is to be useful to a manager in making a decision, he must receive it before the decision must be made. If it is to be useful in planning future operations, it must be received well in advance of the period being planned. If it is to be used in controlling current operations, it must be received at once. A weekly report of actual and standard materials usage received on the third day of the week following that

[1] Rudyard Kipling, chapter heading for "The Elephant's Child" in *Just-So Stories* (New York: Doubleday, Doran & Company, Inc., 1907), p. 85.

covered by the report is too late. It should be available on the morning of the first day of the following week. A monthly summary of operations received at the middle of the following month is too late. It should be submitted within the first five days of the next month. It is entirely appropriate to accept a tolerable degree of inaccuracy as the price of promptness. If more precise data can be reported by delaying a report for a few days, the loss of time may well outweigh the gain in precision. The use of high-speed computers in business has greatly facilitated promptness in reporting. Computations and summaries that formerly required days for manual preparation can now be prepared by machines in minutes.

Timeliness is not merely a matter of promptness, however. Timely reports should be received when needed and only when needed. Too many reports can be just as bad as too few. Daily reports to department foremen of materials usage and labor efficiency may be both feasible and desirable. They permit foremen to take corrective action as soon as the need for it appears. On the other hand, daily profit reports for a company would be considered excessive in most cases. Regular reports should be prepared as often as management actually needs them and no more often. Irregular, or special, reports also should be submitted when needed. Ideally, the reporting system should be so structured as to provide managers with reports for special purposes whenever they are pertinent, not merely when managers request them. For example, suppose that a factory manager requests a report as to the profitability of replacing a particular machine. The report submitted indicates that replacement is not presently profitable. The internal information system should not drop the matter at this point. It should be so designed as to keep a constant watch on this replacement question. When replacement of the machine would be profitable, the system should recognize the fact and submit an appropriate report to the factory manager without his having to ask for it. In other words, the reporting system should provide for automatic feedback of relevant information to management.

Clarity

It should go without saying that reports to management should be clear and understandable. Yet, this most obvious of reporting requirements is so often missed. The author has heard so many business executives and partners in public accounting firms complain that junior executives and accountants cannot prepare readable reports that the problem assumes almost alarming proportions. As most reports are prepared in preliminary drafts by hand, a neat and legible handwriting can hardly be overemphasized. Grammatically correct and structurally attractive written English is essential to intelligent communication in business or elsewhere. Most importantly, of course, clarity involves making the point of the report clear at once to the reader. If a report presents the financial analysis of a proposal to process further a product now sold in a semifinished state, it should be organized around the two alternatives and not around the usual functional or departmental account classification of the firm. Variance reports should highlight variances, not the actual and standard costs from which they are determined.

Conciseness

Conciseness is very closely linked with clarity. Conciseness is not simply brevity. A concise report is both brief *and to the point.* Unnecessary information and explanations are eliminated from reports so that the necessary information stands out clearly. In a report comparing the incremental profits of alternative courses of action, for example, sunk costs ought not appear. Reports to management should be as short as possible, consistent with the need for completeness. A manager's time is valuable. Typically he is hurried. Long reports slow him down. Worse, long reports may force him to scan quickly and thus, perhaps, to miss important points. In his capacity as Prime Minister and Minister of Defence during World War II, Sir Winston Churchill often required subordinates to submit reports to him on a single sheet of paper.[2] The effectiveness with which he discharged his wartime responsibilities argues well for wider adoption of this practice.

Written Reports

As a general rule, all formal reports to management should be in writing. Oral reports should be limited to informal or emergency communications. (A written report that the storeroom is on fire ought not be necessary.) Oral reports are inconvenient and unreliable. They demand that the person to whom a report is directed receive, digest, and evaluate the report at the moment it is presented to him. Further, they leave no evidence of their having been made. They cannot be proved later or referred to again. Sir Winston Churchill insisted upon transacting all official business in writing and disavowed responsibility for oral directives attributed to him unless they were confirmed in

---

[2] Winston S. Churchill, *Their Finest Hour* (Boston: Houghton Mifflin Company, 1949), pp. 166 and 168.

writing.[3] Such a requirement facilitates fixing responsibility for reports and prevents subsequent misunderstanding of or disagreement about what was reported.

The requirement of written reports should not preclude oral discussion of them, of course. Extensive discussion of operating reports by members of a budget committee, for example, may be extremely useful in more effective and profitable planning of future operations. Department foremen should be encouraged to discuss reports of their operating performances with plant managers and with members of the accounting department. Such discussions can foster improved understanding and acceptance of reports and their objectives, enhanced rapport between operating personnel and management, and, ultimately, improved operating efficiency.

Responsibility Reporting

Operating reports should be developed according to areas of responsibility. Reports on the operating performance of a particular supervisor should cover only those items for which he is responsible or should clearly distinguish between such items and those for which he is not accountable. Departmental expense reports, for example, should distinguish between costs that are controllable and those that are noncontrollable at the level of the department supervisor.[4] Otherwise, the manager reported on is likely to develop antagonism toward the reporting system, the accounting staff, and the higher management that reviews the reports. And higher management's review of operations would be impaired by a lack of distinction between controllable and noncontrollable costs.

The level of responsibility to which a report is directed should dictate to a considerable extent the form and content of it. To illustrate this idea, let us consider only the operating costs incurred in a single department during a month. The cost report submitted to the department supervisor should detail the individual cost items, classified as controllable and noncontrollable. It should indicate both actual and budgeted costs for the month and, possibly, the year to date and the resultant variances. If preferred, noncontrollable costs might be omitted from the report altogether. The report submitted to the plant manager will include cost data for all of the departments in his plant. These data may be summarized simply by broad functional classifications (materials, labor,

---

[3] *Ibid.*, p. 17.

[4] See Table 9–2 in Chapter 9.

and overhead), by their variability or fixedness with respect to volume, and by controllability. The report submitted to the vice-president for manufacturing may include summaries of cost data from several plants. The data for individual departments within a plant may not be identified separately at all at this level of responsibility. If the vice-president is not the one to take action to correct excessive materials usage in a department (or any other deviation from budgets or standards), there is no point in cluttering his report with such detailed information. The reporting of variances from standard by responsibilities was discussed at some length in Chapter 11.[5] The reader may wish to review that discussion at this point.

Although reports of operations directed to lower levels of management should clearly distinguish between controllable and noncontrollable data, they need not omit the latter. As a matter of fact, inclusion of information which is beyond a manager's present scope of responsibility may be a useful technique for expanding his perspective of the firm's operations and, thus, helping prepare him for broader managerial responsibilities in the future. Also, reports to a manager of the operating results of other divisions as well as his own may help to stimulate healthy competition among divisional managers. This may be particularly beneficial in connection with sales divisions. Care must be exercised, however, to ensure that such competition does not result in improved divisional performances at the expense of optimal company profit.

Reporting Exceptions

The concept of management by exception was mentioned earlier in this volume.[6] It is an approach to management which focuses attention on situations and operations which deviate from plans or from normal conditions. It is predicated upon a belief that management's limited and costly time is best spent in matters requiring corrective action or other improvement, not in reviewing satisfactory performance. Regular reports of operations, therefore, should be so constructed as to draw management's attention to exceptions. In a variance report, for example, special treatment should be given to variances which are beyond the established range of tolerance; for these are the variances which call for managerial action. This may be accomplished by placing such variances in a special column in the report or by putting some identifying mark next to them. The importance of reporting exceptions does not mean

[5] Pages 270 to 273.

[6] See Chapter 5, page 131.

that satisfactory operating results are unimportant. Management, naturally, wants to know the results of operations, whether good or bad; but the bad results should be clearly identified. The reporting of exceptions obviously is one of the most critical features of reports prepared specifically for purposes of control.

Report Retention

There seems to be a pack rat instinct in human nature that manifests itself in business offices as well as in private homes. Once a report has been prepared and submitted, it is almost invariably filed. Once filed, the chance of its being thrown away all but disappears. Eventually, the report may be microfilmed and the original copy discarded in order to save storage space; but it remains a part of the company's archives. There should be a general rule in business firms that nothing is retained unless there is some real possibility of its further usefulness. Alternatively, there might be some system of short-term filing for items of only temporary significance, the short-term file being cleared out on a regular schedule. Many reports must be retained for some specified period of time in order that their data may be included in subsequent summary reports. Other reports may have some legal significance and should be retained for a period governed by the applicable statute of limitations. Finally, some reports, such as annual financial statements, may be retained permanently as part of the history of the firm. Reports of clearly temporary usefulness, however, should be discarded as soon as their utility has been exhausted. Daily materials usage reports, for example, are unlikely to be of further significance (except, perhaps, as support for later summaries) after the end of the next day.

FORMAT OF REPORTS

Universally standardized report forms do not exist nor would it be desirable if they did. The organizational structures, operations, and managerial philosophies of business firms differ considerably. Reports should be adapted to fit the peculiar characteristics of each individual firm. Within a single firm, however, standardization of report forms, within reasonable limits, is desirable. It fosters economy in report preparation and facilitates comprehension of reports. Standardization, of course, is possible only for regular reports. Limited standardization is possible for some special reports, but there must be adequate room for variations necessary to fit the individual situation. Requests for capital investments, for example, may be submitted to top management on standard forms; but their contents are likely to vary considerably.

Tabular Reports

Most accounting reports are prepared in tabular form. They typically contain one or more columns of data and frequently present combinations and/or comparisons of information. Financial statistics lend themselves to tabular presentation, and there is every reason to expect that most accounting reports will continue to appear in that format. A review of the various reports illustrated in the tables throughout this book will show almost all in the tabular form. This preponderance of practice should not preclude experimentation and change in report forms, of course. For some purposes, tabular reports may advantageously be supplanted or, at least, supplemented by other forms.

Graphic Reports

The use of graphs and charts is becoming increasingly popular in all types of reports. Relationships between two quantities (e.g., actual cost and budgeted cost) can be shown more clearly and vividly in many cases by two lines on a graph than by a comparison of dollar amounts. Graphs also lend themselves particularly well to presentations of comparative data intended to depict trends and other quantitative relationships over time.

Figure 19–1 is an illustration of a graphic report of the materials usage variance in a production department over a period of three months. It is a cumulative report, one that is added to daily and is completed only at the end of the quarter. This report is prepared for the plant superintendent, who uses it as a quick review of the operating performance of the department supervisor in one important area of his direct responsibility. Its cumulative content facilitates evaluation of the department's efficiency over time and of the results of efforts to correct prior variances. Separate daily reports of materials usage may be submitted to the department supervisor. Alternatively, as the variance data in Figure 19–1 are developed and entered daily, the same report could be presented to the department supervisor. The report in Figure 19–1 shows variances as percentages of standard usage rather than as physical amounts or dollars. The center line represents standard usage per unit of output. On either side of this line there is a line indicating the boundaries of the range of tolerable variances. Notice that the tolerable excess usage (2.0% of standard) is greater than the tolerable amount below standard (1.0%). This may be explained by the need to maintain product quality. If materials usage falls below the minimum, product quality may be so impaired that the units produced that day must be rejected.

FIGURE 19–1

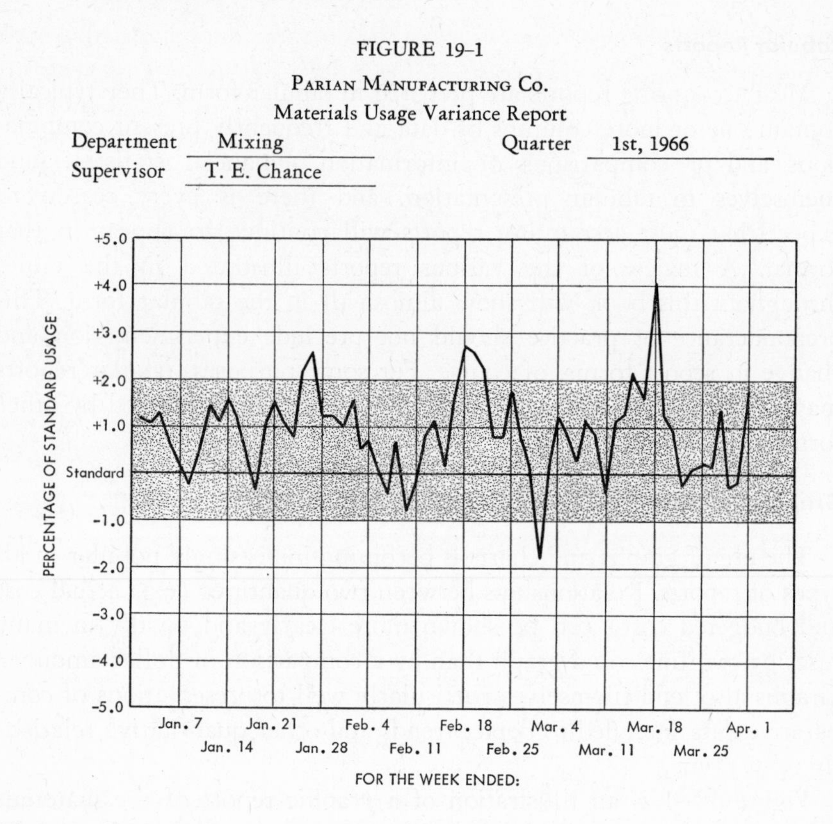

The area between the two lines bounding the range of tolerable variances is shaded on the graph so that variances outside that range—the exceptions requiring specific corrective action—are more readily identified.

Graphic reports, of course, are not always preferable to those in tabular form. Indeed, current reporting practices would seem to suggest just the opposite. Graphs tend to be less precise than tabulations. Further, they become increasingly difficult to read as additional data are reported in them. For simple reports, such as that in Table 19–1, and for long-term trend analyses, such as the growth or decline of the rate of return on investment in a firm over many years, graphs are especially appropriate. Probably their greatest advantage is that they enable the reader to grasp broad relationships or patterns quickly.

Narrative Reports

Although most accounting reports emphasize quantitative data, there is no reason why they should not also include textual material of a narrative or descriptive nature. Budget review reports, for example, might well include brief narratives of the operations for a period of time and the reasons for variances from the budget. Special reports covering such things as equipment replacement analyses, product line profit comparisons, and make or buy decisions ought to include some explanations of other pertinent factors which cannot presently be quantified. Quantitative information must be placed in its proper context, and this is properly the task of the written word. Almost anyone can fill in blanks with numbers, but this is not the essence of report writing. The good report writer can add succinct explanatory comments which give depth and meaning to the numbers. And management reports are nothing without meaning.

QUESTIONS FOR DISCUSSION

1. Discuss the relative advantages and disadvantages of tabular and graphic presentations of financial data in accounting reports.
2. What general rules may be stated for the frequency of issuance of regular reports?
3. Describe what you believe to be a good format for a monthly report of overhead costs incurred in a production department. If the data in the report would be classified, explain the reasons for the classifications. If any comparative data are included, explain what comparisons are made and why.
4. You are employed in a large, multiproduct firm that frequently must make decisions respecting product prices. You have been asked to draft a standard form on which the relevant financial data for pricing decisions can be reported to managers responsible for pricing. Describe the content of the form you would prepare and discuss its usefulness to management.
5. Are the data reported in the income statement which is usually included in the corporation's published annual report useful to the corporation's management for purposes of decision making? Explain your answer and discuss fully. If you feel they are not useful to management, of what value are these published data?
6. Variance reports were discussed in Chapter 11 as well as in the present chapter. What would you consider to be the basic guidelines for an effective variance report?
7. "*Resolved:* All reports submitted to the president and/or to the chairman of the board of a large industrial corporation should be no more than one page long." Do you concur with this resolution? Discuss fully.
8. Prepare a flow chart outlining the steps and procedures to be followed by a corporation's accounting department in preparing and distributing all types of financial reports.

APPENDIXES

Appendix A

CASES FOR ANALYSIS AND DISCUSSION

SMOG HARBOR REFINERY

(This case may be taken up after study of Chapters 2, 3, and 4.)

Late in 1965, the Contour Oil Company completed construction of a major oil refinery at Smog Harbor, California. The total cost of the refinery was $60 million, and the facilities are expected to have an economic life of 15 years. The maximum productive capacity of the refinery is 6 million barrels of crude oil per year. However, during 1966, the first year of operations, it is estimated that actual production will be only two thirds of capacity.

Refinery operations will be largely automated. Hourly employees for the first year of operations have been planned as follows:

Position	*Number*	*Hourly Wage*
Refinery operator	250	$3.60
Maintenance man	80	2.75
Watchman	40	2.00
Shipping-dock worker	75	2.80
Boat crewman	12	3.00

There will be 255 eight-hour working days in each year. Refinery operators run the refining machinery. Maintenance men perform routine repair and maintenance work on buildings and equipment. Shipping-dock workers load tank trucks which carry finished products to Contour Oil Company's bulk stations for further distribution. Boat crews assist tankers delivering crude oil to the refinery and tend the subsurface pipeline from the offshore tanker anchorage to the crude oil storage tanks. In addition to hourly wages, the following monthly salaries are anticipated:

Administration	$120,000
Refinery foremen	15,000
Shipping-dock foreman	750
Boat captains	1,750

The only significant raw material used by the refinery will be crude oil. It is expected to have an average cost of $.48 per barrel, delivered.

On the basis of its experience with other refineries, the company has estimated that other refinery overhead and operating expenses will be as follows:

Variable overhead	$.15 per barrel of crude oil
Fixed overhead (excluding depreciation)	$175,000 per month
Miscellaneous administrative expenses	$80,000 per month

Although the refinery is a "modern" one with pollution control devices, emission of air pollutants from time to time is inevitable. A county ordinance requires that the refinery be shut down after any 12 hours of pollutant emission until the situation is corrected. The company's labor agreement requires that all hourly employees be paid in full if they are on the premises during such shut-down periods.

Required:

1. Should Contour Oil Company use a job order or a process cost system for this refinery? Explain.
2. Should the output of the refinery be costed by the absorption costing method or by the variable costing method? Explain.
3. Should the wages of the shipping-dock workers be accounted for as direct labor? Explain. If not as direct labor, how should they be classified?
4. How should the wages and salaries of the boat crewmen and captains be accounted for?
5. During 1966, the refinery was shut down because of air pollutant emission for a total of 19 working days. How should employees wages paid for these 19 days be reported in the company's annual report?

SLICKO MANUFACTURING CO.

(*This case may be taken up after study of Chapters 5 through 8.*)

The Slicko Manufacturing Co. produces and sells snow blowers, powered by 4.5 hp. gas engines. Sales of the snow blowers have always shown a marked seasonal pattern. The sales forecast for 1967 reflects the typical seasonal distribution of sales.

Quarter	*Unit Sales*
1st	5,000
2nd	5,000
3rd	60,000
4th	30,000

To meet sales demand, the company has, in the past, followed the practice of producing expected sales volume one quarter in advance. This policy has resulted in peak production activities in the spring and summer and very little output during the fall and winter.

Late in 1966, the company signed its first union agreement, which includes a union shop provision. At the time of this signing, the work force was at its seasonal low level of 150 hourly employees. In past years, the seasonal high level of employment was 1,200 factory workers. The union agreement provides that employees who are on the payroll for 90 days or longer cannot be laid off without two weeks' notice and two additional weeks' severance pay.

The standard production costs of one snow blower, after inclusion of the recently negotiated wage rate, is as follows:

Materials:	
Frame	$ 14.40
Engine	39.60
Rotor assembly	13.50
Wheels (3 @ $1.50)	4.50
	$ 72.00
Labor (12 hrs. @ $2.25)	27.00
Overhead:	
Variable (12 hrs. @ $.75)	9.00
Fixed (12 hrs. @ $1.00)	12.00
	$120.00

The company's finished product storeroom will accommodate no more than 8,000 snow blowers at one time. The inventory of finished product at December 31, 1966, consists of 1,000 units. When needed, additional storage space may be rented at a rate of $2,500 per quarter or any fraction thereof for space to accommodate 5,000 finished snow blowers. Construction of a new warehouse would take at least ten months. The company's management is confident that sufficient storage space can be rented in 1967 to meet the firm's needs.

There will be 250 eight-hour working days in 1967.

Required:

1. Identify and discuss the principal problems facing the company in the planning of production for 1967 and subsequent years.
2. How should the company schedule production in 1967 so as to meet sales demand and minimize total costs?

SENTINEL SEATING CORPORATION

(This case may be taken up after study of Chapters 9 through 11.)

The Sentinel Seating Corporation manufactures armchairs for classroom use. The standard cost of manufacturing one chair is as follows:

Raw materials:		
Steel (8 lbs. @ $.67)	$5.36	
Wood (2 bd. ft. @ $.20)	.40	
Chrome casters (4 @ $.06)	.24	$6.00
Direct labor:		
¾ hr. @ $3.60		2.70
Overhead:		
Variable (¾ hr. @ $.80)	$ .60	
Fixed (¾ hr. @ $1.20)	.90	1.50
		$10.20

The standard overhead rates above are derived from the following flexible budget for indirect manufacturing expenses:

	Variable Cost per Labor Hour	*Fixed Cost per Month*
Indirect labor		$20,000
Labor-related costs	$.54	3,000
Indirect materials	.11	
Power and light	.05	5,000
Depreciation		18,000
Taxes and insurance		2,000
Repairs and maintenance	.10	12,000
	$.80	$60,000

For the past five years, the corporation's sales and production have grown steadily, if not spectacularly. Actual output, in units, during this period is summarized below.

Year	*Units*
1962	780,000
1963	810,000
1964	850,000
1965	880,000
1966	900,000

After the first six months of 1967, it appears that total output will rise again for the sixth consecutive year. Output for the month of June, 1967, totaled 80,000 chairs.

A total of 325 tons of steel was purchased during June, 1967, at an average price of $1,500 per ton. Materials usage reports indicate that 324 tons were used in production during the same month. Two hundred thousand board feet of wood were purchased for $.14 per board foot. All of this wood was consumed in production during June. It was a very green wood and proved to be difficult to work with. In addition, cracking and warping in the production process was far in excess of normal. Four thousand hours of rework time were required for chairs on which the wood originally installed proved defective and had to be replaced prior to shipment. Five hundred cases of brass casters were purchased at an average cost of $24 per case. Each case contains 600 casters. These brass casters were purchased because of a temporary market shortage of the chrome casters. They are substantially similar to the standard item, although they tend to have a somewhat shorter life in service. Two hundred cases of chrome casters (600 casters per case) and 335 cases of brass casters were used during June.

Production workers recorded a total of 62,000 direct labor hours in June 1967. Of these, 56,000 were straight-time hours at the rate of $3.72 per hour, and 6,000 were overtime hours at one and one-half times this hourly rate. Employees were granted a $.12 per hour wage rate increase in the new labor agreement signed on April 20, 1967.

The actual overhead costs incurred during June included the following:

Indirect labor	$24,000
Labor-related costs	39,870
Indirect materials	7,450
Power and light	7,500
Depreciation	18,600
Taxes and insurance	2,000
Repairs and maintenance	15,220
	$114,640

The president of the corporation has recently expressed concern that cost control in the factory is not tight enough. He has called a meeting of the policy committee for July 16 to discuss the situation, to determine whether a problem really exists, and to consider remedies if it does. The controller, a member of the policy committee, has been directed to provide appropriate financial information for purposes of this meeting.

Required:

Prepare for the controller an analysis of production costs during the month of June, 1967, as an illustration of factory costs. Indicate which costs, if any, were excessive during June; and identify reasons for such excess costs where possible. Suggest steps that might be taken to control excessive costs in future months.

ASBESTONE PAINT COMPANY

(This case may be taken up after study of Chapters 13 and 14.)

In 1936, William Henry developed and patented a heat resistant paint which had the additional properties of being long wearing and easily cleaned. Henry found a ready market for this new paint among the manufacturers of ovens and other equipment used under conditions of extreme heat. At the outset, Henry and six employees produced and delivered this paint in the Chicago area only. By 1939, however, it was evident that a broader market for the product existed and could be served only by a major expansion of production and distribution facilities. Accordingly, Henry incorporated under the name Asbestone Paint Company and constructed a large plant in South Chicago. An expanded sales force began distribution of the paint under the trade name "Asbestone" throughout the East and Midwest.

In 1950, Henry obtained a patent on a graphite-base industrial lubricant, subsequently marketed under the trade name "Glideze." The combined demand for this new product and for "Asbestone" soon overtaxed the capacity of the South Chicago plant. In 1954, a new plant was completed in Streator; and all paint production was shifted to that location. For a while, the South Chicago plant was operated considerably below capacity. However, by 1958, it became necessary to produce paint there as well as in Streator.

In 1962, the company introduced a lightweight heat-proof liner for use in ovens, kilns, and similar equipment. This liner, called "Heatrap," proved to be a good seller, especially to firms that could also use "Asbestone." By the end of 1966, it was apparent that the combined capacities of the two plants would not be adequate to meet sales demand in the following year. After considerable discussion, the board of directors agreed to construct a large new plant in South Bend. When this plant is completed, the old South Chicago factory will be sold. The South Bend plant cannot be ready for production until the spring of 1968, however. Hence, it will not help solve the immediate problem of meeting demand in 1967.

Sales in units of products for the ten years prior to 1967 were as follows:

Year	*Asbestone (gallons)*	*Glideze (pounds)*	*Heatrap (sq. yds.)*
1957	2,500,000	500,000	
1958	3,000,000	600,000	
1959	3,120,000	640,000	
1960	3,245,000	695,000	
1961	3,375,000	735,000	
1962	3,630,000	800,000	600,000
1963	4,170,000	850,000	2,000,000
1964	4,916,000	880,000	3,000,000
1965	6,068,000	960,000	5,000,000
1966	7,426,000	1,025,000	6,000,000

Sales for 1967 have been budgeted as shown below.

Asbestone	9,000,000 gallons
Glideze	1,100,000 pounds
Heatrap	7,000,000 square yards

Standard production lots, factory time, and direct costs for the three products are as follows:

	Asbestone	*Glideze*	*Heatrap*
Standard production lot	100 gal.	50 lbs.	1,000 sq. yds.
Direct labor hours	16	16	80
Standard wage rate	$2.50	$2.50	$2.50
Materials cost per lot	$436	$41	$60

The flexible budgets for overhead in the two plants are summarized thus:

	South Chicago Plant	*Streator Plant*
Variable overhead per direct labor hour	$.75	$.80
Fixed overhead per year	$1,200,000	$3,600,000

The annual productive capacity of the South Chicago plant is 600,000 direct labor hours. Capacity at the Streator plant is 1,500,000 labor hours per year. Both plants are capable of producing any or all of the three products.

Inventories of finished products and work in process at December 31, 1966, are the minimum stocks required for continuous sales and production operations.

The corporation's income statement for 1966, by products, appeared as follows:

	Asbestone	*Glideze*	*Heatrap*
Sales	$60,150,600	$3,177,500	$3,000,000
Standard cost of goods sold	38,954,500	2,656,200	3,017,200
Gross profit	$21,196,100	$ 521,300	$ (17,200)
Selling expenses	$ 7,815,060	$ 417,750	$ 400,000
Administrative expenses	2,700,000	150,000	150,000
	$10,515,060	$ 567,750	$ 550,000
Income before tax	$10,681,040	$ (46,450)	$ (567,200)
Income tax (40%)	4,272,416	(18,580)	(226,880)
Net income	$ 6,408,624	$ (27,870)	$ (340,320)

Direct selling expenses average 10% of sales. All other selling and administrative expenses are regarded as fixed.

Required:

1. What, if anything, might the corporation do to increase its output to meet expected sales demand in 1967?
2. If output cannot be raised to meet demand in 1967, what action should the corporation take?

BEAN BLOSSOM PAPERBOARD COMPANY

(This case may be taken up after study of Chapters 13 through 16.)

The Bean Blossom Paperboard Company built its present plant in Bean Blossom, Indiana, in 1948. The total original cost of the plant, including land, building, and equipment, was $650,000. The estimated economic life of the building and equipment was set at 25 years, with no significant terminal salvage value. Now, early in 1966, the company's management is considering the construction of a new plant closer to Indianapolis.

Until World War II, Bean Blossom was a sleepy farming community basking in the sunny hills of Brown County. During the war, however, it became the site of a large ammunition depot, employing several hundred civilians from the surrounding area. Two years after V-J Day, the ammunition depot was closed and the land offered for sale. C. W. Graves, having returned to his native Nashville after the war, saw the potential of a relatively low-cost paperboard plant on the site of the old depot. His bid of $30,000 for the land was accepted by the government, and he began making plans for the construction of the factory. The building was completed and equipment installed early in 1948, and operations commenced with a payroll of about 120 persons.

Initial labor costs in the plant were quite low, as there was no other industry in the area to absorb the workers idled by the closing of the ammunition depot. After a short training period, these workers proved efficient and content to work for wages considerably lower than the level then obtaining in the Indianapolis area. By 1965, the company's payroll had expanded to over 500 persons; and the initial wage advantage over the Indianapolis location had all but disappeared. The latter change was due partly to the southward movement of industry and partly to the organization of the company's employees in 1958 by the International Paperboard Workers.

During 1965, the company's sales outstripped the capacity of the plant. Some sales, totaling $1,500,000, had to be made by subcontracting the work to paperboard manufacturers in Indianapolis. These orders were shipped directly to the customers from the subcontractors' plants. No uncompleted subcontracts remained outstanding at December 31, 1965. Mr. Graves has estimated that sales volume in 1966 will be 10% higher than in 1965 and that it will continue to rise thereafter at an annual rate of about 5%.

Preliminary studies indicate that the construction of a factory in Indianapolis would cost $1,800,000 on land leased for thirty years at an annual rental of $4,000. Machinery and equipment would cost $900,000. The building would have an estimated useful life of thirty years. The machinery and equipment would have a life of fifteen years and a terminal salvage value equal to the estimated cost of removal. This plant could be ready for operations at the beginning of 1967. Its capacity would be expected to meet sales demand through 1981, after which expansion of the factory would be expected.

Labor costs in Indianapolis would be approximately 5% higher than in Bean Blossom. Variable shipping expenses would be about 10% lower, however. Other current operating expenses would remain very nearly the same as at present. The Bean Blossom plant, including land, could be sold early in 1967 for about $60,000.

Summarized operating statements for the company for 1965 are shown below.

BEAN BLOSSOM PAPERBOARD COMPANY
Income Statement
For the Year Ended December 31, 1965

Sales		$10,000,000
Cost of goods sold (Schedule A)	$6,810,000	
Less overapplied overhead (Schedule B)	50,000	6,760,000
Gross margin		$ 3,240,000
Selling and administrative expenses (Schedule C)		1,590,000
Income before tax		$ 1,650,000
Income tax (40%)		$ 660,000
Net income		$ 990,000

Schedule A: Cost of Goods Manufactured and Sold

Raw materials	$ 1,700,000
Direct labor	2,550,000
Variable overhead applied	850,000
Fixed overhead applied	510,000
Current production costs	$ 5,610,000
Cost of goods produced by subcontractors	1,200,000
Cost of goods manufactured and sold	$ 6,810,000

Schedule B: Overhead Incurred and Applied

Variable overhead costs incurred:	
Indirect labor	$ 150,000
Labor-related costs	270,000
Indirect materials	180,000
Power	80,000
Maintenance	170,000
	$ 850,000
Variable overhead applied	$ 850,000
Fixed overhead costs incurred:	
Depreciation	$ 26,000
Taxes and insurance	34,000
Repair and maintenance	400,000
	$ 460,000
Fixed overhead applied	510,000
Overapplied fixed overhead	$ 50,000

Schedule C: Selling and Administrative Expenses

Sales commissions	$ 500,000
Shipping expenses	255,000
Promotion expenses	235,000
General administration expenses	600,000
	$ 1,590,000

Both variable and fixed overhead are applied to production at normal rates per direct labor dollar. Mr. Graves has estimated that the company's effective cost of capital is 7% after income taxes.

Required:

1. Identify and discuss the important facets of the plant construction decision confronting the Bean Blossom Paperboard Company in 1966. Before making a decision, what additional information do you believe the company's management should have?
2. If you were asked to advise the company on the profitability of the proposed new plant, without further information, what recommendation would you make? Support this recommendation with appropriate financial analysis. What do you consider the most significant shortcomings of your analysis?

NOANK LIVE LOBSTERS, INC.

(This case may be taken up after study of Chapter 17.)

Schooner Harbor has long been one of the most popular seafood restaurants in eastern Connecticut. It is most famous for its boiled-live lobster with a special butter sauce made from a secret recipe. The national reputation of this particular dish has led to numerous requests from restauranteurs all over the country for the right to serve it in their establishments under the Schooner Harbor name. Several years ago, the proprietor of Schooner Harbor sensed in these requests an opportunity for very lucrative additional business at the cost of a fairly modest investment.

Thus, the proprietor set up a separate corporation, Noank Live Lobsters, Inc., to pack and ship live lobsters and jars of sauce. Sauce is prepared in the restaurant's kitchen and put into 2-pound jars. It is then transferred to a packing plant purchased especially for the new corporation. In the packing plant, twenty live lobsters and three jars of sauce are packed in specially designed cases. All cases are packed for specific customers' orders. The cases are then taken by company-owned trucks to New York for delivery to local restaurants, or for air shipment to out-of-town buyers.

Shipments of live lobsters have increased steadily since this business was begun, until, today, the packing plant is operating at its practical capacity. Even so, orders frequently must be delayed because of a backlog of demand. Initially, orders were received only from "exclusive" restaurants in large cities. Recently, however, orders have started to come in from a wider variety of restaurants. Some chains of restaurants have asked the company to ship large orders at reduced prices. Thus far, the proprietor has not been able to fill any such orders because of the heavy demand from regular customers. However, he has begun to wonder whether he may not have conceived the live lobster shipping business on too small a scale. He currently is considering the feasibility and financial advisability of shipping large quantities at special prices, and of shipping to a wider variety of customers. Realistically, the latter course of action would have to involve lower basic prices.

Each case of live lobsters is now sold for $80 plus air freight charges from New York. This price was arrived at by assuming that restaurants serving Schooner Harbor lobster and sauce would price the item at $6.00 per serving and that they would be willing to pay an average of $4.00 per serving for the distinction of including the dish on their menus. Information from present customers suggests that most do charge about $6.00 for the dish. The costs of producing, packing, and transporting the lobsters have been estimated by the proprietor as follows:

Cost of packing case (empty)	$3.60
Cost of 2-pound jar (empty)	$ .03
Packing labor per case	$ .80
Cost of sauce:	
Ingredients per pound	$1.10
Labor per pound	$ .20
Trucking costs per month	$800
Packing plant overhead per month (wholly fixed)	$500
Cost of lobsters (see below)	

The cost of lobsters varies widely, depending upon seasonal changes, weather, and market conditions. Within a single year, the cost may range from $.75 to $1.50 per lobster.

Several restaurants which price their meals considerably below those sold in the corporation's present customers' establishments have indicated that they would be eager to buy if the price could be reduced to $3.00 per lobster or less. One restaurant chain has offered to purchase regularly in quantities of at least fifty cases per order at a price of $50 per case. The proprietor of Schooner Harbor believes similar arrangement could be made with other chains.

Required:

1. Evaluate the corporation's present pricing system.
2. Define the decisions facing the proprietor in connection with the growing demand for live lobsters and sauce. Suggest approaches to the solution of each of these decisions.
3. If the proprietor does decide to reduce the price and to offer quantity discounts, would the prices of $3.00 per lobster and $50 per case to chains for large orders, as suggested by potential customers, be satisfactory? Discuss.

Appendix B

TABLES OF PRESENT VALUES

THIS APPENDIX contains three tables of discounted present values of amounts to be paid or received in the future. These tables are based upon compound interest principles. They are included here primarily for use in the solution of problems in this text. They do not purport to be a complete set of compound interest tables useful to business managers and accountants. Each of these tables contains three basic data, interest rates, time periods, and present values of $1. Given any two of these data, the third can be found in the tables, unless either the time period or the interest rate is beyond the limits of the tables. For most of the problems in this book, the interest rate and the time period will be given; the quantity sought will be the present value of some future cash receipt or payment. For some problems, the present value and the time period may be given, the interest rate being the unknown quantity. As a practical matter, the time period would seldom be unknown; but it could be found easily enough if the interest rate and the present value were given.

Although these are tables of the present value of $1, they can be used quite easily to determine the present value of any amount. The tabulated present values of $1 are often referred to as *present value factors.* These factors can be used to determine the present value of any dollar amount by simple multiplication. For example, the present value of $100 is simply 100 times that of $1; the present value of $.50 is half that of $1. The nature and the usage of each of the tables will be explained briefly in the sections that follow. Additional illustrations of their use will be found in Chapters 15 and 16 of the text.

Table B-1

Table B-1 is a table of present values of annuities of $1 to be paid or received in a steady stream throughout each of a given number of future periods. The word "annuity" suggests that the time periods involved be years, but this is not necessarily the case. The time period may be of any designated length, although most often it will be a year.

For most of the problems in this book, annual amounts received will be in the form of revenues or cost savings and amounts paid, in the form of expenditures or revenues foregone. As revenues and expenditures normally occur regularly throughout a period rather than only at one point of time in the period, Table B-1 is based upon the concept of continuous discounting. The annuities discounted by means of this table are assumed to be received or paid in a steady stream during each year of their lives. Further, cash receipts are assumed to be reinvested as soon as they are received; and cash paid out is assumed to have been invested productively up to the time of its disbursement. Generally speaking, these assumptions are valid and fairly descriptive of the ordinary operating receipts and payments of a business. If a particular annuity involves annual lump-sum payments or receipts rather than a steady cash flow during the year, it cannot be discounted by use of Table B-1. Table B-3 can be adapted quite easily for this purpose, however.

An inspection of Table B-1 will show that the present value factors increase at a decreasing rate as the number of time periods increases. Each additional period involves an additional cash receipt or payment, but the successive present values of such additional amounts decline. Thus, the present value of the additional cash flow in the tenth year is less than that of the additional amount in the ninth year, etc. The total present value of the annuity continues to increase, however. For any given period of years, the present value of the annuity decreases as the discount rate increases; there is an inverse relationship between the discount rate and the present value of a future cash flow.

To illustrate the use of Table B-1, assume that a firm has an opportunity to purchase a machine that will result in out-of-pocket operating cost savings of $15,000 per year for 12 years; the machine would have no terminal salvage value. Future cash flows are to be discounted at an interest rate of 9%. The projected annual cost saving of $15,000 is a 12-year annuity, the present value of which may be found from Table B-1. Enter Table B-1 at the column for 9% and the line for 12 years. The present value factor found at the intersection of the 9% column and the 12-year line is 7.3377. Multiply this factor by $15,000 to obtain a present value of $110,065.50 for this annuity. At a discount rate of 9%, a commitment to receive $15,000 annually in a steady stream for 12 years is presently worth $110,065.50. This is the maximum amount that the firm would be willing to pay to obtain the projected cost savings. Hence, the machine will be purchased only if its cost is $110,065.50 or less.

If an annuity will be received or paid over several future years not beginning with the first year, its present value can still be found from Table B-1. Suppose, for example, an investor can purchase an annuity which will pay him $10,000 per year for 15 years, starting in the eleventh year hence. The tabulated present value factor for fifteen years is for the first fifteen years in the future and, thus, not appropriate here. This annuity will be received during the eleventh through the twenty-fifth future years. Its present value factor is found by subtracting the factor for the first ten years from that for the first twenty-five years. The remainder is the factor applicable to the eleventh through twenty-fifth years. If the appropriate discount rate is 10%, the present value of this annuity is computed as follows:

Present value factor for 25 years	9.1790
Present value factor for 10 years	−6.3213
Present value factor for 11th–25th years	2.8577
Face amount of annuity	×$10,000
Present value of annuity	$28,577

If the life and the present value of an annuity are known, the discounted rate of return (cf., Chapter 15) to be earned by purchase of the annuity may be found from Table B-1. For example, if we know that the present value of an annuity of $1 for 20 years is $7.58, we have but to enter the 20-year line of Table B-1 and look for a present value factor of 7.58 therein. We find it (7.5782 actually) in the 12% column; therefore, 12% is the discounted rate of return on the purchase of the annuity. Suppose, now, that the annuity is one of $12,000 per year for 10 years and that its present value is known to be $93,000. As the table is for an annuity of $1, not $12,000, both the annual amount of the annuity and the present value thereof must be divided by $12,000. An annuity of $12,000 for 10 years with a present value of $93,000 has the same discounted rate of return as an annuity of $1 for 10 years with a present value of $7.75 ($93,000 ÷ $12,000). In Table B-1, we find that a present value factor of 7.75 for a 10-year annuity falls between the tabulated amounts for 5% and 6%. For many purposes, this may be sufficiently precise. If a more exact rate of return is desired, it may be computed by interpolation.

Interpolation. The discount rate for a present value factor which falls between two tabulated factors may be determined by interpolation. The mathematical process of interpolation is illustrated below for the $12,000 ten-year annuity described in the preceding paragraph. Its present value factor of 7.75 falls between tabulated factors of 7.8692 for 5% and 7.5198 for 6%. The total interval between these two tabulated factors is .3494 (7.8692 − 7.5198); this factor interval corresponds to a discount rate interval of 1% (6% − 5%). The interval between 7.8692 and 7.75 is .1192, and this corresponds to the interval between 5% and the exact discounted rate of return for the annuity in question. The difference between 5% and the exact discount rate is computed as follows, the difference being represented by x:

$$\frac{x}{.01} = \frac{.1192}{.3494}$$

$$\frac{x}{.01} = .344$$

$$x = .01(.344) = .00344$$

The exact discount rate (r) for this annuity then is equal to 5% plus x, or

$$r = .05 + .00344 = .05344.$$

By interpolation, the discount rate for a present value factor of 7.75 for a 10-year annuity of $1 (or for a present value of $93,000 for a 10-year annuity of $12,000) is found to be 5.344%.

Table B-2

Table B-2 contains the present values of amounts to be paid or received in a steady stream during only one future year. Like Table B-1, it is based upon the concept of continuous discounting; but the cash flows discounted in this table occur during a single year only. The basic mechanics of using this table are the same as those for Table B-1. Assume that a firm has an opportunity to purchase a machine with a life of five years and no terminal salvage value. The machine will cause an annual out-of-pocket operating cost saving for five years, but the successive annual cost savings will decrease in amount; they will not be in the form of a level annuity for five years. The cost savings expected are as follows:

Year	*Cost Saving*
1st	$20,000
2nd	16,000
3rd	12,000
4th	10,000
5th	8,000

Because these savings are not in the form of a level annuity, no single present value factor can be used to discount them. Each annual cost saving (cash inflow) must be discounted separately. Assuming that the appropriate discount rate is 8%, these cost savings have a total present value computed as follows:

Year	*Cost Saving*	×	*Present Value Factor at 8%*	=	*Present Value*
1st	$20,000		.9610		$19,220
2nd	16,000		.8872		14,195
3rd	12,000		.8189		9,827
4th	10,000		.7560		7,560
5th	8,000		.6979		5,583
					$56,385

If either Table B-1 or Table B-2 alone were given, the other could be developed from the one available. Notice that the first lines (the lines for the first year in the future) of the two tables contain identically the same present values. Each present value factor in the second line of Table B-1 is equal to the sum of the first two factors for the same interest rate in Table B-2. The factor for three years in Table B-1 is the sum of the factors for the first three years in Table B-2, etc. Conversely, the factor for the second year in Table B-2 is the difference between the factors for two years and for one year in Table B-1, etc.

Table B-3

Table B-3 is unlike the first two in that it contains present values for lump-sum cash receipts or payments at some moment in the future. As the cash flows here are momentary rather than steady, continuous discounting is not appropriate. Hence, Table B-3 is based upon the concept of discrete discounting. The basic mechanics of its use, however, are the same as those for Tables B-1 and B-2. For example, the present value of a payment of $1 eighteen years in the future at a discount rate of 15% is $.0672 (the factor at the intersection of the 15% column and the 18-year line). If the payment were $10,000, the present value would be $672 ($10,000 × .0672).

Sometimes a business enterprise will anticipate a series of equal periodic payments in the future, as in the case of rental payments. The present value of such payments may be determined from Table B-3 also. Assume that a company enters into a ten-year lease agreement for a building. It agrees to pay annual rental of $40,000 on the first day of each of the next 10 years. This amounts to an initial payment of $40,-000 and an annuity of $40,000 payable annually in lump sums at the end of each of the succeeding 9 years. (The first day of the second year is the end of the first year, etc.) Rather than to multiply 9 annual $40,000 payments by 9 separate present value factors, it is easier and quicker to add the first 9 tabulated factors in the appropriate interest rate column in Table B-3 and multiply their sum by $40,000. As the first year's rental must be paid at once, there is no time lapse and its present value is equal to its face value. Assuming a discount rate of 6%, the total present value of these rental payments if computed as follows:

Time of Payment	*Face Amount* ×	*Present Value Factor at 6%* =	*Present Value*
Immediately..................	$40,000		$ 40,000
End of each of next 9 years.....	40,000	6.7476	269,904
			$309,904

The present value factor 6.7476 is the sum of the first 9 factors in the 6% column of Table B-3.

TABLE B-1

Present Value of Annuity of $1 Received or Paid in a Steady Stream throughout *n* Years in the Future

n	5%	6%	7%	8%	9%	10%	11%	12%	13%	14%	15%	20%	25%	30%	40%
1	0.9754	0.9706	0.9658	0.9610	0.9563	0.9516	0.9470	0.9423	0.9377	0.9332	0.9286	0.9063	0.8848	0.8640	0.8242
2	1.9032	1.8847	1.8663	1.8482	1.8303	1.8127	1,7953	1.7781	1.7611	1.7444	1.7279	1.6484	1.5739	1.5040	1.3767
3	2.7858	2.7455	2.7059	2.6671	2.6291	2.5918	2.5553	2.5194	2.4841	2.4497	2.4158	2.2559	2.1106	1.9781	1.7470
4	3.6253	3.5562	3.4888	3.4231	3.3591	3.2968	3.2361	3.1768	3.1190	3.0628	3.0079	2.7533	2.5285	2.3294	1.9952
5	4.4239	4.3197	4.2187	4.1210	4.0263	3.9347	3.8460	3.7599	3.6765	3.5958	3.5175	3.1605	2.8540	2.5896	2.1616
6	5.1835	5.0387	4.8993	4.7652	4.6361	4.5119	4.3923	4.2771	4.1660	4.0592	3.9561	3.4939	3.1075	2.7824	2.2731
7	5.9061	5.7159	5.5339	5.3599	5.1934	5.0342	4.8817	4.7359	4.5959	4.4621	4.3336	3.7669	3.3049	2.9252	2.3479
8	6.5935	6.3536	6.1256	5.9089	5.7027	5.5068	5.3202	5.1428	4.9734	4.8123	4.6586	3.9904	3.4587	3.0310	2.3980
9	7.2473	6.9542	6.6773	6.4157	6.1682	5.9344	5.7130	5.5037	5.3048	5.1168	4.9383	4.1734	3.5784	3.1094	2.4316
10	7.8692	7.5198	7.1917	6.8835	6.5936	6.3213	6.0649	5.8238	5.5958	5.3815	5.1790	4.3232	3.6717	3.1675	2.4541
11	8.4608	8.0525	7.6713	7.3153	6.9824	6.6714	6.3801	6.1077	5.8514	5.6116	5.3862	4.4459	3.7443	3.2105	2.4692
12	9.0236	8.5541	8.1185	7.7139	7.3377	6.9882	6.6625	6.3595	6.0758	5.8116	5.5645	4.5463	3.8009	3.2424	2.4793
13	9.5589	9.0265	8.5354	8.0819	7.6625	7.2748	6.9155	6.5828	6.2728	5.9855	5.7180	4.6285	3.8450	3.2660	2.4861
14	10.0681	9.4714	8.9242	8.4216	7.9593	7.5341	7.1421	6.7809	6.4458	6.1367	5.8501	4.6958	3.8793	3.2835	2.4906
15	10.5525	9.8904	9.2867	8.7352	8.2306	7.7688	7.3451	6.9566	6.5977	6.2682	5.9638	4.7509	3.9060	3.2965	2.4936
16	11.0133	10.2850	9.6246	9.0247	8.4785	7.9811	7.5270	7.1124	6.7311	6.3825	6.0617	4.7960	3.9268	3.3061	2.4957
17	11.4516	10.6567	9.9397	9.2919	8.7050	8.1732	7.6900	7.2506	6.8483	6.4819	6.1459	4.8330	3.9430	3.3132	2.4971
18	11.8685	11.0067	10.2335	9.5386	8.9120	8.3470	7.8360	7.3731	6.9512	6.5683	6.2184	4.8633	3.9556	3.3185	2.4980
19	12.2651	11.3363	10.5074	9.7663	9.1012	8.5043	7.9668	7.4818	7.0415	6.6434	6.2808	4.8881	3.9654	3.3224	2.4986
20	12.6424	11.6467	10.7628	9.9765	9.2741	8.6466	8.0840	7.5782	7.1208	6.7087	6.3345	4.9084	3.9730	3.3253	2.4990
21	13.0012	11.9390	11.0009	10.1705	9.4322	8.7754	8.1889	7.6637	7.1905	6.7655	6.3807	4.9250	3.9790	3.3274	2.4993
22	13.3426	12.2143	11.2229	10.3496	9.5767	8.8919	8.2829	7.7395	7.2517	6.8149	6.4205	4.9386	3.9836	3.3290	2.4995
23	13.6673	12.4736	11.4299	10.5150	9.7087	8.9973	8.3671	7.8068	7.3054	6.8578	6.4548	4.9497	3.9872	3.3302	2.4996
24	13.9762	12.7178	11.6229	10.6676	9.8294	9.0927	8.4426	7.8665	7.3526	6.8951	6.4843	4.9588	3.9900	3.3311	2.4997
25	14.2700	12.9478	11.8029	10.8085	9.9397	9.1790	8.5102	7.9194	7.3940	6.9275	6.5097	4.9663	3.9922	3.3317	2.4998

TABLE B-2

Present Value of $1 Received or Paid in a Steady Stream throughout the *n*th Year in the Future

*n*th year	5%	6%	7%	8%	9%	10%	11%	12%	13%	14%	15%	20%	25%	30%	40%
1st	0.9754	0.9706	0.9658	0.9610	0.9563	0.9516	0.9470	0.9423	0.9377	0.9332	0.9286	0.9063	0.8848	0.8640	0.8242
2nd	0.9278	0.9141	0.9005	0.8872	0.8740	0.8611	0.8483	0.8358	0.8234	0.8112	0.7993	0.7421	0.6891	0.6400	0.5525
3rd	0.8826	0.8608	0.8396	0.8189	0.7988	0.7791	0.7600	0.7413	0.7230	0.7053	0.6879	0.6075	0.5367	0.4741	0.3703
4th	0.8395	0.8107	0.7829	0.7560	0.7300	0.7050	0.6808	0.6574	0.6349	0.6131	0.5921	0.4974	0.4179	0.3513	0.2482
5th	0.7986	0.7635	0.7299	0.6979	0.6672	0.6379	0.6099	0.5831	0.5575	0.5330	0.5096	0.4072	0.3255	0.2602	0.1664
6th	0.7596	0.7190	0.6806	0.6442	0.6098	0.5772	0.5463	0.5172	0.4895	0.4634	0.4386	0.3334	0.2535	0.1928	0.1115
7th	0.7226	0.6772	0.6346	0.5947	0.5573	0.5223	0.4894	0.4588	0.4299	0.4029	0.3775	0.2730	0.1974	0.1428	0.0748
8th	0.6874	0.6377	0.5917	0.5490	0.5093	0.4726	0.4385	0.4069	0.3775	0.3502	0.3250	0.2235	0.1538	0.1058	0.0501
9th	0.6538	0.6006	0.5517	0.5068	0.4655	0.4276	0.3928	0.3609	0.3314	0.3045	0.2797	0.1830	0.1197	0.0784	0.0336
10th	0.6219	0.5656	0.5144	0.4678	0.4254	0.3869	0.3519	0.3201	0.2910	0.2647	0.2407	0.1498	0.0933	0.0581	0.0225
11th	0.5916	0.5327	0.4796	0.4318	0.3888	0.3501	0.3152	0.2839	0.2556	0.2301	0.2072	0.1227	0.0726	0.0430	0.0151
12th	0.5628	0.5016	0.4472	0.3986	0.3553	0.3168	0.2824	0.2518	0.2244	0.2000	0.1783	0.1004	0.0566	0.0319	0.0101
13th	0.5353	0.4724	0.4169	0.3680	0.3248	0.2866	0.2530	0.2233	0.1970	0.1739	0.1535	0.0822	0.0441	0.0236	0.0068
14th	0.5092	0.4449	0.3888	0.3397	0.2968	0.2593	0.2266	0.1981	0.1730	0.1512	0.1321	0.0673	0.0343	0.0175	0.0045
15th	0.4844	0.4190	0.3625	0.3136	0.2713	0.2347	0.2030	0.1757	0.1519	0.1314	0.1137	0.0551	0.0267	0.0130	0.0030
16th	0.4608	0.3946	0.3379	0.2895	0.2479	0.2123	0.1819	0.1558	0.1334	0.1143	0.0979	0.0451	0.0208	0.0096	0.0021
17th	0.4383	0.3717	0.3151	0.2672	0.2265	0.1921	0.1630	0.1382	0.1172	0.0994	0.0842	0.0370	0.0162	0.0071	0.0014
18th	0.4169	0.3500	0.2938	0.2467	0.2070	0.1738	0.1460	0.1225	0.1029	0.0864	0.0725	0.0303	0.0126	0.0053	0.0009
19th	0.3966	0.3296	0.2739	0.2277	0.1892	0.1573	0.1308	0.1087	0.0903	0.0751	0.0624	0.0248	0.0098	0.0039	0.0006
20th	0.3773	0.3104	0.2554	0.2102	0.1729	0.1423	0.1172	0.0964	0.0793	0.0653	0.0537	0.0203	0.0076	0.0029	0.0004
21st	0.3588	0.2923	0.2381	0.1940	0.1581	0.1288	0.1049	0.0855	0.0697	0.0568	0.0462	0.0166	0.0060	0.0021	0.0003
22nd	0.3414	0.2753	0.2220	0.1791	0.1445	0.1165	0.0940	0.0758	0.0612	0.0494	0.0398	0.0136	0.0046	0.0016	0.0002
23rd	0.3247	0.2593	0.2070	0.1654	0.1320	0.1054	0.0842	0.0673	0.0537	0.0429	0.0343	0.0111	0.0036	0.0012	0.0001
24th	0.3089	0.2442	0.1930	0.1526	0.1207	0.0954	0.0755	0.0597	0.0472	0.0373	0.0295	0.0091	0.0028	0.0009	0.0001
25th	0.2938	0.2300	0.1800	0.1409	0.1103	0.0863	0.0676	0.0529	0.0414	0.0324	0.0254	0.0075	0.0022	0.0006	0.0001

TABLE B-3

Present Value of $1 Received or Paid in a Lump Sum at End of *n* Years in the Future

n	5%	6%	7%	8%	9%	10%	11%	12%	13%	14%	15%	20%	25%	30%	40%
1	0.9512	0.9418	0.9324	0.9231	0.9139	0.9048	0.8958	0.8869	0.8781	0.8694	0.8607	0.8187	0.7788	0.7408	0.6703
2	0.9048	0.8869	0.8694	0.8521	0.8353	0.8187	0.8025	0.7866	0.7711	0.7558	0.7408	0.6703	0.6065	0.5488	0.4493
3	0.8607	0.8353	0.8106	0.7866	0.7634	0.7408	0.7189	0.6977	0.6771	0.6570	0.6376	0.5488	0.4724	0.4066	0.3012
4	0.8187	0.7866	0.7558	0.7261	0.6977	0.6703	0.6440	0.6188	0.5945	0.5712	0.5488	0.4493	0.3679	0.3012	0.2019
5	0.7788	0.7408	0.7047	0.6703	0.6376	0.6065	0.5770	0.5488	0.5220	0.4966	0.4724	0.3679	0.2865	0.2231	0.1353
6	0.7408	0.6977	0.6570	0.6188	0.5827	0.5488	0.5169	0.4868	0.4584	0.4317	0.4066	0.3012	0.2231	0.1653	0.0907
7	0.7047	0.6570	0.6126	0.5712	0.5326	0.4966	0.4630	0.4317	0.4025	0.3753	0.3499	0.2466	0.1738	0.1225	0.0608
8	0.6703	0.6188	0.5712	0.5273	0.4868	0.4493	0.4148	0.3829	0.3535	0.3263	0.3012	0.2019	0.1353	0.0907	0.0408
9	0.6376	0.5827	0.5326	0.4868	0.4449	0.4065	0.3716	0.3396	0.3104	0.2837	0.2592	0.1653	0.1054	0.0672	0.0273
10	0.6065	0.5488	0.4966	0.4493	0.4066	0.3679	0.3329	0.3012	0.2725	0.2466	0.2231	0.1353	0.0821	0.0498	0.0183
11	0.5770	0.5169	0.4630	0.4148	0.3716	0.3329	0.2982	0.2671	0.2393	0.2144	0.1921	0.1108	0.0639	0.0369	0.0123
12	0.5488	0.4868	0.4317	0.3829	0.3396	0.3012	0.2671	0.2369	0.2101	0.1864	0.1653	0.0907	0.0498	0.0273	0.0082
13	0.5220	0.4584	0.4025	0.3535	0.3104	0.2725	0.2393	0.2101	0.1845	0.1620	0.1423	0.0743	0.0388	0.0202	0.0055
14	0.4966	0.4317	0.3753	0.3263	0.2837	0.2466	0.2144	0.1864	0.1620	0.1409	0.1225	0.0608	0.0302	0.0150	0.0037
15	0.4724	0.4066	0.3499	0.3012	0.2592	0.2231	0.1921	0.1653	0.1423	0.1225	0.1054	0.0498	0.0235	0.0111	0.0025
16	0.4493	0.3829	0.3263	0.2780	0.2369	0.2019	0.1720	0.1466	0.1249	0.1065	0.0907	0.0408	0.0183	0.0082	0.0017
17	0.4274	0.3606	0.3042	0.2567	0.2165	0.1827	0.1541	0.1300	0.1097	0.0925	0.0781	0.0334	0.0143	0.0061	0.0011
18	0.4065	0.3396	0.2837	0.2369	0.1979	0.1653	0.1381	0.1153	0.0963	0.0805	0.0672	0.0273	0.0111	0.0045	0.0007
19	0.3867	0.3198	0.2645	0.2187	0.1809	0.1496	0.1237	0.1023	0.0846	0.0700	0.0578	0.0224	0.0087	0.0033	0.0005
20	0.3679	0.3012	0.2466	0.2019	0.1653	0.1353	0.1108	0.0907	0.0743	0.0608	0.0498	0.0183	0.0067	0.0025	0.0003
21	0.3499	0.2837	0.2299	0.1864	0.1511	0.1225	0.0993	0.0805	0.0652	0.0529	0.0429	0.0150	0.0052	0.0018	0.0002
22	0.3329	0.2671	0.2144	0.1720	0.1381	0.1108	0.0889	0.0714	0.0573	0.0460	0.0369	0.0123	0.0041	0.0014	0.0002
23	0.3166	0.2516	0.1999	0.1588	0.1262	0.1003	0.0797	0.0633	0.0503	0.0399	0.0317	0.0101	0.0032	0.0010	0.0001
24	0.3012	0.2369	0.1864	0.1466	0.1153	0.0907	0.0714	0.0561	0.0442	0.0347	0.0273	0.0082	0.0025	0.0007	0.0001
25	0.2865	0.2231	0.1738	0.1353	0.1054	0.0821	0.0639	0.0498	0.0388	0.0302	0.0235	0.0067	0.0019	0.0006	....

INDEX

INDEX

This book has been set in 12 point Garamond #3, leaded 1 point, and 10 point Garamond #3, leaded 1 point. Part numbers and titles, and chapter numbers and titles, are in 18 point Spartan Medium italic. The size of the type page is 27 × 46½ picas.